The Development
of a
Modern Navy

French Naval Policy
1871–1904

by
Theodore Ropp

Edited by
Stephen S. Roberts

Naval Institute Press
Annapolis, Maryland

Photo Credits:

Marius Bar: p. 15 (4773), p. 223 (264), p. 247 (5162), p. 268 top (5092), p. 278 (260), p. 286 (230/2214), p. 288 (230/2759), p. 330 (230/2608), p. 332, p. 346, p. 349 (6877).

Naval Historical Center: p. 9 (75901), p. 17 (74921), p. 29 (88651), p. 36 (74894), p. 38 (00032), p. 39 (74839), p. 40 (74975), p. 50 (64455), p. 56 (74895), p. 59 (74911-A), p. 72 (88720), p. 82 (88710), p. 83 (88685), p. 85 (88704), p. 93 (66056), p. 96 (74805), p. 98 (64446), p. 99 (64451), p. 100 (88816), p. 103 (61616), p. 107 (66086), p. 108 top (74873), p. 108 bottom (88804), p. 115 (70392), p. 129 (74961), p. 130 (66031), p. 133 (88794), p. 135 (65763), p. 149 (75911), p. 151 (57808), p. 172 (66050), p. 173 (74856), p. 174 (74813), p. 175 (64376), p. 188 top (88780), p. 188 bottom (64375), p. 189 top (64201), p. 207 (76905), p. 209 (52869), p. 222 (82700), p. 225 (74883), p. 237 (64369), p. 249 (88803), p. 253 (64465), p. 255 (63905), p. 275 (60428), p. 285 top (64438), p. 298 (47877), p. 309 (52622), p. 311 (64365), p. 318 (92337), p. 342 (64366), p. 344 (66068).

Ship Plan Credits:

Archives de la Marine: p. 70 (8DD-1), p. 287 (8DD-1).

L'Association des Amis des Musées de la Marine: p. 189 bottom (*Triton,* No. 48: 16), p. 224 (*Triton,* No. 45: 14), p. 279 (*Triton,* No. 45: 15), p. 289 (*Triton,* No. 44: 13), p. 319 (*Triton,* No. 55: 7), p. 331 (*Triton,* No. 42: 15).

Le Yacht: p. 268 bottom, p. 285 bottom, p. 333.

Library of Congress Cataloging-in-Publication Data

Ropp, Theodore, 1911–
    The development of a modern navy.

    Bibliography: p.
    Includes index.
    1. France. Marine—History—19th century.
2. France. Marine—History—20th century. 3. France—
Military policy. I. Roberts, Stephen S. II. Title.
VA503.R6 1987   359'.00944   86-31303
ISBN 0-87021-141-2

Printed in the United States of America

Preface

THIS BOOK became a classic long before it was published. It was written in 1937, around the same time as two other naval history classics, James Phinney Baxter III's *The Introduction of the Ironclad Warship* and Arthur J. Marder's *The Anatomy of British Sea Power*. Unlike Baxter and Marder, Theodore Ropp never revised his dissertation for publication, concentrating instead on a highly successful teaching career at Duke University. Even so, his work became well known to specialists as the only thorough study of Europe's second largest navy in one of the most crucial periods in its history—the one in which it adapted to modern technology and democratic politics. Ironically, the mere existence of the dissertation in the Harvard archives may have deterred further research on the topic that it already covered so thoroughly, for after fifty years it still lacks any worthy competition. The Naval Institute Press is pleased finally to make this important work generally available, in an edition prepared for it by another expert in French naval history, Stephen S. Roberts.

Ropp's broad approach to his topic makes his work far richer than its title indicates. His examination of French naval policy led him to analyze other aspects of late-nineteenth-century France, especially the colonial movement and selected sectors of the economy. More important, he gave over major sections of the work to a relatively complete discussion of the development of other contemporary navies, notably the British and the Italian. The influence of Ropp's mentor, the great diplomatic historian William L. Langer, ensured that the diplomatic events and the great political personalities of the day also received solid treatment.

The richness of this book resulted from the fact that Ropp was one of the first to employ a new approach to the study of naval history, an approach that is now generally accepted. Influenced by the seemingly inexorable series of events that had led to World War I and by the awareness of another approaching worldwide catastrophe, he and contemporaries such as Marder felt that traditional naval histories, which focused on personalities and battles, were inadequate, and that maritime history could only be understood if scholars also examined institutions and peacetime policy formulation. His work helped to show that in a modern society, even purely technical decisions could have a major influence not only on hardware but on overall national policies and even on relations between states.

Instead of just narrating the development of French naval policy during three decades of peace, this book concentrates on four more general factors, which appear to have been the main elements in the navy's experience. First, it focuses on the mechanics of the arms races of the period. Both the Franco-Italian and the Anglo-French naval competitions provide insights into the workings of arms races not offered by the much-better-known rivalry between England and Germany. The Italian Navy sought to compensate for inferior numbers of ships by creating vessels individually superior to those possessed by France, while the French used administrative organization and strategic and tactical theory as well as technology in a similar manner against England. This factor is closely related to the second: the larger issue of the effects of technical change and strategic theory on the naval balance of power. Every change in European naval strength, whether on the part of England, the powers of the Triple Alliance, or Russia, had a direct effect on the naval position of France.

Of particular importance in the French case is the third factor: the relationship between public opinion and national defense in a democracy. With the advent of the French Third Republic in 1871, public opinion suddenly took direct control of a field that previously had been the preserve of a guild of experts. The French people, ill-trained as yet in the mechanics, if not in the theories, of self-government, with practically no economic interests beyond the seas, were brooding in 1871 over their defeat by Germany, a disaster that had seemed to come from an overemphasis on sea and colonial power. This narrowly continental people was served by a closed corporation of naval officers and men who were as unfit to educate the public in the new need for sea power as the public itself was unsuited to comprehend their teaching. The intervention of the Chamber of Deputies and the press in naval matters reached a high in the mid-1880s and remained there for over a decade, producing problems in naval organization, strategy, and technology that were extremely far-reaching and complex.

Perhaps the most original—and least understood—achievement of the French Navy in this period was the fourth factor: the development of a "strategy of the weak" as a rival to the theory of Alfred Thayer Mahan. Mahan produced a classic synthesis of naval theory based on the experience of the eighteenth century, in which the most numerous battle fleet generally controlled all the sea, allowing it to give effective protection to its own commerce and colonies and to destroy the commerce and capture the colonies of weaker powers. In France the need to face both the superior power of England and the inferior power of Italy caused a profound examination of the questions of naval strategy and war at sea. Against Italy the theory based on the British experience would suffice, but against Britain the French could not resign themselves to a naval theory in which France would, by definition, succumb. For some French leaders the issue was survival itself; the loss of France's first colonial empire to the English was still very much on their minds, and at this time they were building another, which they saw as France's last hope against her economically stronger rivals.

The alternative theory eventually developed by the French held that in modern times, command of the sea by a larger fleet was limited both geographically and strategically. In certain zones (notably the Mediterranean) a weaker navy could defend its own communications and colonies. In addition, it could find ways to force the stronger to supplement the indirect protection given to its seaborne commerce by the existence of its superior battle fleet. The aim was to compel the enemy to provide direct protection to his trade proportional to the importance of that commerce in his national life—a task that might prove impossible or prohibitively expensive. Desperately, courageously, and often far too optimistically, the French sought to develop a strategy that would enable the weak to bring the strong to terms.

Since the archives of the Ministry of Marine for the years 1871–1904 were not open to the public at the time this research was undertaken, this study is based on materials found in the technical press, which contained much valuable information because they appeared before the beginning of the modern period of secrecy in naval affairs; in the Harvard Library's special collection of periodical and newspaper material on the French Navy of these years; and in the materials in the library of the French Navy's historical service. The Harvard collection of contemporary periodical and pamphlet literature, once the property of Olivier F. Guihéneuc, a civil employee of the Ministry of Marine, is probably the best single group of printed materials to be found outside the library of the Service historique. Free access to the latter was provided by a Sheldon Fund fellowship, which allowed completion of the research in France.

Besides the help of Professor Langer, under whose general direction this study was done, the author would like to acknowledge the suggestions of Professor Baxter, and also of Assistant Professor Opdyke of the Harvard Department of Fine Arts. The latter kindly provided access to the Guihéneuc collection of photographs of French men-of-war, which became his personal property at the time when, through his intervention, the Guihéneuc pamphlet and newspaper collection was sold to the Harvard Library. The staff of the United States Naval War College at Newport permitted the use of materials there. In France, Commandant Barbier of the Service historique; M. Benoist, its librarian; M. Braibant, its curator of manuscripts; and Professor Reussner of the School of Naval War all assisted in finding materials and in providing introductions to naval officers, notably Commandant René Jouan and Admiral Raoul Castex. The late Admiral W. S. Sims, American attaché to France and Russia at the time of the Fashoda crisis, provided his extremely interesting impressions of the French Navy of that day. As the last of the major figures in the gunnery revolution of those years, he also helped untangle the difficult technical points in this area.

The editor became closely familiar with the Ropp dissertation during his undergraduate years at Harvard, and in 1976 he received a Ph.D. for a dissertation on a slightly earlier period in French naval history, 1818–1852. His intent in editing the work was to make the types of changes an author normally makes when converting a dissertation into a book: tightening up the organization, clarifying obscure historical references for the general reader, et cetera. In doing so, he took pains to ensure that all of the ideas and as much of the writing as possible remained those of the author. He made no attempt to update the research, as his own extensive work in the archives that had been closed to Ropp persuaded him that additional sources would not lead to any significant changes in the volume. He did, however, add an appendix based on archival sources and a supplementary section in the bibliography listing the main works that have appeared on this subject since Ropp completed his own.

Most of the photographs in this volume are from the collection of the U.S. Naval Historical Center, which has acquired over the years many of the photographs gathered during the 1880s and 1890s by the Office of Naval Intelligence. The rest of the photos are from the excellent collection of Marius Bar in Toulon, France. Most of the plans are published courtesy of the Amis des Musées de la Marine in Paris.

The editor wishes to thank Norman Friedman and Professor Kenneth Hagan for helping to make this project a reality and Sue Goetz Ross for her encouragement during the long period in which it was in gestation.

Contents

The Development of a Modern Navy ❧

One

~~~~~~

Introduction: The Second Hundred Years' War

IN THE late nineteenth century the French Navy entered the modern industrial age. It had to adjust to massive changes in technology, strategic
thought, and political environment while attempting to compete with the
overwhelming naval and economic strength of England. It accomplished
this in two phases—a relatively passive period of recovery under the new
Third Republic after the fall of Emperor Napoleon III in 1870, and a period
of active rivalry with Italy and England from the mid-1880s to the turn of the
century. The prelude to this effort was the navy's experience under the empire of Napoleon III (1852–70). This, in turn, can only be fully understood
in the context of the more remote historical past, particularly the long naval
rivalry between France and England sometimes referred to as the second
Hundred Years' War.

In the middle of the seventeenth century the naval powers of northern
Europe began a three-cornered struggle to control the sources of wealth
first opened by Spain and Portugal. All three powers—France, Holland, and
England—had united their merchant marine, navy, and colonies into a
single naval-colonial system in which many officers and most seamen transferred freely between the war and the merchant fleets. The three rivals differed little in their internal organization, but the navy's place in the life
of the three nations and the methods of warfare adopted by each varied
considerably.

Holland was originally the most prosperous, but she was eliminated because her position on the continent forced her to defend herself on land as
well as on sea. Holland depended on her trade for national existence, and
as a consequence the relations between her navy and public opinion were
very close, as in England in more modern days. At times, the influence of

public opinion was so strong that it took effective control of the conduct of naval operations.

In France the conditions of sea power were totally different. Around the same time that Louis XIV's minister of war, François-Michel Le Tellier, marquis de Louvois, and his great military engineer, Sébastien Le Prestre, marquis de Vauban, organized France's professional army, his minister of marine, Jean-Baptiste Colbert, created a professional navy to serve as an instrument of policy abroad. The navy, the colonies, and the merchant marine became a single professional organization controlled by the state and forming one of its organs. They were the main elements of an integrated colonial system, whose purpose was to enhance the prestige of the state and help finance its wars against internal and external enemies. The navy, like the palace at Versailles, was a symbol of the power of the state and of the personal ambitions of its monarch. The abundant resources of seventeenth-century France usually enabled her to pay her bills, and whenever the schemes of the central government included colonial ventures, a powerful navy was generally the result.

The French Navy thus began life as a luxury of the central government that was of no importance in the life of the people at large or in the defense of their interests. Its hold on national opinion was insignificant. Its officers and men became a closed corporation, drawn from a limited number of noble families and coastal towns. In this respect, it was similar in some ways to the state-run Gobelins tapestry-making enterprise. In times of peace or financial hardship, the navy tended to be one of the first areas in which the government tried to save money. At such times it survived largely because the state was expected to keep up appearances and felt it had a definite duty to maintain the personnel it had trained for this special profession.

England occupied a middle position between her rivals in all respects but her geographic insularity. She was naturally poorer and less populous than France but more wealthy than Holland. Though her national economy did not depend on the sea, sea trade and consequently the interest of the public in the navy were much more significant than in France. The English public employed its navy as the continental powers employed their professional armies: it paid the bills, applauded successes like those of Admiral Horatio Nelson, and punished obvious failures—Admiral John Byng was shot for losing Minorca in 1756. Though keenly interested, the public was hardly ever powerful enough, as in Holland, to interfere seriously in the actual conduct of operations. The officer corps, though a closed corporation, was less associated with specific localities than in France and less national than in Holland. The men came from the nation at large, although only from certain economic levels of the population.

In spite of a tendency of later historians to exaggerate economic factors, the essential explanation for English success was purely and simply geographic. Thanks to the barrier of the English Channel, the English could concentrate all of their resources into a single armed force, the navy, which could secure most of the objectives of the confused struggles of the eighteenth century. It could defend England's own territory while supporting efforts to acquire either the continental or colonial symbols of dynastic prestige for which the European states were striving. In the beginning, the English intervened indiscriminately in Europe and beyond the seas, and only after experience had shown that continental territory was next to impossible for them to hold did they begin to confine their attention to colonial projects. Even in England, the navy in the beginning was partly an instrument of prestige and national glory.

England ultimately won control of much of the decaying Spanish and Portuguese overseas empires because of the general military supremacy she maintained on the sea routes leading to them. Her key advantage was that the sea routes from both France and Holland to the outer world passed sufficiently close to Britain to be effectively controlled by the forces commanding British home waters—which were always British. England envisaged three general types of maritime operations: war on the high seas to defeat or blockade the enemy's battle fleet and secure the command of the seas around Britain; attacks on and defense of commerce; and combined naval and military expeditions. The command of British home waters was always the primary British objective. Not until France's navy was blockaded in its ports did England normally detach large numbers of ships to pursue objectives on the continent or in the colonies or undertake the direct protection of her commerce. Command of British home waters (which were considered to include part of the North Atlantic and the Straits of Gibraltar) was important above all because it kept French armies from English soil. It also limited French ability to attack British commerce and colonies while cutting off all French maritime communications. By focusing on this objective, England remained dominant at sea throughout the series of wars in this period, although she never defeated the French nation. Even the loss of her most valuable single colonial possession, the thirteen North American colonies, did not seriously injure her.

In the long series of wars from 1688 to 1815, France wavered between three general strategies, each of which can be associated with one of the three traditional kinds of naval operations. Normally, she first focused on the Channel. By great efforts at building up the navy in peacetime, an alliance with Spain, and skillful strategic combinations, the French attempted to gain approximate equality in the Channel to permit launching an expedition to Ireland or Jacobite Scotland. Occasionally they achieved an uneasy equilibrium, but England always renewed her forces, Spain always proved an unsatisfactory ally, and the French ended up abandoning the objective of Ireland or Scotland for others that looked more practicable. The French objectives were as limited as those of the English, and not until Napoleon formed an invasion flotilla at Boulogne in 1805 did France contemplate attempting a blow at the heart of Britain.

Because English ships were certain to be concentrated in the British seas, the French occasionally resorted to a temporary concentration in an area removed from the center of British power, avoiding local English forces or defeating them if they were inferior. The campaign of Pierre-André, bailli de Suffren de Saint-Tropez, in the Indian Ocean in 1782–83 took advantage of the absence of preponderant British forces from a very important secondary objective, India. In his expedition to Egypt in 1798, Napoleon avoided the English Mediterranean fleet and attacked a peripheral region that he thought was becoming vital.

Direct war on commerce, with deliberate avoidance of battle, became the principal strategy for the French after both of the previous approaches had failed. As with an expedition against Ireland or one of the English colonies, the object of this strategy was not to bring about the collapse of the English nation but to do as much harm as possible with the limited means left at France's disposal. By this stage in the war, the major portion of England's navy would be blockading the French battle fleet in its ports, and British commerce would be passing practically unprotected on the seas. For France, detaching ships from her immobilized battle squadrons and idle merchant marine to attack this trade seemed the only logical course. A series of initial successes was sure to follow, producing a crisis in the City of London. The French would then send out more ships from the battle fleet as the English detached ships from the blockade for convoy and patrol. The single French corsairs would band together to overwhelm the English convoys, and both raiding divisions and convoys would soon reach considerable size while the French battle fleet atrophied in port. The whole English naval force, now practically freed from the need to maintain the blockade, would use its superior numbers to track down the corsairs as mercilessly as it had formerly blockaded the battleships. Since the corsairs, as well as colonial expeditions, were forced to pass through the same area the battle fleets had already given up as hopeless, their ultimate success was no more likely than that of the battleships. By 1815 Britain had mastered the threats from France's battle fleet and commerce raiders and had gained complete control of Europe's communications with the outer world.

During the rest of the nineteenth century, England became the leader of Europe's economic activity by adding the raw materials of the world beyond the seas to the coal and iron she found at home. The character of maritime trade itself changed, and while the military control of the British seas remained the basis of Britain's defensive system, her economic existence finally became dependent on the regular flow of her shipping. The continental nations gradually developed the same type of economy. The connection with the outside world became as vital to some of them as to England, and its maintenance became an important factor in their continental positions.

At sea, the methods of the industrial revolution challenged the old bases of sea power. The traditional officer corps were overwhelmed by new inventions and corresponding changes in the nature and techniques of naval war, and the naval power of the state became even more a function of its industrial system. Naval strategic geography itself changed, as the single Atlantic seaway to the West and East Indies gave way to a multiplicity of land and sea connections between Europe and the outer world. Finally, even in England, the problem arose of educating the rulers and an ever-widening public about the need to protect those connections.

On the continent, the nineteenth century converted the navy into a fuller partner with the army as a real part of the national defense. As the rivalries on the continent (in which England participated) became more bitter toward the middle of the century, the continental powers one by one faced the problem of confronting England over issues that were no longer those of prestige but those of national existence. Each faced the same problem: to oppose the greatest of naval powers with forces that were by definition inferior. In the classic words of two French maritime historians, they were motivated by *notre éternel désir de rendre le faible plus fort que le fort* (our eternal desire to render the weak stronger than the strong).[1] Solution of this problem was no longer a luxury, it was a necessity. The effort to solve it dominated the history of the French Navy for the remainder of the century.

Two

The Navy of Napoleon III

UNDER THE empire of Napoleon III (1852–70), the French Navy made its first concerted effort to use the new achievements of the Industrial Revolution to challenge England at sea. These two decades saw the introduction of many new weapons and theories, and also provided a testing ground for them in the Crimean War (1853–56), the wars of national liberation in Europe (Italian unification in 1859–60, Schleswig-Holstein in 1864, the Seven Weeks' War of 1866, and the Franco-Prussian War of 1870), and the American Civil War (1861–65). This period provided the background for naval developments for much of the remainder of the century, because naval thinkers required a long time to assimilate the meaning of the new weapons and because the long period of peace that descended on Europe after 1870 made it impossible to test hypotheses empirically.

THE PRESTIGE FLEET

The rebirth of the navy in France after the Napoleonic Wars was the direct result of France's humiliation by England in the Near East crisis of 1840, in which France's ally, Egypt, was defeated by British sea power. When the crisis came, in spite of diligent naval construction since 1820, the French Navy was not ready, and extraordinary crisis expenditures only proved that a fleet could not be improvised on short notice. According to the French naval program of 1837, the navy was to keep twenty of its forty ships of the line "in reserve" on the building ways, about 90 percent complete, because their timbers stayed better preserved on land than in the water. Preparing such ships for sea proved to be a difficult and time-consuming operation. In addition, the supply depots were nearly empty, and even trained officers and men were lacking. Throughout the next four years, François-Ferdinand-

Philippe d'Orléans, prince de Joinville, a son of King Louis Philippe (1830–48) who had made the navy his career, carried on a continuous agitation for the navy. In 1846 Parliament voted a special law of 93 million francs for its rebuilding.[1]

Though public opinion favored a large number of fast, light vessels for destroying the commerce of England, the navy's leaders—Admirals Victor-Guy Duperré, Albin-Reine Roussin, Julien-Pierre Lalande, and the prince de Joinville—succeeded in obtaining a Squadron of Evolutions, a squadron of seagoing ships of the line maintained in permanent commission in the Mediterranean for training in gunnery, tactics, and squadron navigation. In spite of criticisms of naval administration by some members of the Chamber of Deputies (the popularly elected house of the French Parliament), Adolphe Thiers, prime minister during the 1840 crisis, overcame all opposition to naval expansion, insisting that "France must have a fleet that can make her respected." The deputy who reported to the Chamber on the 1846 law added:

> If France is condemned by her numerical inferiority in sailors to admit that there is a power that can have more sailing ships than we can, the difference could disappear if we use another force [steam] which the industrial genius of France can and must create.[2]

Though economic motives were present in the French naval revival, the behavior of Thiers and his English rival, Lord Palmerston, indicates that it succeeded primarily because the bourgeoisie had adopted the archaic dynastic idea of chasing after glory. The bourgeois was just beginning to cut a figure in the fields of culture, society, and policy, and he found that he could also afford the luxury of a navy. In the early years of the revival, the navy was still largely an instrument of prestige. Its ambition was near equality to England in numbers of ships and superiority in technical skill.

Napoleon III further developed these characteristics. While French economic interests continued to expand, the prestige character of the navy developed even faster. In acquiescing in the coup that made Napoleon III emperor in 1852, the French sold their liberties for prosperity and glory. Though the navy was a valuable accessory to prosperity, it became under Napoleon III the principal instrument of glory. Napoleon discovered, as had the great English prime minister William Pitt years before, that glory was cheaper beyond the seas, almost as brilliant, and a great deal less dangerous.

In 1857, to conserve its excellent naval position after its victory in the Crimean War, France adopted a new fleet program that shows clearly its military ideas. The Program of 1857 provided for three fleets: one of battleships to uphold France's position in Europe, one of ships for foreign stations to make her respected abroad, and one of transports and gunboats either to conduct colonial expeditions or to land and support troops in another Crimean War. This program was modified in 1863 and 1865 as the result of the introduction of armored ships, but its general arrangements remained essentially unchanged. It provided for a formidable force, almost numerically equal to that of England.[3]

TECHNICAL EXCELLENCE

The French Navy also redoubled its efforts to attain superior technical efficiency. It gave its officers the most advanced scientific training in Europe, and it supplemented the simple common sailors, conscripted from the merchant navy, with volunteer specialists. The common deckhand was now only a convenient source of muscle, and brevetted gunners, riflemen, topmen, signalmen, engineers, mechanics, and stokers, all carefully trained in special schools, became the backbone of the crews. Squadrons of Evolutions spent much time at sea studying the tactical opportunities offered by the new weapons. The three principles of the French Navy under Napoleon III, as under the prince de Joinville, were near equality in numbers, superior fighting efficiency, and the bold adoption of every new step forward.

The French Navy counted modern science as one of its major weapons for two reasons: each revolution in naval warfare gave France the prospect of temporary numerical equality and even superiority to England, while historically French naval architects had usually been superior to their English counterparts. (British constructors often modeled their designs on ships captured from France, and as late as 1850 over a third of the ships of the British fleet were based on such designs.)[4] Strongly organized as autonomous services with excellent preliminary and professional training, the two technical corps of Naval Constructors and Naval Artillery were in essence groups of scientific specialists for getting the jump on the English.

The French Navy in these years was an engineers' and scientists' fleet dominated by its corps of naval constructors, the Génie maritime. Recruited from the top students at the Ecole polytechnique, which gave the best general scientific training in Europe, French naval constructors attended the foremost naval construction school in Europe and completed their training by practical work in the arsenals.[5] Thorough scientific training before the commencement of practical education was a feature common to both the technical corps and the navigating officers. Under Napoleon III, a single individual who enjoyed the emperor's confidence headed each of the technical corps, and the two corps formed a small, coherent centralized group of a few hundred officers with wide scientific training and practical experience. The head of the Génie was Stanislas-Charles-Henri Dupuy de Lôme, famous for designing France's first fast steam battleship and her first ironclads. The head of the artillery was General Charles-Victor Frébault.

English ship designers, on the other hand, were not part of any special organization, and for a long time they were nothing but glorified dockyard

The ironclad Surveillante *(launched in 1864), of the* Flandre *class. A near sister to the first ironclad battleship, the* Gloire, *she was one of the first generation of battleships designed by Dupuy de Lôme with wooden hulls and armament on the broadside.*

foremen. The English still educated their constructors according to the old rule of practice before theory, and only established a special school for them in 1864.[6] Even then, all the students, regardless of their preliminary education, went through the lower grades as arsenal workmen. Finally, in 1883, after the Italian, Russian, and German navies had formed constructors' corps like the Génie, the leading British constructor persuaded the Admiralty to follow the French ideas.[7]

In these conditions, it is not surprising that the French were generally successful in keeping technically ahead of the British. The ironclads of Dupuy de Lôme were only the culmination of the series of naval technical revolutions that had been foreseen in the 1840s as a major element in French success against England. Dupuy de Lôme's *Napoléon,* the first fast steam line-of-battle ship; his *Gloire,* the first seagoing ironclad; and his colleague Camille Audenet's *Couronne,* the first capital ship with an iron hull, were important landmarks in this evolution. The French capitalized on this technical success by ordering a large number of the new ships, and Dupuy de Lôme's completed fleet comprised sixteen homogeneous broadside battleships of the *Gloire, Couronne, Flandre,* and *Solférino* classes, completely covered with 4½-inch plating, which was practically invulnerable to the guns of the day. The heterogeneous collection of nineteen first-generation British broadside ironclads begun between 1859 and 1863 was little more than equal to it.

In the later 1860s, however, the English gradually recovered their threatened supremacy. In conception of plans French genius in engineering was a real source of strength, but in execution of those plans France was unable to compete with the financial and industrial resources of England. The delays and difficulties due to French industrial deficiencies were notable, even after the French decided to build nearly all their ironclads with wood hulls because of the backward condition of the French iron industries. The other materials furnished by French firms were costly and constantly unsatisfactory, and the enormous expenses of building the fleet were more than French finances could stand. The navy's budget rose from 158 million francs in 1858 to 219 million in 1864. By the end of the 1860s the navy was beginning to decline, along with the whole prestige system of Napoleon III. The first great modern naval race was ending with the complete victory of England.

ORGANIZATIONAL REFORM

In 1869 the French liberals regained a share in the government after a successful campaign against the more authoritarian aspects of the empire of Napoleon III. One of their demands was a general reduction in naval expenditures, or, if that was impossible, internal reforms in the navy's organization to put it on a businesslike basis. In spite of the introduction of the new weapons, the French had not attempted any reform of the naval administration, and as a result the ancient organization of the old monarchy and the Napoleonic era was administering a modern industrial system.

From the very beginning, a powerful movement to reform the navy's organization had accompanied the effort to rebuild the navy. One of the first results of the liberal triumph in the revolution of 1848, which replaced the monarchy of Louis Philippe with the Second Republic, was a step in this direction. The new republic was not hostile in principle to the naval revival, for it was mixing furiously in other people's business all over Europe, but before spending any money on the navy it organized a grand, general parliamentary investigation. Napoleon III dissolved the parliamentary commission before it could bring in its report, but the general tone of its sessions was unfavorable to the existing system of naval administration. The liberals were convinced that without a thorough reform of the organization, efficiency was impossible. This became their recurrent complaint during the rest of the century. As late as 1913, an expert on the subject wrote that "the navy is a department of generally organized disorder, and no matter how many millions we may expend, there will be no navy as long as we continue the present system . . . of organization."[8]

In liberal circles everywhere in Europe, the movement for lightening the "unproductive" burdens of armaments was related to a similar drive for general governmental efficiency. In the short period of the Liberal Empire (1869–70), however, the general move toward reorganization did not have time to succeed, and the only accomplishment was an immediate general reduction in naval expenses. The liberals forced the retirement of Dupuy de Lôme, whose ships had become a symbol of the emperor's useless ambition, and they cut as much as they could from the budget. But these cost-cutting efforts had little impact because they were not followed up by basic reforms.

Liberal reform failed in France at the very time that a similar movement in England was largely successful. Even before the humiliation of England's chief rival, France, by Prussia in the war of 1870–71, Hugh Childers, first lord of the Admiralty in the first ministry of the great English liberal William Gladstone, succeeded both in reducing total expenses and in carrying through a general reform of the navy's administration. Although his claim to have reduced only "unproductive expenditures" was largely a myth, the damage he did to immediate naval efficiency (for which he was much criticized) could be made up, while the influence of his general reforms endured.

His changes in the naval administration completed the work begun during the great liberal reforms of the early 1830s. The first lord became a real, responsible cabinet minister, and the other lords, who had formerly collectively controlled a group of subordinate technical bureaus, individually received control of specific departments. Childers placed the entire manufacturing system of the fleet, including its design and construction, in a single service, which he removed from a position subordinate to the naval members and placed on an equal footing with them. He divided the whole British navy into four sections. The three sea lords controlled the operational fleet, the controller managed the fleet under construction, the civil lord handled naval works and shore installations, and the financial secretary, who was not a member of the board, was a head bookkeeper charged with purchasing and contracts. There were no other technical services, and the only forum for discussing decisions was the board itself. In such discussions, representatives of both military and civil interests were always present, and the naval lords' retention of the power of resignation curbed the absolute power of the minister (the first lord).

For the administration of its navy, the country of parliamentarianism and decentralization adopted a highly centralized system.[9] From the dockyards, Childers demanded efficiency in construction, and he closed two arsenals entirely in order to specialize and rationalize those that remained. A system of modern accounting enabled him to see what was going on. He abolished scores of minor offices and establishments completely, and he placed extra officers on half pay or retired them. But when he suggested replacing the militarily useless ships that were "showing the flag" on foreign stations with a system of flying squadrons that would represent a real military force and give their crews needed training in squadron navigation, the diplomats fought him successfully and the project was abandoned.[10] Childers did not build the modern British fleet, but he cleared the ground for one. Even if the navy after his retirement returned to its comfortable traditions, it had received from him and the reviled Gladstonian liberals the foundations of a modern organization.

WAR LESSONS: FLEET ACTIONS

Despite its archaic organization, the French Navy in the mid-1860s practically attained its objective of near numerical equality with England and superiority in technology and tactical training. The experiences of the wars of this period were doubly important for France. They had an immediate impact on the technical characteristics of the ships of the last period of the empire, and they were equally influential in the 1870s and beyond, when the French Navy had to reinterpret the same experiences from the position of a *marine des pauvres,* a poor man's navy.

Of all the wars of these years, the American Civil War was by far the most significant. By land and by sea, the improvised naval forces of the Union first blockaded and then cut in two the entire southern people. In spite of the South's desperate efforts to break the blockade, the Union captured nearly every southern outlet to the sea. Supplying his army from these ports, Sherman delivered the final blow to the southern rear as Grant made his terrible frontal attack on Richmond. In this prototype of the modern war of exhaustion, both the successful improvisation of a fleet by a superior financial and industrial power and the use of combined naval and military operations made a great impression in Europe. The four efforts of the South to break the blockade—the exploits of the successful blockade runners, the engagements of the ironclad *Merrimack* in Hampton Roads, the destructive career of the commerce raider *Alabama,* and the Confederacy's invention of underwater attack by means of primitive submarines and mines—were not of immediate interest to France but were important in later naval theory.

The Battle of Lissa between Austria and Italy in 1866, the only major fleet action during this period, reintroduced the ram into naval warfare and thereby became a key event in naval tactical history. The sureness and freedom of movement given by steam propulsion had suggested the idea of using the ship itself as a weapon long before ships became invulnerable to shot. In France, Admiral Nicolas-Hippolyte Labrousse had proposed a ram steamer as early as 1840, and Dupuy de Lôme had given a ram to the largest of his first-generation ironclad designs, the *Solférino* class, in 1860.[11] Against the new invulnerable ironclads, the ram appeared to be the only way of bringing about a decision. At Lissa the Austrian admiral, Wilhelm von Tegetthoff, went into action with the deliberate intention of using the ram, and his flagship *Ferdinand Max* succeeded in ramming and sinking the Italian flagship *Re d'Italia.* This action confirmed the ideas of the experts and started a flood of wonderful tactical elaborations. These, however, overlooked the fact that Austrian gunfire had almost completely stopped the *Re d'Italia* before Tegetthoff rammed her.[12]

The French, who led in the reintroduction of the ram, were naturally the most thorough in erecting a system of ram tactics. The semiofficial account of the battle declared that "the ram is today the principal arm of combat by sea and the *ultima ratio* of maritime warfare."[13] The official tactics of the Squadron of Evolutions at the outbreak of the war with Prussia in 1870 were based on the ram's supremacy:

> The same lesson has come to us from Lissa as from the banks of the Chesapeake [Hampton Roads], and the very day when the ship itself entered the battle with its entire mass, the decline of the artillery began. Our foundries, it is true, have not had their last word, but in the relative situation of the ship and the gun, not an admiral will dare to turn his broadside to the enemy. . . . Even if the gun has recovered some effect when it strikes perpendicularly and at close range, it is completely powerless against an oblique surface. We must win victories by the ram, we must defend ourselves against it. At the approach of the enemy, an armored ship can only silence its guns; . . . the feeble advantage due to their uncertain fire . . . will not be worth the danger of a cloud of smoke . . . at the moment when the ship's safety depends upon the precision of her maneuvers.[14]

Though the artillerists "had not yet had their last word," the uselessness of even the new guns in the oblique angles and rapidly varying distances of ram combat relegated them to a secondary role. The ram was the principal arm; the gun was only to prepare the way for it.

The line abreast now became the usual formation for battle.[15] Since the number of guns that could fire over the bows of a ship was necessarily very limited, the cult of the ram strengthened the demand for larger-caliber guns. A small, short ship could easily outmaneuver a longer and faster vessel, and small displacements, moderate speeds, and rapid turning became as important in new battleship designs as the ability to fire the guns in line with the keel. Finally, as a partial defense against the ram, the new ships were divided into a number of watertight compartments.

These requirements led to the development of the first true coastal battleships. The *Monitor,* famous for defeating the *Merrimack* at Hampton Roads, was still just an armored floating fort. It could move from place to place to supplement or to bombard coastal fortifications, but it could fight a battleship only when the latter chose to let it. In 1863 Dupuy de Lôme designed the first coastal battleship, the armored ram *Taureau,* specifically to attack other warships at anchor or in narrow passes. He put guns in her only as a concession to the artillerists and with the sole function of preparing the way for the ram. In the original design, he placed the guns in a fixed turret where they could fire only parallel to the ship's axis.[16]

The revival of the gun began around 1864, and until then, in the absence of the ram, armored navies were practically helpless against similarly armored rivals. At Kinburn during the Crimean War, the Russian smoothbore guns had made depressions less than an inch deep in the 4½-inch armor of the French floating batteries.[17] Responding to this challenge, artillerists tried to solve the problems of gun, projectile, powder, and carriage simultaneously. For smashing the new armor, England and the United States first tried enormous smoothbores, which the United States eventually adopted in the form of the 15-inch Dahlgren. The French, with an equal lack of success, attempted to punch through armor with small bolt-shaped projectiles. Only in 1864 did England and France both reach a provisional solution in the form of rifled breechloaders, and they soon placed guns on the ships that, according to proving-ground tests, had some chance against armor.[18] Six years later the French carried their original experiments to a more definite conclusion and developed the Model 1870 guns, which were the real forerunners of modern French naval artillery.

The Naval Artillery Corps, which constructed these guns, was, like the Naval Constructors Corps, an autonomous part of the navy. Its officers received their education at the Ecole polytechnique and were responsible for the design and construction of all French naval artillery. The Artillery Corps carried out its work in a very scientific manner. It tested every theory on the proving ground at Gâvres according to three general principles laid down by the trials commission there: never fire a gun uselessly, always reckon beforehand all possible *a priori* data, and test all theories to their utmost possible limits.[19] The trials eventually developed a complete logical system of artillery whose basic empirical principles were applicable to all sizes of guns. Progress in any direction was solidly based on a multitude of previous experiments. On these principles the French Army developed its famous "75" after the Franco-Prussian War, and throughout this period French guns never caused the death of a gunner in service.

The breech-loading Model 1870 was, like its contemporaries, a smashing rather than a piercing weapon. It had an iron body with a steel inner tube and was strengthened on the outside with steel bands. (At this time Alfred Krupp's breechloaders were the only all-steel guns.)[20] While the first major product of the efforts of the Commission of Gâvres was thus imperfect, the effects of the patient experiments on explosives, projectiles, and armor were to become extremely important, and the original attempt to pierce armor rather than smash it ultimately emerged triumphant.

By 1867 all the leading maritime countries had guns in service that could smash the early 4½-inch iron armor. Their tremendous destructive effect caused a curious reaction against the use of armor in general, called *décuirassement* (disarmoring).[21] As in the case of a ball thrown against a window, the effect of a successful smashing blow against armor was greatly increased by armor fragments sprayed into the ship by the projectile. Under these conditions, no protection at all was decidedly better than one that was ineffective, and the logical solution was to abandon armor altogether.

Sir William Armstrong, England's leading gun designer, claimed that the development of the new guns had produced a second nemesis for the invincible ironclad in the form of a swarm of unarmored gunboats whose protection consisted of their number and speed. According to Armstrong,

> It is not too much to say that for the cost of one ironclad we could have three unarmored ships of far higher speed, and carrying collectively three armaments, each equal to that of the armored vessel.[22]

For coast defense Armstrong began building a series of "flatiron" gunboats, little larger than the battleship-sized guns they carried. The notion that an unarmored "freely penetrable" cruiser or merchant ship carrying a few heavy guns would have a good chance against an armorclad also became popular. These theories completely overlooked the original purpose of armor, which had been to keep out explosive shells rather than solid shot. Instead, they made the return to the *belle marine en bois,* the good old wooden navy, into a significant sentimental current.[23]

These new dangers resulted in two immediate changes in battleship design. Naval architects obtained better protection by thickening the armor on the waterline and by concentrating the guns in an armored box amidships. By leaving the ends of the ship above the waterline unprotected, they took a first step toward *décuirassement.* At the same time, they provided end-on

The ironclad battleship Suffren *(1870). A belt-and-battery ship designed by Dupuy de Lôme with two barbettes on each side of the upper deck above an armored broadside gun battery.*

fire in some ships by cutting away the upper works of the hull fore and aft of the armored box so that the guns in the corners of the box could fire past them. Another technique adopted to provide end-on fire was to place open circular armored redoubts or "barbettes" on the upper deck with guns on turntables inside them firing over their edges. French designers preferred to use barbettes for end-on fire, and in 1870 France had in various stages of construction seven "belt and battery" ships with an armored battery amidships on the lower deck and barbettes above it. Many naval officers, however, viewed this type as only a provisional solution and believed that ultimately the ram and the gun were both likely to make the battleship obsolete.

COASTAL WARFARE

The development of coastal warfare only added to the general confusion. The idea of making war directly on the enemy's coast had received a great impetus as soon as steam permitted inshore navigation, and the experiences of the American Civil War confirmed ideas derived from the Crimean War concerning its utility. In all but one of the fourteen wars between 1857 and 1893 in which naval operations figured, the command of the sea itself was not disputed and the forces of the superior navy were free to operate against the enemy's coasts.[24] This involved hitting the enemy's territory in a way the continental mind could understand, an important consideration as public opinion became more involved in naval strategy.[25]

After constructing its initial battleship fleet, and as growing tensions with Germany revealed the possibility of a serious continental war, France turned its attention to ships for coastal warfare. Between 1859 and 1867 France built eleven descendants of the floating batteries that had bombarded the Russian forts at Kinburn during the Crimean War. The designers of these ships crowded as many guns and as much armor as possible into a limited space and then gave the mass just enough steam power to move. Floating batteries soon lost favor owing to their lack of seaworthiness.

In the later 1860s inventors deluged the Conseil des Travaux de la Marine (literally the Council of Works of the Navy, a group of senior officers that advised the minister of marine on ship design and other technical matters) with projects for coastal matériel. The economizing tendencies of the legislature made it possible to pursue only one of these, a diminutive form of Armstrong's flatiron gunboat designed by Lieutenant Jérôme-Eugène Farcy, which was hardly larger than a floating gun carriage and which carried a single big gun for bombardment. The French also bought two American coast-defense ships, the casemate ship *Dunderberg* and the monitor *Onondaga*. The whole collection was admirably described as a *flotille de siège garde-côtes* (coast-defense siege train), and its mission was to repeat the offensive triumphs of the Crimean War.[26]

Coast-defense battleships of the Cerbère *class at Cherbourg in 1875. From left to right are the* Cerbère *(1868),* Bélier *(1870), and* Tigre *(1871). They combined a rotating turret with the strong ram of the earlier* Taureau.

The French spent much effort on light-draft coastal battleships to support these coastal forces. Dupuy de Lôme's *Cerbère* was similar to the ram *Taureau* but added guns in an armored turret as in the American *Monitor* and had improved seakeeping qualities. Unlike the *Monitor,* the *Cerbère* had a turret that rested on a barbette, which protected the rotating mechanism and ammunition supply—an arrangement that became standard after around 1890. While the *Cerbère* retained many of the limitations of her predecessor, later so-called coast defense ships were neither armored rams nor floating forts but light-draft battleships able to operate on German as well as French coasts.

France, England, and the United States originally developed the ram, the unarmored gunboats, and the coast-defense battleships primarily for offensive use. The ease with which these could be used defensively, however, was readily apparent. In groups close to a friendly coast, they could be truly formidable antagonists for a battleship. The appearance of each was the signal for new predictions of the end of the battleship. Their cheapness, their novelty, and their immediate defensive utility readily won them public support.

The panics in England during the French Second Empire were abundant

lence of the instinctive reaction of the moneyed class to seek direct de-
ses for threatened possessions. As the English merchants hastily moved
to counter the monsters of Dupuy de Lôme, the thought of protecting their
overseas communications all but vanished. The British Parliament's first
concern was to armor the islands. Open points along the coast, like Harwich
and Dover, were made safe against a landing. A ring of detached outworks
similar to those around Paris defended London, and the naval dockyards
were given defenses against military and maritime sieges. While the ghost
of Lord Barham (the first lord during the Napoleonic Wars) looked on
aghast, the new popularly elected Parliament took over the job of determining the strategy of the British navy.

A fort for his direct defense and an ironclad sitting like a watchdog in the
harbor appealed as much to the prosperous bourgeois as did the cheapness
of these means of defense. Both military men and other interested parties
exploited his inexperience. The argument was made that

> if a port is left to the protection of seagoing ships . . . a slight error in
> judgment might cause their removal at a critical time. . . . But if the ves-
> sels to protect the port cannot put to sea, they are sure to be at their
> posts when wanted.[27]

The professional army and navy men were not solely responsible for the
manipulation of public opinion. The creator and proponent of many of the
new weapons was that most characteristic figure of the Industrial Revolution—the inventor. Only in the industrial era have private individuals outside the regular technical services not only manufactured weapons but designed them and offered advice as to their use. Inventors were accustomed
to appealing to the public for support, and they thoroughly understood the
ways to work upon it. For an Armstrong, a Krupp, an Ericsson, or any other
enthusiastic mechanical engineering genius with but a lay knowledge of
naval strategy, the education of the public concerning the backwardness of
the old men of the sea was both a patriotic and a personal duty. Just at the
time that Parliament made its first effort in strategy, it forced the Admiralty
to build a battleship, the *Captain,* to the design of a private inventor with
strong political connections. By the mid-1860s, public opinion in England
was playing a part in every field of policy, ship construction, and strategy.

In England, the question of the role of the public in the first two of these
areas was soon resolved. Public ideas on naval administration and industrial
production were sound, and sooner or later the navy, as it did under Childers, had to accept them. On technical issues the public burned its fingers
in the tragic affair of the *Captain,* which capsized with heavy loss of life
soon after commissioning because of faulty construction. As the 1870s began, the public and the experts were ready to concentrate on the third area
and work out together a general system of diplomacy and naval strategy. In

France, resolution of the public role in all three areas remained a problem for the future.

GRIVEL AND THE ORIGINS OF MODERN FRENCH NAVAL THEORY

French engineers had succeeded in finding ways to meet England at sea, but they badly needed a unifying set of ideas on how to use them. Like many other technical revolutions, this one had gotten away from its authors. Instead of seeing a single logical next step, the French found themselves offered several panaceas. The ideas and the confusion of the latter half of the 1860s are conveniently summarized by the real founder of modern French naval theory, Captain Baron Louis-Antoine-Richild Grivel. Grivel's 1869 work on naval war and the new inventions, though still devoted largely to technical considerations, was the theoretical point of departure for the new epoch. In it he added conclusions from his personal experiences in the Crimean War and later years to a synthesis of older principles, which were largely contained in a similar work by his father. No single person could better have represented the fusion of old and new in the set of ideas that eventually became known as the Jeune Ecole (Young School).[28]

Grivel classified naval operations in the traditional categories of war on the high seas, on coasts, and against commerce. He had a perfectly sound idea of the relationship between the latter two and the first, which Mahan later called "command of the sea." For Grivel, the reason for attempting to obtain control of the high seas was the freedom it gave to carry on secondary—but decisive—operations against an enemy's coasts or commerce. Naval strategy consisted of choosing between the various strategic theaters of operations. By gaining command of the great highroad of the sea, one side automatically restricted the other to the defensive and gained the freedom to choose between the enemy's coasts or his commerce or to attack both at once. The reason for defeating the enemy's battle fleet, according to Grivel, was "to acquire an influence and supremacy on the great roads of the sea, which will open the way for coastal and commercial warfare."[29]

> As soon as one becomes preponderant at sea, one's maritime strategy can, with relative security, give itself a sort of *carte blanche* . . . to choose between the operations which constitute maritime warfare . . . blockade the littoral of [the enemy], sweep from the seas its foreign trade, and undertake a major diversion in its rear.[30]

Grivel did not use the term "command of the sea," but he stated its fundamental nature. The sea is a road, the control of which is a necessary preliminary to attacking the enemy's and defending one's own coasts and commerce. In the case of war with a continental power, whose navy would be inferior or equal to the French, France should attempt to obtain this advantageous position.

> Mistress of the sea, could not France at will blockade the numerous
> ports of the North German Confederation . . . actively pursue the Con-
> federation's commercial shipping on the seas . . . [and] attack the enemy
> shore in the Baltic or the North Sea, creating there diversions large
> enough to give powerful support to the operations occurring at the
> same time on the Rhine?[31]

Against Prussia, it was reasonable to expect to attain command of the sea,
but England was an opponent of an entirely different nature. According to
Grivel, the whole idea of attaining equality with England by achieving in
peacetime near equality in numbers and superiority in training and ship
designs was an illusion. Historically this method had failed, and to those
historical failures France had added another defeat in the naval race of the
1860s. The greatest of modern naval constructors using the greatest financial resources France had ever thrown into the naval struggle had failed.
Even before the collapse of Napoleon III, France had again been defeated
by England, though nominal peace was maintained.

The officers who could see that the invincible ironclads of Dupuy de
Lôme were no longer omnipotent were ready to abandon the cult of technical progress that had produced them.

> Should not fleet warfare, or the warfare of the big battalions . . . be reso-
> lutely avoided as ruinous for the nation that is less rich in sailors and
> ships as well as in the means of renewing them? . . . It is on account of
> France's failure to understand such a clear situation that she has suffered
> all the maritime defeats of her history. . . . Regardless of the inventions
> that may appear, in the past or in the future . . . it is not within the
> power of any human force to displace suddenly . . . a well-established
> naval preponderance . . . based on the customs, the geographic situa-
> tion, and the vocation of a people. . . . Our navy cannot permit itself any
> illusions regarding an inequality so clearly revealed by geography, his-
> tory, and statistics.[32]

In the face of this situation, it was necessary to attack England economically.

> Commercial warfare, the most economical form of war for the poorer
> fleet, is at the same time the one best suited to restore peace promptly,
> in that it strikes directly . . . at the very sources of the prosperity of
> the enemy.[33]

Defensively, in any case, "there remains for every proud nation the common duty of defending vigorously her base of operations, maritime frontiers, and ports."

Grivel realized that war on the high seas, the prerequisite for decisive
operations against continental coasts and commerce, was impossible against

England. Even Dupuy de Lôme was powerless against the laws of economics. But adoption of the alternative of direct attack on the English coasts and commerce without command of the sea was unfortunately contrary to Grivel's own statement of the fundamental laws of naval warfare. Solving this dilemma was the basic problem that the Jeune Ecole of the 1880s set for itself, and Grivel himself did little more than state it. He narrated at great length the story of various coastal and cruiser operations, but mere description did not prove the theory.

Grivel and his successors in the Jeune Ecole who advocated cruiser and coastal warfare against England in lieu of high-seas warfare did not see that their situation was the same as that of Dupuy de Lôme. Dupuy had failed to demonstrate that modern progress could be used to overthrow England on the high seas, and the Jeune Ecole also had to show that even newer conditions had changed the old historical truth that it was impossible to attack the English coasts or commerce without first having command of the Channel. Although historical arguments were worthless, both sides worked them to exhaustion. The claim of the Jeune Ecole that France had never been able to win command of the sea from England was true, but the argument of the traditionalists that French coastal and commercial operations had always failed was equally true. The essential factor was the new conditions of coastal and cruiser warfare as applied to the specific case of England. Since the weapons used for these types of warfare were those in which changes next occurred, the arguments of the Jeune Ecole began to seem more plausible in the 1870s and 1880s. However, Grivel's writings were too early to contain much more than a statement of faith in the new methods.

The arguments in favor of coastal and cruiser warfare would probably have completely triumphed in France, as in the United States after the Civil War, were it not for another great difficulty, which Grivel met more successfully than any of his successors until 1900. France did not face one kind of enemy but two, and to adopt a matériel solely for use against England was to abandon the navy altogether as a weapon against a continental rival. Because of the need to design the navy for use against two types of foes, radical solutions were impossible, and Grivel, the founder of the Jeune Ecole, did not propose any important changes in the general composition of the fleet. From the beginning, he saw that the only possible solution for France was to retain all the elements of her fleet but to use them differently according to the enemy she faced. Against a continental power she would seek command of the sea. Against England the same forces would undertake different operations. "Would not fleet warfare become the exception, while the system of distant cruising and coast defense remains the rule?"[34] However, "without a battle fleet, [there is] no offensive coastal war nor effective protection for the nation's ports, [and] little opening for cruiser warfare."[35] To the partisans of more radical ideas, this solution was too insipid. In reality, it was the one that was reached again only in 1900. It would at least give the navy a "tactics in harmony with its means" against both the continental nations and England.[36]

Finally, to gain acceptance of these ideas, Grivel asked his fellow officers to appeal to public opinion, saying that the experts should take the nation into their confidence.

> The navy seems to remain in France a sort of poetic legend. It is loved without understanding. . . . In the press, at the rostrum of the Chamber, in books, and in our daily conversations, let us work for the naval education of our nation![37]

This also was an essential characteristic of the naval officers who were members of the Jeune Ecole—they understood at least vaguely the growing importance of public opinion. Although in many ways Grivel's ideas were sounder than those of his successors, he failed to attract public support in technical matters because he attempted to avoid too radical solutions and, more generally, because he failed to see the need for a preliminary reform of the navy's organization. In addition, his belief that his strategy offered a cheaper mode of warfare was unsupported.

Later experience showed that in dealing with public opinion, the enthusiasts who preached the complete abandonment of the capital ship, with its corollary of a fleet built solely against England, were on dangerous ground. They preached a policy of coast defense and cruiser warfare against England; the unexpected result was always coast defense against Germany and nothing at all against England. Perhaps the explanation was that even after France's worst crisis with England in this period (the Fashoda crisis of 1898), the public was never really convinced of the "inevitability" of war against this particular "hereditary enemy." After the Franco-Prussian War, most saw Germany as the main threat.

The Franco-Prussian War

In July 1870 the Prussian chancellor, Otto von Bismarck, provoked Napoleon III into starting the Franco-Prussian War, which ended in the downfall of the second French empire and the creation of the second German reich. The general objectives of the French Navy in a war with Germany as defined in the 1860s were to defeat the German ironclads, destroy the unfinished German naval bases of Wilhelmshaven and Kiel, blockade Germany's coast, destroy her commerce, and land an army corps in her rear. The French Navy greatly outnumbered the German: France had some 400 vessels (including 34 armored) and 28,000 men against 34 vessels (including 5 armored) and 6,200 men. However, the suddenness of the outbreak of war caught the navy, like the other organs of the empire, by surprise, and neither in its construction of ships for coastal operations nor in its preparation for combined operations with the army was the navy completely ready.[38]

Careful studies of the German coasts had led the French to conclude that, except in the Baltic, a landing was practically impossible. For operations in the Baltic, an alliance with Denmark was almost indispensable. While a mixed army and navy commission studied the problem of transporting an army corps, Captain Louis-Marie-Victor Palasne de Champeaux was sent to work for the alliance. He reported that Danish cooperation was practically assured, confirmed the studies of the German coast, established the essentials of an advanced base in Køge Bay, let contracts to Danish merchants for provisions and coal, and got ready to buy the goodwill of the press. The rest was left to diplomatic action.[39]

But these were only preliminary studies, and though the navy's situation was better than that of the army, a complete plan and complete matériel for immediate offensive action against the German coast were lacking, in part because of budgetary troubles. In addition, the corps of the navy's higher officers proved to be not much more cohesive than that of the army, and there was a disgraceful struggle for the command of the combined expedition between the minister of marine, Admiral Charles Rigault de Genouilly, and the commander of the Channel fleet, Admiral Louis-Edouard Bouët-Willaumez, in which the emperor himself was forced to intervene.[40]

Mobilization was extremely slow. Although the few German cruisers that happened to be abroad were easily blockaded, the opportunity to destroy the mass of the German fleet, which happened to be in dry dock in England, was missed completely; nobody was even sent to observe it. Meanwhile the Squadron of Evolutions was kept in the Mediterranean to safeguard the transport of troops from Algeria to France against purely imaginary Germans.

At the end of July the navy was ready to begin the combined operation, but by that time all hope of a successful land campaign on the Rhine had vanished and there were neither troops for an expeditionary force nor any chances of alliance with the Danes. Even so, the fleet set out, without its troops and transports, for a futile cruise off the low and stormy German coast. For twenty-five days in the North Sea and thirty-six in the Baltic, two French fleets "blockaded" the German ports in one of the most useless demonstrations in French naval history. Even at Heligoland, an island off the west German coast still owned by England, in the lee of which the French ironclads painfully coaled, merchantmen stopped to take on pilots almost as in time of peace. The big ironclads with their delicate machinery had trouble just keeping at sea, while the "blockade" itself was not enforced. Fear of trouble with England kept the French from interfering with German commerce under the British flag, and all that was really accomplished was the shutting up of a few German merchantmen in their own or neutral ports. Without a landing force or suitable matériel for forcing the harbor approaches, it was impossible to get at the German fleet, which remained in Wilhelmshaven after its hasty return from England. Bombardments of the few open commercial ports that existed would only have led to reprisals against French ports.[41]

When winter came on, even this was abandoned, and the fleets returned to Cherbourg to be stripped of their men and supplies for the general defense. Cruisers were kept observing the German fleet, the entrance to the Channel, and the Irish coast; and the German cruiser *Augusta,* which tried to repeat the exploits of the *Alabama,* was chased into the Spanish port of Vigo. The only naval action of the war was a fight between the French aviso (dispatch vessel) *Bouvet* and the German gunboat *Meteor* off the coast of Cuba.

In spite of the navy's services in assuring the free flow to France of American arms, on which all of France's efforts during the remainder of the war depended, none of the exploits the public had been led to expect were accomplished. The German fleet and arsenals remained intact, there was no landing on the German coast, and Denmark remained neutral to the end of the war. The failures of the imperial army and diplomacy had undermined the navy's plan, and the inglorious blockade of the German coast appeared to be the navy's sole contribution.[42] The British foreign secretary, the earl of Granville, had the happy idea of ending once and for all the dangers of French competition and suggested that England purchase the helpless ironclads *en bloc.*[43]

Only the navy's services on land saved it from a wave of public indignation equal to that in Italy after the ignominious defeat at Lissa in 1866. In the retreat from the Rhine and during the siege of Paris, the comparatively small group of naval officers and men was almost the center of French military resistance after the great collapse of the imperial army and the abdication of Napoleon III. These specially trained riflemen and artillerists were most valuable in the formation of the new armies from raw militia and the debris of the beaten regular army. The forts of the outer defenses of Paris were given to the navy (which organized each fort exactly like a ship), the city's defenses were organized by a committee of higher officers, and the presence of the naval troops did much toward prolonging the siege. According to one account,

> The men were well disciplined, cool, hardy, and did their work without bragging; the officers were able, chivalrous gentlemen. It cannot be said that the jealousy cherished by military men towards the sister service was much allayed by a campaign in which their own defects came out so conspicuously beside the merits of their rivals.[44]

Outside Paris, the navy also played a large part in organizing and equipping the new armies. In all, the navy furnished 55,300 officers and men,

1,032 guns, 29,300 rifles, and much other equipment to the army. The resources of the navy's arsenals were exhausted in the desperate final resistance on land.[45]

The navy emerged from the war in the strange position of having accomplished little on the sea while winning on land the admiration of the whole population, and from this can be dated the peculiar popularity that the navy subsequently enjoyed in Paris. Although lacking a true recognition of the importance of sea power, the average Frenchman showed himself ready to maintain the navy as a tribute to the attainments of its personnel. In spite of its lack of success upon the sea, the navy was never more popular than after 1871, and its officers were given important political positions in the new Third Republic, which replaced the empire of Napoleon III.

Three

~~~~~~

The Program of 1872

IN SPITE OF the popularity of its officers and men and the fact that its matériel remained physically intact, the French Navy entered a very precarious period after 1871. France had to pay an enormous indemnity to
Germany as part of the terms of peace, and the paramount task of re-
constructing the army absorbed her remaining resources for many years. In
addition, there was a resurgence of the old feeling that a maritime and colonial policy brought on disasters that its instrument, the navy, was powerless
to avert. The navy's supporters had to admit that, even had it been technically perfect, it could have done little to prevent the defeat. The two factors that combined most often to stunt French naval development—lack
of money and lack of public interest in naval affairs—were thus both enhanced by the war. When the navy began drafting its postwar building program in 1872, it found that political and military conditions had changed
drastically since the days of Dupuy de Lôme and Napoleon III.

ATTITUDES AFTER 1870

In the 1870s the feverish naval construction of the 1860s slackened or
even halted, not just in France but everywhere, because of the return of a
general peace and also because of a general distrust of navies. Of the two
powers that had brought about the naval revolution, one, France, had been
beaten disastrously, while the other, America, had turned away from the sea.
Germany, a power with an insignificant fleet, attained the undisputed military dominance of Europe and continued to show little interest in its navy.
The settlement in 1872 of the legal claims arising from the exploits of the
Alabama eliminated the tension between the United States and England.
England was thus permitted, and France forced, to live throughout the de-

cade on their naval capital. One result was that thirty years after France had started to contest English sea power by means of technical innovation, the English navy was again "equal or superior to all the fighting navies of the world put together."[1]

One additional reason for the general distrust of navies was the technical uncertainty that prevailed throughout the 1870s and 1880s. The navy built by Dupuy de Lôme in the 1860s and the one built by the British after 1889 consisted of a relatively small number of classes of ships, which were generally homogeneous. The fleets of the period in between were some of the strangest collections ever assembled, reflecting not only a rapid series of technical inventions but a state of near anarchy in the ideas of naval architects. England's policy was to wait passively until a new ship type appeared abroad and then build two bigger ones like it. France adopted a somewhat similar policy because she was too poor to embark on radical experiments. Britain's leading naval constructor explained in 1876 that

> the introduction of the screw propeller into the Navy in 1844 made a magnificent Navy obsolete; the realization of the terrible effects of shell fire in 1854 again rendered our grand screw line-of-battle ships and frigates things of the past. . . . We are bound to take care not . . . to neglect the signs and warnings that are given us. It is my duty . . . to detect at once the appearance of a new peril for the ships, or a new source of power for them.[2]

The results of this policy were often astounding, particularly when the appearance of the torpedo during the 1870s added to the confusion. As in the case of the unarmored gunboat and the ram, the torpedo's inventors made extravagant claims for it.[3] It was still so unknown and mysterious in the early 1870s that the statements regarding it were largely theoretical, and it was freely adopted by advocates of the other enemies of the battleship.[4] Indeed, gunboats, rams, and the torpedo were supported with the same enthusiasm, with the same general arguments, and even by the same people.

At the beginning of the 1870s, there was a vague general feeling among the experts that the battleship was finished, though none of them was quite sure of the way in which its end would come about. Even those who were not yet partisans of a particular new weapon often agreed with the general conclusion that the capital ship had seen its day. A book on armored ships by the secretary of the Conseil des Travaux, Paul Dislère, was written "to preserve their trace and to record, if only as a memory," the chief facts regarding their construction.[5]

In this period of general indecision, the only consistent feature was a reasoned distrust of large displacements. The ram and the necessities of coastal navigation were chiefly responsible, but an idea that occurred again and again was fear of any radical decision. Navies took care not to go too far or too fast in any direction, not to place too much money in a single ship, or in a single type, or in a definite program. A new invention would certainly render a new ship obsolete. Whether or not this idea was justified, it was certainly different from the confident acceptance of successive changes that characterized Dupuy de Lôme and his era. After 1870, every increase in size of battleships was followed by a reaction, and a typical English battleship of the mid-1880s, the *Collingwood,* was not much larger than the first English ironclad.

German Naval Policy

Some of the first new naval ideas of the 1870s came from Germany. While Germany's navy was insignificant compared to its army, it had a strong influence on naval policy in the early 1870s, particularly in France. Foreign observers who studied the work of the German General Staff after its great victory over France and its subsequent actions in the early 1870s discovered a new kind of navy, one clearly subordinate to the army and specially designed for coastal defense. It was an entirely different kind of naval force from the splendid collection of battleships and transports of the fallen French empire. For one thing, the spreading of culture to remote islands and the giving of balls for consuls abroad were not among its functions, and it did not need to maintain a large overseas station fleet. The new empire's prestige rested on more solid foundations at home.

The German navy was simply another arm of a rational system of national defense. Strategically, the chief of the General Staff, General Helmuth von Moltke, organized the navy as he organized a defensive sector on land: the navy was merely the part of the army that happened to watch the sea frontier. On land, three elements formed a defensive system: a number of strongly fortified points each containing an army, the strategic railways connecting them, and a cavalry force to observe and delay the enemy's concentration. Moltke envisaged coastal defense in an exactly similar way. Coastal observers would tell the commander of the danger, the fleet would issue from its fortified bases to delay or prevent the landings, and army divisions concentrated by rail would thrust the enemy backward.[6] On sea as on land, rapid and paralyzing concentration of superior force was the key to German military greatness. Fixed defenses were only to prevent a *coup de main* while the mobile forces were gathering.

Because of the nature of the German coasts and ports, only four points required really serious defenses: the all-important mouth of the Elbe and Weser and the ports of Kiel, Stettin, and Danzig. In the late 1890s there were only nine points on the 1,300 kilometers of the German coasts that were classified as fortifications.[7] From the very beginning, the acquisition of the English-owned island of Heligoland off the German coast and the construction of a canal at Kiel to connect the Baltic and the North Sea were recog-

The German coastal battleship Bayern *(launched in 1878). Referred to as an* Ausfallkorvette, *she was part of Germany's new coast-defense scheme and carried a main battery of six guns, four of which could fire forward.*

nized as necessary to the fully satisfactory completion of the defensive scheme.[8] The mobile sea forces that operated from the defended points while land forces were held ready to prevent a landing were easily assembled using the types of ships and weapons developed for coastal warfare during the 1860s.

Before the war, the North German Confederation had adopted a modest program of ten relatively large armored vessels, but the victory was immediately followed by a reduction to eight for the new German empire, and the modified program dragged on with a constantly diminishing level of enthusiasm for high-seas forces. British anxiety, which initially was considerable, was allayed in the course of a very few years, and even the French soon recognized that the German navy was not a serious danger.[9]

Instead, in the 1870s Germany began building a series of *Ausfallkorvetten* (sortie corvettes), which were small but powerful copies of the type of ship that Britain and France had developed for offensive coastal warfare, the misnamed coast "defense" battleships. Plans for the first four ships of this type, the *Sachsen* class, were begun in 1872.[10] According to the new ideas, these ships were to be supported by a number of armored gunvessels that would defend the minefields and thus delay the enemy's advance long enough for the mobile forces to gather. The fleet contained practically no other light forces and no cruisers except unarmored corvettes. The latter were scattered sparingly on foreign stations and supplemented at home by the well-developed coastal telegraphs, which told of an enemy's advance. The eyes of the German fleet were practically stationary, because in home waters the cruisers merely supplemented the coastal observation posts. The big ships were distributed in their bases like a garrison facing the sea.

One weakness was that the Germans completely neglected squadron tactics. They drilled their sailors like an army on shore for most of the year, and took the ships out in the summer for rudimentary sea exercises. In 1882 these consisted of firing broadsides into an old hulk at a range of 200 to 500 yards. In the same year, two efforts to visit Russia only succeeded in getting the ships as far as Königsberg.[11]

The Germans' greatest progress was in the improvement of their arsenals and in providing means for the upkeep and construction of their fleet without recourse to materials from abroad. In 1870 Germany still had no drydocking facilities for her large foreign-built ironclads. Failure and waste were inevitable at the start of the drive for industrial independence, but the result of this period of slow development and experimentation was that after 1898, Germany was able to build rapidly and without a major construction error the entire High Seas Fleet that contested Britain in World War I.

Germany's policy of a mobile coast defense on land and sea, a product of the army's domination of strategy, was a logical adaptation to defensive purposes of the matériel developed for offensive coastal warfare in the American Civil War. It was not the result of pressure from panicky public opinion but the reasoned policy of the military masters of Europe in accord with the principle of the greatest economy of forces under a unified command. It was a perfectly logical reply to Napoleon III's collection of transports and their accompanying doctrine of combined operations. It effectiveness came from the growth of land transportation and its new advantages over transport by sea, which was one of the most important military phenomena of the century. In this period, the only major power attacked successfully by a combined expedition was Russia, the power least well supplied with land communications. In addition, these attacks occurred precisely at points— the Crimea and the Far East—where Russian land transportation was particularly inadequate.

French Reaction to the War

In the early 1870s the situation of the French Navy was very precarious, despite the popularity of its personnel. At this time a formidable movement began for making the navy a branch of the army, and in spite of its historic traditions, it is probable that only the laurels of the siege of Paris and the discredit into which the army itself had fallen enabled the navy to escape the fate of the fleets of the other continental powers.

> We do not have the means (and who does?) to be a first-class power at the same time on land and at sea. But it is indispensable that our army

be strong enough to fight that of Germany. . . . To think that with the twenty-five million francs a battleship costs, we could buy and maintain the horses we need in order to have as much cavalry as the Germans, and that a division of cavalry will weigh more in the balance than the most formidable battleship.[12]

To the end of this period, the great majority of the French public regarded the navy as an expensive luxury that was kept up for the purpose of French prestige but which added nothing important to real national defensive power. The financial needs of the army and distrust of naval power itself were never stronger than after 1871. The result was, in the short term, drastic budget cuts, and, in the longer term, a profound influence on the development of French naval thought.

In reducing the navy's 1872 budget by a sixth, the able minister of marine, Admiral Louis-Pierre-Alexis Pothuau, summarized the principal emotions of the time. Noting that the navy had to sacrifice itself on the altar of the *Patrie,* he stated, "I am going to be obliged to reduce our unfortunate budget. All our efforts must be concentrated on land. Indeed, what good will a navy be to us now?"[13]

Other people had more radical proposals. One group wished a pure and simple liquidation of everything not useful for coast defense, and there was talk in the National Assembly of limiting the whole naval and colonial budget to 60 million francs instead of the 148 million requested. The navy would receive about half of that amount, leaving it at about a fifth of its former status. A second group, which included many naval officers, wished to adopt the post–Civil War American solution of saving nothing but the personnel, who were to be trained by retaining some sailing vessels. While these people did not advocate France's permanent retirement from the sea, they pointed out that most new ships were apparently doomed to rapid and catastrophic obsolescence and proposed limiting construction in the near future to floating batteries and gunboats. When naval constructors had finally decided on a new type of warship, the personnel would be ready to man it. In the meantime, in the unlikely case of trouble with England, a formidable fleet of commerce destroyers could be improvised from the merchant marine. This, the view of Admiral Théophile Aube, who later became the founder of the main reform movement of the period, the Jeune Ecole, clearly expressed the nostalgia for the *belle marine en bois,* the good old wooden navy.[14]

Neither of these theories was accepted by the Assembly, where a special investigating committee cleared the navy of all blame for the disaster of 1870. Even its failures in the Baltic were due to material causes.

> The mind is indeed confounded when it sees this formidable squadron, entirely composed of large vessels, sent to the Baltic, whose coast is accessible only to ships with a very light draft, even though it was not pos-

sible to add to the expedition the gunboats and other small craft that would be indispensable for any landing. . . . The fleet returned without having been able to fire a shot. . . . If it was condemned to inaction, this was not its fault. The courage of its leaders and sailors [on land] prove what it could have accomplished if the expedition had been better conceived.[15]

The report noted that the navy had completely protected the nation's communications and furnished important material aid to the army.

In this and later reports of the Budget Committee (the committee of the legislature responsible for reporting on each section of the annual budget), the parliamentary policy for the navy was formulated. The deputies were convinced of the necessity to retain the overseas stations "wherever the interests of our country require it, to conserve our political influence abroad and to favor the development of our commercial relations."[16] However, they asked the minister to modify the program of 1857. In other words, they favored the continuation of the old navy for maintaining "our political influence abroad," but on a more modest basis.

Again and again in the next several decades, the idea appeared of limiting the navy's expenditures to a certain unvarying, "normal" level. For example, in 1882 the Budget Committee wanted to set a fixed legal annual total that the navy should never exceed. In England, where the navy was perceived to be a real instrument of national defense and therefore a necessity, its cost varied with the diplomacy and resources of the country. French naval programs, however, as far as Parliament was concerned, were always based on an attempt to attain a stable expenditure on a highly desirable luxury, just as the prosperous businessman gave a fixed amount each year to support culture.

After fixing the amount of the navy's expenditure, Parliament returned to the old attempt to see it effectively administered. The politicians called the attention of the navy to certain reforms that they regarded as desirable. Their suggestions, modest enough, were obviously based on Childers's reforms in England. The one on which they were most insistent was a reduction in the size of the navy's personnel, particularly the officers' corps. In spite of the adverse opinion of the Council of Admiralty (the navy's senior advisory board), the deputies favored the "radical measures" of lowering the age limits for active service or of adopting a scheme of voluntary retirement.[17] Their other suggestions were reducing the number of bureaus in the central administration to three (personnel, matériel, and accounts), giving more naval construction to private industry, and limiting the minister's power to appoint officers to commands. Though several deputies wished to replace the foreign stations by flying squadrons, and though one admiral suggested reducing the number of arsenals, neither of these reforms gained the approval of either the minister or the committee.[18] The result was a relatively modest program of purely administrative measures.

The fate of this program of reforms was quickly decided. The Council of Admiralty categorically refused to accept a reduction in the number of officers except by the usual methods of retirement. In addition, while one of the seven naval departments in the Ministry of Marine and Colonies was suppressed, there was no other attempt at administrative reorganization. No naval officer, even a minister of marine, could be expected to deprive his old comrades of the sinecures due them for their long and faithful service to the state, and even had he so wished, he could not have procured the necessary support at this particular time. But by "saving the interests of the personnel," Pothuau relinquished an opportunity to reduce one of the navy's largest and least productive expenditures, meaning that cuts had to be made instead in the navy's productive elements, the fleets in commission and under construction. Finally, none of the new ships was to be built in a private shipyard, and as has already been noted, the suppression of the foreign stations and of the two least productive arsenals had not even obtained the support of the Budget Committee. Extensive economies were made within the old organization, particularly on matériel for new construction, but there were no attempts at general reform.

THE PROGRAM OF 1872: COMPOSITION OF THE FLEET

In accordance with the Assembly's request, Pothuau submitted a general revision of the Program of 1857: the Program of 1872, which became the navy's standard for the next twenty years. He explained that the navy had four general obligations:

> To maintain those stations which, in the different parts of the world, protect our commerce, spread our influence, and make our flag respected;
> To maintain a squadron of evolutions and a certain number of ships of war, veritable classrooms of military instruction where the navy's organization and discipline are conserved and developed, precious instruments of the nation's power, always ready to be thrown into the balance in questions that touch the real and serious interests of France;
> To repair and renew ceaselessly a matériel that every day becomes more costly;
> Finally, to sustain the schools from which will come the specialists who are the strength of our crews.[19]

According to this description, the navy's first duty was to preserve French prestige. Instead of cutting down on its representation abroad as later navies were to do in similar circumstances, it retained its foreign squadrons and was left with but one active organized force in European waters—and that for training the personnel. Of French warships in commission on 1 June 1872, only eleven, "the indispensable minimum for the performance of tactical evolutions," were in the Squadron of Evolutions, while eighty-one were on foreign stations or employed in coastal police duties. Although the mere comparison of numbers is not fair, the fact that there were twenty overseas stations all over the world plus some special services indicates the degree to which the old ideas survived.[20] Wherever an imperial vessel or squadron had paid an annual visit to a local chief, the honor of the republic demanded that its navy do likewise. The republican navy thus retained two of the attributes of its predecessor: an orientation toward prestige, and an emphasis on training its personnel rather than building up its matériel.

The new program abandoned, however, two other characteristics of the imperial navy—the attempt to reach equality with England and the faith in technical progress. The normal composition of the future fleet was set at 157 active units, and the value of this fixed capital, which the Budget Committee had asked the minister to determine, was roughly 400 million francs. This force represented the useful elements of the fleet that had been left by the empire. All the rest of the old fleet that could not be used for schools or other nonmilitary purposes, numbering some two hundred ships, was condemned. The program provided for replacing ships when they reached the age of twenty years, and on this basis, including allowances for depreciation, the amount needed per year to maintain the fleet's fixed capital was determined to be 64 million francs. The budget of 1872 could only allot 49 million to this purpose, but Pothuau expressed the hope that this deficit could be made up in the future.

Although a number of ships left unfinished by the empire needed to be completed, the program provided for laying down some new units to bring the fleet up to its programmed strength and to replace some of its oldest ships. These ships were to be "equal to their most perfected analogues in rival navies."[21] The fact that they were not to be superior indicated that Grivel's theory of the illusion of the continual search for technical perfection had been tacitly adopted.

The program itself contained still another change—the transport fleet of Napoleon III, which was to have reached ninety-four ships under the Program of 1857, had practically disappeared, and the twenty-five transports that remained were kept only for carrying troops to the colonies. The events of 1870 had suggested the uselessness of trying to repeat the successes of the Crimean War, and this part of the fleet was the first to fall to the economizing axe.

The new program thus retained its foreign stations in all their glory, and with them its personnel, but it abandoned the hope of attaining numerical near equality with England and technical superiority to her as well as the transports needed for operations on the continent itself. One might ask whether there was anything left of the old imperial navy but the tinsel. The memorandum introducing the program itself gave the answer. "The adoption of armored ships, appropriate to the attack and defense of coasts, and of fast ships for cruising in time of war, will allow us to constitute our naval establishment on these new bases without weakening it."[22] These ideas, like the abandonment of technical superiority, were also essentially those put forth by Grivel. The program relied on coastal warships for offensive operations against Germany and defensive operations against England, and it counted on cruisers for the offensive against England.

Although the Program of 1872 had been adopted by the navy at the request of the Budget Committee, it was not considered by the cabinet nor formally voted into law by the Assembly. Legally, it was only an explanation of the navy's intentions that accompanied the budget of 1872. As a result the navy was considered to have given a binding promise, while the Assembly and public opinion were not bound at all.

THE PROGRAM OF 1872: MATÉRIEL

The fleet of the new program was divided into three parts, each corresponding to a type of warfare—on the high seas, on coasts, and on foreign stations. The main emphasis was on the latter two, and even the designs of the program's high-seas battleships were heavily influenced by the requirements of coastal warfare.

The purpose of coastal warfare was a vigorous offensive against Germany. Even full-sized battleships were to participate, and in their designs light draft and suitability for the Baltic were primary considerations. Coastal battleships were to possess a "geographical aptitude" for an offensive in those waters, and though their defensive utility against England was seen, it was a minor consideration for their designer.[23] They were still to be accompanied by a floating siege train of armored and unarmored gunboats.

In spite of the official abandonment of the transports and the sad experience of 1870, French faith in the efficacy of regular maritime sieges and expeditions died very hard.[24] Like the cult of the ram, it long outlasted the invulnerability of armor that had begun it. The French explained the failure of 1870 by the lack of suitable matériel, not by the weakness of the concept. After obtaining command of the sea, the French Navy was to start reducing some great maritime fortress.[25] Though most of the transports had been sacrificed as the forces on land became larger, the navy clung to the remainder while completely neglecting merchant ships, which were the only means of throwing a really formidable force on the enemy's coasts.

The design of the first battleship of the new program, the *Redoutable,* was relatively conservative. Her armor was arranged on the belt-and-battery system, like the battleships of the later empire. Her guns were distributed so as to maximize end-on fire, and her high freeboard enabled her to fight in all weather. Because, according to her designer, "in our epoch a battleship must more often operate on coasts than on the high seas," she was given full sail power (a response to the arduous coaling operations off Heligoland), moderate speed, and relatively shallow draft.[26] She retained a number of

Two ships of the French Program of 1872 moored at the Brest arsenal: the battle-ship Redoutable *(1876) and the second-class coast-defense battleship* Tempête *(1876). Most of the* Redoutable's *main armament was contained in a large armored battery amidships surmounted by barbettes, while the* Tempête's *was mounted in a single turret.*

smaller guns for bombarding fortifications. Her design is significant in that, except for her armor layout, she incorporated all of the characteristic features of later French battleships: high freeboard, moderate size and speed, some heavy guns mounted in barbettes on deck, and a large secondary battery. Most of these, in turn, came originally from the need to operate in the Baltic.

That this comparative conservatism was due to a reasoned policy and not to a lack of ability on the part of the Génie is shown by the adoption of steel as the principal material for her construction. The program of 1872 definitely ended the construction of battleships with wooden hulls, which had been a feature of all but a few of Dupuy de Lôme's ironclads. (Wood was retained for most cruisers, partly out of false economy and partly because life in the early iron ships on tropical stations was practically unbearable owing to inadequate ventilation.) Although the program specified iron, the designer of the *Redoutable* proposed the immediate introduction of steel, which he estimated would reduce the weight of the hull by at least 10 percent.[27] The *Redoutable* and the first two coast-defense ships of the program, the *Tonnerre* and *Tempête,* which were laid down in July and August 1873, marked the definite change from iron to steel in French naval shipbuilding.

This shift occurred two years before the first use of steel by the British Admiralty. Even merchant shipbuilders in England were held back by the timidity of the Admiralty, although the "decidedly inferior" quality of English steel was probably also a factor. French arsenal workers at this time were more capable of handling the new material, and the shift to steel ushered in a new era of French superiority in workmanship and in the technology of ship construction.[28] Conditions in 1873 were the exact reverse of those that had prevailed during the period of Dupuy de Lôme, who had lost his battle against England's industrial strength.

The confusion in the ideas regarding battleship design in this period was dwarfed by the anarchy in cruiser policy. While the *Redoutable* and her consorts, which were remarkably successful in service, marked the birth of the modern battleship, the modern cruiser did not yet exist even in theory. The fleet that showed the flag on foreign stations in peacetime was expected to carry out commerce-raiding in time of war, but the then-current concept of commercial warfare was fundamentally unsound. In addition, the idea of using cruisers as scouts for the battle fleet was completely lacking.

As in the case of coastal warfare, the need to "show the flag" and support the interests of civilization and Catholicism overseas had, over the years, called forth an entire specialized fleet, the station fleet. The ultimate solution, building bases overseas from which ships suited for European waters could operate, was still several decades in the future.[29] As long as no other European power could send its ships to India or China, and as long as countries outside Europe could not build really formidable navies, the foreign stations were as distinct a geographic theater as the Baltic.

At the head of the station fleets were the "station battleships," a ship type developed under Napoleon III as the successor to the large wooden frigates that had previously been the flagships of squadrons overseas. The mission of these ships was to match similar English ships overseas and to fight the smaller armored ships that "backward" powers were just beginning to add to their navies. In design, they were reduced copies of European battleships with slightly inferior armor and armament and full sail power, the latter necessary because of the cost of coal and the lack of coaling stations overseas. They were similar in tonnage to coast-defense ships, but were otherwise entirely different: the station battleships had greater range, but would not have been able to stand up to the heavier guns and armor of the coast-defense ships. Too slow to run and too weak to fight battleships designed for service in Europe, they were practically useless when taken out of their geographical environment. As the *Bayard* demonstrated in France's war with China in 1884, however, they were well adapted to their intended purpose of carrying out a long campaign far from a friendly base against a

The station battleship Bayard *(1880) in the Far East, where in 1884–85 she served as Admiral Courbet's flagship during France's war with China. All four of her big guns were in barbettes, one on each side of the bridge and two on the centerline abaft the funnel.*

secondary navy. Construction of thirteen of these ships was begun under Napoleon III, and four more very similar ships were begun under the Program of 1872 in the 1870s. They were supported on the stations by a considerable fleet of unarmored cruising ships and gunboats.

The idea of using the station fleets for commercial warfare was an old one restored to favor by the success of the Confederate raider *Alabama*. In a twenty-one-month cruise covering much of the globe, this comparatively weak steamer with auxiliary sail power took more than sixty prizes. All of the Confederate raiders together captured only 5 percent of the total American merchant fleet, but their activities caused the transfer to neutral flags of another 32 percent of the world's second-largest merchant marine.[30] They did not accomplish their military objectives of breaking the Union blockade of the South or interrupting sea communications that were genuinely vital to the Union.[31] However, like the *Monitor* and the Battle of Lissa, the Confederate raiders had an enormous influence on naval thinkers of the time, and the attempt to reproduce the *Alabama*'s exploits, or defend against them, became one of the dominating ideas throughout the remainder of the century. After the *Alabama,* commerce protection gradually became a factor in English naval policy equal in importance to the control of the Channel against invasion, while repeating the raider's successes became a main objective of her rivals. Even at the beginning, advocates of commerce-raiding based their hopes on the modern idea that a relatively small number of captures would be followed by panic, but initially they also focused more on doing a large amount of indiscriminate damage than on bringing about the military collapse of Britain.[32]

The initial reaction of the major navies in the late 1860s to the revival of commerce-raiding was to increase the speed, and therefore the size, of their cruisers. The American *Wampanoag* was to be the first of seven ultra-fast *Alabama*s, while the English built the *Inconstant* and two similar ships to catch them. This effort was soon regarded as a mistake—the 5,780-ton *Inconstant* was almost as large and as costly as a battleship and carried an enormous armament of battleship guns but was entirely unarmored. In addition, the machinery of many of these ships proved delicate and expensive to operate.[33] France's plans to follow this trend were interrupted by the war of 1870, but under the Program of 1872 she built two large, fast cruisers, the *Duquesne* and the *Tourville*, which shared the shortcomings of their foreign contemporaries.

Sails were considered indispensable, even in these large cruisers, since the *Alabama*'s endurance had been due to her sails.[34] Smaller cruisers retained the sails but abandoned high speed under steam. In the program of 1872, first-class cruisers were given 17 knots, second-class cruisers 16, and third-class cruisers only 15. Later in the 1870s, speed came almost to be regarded as the least important military quality of a cruiser, and all countries returned to simple wooden corvettes. Grivel noted that great speed was indispensable in a cruising ship, but that it was the most expensive of tactical superiorities. The British designer Nathaniel Barnaby felt that "working

The first-class cruiser Tourville *(1876) in a foreign port in the 1880s. She was designed for high-speed warfare on the overseas trade routes, but was expensive to operate.*

The second-class cruiser Lapérouse *(1877) at Algiers in 1886. Typical of French cruisers of the 1870s, she carried a heavy armament of fifteen 5.5-inch guns but was relatively slow and had a wooden hull.*

speeds over 12 to 13 knots" were generally "too dearly bought."[35] Artillery, however, was rated as highly important, by Grivel and others. The idea that a heavily gunned unarmored ship had a fair chance against an armored one resulted in even the smaller wooden cruisers being loaded with artillery, further slowing them down.[36] Though the idea of seeking a large radius of action was sound, the sacrifice of speed for armament was the direct opposite of later cruiser policy, as was the phenomenon in the Program of 1872 of the weakest ships also being the slowest.

In Grivel's theory, and in the Program of 1872, the cruising and station fleets were the same.[37] The idea of building a fleet for striking a decisive economic blow had not yet arisen, and neither had the idea of waging cruiser warfare in European waters according to a definite plan. (The later successes of the *Alabama* and all of those of the next most successful Confederate raider, the *Shenandoah,* consisted of wanton damage inflicted far from the real centers of American trade.) In addition, the fusion of the commerce-destroying and the foreign-service fleets left both at the mercy of the first fast cruiser to come along with dry docks and coaling stations to work from. The whole fleet of station battleships and unarmored wooden cruisers was doomed to faster oblivion than any other part of the navies of the 1870s.

The other traditional function of cruisers, scouting for the battle fleet in European waters, was in theory to be performed by avisos (dispatch vessels), whose most interesting characteristic was that they were slower than battleships. They were also overloaded with big guns to be used in bombarding fortifications.[38] In the Squadron of Evolutions in 1872, one aviso was attached to each division of three battleships, while one larger cruiser linked the two divisions. The only feasible use for these vessels was to examine the possibilities of a bombardment or a landing—finding an enemy at sea was beyond them. If the eyes of the German coastal defenses were merely stationary observation points, the French fleet was almost totally without them.

In 1875 a young naval constructor, Emile Bertin, who ultimately proved to be a worthy successor to Dupuy de Lôme, submitted a proposal for a fast cruiser of 1,280 tons. In rejecting it, the Conseil des Travaux summarized the ideas of the time regarding cruising ships, stating that 15 knots was sufficient speed and that cruisers should be more heavily armed and protected. They concluded that the plans might do for a fleet scout or a carrier of orders "if the creation of such a type were thought necessary."[39] In both concept and execution, the fast cruiser was wholly the work of the years after 1870. In both its battleships and its cruisers, speed was the most neglected element in the Program of 1872.

EXECUTION OF THE PROGRAM

Because most of the existing French fleet had been built of wood and much of it dated from a relatively short period during the 1860s, it was absolutely necessary to maintain the rate of new construction called for in the program. The work of nature on wooden hulls was inexorable. If the ships under construction in 1872 plus the *Redoutable* were all completed by 1878, France would have nineteen battleships, including all but the five earliest wooden ironclads. However, by 1883 eleven more early ironclads were expected to have become unserviceable, and without a very considerable expenditure of effort and funds during the late 1870s and early 1880s the whole French fleet would rot from under its majestic admirals.

The Program of 1872 had been elaborated by a group of moderate naval officers who had considerable influence in the government of Adolphe Thiers, the first president of the Third Republic, and in the elected National Assembly. It was executed by a group of more conservative officers whose influence in the cabinet was reduced when Thiers was ousted in 1873 in favor of a reactionary government dominated by the army. The navy's new leaders were also less suited to appeal to the Assembly and less likely to undertake general reform.

Under Pothuau and Thiers, the budget of 1872, which allotted to new construction only 49 million of the 64 million francs required by the program, had been regarded as a transitional one whose shortages would be made up in future budgets. After the change of minister and cabinet, however, this reservation of the navy was forgotten and the reduced amount was regarded as normal. The Assembly ignored the navy's requests for the rest of its credits but blamed it for its failure to carry out the program. They thus followed what became a characteristic tendency of the French public to make demands on the navy while withholding the financial means to attain them. Indeed, the attempts of French officers to produce miracles have been noticed much more often than the fact that the French public has expected them.

The program started out 15 million francs in arrears, and the budgets of the next two years each left a similar deficit, the total arrears being reduced to 25 million francs by special loans.[40] In addition, even if the credits originally requested had been granted, they would have been insufficient to complete the program. Pothuau's estimates proved entirely too optimistic, and the rising costs of labor and raw materials combined with the increasing complexity of the warships themselves to raise the cost of the ships.

Under these conditions, the first of the conservative ministers of marine, Admiral Charles-Marius-Albert de Dompierre d'Hornoy, and his successors made desperate efforts to obtain more money. Dompierre d'Hornoy warned the Assembly of the impending disappearance of the wooden ships and of the immediate need to either revise or complete the program and asked for an increase in the annual special loan from 10 million to 23 million francs in 1876. Both he and Pothuau made impassioned personal appeals in support of a special allocation of at least 20 million francs.[41] The motion lost by a great majority, and similar attempts during the succeeding years were equally futile. In 1876 the minister of finance, amid great applause, asked the Chamber of Deputies not to consent to any such additional spending.[42] The completion of the program was put off until 1885; no one pointed out that this was practically equivalent to abandoning it.

Under the conservative government and admirals, the French Navy was not even offsetting its estimated annual depreciation with new construction. Instead, the "indispensable minimum" was still further reduced. In 1874 only ninety-four ships were commissioned, and the Squadron of Evolutions was amputated still further. The pressing appeal "to reappear on the seas, protect our nationals, take our part in the affairs of the world, and accentuate our foreign intervention, so that people again shall seek the protection of our flag, those folds of honor and moderation," had not the slightest effect.[43] The Budget Committee no longer suggested reform, and even the cuts in the officer corps were restored. Missionaries and impoverished bishops were given free transportation overseas, and a new naval station was established on the east coast of Africa. Both the ideas and the matériel of the navy were in a state of decay.

Four

~~~~~~

The Heritage

Although the wooden-hulled ships built under Napoleon III were doomed to disappear relatively quickly, the other main element of the navy's heritage, the excellence of its personnel, continued to be a source of strength. Under Napoleon III the navy had been run to a large extent by its technical services, notably Dupuy de Lôme's Génie maritime. With the fall of the empire, control returned to the regular officers, but they too were in many respects the ablest in the world. These officers had to contend with numerous problems, however, notably the stagnation and inefficiencies produced by postwar austerity and the archaic organization of the navy's administration and its arsenals.

The Officer Corps

The superiority of French officers was due chiefly to their education. Regular schools for naval officers had originated in France, and the tradition of naval education continued to be strong during and after the Second Empire. Prospective officers entered the school ship *Borda* around the age of sixteen and received five years of training in the technical aspects of the naval profession. This training was well integrated with the excellent secondary education given in French lycées, and intensive specialization in narrowly naval subjects came late in the curriculum compared to similar programs abroad.[1]

In Britain, though the navy's educational system had greatly improved since the days of Elizabeth I, when young gentlemen were apprenticed to a captain to learn the arts of navigation and command, it was still very backward. In the 1850s cadets were placed on ordinary seagoing ships under universally incompetent naval schoolmasters to receive their general education, and midshipmen performed the most menial duties on board ship or wasted their time on the fine points of navigation.[2] In the 1870s things were much better, but the old idea of catching them young remained. Prospective officers entered at the age of twelve and spent two years in a training ship and five as midshipmen. The Admiralty strongly opposed admitting a youngster from the public schools, stating that

> it is in our opinion essential that he should receive practical training in seamanship while still a boy. To abandon this for the sake of a more perfect theoretical training would be, we are convinced, a fatal mistake.[3]

This system, perfect for teaching the minutiae of life at sea, was remarkably ill-suited to the needs of modern warfare. Because the general education of the cadet was so poor, he lacked the foundations for future progress. One foreign observer concluded that "the high scientific and professional attainments of many English naval officers are not in consequence, but in spite, of their early education."[4]

The French system was not perfect—the old admirals longed to train the young in "military spirit" and "love of combat" without tackling the hard scientific aspects of the profession—but it was far superior to the English.[5] The idea of training officers on a ship was retained, but not with the same devastating results as in England. Training was largely transferred to laboratories ashore, and the training ship *Borda* became merely a floating dormitory to satisfy the old tradition. This did little harm, though life was fearfully dull because of it. Discipline was very severe but not arbitrary, and it was gradually lightened through the years to give more variety and recreation.[6] The French used the tutorial method of instruction, which was very expensive, but this part of French overhead was fortunately not cut down, and its technical results were a major factor in French naval recovery. Further changes were along lines already established, namely, to make the age of entrance still higher and to leave still more to the secondary schools. German cadets, however, whose training was the best given in any European navy, did not enter the naval academy until the age of nineteen, after all of their general education had been completed, and some commentators believed that the French were still commencing their technical training too young.[7]

Perhaps the most important problem in the French officer corps was the conflict between the young officers and the old. A similar conflict in Britain was largely a product of education and outlook: when young officers finally began to receive better training in the 1890s, they found that the capacities of their superiors were often discouragingly low. The older men in the British navy were often mentally incapable of comprehending change, and reformers such as Admiral Sir John Fisher knew it. The same conflict in France was more personal in nature, and was based primarily on two complaints: lack of opportunity for promotion, and favoritism in the few promotions that were made.

The lack of opportunity for promotion resulted in part from the period of peace and retrenchment that followed the war of 1870–71. It was compounded by the failure to follow the Budget Committee's suggestion in 1872 for an immediate reduction in the number of higher officers. But its most basic cause was the transition from sail to steam. As we have seen, the smaller ships of the modern steam navy were developed later than the armored battleship, and the many ships of the days of sail were replaced during a transitional period by a few big ironclads with relatively few supporting ships. The fleets of the early 1880s no longer had enough ships to provide commands for all the officers who were eligible for them, and officers were assigned posts of lesser responsibility in order to get the proper amount of service at sea. Captains received positions once filled by commanders, and the latter in turn got those to which lieutenants had once been appointed. Officers would often be a dozen years at sea before serving as officer of the watch on a ship of any importance. In an age when modern staff work was wholly undeveloped, the mastless seagoing ironclad threatened to make the young officer's whole life one of watch-keeping and deck drill at the very time that budgetary retrenchment cut down the chance for advancement. Every one of the older navies faced the problem, and some, notably the American, were no more successful in solving it than was the French.

In Britain, however, Childers's solution to the problem of large numbers of idle officers on the active list was drastic but effective. He reduced almost immediately the number of active officers to that required for the modern fleet by offering voluntary retirement with a high pension and an advance in rank as an alternative to remaining idle on half pay. The higher commanders fought him step by step, and even his own supporters complained of the expense involved, but some injustice to the older officers was inevitable if the problem was to be solved. The system that Childers had the courage to inaugurate became in the 1890s, like his other reforms, one of the most important factors in England's naval revival. It enabled the Royal Navy to compete with the newer navies, particularly the German with its draconic retirement system. It also assured England one of the youngest active officers' corps and the best reserve of officers in Europe.

The Admiralty treated its officers in a typically businesslike manner. It was rough with them and paid them little when they were young but held out an opportunity for rapid advancement. Because most of the higher officers were young and active, seniority was a feasible system of giving higher commands. The French regarded Childers's much-criticized reforms as an important aspect of British naval power.[8]

In France the problem of finding suitable assignments for officers was even more serious than in England. In 1873 only 22 out of 118 captains, 52 of 264 commanders, and 227 of 721 lieutenants were serving afloat.[9] However, an immediate reduction of the number of higher officers was out of the question. The Budget Committee's demand to this effect in 1872 met with the immediate opposition of both the minister of marine and the higher officers. Many of the latter were members of the National Assembly, and they united in bitter opposition to the idea.[10] Even had it been politically possible, a rational plan of retirement would have cost too much for the budget.

Instead, the navy adopted the policy of making only one promotion for every two vacancies that occurred. It thus preserved the interests of the navy's chiefs and sacrificed those of their subordinates—the older officers were retained until age carried them off, while promotions came to a standstill. In 1872, for the first time in years, no graduate of the Ecole polytechnique chose to become a line officer in the navy. The conservative minister Dompierre d'Hornoy alleviated this impossible situation somewhat by making four promotions for every five vacancies, but this left the list of officers as full as ever. The older men stayed at the top while the younger men vegetated at the bottom. By the 1880s the congestion in both higher and lower ranks was almost unbelievable. French naval officers became the oldest in Europe: in 1894 the average age of a French lieutenant was 52.3 years against 41.3 in Germany and only 32.2 in England. Although the lower-ranking French officers were relatively well paid, they were denied almost all hope of advancement.[11]

Another related problem was the physical incapacity of many of the higher officers. Many posts in the cumbersome administration in France were filled by men whose health had been broken in colonial service. When a crisis in relations with China led to war in 1884, there was also a crisis in the officers' corps. Despite the large number of admirals nominally available, it was rumored that only two, Amédée-Anatole-Prosper Courbet and Pierre-Joseph-Gustave Pierre, were fit to take command. In some ways, the lack of an adequate system of retirement was as hard on the older men as on the younger.[12]

The fate of an attempt to remedy some of the worst of these conditions was typical of French naval politics. A proposal for voluntary retirement was fought in the cabinet, the Chamber, and in their final stronghold, the Senate, by the older officers with the help of an army group who feared a similar measure. The bill was first presented on 6 July 1880 by the minister of marine, Admiral Jean-Bernard Jauréguiberry, and resubmitted by almost every new minister who followed him. The bill took ten years to get out of committee and was not passed by the Chamber until 21 December 1891. The Senate then completely emasculated it by restoring all the old age limits. On

2 June 1896 a law was finally passed providing for voluntary retirement of a lieutenant with fourteen years in that grade. Nothing at all was done to clear away the dead wood at the top. Two years later, on 15 December 1898, a new bill started the process all over again.

The inevitable dissatisfaction among the younger men was intensified by blatant favoritism in the awarding of the few available promotions. This was commonly blamed on the great naval families, which in previous centuries had ruled the navy from the great port cities (Brest, Toulon, Cherbourg, Rochefort, and Lorient) and which allegedly were reserving promotions for themselves. As in the army, social connections played a large part in advancement, even under the Republic, but by the later nineteenth century, personal connections were far more important than family connections.[13]

Throughout the first half of the century, increasing numbers of the lower landed nobility and the upper middle class had come into the navy. The navy offered a prestigious career for second-generation bourgeois and an honorable employment for nobles of declining fortunes for whom the military academy at St. Cyr was too expensive. The interest of Napoleon III in the navy attracted his supporters in the upper bourgeoisie into the service. As in England, the hereditary naval families had never been among the great aristocracy, and the social amalgamation of the new elements (which did not include self-made men from the lower classes) was easy. The result was the end of the traditional monopoly of the navy by the naval ports and the first step toward producing a truly "national" navy.

Although the members of the older nobility remained, they were gradually outnumbered by newcomers who had risen by a combination of merit and personal connections. In the great naval activity of the Second Empire, there were many opportunities for ability to rise to the top. Admiral Laurent-Joseph Lejeune began his career as a common sailor, and Admiral Georges-Charles Cloué was the son of a desperately poor Paris clothing worker without any family connections at all.[14]

In the years after the fall of the empire, the proportion of cadets from naval families remained relatively constant, but the number of promotions and the chances for distinction grew less.[15] The importance of personal sponsorship remained unchanged and, under the new conditions, led to a great deal more injustice. Under the navy's promotion system, officers were chosen by their immediate superiors for a table of advancement, from which a committee of higher officers filled the vacant posts. But since the committee was not required, as in the army, to exhaust nearly all the list, getting on it gave no guarantee of promotion. When the officers on the committee were faced with a long list of men of equal ability, they naturally tended to pick those they knew. Thus men who had occupied staff positions in Paris or who had served under one of the members of the committee were almost certain to advance, while those who had served with ability on foreign stations could be on the list year after year and never advance. The same system was used to award officers command of ships, with similar results: many of the heroes of the Tonkin expedition of the early 1880s were completely neglected by the boards in Paris.[16] The situation eventually became so bad that even the conservative newspaper *Le Temps* began commenting on the extraordinary abilities of the sons of admirals and ex-ministers. After 1890 the whole system was considerably revised, but by then much damage had been done.[17]

POLITICS AND THE OFFICER CORPS

One of the most important results of this system was the personal character of the public debate over naval strategy in France in the 1880s and 1890s. In all countries, the younger officers welcomed the advent of torpedo and cruiser warfare as offering new opportunities for individual initiative and daring at the very time that the mastless ironclads were routinizing naval life. In France, the opposition of the senior officers to these new forms of warfare, at the very time that these officers were stifling other opportunities for advancement through means that verged on the scandalous, appeared to be one more element in a great reactionary conspiracy. As a result, some naval writers took up the new ideas in part as weapons against the establishment. For example, Lieutenant Emile-Charles-Eutrope Duboc, one of the heroes of Tonkin ignored by the committees in Paris, became one of the leading publicists of the Jeune Ecole. In turn, some politicians adopted the new naval ideas as weapons against their enemies on the right in the Chamber. The result, by the 1890s, was a relatively rare phenomenon—the politicization of naval strategy.

Although the polemics of the late 1880s and 1890s gave the impression that the navy was a bastion of political conservatism, this was not the case. Like the French upper middle class and lower nobility in general, and also because of their close connection with Napoleon III, many naval officers were Bonapartists, rather less reactionary than the monarchists in the army and much more willing to cooperate with the Republic that had succeeded the Bonapartist empire. In any case, ever since the great purges of the Revolution, the navy had not taken part in national political life. The sole aim of the naval chiefs, regardless of their private political convictions, was to keep the navy intact, not preserve or support a given political order. Unlike the army, the navy did not respond when a "man on horseback," General Georges-Ernest Boulanger, arose as an alternative to the democratic republic in the mid-1880s.

However, two indefinable but very important characteristics of the navy's officer corps played an important psychological role in the relations of the navy with the politicians in the 1890s. Whatever their intellectual sympathies with the moderate parties, the majority of French officers acted and looked aristocratic. Even those of "democratic" origins were extremely reserved in their personal contacts with their "inferiors." This characteristic was not uncommon in the second-generation bourgeois, and it fitted well with French naval tradition. The "air" of French officers and the distance between officers and men were always particularly noticed by English and American observers.[18] Politically, it clearly made a difference. It was difficult enough to make the *parvenu* lawyer-politicians in the Chamber understand the importance of the navy without adding this personal barrier.[19] Perhaps of equal importance, the methods used to handle the traditionally obedient and simple Breton deckhand were wholly inappropriate to the intelligent specialist required to run the new weapons.

Another personal characteristic of the older French officers that was also often wholly unconnected with their political views was the fact that most were Breton and Catholic. In addition, the close relationship between missionary Catholicism and French colonial expansion made even skeptical officers conform to the particularly pompous form of Catholicism in vogue on foreign stations and in Breton ports (notably Brest). Although this had little to do with the clericalism and reaction that republican politicians sought to root out of French society in the 1880s and 1890s, it was a fertile source of irritation between the navy's chiefs and left-wing politicians and publicists. Admiral Louis-Henri comte de Gueydon, although perfectly loyal and relatively moderate, was a stern disciplinarian and a very devout Catholic in his private life. Admiral Jauréguiberry, another moderate who became minister of marine, was a Protestant and conducted public prayer meetings while he was maritime prefect at Toulon in the 1870s. Admiral Abel-Nicolas Bergasse Dupetit-Thouars, when maritime prefect at Cherbourg in 1885, followed an Easter procession in full uniform, candle in hand. The next year the government tried politely to dissuade him from repeating this scandalous conduct, and this time his whole staff accompanied him. Ironically, it was Gueydon, this incarnation of the old naval aristocracy, who laid the foundation of the French torpedo boat establishment at Cherbourg and helped shape the ideas of one of the best thinkers of the Jeune Ecole, Admiral François-Ernest Fournier.

The situation of naval officers in France was thus a very complex one, in which technical, political, social, and even psychological elements played a part. Although unrivaled technically, these officers were generally unable to bridge the gulf that separated them from many of the elements of French society, and they were ill equipped to appeal to public opinion. In addition, the officer corps was split, for the failure in the 1870s to reduce the number of higher officers and solve the problems of promotion and pensions created a group of dissatisfied younger officers and gave rise to many charges of favoritism. The navy was also not much better fitted than the army to find a satisfactory solution to the problems of the relations between officers and men. One result was that all these personal problems fueled the debate over strategic doctrine. The proponents of the ideas of the Jeune Ecole were joined by civilians demanding organizational reforms, by socialists wishing better treatment for the men, by politicians who detested the haughty clerical admirals, and by those who merely thought the navy too expensive.

THE CREWS

Except for some specialist volunteers, the crews of the French ships were composed of common sailors from the *Inscription maritime* instituted by Colbert in the seventeenth century. Colbert's original purpose had been to replace the brutal methods of the press gang with a more stable and efficient system for manning his new fleet. All Frenchmen who followed the sea were enrolled (*inscrits*) on the register, and all were legally obligated for certain services in the navy. Fair pay, good food, and just treatment, with pensions for the wounded, old, and widows, were the humanizing features of this legislation. Throughout the period of the wars with England, life in the French fleet bore no resemblance to the horrors of the English navy.

Crew members demonstrating their trades aboard the torpedo aviso D'Iberville *(launched in 1893). Represented are engineers, quartermasters, signalmen, gunners, and deckhands. The bridge of this ship was between the two funnels.*

Easily adapted to modern universal military service after the French Revolution, the *Inscription maritime* remained the basis of the French naval recruiting system. In return for the obligation to serve, the *inscrits* received certain privileges from the state. The most important were a monopoly of all the maritime industries of France and a pension after 300 months of service in either the war or the merchant fleets. Although this system was seriously threatened in the name of economic liberalism in the days of Napoleon III, the only major victory of its opponents was the removal of workers in the shipbuilding industries. A similar attack in the 1890s changed only some minor details.[20]

Italy, Spain, and Austria simply copied the French system, and only Germany was able to improve it greatly.[21] There, recruits were chosen by the navy from certain categories in the general army levy, such as sailors, mechanics, stokers, and electricians, making an expensive separate organization unnecessary. The insurmountable obstacle to this solution in egalitarian France was the absolute necessity for naval service to be at least a year longer than army service, which meant that the monopolies and pensions had to be retained as compensations.

The navy's petty officers and most of its skilled ratings came from two sources. Some were reengaged *inscrits* who had already fulfilled their legal service requirements. Others were long-term volunteers drawn from the general population.

The average cost per man on board ship was considerably less in France than in Britain, but the pensions consumed much of the savings.[22] French sailors were better fed but more poorly housed than the English.[23] French ships also tended to have larger crews and were more wasteful of labor—the British Admiral-class battleships had around 475 men each, while the contemporary French *Marceau* type had around 600.[24] The extra men in French ships often represented a residual tendency to rely on muscle instead of mechanical power. These factors, along with the expense of constantly educating new recruits, made the financial advantages of compulsory service mostly illusory. Only in the number of their reserves were the continental systems better than the English system of volunteers.

The men furnished by the *Inscription* were from the fishing population of the port towns. Although the fleet itself was concentrated in the Mediterranean, it was manned, as for centuries past, by Bretons. In 1892 Brest alone furnished 46 percent of the new *inscrits,* and Brest and Lorient together furnished 64 percent.[25] The Bretons were good seamen and easily disciplined, but as the machinery of men-of-war became more complex, they became less satisfactory. The backward primary schools for the French fishing population gave them only rudimentary instruction, and many spoke Breton but not French when they were called to commence their service. (In 1878, 14 percent were absolutely illiterate, 17 percent could read and write a little, and 23 percent could read and write but not calculate.)[26] They were generally strong and fairly intelligent, but were particularly lacking in mechanical aptitude because of the poverty of their origins.

Though the crews of French warships were very good, they required an expensive system of training. Schools for men and petty officers were highly developed. Neither the English with their long term of service nor the Germans with their good primary education had as serious a problem. Instead of drawing on the merchant marine for trained sailors as did the English, the French Navy educated men who later served in the merchant marine, thus reversing Colbert's original intention. Despite its expensive organization, the *Inscription* furnished only the basic common labor for the fleet and was far from being a perfect way to man a modern navy. As in the case of the officer corps, the splendid naval tradition also had its disadvantages.

THE CENTRAL ADMINISTRATION

Another heritage of the past was the navy's unreformed Ministry of Marine. It too had come down from Colbert, and its nonmilitary functions, notably the colonies, the fisheries, and the merchant marine, were a remnant of his naval-colonial-mercantile system.

The chief characteristic of the internal organization of the ministry was that its many organisms all depended on a single head, the minister himself. The minister made all the decisions, the councils advised him, and the bureaus executed his orders. If, for example, a new gun was to be adopted, the first step was for the technical artillery service to prepare designs for it. The minister then consulted one of several councils of naval officers as to the desirability of the change, examined with the directors of matériel and accounts its financial consequences, and determined from the director of personnel its effect on the size of the crew. With all these factors in mind, he made his decision and gave orders to the services for its execution.

This was an excellent system for the careful consideration of a small number of questions of principle, provided that changes were few, leisurely, and general in nature. Yet by the 1870s the Conseil des Travaux, which handled naval construction, the Council of Admiralty (later the Superior Council), which deliberated general questions, and the Inspectors General, experienced officers who were consulted on other technical matters, were flooding the minister with technical "advice," to which his consent was usually automatic. He had the option, however, of ignoring it—legally the councils were purely consultative. In addition, they were neither legally nor financially responsible for the results of their recommendations.

In the area of naval construction, the often automatic consent of the minister and the lack of responsibility of the councils had serious results. After the departure of Dupuy de Lôme, no central bureau closely supervised the preparation of designs and plans for ships, and it became impossible to fix responsibility for them. The first step in the normal process of designing a ship was for the ministry to provide a preliminary list of specifications for armor, speed, and guns. The Conseil des Travaux approved it if it appeared suitable for further work. Several engineers then drew up more detailed plans, and the Conseil and the ministry generally approved the best of these, with changes. The minister then ordered the start of construction, and all major changes in the design that were made during construction were submitted to the Conseil.

A major problem with this system arose because some French ships took a long time to build. The Conseil that approved the original plans of the battleship *Magenta* in 1880 was composed of different members from that which decided a couple of years later on the artillery that she ultimately carried. Half a dozen councils and ministers eventually had a share in her construction. When she was completed in 1893 and found to be defective, who was responsible? Three of the ministers were dead and most of the council members retired, while the original author of the plans had had his ideas mutilated beyond recognition by the various changes.

Another problem with the Conseil was that it was unaware of financial considerations and often proposed solutions that were technically perfect but financially impossible. Composed as it was of older officers, it was generally a veritable bulwark against progress. Sometimes the results were good and sometimes they were bad, but an ardent reform-minded minister like Aube (1886–87) or Edouard Lockroy (1895–96, 1898–99) was not required to take its advice at all.

The executive administration of the ministry consisted of four major bureaus (besides the colonies): matériel, personnel, accounts, and administration. (The latter was a miscellaneous bureau covering the *Inscription,* fisheries, wages, and hospitals.) The Bureau of Accounts was a typically French bureaucracy; instead of being merely an auditing group, it controlled a whole separate corps of accountants spread throughout the navy. The result of its efforts was that a year after a naval constructor spent his money, he got from Paris a report telling him what an English constructor, who kept his own records, knew the next day. At the top of the administration was the personal secretariat, or *cabinet,* of the minister.

Thus, while the English naval administration had two major and two minor divisions, the French had two large and several minor councils, the inspectors general, four major and two minor bureaus, the *cabinet,* the colonies, and the five naval prefectures (one for each of the naval ports), all directly responsible to the minister. The only way the system could creak along at all was under a group of men who knew all its branches equally well and who were united on major questions of doctrine. It was badly in need of reorganization. In the meantime, it was very difficult for a single man to speed up this complex machinery, but very easy for him to create considerable disorder.

The admirals who controlled the ministry in the 1870s at least partially filled these requirements—they knew the system and were fairly united on doctrine. Until 1888, not a single minister of marine had been a civilian: it was as if the admirals designated one of their number as an ambassador acceptable to the Chamber and the government, exactly as they detailed other officers to various commands. The general career pattern was for an officer to become chief of staff to the minister, then maritime prefect at Toulon or Cherbourg, commander of the Squadron of Evolutions, and, after retirement at age sixty-five, minister of marine. The navy was essentially run by a small group of the more vigorous senior officers, and the minister was simply the one who was given the thankless task of wringing money from the reluctant cabinet and Chamber. Even after 1888, the civilian ministers were, for the most part, so lost in the various details that they could not do without the admirals. The major shortcoming of the admirals was that, although they were excellent at routine matters, they could not undertake reform and had little chance of establishing good relations with Parliament, the cabinet, or public opinion. As long as reform was not mentioned, the admirals, with their wide experience in naval administration, were able to keep the navy operating.

The admirals who assumed the direction of the navy after the fall of Napoleon III in 1870 were comparatively moderate. These officers, who had taken part in the defense of Paris, also played an important role in the general politics of the government of Adolphe Thiers. The minister, Pothuau, was only one of a number of naval chiefs who loyally supported Thiers: Captain (later Admiral) Constant-Louis-Jean-Benjamin Jaurès played a leading part in holding the moderates together, and Admiral de Gueydon was sent to put down a native revolt in Algeria. All of these moderates were able and popular with the National Assembly.

With the fall of Thiers in 1873, the army returned to power in matters of general policy. Within the navy itself, power fell into the hands of reactionary leaders. They were totally unsuited to appeal to public opinion, and their administration of the navy was less active, less open to reform, and more pervaded with family and political favoritism. The minister of marine took very little active part in general politics, and he was generally one of the old royalist, clerical nobles who sat quietly in a corner of the Assembly.

Still worse, the reactionaries carried their political views into the operation of the navy and broke a number of liberal officers for no reason other than their private republicanism. The most notorious cases were those of a number of captains who had played an important role in the war and had risen provisionally to the rank of general in the army. Returned on the conclusion of peace to their former naval rank of captain, they expected to be promoted by seniority as the positions above them became vacant. Under the reactionaries, some of these men were publicly passed over. The outstanding examples were Captain Auguste Gougeard, the hero of the battle of Le Mans and later a minister of marine, and the brothers Du Temple, one of whom was an important inventor of steam machinery. In addition, a number of rear admirals, including Aube, were not given turns at command for similar reasons.[27] On the other hand, the rather dubious war record of the aristocratic Captain Charles-Marie Duperré (who left the country with the empress in 1870 and was interned) did not, so far as the republicans could see, hinder his advancement in the slightest. The discontented younger officers found some support among embittered older officers because of these conditions, providing additional strength and a leader (Aube) to the reform movement that became known as the Jeune Ecole.

The Dockyards

The other essential part of the navy's heritage, besides its personnel, was its industrial base. The fleet's industrial system in the 1870s remained as it had been during the empire, centered in the five great naval ports. The most important of these arsenals were Toulon, the only naval port in the Mediterranean; Cherbourg, the "sentinel of the Channel"; and Brest, at the tip of the Breton peninsula. The other two, both historical accidents, were Rochefort, a legacy of the Wars of Religion of the late seventeenth century, and Lorient, the former headquarters of France's East Indies trading company. Despite differences in size and location, each of the ports had the same three general responsibilities: the administration of a district called a maritime prefecture, support and maintenance of the fleet, and construction of warships. In the case of Rochefort and Lorient, this resulted in wasteful duplication, but their specialization or closure was rejected by the Budget Committee. The role of private industry was limited to furnishing raw materials, despite the recommendation of the Budget Committee that more ships be built in private yards. The navy also had three secondary establishments that supplied certain key parts of new ships: Ruelle built guns, Guérigny provided anchors and chains, and Indret supplied steam engines and boilers.

The internal organization of the ports had not been reformed significantly since the age of sail, and it was still structured to support a relatively small fleet in service backed by a large reserve of ships on the building ways ready for launching and rapid completion. As late as 1840, France was still following a system that originally had been developed by Venice: half of her navy was in "dry land" reserve, incomplete on the building ways with its fittings and stores in warehouses. By the 1870s the policy of keeping a reserve of ships on the ways had vanished, but the industrial system optimized for the simultaneous, slow construction of a relatively large number

The Brest dockyard in the early 1880s. The transport Tage *(launched in 1847, originally a line-of-battle ship) is passing through the swinging bridge. The hulks and service craft in the foreground are typical of navy yards of the period. Among them are three early torpedo boats: the large* No. 27 *and two smaller Thornycrofts of the* No. 8 *type.*

of ships remained. The maritime prefect (the civil director of the dockyard) still supervised two commissaries, one for labor and one for materials. The latter bought the simple materials—wood, masts, canvas, and a little iron and copper—and issued them to the construction service. The duty of the former was to keep the permanent force of carpenters and blacksmiths occupied as economically as possible. To accomplish this, a large number of ships were kept on the ways to absorb their labor when hurried new construction or repairs were not needed. When the fleet entered port, labor was shifted to repair work, and new construction stopped entirely. Admirably fitted to the simple days of sail, these principles were still the foundation of French arsenal organization at the end of the nineteenth century.[28]

The red tape associated with this system was formidable. Constructors directing work on a new ship had to negotiate through the prefect for materials from the warehouses, and these central magazines became battlegrounds for all the services in the arsenal. Typically the French adapted not by reforming the system, but by making piecemeal changes. In this case they speeded up the supply service by gradually establishing a lot of submagazines. To avoid having to ask for a new supply of standard objects every day, a constructor would order a great number from the main magazine at one time and then store them in a little subwarehouse where he could get them quickly when needed. The result was that, eventually, the general magazine existed only on paper. To order the materials, the constructor duly sent a form through the prefect to the submagazine, which would inform the fictitious general magazine that the object was needed. The object would be delivered directly from the submagazine to the ship, but the records would solemnly tell of its voyage from the general magazine to the submagazine to the constructor. The number of men and the tons of paper employed in this system were staggering—in a single year, the arsenal at Toulon had to present 14,332 different records simply to tell of its doings with its own magazine.[29]

Even worse than this red tape was the actual waste of materials that resulted from this archaic system. In the days of sail, one of the duties of the director of the theoretical general warehouse was to keep the supply of each item up to its allowed limit. When the stock of cordage, wood, or anchors was getting low, he was empowered and expected to replace them. The refilling of the magazine thus took place almost automatically. Material was also produced for stock to give work to foundries during periods of retrenchment. For an age in which maritime equipment remained about the same, this system was fairly efficient, but in an age in which the number of standardized products was rapidly diminishing, it quickly produced warehouses full of useless objects.[30]

Childers resolved similar problems in England by establishing a central purchasing department, which contracted with industrial firms for immediate production to order of needed spares. It was still essential to maintain stocks of ammunition and fuel, but stockpiling spare parts and other "naval stores" as in the days of sail proved to be highly wasteful in an era of rapid technological change. France, however, continued to maintain a decentralized supply system, consisting of a purchasing department in each port with a lot of additional appendages.

The degree of control over naval construction was further confused by the position of the maritime prefect. Although this had originally been a civilian post, it had taken on so many military functions over the years that in the nineteenth century the incumbent was always a vice admiral, comparable in rank and powers to the governors of the great fortresses on the eastern frontier with Germany. His authority in industrial matters was mostly theoretical, however. He spent most of his time arbitrating questions of detail between his seven continuously squabbling bureaus, and on technical matters he had insufficient time or interest to be more than a rubber stamp for his constructors. In case of dispute, the telegraph made it easy for the constructors to bypass him and appeal to the minister. The minister, in turn, referred the matter to the ministry's Bureau of Matériel, which was composed of colleagues of the constructors in the ports. After several such conflicts, even the most stubborn prefect was easily subdued. However, the constructors always hid behind his authority when they made mistakes.

The result was a highly inefficient industrial system in the French naval dockyards. In each port, there was no special organization solely responsible for the production of warships. There were instead two organizations, construction and matériel, coordinated by a prefect whose time was taken up with a whole variety of other functions. In addition, the outdated practice of simultaneously working slowly on a large number of ships was continued, and in allocating new work it was always necessary to give each arsenal its "share."

These practices violated one of the primary laws of the industrial age—that obsolescence begins at the time a design is made, not at the time the equipment is completed for use. Once again, the French responded not by reforming the system but by making piecemeal changes. They continued to build many ships simultaneously, but they tinkered with their designs during construction to eliminate features that had become obsolete or to add new features. In 1872, in spite of limited funds and although five battleships previously ordered had hardly been begun and three more still needed to be completed, Pothuau laid down three new battleships. In 1880–81 four first-class battleships, the *Hoche, Marceau, Magenta,* and *Neptune,* were laid down simultaneously despite a sizable backlog of construction. In 1888 the *Hoche* and *Neptune,* with two ships begun in 1878, were still completing, and the *Magenta* and *Marceau* were less far advanced. This was not caused by the size or complexity of these ships, for four armored gunboats and a torpedo cruiser of about 1,200 tons begun in 1882 were in the same condition.[31] A similar situation existed in England and was only liquidated by concerted efforts between 1886 and 1889.[32]

Tinkering with designs became so bad that ships were begun before their designs were completely settled, and every gadget invented during their construction was immediately incorporated into them. The adventures of the *Magenta* in the Conseil des Travaux make one wonder how she was ever built at all. As first approved on 7 October 1880, her design called for a ship of 9,800 tons and 14.5 knots that carried three 13.4-inch guns on the centerline. The contract for her hull was signed on the basis of these plans on 26 December 1880. The next year the Conseil changed the armament to two 13.4-inch and two 10.8-inch guns arranged in a lozenge pattern. This increased the Conseil's enthusiasm, and in the course of the next few years it replaced the two 10.8-inch guns with 13.4-inch, added 716 tons to the displacement, lengthened and broadened the ship, increased her speed to 16 knots, gave her military masts, torpedo nets, searchlights, and an armored conning tower, and finished her off with a battery of small quick-firing guns. Somewhere in the middle of this process the contract for her machinery was signed on 23 April 1883. When completed in 1890, the *Magenta* was

The battleship Neptune *(1887). A sister of the* Magenta, *she was encumbered by the same high superstructures and heavy masts that caused Parliament to investigate her sister during the 1890s.*

300 tons overweight and her initial stability had been decreased by about a third. It took ten months to get her ready for her trials, which resulted in the development of a new method for working her guns. In November 1893, perhaps in honor of her thirteenth birthday, she was finally commissioned.[33]

The British did not tinker as much with their ships during construction, but they made up for this with their repair practices. As soon as a British ironclad was paid off after a period in commission, the dockyard started tearing her apart to improve her. Since a ship was torn down as soon as she entered the yard and reconstruction did not begin until the ship was signaled as needed, a sudden demand for ships, as in the war scares of 1878 and 1885, produced a veritable panic in the arsenals.[34] Repairs in France were a little more rapid but equally useless, and they were accomplished only by stopping all new construction. In addition, in both countries the arsenal foremen and ship captains were free to make innumerable petty changes in cabins, steam pipes, and the like, which made no difference whatever in the ship's efficiency but were very expensive.

In general, during the 1870s, ship construction and repair in France was neither slower nor more wasteful than in England. The *Redoutable,* which was built in five and a half years, was built no more slowly than her foreign contemporaries. Only in the late 1880s, when England began building battleships in less than three years while France was taking ten or twelve, did the French practices become a military weakness. In addition, during the 1870s and early 1880s the costs of warship construction were about equal in the two countries, although France was wholly unable to compete in merchant ship construction.[35] The ability of the French dockyards to compete was probably due to their superior machine tools. Because of the recent introduction of these tools, the French dockyards in the late 1870s and early 1880s were in the position of Germany in 1900: their newly equipped shops were competing with English tools and methods that were becoming obsolescent. This enabled the French arsenals to produce as cheaply as the English despite the higher costs of their materials.[36]

The French arsenal workers, like the carpenters of the sail navy, were a relatively stable body of highly skilled craftsmen who were employed whether there was work to be done or not. Their number was larger in France than in England but their pay was lower; the chief consolation of the French workers was the hope of a pension. Hours were very long (nine to twelve hours in France, ten hours in England). Along with its new machinery, the French Navy enjoyed an unusually abundant supply of cheap labor.[37] English labor later achieved superiority owing to the use of piece-work, higher pay, shorter hours, and a flexible hiring service, but these practices only took effect after 1888. Until then, the arsenal worker in both countries was a veritable *fonctionnaire,* working a little and paid a little but satisfied with his secure position.[38]

The workers and the entire population of each port town were united by common interest in solid opposition to any change, which made the deputies from dockyard *départements* like Morbihan and Var even more formidable than the "dockyard Members" in England. They were too few to conduct raids on the Treasury, and their annual motion to raise the salaries of the arsenal workers was only a conventional gesture. However, like other similar little groups in the Chamber, they were marvelously successful in blocking reform. By fighting all reformers to a standstill on issues like the specialization of the ports, they ultimately probably cost the navy more than did the well-publicized rapaciousness of private arms suppliers like Creusot.

As in all sectors of French labor, the old corporate ideas were still very strong among the arsenal workers. In spite of regulations that were supposed to ensure the contrary, the workers were almost exclusively sons or relatives of persons already in the shops. One of their chief aims in life was to have the monopoly of their trade and to pass it on to their children as the French peasant did his soil. In spite of demands for labor in the rest of France, they preferred security to migration, and one of the most characteristic demands of their syndicates was the practical exclusion of outside labor from the dockyards. Their resistance to change was typical of the way in which the navy as a whole resisted reform of its organization and its personnel.

Five

New Factors: French Maritime
Industries

Despite the richness of its heritage, the navy left to France by Dupuy de
Lôme and Napoleon III had not fully entered the modern industrial
age. The fleet of the mid-1870s had armored battleships but lacked the
other two categories of ships that became so important in the late nineteenth century—fast cruisers and the torpedo flotilla. In addition, the navy
lacked a rational organization and had not solved the problem of its relations with public opinion and the politicians of the new republic. Finally, its
personnel were trained but not organized for war, and the navy, with its
multitude of nonmilitary missions, was still not completely or exclusively
an instrument of national defense.

Several changes during the late 1870s and 1880s thrust the French Navy
squarely into the modern era. The later 1870s in France were marked by a
strong military and economic revival and were followed by a period of vigorous colonial expansion in the early 1880s. Three specific factors were of
particular importance to the navy: the development of private maritime industries; the appearance of new naval rivalries, notably between France and
Italy and between England and Russia; and a burgeoning colonial rivalry
between France and England. Of these, the most essential was the development of the industrial and technological base that enabled France to compete with her new rivals.

THE MERCHANT MARINE

The two basic industries that were the foundation of French naval power,
the merchant marine and the steel industry, were closely connected. The
Chevalier-Cobden treaty, which tore down the tariff barriers between France
and England in 1860 in the name of economic liberalism, was a serious

blow to both of them. Neither France's merchant marine nor its metallurgical industry were then equal to those of England, and the immediate results of English competition were disastrous. The Third Republic ultimately restored protective legislation for both, but their histories in the intervening years differed.

The merchant marine had not occupied a brilliant place in French economic life, but the decline of the American merchant marine during and after the Civil War left the French the second largest in the world. French foreign trade reached a high point in 1865, and in that year about 40 percent of French commerce was carried under the French flag. The revival of the French merchant marine had been under way for many years, and it had been one, though not the chief, reason for France's naval awakening after 1840. Under Napoleon III the protection of French commercial shipping was an important function of the navy, and in 1870 the navy expended considerable effort in blockading in neutral harbors the few German warships that happened to be abroad.[1] However, the abolishment in 1866 of the whole system of preferential port dues, which had come down from Colbert, started the decline of the French merchant fleet. The crisis caused by the war with Germany accelerated the decline, and by 1879 the French merchant marine had again sunk to third place behind America and was carrying only 27 percent of French commerce.

In 1872 Thiers tried to cope with this problem by placing a surtax on foreign flag ships using French ports, but the vigorous protests of England at this violation of the treaty of 1860 and a reported threat to send an English squadron to Le Havre caused it to be hastily abandoned.[2] After 1872 the great prophet of the revival of protection, in the form of a direct subsidy for the merchant fleet, was Dupuy de Lôme. After his retirement from the navy he worked unceasingly to bring it about.[3] Finally, following a long series of investigations, a law of 1881 established direct navigation bounties for French-owned merchant ships and produced a vast mushroom growth in French merchant shipping. At the same time, a major program of public works initiated by the government of Louis de Freycinet led to sizable investments in seaport development and a boom in the economy as a whole. By 1887 French commerce carried in French ships had risen to almost 37 percent, nearly the level reached during the Second Empire.

But the maritime revival of the 1880s proved to be a flash in the pan. To begin with, the law of 1881 was badly drafted. It was to run for ten years, and in order to get bounties for as much of that time as possible, shipowners immediately rushed to order new shipping.[4] As a result, the new construction was concentrated in the years 1881–85 and stopped completely after that. More significant was the character of the new ships that were built. They were almost entirely in two classes: fast mail and passenger liners to serve the Far East, Brazil, America, and certain Mediterranean ports; and small ships for the local trade between Algeria and France and along the coasts. In spite of the new law, the French did not build ships in the great middle category, the tramp cargo steamer, and try to break into the common carrying trade.

The shape of this new merchant marine was the basis of one of the most characteristic ideas of the Jeune Ecole as it developed in the early 1880s. Because French maritime trade was primarily in luxury goods and services, France was practically invulnerable in commercial warfare with England. Even a complete temporary stoppage of French trade would not be a serious loss to the nation. The liners would not be missed as merchantmen and would make excellent auxiliary cruisers, and the small vessels that made up the rest of the French merchant fleet were not worth serious protection. Thus, in contrast with the later experience of Germany, the revival of the merchant marine in France did not lead to any great new sentiment for the creation of a high-seas fleet for its protection. Quite the contrary— the Jeune Ecole was ready to accept the loss of all of France's maritime trade in a war with England.

THE STEEL INDUSTRY

Under Napoleon III, France's metallurgical industry, like its merchant marine, was old and respectable but not a brilliant performer. During the 1860s the navy continuously suffered from high-priced and mediocre raw materials. In spite of the navy's efforts, the French iron and steel industries remained far behind the English, both in commercial strength and in the quality of their products. In the 1860s the French iron industry was concentrated in or near the upper Loire valley, and most of the old firms, like that of Le Creusot, were engaged in all forms of commercial iron production. When France was at war they temporarily turned to war materials, but in peacetime they made ordinary commercial products. The armor of Dupuy de Lôme's ironclads was made of wrought-iron plates not greatly different from material produced for civilian use. There were no private gun factories—both army and navy guns were constructed in the foundries of the state.

The removal of the tariff barrier was as disastrous for the metallurgical industry as for the merchant marine, and between 1866 and 1870 the ironmakers were in a state of near collapse. The stronger firms, in a desperate effort to meet the competition, improved their equipment and launched themselves into the then unknown field of steel production. By 1870 the Bessemer process for producing steel was as widespread in France as in England, and the new open-hearth furnace of Pierre Martin was just being introduced.[5]

When the Franco-Prussian War began in 1870, the French metallurgical industry broke down completely, and the new armies formed to defend

Paris and the interior of the country were equipped by England and America. The French companies rapidly came to the government's aid, but only with improvised methods. The crisis was particularly severe in the area of field artillery, where the all-steel guns of Alfred Krupp were far superior to the French Army's iron model. The excellent new French Model 1870 steel-tubed naval guns had not yet entered quantity production, and when this was attempted during the war the French companies were unable to satisfy the demand for gun tubes. For a short time after the war, French gun steel was ordered from the English firm of Firths.[6]

For naval guns and for the new army weapons copied from them, good steel was essential, and one of the chief efforts of the military reconstruction after the war was to develop sources of better steel. The iron firms of the Loire, particularly Creusot and St. Chamond, were encouraged to begin gun steel production. With government aid, they adopted the best machinery used by the leading English firms.[7] As the success of the *Redoutable* clearly showed, the French were ahead of the English in commercial steel by 1875. By 1876 French industry had succeeded in producing tubes for guns, steel shells, and steel armor, not by the costly Krupp crucible method but by treating materials in an ordinary open hearth; and two firms, Terrenoire and Firminy, were pioneering the use of manganese and chrome as additives.

The late 1870s, however, were the high point of the steel industry in the Loire. At the very time that the transition from iron to steel brought prosperity back to the Loire valley, the opening of the great ore fields in Lorraine and the discovery of the Thomas process for exploiting them began a second crisis more serious than the first. To make things worse, the supply of raw materials in the Loire began to fail, and the French commercial iron and steel industry soon left the valley entirely. In 1886 Creusot abandoned rail production, ending its career as an ordinary steel company.

To meet these conditions, the firms left in the Loire had to specialize in endeavors in which raw material costs were relatively unimportant. As a result the Loire became the center of French arms manufacture. Pig iron was made in the Pyrenees or near the Mediterranean coast from Algerian ore and shipped to the Loire, where the firms held their own through increased mechanization and painstaking research in metallurgical science. The necessity for private industry in the Loire to resort to efficiency and science in order to compete against England and Lorraine was as important to the development of superior guns, projectiles, and armor in France as were the activities of the navy's own experimental organization, the Gâvres Commission.[8]

Throughout the 1870s and the early 1880s the English steel-makers lagged behind the French. Heavy investments in ironworks made the English slow to change to steel, and a good supply of ore suitable for the Bessemer process made them reluctant to adopt the open-hearth process.[9] Just as modern tools allowed the French naval arsenals to compare favorably with the British dockyards, the equipment of the Loire companies (often made in England), which dated from the 1870s, allowed them to compete with English firms using equipment from the 1860s. In addition, like the arsenals, they possessed an abundant supply of cheap skilled labor, which they managed paternalistically—in 1899 a third of Creusot's 15,000 men had been with the company for twenty years and a fourth for twenty-five.[10] The fierce competition and technical abilities of the Loire firms brought about a temporary equality in price and superiority in quality in comparison with England during the early 1880s despite higher costs in France for raw materials and transportation. This was prolonged almost to the 1890s by otherwise unfavorable economic conditions: the collapse of Freycinet's public works scheme and of the accompanying armaments boom.[11]

ARTILLERY AND ARMOR

French naval artillery and armor benefited significantly from the technical skill of the French firms, which participated in the experiments conducted by the navy's artillery officers. The artillery officers, however, retained full control of the development process. They carefully analyzed each new idea and integrated the successful ones into the single scientific system that guided artillery design. In addition, they did not accept the products of private firms on the basis of inventors' descriptions of their merits, but subjected them to rigorous testing.

The Gâvres Commission continued to play the central role in both development and quality control of French guns and armor, and its continuity was a major source of strength for the navy. England relied upon competitive trials every two or three years in which manufacturers would submit special test shells or armor plates. The trials were highly publicized and were attended by the press and many dignitaries. Contracts were awarded for the ones that proved the most successful, and there would then be no further trials until the Admiralty wished to let another big contract. Gâvres, on the other hand, followed a continuous routine, which included selecting from every lot delivered to the navy the shell or plate that looked the worst and subjecting it to firing trials. If it failed, the whole lot was rejected or the maker was fined; if it proved unusually good, he received a bonus and the standard for all future shells or plates was raised to the new level. In either case, all the facts concerning the gun, the armor, and the projectile were recorded for reference during future trials. Tests of important new developments could always be worked into the routine program.

This process was slightly more expensive and a great deal less spectacular than the English system, but it provided a continuous incentive for progress as well as a large body of accurate data on which the progress could be based.[12] Even the reputation of an individual manufacturer was much more solidly founded than it was when everything was staked on a few isolated plates.[13] Protected because flaws could easily be seen or tested after delivery of a lot, France depended entirely on private firms for projectiles and armor plate, and in return the companies of the Loire played a large part in their technical development.

The chief developments in the first half of the 1860s had been in armor, and the main product of the later 1860s had been the Model 1870 gun. After the war, the still uncompleted experiments on projectiles were resumed. Through the 1860s France had tested its projectiles by firing them at right angles to the armor plate (the technique used until the 1890s in England). In 1869, however, just as French projectiles were beginning to equal those that could be purchased abroad, France shifted to testing with oblique fire, probably because of the general belief in ram warfare.

By 1872 this change in the method of testing had already led to four important results: final abandonment of the cylindrical shape, the superiority of the French pointed shot over the longer English form, the superiority of steel to iron projectiles, and the realization that the ideal projectile would be a hollow shell filled with explosive. By abandoning massive cylindrical shot, the French were the first to resume the attempt to pierce armor rather than smash it, and their attention turned to the steel armor-piercing shell. Two years later, more tests confirmed these principles, and the commission asked that studies with picric acid explosives be continued. The French naval artillery had thus decided by 1874 on the principle of the high-explosive armor-piercing steel shell.

The long story of the subsequent implementation of this principle is an excellent example of experimentation by French firms under the control of the commission. The first cast steel projectile made by the firm of Terrenoire was successfully tested in 1875, and regular production began in 1877.[14] The next advance was the steel shell developed by Holtzer, which was tried in 1884. For this test the commission purchased an English 16-inch armor plate supposedly capable of resisting the French 13.4-inch gun. The new Holtzer shell went completely through it and was picked up unbroken 150 yards beyond.[15] A preliminary scientific appreciation of the nature of the problem and the close cooperation of the commission with the steel firms had brought about a successful steel shell by 1884.

In contrast, the English had not even begun experimenting with steel projectiles in 1884.[16] They had rejected Joseph Whitworth's scientific system of breech-loading artillery in the 1860s, and his later efforts to obtain firing trials at oblique angles with steel projectiles met with no greater success. The French, on the other hand, showed great respect for Whitworth's unaided efforts, and it was at Gâvres that his projectiles were first tried.[17]

In armor manufacture, the French also took the technological lead by the mid-1880s. In the first of a series of trials that began in Italy in 1876, the wrought iron used in the early ironclads was finally abandoned, leaving Creusot solid steel and English compound armor (a hard steel face welded to a soft iron back) in the competition. Because of the irregularities of the early steel, the results of the contest were at first in doubt, and after a notable victory of compound armor at Gâvres in 1880, three French companies took out the English patents. After 1882, however, steel steadily gained the upper hand. Though the French makers of compound armor were given a few orders to compensate them for their investment in expensive patents and factories, solid steel armor was definitely adopted in France by 1884. The English continued to use compound armor. Thus the Loire companies followed up their success in producing the first steel warships by making the first steel shells and the first steel armor plate.[18]

The private manufacture of guns in France dated only from the beginning of the Third Republic. Thiers and many of the moderates in his government felt that the only way to avoid a repetition of the artillery crisis of 1870 was to set up a French rival to Krupp and Armstrong, and they encouraged Creusot and St. Chamond to undertake the manufacture of completed guns. (It was also reported that they were interested financially in the new project.)[19] By 1884 France had two large private gun factories, Creusot and a new plant owned by the Forges et Chantiers de la Méditerranée and run by Gustave Canet, a gifted engineer who had received his training at Armstrong's. There was also a third large plant at St. Chamond, which produced all of the necessary parts for guns and could assemble them in case of war, and three smaller ordnance firms.[20]

Yet the navy continued to make its own guns. In contrast to the liberals who championed private arms manufacture, the more conservative naval artillerists saw private companies as good suppliers of parts but refused to deliver the government into the hands of a single great firm like Armstrong or Krupp and buy completed guns from it. They bought parts, which like shells and armor could be watched during fabrication and examined after receipt, but they insisted on assembling the guns in the naval ordnance plant at Ruelle. They felt that in the delicate construction of a heavy gun, workers and inspectors in a profit-seeking firm all had an interest in concealing slight flaws that would not interfere with the gun's firing trials, while in the government plant every effort to conceal a fault was punished severely.[21] The private firms built very good guns, which were practically copies of the regular naval models and which were assembled from regular naval parts, but the French Navy bought few of them.

Shipbuilding and Export Sales

Conditions in the private firms that built warships and their engines depended on three basic factors—the state of the merchant marine and the steel industry and the degree to which the navy was expanding. All of these factors fluctuated together between the 1860 Cobden treaty and 1886, producing even more spectacular fluctuations in the French shipbuilding industry.

At the time of the Cobden treaty, the government stopped giving a bonus for the construction of ships in French yards and new orders ceased. Merchant tonnage built in French yards fell in fifteen years from 65,000 to 12,000 tons, of which only 3,500 were steam-propelled. Foreign orders for warships (which had come largely from Italy and Spain) vanished with the end of the first rush to build ironclads in the mid-1860s.[22] Of the four companies that had formerly participated in warship construction, only the largest, the Forges et Chantiers de la Méditerranée at La Seyne, was able to survive at all. It bought out the yard at Le Havre, which had gone bankrupt, and from 1870 to 1886 it monopolized the few foreign orders that were left to France. The firms at Bordeaux and Nantes were moribund and were unable to participate in the orders given to private builders in an effort to revive the industry after the liberals returned to power in 1876. With the sole exception of La Seyne, whose signs of life were due to its owning Canet's gun plant at Le Havre and the desperate efforts of the republicans to keep it going, the French warship-building industry was dead.

In 1881 new legislation reestablished the bonuses for both shipbuilders and shipping companies as quickly as they had been taken away in the 1860s, and there was an immediate rush to build new merchant ships. In 1884 French-built merchant tonnage rose to 57,000, of which 70 percent was steam. The boom ended as suddenly as it had begun, and the tonnage built in 1885 fell to 16,000, of which only 30 percent was steam. For the navy, which had just succeeded in reviving the company at Bordeaux (the Société des Chantiers et Ateliers de la Gironde) and in reorganizing that at Nantes (the Ateliers et Chantiers de la Loire), this was a real disaster, particularly since it was then absolutely unable to give them government orders. The Loire steel firms, with their newly developed plants for armor and shells, were in similar straits, because the crisis that followed the loss of the commercial market to Lorraine and the collapse of the Freycinet public works scheme had come to a climax in 1885. In spite of their technical ability, many of the firms that had developed the new war materials and that had been forced to specialize in them were practically bankrupt.[23]

The only possible solution was to go after foreign orders. In 1886 the prohibition on the export of guns was removed, and with financial backing from Paris, Creusot formed a syndicate of the yards of La Seyne, the Loire, and the Gironde for the exploitation of the export market. This brought together all of the French warship-builders except Jacques-Augustin Normand, the leading torpedo-boat builder, into a powerful organization for international trade, although they remained competitors in the domestic market.

TABLE 1

THE INTERNATIONAL TRADE IN WARSHIPS
(NOT INCLUDING TORPEDO CRAFT)

	England	France	Germany	Italy	USA	Others
			TONNAGE LAUNCHED FOR SALE ABROAD BY:			
1863–66	67,350	31,600			4,200	
1867–70	33,480	19,460				2,030
1871–74	35,620	1,540				2,300
1875–78	29,090	12,170			1,230	
1879–82	16,930	4,300	16,260			
1883–86	40,830		6,720		1,200	6,480
1887–90	23,780	49,260	9,150			
1891–94	25,900	4,680	3,240	1,200		5,560
1895–98	135,310	12,370	13,480	29,280	10,180	
1899–1902	82,690	35,010	28,570	450	21,200	3,200
1903–6	54,370	11,750	8,770	17,800	3,300	
1907–10	56,630	450	5,150	9,950		6,900
1911–14	123,120	5,200	12,900	900	61,850	

From 1884 to 1890 the spectacular entry of French private companies into the international arms trade revealed to the world, and particularly to the English, the great revival in French sea power that had taken place since 1870. In that period the French Navy, the steel companies, and the shipyards had solved numerous technical problems, with the result that French ships were well built and carried better armor, guns, and projectiles than the English. Until the mid-1880s this was known only to specialists, since the tables that were published comparing the world's navies could not show factors such as quality of design and manufacture. In the four years between 1883 and 1886, French firms did not launch a single foreign warship, while England built around 40,000 tons. In the next four years, however, France launched 49,260 tons to only 23,780 for England.

Much of this tonnage was obtained by official naval missions to Japan and Greece. France had old connections with both of these navies, but the sudden revival of these ties in 1886 was a significant diplomatic as well as commercial success. Britain had always been the principal adviser to the personnel of the Japanese navy, but it was France that organized the Japanese arsenals. Between 1865 and 1876 French engineers under François-Léonce Verny transformed a nearly empty beach at Yokosuka into a fully equipped naval arsenal, built several ships and repaired over 300 vessels there, and trained the native personnel that eventually took over the yard.[24]

When Japan started a serious naval building program following the French war with China in 1884, she purchased two cruisers from Armstrong in En-

Projet de Croiseur rapide
à flottaison cuirassée

Echelle 1 : 0.01
Coupe Longitudinale

The protected cruiser Unebi (1886), built at Le Havre for Japan. She carried four 9.4-inch guns to compete with the two 10-inchers on cruisers sold by the British Armstrong firm, but produced a setback for French industry when she was lost owing to unknown causes on her delivery voyage.

gland and was regarded as a good prospective customer. At the very beginning of the new program, however, French diplomats, the Paris banks, and
the arms syndicate took it right out of English hands. In 1886 the Japanese
chose the talented French naval engineer Emile Bertin to take over the
Yokosuka yard and introduce the technique of building steel ships. In the
process, Bertin reorganized the entire matériel of the Japanese navy, and
most of the fleet that won the Battle of the Yalu in 1894 against China was
built to his designs. Some of the ships were ordered and built in French
yards, including two unusual large protected cruisers, each with an enormous 12.6-inch, 66-ton Canet gun. Others were assembled in Japan from
components fabricated in France, while still others, including a copy of
the two large French-built cruisers, were built entirely in Japan on French
plans.[25] Until Bertin's return to France in 1890, the French controlled the
matériel of the Japanese navy, despite incidents such as the mysterious disappearance of a smaller French-built cruiser, the *Unebi,* on her way out to
Japan in 1887. British firms finally regained the Japanese naval market after
the Sino-Japanese War of 1894–95 as a result of the French diplomatic attitude toward Japan and the stipulation of the British bankers that the funds
they loaned China for the indemnity to Japan had to be spent in England for
naval construction.[26]

The French got off to a similar start in China when in 1866 Prosper Gic-
quel, a former French Navy lieutenant serving in the Chinese customs service, obtained a contract to create a naval arsenal at Foochow. By 1874,
when he turned the yard over to the Chinese under the terms of the contract, it was completely equipped and had produced fifteen naval steamers.
During the 1884 war with China, however, a French fleet under Admiral
Courbet destroyed the Foochow arsenal, and despite great pressure on the
Chinese, Creusot was unable to begin this profitable cycle all over again.

In Greece, because of French support in diplomatic crises in 1878 and
1884, the French syndicate received large orders for ships including three
powerful light-draft battleships. In addition, the French sent a naval mission
to choose the sites for Greek naval arsenals. The active work of this mission
in the Greek islands was one of the reasons why the British looked with
great suspicion on the Dual Alliance of the early 1890s between France and
Russia, a country that also had ambitions in that part of the Mediterranean.

Elsewhere, the French syndicate received orders from Spain for a first-
class battleship, the *Pelayo,* and from Russia for a fast first-class cruiser, the
Admiral Kornilov. Perhaps most impressively, it won a great victory in an
"open" competition for the contract for the Chilean coast-defense battleship
Capitan Prat. Chile, Armstrong's most faithful customer, sent a special mission to select the designer and builder of the battleship. The mission was
wined and dined all over Europe while an advisory council of the re-
nowned English constructor Sir Edward Reed and a French and a German

The Spanish battleship Pelayo *(1887), fitting out at La Seyne, where she was built. The mast and funnel of another La Seyne product, the Japanese cruiser* Itsuku-shima *(1889), are behind her.*

constructor ensured fair play.[27] The ship herself, the first battleship ever equipped throughout with electrical machinery (in which at this time the French excelled), was considered even by the English to be the ideal coast defender.[28]

In spite of the government's efforts to exert its influence in connection with most of these orders, there is much evidence that the chief reason for the French success was the loans offered by the Paris banks. The prices for French-built warships were generally in line with their English contemporaries (although French prices for armor were lower), but because of the depression in the steel industry and in shipbuilding, the financial backers of the consortium offered favorable terms to secure the contracts.[29] As a result, France gave England the first real competition in naval shipbuilding that it had experienced since before 1870.

Other signs of French superiority appeared in contracts awarded for armor and artillery. In 1884 Italy, the most progressive of the naval powers in matters of technology, concluded a contract with Creusot for the erection of a steel armor plant; and a special American committee, the Gun Foundry Board, adopted the whole French system of ordnance and armor. The Americans concluded that in France "there have been produced, within a comparatively short period, the finest gun factory in the world, victorious steel shells, and equally superior solid steel armor," and they recommended "in inaugurating the manufacturing of war material in our own country, a conformity as close as circumstances will permit to the plans which had proved so successful in France."[30] Russia also adopted steel armor and shells at that time.

By 1886 English experts and public opinion had finally become convinced of France's technical progress. The shift of Italy, America, and Russia to an essentially French system of armor and artillery occurred while England was experiencing a major crisis in the manufacture of guns and produced much condemnation of the unhappy directors of the Woolwich arsenal who were responsible for England's policies.[31] In 1886 an English firm, John Brown, bought the Creusot process; another firm, Firths, came to terms with Holtzer; the Admiralty ordered 400 French projectiles; and the Ordnance Committee unanimously adopted the principle of steel armor and shells.[32] The English did not catch up right away. They were not able to make steel armor until 1891, and the trials of the compound armor for the ships ordered under the 1889 Naval Defence Act revealed continuing problems with English shells. In both of these trials, the English shells broke up while the French stayed in the target. Finally a French shell went clear through the target and was picked up unbroken on the other side, duplicating for English benefit (and French amusement) the results of the Gâvres trials of exactly six years before.[33] As they entered the 1890s, the French industries remained fully competitive with the English.

Six

New Factors: Italy and Russia

Aₐfter the 1870 defeat, France continued her navy, as one historian remarked, *sans trop savoir pourquoi* (without really knowing why).[1] With its prestige-oriented organization and despite its highly trained personnel, the navy vegetated under its conservative chiefs. Two new naval rivalries arose during the 1870s, however, forcing it to respond to some important new ideas. First, France and the newly independent state of Italy came to see each other as potential foes after a series of diplomatic disputes and entered into a vigorous naval arms race in which the main feature was the imaginative use of technology by Italy to compensate for inferior resources. Less important but still significant were the efforts of Russia to compete with England at sea by developing new means of cruiser warfare.

The Italian Naval Revival

After the effervescence of the 1860s had died down, the next steps in the development of the modern navy were taken by Italy. The Italians integrated into their new policy three ideas developed by other navies—the French emphasis on engineering progress, the rational English naval organization, and the German defensive strategic system. They added one idea of their own: the clear perception that against her principal enemy, Italy would necessarily be weaker at sea because of inferior resources. This was a big change from the previous policy of the Italians, according to which they expected to be superior to their main rival, Austria, and could afford to copy both the strategic ideas and the fleets of Britain and France. The Austrian defeat of the Italian fleet at the Battle of Lissa in 1866 had discredited this policy. For the next six years the Italian people were not hostile to the navy but completely indifferent to it. The taxpayer's dream of improvising a fleet from the merchant marine and using ships as floating forts for the defense of harbors was very popular.[2]

The French did as much as anyone to trigger Italy's naval revival. Under Napoleon III, the political right intervened clumsily on the side of the pope in his dispute with the new secular Italian state over the possession of Rome, while the left equally irresponsibly sent aid to Italian republican adventurers. Thiers clearly indicated the Roman policy of the new French republic by sending the paddle frigate *Orénoque* to Civita Vecchia to demonstrate support for the pope after Italy occupied Rome in 1870. This caused the first great outburst of public opinion that led to the creation of the modern Italian Navy. In 1872 the Budget Committee of the Italian Chamber proposed a vast new naval program, the money for which would be obtained in part from selling the ships of the old fleet.[3] When the minister stated that only financial considerations kept him from asking for more money, the Chamber voted an order of the day asking him to propose the needed sums.

France's blunders not only prompted this revival but also helped define the primary purpose of the new fleet—to defend the Italian coasts against the French Mediterranean fleet. The orientation, not toward expansion in the Mediterranean but toward defense of Italy's coasts, comes out clearly in the conclusions of the great Permanent Commission that drew up a general plan for Italy's defenses.

> Superior at sea but inferior on land, we could not prevent the invasion of our territory. Even the most powerful army unaided by a fleet, however, would be unable to guarantee our extended coasts or defend our islands against enemy attacks. Our army itself would not possess the necessary freedom of action if it were menaced at its bases.[4]

Many of the ideas of the Piedmontese who directed the new Italian state were based on those of the Germans. The Italian leaders felt that the army was the only offensive weapon of the state since wars were decided on land, but they saw that the help of the navy was necessary to give the army freedom of action for its land operations. As in Germany, they left the army in complete control of all military operations and limited the naval command to the tactical execution of orders from the army.[5] This subordination to the army shows the close functional similarity of the Italian and German navies. The Italian system also had the other main features of the German one—the "light cavalry" of coastal observation points, telegraph system, and dispatch boats and the "heavy cavalry" of coast-defense ships or *Ausfallkorvetten* to issue from bases to delay and disorganize the enemy's assault until the land forces, concentrated by rail, could deliver the paralyzing blow.

Although the purposes of the Italian and German navies were similar, the two fleets differed greatly because the Italian coasts presented an entirely different defensive problem from the easily defended German shores. Italy,

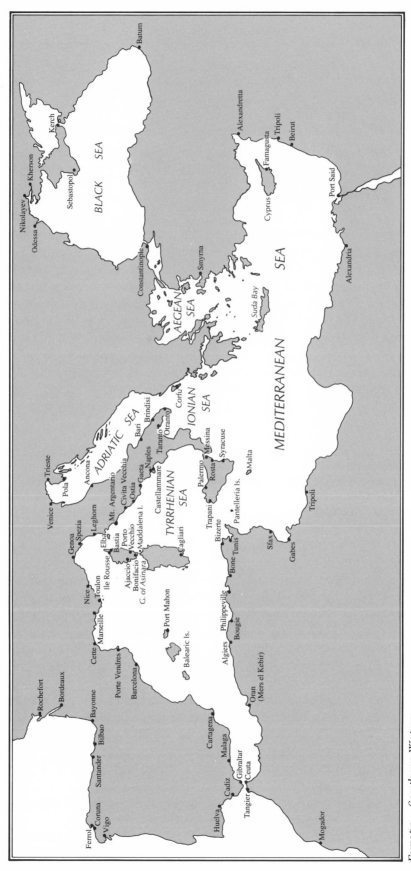

Europe—Southern Waters

as a peninsula, was by definition particularly vulnerable to naval attack, and she had a large number of defenseless coastal cities and a primitive internal transportation system, which, unlike the German railroads, could not support rapid army operations. From the maritime point of view, her defensive problem centered on four strategic basins—the Ligurian, Tyrrhenian, Ionian, and Adriatic seas, of which only the first two were threatened by France.

The Ligurian Sea, extending from the French border to the island of Elba, was directly open to the French base at Toulon but offered only three military objectives—Genoa, Leghorn, and the coastal railways. At Genoa the commercial port could be seriously damaged by a naval bombardment, as could the major shipyards of Ansaldo (in Sestri Ponente) and Odero (in Sampierdarena), but the land fortifications could not be reduced without the help of an army. Leghorn, with another major shipyard belonging to Orlando, was poorly defended, but a landing by an army for an advance up the Arno River to Florence was possible only in the immediate neighborhood of the city. In addition, both Genoa and the mouth of the Arno were connected with the fairly well-developed northern Italian railway system.

In the larger Tyrrhenian Sea, the strategic problems were much more complicated and important. This basin has four entrances of varying widths: the channel between Corsica and Italy (partially closed on the Italian side by Elba and the point of Monte Argentario), the Strait of Bonifacio between Corsica and Sardinia, the wide passage between Sicily and Sardinia, and the Strait of Messina. It also contained two points of greater importance than either Genoa or Leghorn—the kingdom's capital, Rome; and its largest city and second largest port, Naples. Rome was open to attack by forces landed at Civita Vecchia, Ostia, or Gaeta. The Italians correctly regarded Naples as completely at the mercy of a superior fleet.[6] The maritime region of Naples included, besides the city, the navy's gun factory, an arsenal, and major private shipbuilding firms including Armstrong's works at Pozzuoli, the Castellammare shipyards, and the engine works of Pattison and Guppy. Serious as threats to Genoa, Leghorn, or Rome would be, the Bay of Naples was the Achilles heel of Italy.[7]

Still more important, neither Rome nor Naples was well supplied with railways, and those that did exist in the peninsula were completely inadequate for mobile land defense. All of the Italian railways were then single-tracked and lacked both terminal facilities and rolling stock. The mountains running down the center of the peninsula were so rugged that even with double engines, the crucial interior line from Bologna to Florence and south to Rome could carry only half as many troops per day as an average line. Faced with an impossible problem, the Italians opted for concentration in the north; they kept nine tenths of their artillery and stores in the northern part of the kingdom and brought the men from the peninsular region to their matériel. This allowed the Italians to get their forces together in the north in four or five weeks, but it would have produced chaos had they tried to reverse the process to meet an attack in the south. It was estimated that six days would be needed to move the infantry of an army corps and some of its artillery and cavalry south over the Bologna line, compared with twenty-four hours for a similar movement by an entire corps in Germany.[8]

Italy lacked the most important part of the German system, its railways, and also did not enjoy another advantage of the Germans, the sandbanks that made it difficult for ships to approach the coasts closely enough to bombard them. As a result, the transports that France had found to be useless against Germany were still a serious threat to Italy.[9] More men could be embarked at Marseilles and Toulon than in France's northern ports, the distances to be crossed were shorter, and more points in Italy were open for landings. The French had shown what they could do by transporting 100,000 men to Genoa in 1859 to help Italy win her independence and by their efficient colonial expedition to Tunis in 1881.

Even the Italian imagination was more vivid than the German, and the 60,000 men in two successive contingents in French plans became 130,000 in a single trip in the Italian horror stories. The Italian government was eventually forced to leave a third of its active army on its western coast, at Rome, Naples, and La Spezia; and the German general Moltke regarded its entire force as practically paralyzed by the mere threat of a seaborne expedition. The remainder of the Italian Army was tied down by the phobia of a French attack through the Alps—the Italians planned to let the enormous French forces come through the passes and then crush them around Turin.[10] The bombardment-invasion propaganda of the 1870s was one of the reasons for the continuous scares of the 1880s, when it was impossible for two French transports to put in to Toulon together without Italy complaining to Germany and Britain about it.

In the early 1870s Italy developed its own Young School, a group of younger officers who developed a new strategy and were largely able to implement it. They realized that the Italian peninsula, unlike the German coast, could not be defended without a navy of seagoing ships. The initial objective of their officially sponsored propaganda, like similar writings in England during the 1860s, was not to sell sea power and colonial expansion to the middle class but simply to prove that the cheap floating batteries that were so popular were useless. They used techniques ranging from history to the scare novel—one novel was officially printed in 1872 by the minister of marine for distribution to the Chamber.[11] They also spread their message in the same middle-class periodicals that had supported the efforts of Count Camillo Cavour to unify Italy. In the process, the dull official navy magazine *Rivista marittima* became the best informed and the most active naval periodical in Europe. They also adopted the English lecture method of arousing public opinion, assisted by the vice president of the British Royal United Service Institution.[12]

The revival had two outstanding leaders: Benedetto Brin, a naval engineer, and Admiral Simone Pacoret de Saint Bon, a strategist and parliamentarian. Both were able to work with the Chamber, where two other old sea dogs turned minister of marine, Admirals Guglielmo Acton and Augusto Riboty, had failed. Saint Bon belonged to the extreme right, while Brin was minister for the leftists, but the unity of strategic views in these men of very different political persuasions gave the navy a unity of direction that was nearly unique in Italian politics. Their first period of power, from 1872 to 1877, laid the foundations of the modern Italian Navy.

Benedetto Brin was the most remarkable naval engineer in Europe after Dupuy de Lôme. In some ways he may be regarded as Dupuy's successor, for just as France was abandoning the cult of technical progress, Brin made the Italian Navy a test tube for new technical ideas. Like Dupuy de Lôme's navy, his was an engineer's fleet. He did not hesitate to take on powerful opponents; he had so little use for the British navigating traditions followed by the line officer corps that one of his first efforts was to try to reform the naval academy of Leghorn. (The line officers ultimately combined with conservative local interests to produce Brin's fall.) He was a close personal friend of the great Italian artillery officer Carlo Felice Albini and of Andrew Noble of the Armstrong firm. His ideas were strongly influenced by foreign industrialists, particularly Armstrong, the partisan of big guns and the abolition of armor.

Brin was the founder of the modern Italian warship-building industry. In his effort to create Italian heavy industry for shipbuilding, he depended largely on foreign companies, which naturally were mostly British. At the beginning, Armstrong's gun factory at Pozzuoli was the chief example of an Italian subsidiary of a foreign naval firm, but after a series of dismal efforts to copy foreign products the leading Italian machinery firms were also forced into "partnerships" with British builders. Ansaldo at Genoa became a technical subsidiary of Maudslay, the English builder of steam machinery; Guppy of Naples accepted the help of another such firm, Hawthorne; and Pattison at Venice built torpedo boats from Thornycroft's plans. The large English investment in Italian warship-building had political implications: it was the economic basis of the movement for Anglo-Italian naval cooperation as well as for English loans to finance Italian naval expansion.

The Italians chose their industrial supporters carefully, however, and in fields where Britain was not the best, they invited others to the feast. As a result, Italy opened herself to the experiments of all Europe's naval inventors. Schwarzkopf of Berlin set up a torpedo factory at Venice, and Italy procured her steel-making capability from the supposed future enemy,

France. After the continued victories of French steel armor, shells, and hull plates, the Italian government in 1884 gave Creusot a loan of 12 million lire to organize at Terni the first modern steelworks in Italy.[13]

Although this system of subsidiaries and disguised partnerships delivered Italy to the tender mercies of foreign builders, it was at least better than direct construction abroad.[14] Although Brin attacked the British-style naval education in Italy, he replaced the French-style arsenal organization with that of Childers, and modern methods were gradually introduced into the Italian dockyards. In spite of the original ignorance of the Italian workers, the quality of their production was soon equal to that obtained from abroad.[15]

The new Italian Navy was particularly unfortunate in the location of its bases. Only the least important of the old ones, Venice, could still be used, and it was badly silted up. The other two, Genoa and Naples, could not be protected from bombardment. The transfer of Genoa's arsenal to the position chosen by Napoleon for it, La Spezia, had begun before 1872 and was practically completed by the start of the serious Franco-Italian rivalry. This position, the Toulon of Italy, secured the command of the whole Ligurian basin and provided partial protection of the northern entrance to the Tyrrhenian Sea. The only solution to the problem of defending the arsenal at Naples was also to move it, and the reformers proposed a new base at Taranto. For Naples, which had already lost its independence and a great part of its trade when Italy was unified, the move seemed the final blow to its former glory. During the erection of the base at Taranto, the government gave in to the local interests and decided to keep the old Neapolitan arsenal in operation, although ships were not to be based there.

A more important weakness of the new base at Taranto was that it was not in the Tyrrhenian Sea at all. The seemingly simple proposal to transfer the Naples arsenal there revealed that the naval reformers, who mostly came from northern Italy, had an additional theme in their plans—hazy ambitions in the eastern Mediterranean and the Balkans. By pursuing the shadowy advantage of having an offensive base near the Levant, Italy left herself without a defensible base in the vital Tyrrhenian Sea. The gaping Sicily-Sardinia passage led straight to the heart of southern Italy, which was not defended by any of Italy's three bases at Spezia, Venice, or Taranto. The weak spot in the Italian program was the result of a double concession to local Neapolitan interests and to the Balkan megalomania.[16]

ITALIAN SHIP DESIGN: THE *DUILIO*

In Italy as in Germany, naval bases were "sortie ports" for ships defending the coasts.[17] However, the Italian equivalents of the *Ausfallkorvetten* could only be high-seas battleships. Battleships could bombard Italian coastal towns or cover a landing, and Italy was forced to meet them with battleships. Since she could not attain numerical equality, she was forced to depend on the superiority of the individual ships. But in spite of the later claims of the Italians that they had built a Mahanian fleet before Alfred Thayer Mahan and Philip Colomb, they did not grasp the essential idea of command of the sea, which even then was inherent in the French and British tradition. The Italian ships were not a fleet designed to destroy the enemy's forces by an immediate offensive, thereby preventing a landing or a bombardment. Instead they were a collection of individually powerful units that would wait passively until the French were in the midst of a coastal operation, like the one the Italians themselves had rashly attempted at Lissa. The Italian Navy of the 1870s, like the German, was not a single fleet with several bases but scattered ships garrisoned at threatened points. It was a group of giant coast-defense ships whose sole function was to prevent not even a bombardment, but a landing.

Brin developed his battleships, which were intended to be more powerful than any the French could send against them, from the most powerful English battleships then in existence. While the French *Redoutable* was a direct descendant of the ship of the line with her tall sides studded with guns, the British had embarked in a new direction. They had been greatly impressed by the big American monitors, one of which, the *Miantonomoh,* had visited Europe after the Civil War. In 1869 they laid down the *Devastation,* the world's first mastless seagoing ironclad, which abandoned sails entirely and, despite her low freeboard, was capable of crossing the Atlantic. She carried her four heavy guns in two turrets, one at each end of a thickly armored breastwork that rose above the main deck in the central portion of the ship.

The *Devastation* was still unfinished when the *Captain,* a low-freeboard turret ship with a full sail rig, capsized and provoked an investigation of the whole subject of Admiralty ship designs. Though the Committee on Designs finally accepted the *Devastation* as stable, the chief result of its discussion related to an entirely different matter. Armstrong and the British opponents of armored ships used the opportunity to give their case a detailed public airing. They claimed that a successful smashing blow would carry a large amount of debris from the shattered armor into the ship, and they concluded that no armor at all was safer than armor that could be penetrated. Although the committee refused to do away with armor altogether, it adopted the chief idea of its opponents: that armor was worse than useless unless it was impenetrable to solid shot from the largest guns. The committee recognized that it was rapidly becoming impossible to put invulnerable armor both on the hull at the waterline and over the guns, and it concluded that a different method would have to be found for either keeping the ship afloat or protecting the guns. The armor taken from one could be used to make the other invulnerable.[18] The ship armored only at the waterline would be essentially an armored ram, the one armored only over the guns primarily a gun ship.

Brin, a friend of the artillerists Armstrong and Albini, naturally favored the second alternative and designed two ships, the *Duilio* and *Dandolo,* which were to combine the heaviest guns, invulnerable armor to protect them, and the highest speed afloat. Brin altered the *Devastation*'s central breastwork and the armored hull sides below it into a citadel covered with twenty-two inches of solid steel, surmounted by equally well-protected turrets. He compensated for the additional weight by omitting all of the armor from the waterline at the ends of the hull. Instead, beyond the ends of the central armored citadel, he provided only an underwater armored deck surmounted by a belt of small watertight compartments designed to localize flooding from any hits. Some of these cells were filled with coal and others with cork or stores. The general plan thus consisted of an invulnerable armored box in the center and an underwater armored deck with a cellular life preserver on top of it at the ends.[19]

The guns were to be the biggest that Armstrong could make, and the ship was begun before their size was determined. The *Devastation*'s guns, built by the Admiralty at Woolwich on Armstrong's principles, were 35-ton weapons, but when Armstrong's original design of 60 tons was met by Woolwich with 80, Armstrong jumped to 100. In the process of increasing gun size from 35 to 100 tons, Armstrong increased the caliber from 12 to 17.7 inches,

Benedetto Brin's first masterpiece, the Italian battleship Duilio *(launched in 1876). The armor of this unusually large and fast ship was concentrated in a citadel enclosing the bases of the funnels and turrets.*

The turret-mounted 100-ton, 17.7-inch muzzle-loading guns of the Duilio. *The guns were loaded through armored ports in the deck, two of which are visible near the turret on the right.*

the weight of the projectiles from 700 to 2,000 pounds, and the amount of wrought-iron armor that could be penetrated at 100 yards from 12 to 37 inches. In 1876 the first of these monsters was successfully tried at Spezia. These guns reflected no new principles of gun design; they were still muzzle-loaders with a steel body strengthened by iron bands. They were mounted in twin turrets arranged diagonally, the forward one to starboard and the after one to port. This was supposed to allow all four guns to be fired ahead, astern, or directly on either broadside, while at least two could fire in any direction. The enormous mass of the guns was worked by hydraulic machinery, and they were loaded by poking their muzzles into armored holes in the deck, behind which were the necessary rammers and ammunition.

While the guns and the partial abandonment of armor were the ideas of Armstrong, Albini, and Brin, the speed of the ships was due to Saint Bon. The *Duilio* and *Dandolo* were designed for 15 knots, two knots faster than any contemporary battleships. Saint Bon and the Italians in general were the first to see the tremendous importance of speed for the weaker ship or navy. Grivel had recognized it in theory, but in practice speed was always the first quality to be sacrificed by naval architects or cost-conscious politicians. Saint Bon placed it on an equal level with armor and protection in the belief that the strongest ships of a weaker navy must have the power of forcing or avoiding battle. His battleships were to use their speed not only to outrun a stronger opposing force but to catch and defeat unwary fragments of it.

An active defense relying on speed was a particularly appropriate response to the French Navy, because speed was the most neglected element in French ship designs. As long as the *Duilio* and *Dandolo* were "in being" and ready for action, they would fulfill their purpose because the French would not dare to launch a major maritime expedition. In the meantime, the whole French Squadron of Evolutions would find it very difficult to catch one of them, and the Italians might succeed in overtaking and destroying some isolated French ships that, although more numerous, were slower and weaker than their opponents.

Italy's vague Levant ambitions were reflected in the final characteristic of the new ships, their range of action. They were given the enormous steaming range of 5,000 to 6,000 miles, ostensibly to protect the long Italian coast but really to be able to act throughout the eastern and western Mediterranean in accordance with Italy's new expansionist aims. Italy's designs in Tripoli, Tunis, the Balkans, the Aegean, and Morocco could be supported by the home navy; the fact that Italy was not burdened with foreign stations did not result from a lack of colonial ambitions but from the capabilities of its new ships.

RESPONSES TO THE *DUILIO*

The Italian high-seas *Ausfallkorvetten* were larger, more heavily gunned, and faster than any ships that had previously existed, and both in England and in France the public demanded that something be done about it. The Admiralty, as usual, simply built a bigger ship like the Italian ones. The *Inflexible,* even down to the diagonal arrangement of the guns, was copied from the *Duilio,* except that the British did not adopt high speed. As on the *Duilio,* the armor of the *Inflexible* was concentrated on the central citadel, the underwater deck, and the cellular layer above it. Britannia could not properly rule the waves if foreign ships had bigger guns, and Woolwich built 80-ton muzzle loaders for the *Inflexible* and prepared designs for guns of 160, 190, and 220 tons.[20]

From the beginning, this concept was violently attacked by Sir Edward Reed, whom the new ship's designer, Nathaniel Barnaby, had just displaced as chief constructor. The whole controversy turned on the amount of punishment the ship could take without sinking; questions such as whether the ship could conserve her speed or maneuvering qualities or the wisdom of giving her such enormous guns were not addressed. A special investigation finally decided in favor of the system, concluding that even if the cellular layer was completely blown away, the citadel would keep the ship afloat, although she would then be in a very critical condition.[21] The soft-ended protection scheme was only tested once in action, in two Chinese battleships that participated in the Battle of the Yalu in 1894. Each ship was hit near the waterline over 200 times but was able to get back into harbor.[22]

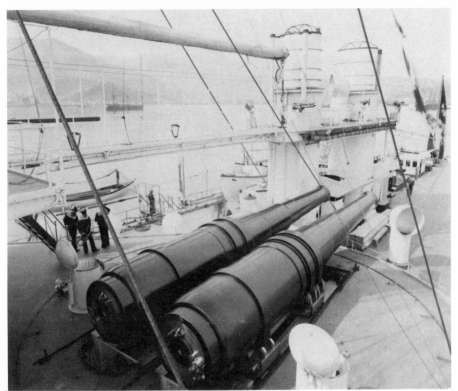

*The barbette-mounted 100-ton, 17-inch breech-loading guns of the Italian battle-
ship* Lepanto *(1883). This ship and her sister* Italia *had four of these guns on two
turntables in a single giant barbette amidships.*

Neither the *Duilio* nor the *Inflexible,* however, fully adopted either of the
two extreme proposals put before the Committee on Designs; neither took
all the armor from either the guns or the waterline. In 1876 Brin began construction of two even larger and faster ships that did away with waterline
armor, the *Italia* and *Lepanto.* These ships were entirely unarmored except
for an underwater deck running the length of the ship, a big barbette containing the four 100-ton guns, and ammunition tubes between the deck and
the barbette. The purpose of the deck was to protect the engines and
boilers, and the ship was kept from sinking solely by the cellular layer of
watertight compartments above it. The result of this extreme *décuirassement* and of the great size of the ships (nearly 13,900 tons) was extreme
speed: 17 knots in the *Italia,* 18 in the *Lepanto.*

The period of Italian innovation in battleship design came to an end after
the 1878 Congress of Berlin, when Italy's attention turned to her irredentist
claims against Austria in the Tyrol and to her ambitions in the Balkans. Due
to the new focus on the Adriatic, the new ships began to be regarded with
disfavor. The Austrian Navy was building a considerable number of small

battleships for Adriatic waters—it launched seven ranging from 3,600 to 7,000 tons between 1871 and 1878. In addition, the personnel of the little fleet that had won at Lissa were the best in Europe. The *Duilio* could not even enter the dockyard at Venice, and the need for smaller ships resulted in a reaction against Brin's ideas. In addition, cautious navigating officers in Italy and in other countries opposed the enormous size of Brin's creations.

At the end of 1879, Admiral Ferdinando Acton became minister of marine and restored power to the line officers. He took a sort of plebiscite among all the higher regular officers, which showed that the vast majority favored ships of 15 knots and 8,000 tons. Though Brin and Saint Bon defended their policy in a bitter three-day debate in the Chamber, Acton was upheld. Eventually the Italians laid down three compromise ships of the *Ruggiero di Lauria* class, which returned to the principles of the *Duilio.* Although smaller, slower, and more heavily armored than the *Italia,* they were still faster than any of the French battleships and still carried four 100-ton guns.[23] Brin's fall, however, marked at least a pause in Italian naval expansion.

RUSSIA AND CRUISER WARFARE

Cruiser warfare was largely ignored in the 1870s. French cruisers at this time were mostly station battleships or smaller ships that were slower than battleships and burdened with heavy artillery for coastal bombardment. In Italy, however, Saint Bon laid the basis for the modern fleet scout when he adopted the principle that any weak ship, including a scout or cruiser, must be faster than any ship stronger than it. Italy built only three cruisers in the 1870s, of which one, the 2,300-ton wooden sail-equipped *Cristoforo Colombo,* was two or three knots slower than the battleships and was designed to be sent on foreign missions. The two others, the *Staffetta* and *Rapido,* were smaller and mastless, had unsheathed iron hulls, and were designed to make 17 knots. The secretary of the French Conseil des Travaux, Paul Dislère, was so astonished at Saint Bon's error in trying to make "mere avisos" faster than battleships that he could find no suitable comments besides predicting that they would fail to make their speed (in which he proved correct).[24]

The purpose of these ships was to provide a part of the German coast-defense system that Italy still lacked—the "light cavalry" to tell of the approach of the enemy. They were thus dispatch boats rather than scouts, but they were still the first small ships designed to be faster than anything more powerful, and they foretold the path that cruiser development was to take. The British experimented with a similar idea in the 1870s. When they abandoned the effort to combine high speed under steam and a full sail rig as they had done in the *Inconstant,* they built two lightly rigged unsheathed steel "dispatch boats," the *Iris* and *Mercury,* which resembled the Italian ships but were much larger.

Throughout the 1870s France, like Italy and Germany, had not the slightest intention of going to war against the world's greatest commercial power, England. Indeed, Britain and France continued the free exchange of military and technical ideas that had begun at the time of the Crimean War, and French visitors were regularly shown complete Admiralty plans of new warships.[25] The continental countries mentioned Britain as an enemy only in the wildest of hypotheses, and neither the German nor the Italian navy produced any advances in the theory of commercial war while France did little to develop her capabilities. Only Russia was forced to consider the problem of opposing Britain. Also greatly influenced by the Germans, she was the sole exponent of a naval policy that combined coast defense and commercial warfare.

Russia's efforts in coast defense were undistinguished. She had experienced a craze for monitors in the mid-1860s when the western powers seemed ready to intervene in a revolution in Poland, but thereafter construction of coastal battleships slowed. In the 1870s she launched two bizarre coast-defense ships with circular hulls designed by Admiral Andrei A. Popov, and except for these and the *Petr Veliki,* a bad copy of the *Devastation,* she did not launch a single battleship until 1886. Although Popov and Russia's leading naval tactician, Admiral Grigori Butakov, were known to the outside world, her navy was inferior even to the Turkish when the two fought in 1878. The attitude of England during the 1878 war caused the first signs of a revival in the form of feverish fortification of the Black Sea ports.

From the visit of a Russian cruiser squadron to San Francisco during the Polish crisis of 1863 through the Anglo-Russian naval scares of 1878 and 1885, the only serious naval measures taken by Russia were for commercial warfare. Since her only base for commerce-raiding operations was Vladivostok in the Pacific, and since the experiences of the *Alabama* and *Shenandoah* had caused commercial warfare to become identified with war on foreign stations, it is not surprising that Russia's larger cruisers were of the ordinary station type. The 4,600-ton *General Admiral* and *Gertsog Edinburgskiy,* launched in 1873 and 1875 and popularly supposed to be the world's first armored or "belted" cruisers, were nothing but mediocre 12-knot sailing station ironclads with armor restricted to the waterline belt. Their survival depended on the lack of docks and coal in distant seas, which made it impossible for bigger ships to get at them.

Russia's effort in her crisis with England in 1878 to improvise around these two ships a force of unarmored cruisers was much more interesting. After the failure throughout the 1870s of the other powers to create high-speed sailing *Alabama*s, and with little time to put together a raiding force, the Russians bought German, American, and even English merchant ships and converted them into auxiliary cruisers for their new "Volunteer Fleet." Two of the ideas behind this fleet, the success of the North in improvising a fleet during the American Civil War and the notion that an unarmored ship with a big gun might unexpectedly disable an armored ship, were none too solid. However, with respect to speed, even an ordinary passenger ship was superior to most cruisers in the 1870s. Warship designers were just abandoning the attempt to combine speed under steam with a full sail rig, and they had not yet begun to tackle the problem of designing engines suitable for cruisers. In this transition period between the attempt to reproduce the *Alabama* and the creation of mastless cruisers, even average merchantmen enjoyed an unusual superiority in speed over most warships. Though the ships of the Volunteer Fleet later became nothing more than freighters for a government line to Vladivostok, at the outset they were at least as fast as most of the warships England could send against them. Their acquisition, particularly the vigorous purchasing activities of the Russians in the United States, nearly created a panic in England.[26]

The English supposed that the danger of armed merchantmen had been entirely settled by the abolition of privateering in the Treaty of Paris in 1856.[27] Privateering, or cruiser warfare by licensed private individuals who retained the profits from the sale of the prizes, had been ended by legislation against bringing prizes into neutral ports and against fitting out raiders there. Destroying prizes at sea to keep them from being recaptured on their return to blockaded home ports took the profit out of the venture. The Confederacy, the last state to attempt privateering, soon abandoned it for government commerce-destroying.[28] But in 1878 the British rudely awoke to the realization that as far as war on their commerce was concerned, government-owned auxiliary merchant cruisers would have exactly the same effect as privateers, and if they could be fitted out in foreign ports and transferred and armed at sea (as the Russians were doing in America with the help of Philadelphia bankers), even the danger of neutral support for commerce raiders was not ended.[29] War against commerce by means of government auxiliary cruisers might prove as effective as that waged by privateers.

Russia's aim in a maritime war was to avoid battle at all costs and concentrate on commerce-destroying. Ships would be stopped and searched, their coal and valuables confiscated, and the ships themselves destroyed instead of being taken to a neutral port. Prisoners would be put on board the next convenient neutral ship. The Pacific was to be the main field of action, and Russian ships were equipped with charts of the routes followed by English commerce.[30] But the attack was still at the periphery of the British Empire, and the Russian theory essentially duplicated the policy of the *Shenandoah* of doing a lot of indiscriminate damage.[31] Their general ideas were expressed in a famous scare story of 1887, *The Russian's Hope, or Britannia No Longer Rules the Waves,* a magnificent Slavic tale of the exploits of a new cruiser in the Indian and Pacific Oceans.[32] She easily eluded the old, slow

British cruisers and destroyed all the shipping in Bombay in one superb coup by flooding the harbor with oil and then setting fire to it. Though the Russians built three more larger and faster armored cruisers and two regular unarmored cruisers before 1885, they still placed much trust in converted steamers.

Although the Russian cruisers were only belated *Alabama*s, the British navy had to start from scratch to find a way to destroy them. The simplest means of commerce protection was to run down each enemy cruiser, and the big, fast unarmored cruisers built in the late 1860s and early 1870s—the *Inconstant, Shah,* and *Raleigh*—were designed to chase the fast American *Wampanoag*-class cruisers. As with battleships, the standard British reply to new foreign ships was to build more, bigger ones, and they laid down a large number of armored cruisers to answer the Russians. This hound-and-hares, bigger-and-better policy was Britain's chief means of commerce protection in the 1870s.

Sir Edward Reed, the naval constructor turned critic, was even opposed to unarmored cruisers for chasing: the "moral power" of England could only be sustained by armored ships.[33]

> What I feel sure of is that with less than half a dozen 20-knot armour-clads, each with a large coal capacity, we might sweep the seas of everything that can assail our commerce. . . . What power, what security, what mastery of the seas, what national pride and honor would they not confer upon us![34]

This "moral power" for commerce defense was less ridiculous in the 1870s and early 1880s than it later seemed, because the retention of sails on unarmored cruisers so compromised their speed that one big armored ship might eventually catch three or four little unarmored ones. It was, however, nearly the only means England had of protecting her commerce. The British built a dozen belted cruisers beginning with the *Shannon,* ordered in 1873. In the later *Imperieuse* and *Orlando* classes they gradually took the important steps of abandoning sails and making the ships faster than regular battleships. But all of these miniature battleships, with their excessive concentration of armor and big armor-piercing guns, were still too weak to fight battleships and too slow to catch fast cruisers. One critic wrote that they resembled "a bandit of melodrama, hung about with swords and pistols and carbines innumerable," instead of soldiers of any purpose.[35]

The British efforts to catch the Russian converted liners resulted in two other moves forward. The more important of these was the development of dry docks and coaling stations outside of Europe, which began to make it possible to send ships overseas that had been designed for service in home waters and to suppress two features previously required in station cruisers: sails and the wooden sheathing that protected their bottoms from fouling.

The examination of British coaling stations by the Carnarvon Commission after the Russian war scare of 1878 was the beginning of the end for the old station fleets. The agitation during the scare laid down all of the main elements of naval defenses outside Europe, including coaling stations, telegraph cables, dry docks, and colonial fortifications. In response to the Russian threat in the eastern Mediterranean and the Pacific, the English initially confined their efforts almost entirely to the direct route to the Far East via Suez. They gave considerable attention to the Indian and Pacific Oceans, Aden, Bombay, Singapore, Hong Kong, British Columbia, and Australia, while they largely ignored the Cape of Good Hope.[36] In the Mediterranean they did much work at Malta, remedying shortcomings that had caused much concern in the 1878 scare, but showed very little interest in Gibraltar. Cyprus, which the British won in 1878 in return for giving France a free hand in Tunis, proved to be a complete disappointment, and the expedition that sailed to occupy Egypt in 1882 assembled at Suda Bay in Crete.[37]

The other major move forward made by the English at this time was to give the smaller ships of the station fleet some serious protection in the form of a light armored deck and a cellular layer, features that could not be fitted to merchantmen. The first of these new "protected" cruisers, the *Comus* class, were still masted, sheathed, and slower than their more powerful enemies. In 1880, however, the improvement in British coaling stations resulted in Britain ordering four ships of the *Leander* class, which had no sheathing, and in 1883, four ships of the *Mersey* class, which were similar but practically mastless. Both of these later classes were faster than contemporary battleships and at least as fast as the best of the new belted cruisers.

The only better cruiser then in existence was Sir William Armstrong's *Esmeralda,* completed for Chile in 1884. In this ship, the comparatively large number of small guns mounted on the broadside in typical British cruisers were replaced by two 10-inch, 25-ton breech-loading guns, one at each end, plus three 6-inchers on each side. Mastless except for signal poles, making 18 knots on a displacement of 3,000 tons, protected by an armored deck, cellular layer, and shields over her guns, the *Esmeralda* in concept was a little station *Italia.* The appearance of a ship like this on foreign stations made the majestic wooden station fleets obsolete even against the "savages." England had nothing as good as the *Esmeralda* and also lacked a rational system of commerce defense, but with nine belted and eight reasonably fast protected cruisers and the beginnings of a seriously defended chain of coaling stations, she was fairly well able to take care of the Russians by the late 1880s and possessed the nucleus of a modern fleet for foreign station commerce protection.

Despite this progress the Admiralty, like the Russians, depended greatly on converted merchantmen for service as fast unarmored cruisers in wartime. Britain's merchant fleet was actually considered a source of military strength instead of the weakest point in the imperial system. Some enthusiasts even claimed that a group of merchant ships could beat off cruiser attack by ramming, and that merchantmen in groups could easily protect themselves.[38] In order to have more armored ships to scare the enemy into submission, Reed opposed all construction of unarmored ships. His successor, Barnaby, agreed with this misconception (they disagreed on everything else), writing about merchant ships that "so long as they can be fought bows on, they will compare favorably for ordnance, for the ram, and for the torpedo with unarmored ships of war."[39]

But commerce protection by means of merchant ships proved to be more difficult than it looked. In 1853 the Admiralty had flatly refused to give any subsidies to fast ships in the form of postal contracts; now it led in encouraging merchant builders to meet its requirements.[40] No one pointed out until later that the taking up of so many ships would itself be a formidable blow to the carrying trade. The Admiralty continued to believe in its great reserve of cruisers until the second Russian scare in 1885, when, at a cost of 783,000 pounds, it took over fifty merchant steamers only to find that none had any of the necessary structural features and that there were no guns or gunners for them. It could also be very expensive: 55,000 pounds were spent in tearing out the cabins of the Cunard liner *Oregon,* then the blue ribbon ship of the Atlantic.[41] Only one ship was ever fully equipped, and the Admiralty learned that ships, like big guns, could not be improvised overnight.[42] In 1887 Parliament voted the first regular subsidy for merchant ships built with features making them suitable for use as cruisers; and these ships, along with their pre-installed gun mountings, their guns in depots on shore, and a certain number of reservists among their officers and crews, replaced the unorganized efforts of 1885.

In answer to the Russians, England had begun to develop a fairly effective matériel for the defense (and attack) of commerce—modern fast cruisers and the chain of coaling stations needed to support them. But the Russian policy of causing indiscriminate destruction in the most distant parts of the empire was not nearly as dangerous as the later French policy of concerted commercial warfare in European waters to bring about the military collapse of England. In addition, the crude British defense method of shadowing each enemy cruiser was ill adapted to meet serious attacks near home. Ultimately, the struggle in distant waters was still over the ancient question of prestige, not national survival. For Prime Minister Benjamin Disraeli and many of the other statesmen of his time, the British Empire was "a makeweight in the councils of Europe," and safeguarding the road to India was above all a matter of British prestige.[43]

Seven

The Revival of French
Naval Matériel

THE RESPONSE of the French naval constructors to the innovations of Benedetto Brin began to appear in the late 1870s. Instead of simply copying some of the Italian ideas as the British did, the French engineers built on their own experiments with armor and guns to produce a type of battleship that was a distinctive mix of previous French practices and new technology. In the process, they began construction of a new fleet that caused considerable alarm in England when its proportions became known in the mid-1880s. With responsibilities extending far beyond the Mediterranean, the French did not limit themselves to a response to Brin's battleships but also took another look at cruiser warfare and participated in the development of an important new weapon, the torpedo.

THE FRENCH RESPONSE TO ITALY

The French initially disregarded the Italian innovations in ship design and followed the lead battleship of the Program of 1872, the *Redoutable*, with two more of the same type, the *Dévastation* and *Courbet*. They did not begin their answer to the *Duilio,* the *Amiral Duperré,* until 1877, although they built her (at La Seyne) in the then-remarkable time of less than five years. This ship was not a copy of the Italian type but a development of French ideas. After unhappy experiences with two low-freeboard American ironclads purchased in 1867, the Conseil des Travaux consistently rejected all proposals for mastless turreted ironclads derived from the monitor type.[1] The new ship's design reflected the absolute insistence of the French on seakeeping qualities, which led to the ultraconservative step of retaining sail power but also resulted in desirable features such as big guns carried

The French answer to the Duilio: *the battleship* Amiral Duperré *(launched in 1879). Her armor was concentrated in a narrow strip around the hull at the waterline and in her four barbettes.*

twenty-six feet above the water. (The *Duperré*'s sails were removed before the ship was completed.)

The *Amiral Duperré*'s armor scheme was the result of an intensive debate. Between 1867 and 1873, while Armstrong was airing his ideas in England, the Conseil des Travaux was controlled by Admiral Philippe-Victor Touchard, the leading advocate of *décuirassement*. Under Touchard in 1871 and 1872 the Conseil explored two of the alternatives proposed to the British Committee on Designs by the opponents of armor: it accepted as a basis for further study a proposal by the naval constructor Emile Bertin for a cruiser protected only by a cellular layer, and it tentatively approved the suppression of the armor over the guns on two station battleships then under construction in order to thicken the armor on the waterline. (The director of matériel also proposed similar changes to two first-class battleships, but the Conseil demurred.)[2] The next year Touchard lost control and neither scheme was adopted, but the Conseil accepted the necessity of rendering invulnerable the armor that was retained. To make this possible, the Italians and the English had deleted armor from part of the waterline; the French took it from the side above the waterline. The *Duperré* retained a complete belt extending 320 feet from stem to stern, 22 inches thick, but only 8 feet high. Flush with the top of the belt was an armored deck, and the stability of the ship and the protection of its machinery thus depended on a shallow, closed-top armored box the length of the ship. Above the belt, the sides of the ship, like the ends of the *Duilio,* were unarmored in order to concentrate the armor where it was essential.

The heavy guns were placed in armored barbettes on deck connected to the protected portion of the hull by tall armored towers. The *Duperré's* four 48-ton guns—one-half the size and power of the *Duilio's*—were arranged in four barbettes, two abreast forward and two on the centerline aft. These guns, in their open-topped armored towers, were more easily worked but less well protected than those in the Italian turrets. In addition, unlike other contemporary designs, the *Duperré* had a considerable number of intermediate-caliber (5.5-inch) guns on the broadside, entirely unprotected.

The differences between the French and Italian protection schemes were due to the strength in France of the cult of the ram. Brin wished to keep his ship afloat and firing its guns; the French wanted to retain mobility because of their belief that as long as a ship could move, there was hope of victory through ramming. A complete waterline belt was thought to protect mobility better than the citadel system, for a single shot in the unprotected bow of the Italian ship near the waterline from even a little gun might reduce its speed and ability to turn.[3] If such a ship were rammed in either end it would almost be cut in two, and ramming would be dangerous itself when the ram was not supported by a solid structure like an armor belt. Subsequent experience bore out some of these concerns: the British battleship *Victoria* lost her ability to maneuver and ultimately foundered after being rammed accidentally in the bow in 1893, and the Chinese battleships at the Yalu a year later, while remaining afloat, could only manage four knots at the end of the battle and could easily have been finished off by either the ram or the torpedo.

France also continued to follow her own principles of gun design. The enormous increase in the size of guns came just as steel was being adopted as the sole material for gun construction. Italy and England built their first large guns on the older system using iron, and they began the change to steel only after guns had reached the 100-ton size. In France, in spite of the opposition of the gunnery specialists, the navy first changed to steel and then worked toward larger sizes, although more slowly than abroad.

Both in France and abroad, the change to steel guns was made possible by the production of better-quality steel and by important new principles discovered around 1870 in the manufacture of powder. The improvements in powder were made possible by the development of a means of measuring pressures in the bore of a gun during a test; formerly the only method had been to step up the charges until the gun burst.[4] The Model 1870 guns used the same black powder as propellant that guns had used since the Middle Ages. It was cheap and practically foolproof, but owing to its rapid burning, the gas that propelled the projectile was produced all at once, kicking rather than pushing the shell out of the muzzle and causing enormous sudden stresses in the gun. As a result, the Model 1870 guns, like their predecessors, were relatively short (typically of 18 calibers, or with a bore 18 times as long as its diameter) and with a thick mass of metal around the breech. The quick-burning black powder was the chief cause of the bursting of most of the original steel guns. Later powders burned slowly and more evenly, with a minimum of pressure at the start and a gradual increase as the shell accelerated toward the muzzle. This improvement, coupled with the introduction of more homogeneous steel, made possible the change to all-steel guns.

The first step was simply to replace the iron body of the Model 1870 gun with a steel one. Immediately after the war of 1870, twenty experimental steel guns built in this way proved successful. Largely for reasons of economy, however, the navy decided to retain the satisfactory iron produced by the navy's foundry at Ruelle, and the 38-ton guns designed for the French *Dévastation* class and some coast-defense ships to match those in the British *Devastation* were still of this cheaper construction. The Gâvres Commission continued to find fault with French steel, and late in 1874 the commission and the Conseil des Travaux agreed that the answer to the Italians should be larger weapons of the iron model.[5] In spite of this, the minister of marine, apparently under pressure from the steel manufacturers, decided to adopt steel.

Three years after the founding of the new private gun works in France, the steel men thus won a great victory over the naval artillerists, which the latter never forgot. The Model 1870 gun had required such careful construction that private companies could not build it, and its low price would have made it impossible for them to make a profit. In order to take advantage of the greater strength of steel, it was necessary to produce a new design to enable the same gun to be built of the new material. The modified Model 1870 guns were naturally no better than those that they replaced— except to the steel-makers. In the meantime, at the very beginning of the big gun race, the French were delayed by the shift from iron to steel guns.[6]

The glowing accounts of the wonders coming out of Armstrong's works greatly excited public opinion and caused the new French design to be rapidly pushed to completion. The 48-ton, 13.4-inch Model 1875 guns built to this design were installed in the *Duperré* and all of the ships originally designed for the 38-ton, 12.6-inch gun. After the trials at La Spezia in 1876, however, the deputies in the French Parliament became even more alarmed about the Italians, and France entered the race for bigness more enthusiastically. The minister of marine assured the Chamber that French 100-ton guns were just around the corner, and two new ships, the *Amiral Baudin* and *Formidable,* were to be built to carry them.[7] The formerly conservative

The battleship Formidable *(1885). The secondary battery of 5.5-inch guns was soon supplemented, as shown here, by four 6.4-inch guns in sponsons to augment end-on fire, which was weak owing to the location of all three big guns on the centerline.*

Conseil wanted to go to 120 tons and, like Barnaby, "could see no limits, except those of our methods of manufacture and our money."[8] But since the *Baudin* class retained the intermediate armament of 5.5-inch guns, they could carry only three of the monsters.

In the new ships, which were without sails, the guns were placed on the centerline to fire on either broadside. The armor scheme was similar to that of the *Duperré,* and these two ships, with their narrow but complete waterline belt, protective deck, and (as initially designed) three barbette-mounted 100-ton guns, were the final French answer to Brin's *Duilio* and *Italia.* France had gotten a late start in the gunnery race owing to the decision of the minister to change from iron to steel, but public opinion was responsible for subsequently hastening the process of the change to steel and the jump in the size of the guns. There were as yet no objections to the principle of Armstrong's tremendous cannon.

The French managed to avoid excessive alarm about the Italians during the first period of Italian naval activity. Between 1872 and 1878, Brin launched three battleships—the *Duilio, Dandolo,* and *Italia*—and began a fourth, the *Lepanto.* Though the Italian naval budget had nearly doubled since 1870, it was still no more than a quarter of the French.[9] French observers regarded the new Italian Navy as a serious but not a dangerous rival, and they did not take seriously Italian hopes of reaching the levels set in a "basic" ten-year program adopted in 1877.[10]

THE FRENCH REVIVAL AT ITS PEAK

One result of the French efforts to respond to Italian naval construction was that during the second ministry of Admiral Pothuau (1877–79), most of the backlog of ship construction in the dockyards was cleared up. The arsenals needed work, and thanks to Freycinet's program of funding public works by loans, more money was available for building new ships. The leftist deputies in Parliament wanted to institute some reforms before new ships were laid down, but the rotting away of the first generation of ironclads made prompt action essential and the work of replacement began.

Despite the efforts of the reformers, the structure of the fleet as established in the Program of 1872 was not changed.[11] A factor of major significance in the naval situation in 1879 and 1880 was the relative clearness of the French diplomatic horizon. Tension with Germany had nearly disappeared, Italy was occupied in bickering with Austria, and the republicans in power in France favored cooperation with England. The lack of pressing diplomatic problems and the need for immediate action made it easier to follow the line of least resistance and simply replace the disappearing ships rather than reconsider France's entire naval policy. In a five-day discussion in 1879, the Council of Admiralty developed no new general program, and the only change it made was to replace some of the small craft in the 1872 program with torpedo boats.[12] The ships that were rotting were practically all battleships built in the 1863–66 period, along with a few station and coastal ships, and the council did not review the cruiser problem. As in 1872, a large number of ships were laid down simultaneously, but they were begun as routine replacements for the older ships in the fleet of 1872 before the danger from either Italy or England became apparent.

Most of the new ships were developed from either the *Duperré,* with four big guns and sails, or the *Baudin,* with three still larger weapons and no sails. They fell into the traditional high-sea, station, and coast-defense categories. In 1880 four new battleships—the *Hoche, Magenta, Marceau,* and *Neptune*—were begun. As originally conceived, all had the same high freeboard, armored waterline and barbette towers, moderate speed, secondary 5.5-inch armament, and three 100-ton guns as the *Baudin.* The four new armored station ships of the *Duguesclin* and *Bayard* classes were small-scale *Duperré*s with four barbettes and auxiliary sails.

The only new ships whose design broke with past practices were the four coast-defense ships of the *Indomptable* class. The six 5,000-ton coast-defense ships of the 1872 program were designed as descendants of the armored rams and monitors of the 1860s. They were low-freeboard ships with a single turret forward whose guns would prepare the way for ramming. The new, heavier, and more powerful German *Ausfallkorvetten* of the 7,600-ton *Sachsen* class rendered them obsolete. The German ships were not designed around the ram but were small citadel battleships, and they created a considerable problem because they appeared just as the increase in tonnage and draft necessary to meet the Italians made it impossible for the new first-class French battleships like the *Duperré* to operate in the Baltic as comfortably as the *Redoutable*.

The French decided to follow the German lead, and in early 1876 they redesigned the last two of the 1872 coast-defense ships, the *Furieux* and *Tonnant,* as small battleships with increased freeboard and with a gun at each end in barbettes. In 1877 they designed the *Indomptable* class as small battleships based on the *Baudin* but cut down for the Baltic by lifting out the middle barbette.[13] The new ships resembled earlier coast-defense ships only in their relatively low freeboard at the ends and in their lack of steaming radius. Instead of a single bow turret, they had single barbettes fore and aft with a 76-ton, 16.5-inch gun in each. Compared to contemporary battleships, they were almost as fast, carried more armor for their size (2,670 tons on the 7,200-ton *Indomptable*), and had only one less big gun. If they were counted as battleships, France had under construction eight of the new type that she had developed to meet the Italians, in addition to three whose construction was further advanced—the *Duperré, Baudin,* and *Formidable.*

Before 1886 the French made only one major change in these designs: France, the last of the three powers to adopt the 100-ton gun, was the first to abandon it. The Model 1875 gun, which had been adopted against the wishes of the naval artillerists, almost immediately began to give trouble.

The coast-defense battleship Furieux *(1883). Her original design closely resembled that of the* Tempête, *but she was completely redesigned as a barbette ship with a 13.4-inch gun at each end.*

The coast-defense battleship Requin *(1885) as originally built. This and the other three ships of the* Indomptable *class had the largest-caliber guns (16.5-inch) ever put into a French battleship.*

The first of the very large versions of this model, the 76-ton, 16.5-inch, 22-caliber gun for the new coast-defense ships, failed as the artillery men had predicted because of the still-uncertain quality of the steel used. One gun built of Creusot parts was rejected six times in succession and two failed at the muzzle during their firing trials. So many troubles of all kinds were encountered that by 1879, before any of the 76-ton guns were in service, the French had abandoned the attempt to build one of 100 tons.

Instead, they started in the totally different direction of trying to make better use of the power of the new French slow-burning powder.[14] The result of the first experiments by the Gâvres Commission with powders of this type was a new gun of the same weight as the troublesome 76-ton weapon but of different proportions. It was a 14.6-inch gun of 75 tons and 28 calibers designated Model 1875–79. The French then went all the way to the sound principles of 1870 and decided to try to equal the penetration of the 100-ton gun by taking advantage of the higher shell velocity given by a longer and lighter gun using the new powder. In 1880 they developed a 52-ton gun of 13.4 inches in diameter and 28 calibers in length, which, though its projectile was naturally smaller, succeeded in obtaining a penetration as good as that of the English and Italian weapons of twice its weight. Compared to the Model 1870 gun, the new Model 1881 had its chamber enlarged to make maximum use of the new powders. None of the Model 1870 guns so enlarged ever failed in service. Indeed, the only French gun that ever did was a Model 1875 on the *Duperré* that blew out its breech because of a similarly increased charge. The gun had been in service for seven years at the time of the accident, and nobody was killed. By 1881 the reign of the

The battleship Hoche *(1886). She is shown under way with her low ends awash after an 1894 refit in which one military mast and some of her superstructure were removed.*

big guns was only an unhappy memory in France, although those involved never forgot the lesson concerning the intervention of public opinion in matters of artillery.[15]

Of the six battleships that had been designed for three 100-ton guns in centerline barbette towers, the *Baudin* and *Formidable* were well along in construction and could not be changed, although they were given the new 75-ton Model 1875–79 guns instead of the proposed 100-tonners. The plans for the other four as approved in late 1880 provided for three of the even smaller 52-ton guns instead of the 100-tonners in the original concept, but during the next two years these ships were entirely redesigned. In three of them, four barbettes arranged in a lozenge pattern (one at each end and one on each side amidships) replaced the centerline arrangement of the main armament, which had always been warmly criticized by the partisans of the ram.[16] These ships ended up with four 52-ton guns, France's final answer to Armstrong's 100-ton blunderbuss. The fourth of the new ships, the *Hoche,* was built with turrets instead of barbettes at the ends and an armament of two 52-ton and two 28-ton guns.

The rearrangement of the guns on these ships made them particularly well suited to fighting end on. They could train three guns ahead or astern, the armor on the forward three barbettes gave good protection against shot coming from ahead, and their complete armor belt protected their ability to maneuver. They were much more vulnerable on the broadside: their secondary guns and the bases of the barbettes were badly protected, and the top of the armor belt was so low that there was danger of water getting over it into damaged areas of the ship. The earlier *Baudin* and *Formidable* and the four coast-defense ships were even less satisfactory in this respect, since their artillery, being on the centerline, was placed to fight on the broadside, but the hulls were not protected accordingly.

By 1882 the French were thus building a large number of new battleships of the single type they had evolved in answer to the *Duilio.* Though their guns were different, all seven were of about the same tonnage and would form a relatively homogeneous fleet. Even without adding the four coast-defense ships also under construction, France was building a very formidable fleet. The original reason for this effort was merely to replace earlier ships to maintain the level of sixteen battleships established in the Program of 1872—the ten steel battleships and six earlier ships begun by Napoleon III and launched in the 1870s. But because it coincided with a period of slow construction in England, the French effort had the potential to make France almost equal to England in ships of the latest type.[17]

England had a much larger number of battleships built to designs predating the *Duilio,* including some purchased during Britain's crisis with Russia in 1878. The liberal government chose to patch up these ships instead of laying down new ones "whose fighting efficiency in the near future is open to doubt."[18] For ramming, these stout iron hulls fitted with new engines and boilers seemed just about as good as new ships, and many French officers regretted that Dupuy de Lôme's use of wood hulls made it impossible for France to follow the English example of patching.[19] But to the partisans of either the gun or the torpedo, these old ships with their thin side armor, light guns, and few watertight compartments were as obsolete in England as in France.

Of the new type of battleship, England was building only the *Inflexible,* four smaller ships patterned on her that were hardly larger than the French coast-defense ships, and six ships of the new "Admiral" class based on a defective design. "In the sort of despair that possessed us" in 1880, the designers of the Admiral class managed to combine the chief weaknesses of the *Inflexible* with all the worst features of the French *Indomptable,* upon which the new British design had initially been based.[20] The armor scheme of the new ships combined the soft unprotected ends of the *Inflexible* with the low belt of the *Indomptable,* while the layout of the guns essentially duplicated the *Indomptable* with a barbette at each end and a few secondary guns amidships. The Admirals were thus Italian at the ends and French in the middle, except that they retained the low freeboard at the ends of the French coast defenders, which made them bad sea boats. They were weak for end-on fighting because of their unprotected ends and the centerline location of their main armament, while on the broadside they were almost as poorly protected as any of the French ships.

In their armor, their guns, and many of the details of their construction, the new French ships were better than the British, and the French replacement program seemed about to recover for France the old position of near equality in numbers of ships and superiority in individual units that had been the ambition of Napoleon III and Dupuy de Lôme. Many historians have minimized the material factor in the British naval scares of the 1880s and have found sufficient explanations in the general diplomatic and political situations.[21] However, the French ships actually under construction were nearly as numerous and were advancing as fast as the British, while the French armor, guns, and projectiles were better. In addition, under the Freycinet system of funding public works by loans, French naval expenditures were increasing. After a short period of decline, the ordinary expenses of the navy steadily rose from 181.2 million francs in 1879 to a new high of 217.2 million in 1883. The two weak points in the French position only became apparent later: the program had not been adopted with opposition to England in mind, and its financial basis was unsound.

PROBLEMS WITH GUNS ABROAD

The French were interested spectators to the later trials and tribulations of the British and Italians with their oversized naval artillery. There was little difference between the Italian Armstrong guns and the Woolwich model, and both Italy and Britain went through the same evolution. The trouble began in 1879 with the explosion in the British battleship *Thunderer* of a 38-ton gun, the model that had served as the point of departure for the jump to 100 tons. Forty-seven men were killed or wounded. The official British explanation for the disaster was that the gun—one of two in the turret—had missed fire on the previous salvo and that a new charge had been rammed in on top of the first one. After a long series of tests, the investigating committee double-loaded the second gun from the same turret, and the fragments of the gun after this second explosion corresponded fairly well with the remains of the first.[22] A year later one of the *Duilio's* guns failed at the same place, and the Italian committee adopted a similar explanation. They likewise reassured their officers by bursting a 100-ton Armstrong gun by double-loading.[23] This trial was hardly over when a second Armstrong gun split into two pieces from a small practice charge of powder and the three remaining guns of the *Duilio* were found to be defective.[24]

With the new powder, the demand for longer guns, and the danger that a careless sailor would swab out a muzzle-loader and reload it without noticing that a ton and a half of powder and projectile were in the bore, the English and the Italians could no longer delay the change to breech-loading guns. (The French had used breechloaders since the 1860s.) The British designed their first new breech-loading guns to have the system of mixed iron and steel construction used for the muzzle-loaders, but the press informed the authorities that the French had been building all-steel guns for five or six years. Woolwich then decided to start all over again and copy the latest

The British battleship Benbow (1885), *of the Admiral class, showing off one of her two 16.25-inch guns. Side armor was restricted to a relatively small patch amidships.*

long steel breech-loading continental guns, just as the Admiralty copied major foreign innovations in ship design. About 1882 the British made three major changes simultaneously, combining the best features of the continental system with British improvements. The overall design of the new steel gun and its breech mechanism were French with British changes, and the method of construction was copied from Krupp in Germany. In addition, a large number of the new guns were to be constructed at once. The only French comments were that the British had made some important changes in the borrowed features, that the British "improvements" weakened the guns at the breech, and that the British effort was not supported by "the only unanswerable argument in artillery, a record of firings in trials *à outrance* [to destruction] undergone by several of the new large-caliber guns."[25]

Even more important, the reduction in the caliber of battleship guns that accompanied these changes proved to be only temporary in England. England followed the *Inflexible* with four smaller ships built on the same pattern and designed for 38-ton muzzle-loaders. In two of these, the *Colossus* class, 45-ton breechloaders were substituted after the *Thunderer* accident. However, the Admiralty was only waiting until Woolwich could build the new breechloaders bigger, and instead of attempting to reproduce the French effort to reach higher velocity and equal piercing power with a smaller gun, they renewed the chase after the Italians. The six ships of the

Admiral class followed the *Colossus,* and of these the first, the *Collingwood,* carried four 12-inch, 45-ton guns, four carried four 13.5-inch, 67-ton guns, and one, the *Benbow,* carried two giant 16.25-inch, 110-ton weapons.

The real trouble began when the British tried to fire their new hybrid guns. There was a long delay in the guns' manufacture, and many were rejected on the proving ground. (One firm alone had five big guns condemned.)[26] The new guns entered the fleet in 1886, and beginning with one in the *Collingwood* in that year, they failed with truly remarkable regularity. In some cases, the British projectiles burst in the bore—four out of fifty-four projectiles in one ship malfunctioned in this manner, and such accidents disabled at least five heavy guns.[27] The liners failed in other guns, including three 67-ton and five out of twenty-six 9-inch guns. Both of the 110-ton guns in the *Victoria* (a ship built immediately after the "Admirals") split at the muzzle and had to be shortened. Some guns (including the 110-tonners and ultimately all of the 9-inchers) lacked longitudinal strength and began to droop at the muzzle. Finally, if something went wrong with the hydraulic machinery, it was impossible to work the guns; at one practice the *Hero, Inflexible,* and *Colossus* were put out of action at the first round.

Of all the now-forgotten matériel incidents that caused the British to worry during these years, these were by far the most important. "The real serious deficiency," wrote the prime minister, Lord Salisbury, to the queen, "is *the want of big guns.* This deficiency paralyses a certain number of vessels, about a dozen, and makes the Navy weaker than it otherwise would be."[28] The "about a dozen" varied from time to time, but in 1889 they included six new first-class battleships—the *Anson, Howe, Camperdown, Sans Pareil, Victoria,* and *Trafalgar.*[29] This was exactly 40 percent of the post-*Duilio* British fleet.

The danger was so grave that instead of being exaggerated in the press and in Parliament, it was minimized. Some ships were actually sent to sea with unsafe guns, and their captains had orders not to fire them with battle charges.[30] None of the guns had ever been thoroughly tested, and nobody knew how many rounds they would last. Though the trouble really began with the hasty changes of 1882, it became clearly apparent only after 1886. The experts who had seen French shells go clear through British armor knew that French steel projectiles and armor were greatly superior to the British, but even the public could tell that a ship with its guns in the factory was not a fighting unit.

Italy had no more notable tribulations after the failure of the gun of the *Duilio,* but many French officers claimed that the Italians were afraid to fire their guns with battle charges. Their guns shared all the faults of the Armstrong system, and since their ships carried nothing but 100-ton guns, their entire fleet was subject to all of the general weaknesses of this huge artillery.[31]

The danger of a slight injury to the hydraulic system completely immobilizing the gun has already been mentioned, but even when the guns were working properly, their rate of fire was incredibly slow. With ninety men serving them, they took from ten to twenty minutes to load and fire a single round. After each shot, the enormous mass of the gun had to be moved to its special loading position, washed out, loaded, and repointed. It was perfectly possible that if the shot missed, the smaller French guns, loading and firing two or three times as fast, might put the Italians out of action or that the French ships would be able to close and ram between rounds. Thus if the *Duilio* did not happen to sink her opponent on the first discharge, a combat with either artillery or the ram might end disastrously for her.[32] Although the later 110-ton English guns could be worked faster, the danger of an injury to the machinery remained. The smaller guns on the French ships could always be worked by hand if necessary.

TACTICS

Today the ships designed during this period, with their practically unarmored sides and enormous guns whose sole purpose was to try to hit one of the little patches of armor opposite them with a solid shot, seem about the strangest warships that were ever put afloat. One wonders what would have happened had anyone tried to use such ships in a battle. It is practically impossible to tell, for the science of naval tactics was next to nonexistent. The two prevalent tactical notions, an artillery duel between two parallel lines and a ramming melee, were completely incompatible. Ship designers in both Italy and Britain had followed to its logical conclusion the unsound principle that armor was useless unless it was impenetrable, and in doing so they had produced long, heavy, soft-ended ships that were best suited for fighting with the gun.[33] The fighting officers in these navies, however, had made absolutely no progress toward the use of the new matériel, developing neither new principles of gunnery nor new gunnery tactics. In Italy an engineer had tripled the size of the guns in the navy's battleships, but the vast majority of the English-trained line officers continued to believe in and study ramming tactics.[34] In England the 110-ton guns of the *Victoria* were aimed by the methods of Horatio Nelson, and if the works on naval tactics can be believed at all, officers expected to use the soft-ended, heavily gunned *Inflexible* for ramming.

French ship design was more consistent with ramming tactics. The French showed concern for the ships' mobility by armoring the entire waterline, and they kept their ships much shorter than those of the British and the Italians. The design of the *Baudin,* with three weapons on the centerline, was the only departure from gun layouts consistent with ramming tactics. However, when even the smaller French guns were fired directly forward, the blast generally ruined the boats, paint, and skylights. (In England, when the *Sans Pareil* fired her guns right ahead, the deck itself was caved in and a man who had not been evacuated from the front end of the ship was killed.)[35] The cult of the ram was more deeply rooted in France than in any other European navy. It was said to be especially suited to the descendants of the ancient Gauls, and with one exception, all of the French writers on tactics agreed that the ram was the chief weapon of naval warfare.[36]

The new signal book that the French adopted in the 1870s was, in fact, a perfect example of the small amount of change that resulted from the introduction of the new weapons. The war of 1870 had prevented following up the tactical proposals worked out in the Squadron of Evolutions before 1870 in response to the Battle of Lissa. Instead of beginning all over again, a Tactics Committee in 1876 merely approved these proposals. Thus, in the year of the Spezia trials of the 100-ton gun, the French fleet simply took its 1870 tactics out of cold storage, and the new official instructions published in 1879 were the actual code worked out after Lissa.[37] The very country in which tactical study had formerly been most advanced did not even seriously examine the possible consequences of a tripling in the power of naval artillery. Even more uncritically than the English or the Italians, the French accepted ideas developed for the completely armored ironclads of Dupuy de Lôme with many small guns as sufficient for the new scantily armored ships carrying a few much larger guns.

According to the prevalent tactical ideas, an ideal battle was to begin with a gunnery duel at long range, while each side rushed full speed toward the other. For this preliminary cannonade, the ships practiced all sorts of pretty evolutions in squares, triangles, and lines ahead and abreast.[38] The sole purpose of these formations was to ensure that the ships arrived at the battle together and in good order. These maneuvers were all that was left of naval tactics. The French committee did not prescribe any particular method for battle. "Only one condition is essential, the bows must be turned toward that side from which will come the attack."[39] The melee when the two lines met, after all, was the real battle. Only eleven of the 183 articles of the code were devoted to battle tactics, and these were no more than the vaguest general instructions. As long as the ram was the chief weapon and the melee the major part of the battle, squadron tactics, or unified action under a single chief, was impossible at least during the decisive period of the action.

> The admiral has ordered "Advance!" and he rushes toward the enemy.
> . . . They advance in good order. . . . But once the ranks are broken, the
> signal book is closed and the responsibility of the Captains commences.[40]

Scientific preparation for these grand free-for-alls was useless. The new armored knights were reduced to the crude methods of a medieval tournament. The image of close-quarters confusion became a key element in the public's idea of a naval battle and in the theories of later opponents of the battleship.[41]

The hope of striking a gigantic and decisive blow from the ram or a monster cannon had completely replaced the older attempt to defeat the enemy by combining well-directed minor efforts.[42] The possibilities of completely destroying an opponent by a lucky blow of the ram, or an equally lucky hit with a one-ton projectile, were obviously attractive, and Brin's ships were protected against, and built to deliver, a single knockout blow. This "one-punch" theory of battle was the fundamental idea behind naval ship design throughout the period.

French Cruisers and Commercial Warfare

In France in 1872 the station fleet and commerce-destroying fleet were one and the same, and during the years of friendship with England after the war of 1870, French cruiser policy stood still. France's efforts to emulate the British *Inconstant* and produce a large, fast, fully rigged cruiser were limited to three ships of the Program of 1872: the *Duquesne,* the *Tourville,* and

The first-class cruiser Naiade *(1881). This was one of five ships, including the* Dubourdieu *and the canceled* Capitaine Lucas, *ordered in the late 1870s with wooden hulls, low speed, and no armor. As fighting ships, they were little better than the steam frigates of the 1850s.*

The first-class protected cruiser Sfax *(1884). A vast improvement over the* Naiade *type, she had a steel hull, a protective deck, and good speed. She was France's first modern cruiser since the* Tourville *of 1876.*

The first-class protected cruiser Cécille *(1888). She is shown at Villefranche with the battleship* Courbet *(1882), one of two improved versions of the* Redoutable *begun in the mid-1870s.*

the slightly smaller *Duguay-Trouin*. These were no better and no worse than their contemporaries, and like them were too expensive to be reproduced in quantity. The French launched around two dozen unprotected fully rigged corvettes of various sizes after 1870, but these, like similar foreign ships, were useless for wartime employment. The best of the station battleships were two begun under Napoleon III and four little *Duperrés* built in the late 1870s, but these, with a speed of 13 knots, were still slower than battleships.

In 1878 the Conseil des Travaux approved specifications for sixteen-knot protected cruisers of about 3,000 tons for commercial war.[43] Somewhere in one of the changes at the ministry this good resolution was lost sight of, and by 1881 there were four more fully-rigged wooden cruisers reminiscent of the old frigates under construction. A fifth, the *Capitaine Lucas,* was just about to be laid down when Emile Bertin's frantic protests awoke the Conseil to the existence of the English protected cruisers. After a long discussion, the *Capitaine Lucas* was replaced by the first French cruiser with a protective armor deck, the *Sfax.* Though still fitted with a full sail rig, she made the unheard-of speed of 17 knots.[44] In 1885, while she was completing, two larger, faster, rigged cruisers of the same general type, the *Tage* and *Cécille,* were ordered.[45] These three comprised the entire French commerce-destroying fleet of the mid-1880s.

More typical of the French cruising fleet was the *Dubourdieu.* The last of the four wooden sailing cruisers built in the late 1870s and early 1880s, she was launched in 1884 and made 13.7 knots on her trials in 1886. She spent the next two years in France being fitted with admiral's quarters, and in 1889 she made her maiden voyage as flagship of the Pacific Station. The powers at whose ports she touched were Hawaii, under the protection of the United States; Chile, whose *Esmeralda* could have blown her out of the water in fifteen minutes; Peru; and Tahiti. There was no more fitting monument to the prestige ideas of the old French Navy. "To satisfy the needs of a useless station, the French navy creates a type of warship whose inferior speed could expose it to great perils in time of war. . . ."[46] Even the conservative Admiral Jules-François-Emile Krantz is supposed to have remarked sadly to the president of the Republic, "*Ce n'est qu'un beau logement*" (she is nothing more than nice accommodations).[47] It was ironic that the power that had supposedly renounced the idea of equaling England on the high seas in order to threaten her by commercial warfare had, in 1886, almost equaled her in battleships but had only a single modern cruiser for commerce-raiding. Although English commerce was practically unprotected, France possessed almost nothing but merchant cruisers and small scouts for attacking it.

With regard to merchant cruisers, the French position was better. Although the Conseil wisely opposed a suggestion to arm some of the older merchantmen, a clause in the subsidy law of 1881 provided a further bonus for all new ships built to navy specifications.[48] By 1884 a well-organized system for converting a small number of liners had been set up. Although suitable ships were relatively few (only nineteen were on the list in 1897, of which not all qualified), at least the guns were real and the gunners knew how to use them. This system of construction for subsequent conversion was greatly in advance of the British idea of taking over a large number of ordinary liners at the outbreak of trouble and quickly making cruisers of them. This was the only part of French commercial warfare policy that was equal to that of the British. Even though France in the 1880s stopped building useless ships for the special purpose of upholding the honor of France and her missionaries overseas, she did not develop a policy for defending her colonies for another fifteen years.

THE DEVELOPMENT OF TORPEDOES AND TORPEDO BOATS

Russia astonished the naval world in 1877 and 1878 by ordering 110 little torpedo boats for the defense of her Black Sea ports against Turkey. Strong coast defenses were, in fact, the necessary corollary of limiting high-seas offensive capabilities to commerce-marauding in distant waters, but she was the first to adopt the torpedo on such a large scale.

Early torpedoes were divided into two categories, fixed torpedoes (now called mines) and mobile torpedoes. Both types began to be used in the American Civil War. Ingenious Americans, including David Bushnell, Robert Fulton, and Samuel Colt, had always led in their construction, although most experiments before the Civil War had consisted of placing a charge beneath a stationary hulk and blowing it sky-high for the edification of numerous spectators, without in any way advancing the development of naval science. Only in 1862, with the organization of the Confederate States Submarine Battery Service under the inspiration of the world's greatest oceanographer, Matthew Fontaine Maury, did the history of submarine warfare really begin. The Confederates had no special equipment, no trained men, and no special scientific knowledge whatever, but in the course of the Civil War they damaged twenty-six vessels and seriously injured or sank nine by mining. Two of the amazing devices the Confederates invented were of particular importance. One was the portable or spar torpedo, a keg of explosives on the end of a pole to be carried by a small, swift boat against the side of an enemy ship. The other was the contact mine, designed to explode when a ship happened to touch it. Confederate observation mines, which were detonated by observers ashore when an enemy ship passed over them, were generally failures due to poor knowledge of electricity, and the success of the Confederates' generally crude methods depended greatly on the shallowness of southern waters and coasts and on the lack of friendly shipping. Nonetheless, they were able to close their harbors almost completely.[49]

In Europe after 1865, both England and France carried on active experimentation. In England the scientific study of the phenomena of underwater explosions began with tests against the iron paddle sloop *Oberon,* while Captain James Harvey invented a special towing torpedo. The Harvey torpedo was kept in tow at the side or rear of a ship (often a battleship) and was suddenly whipped out to hit an approaching enemy. In France a special committee was appointed in 1866. Admiral Viscount Octave-Pierre-Antoine-Henri de Chabannes-Curton La Palisse carried out a series of successful experiments with an ordinary ship's boat armed with a spar torpedo, and by 1869 a permanent torpedo station and school was opened near Rochefort at Boyardville.[50] Both spar or towing torpedoes could be used on little boats for the mobile defense of a harbor, but their use on a ship's boat, which could be carried to the scene of operations, or on a battleship itself, were the first efforts to use them in offensive operations.

English and French defensive preparations were less satisfactory than their offensive experiments. Neither power could expect to close its ports entirely with torpedoes, and two of the major French bases could not be well defended by them. Cherbourg could be bombarded from the open sea, and Brest had a long and narrow channel with strong currents and very high tides, which made torpedo work particularly difficult. Germany and Austria, whose coastal geography and lack of friendly shipping more nearly approached Confederate conditions, made much more progress in the defensive use of torpedoes. For the Austrian port of Pola, Baron von Ebner devised the first complete defensive mining system. Both his contact and observation mines were fairly satisfactory, and their combination into a dangerous zone of contact mines and a passage of observation mines which could be opened or closed at will was the basis of later defensive systems.[51] In 1870 extensive German contact mining effectively prevented all French attempts to force the German coastal passes, but the laying and recovering of these mines reportedly cost the Germans 150 officers and men.[52]

The chief types of underwater weapons in existence in 1872 were spar and towing torpedoes, fairly good observation mines, and very unreliable contact mines. These were the basis of numerous vague and sensational rumors and of the general idea of many officers that against the combination of the torpedo, the ram, and the small gunboat armed with a big gun, the battleship had little chance of survival. One of the most important elements in submarine warfare, the fear of finding an invisible and deadly opponent almost anywhere, was already fully apparent in the Franco-Prussian War, and the torpedo's cheapness and usefulness for coastal defense greatly appealed to public opinion even in the 1860s. The news of de Chabannes's experiments was followed by a sensational debate in the legislative chamber: Marie-Aimé-Philippe-Auguste Le Coat, viscount de Kervéguen, demanded the complete suppression of the costly battleships, and Dupuy de Lôme himself had to be brought in to reply to him.[53]

After the war, although France reopened the school at Boyardville in 1872 and reestablished the Commission des Défenses sous-marines there under Admiral Siméon Bourgois, she remained far behind in torpedo work until 1877 or 1878. The lead was taken by small powers that could not afford sea-going forces for coastal defense. French coastal defenses were behind those of countries like Denmark, and much of the organization of French defenses seems to have been based on studies made in Holland. France was the last power to replace black powder in its torpedoes by high-explosive charges; she had much trouble with most of the devices she experimented with; and she was nearly the last to adopt the automobile torpedo, the only new type of torpedo that appeared after 1870.[54]

The automobile torpedo began as a little petroleum-burning steamboat guided by ropes from the shore. Although Robert Whitehead did not originate the idea, this clever English manager of an engine works in Fiume, Austria, contributed all the mechanical devices that made it work. He suppressed the ropes, replaced steam with compressed air, and finally decided to try to make the device run underwater as an invisible submarine weapon attacking heavy ships under their waterline armor. The "balance chamber" that enabled the torpedo to keep at a constant depth below the surface was Whitehead's "secret." It was never patented or successfully pirated, perhaps because of the great number of "infallible, complete" descriptions published and self-styled ex-mechanics from Fiume who offered their services to every navy in Europe. In 1869 Austria purchased the secret and gave Whitehead the right to sell his torpedo abroad. After his success in selling it to England in 1871, the rest of the European powers quickly adopted the invention. Each was given a torpedo and a set of drawings and was allowed to send a certain number of officers to Fiume.

Although France had been negotiating with Whitehead in 1868, the conversations were cut short by the 1870 war. Not until 1872 did the reports of his other successes get him a trial. His glowing prospectus also played a role—he claimed that at ranges between 180 and 600 yards "no well-launched torpedo" would miss a stationary target, whether the firing ship was moving or not, and that within another 200 yards there was "every assurance" of hitting.[55] In January 1873 Whitehead came to France with his torpedo, and after successful trials and considerable haggling over the price, the navy decided to purchase the secret for 288,000 francs. The "Secret Treaty of April 1873," as it was always called in the navy, was not a contract between Whitehead and the ministry but a regular treaty with the naval representatives of the French Republic.[56] Five officers were to be sent to receive the plans and torpedo, and two were to be taught its manipulation. The government was given all the rights of manufacture in France and agreed to keep the secret from all foreign countries.

It now remained to put the weapon to use. The experiments of the next six years are sufficient explanation of some of the experts' reservations with regard to the wonders that the lay enthusiasts of the torpedo later promised. Even while urging the new torpedo's acceptance, the Boyardville commission had noted that Whitehead's "complete assurance" at 600 to 800 yards was "very exaggerated" and "infallibility" up to 600 yards was "equally exaggerated." The French had bought an experimental weapon that was fairly good up to 200 yards (with a speed of 9 knots at that distance), and though this was remarkable enough, the Whitehead was far from being an actual instrument of warfare.[57]

The first idea of the French was not to use the Whitehead defensively (except at Brest, where mining was almost impossible) or on a light ship, but to fit it to battleships as an extension of the ram to help deliver a single big blow in a squadron combat. As first tried on the coast-defense ship *Tigre,* it was placed in a simple underwater shell and ran out of the ship under its own power when the screws were released. Tested at Brest, the torpedo was so slow that it was practically impossible to hit an object moving in the channel, and it was almost necessary to stop the *Tigre* to prevent her from running over and damaging her torpedo after release. After long consideration, the Boyardville commission decided to abandon the *Tigre* and try the torpedo on a ship's boat or any craft up to 200 tons that could "stop quickly" to let the torpedo get clear.[58] But the underwater installations proved so cumbersome that it was impossible to apply this idea, and by 1875 experiments on Whitehead torpedoes in France had nearly come to a standstill amid complaints about their weight, cost, and uncertainty.[59] In the same year, most of the officers in Austria and Italy, in spite of the perseverance of their ministries of marine, were similarly convinced that the Whitehead was a failure.[60] In England, where the submerged tube was also the original method of launching, the attempt to use the Whitehead from battleships ended in frustration as well.[61]

The Whitehead was still an expensive and uncertain spar torpedo at the end of an imaginary hundred-yard pole, and the much simpler and cheaper spar and towing models were in the meantime making far better progress.[62] Harvey's towing torpedo, considerably modified at Boyardville after 1872, was the favorite for squadron action. Every large ironclad was equipped with one on each side, and if the enemy turned away when the French ship tried to ram her, one of the towing torpedoes that stuck out like antennae fifty feet or so from her flanks would be almost certain to deliver its blow. The towing torpedo was unique in that it was more successful against mobile than stationary targets, since a moving target that hit the tow line at any point would pull the torpedo into it. In 1878 the cruiser *Desaix,* sixty feet from the target ship *Arrogante* with both moving at 8 knots, successfully exploded her torpedo over two thirds of the time.[63] The first regular torpedo tactics were issued for the towing model in 1875—it was to be towed closely behind the ship and suddenly let out when the enemy came into range—and it was the first torpedo that was successfully tried in maneuvers for a squadron action.[64] In 1877 towing torpedoes were already so effective that the commander in chief reported that the ram and torpedo "tended to neutralize each other; [the torpedo] is destined effectively to hold at bay any enemy who desires to use his ram." The Harvey torpedo was thus the beginning of the end for ram warfare.[65]

The spar torpedo, the simplest of all, was obviously not suited for use in larger vessels. The problems of keeping the torpedo from bouncing off the target and of getting it under the target's armor belt deep enough to keep the explosion from swamping the attackers were relatively easy to solve. The main effort went into finding some way, by invisibility or speed, to get the boat up to the enemy. In the American Civil War, both William Barker Cushing for the Union and the "David"-type submersibles of the Confederates had adopted "creeping" tactics, and the total failure of the French to develop a high-speed boat before the English did was largely due to their concentration on similar tactics. The French were intrigued by three ideas— the search for stealth and invisibility, the ability to put the torpedo on a boat little enough to be carried to the scene of action, and the concept of the submarine. Even in periods of relative inaction in submarine development this great dream of French naval engineering kept reappearing, and the first torpedo boat proposed by Admiral de Chabannes in 1865, with its armored deck and conning towers and its ballast tanks for submerging at the moment of attack, shows this influence very clearly. (It would certainly have perished from the explosion of its own torpedo, just like the Confederate "David" that sank the Union sloop *Housatonic.*)

The first boat actually tried by the French was designed by the engineer Charles Brun, who along with Admiral Bourgois had built the experimental submarine *Plongeur* in 1859. Brun's boat, tried in 1870, suffered from the effort to combine small size, armoring, and submersibility—it was only twenty feet long, unstable, unsubstantial, and slow.[66] The next boat, though larger, practically reproduced the de Chabannes plans. It had a silent petrol motor, compact Belleville boilers, and a turtle-backed, nearly submerged shell on top. Though solid and stable enough, the best it could do was five knots, and the motor could be made silent only by closing the ventilators, with disastrous effects on the crew.[67] After the failure of this boat, the French tried a smaller one on which they closed the ventilators and did without the crew—it was directed by two miles of wire.[68] The problem of creeping up on the enemy was still unsolved, and although "a submarine boat" was the "great desideratum," the Boyardville commission reluctantly turned to fast steam surface craft.

By this time the French Navy and the British Admiralty (whose first torpedo boat, the *Vesuvius,* was also a low-speed semisubmersible) were fully two years behind an English private firm. In 1873 the English boat builder

John I. Thornycroft produced a 15-knot, 8-ton steam launch equipped with a towing torpedo for the Norwegian navy, and in the next two years his firm and that of Alfred Yarrow built similar and better boats, fitted with spar torpedoes, for Austria, Argentina, Sweden, and Denmark.[69]

Immediately after the failure of the French petroleum boat, the French naval engineer Louis de Bussy was sent to England, and in the same year as it decided to build the *Duperré* and change to all-steel ordnance, the ministry ordered seven fast torpedo boats. Two were to be fitted with a new-model Whitehead torpedo that traveled at 20 knots instead of 10, and the other five, like the Thornycroft boats, were to use spar torpedoes. The boats were to be of steel strong enough to keep out rifle fire, sixty feet long, noiseless, with a speed of 13 knots, and seaworthy enough to go six miles outside Cherbourg.[70] They were thus strictly for coast defense, and they could not be carried into a squadron action. Two each were ordered from Thornycroft and the French firm of Claparède (at St. Denis, just outside of Paris) and one each from Thornycroft's competitor, Yarrow, and the arsenals at Rochefort and Brest.

In the trials at Cherbourg, the two Thornycroft boats (*No. 5* and *No. 6*) traveled fifty-four miles in a continuous three-hour run; their plates were only dented by rifle bullets at fifteen feet; and in an attack on the old hulk *Bayonnaise,* one of them ran right into the target at 12 knots with a thirty-five-pound charge of guncotton without either the collision or the explosion seriously damaging the little boat. The Yarrow and the Claparède spar boats were less solid and four knots slower, and the spar boat from Rochefort and both Whitehead boats were failures. But at last, thanks mainly to private invention and amateur ingenuity, the fast surface torpedo boat was begin-

A "torpedo steamer," probably torpedo boat No. 4, *built in 1875 for the French government by the British firm of Yarrow. She carried a primitive spar torpedo.*

ning to look promising. While the naval experts were longing for the *belle marine en bois,* a group of Americans with some wire, beer barrels, and gunpowder; an expatriate English mechanic; and a London boat builder were changing naval warfare.

In 1877, just after the British Admiralty ordered its first Thornycroft boat, the Russians ordered 110 torpedo boats (mostly to Yarrow plans) for use in their war that had begun earlier that year against the Turks. The boats, built amid tremendous fanfare, were sent by rail from St. Petersburg to Sevastopol, where a few arrived before the end of the war early in 1878. It was wonderful advertising and, like the Russian conversion of merchant ships into the Volunteer Fleet, very impressive, but the results were inconclusive. During the war, under the dashing Lieutenant Stepan O. Makarov, a group of steam launches fitted with torpedoes had delivered large numbers of brave and unorganized attacks with a practically uniform lack of success. The towing torpedo was found to be worthless, the Whitehead was tried only twice, and most of the spar torpedoes exploded on outlying booms. A couple of minor Turkish vessels that were keeping a somnolent watch were the total bag of much random bravery. Despite the lack of searchlights and quick-firing guns, even an alert lookout foiled most of the attacks. The British officer serving with the Turks pointed out that the lack of previous organization and training was more responsible for the failure than the weapon itself.[71] The British public, however, preferred to believe the much-quoted accounts of this officer's superior, Hobart Pasha, who told them that England had nothing to fear from the torpedo. "Were it not so," he stated as his final clinching argument, "one might almost say that naval warfare would soon come to an end altogether."[72] To a good Briton, he pointed out, it was inconceivable that blockades, attacks on the enemy's harbors, and cruising off his coasts would ever become impossible. His interpretation of the Russian failure was apparently convincing. In 1877 and 1878 the Admiralty bought twelve larger boats, in 1880 it purchased thirty-four small ones for harbor work and for carrying on battleships and cruisers, and from 1881 to 1884 it bought no torpedo boats at all.[73]

While the developments in naval matériel during the 1870s had little immediate impact on internal politics, international rivalries, or even naval theory, they played a key role in the turmoil that developed after 1885. Brin's and Saint Bon's ingenious response to the problem of defending the Italian coasts from serious attack, particularly their adoption of the big gun, their search for invulnerable armor, and their effort to make quality in ships take the place of numbers, caused the change from the completely armored ships of Dupuy de Lôme to the almost unarmored monstrosities of the late 1870s and early 1880s. The *Duilio* differed nearly as much from the *Redoutable* as the latter did from the *Gloire.* The response to these changes, particularly France's undertaking a substantial building program while England patched up its obsolete ships, was one of the chief reasons for the British alarm at the French Navy in the mid-1880s.

Another major reason was the changing diplomatic situation. The French program had begun simply as an effort to replace rotting wooden ironclads at a time when the French government was friendly toward England, and Italy was embroiled with Austria. It was continued and completed, however, in a period of intensifying Anglo-French colonial rivalry and renewed diplomatic antagonisms between France and Italy, Britain's friend. Within France the problem was compounded by the fact that the torpedo helped make naval strategy an issue in partisan politics. The great changes before 1885 were in naval matériel; the next fifteen years were occupied in sorting out the implications of these changes for naval organization, theory, and tactics as well as for internal politics and the international balance of power.

Eight

The Navy Under the Republicans

T HE ADVANCES in French naval matériel during the late 1870s and early
1880s were accompanied by important developments in naval policy
and politics. The naval reform movement reemerged in Parliament in 1878
with demands for reform of the navy's archaic administration and suggestions for a new naval strategy. Three years later a reform-minded minister of
marine, Auguste Gougeard, attempted to implement some major changes.
While his ministry was too short to see these through, Gougeard together
with the parliamentary movement laid a firm foundation for the more drastic reform efforts of the Jeune Ecole later in the decade. They also helped
increase the navy's interest in torpedo warfare, which made major advances
during the period.

THE LIBERALS REPLACE THE CONSERVATIVES

At the end of 1877 the liberal republicans in the Chamber of Deputies
wrested control of the government away from the conservative monarchists
who had dominated it since the resignation of Thiers in 1873. The conservatives had considerably augmented naval expenditures during the last two
years of their rule by means of a complex system of special credits. The
republicans brought back to the Ministry of Marine Admiral Pothuau, the
author of the Program of 1872, and pushed the construction of ships still
more actively.

The most interesting aspect of the republican victory, however, was the
immediate revival of the old liberal demand for general reform of the navy.
In the five years since the drawing up of the Program of 1872, the navy's
leadership had made no effort whatever to implement the reforms requested by the Assembly's Budget Committee. In 1877, when the first phase

of the program should have been approaching completion, the full impact of the disappearance of the first generation of wooden-hulled ironclads and the arrears in the new program was becoming apparent. If the navy were not to vanish entirely, its leaders would have to ask Parliament for more money.

As if to forestall such a demand, the republicans took the offensive in the very first session after their triumph. Instead of registering a perfunctory approval of the minister's plans, the reporter of the Budget Committee, Etienne Lamy, undertook a thorough examination of the whole naval situation. His report was more than the personal effort of a young and unknown deputy—it was a general summary of the whole liberal case against the navy. It clearly stated what can be called the parliamentary naval theory, which remained in opposition to the official theory throughout the rest of the century.

Lamy advised the Chamber to remember, before it granted money for a new naval program, that the failure of the navy to build the ships called for under the Program of 1872 was not the first such sad experience but the latest in a whole series of failures.

> Never has the nation refused the navy the resources it has demanded for the realization of its programs; never have its programs been realized. . . . So persistent an evil has permanent causes and indicts the very organization of the navy. These causes must be found and destroyed or, far from being able to save the institution by augmenting the expense, we will continue to augment the expense without saving the institution.[1]

Lamy asserted that the naval administration, in pursuing its policy of "saving the interests of the personnel," had simply become a means of supporting its clerks, officers, and arsenal workers. His specific proposals, discussed in a previous chapter, included reduction of the number of bureaus in the central administration, better accounting, rationalization and specialization of the industrial system, and the sponsorship of ship construction in private yards. The demand for efficient organization was thus still the basis of the parliamentary case against the navy, and the Chamber and Lamy were recommencing the struggle that Childers had won in England exactly a decade before.

The novelty of Lamy's report was not the charge against the naval administration but the entry of the Budget Committee into the field of naval strategy. As Lamy correctly pointed out, the failure of the Program of 1872 and the decay of the wooden-hulled ironclads had left France faced with fundamental problems:

> France hoped she had saved in her fleet a force for the future. . . . Here, as elsewhere, the Empire had raised appearances of grandeur but left

only ruins, and, after so many years and so much money spent, the fleet is still to be created.

What was needed was not a reform of details but a reevaluation of the entire navy starting from basic principles. For example,

> Just as for matériel, the size of the navy's personnel should be determined from the composition of the fleet that the state desires to maintain. The personnel should be capable of assuring all the necessary services, and should be limited to the size required by those services.[2]

In creating a new navy, France, like Italy, first had to decide on the purpose of the naval organization and then on the means for accomplishing it. The Program of 1872, according to Lamy, had lacked such a clear definition of its objective, and the mere retention of a certain respectability abroad was no longer a sufficient purpose.

> Until recent years, there were only two military powers in Europe. . . . These days are no more. . . . Three peoples, who have achieved grandeur in recent events, border on the sea . . . and have loudly announced their naval programs. . . . It would suffice for two of these navies, nonexistent twenty years ago, to unite for France to lose numerical superiority. . . . Today there is no security for [France] if she does not make herself capable of standing up to a coalition of two of them.[3]

The report thus proposed a new standard, the ability to match any two continental navies, to replace the vague ambitions of Napoleon III. But what kind of fleet was needed? The high-seas fleet, whose "appearance of grandeur" had been so deceiving, was disappearing. Could France afford another? The cost of Napoleon III's battleships and their complete uselessness in the tragedy of 1870–71 left no answer for Lamy but the negative.

> They were powerless to maintain the blockade of the enemy's coasts and returned to French ports in the very middle of the conflict. They only began to render services when they disembarked their crews. . . . The construction of battleships is so costly, their effectiveness so uncertain and of such short duration, that the enterprise of creating an armored fleet seems to leave fruitless the perseverance of a people. In renouncing warfare between battle fleets, a nation does not abdicate if it can produce, after having assured the defense of its coasts, ships with powerful engines and strong artillery, able to remain at sea for an extended time, and destined for commercial war.[4]

Lamy's strategic theory contained three basic ideas: first, that France needed a two-power continental defensive naval standard; second, that Napoleon's big battleships were another part of the useless imperial facade;

and third, that coastal battleships and cruisers were cheaper than a high-seas fleet. These, along with Lamy's demand for administrative reform, were all ideas with strong popular appeal. In combination, however, they produced a strategy that was incoherent in that its means did not match its ends. The coast-defense and cruiser policy had traditionally been a last resort against England, but Lamy did not even take England into consideration as a possible opponent. Instead, Lamy proposed using such a fleet to maintain a continental standard whose nature was also exceptionally thin and shadowy.

A continental two-power standard made sense for France after the conclusion of the Triple Alliance between Germany, Austria, and Italy in 1882, since it would ensure the defense of French coasts against Germany and the security of French communications with Algeria against Italy. When Lamy wrote in late 1878, however, neither of these had yet been threatened. Lamy himself was a prophet of colonial expansion in the eastern Mediterranean, and his strategic scheme was simply an outgrowth of public uneasiness over the naval efforts of Italy, Germany, Austria, and Russia which coincided with a new series of crises and wars in the Balkans and the Middle East. The deputies were watching, passive and confused, a new act of the eastern drama in which their emperor only twenty years before had played the leading role. Lamy and the public did not seem to know which two navies were threatening France's eastern interests, but they wanted the navy to give less attention to distant places like the Fiji Islands and more to the eastern Mediterranean, where, under the Program of 1872, the Levant Squadron had been replaced by a single gunboat with the impressive title of the "Station of Constantinople and the Danube." Lamy's two-power standard was less a defensive strategy providing for the abandonment of the prestige fleet than a call for reconcentration in the Levant.

The other two of Lamy's ideas were totally irrelevant from the point of view of strategy but highly important for the political future of the navy. The idea that a coast defense and cruiser force was cheaper than a high-seas fleet had a long tradition, going back through Grivel to Louis and Jérôme de Pontchartrain, the ministers who in Louis XIV's later years presided over the decay of Colbert's fleet. Lamy's other idea, the linking of battleships with the fallen empire, was newer and proved to be a fertile source of confusion, for it tacitly associated the big ships with political conservatism. The idea found immediate appeal because of the conflict between the politically and navally conservative higher officers and the more progressive younger men. French liberals soon came to identify the navy's majestic battleships with the equally majestic admirals who advocated them, and many adopted the bizarre notion that battleships *per se* were unsuitable to a democratic republic.

Lamy's report was a landmark in French naval history because it was the first parliamentary document to propose a complete program of naval organization, strategy, and ship construction. It also shared most of the strengths and weaknesses of such parliamentary efforts. In the field of naval organization, Lamy's views were perfectly sound. In strategy, his uneasiness about the situation in the Mediterranean was closer to political reality than were the views of the older officers. However, the ships he proposed, coast-defense vessels and cruisers, would not have attained what seems to have been his objective. Finally, his reasons for supporting those types of ships—cheapness and suitability to a republic—were irrelevant and soon led to a disastrous politicization of naval strategy.

This wholesale criticism from the usually passive Budget Committee created a considerable sensation, and an impressive Parliamentary Mixed Commission was appointed in 1879 to look into the charges. Including the minister of marine, it had no less than thirty-three members, and it set out to complete the work begun by a similar commission after the revolution of 1848. Italian competition and the decay of the old fleet made it impossible to wait for the new Mixed Commission to finish its investigation, and the navy began some new ships, including the four large battleships of the *Magenta* class described previously, to replace the ones reaching the end of their lives. By beginning a large replacement program, the navy effectively evaded a discussion of Lamy's two-power standard and rejected the policy of a fleet of coast-defense ships and cruisers while leaving the Mixed Commission to debate Lamy's demands for reform of the administration. Instead of leading to a new naval policy, the new ships fastened the naval, diplomatic, and financial conditions of 1879 and 1880 on the following decade, just as the ships left unfinished by Napoleon III had helped to fasten the ideas of the imperial navy on the navy of the Republic during the 1870s.

The Mixed Commission conducted a bulky investigation of the Ministry of Marine and the arsenals and even published some of its proceedings. Just like the Commission of 1849, however, it was dissolved before it could report its conclusions. It fell, owing not to a coup d'état as in 1849, but to the sovereign indifference of French public opinion. In the elections of 1881 several of its members were defeated, and nobody in the new Chamber ever bothered to appoint new ones or to call the commission together again. It expired peacefully in the ordinary round of French politics, leaving the major portion of its proceedings in the archives. These reveal that its recommendations would have followed four general principles: the arsenals were to be subdivided into three departments (the fleet, construction, and provisions); all five naval ports were to be retained; coast defense rightly belonged to the navy; and a rational system of accounts should be adopted.[5]

The Gougeard Ministry

The work of the Mixed Commission was not entirely in vain because the elections of 1881 brought one of its members to the Ministry of Marine. The cabinet of the great radical politician Léon Gambetta lasted only a little over two months, from 14 November 1881 to 27 January 1882, but it was a milestone in the history of the navy. Externally, it came at the moment when renewed colonial rivalry was ending the period of friendship with England that had prevailed during the 1870s. Internally, Gambetta's choice as minister of marine of Auguste Gougeard, a retired navy captain who was the most notable of the republican officers not promoted after 1872, marks the transition from the old navy to the new.

Of all the men in Gambetta's "great ministry," Gougeard was the "one who came to power with the clearest idea of his task."[6] He was the man who best knew the navy's complex administrative machine and who was also thoroughly convinced, perhaps from personal motives, of the need to make many of the changes that civilians such as Lamy wished to impose. There was no other French naval reformer, before or after, who was not either a civilian, like Edouard Lockroy, trying to reform a machine he did not understand, or a military man, like Admiral Aube, who knew the machine but could not see the necessary changes. In the development of that peculiar mixture of civilian and military ideas known as the Jeune Ecole, Gougeard was the most important figure between Grivel and Aube.

Gougeard's ministry drew its ideas from the Lamy report in that its chief aim was the reform of the navy's administrative organization. It also drew on the work of the Mixed Commission, of which Gougeard had been an active member.[7] His two-volume study on the arsenals published in 1882 was in many ways a one-man unofficial report of the work of the whole commission.[8] As in the case of Grivel, who owed much to his father, and Lamy, who summed up a whole series of parliamentary complaints, Gougeard's work was much more than the result of one man's experience.

Though Gougeard based his proposals on the commission's investigations, he did not hesitate to change its recommendations on a number of important points as a result of his own studies. During the period in the 1870s when he was passed over for promotion because of his republicanism, Gougeard studied the history of the naval troops he had commanded on land during the war of 1870 and then turned to the general history of the development of French naval organization.[9] Only then did he begin to see how little the system of 1870 differed from that laid down by Colbert in the 1600s.

This led him to study the navies of the other powers, and before his appointment to the Mixed Commission he fully realized the importance of the work of Childers in England and Brin in Italy. In England he saw how an active public opinion had helped change completely a system of naval organization that originally had been much like that of France.[10] In Italy he saw how Brin and Saint Bon had successfully opposed the interests of the largest city in the kingdom, Naples, while in France a few deputies from the much smaller ports of Rochefort and Lorient had been completely successful in blocking every measure of reform. Even worse, Brin had successfully abandoned the French system of organization in use up to then in the Italian arsenals for the one prevailing in England. Armed with a thorough understanding of the history and principles of the existing naval organization in France and of the English and Italian reforms, Gougeard was in an ideal position to exploit the opportunity provided him as a member of the Mixed Commission to investigate the arsenals at first hand and to gain access to the files of the bureaucracy.

Once the origins of Gougeard's administrative proposals are clear, it is necessary only to outline their main points. In the central administration, he proposed replacing the old, illogical division between matériel and personnel by an English-style active fleet, fleet under construction, central purchasing agency or commissary, and service of accounts. All the civilian services, like the administration of the colonies, were to be distributed to the proper civilian ministries. This last, one of his conditions for accepting office, caused the first transfer of the colonies to the Ministry of Commerce, a reform that did not outlive the Gambetta cabinet.[11]

Gougeard's call for a rational accounting system and the assignment of coast defense to the navy rather than the army duplicated two of the points in the commission's program. His proposed organization of the arsenals, like that recommended by the commission, differed slightly from the English model. He proposed creating separate services for the fleet afloat and the fleet in construction to correspond to the new divisions at the ministry, but he retained a general magazine in each port that represented the central purchasing agency. In England the central purchasing agency did nothing but execute the orders that came in from the fleet or the naval constructors, but in France the idea that it should also have a special independent magazine where the services would negotiate to get their stores was very persistent.[12] But all through his proposed organization, a careful separation of the fleet in construction from that in active service replaced the previous division between personnel and matériel.

Gougeard's administrative program was diametrically opposed to that of the commission on only one point—he demanded the specialization of Lorient and the elimination of Rochefort as a naval port. The local deputies had browbeaten the commission as easily as they had the Budget Committee of 1872, but the commission's figures on the inefficiency of Rochefort compared to the other ports suggested that there was nothing to do but close it altogether.[13] Of the other ports, Toulon, already largely occupied with repairs, was to continue in that function; Cherbourg and Brest were to continue construction of new ships in order to have repair facilities available when needed; and Lorient was to specialize in new construction. All the work was to be rationalized, and about a third of the navy's shipbuilding, a modest proportion, was to be given to private firms.[14]

Gougeard had no time to put his organizational reforms into effect. Though his successor, Admiral Jauréguiberry, suppressed a Bureau of Miscellaneous Services in the central administration, ten days later the colonies came bundling back to their old familiar roof in the Ministry of Marine. Lamy's administrative reforms were not carried through, and the navy struggled along with its organization essentially unchanged.

Gougeard also proposed two important military reforms. The one that he made particularly his own was the foundation of a central scientific institution in Paris, the Ecole supérieure de la Marine, to combine the functions of a Naval Institute and a Naval War College. Like the Royal United Service Institution in England and the copy Brin had established in Italy, the new organization was to take the discussion of naval affairs out of the "obscure redoubt of the ministry" where the experts' ideas were subjected to neither criticism nor appreciation. Following the pattern of the army's new Ecole supérieure de la Guerre, it was also to complete the technical education of French naval officers. The Ecole supérieure de la Marine, with a student body of forty or fifty officers at a time, was to be a real institution of higher learning and not a mere staff college.[15]

While the idea of educating naval officers for actual war was clearly important, so was Gougeard's intention of simultaneously educating the public, and he clearly intended his new institution to fulfill both purposes. He saw as clearly as had Grivel the need "to interest the great French public in the affairs of the navy."[16] Edouard Lockroy, the reforming minister who revived the idea and established the school in the 1890s, completely missed the idea that one of its functions was the enlightening of French public opinion. Of all the partisans of the Jeune Ecole, only Grivel and Gougeard saw the necessity of educating the public, not in a particular system of naval tactics, but in the general principles of war at sea.

After the fall of Gambetta's cabinet, the new minister, Jauréguiberry, placed the project before the Council of Admiralty. The council found the idea of higher technical education to be theoretically sound but proceeded to bury it with full military honors. The proposal would be retained for future consideration, but for the present, "experience is the only fit school for a naval officer; naval superiority resides in character, will, and natural aptitude; and these are not acquired by theoretical instruction."[17] Although France was not as stifled by the "seagoing" tradition as was England, most of the older men were still more interested in navigation and saluting than in the hard work of getting ready for war. The belief that the age of naval battles had passed, and the complete degeneration of tactics due to the advent of the ram, were additional factors contributing to the belief that the scientific study of war was more or less useless. Indeed, not all the traditionalists were as polite to the project as was the council. Admiral Krantz later told the Chamber that he was "entirely hostile to that creation," since a young man from the training ship had all the theory that he would ever need. He added that even in the existing schools, he had tried during his term as minister (1887–89) "to diminish a little the scientific baggage that they were given" and provide them more military instruction.[18] He made this comment only two years before Admiral Stephen B. Luce established a Naval War College in the United States with Captain Alfred Thayer Mahan as naval history professor.

Another part of Gougeard's military program did bear fruit, however, with the founding of the first French Naval General Staff. This was the first step toward the careful preparation and organization for war that became an outstanding characteristic of the French Navy during the 1890s. It is not easy to tell to what extent the navy was influenced by a similar development in the army, but a colonial expedition mounted in mid-1881, the occupation of Tunis, clearly played an important role. During the operation the navy had lacked both information and plans, the provision of which was the function of any general staff. Probably as a result of the way the Tunis expedition was conducted, the French Navy went even further and tried to make its chief of staff a kind of subminister for all military affairs. The whole Tunis affair, down to the last detail, was conducted by telegraph from Paris. This was partly due to the personalities of the officers involved—the minister, Admiral Cloué, was a man of great ability and experience while the men commanding the forces were apparently lacking in decisiveness. The major reason, however, was certainly the need to keep the operation closely coordinated with the Foreign Office. Paris again took a central role in the campaign against China in 1884 when the personal factors were absent. The absolute necessity of keeping every petty expedition under the tightest possible control while the diplomats bargained with the other powers, especially England, was reflected in the centralizing function of the new staff.

The first step toward the organization of the French naval staff was taken during the Tunis expedition itself, when the Bureau of Officer Personnel was placed in the minister's private cabinet to give the minister more direct control over operations. Exactly in line with this policy, Gougeard had proposed to create in the cabinet a "Service of Action" to obtain information, prepare plans, and conduct military operations. The minister's cabinet was to "give the decisive impulse to the whole navy; it is the final expression of centralization" for the fleet.[19] This organization was formally set up two weeks after Gougeard's fall. Headed by the chief of staff, it contained three divisions: Foreign Navies, Operations, and Personnel.

One weakness of this organization was that the chief of staff was also chief of the minister's cabinet and was therefore replaced with each change of minister. In addition, because the staff was designed to coordinate colonial expeditions that were really conducted from the Ministry of Foreign Affairs, it had a number of administrative functions in addition to its main tasks of providing information and planning for war. However, the mere creation of special services for information and planning was a great step forward for the navy.[20] Similar organs were soon established in each port, and in 1885 each fleet was given a permanent staff.

Despite its success in introducing the doctrine of careful preparation for war that Germany had so successfully applied on land, the Gougeard ministry was for the most part a missed opportunity. The failure to institutionalize the navy's relations with public opinion and the failure to remedy its defective administrative and industrial organization left the navy's greatest weaknesses untouched just as it entered a new period of conflict, with England and Italy abroad and with political critics at home. The chance of following the example of the English and Italian reforms slipped away, and as Lamy had foreseen, once the contest had fairly begun, there was no further chance for reform.

Gougeard's Tactical Ideas

Renewed colonial rivalry with England brought to the fore the commerce-raiding theories of Grivel, which had been inspired by the adventures of the *Alabama*. Admiral Aube, one of the most fanatical of the original *Alabama* school, favored a ruthless attack on English trade.

> The present power of England is greatly exaggerated. . . . Never was the comparison more true than that of the "colossus with feet of clay" as applied to that immense empire. . . . Twenty cruisers of superior speed, thrown onto the world's trade routes and commanded by men resolved to wage merciless war—true war—would be sufficient to strike her to the heart.[21]

Gougeard, like the leaders of the Jeune Ecole, was an ardent partisan of colonial expansion and concentration as a way to restore French prestige. He was also one of the few men who realized that the British Empire was not as fragile as German and French diplomatic successes were then making it appear. He took issue with Aube on both the theory and the expected results of a strategy based on nothing but commerce-destroying.

> One does not obtain such great results with such puny means. These theories are seductive. They spread easily in public opinion, but they also pervert and mislead it. When we wish to attain an important goal, we must be ready to appropriate the means. . . . In no area on earth can one make something out of nothing, or gain a big payoff by risking only a small stake.[22]

He also noted that against Italy or Germany such proceedings would be "slightly infantile." Without even undertaking a historical argument, he hit on the two weakest points of the commercial warfare theory: the notion that it was cheaper than other kinds of war and its uselessness against France's continental enemies. As for the immediate future, he pointed out that Aube's twenty cruisers and the coaling stations from which they were to operate did not, unfortunately, exist. France could scarcely be expected to enter such a struggle with "the wood cruisers we now possess."

The idea that commerce-destroying alone was both theoretically unsound and immediately impossible led Gougeard to one of his main themes:

> It is necessary to menace England in her most treasured and most vital point, her communications with India . . . and that in a certain measure her own territory should cease to appear to her as an inviolable refuge. It is in the Mediterranean that the destinies of the world will be decided.[23]

Since the Mediterranean was to be the chief field of action, it was essential for France to create several bases in that sea, beginning with Tunis. The next most important field of action would be in the Channel, where France would stage offensive operations, possibly an invasion, from Cherbourg. He noted that "Brest's geographical situation assigns it a less important role than that of Cherbourg and condemns it to serve only as an auxiliary."[24]

Gougeard's policy of an offensive in the Mediterranean combined with the threat of a cross-Channel invasion was appropriate to the actual condition of the French Navy and to the new battle fleet that France had started in 1880 practically without thinking. But, unlike Grivel, Gougeard did not see the possibility of using the battle fleet and cruisers in different ways depending on who was the enemy of the moment (England or a continental power). In addition, if Aube was misled by the emphasis of the British liberals on their trade, Gougeard was equally misled by the conservative Disraeli's emphasis on the route to India, which, while "most cherished," was not actually the "most vital."

Gougeard did not believe in the cult of commercial warfare, but he did agree with the leaders of the Jeune Ecole that the further development of the torpedo had made the battleship obsolete. Recent improvements in the Whitehead torpedo made this view more realistic. In the five years since its failure in the French trials aboard the *Tigre* and in the Russo-Turkish war, both of the Whitehead's main drawbacks, its slow speed and the imperfect method of launching it, had been overcome. Just as the Whitehead was being nearly abandoned everywhere, its makers in Fiume succeeded in doubling its speed and in expelling it from a tube above the water instead of having it swim out under its own power. The torpedo was launched by steam or compressed air, preferably dead ahead from a tube fixed in the boat's bow. (If fired any other way, the torpedo, which dropped into the water at an angle, would be deflected off course by an amount roughly proportional to the boat's movement.) In 1880 the Whitehead's charge of explosive was also doubled.

The scout cruiser Milan *(launched in 1884) at Algiers. She was built for speed, and her main armament consisted of 4-inch guns, one of which is visible on the bow.*

The solution of the problem of firing the Whitehead made the torpedo a real extension of the ram and made the idea of building a special torpedo ship for squadron combat look promising.[25] The English "torpedo-ram" *Polyphemus* was theoretically a high-speed armored torpedo boat to be used in a squadron action. Though seaworthy and successful in her trials, at 2,640 tons she was too large and expensive to be repeated. As had some much smaller and earlier French experiments, she proved that it was impossible to combine nearly submerged navigation, armor protection, and speed without spending such an enormous amount of money that numbers, the other essential attribute of these special craft, were sacrificed. In 1880 the Conseil des Travaux decided not to introduce ships like the *Polyphemus* into the French Navy.[26]

In 1879 the Conseil asked for something "entirely new; a torpedo vessel of large dimensions, very fast, without masts, artillery, or ram, destined to keep the sea with the squadron and to serve it as a special auxiliary."[27] In other words, it wanted a seagoing torpedo ship to fulfill the functions of a squadron cruiser. A year earlier the Conseil had finally realized that it was too much to expect real scouting from 14-knot cruisers and 12-knot avisos and asked for light protected cruisers of about 2,000 tons for scouting and commercial warfare in addition to some larger, fast commerce-destroying cruisers.[28] These two cruiser concepts were developed for different purposes, the former for coast defense and the latter for commerce-raiding. In the first French light cruiser, which was laid down two years later, the coast-defense concept triumphed. The *Milan,* designed by Emile Bertin and proposed by him regularly since its original rejection in 1875, was a scout of only 1,700 tons armed with nothing but torpedoes and light automatic guns.[29]

Although the station fleet still lacked real commerce destroyers, the light cruisers added to the home fleet after the *Milan* became smaller, less useful for commerce-destroying, and even more like torpedo boats. The French

The torpedo cruiser Vautour *(1889), one of four ships of the* Condor *class. She carried five torpedo tubes: one forward on each side abaft the anchor, another pair amidships abaft the gun sponsons, and one aft.*

abandoned the *Milan* type for an even smaller "torpedo cruiser" related to the German *Zieten* of 1876. In 1882 they began four torpedo cruisers of the 1,200-ton *Condor* class and eight smaller "torpedo avisos" of the 320-ton *Bombe* class to replace the old slow scouts and avisos. All of these vessels were also intended to serve as torpedo boats in a squadron action. These hybrids, the answer to the Conseil's request for seakeeping torpedo ships and the first result of the successful use of the Whitehead from a fixed bow tube, ultimately proved to be too large for torpedo boats and too small for cruisers.

Gougeard believed that something very similar to the new torpedo cruiser was the ideal ship of war. He felt that the *Italia* was a great advance in that Brin had abandoned the "chimera of invulnerability" to give her such speed that it would be impossible for the whole French Mediterranean fleet to catch her.[30] Neither the gun nor the ram offered a certain means of sinking such a ship. The only answer was a "true seagoing ship . . . whose principal weapon would be the torpedo."[31] Eight of Gougeard's 1,800-ton protected-deck "torpedo ships" could be built for the price of one *Italia;* the Mediterranean was a sea particularly adapted to them; and a flotilla of such ships coming at an *Italia* from all points of the compass could certainly sink her.

Gougeard's torpedo ship represented merely a further development of the one-punch theory of naval war—Gougeard preferred the torpedo over the gun precisely because he felt the gun could not sink an *Italia.* In addition, his tactics were those of the cheap rams or Armstrong's gunboats of the late 1860s, which were "absolutely certain" of destroying the enemy if a number of them converged on him simultaneously. Gougeard took the interesting step of applying these originally purely defensive weapons to the problem of cutting England's communications with India. In effect, he suggested turning the Mediterranean from a sea into a lake. Unlike the rams and gunboats, his torpedo cruisers were not to wait for the *Italia* to come to the French coasts but were to hunt her down and destroy her in any portion of the Mediterranean. Though he wished to finish construction of the battleships that had already been started, he expected the torpedo ship to replace the armor-clad.

In Italy torpedo ships also enjoyed considerable favor during the 1880s, and even commerce-destroying was greatly in vogue, though nobody seemed to know exactly whose commerce Italy was going to destroy. At this time Armstrong had just produced the protected cruiser *Esmeralda* and was full of enthusiasm for the new type. The Italians, after following Armstrong's craze for big guns, now bought his cruisers with equal ardor. During the 1880s Italy added five large cruisers of around 3,400 tons to her fleet, along with some smaller ones and about a dozen light torpedo avisos like the *Zieten*. In addition, the Italians carefully organized their system of coastal telegraphs and observation points, giving them the main elements of a coast-defense scouting fleet.[32] The English and several other navies also experimented with various types of torpedo ships during the 1880s.

While Gougeard's chief importance lay in his efforts at administrative and military reform, his tactical and strategic ideas mark him as by far the ablest of the ministers of the Jeune Ecole. He was not a naval fanatic in any sense of the word, and his appeals to public opinion were moderate and sane. Finally, and most to his personal credit, he did not identify his proposals with political ideas, even though he was the most outstanding example of the unjust treatment accorded by the monarchist admirals to the republican officers after 1872. In particular, Gougeard did not claim that the torpedo ship was an especially republican instrument of warfare.

Coast Defense

Although the proposal that responsibility for coast defense be transferred from the army to the navy died with Gougeard's ministry, considerable progress was made during this period in developing coast-defense matériel. In the use of mines, the deficiencies of the early 1870s were fully corrected, and the mine defenses adopted for each of the five naval ports in 1877 were judged satisfactory by 1881, even at Brest.[33] Most of the French mines were observation or electro-automatic (rendered automatic from the shore) bottom mines laid in time of peace; those in the deep water at Brest contained as much as 1,700 pounds of guncotton. Active work continued on the form and charges of mines and on minelaying, countermining, mine-sweeping, and the defense of minefields by gunboats, searchlights, and automatic guns. By 1886 plans called for the defensive systems to be completely ready two days after notice was given to lay them.[34] All the continental countries, led by Germany, were also very active in this field, and even the Italians developed excellent defenses where the conditions of their ports permitted them. Defensive mining was now highly developed, even though a satisfactory offensive automatic mine had not yet been produced.[35]

The exception was England, whose mining system, under the Royal Engineers, suffered from the same defects as naval artillery under the War Office. It was "virtually an excrescence" which was not worked into any general plan by the navy.[36] As many as four separate authorities might be responsible for the defense of a single point. For example, the defenses at Malta consisted of a fairway buoy, a controllable torpedo, observation mines, and a boom to keep out torpedo craft, each under a separate authority. Unfortunately the torpedo could not be run out unless the fairway buoy was taken out of the way, and if the observation mines went off they would blow up the boom.[37]

The progress with mines was soon overshadowed by the development of practical coastal torpedo boats. In France a flurry of activity in the late 1870s was followed by further steady development in the early 1880s. The big Russian torpedo-boat program of the mid-1870s had little effect in France, but the success in 1876 of France's two Thornycroft boats led to serious construction of the new type. Immediately after the completion of the trials, the navy decided to order twenty-three more boats, including twelve spar boats directly from Thornycroft, six larger ones from French companies using Thornycroft's plans, three boats with submerged tubes to launch the Whitehead, and two little Thornycrofts to be carried on the decks of battleships "not for operations in a fleet but for *coups de main* on the enemy's coasts."[38] Thus, even before the success of the Whitehead with a fixed bow tube, the French had embarked on a fairly large torpedo boat program.

When the automobile torpedo began to be effective, it was fitted to many of the existing spar torpedo boats while new construction continued. Twelve new boats were ordered in 1878, 11 in 1879, and 7 in 1880 and early 1881. The size of the boats gradually increased, with the first "seagoing" boat of 46 tons, the *No. 60,* being ordered in 1880. Between 1881 and 1883 fourteen more seagoing boats were begun. As a result of this steady construction, France in 1884 with about fifty good-sized boats of various types was second only to Russia, most of whose 115 boats had been bought in 1877. Italy's eighteen boats and England's nineteen placed them behind even Holland, one of several smaller navies that took the torpedo boat seriously.[39]

The most famous of these early "seagoing" boats, the *No. 63* and *No. 64,* were built at the Normand yard at Le Havre, which specialized in such craft. They measured 108 feet in length, displaced 46 tons, and made 22 knots on

Torpedo boat No. 63 *(1883). The successful performance of this boat and her sister,* No. 64, *in a Mediterranean storm made the 33-meter type the model for the "autonomous torpedo boats" that the Jeune Ecole expected would end the reign of the battleship.*

their trials. They were manned by twelve men and one officer, had a range of about 1,000 nautical miles, and were armed with fixed bow tubes. After making the voyage from Le Havre to Toulon without difficulty, they were assigned to the torpedo trial station and then, at the request of Admiral Aube, temporarily in command during the absence of the regular commander, attached to the Squadron of Evolutions. The first small torpedo boats ever assigned to a French squadron, they took part in all its maneuvers and, on the way from Toulon to Villefranche, were able to continue their voyage in a storm that forced two coast-defense battleships to put into port. Although not built for action with a squadron at all, these boats obtained a remarkable success. Though they could not be expected to keep the sea indefinitely with a squadron, the Boyardville Commission found them completely satisfactory for coast defense, in which "seagoing" meant only the ability to withstand occasional high winds. Their chief deficiency was that their fixed bow tubes could not be used except in good weather.[40]

The main change in these boats besides their increased size and seaworthiness was in the method of launching torpedoes. By changing the shape of the muzzle of the tube to resemble an inverted spoon, Whitehead succeeded in making it possible to fire a torpedo from a moving ship at any angle, on the broadside as well as dead ahead. (The spoon-shaped tube made the torpedo drop flat into the water, eliminating deflection caused by the speed of the ship.)[41] Just at the same time, the first scientific investigations of the method of firing a torpedo from a moving ship at a moving object were concluded and firing tactics were developed.[42] The boat, the torpedo, and the method of using the latter from a moving boat against a moving target were at last fairly satisfactory, and by 1884 the Whitehead torpedo had become a practical weapon.

As in the case of the battleship, however, the French had still made relatively little definite progress in the tactical use of the new weapons. The torpedo course at Boyardville in 1885–86 and the reports of the French commission sent to Fiume in 1884–86 give an exact idea of the status of the torpedo just before Admiral Aube became minister of marine.[43] The Fiume commission reported that all the maritime powers, including England, were very active in torpedo work and that Whitehead's factory was so busy that the quality of its work had begun to suffer. The English and German torpedoes, from Woolwich and Schwarzkopf respectively, were better than those from Fiume, and the commission recommended the immediate renewal of attempts to manufacture torpedoes in France.[44] (This had been begun seriously in 1878, when Austria placed an embargo on Whiteheads in order to prevent their sale to Russia, but was abandoned when the torpedoes produced by the navy's factory at Indret proved to be not as good as Whitehead's.) The commission also recommended continuing to buy a few at Fiume in order to keep in touch with the progress of other nations. (This policy of "keeping in touch" was immediately successful—the Fiume commission sent back full drawings of all the latest inventions, including the chief torpedo secret of the Italians, the underwater torpedo tube for their battleships.)

Among foreign navies at this time, England had a few torpedo experts but no real organization, and its torpedo personnel were "very much behind." As before, Germany and Austria were the real leaders, if not in numbers of torpedo boats, at least in their organization. The coming man in the German navy was a torpedo expert, Alfred von Tirpitz, who as captain of the torpedo vessel *Zieten* between 1878 and 1880 devoted himself to developing German torpedo defenses. "Here," he wrote, was "a weapon . . . ready for use in actual war, as important as Paixhans's shells."[45] The head of the German navy, Albrecht von Stosch, recommended just before his fall from power in 1883 that Germany abandon battleship-building altogether and limit new construction to armored gunboats (to defend the minefields) and torpedo craft. His successor, General Georg Leo von Caprivi, staked everything on the torpedo boats.

The German torpedo-boat organization was merely a development from the coast-defense organization of the early 1870s. With the minefields, the new boats were to delay and disorganize the enemy. From the beginning they were grouped in flotillas based in a protected refuge and accompanied by a larger flotilla leader to do their scouting. Coastal telegraphs and fast

The German torpedo vessel Zieten *(1876), the prototype for torpedo avisos and torpedo gunboats in many navies. She had two submerged torpedo tubes, one forward and one aft.*

torpedo cruisers ensured their rapid concentration. The role of the armored ships was reduced even more to that of mobile forts intended to sustain the torpedo boats in their delaying action.[46] Caprivi planned a large number of torpedo cruisers to assist the coastal telegraphs and a flotilla of 150 modern torpedo boats.[47] Since his plan included only one large cruiser and a few gunboats for the colonies, the few offensive ideas the German navy had had under Stosch now disappeared altogether.

Caprivi, like the General Staff, was obsessed by one idea—that a war with France and Russia was inevitable and would come very soon. This meant that there was time to build only torpedo craft and light cruisers, and that the main job of the navy was to completely relieve the army of the threat of a landing from the sea. The outstanding characteristics of the Caprivi period were a fixation on the uselessness of further long-term planning and on the necessity for immediate concentration on coast defense. Its main legacy, however, was not so much the complete disappearance of the idea of offensive high-seas action as the completion of a practically impregnable system of fixed and mobile coast defenses, which became the model for the rest of Europe.[48] Caprivi's modest policy was extremely popular with conservatives, who had feared that the new colonial policy would mean useless foreign stations; with the officers, to whom torpedo work gave a chance of advancement; and with the army and liberals, who hated naval expenditures with equal fervor.

The French commission that visited Fiume reported that the Austrians were probably even better than the Germans in the organization of their coastal torpedo work and that, in addition, the Adriatic was ideal for mine and torpedo warfare. In one of eleven night attacks in the Austrian maneuvers that the commission attended, four battleships were judged out of action.[49] Like the Germans, the Austrians grouped their boats in flotillas accompanied by torpedo avisos like the *Zieten*. However, the Austrian Navy, whose sole idea under Tegetthoff at the Battle of Lissa in 1866 had been to fall on a fleet twice its size with a miscellaneous collection of wooden warships, could not be expected to abandon altogether offensive squadron navigation. In their squadron maneuvers in the open sea, the Austrians practiced for an artillery duel, which would be conducted in parallel lines 2,000 yards apart. One torpedo boat accompanied each battleship, with the mission of dashing out from behind it when the enemy was covered with artillery smoke. The Austrians told the French that similar maneuvers had taken place the previous year in the presence of the emperor at Pola. Thus, three years before France and England began to study the problem of the place of the torpedo boat in naval warfare, the navy that was reputed to have won the Battle of Lissa with the ram had started to abandon the formation identified with ramming, the line abreast, and to develop tactics for using the torpedo in squadron combat.

The German principles of defensive torpedo organization were first applied in France in 1885 by Admiral Bergasse Dupetit-Thouars, the maritime prefect at Cherbourg. He accepted the general idea of grouping the boats into flotillas or *défenses mobiles* around a base or a larger ship that would furnish them with coal, water, and torpedoes. In an inflamed harangue to the officers of the new *défenses mobiles,* the prefect predicted that they would be the "terror of England."[50] But nobody had any very specific ideas regarding the tactics of the flotilla after it sighted the enemy. In a squadron combat, the threat of the torpedo had practically suppressed the ram, and the smoke from the big guns, which would entirely cover the melee, would give torpedo boats a great chance.

Concrete tactics for use in such an encounter did not exist, however. Instead of uniting all three weapons in a single type of ship (the battleship), the French seemed to feel that the future fleet would probably be composed of separate rams, torpedo ships, and gunvessels. Their entire torpedo tactics consisted of the vague general principle of surrounding an isolated ship with a swarm of torpedo boats and of creeping in the smoke of a general melee to get in a lucky hit with the torpedo.[51] In this respect they were definitely behind Germany and Austria—but as definitely ahead of England. In 1884, when Britain had about a dozen torpedo boats in all, most of which were used for picnic parties, one of the leading British torpedo boat builders, Alfred Yarrow, read a paper on the subject at the Royal United Service Institution that aroused considerable comment.[52] The Admiralty responded by immediately ordering two new boats from Yarrow and two from Thornycroft.

DEFENSE OF THE FLEET

While developing means of launching torpedo-boat attacks, navies also tried to develop torpedo defenses for the targets, the battleships. The question was literally one of "the microbe and the giant," to use a phrase popular with the Jeune Ecole, because the fleets of the day were composed of nothing but battleships and large cruisers. (The French Squadron of Evolutions consisted of six battleships, one large cruiser, and two avisos.) The torpedo cruisers and larger torpedo avisos were not yet completed for sea, and they were reassigned as "torpedo-boat destroyers" only after the need for small ships for this purpose had become apparent. For the moment, the battleships had nothing but the slow and unsuitable avisos to help them.

The first anti-torpedo-boat weapons for use on ships were the Hotchkiss and Nordenfelt semiautomatic guns. They were rejected in 1873 as unable to maintain continuous fire on a moving target, and a lighter gun was adopted in 1878, ironically in the midst of the craze for the monster cannon. It fired about fifteen one-pound shells a minute (compared to one round every fifteen minutes for the big guns), and it was balanced on its mounting so that the gunner could follow a moving target directly and judge the accuracy of his aim by the succession of splashes in the water. In the new weapon, the principle of continuous aim, or of pointing the gun like a rifle at a moving target, was as important as rapidity of fire.[53] By 1880 these new light guns, which by then were able to keep a torpedo boat under continuous fire at ranges up to about 2,000 yards, had been adopted for battleships. These ships were also given electric searchlights to point out the torpedo boats at night. In the same year the French began to experiment with torpedo nets—steel nets hung from booms around a battleship—and by 1888 all battleships were equipped with them.[54] At anchor these were reported to provide "absolute protection," while in perfect weather a ship could make seven knots with its nets deployed.[55]

The chief means of torpedo defense for battleships were nets, guns, lights, and such small craft as they could muster (generally their own boats). The problem, however, was not taken seriously until 1885, and the measures taken then tended to justify the confidence of the early torpedo enthusiasts. In 1885 the future British admiral, Sir Arthur Knyvet Wilson, wrote a friend about what he believed was the first real practice ever carried out at night against a target representing a torpedo boat.

> We moored our model six miles off, and when it was quite dark we went to look for it, searching all around ahead of us with the electric light, all the guns, machine guns, and rifles ready for firing. We first had

a false alarm, and the men began blazing away at what I now believe was our own shadow on the opposite side to the electric light. The firing soon stopped, and then we sighted the real target on the other side. Guns, rifles, and machine guns all opened fire at once, an awful din, as you can imagine, and the result was that in a few seconds there was so much smoke that the target could not be seen at all where they thought the target was until I sounded the "cease firing." When we came to examine the target there was not one hit.[56]

The umpires in most naval maneuvers, who judged by volume of fire and sound, would have decreed the destruction of half a dozen targets.

In 1888 the French prescribed the following defenses for protecting a fleet at anchor: a line of light mines to defend against rams, a barrage of spars or masts to stop torpedo boats, an advance guard of light craft and all the ships' boats, searchlights and quick-firing guns on shore to form a luminous zone at the entrance to the anchorage, and nets on all large ships. None of the big guns were to fire under any circumstances.[57] Perhaps motivated by the fact that British ships were still painted white, a color that looked much better in naval reviews than the gray of French and German ships, the future Admiral Wilson even went to the trouble of getting shrubbery to cover his ships (for which some of his enterprising tars came back with half an olive grove). If one could get one's nets, barrages, searchlights, and shrubbery out in time, the problem of protecting a fleet at anchor appeared manageable.

On the other hand, it became evident that the torpedo boat was an almost insurmountable obstacle to the close blockade of a port by unescorted battleships and a very serious danger in a conflict between squadrons. The two greatest perils in such actions were the smoke from the heavy guns and the general dangers of fighting at close quarters. When British battleships bombarded the forts at Alexandria during the occupation of Egypt in 1882, the smoke became so dense that the ships had to stop firing entirely. At Lissa in 1866, smoke covered the whole free-for-all. Even when only small guns were used against torpedo boats, the smoke was often nearly as bad. Nets were as useless for a ship in a squadron battle as for one attempting to prevent fast cruisers from escaping from a blockaded port.

At last, the dream of the pioneer of the torpedo and the submarine, Robert Fulton, of "2,000 torpedo-boats wresting from the English the mastery of the Channel" seemed about to come true.[58] In 1884 the whole question of torpedo boats and battleships was raised in a particularly violent discussion in the Chamber of Deputies, fittingly inaugurating the endless debates of the next twenty years.[59] Like Gougeard a few years before, the minister of marine, Admiral Alexandre-Louis-François Peyron, wished to finish the battleships under construction but admitted that he was so unsure of the future that he would not take the responsibility of laying down more of them. Around this time the French suspended construction of two ships that would have been slightly enlarged *Marceaus*, the *Brennus* and the *Charles Martel.*

All navies seemed to feel that the dim forebodings of the early 1870s were about to be realized and that the ironclad was actually on the way to extinction. For almost five years, battleship construction was nearly abandoned all over Europe.[60] In England the first lord of the Admiralty, the earl of Northbrook, stated that if he were given the money for the new ships demanded by the proponents of a big navy, he would not know how to spend it.

> It would be an extravagance to spend £2,000,000 on the construction of large ironclad ships. The great difficulty which the Admiralty would have to contend with if they were granted £3,000,000 or £4,000,000 tomorrow for the purpose referred to would be to decide how they should spend the money. The difficulty of the present time was whether it was desirable to increase the number of these enormous ships of war; and that it was a difficulty felt not only by our Admiralty but, as he knew, by those who had to conduct the affairs of other countries.[61]

This passage was quoted out of context in later years to demonstrate the incompetence of Northbrook's administration, but in fact it shows perfectly the state of mind prevailing at that time in every navy in Europe. Two years later, the British parliamentary secretary's sole defense for spending more on battleships under construction was that so much had already been sunk in them that they would have to be finished. In introducing the Naval Estimates for 1886, he stated that the two battleships over which controversy was then raging, the *Nile* and *Trafalgar,* would probably be "the last ironclads of this large type that will ever be built in this or any other country."[62]

The need to protect fleets at anchor also caused new activity in developing harbor defenses. Gougeard saw that, at least in major military ports, it was now absolutely necessary to close the greater part of the anchorage against torpedo attack by building permanent moles. With the longer range of naval guns as another great source of worry, the appearance of the torpedo boat reopened the question of the safety of even the strongest of naval bases, just when the mine had apparently eliminated most of the danger of their being forced by a hostile fleet. Even before Gougeard, the French had spent much money on Toulon, and he proposed an immediate expenditure of 100 million francs on harbor defenses (with another 47 million for later improvements).[63] This project, like so many others, was presented by the new minister, Jauréguiberry, after Gougeard's fall. The English and Italian ports were of course in the same vulnerable condition for the same reason, the appearance of the torpedo boat as an effective weapon.

Even before the new weapons raised doubts about the future of the battleship, construction of the ships begun in 1880 was slowed by the financial crisis of 1882 and the collapse of Freycinet's public works scheme. The expansion of the French Navy in the early 1880s, along with many other capital improvements, was financed by loans. When these dried up, the navy was forced to take a major cut in its budget, which fell from 217.2 million francs in 1883 to 171.6 million in 1885. As a result, the whole armored ship-building program nearly ground to a halt. In 1885 the minister of finance responded to the piteous appeals of the minister of marine with a flat refusal:

> However justified the augmentations . . . that you think necessary, what-ever considerations you may invoke, there is a fact of *force majeure* that dominates the whole question, the lack of resources to meet the augmentation of expenses.[64]

The economic recession that followed the crisis of 1882 proved to be severe and long-lived. Economic growth in France stagnated between 1883 and 1896, and bankruptcies and unemployment were common. As parliament and the navy's own leaders considered the future of the navy during these years, they were preoccupied by a problem they had not faced in the "good" years of the late 1870s and early 1880s: a chronic shortage of funds.

Nine

❧❧❧❧❧❧❧❧❧❧❧❧❧❧❧❧❧❧❧❧❧❧❧❧❧❧❧❧❧❧❧❧❧❧❧❧

New Factors: Colonial Expansion

Fᴿᴀɴᴄᴇ once had one of the world's greatest colonial empires, but she lost all but a few scraps of it in the series of wars that ended in 1815. For the next seventy years, France and the other major European powers paid relatively little attention to colonial expansion. Most of the conquests made during this period resulted either from isolated diplomatic crises or from the initiative of a small number of colonial officials and enthusiasts, such as Louis Faidherbe in Senegal. After the Franco-Prussian War of 1870, interest in colonial affairs began to revive, and the Congress of Berlin in 1878 marked the beginning of a great scramble by the powers for new colonies. During the first part of the 1880s, French colonial expeditions in Tunis, China, and Madagascar imposed major new burdens on the navy and, more important, once again pitted France against her old rival, England.

Tʜᴇ Nᴀᴠʏ ᴀɴᴅ Cᴏʟᴏɴɪᴀʟ Eхᴘᴀɴsɪᴏɴ

The navy was intimately involved in the colonial expansion of the new French republic. During this period the relationship between the navy and the colonial movement was closer than in any other European state. Naval officers were among the most ardent supporters of colonialism. Even after the colonial administration was finally separated from the Ministry of Marine in 1893, the navy retained sole responsibility for colonial defense.[1]

Three stages can be distinguished in naval support for colonialism under the Third Republic. In the first, prior to the Tunis expedition of 1881, the primary motivation continued to be prestige, as it had been under Napoleon III, and economic and strategic factors played no part whatever. The occupation of Tunis was perceived as a symbol of France's recovery as a European power, and the older naval officers saw little more in colonies than a new source of glory.

Key figures in the Jeune Ecole, such as the journalist Gabriel Charmes and Admiral Aube, saw colonial activity in a broader context involving both political and economic interests. To them, Tunis was only the first step toward acquisition of the whole North African shore of the Mediterranean. Charmes claimed that France was, next to Turkey, "the first Arab power in the world" and that it would be possible for her to conquer and convert to Christianity the whole of the Arab territories of North Africa and Mediterranean Asia.[2] Charmes offered reasons for the North African conquest that were both economic and historical. These were paralleled by Aube's arguments for French expansion in the Levant:

> [This is] the last act of the uninterrupted conflict of the last thousand years between Moslem Asia and Christian Europe. . . . But here the victory of the Galilean is not only that of the Christian faith and European civilization over Islam and Asiatic barbarism . . . it is first of all the incontestable, striking affirmation of the traditions and political ideas that the old France pursued in the Orient. Perhaps the new France, republican France . . . linked to the France of yesterday . . . is permitted to see in it a promise of her future revival.[3]

The third stage in French Republican colonialism, in which naval strategy became a primary motivation, only took shape after the turn of the century. In the minds of the naval officers who favored colonial expansion in the 1880s and 1890s, prestige was the primary reason for colonial activity, economic gain the second, while naval considerations brought up the rear. By the 1930s, France's leading naval strategist, Admiral Raoul-Victor-Patrice Castex, was giving precedence to strategic considerations. Ironically, Castex claimed that France's empire in the Levant was so poorly positioned strategically that France should get rid of it as quickly as possible.[4]

In the late nineteenth century, glory was much cheaper in the uncivilized parts of the world than in Europe, and the French Navy, instead of confining itself to a two-power standard as Lamy had suggested in 1878, became once more a vast prestige machine, acquiring colonies the French people did not want and defending them by the most ruthless possible methods against an enemy the French people did not wish to fight. It paid a high price for its ambitions, and the ultimate effects of the navy's colonial activities on its readiness for European conflict were little short of disastrous. The large fleet maintained for operations on overseas stations was perfectly useless for combat against a European opponent, while vast sums disappeared in the navy's murky administration as part of France's new colonial effort. In addition, until the administrative union of the departments of the navy and the colonies finally ended in 1893, the minister of marine was completely preoccupied with colonial affairs.

Perhaps most important, the union of the two departments led to persistent efforts to hide the costs of the forbidden fruit of colonial expansion among naval as well as colonial portions of the budget.[5] Besides the regular increases in the allocations to the colonies, considerable additional sums for colonial activities were tucked away in naval chapters, and many regular officers and nearly the whole of the Naval Artillery and the Naval Infantry Corps were eventually entirely occupied in the colonies. Much of the work of exploration and conquest was done by regular naval officers, such as Francis Garnier and Henri Rivière in Tonkin and Pierre Savorgnan de Brazza in the Congo. Where possible, as in the Congo, the work of these officers was presented as a series of little *faits accomplis* to be covered by the regular expenditures for naval personnel and matériel, and only when these little wars got out of hand, as in Tonkin and Madagascar, was the minister forced to ask for special credits to squeeze through. The deputies did not realize that much of the money in the naval budget was going to such places as the Congo instead of the Mediterranean or the Channel until someone like Jules Ferry, the instigator of the Tonkin war, got in over his head.

The Naval Infantry, whose chapter in the budget was acknowledged to be partly for colonial expenses, also had the important duty of garrisoning the naval forts in metropolitan France. In the period of colonial expansion, this corps furnished notable leaders including Alfred-Amédée Dodds (Dahomey), Louis-Alexandre-Esprit-Gaston Brière de l'Isle (Senegal), Charles-Marie-Emmanuel Mangin (Morocco), and Joseph-Simon Galliéni (Madagascar), as well as practically all of the expedition of Jean-Baptiste Marchand that confronted the British on the Nile at Fashoda in 1898.[6] The corps's metropolitan duties, however, suffered accordingly. Because of its colonial duties, the corps could recruit only from volunteers, generally of very poor quality and numerically insufficient. As the demands of the colonies grew, the metropolitan garrisons became nothing but recruiting and recuperating depots for the colonial service. Many of the home regiments were reduced to but 50 or 75 percent of their nominal strength.[7] In wartime, most of them were to be given to the army to form a part of the regular forces. To fulfill the wartime task of providing fortress garrisons of about 5,000 men, the navy by 1898 was maintaining a total force of 82,000 European and native troops and 46,000 reservists at an annual cost of 20 million francs.[8] The great shortcomings in coastal and colonial defense revealed during the Fashoda crisis with England in 1898 were a direct result of this hybrid system.

Things were even worse in the Naval Artillery. This corps, the real virtuoso of the navy, built naval guns, served as the colonial artillery force, and finally was even given responsibility for colonial engineering. It possessed two regiments of mounted batteries, mountain guns, and special companies of sappers and engineers, and it filled out its forces by instructing colonial troops who had never seen a warship. The career of General Gustave Borgnis-Desbordes was typical. He began at Toulon, served in Indochina, and then spent three years in Paris as a general's aide. Returning to the colonies, he led the expedition that linked Upper Senegal and the Niger River and then moved on to Tonkin, New Caledonia, and back to Tonkin. From 1890 to 1899 he was inspector-general of the corps, in charge of all its technical activities, and he ended his career as general organizer of Indochinese defenses. Another successful officer, General Prosper-Jules Charbonnier, described his whole life as a young man as "cut into sections of three years each, filling the most diverse of functions under every climate . . . uncertain in ambitions, contrary in taste, and frittering away life in a thousand unfinished tasks."[9]

The confusion caused by such conditions in the highly technical matters of naval gun construction is obvious, and here, too, the pressing necessities of a colonial policy for which the minister did not dare ask the Chamber for sufficient men eventually weakened the navy itself. The average interval between successive colonial campaigns fell from eight years to two, and promotions were earned in the colonies, not in France.[10] However, the time spent by France's most eminent ballistics expert in the colonies turning out a "Classification of the Woods of Cochin-China" and a "Grammar of the Peulhe language" was certainly largely wasted.[11] As a result, on the only important occasion in which the English artillery ever surpassed the French (the introduction of medium-caliber quick-firing guns in the 1890s), the French were without sufficient men to carry through their experiments fast enough. The logical separation of the Naval Artillery Corps into a technical group of artillery engineers and the Colonial Artillery, suggested in 1884, was not acted on at all for sixteen years and was definitely adopted only in 1909.

For the Naval Infantry, the Naval Artillery, and the whole naval organization, the often deliberate confusion between metropolitan and colonial expenses and forces was ultimately detrimental for both the technical efficiency and the real interests of the service. It put the navy in an utterly false position relative to public opinion, and the tendency to evade, conceal, and falsify recoiled eventually in often-unfounded charges of naval inefficiency. The burdens of French colonial policy must be kept in mind when judging the navy for its failure to keep up with Italy, Germany, and England during the next decades. Indeed, another often maligned service, the British army, also bore a similar burden and similar libels of inefficiency.

THE TUNIS EXPEDITION

At the beginning of the period of Republican colonial expansion, and for much the same motives as in the day of Napoleon III, most French naval officers heartily supported colonial expansion. In the Republic's first major expedition, the supremacy of prestige and political motives over strategic considerations comes out very clearly, although Tunis included a position,

Bizerte, that was eventually seen to be a second Toulon on the southern shore of the Mediterranean. In fairness to the navy, it must be pointed out that France's political leaders who negotiated for a free hand in Tunis at the Congress of Berlin in 1878, and even the English who granted it, concentrated on the role of Tunis in the resolution of the Eastern Question, the principal diplomatic issue of the day, and paid no attention to its strategic significance. The French negotiators also saw Tunis as a symbol of France's recovery in Europe, while England was happy to exchange it for a free hand in Cyprus.

The idea of Italian historians that England gave Tunis to France to prevent it from falling into Italian hands is groundless.[12] The Italian on the spot at the Congress, Francesco Crispi, dismissed the theory.[13] A British participant wrote:

> When Décazes [a French spokesman] wished to set us against the supposed Italian designs upon [Tunis], he used to talk of its being dangerous to us to have Malta in a vice between Sicily and an Italian Tunis, but it never seemed to me that the peril was very close.[14]

In the French Navy, the Machiavellian idea of securing the position behind the back of England was equally missing. The complete ignorance of the potential of Bizerte and the lack of modern ideas on the importance of naval bases are sufficient to explain the total absence of strategic considerations on both sides. The naval aspect of the problem was not mentioned in the preliminary diplomatic conversations.

At the time of the French landing in Tunis in 1881, Bizerte was only another open anchorage on the bleak shores of North Africa. The northern coasts of Tunisia were exactly like those of Algeria, and there was nothing to indicate that Bizerte was any different from the Algerian ports. These, constructed of concrete-block breakwaters, served well enough for commercial purposes but were utterly open to bombardment from the sea. The half century of French possession of Algeria had not resulted in any naval establishments whatever.[15]

But behind the unindented rampart of coastal hills, as a reminder of more prosperous Roman days, there existed a number of depressions or remnants of ancient lakes. The idea of restoring the fertility of the Sahara by letting the sea into one of them had always had considerable appeal, and when Tunis was still a nominal possession of the Turks such a scheme was officially studied by French military engineers for the region of Gabès in southern Tunisia.[16] Whatever the climatic results of such a large-scale endeavor might be, the changing of one of the smaller basins into a naval base protected by a row of fortified hills was an obvious development of this idea.

At Bizerte in 1881, the usual dirty Arab fishing town on the usual open roadstead was connected by a shallow winding river about ten miles long with two large inland lakes. The only difference between these and many other depressions in this region was that they had not yet dried up. In 1845 Lieutenant (later Admiral) Thomas A. B. Spratt of the English navy visited the spot and studied the lakes. The smaller and farther from the sea was a shallow body of fresh water of no importance, save that it took all of the alluvial deposit and left the first lake, which was salt, with a nearly uniform depth of about thirty-six feet. The salt lake, eight miles long and six wide, was hidden from the sea by the usual range of hills.[17] In his report to the Admiralty, Spratt pointed out the possibility of connecting this lake more directly with the sea. This forgotten report, and a letter from Spratt to Lord Clarence Paget in 1864, were the only documents the Admiralty possessed concerning Bizerte.[18]

In the French Ministry of Marine, the Tunis expedition was regarded as just another colonial affair to gain prestige on the cheap, like the affairs of Napoleon III. The whole campaign was carried through with the magnificent lack of preparation that characterized nineteenth-century navies. Although the expedition was precipitated by Italian provocations in Tunis, the French had been contemplating such a move for at least twenty years. Even so, their only plan was a general sketch worked out by the current minister of marine, Admiral Cloué. They had no good map of the Tunisian coast and no specific plans for landings—at each beach, a vessel had to be sent ahead to take soundings.

Not only did the French know nothing about Tunis, their information about the two European navies that might have become involved was equally fragmentary. On 17 April 1881, two weeks after the decision to intervene, Admiral Henri-Jules-François Garnault, commander of the Squadron of Evolutions, knew nothing about either the Italian fleet or its base at La Spezia. He finally received the information on 12 May in a letter of 29 April from the military attaché in Rome. Word about the Turkish fleet had arrived three days earlier. From the time Garnault was ordered "to be ready for any eventuality," a month and two days had elapsed before he had the first official indication of the status of the forces he might have to meet.[19]

Bizerte was chosen as the first of the "strategic points" designated by the government in 1878 to be occupied—because it was the least important! The immediate occupation of La Goulette, the port of Tunis itself, would have risked awakening too many international susceptibilities. There was nothing in the French files on Bizerte except a short note by one of the navy's leading surveyors, Admiral Amédée-Ernest Mouchez.

> Well sheltered from the SW and NW wind, the anchorage is bad with a NNW wind and very bad with one from N. . . . The entrance to the river is narrow and choked with gravel, which forms a rough bar in any slight sea.[20]

The French had nothing like Spratt's report—for them, Bizerte looked like just another mediocre North African anchorage.[21]

The landing proved much easier than Mouchez had foreseen, and its commander, Admiral Alfred Conrad, became enthusiastic in a report dated 5 May over the possibilities of the location.

> The size of the anchorage and of the port that it will be easy to create here could make this point the most important naval station on the North African coast, in view of its situation on the route of all the steamers that go from the Suez Canal toward the Strait of Gibraltar.[22]

Even yet, however, the idea of digging a canal between the salt lake and the roadstead does not seem to have arisen.

The British Foreign Secretary, Lord Granville, who had found the bargain struck at Berlin hard to swallow, raised the question of a naval base after the French occupation of the port had caused the exhumation of Spratt's documents from the files. He obtained from the French the official declaration that

> whatever enterprises private companies may attempt at Bizerte, it does not enter at all into our intentions to expend today the enormous sums and to begin the gigantic works that would be necessary to transform this position into a military port.[23]

This shaky assurance was the only promise that bound France on the specific question of Bizerte. The horses had been traded at Berlin, and the efforts of Spratt to arouse English public opinion were fruitless.[24] The French diplomats had given their assurances very lightly, in ignorance of Conrad's report, and they were subsequently astonished that the English knew about the possibilities of the port. Later the prime minister, Jules Ferry, made an often-quoted statement that "if I took Tunisia, it was to have Bizerte."[25] This, however, was only a typical statesman's claim to prophetic vision when he found that the gold brick was real gold.

Twenty years were to pass before Bizerte became a real factor in the Mediterranean balance of power. Both the diplomatic promises and the opinions of the traditional French naval school on the value of naval bases in general were to blame for the delay. According to Admiral Krantz, "For us, the insufficiency of the fleet can only be corrected by the growth of the fleet; the erection of a few forts and a few moles at strategic points cannot compensate for the numerical inferiority of our combat units."[26] English experts, perhaps whistling in the dark, agreed with him: "The balance of power in the Mediterranean can only be altered by accessions of naval strength. It is not affected by the construction of a war harbor even of the highest rank."[27] According to another, "given a number of hostile battleships, it is not a matter of the first consequence whether they are all in one port or half a dozen."[28]

France gave no promises to Italy regarding a base at Bizerte. The slight importance of Italy in French eyes is shown not only by the lack of information about the Italian navy at the time of the expedition but also by the fact that the advocates of the new possession considered it first with relation to Malta and the British route to India, second as a step on the French road to the Levant, and scarcely at all as the most serious of threats to the Italian peninsula. That Bizerte was not only opposite Malta but also opposite the wide-open gap between Sicily and Sardinia that led to Naples was not fully realized until much later. Though the expedition was triggered by Italian provocations in Tunis, Italy was practically ignored in the diplomatic action that accompanied it, in the consideration of its possible effects on the general European alignment, and even in the estimation of the military value of the new possession. Tunis offers a concrete example of France's attitude toward Italy and her new navy in the period before the summer of 1890, when France suddenly realized that her Mediterranean hegemony had all but disappeared.

In May 1882, Germany, Austria, and Italy concluded the Triple Alliance, which, periodically renewed, ran until 1915. The alliance gave Italy protection from a direct French attack in return for Italian renunciation both of irredentist agitation against Austria and of a possible combination with Russia in the Balkans and the eastern Mediterranean. But it did not give Italy support for her ambitions in the western half of the Mediterranean, and Bismarck carefully assured the French that it was not directed at them. His loyal support of France in both Tunis and Morocco during 1881 apparently convinced the French that the alliance contained no additional dangers for their position in North Africa.

France's perception of England was very different. The opposition of Lord Granville to French actions in Tunis marked England as a determined colonial rival, which was driven home the following year when England outmaneuvered French diplomacy and occupied Egypt. In the next few years, French colonial rivalry with England spread beyond the Mediterranean to nearly every part of the globe.

Ferry's Colonial Operations and the British Reaction

Jules Ferry, who held the office of premier for an unusually long continuous period from February 1883 to March 1885, vigorously promoted French colonial expansion just at the time the rivalry with England was reviving. Sensing widespread opposition to colonial adventures in Parliament, Ferry attempted to achieve his objectives without putting himself in a position where he had to ask parliamentary approval. In the manner of Napoleon III, he eventually had the French Navy carrying on two undeclared wars simul-

The aviso or third-class cruiser Volta *(launched in 1867) in Chinese waters during or soon after Courbet's campaign. Astern is the gunboat* Vipère *(1881) and to the right is a torpedo boat, either* No. 45 *or* No. 46 *(1879).*

taneously, in Tonkin and Madagascar, both behind the back of the public and without sufficient forces for either. As in the case of Tunis, strategic considerations at first played almost no part in either of these operations.

The most famous of Ferry's "telegraph wars" (so called because he personally controlled the forces by telegraph) was the campaign by Admiral Courbet against China in 1884 and 1885 after the establishment of the French protectorate in Tonkin. Courbet first seized as a "gage" the Keelung coal mines in Formosa, while part of his forces watched the Chinese fleet in the Min River at Foochow. His second in command had already bombarded Keelung when news came that Ferry was afraid to ask the Chamber for troops to hold it. Instead Ferry ordered that the vote of a new credit was to be the signal for an attack on the Chinese fleet and arsenal at Foochow. In August 1884 Courbet advanced up the Min, destroyed the fleet, the arsenal, and a large number of Chinese, and was ordered to resume his watching while neutral British ships took the remaining Chinese troops to Shanghai. Ferry decided to strike a blow at Peking, but, deterred by British pressure from taking the northern ports of Wei Hai Wei or Port Arthur as Courbet had wished, he eventually ordered a blockade of rice shipments from the Yangtze region to the north. In the meantime he sent Courbet back to Keelung, which the admiral occupied.

Courbet spent the winter of 1884 blockading Formosa and losing men in the unhealthy harbor of Keelung while asking the government for permission to transfer his fleet to the Pescadores Islands. These, located between Formosa and the mainland, had an excellent strategic position and a good harbor, which would be worth keeping after the war. Four days before the news of the defeat of a French force at Lang Son arrived in Paris and caused Ferry's fall, the minister telegraphed Courbet "to take account of the possibility that we will retain these islands."[29] The supplies at Keelung were transferred, field guns were landed, and buildings were begun for a naval base. It is interesting to note how late strategic considerations were invoked for the retention of this "Gibraltar of the Pacific."

In the end, the war accomplished little besides confirming French control over Tonkin. Ferry's successor evacuated the Pescadores under pressure from the British, who refused a French offer of part of Tonkin in compensation and instead abandoned their own position at Port Hamilton on the southern Korean island of So Do. In June 1885 Courbet, exhausted by the campaign, died on his flagship.[30]

The story in Madagascar was similar to Tonkin except for the ending. Ferry's immediate predecessor sent out an expedition in early 1883 under Admiral Pierre-Joseph-Gustave Pierre and intended to conquer the whole island. Pierre died during the expedition, but his successors, Admirals Charles-Eugène Galiber and Paul-Emile Miot, eventually gained control of most of the Malagasy ports. In particular, the vast bay of Diégo-Suarez, at the northern tip of the island, was occupied on 12 November 1884. The colonialists were able to save this from the debacle following the fall of Ferry. The treaty of 1885 gave France the right to establish a naval base there, although haste in the Foreign Ministry resulted in the boundary being drawn too close to the bay itself.[31]

The incidents of the China and Madagascar campaigns further embittered Anglo-French relations, already poor because of the Egyptian crisis of 1882–83. The British refused to let French ships coal at Aden on the grounds that France was actually at war with China, and the French marauding off the China coast so seriously affected British trade in opium and tea that the London *Times* in a leader on 8 September 1884 practically urged China to declare war on France so England could close its ports to French ships entirely. The rice blockade, which was recognized with suspicious promptness by Germany and Russia, was regarded in England as a trial balloon for making foodstuffs contraband of war.

In 1884 a great public campaign broke out in England over the weaknesses of the Royal Navy. It was largely a French scare, and all the facts of French near-equality in armored ships and superiority in torpedo boats and guns were brought out. On 2 December 1884 the first lord of the Admiralty, the earl of Northbrook, for the first time officially mentioned France as the standard of comparison for the British fleet, and on the same day Lord Brassey submitted in Parliament a program that would give England equality against France and any other power.[32] The other power could not have been Italy, and given the condition of the German and Russian navies, only France seriously entered the British calculations despite the Franco-German colonial entente and the danger of a Franco-Russian alliance. The ships authorized between 1885 and 1888 included four battleships: the *Victoria* and

The British belted cruiser Orlando *(1886). While modern in appearance, this ship and her six sisters retained the outmoded narrow, thick armor belt of the station battleships.*

Sans Pareil, which with two 16.25-inch, 110-ton guns in a single bow turret were among the worst one-punch monstrosities ever built; and the *Nile* and *Trafalgar,* whose design was based on neither the Admirals nor the *Inflexible* but the *Devastation,* which the British had not copied since 1875. Perhaps more important, these programs also included nine first-class belted cruisers of the *Orlando* class to match the latest Russian raiders, eleven smaller protected cruisers "to patrol the narrow seas," five cruisers for the defense of Australia, eight torpedo cruisers, and a torpedo depot ship. The British had begun to think at least of the protection of English commerce in home waters.[33]

FRENCH COLONIALISM AFTER FERRY

The French colonialists regarded Ferry's fall in March 1885 not as a turning point but as a breathing spell. Since no further expansion was possible for the moment, they concluded that their two most immediate tasks were to defend the colonies that had been acquired and to develop a French route to the Indies.

The need for French strong points on the route to the Orient had been shown by England's attitude in the China war. The incidents at Aden had suddenly made Obock, the nearby French foothold on the Red Sea, appear extremely important. Although the French had obtained the position in 1862 in a treaty with a native chief, they only established a coal depot there after the English attitude forced them to. Obock was an open port too close to Aden to be defended, and it suffered from the usual Red Sea climate; one of its chief advocates admitted that the temperature would reach 130 degrees on a "summer day." In 1884, therefore, the French sent an expedition to Shaykh Said on the other side of the straits to look at a harbor where the French had coaled in 1870. During the intervening fifteen years the Turks had moved into the area, but the Foreign Ministry was beginning a diplomatic effort to dislodge them on the eve of Ferry's fall. Proponents claimed that Obock and Shaykh Said would form a "new Gibraltar" that would neutralize Aden and replace it as a coaling port.[34]

But for most French colonialists, Obock was only a way station and Tunis, Madagascar, and Tonkin were to be the key points on the new route to the China Seas. A remarkable little booklet entitled *Les colonies nécessaires* outlined the whole policy of the rival French route to the East.[35] The author was a flag officer closely connected with Ferry's policy—perhaps Ferry's minister of marine, Admiral Peyron, or his successor, Admiral Galiber. (The choice of Galiber, who had just returned from Madagascar, as minister of marine indicated as well as anything that Ferry's fall marked a pause and not a reversal in colonial policy.) The author began his argument by saying that the coming of the new conservative government in England would be the signal not only for a great English naval effort but for an important change in the general diplomatic alignment of Europe. "Russia, now attached to the axis of Berlin, may be pushed aside to make room for her traditional rival," England, meaning that France would face the redoutable combination of Germany, Italy, and England. The only way to avoid this was to keep French naval power "ready to check England. . . . Since France has recovered military equality with Germany, Europe will fix its combinations according to the relative maritime forces of England and France."[36] He explained that

> England's head lies in the British Isles, her body is the great mass of the Indian Empire, while her members encircle the globe. . . . The lines of communication that link England to India, the source of her industrial activity and strength, are the great arteries of her economic and national organism.[37]

The booklet thus elaborated on Gougeard's policy of cutting the road to India in the Mediterranean and indicated that the French effort should be based on three key points, the "necessary colonies." Tunis was needed "to check Malta and to threaten the direct route at the only point where it is vulnerable to us." Madagascar was necessary "to cut the indirect route by the Cape of Good Hope." Finally, Tonkin, "in the China and Indian seas . . . where almost all the wealth and more than half of [England's] merchant fleet are concentrated," would counter Hong Kong and Singapore, cut the route through the Panama Canal, and take India on the flank.

The author said nothing about Brest and noted that Dakar in Senegal was too far from Madagascar to be of much use. So strong was the cult of the *Alabama,* so strong the appeal of the East, that France, located near the very heart of Britain, was hunting for a way to attack her on the periphery of her empire. When the fallen minister, Ferry, rose in the Chamber amid wild tumult to attempt to save at least Diégo-Suarez, he expressed exactly the same ideas:

> In this maritime war, it is not in the Mediterranean, it is not in the Channel that the decisive battle will occur. Marseilles and Toulon will be no less effectively defended in the Indian Ocean and in the China seas than in the Mediterranean and the Channel. . . . The conditions of maritime war have profoundly changed. . . . It is for this that we needed Tunisia; it is for this that we needed Saigon and Cochinchina; it is for this that we need Madagascar, that we are at Diégo-Suarez and at Vohémar, and that we will never leave them![38]

If England did succeed Russia in the German alliance system, the anonymous author suggested that France and Russia working together could contain the combined power of the Anglo-German alignment:

> In every direction in which the inevitable push of the Russian Empire can manifest itself . . . the French army and navy will take in the rear the only powers capable of stopping her traditional march: on our Eastern frontier from France; in China from Cochin-China; and on England's route to India from Madagascar and Tunis.[39]

Tunis, Tonkin, and Madagascar were the stages on the route to the Far East that had been won in the Ferry period, but to the French colonialists this was only the first step. France was not to be an Asian and African but a world naval power like England. The second part of the process would be the cutting of a canal across Panama. New Caledonia, Tahiti, the Windward Islands, and even Easter Island were to be linked by Panama to the French Antilles to form the rest of an all-French line around the world.[40] Admiral Aube's plan was to encircle the globe with French positions: Tunis, Obock, Madagascar, Saigon, Tonkin, Nouméa, Tahiti, Tuamotu, the Panama Canal, and Guadeloupe—with Dakar and Gabon thrown in as flanking positions.[41]

In 1878 it had been necessary to give a morsel to France at the Congress of Berlin; seven years later she was dreaming of equaling the English effort of three centuries. The same men spoke of cutting the Isthmus of Corinth and that of Panama, of building a canal across the Malay peninsula, of a trans-Siberian railroad, and of flooding the Sahara. The naval and colonial movement was closely associated with the resurgence of nationalism in France—Paul Déroulède founded the extremist League of Patriots at this time, in 1882. According to Aube, "Patriotism, in these somber hours, has become a religion that demands Hope and Faith as its theological virtues."[42]

The new colonialism was indeed a religion, and its driving force was fear of English jealousy and greed. When an author wrote of Mayotte, an island of 10,000 blacks and 100 whites in the Indian Ocean, that "if this beautiful colony shares the fate of Mauritius, of India, and of Canada, it shall be a heavy blow to France!" he was not joking, he was mightily in earnest.[43] The editor of a volume to which Aube contributed gave an exhortation that is typical of the movement:

> Let us take up again the work of the seventeenth century. . . . Let Indo-china replace India, let Madagascar become the new East France, let Guiana have a connection with Brazil, and may Africa offer us a compensation for the loss of North America. Our Revival, and Power, and Glory will be assured to France.[44]

Ten

The Jeune Ecole

T HE YEAR 1886 was a key turning point in the history of the navy of the French Third Republic before 1914. In January 1886 Admiral Hyacinthe-Laurent-Théophile Aube became minister of marine, bringing to power the leader of a school of naval thought, the Jeune Ecole, that advocated a type of naval war radically different from that previously accepted. Aube remained minister long enough to experiment with many of his ideas, and when he left office in mid-1887 he left both the navy and public opinion deeply divided over the future of the navy.

THÉOPHILE AUBE

The French Navy in 1885 was described by a colonial writer as being divided into three castes: the ruling class, which spent its time moving from promotion to promotion in the navy of the Seine with short voyages on battleships or honorable positions at Cherbourg and Toulon; the servant class of older officers who had given up hope of advancement but were comfortably settled in obscure positions in the metropolitan ports; and the navigators or pariahs who served primarily overseas.

From the beginning of his active service on a gunboat in the Philippines (1843–47), Théophile Aube, born in 1826 at Toulon, had been one of the pariahs. Except for a taste for describing his travels in the *Revue des deux mondes,* which began on his very first voyage and continued throughout his life, the career of the principal leader of the Jeune Ecole was typical of the navigators.[1] After serving in the Mediterranean during the brief period of the Second Republic (1848–49), Aube spent two years in Senegal with the great proponent of colonial expansion Louis Faidherbe, whose niece he married. He then served four years in the Far East, one at Lorient, eight in

Senegal (whence he was twice invalided home with fever), and two more in the Far East. He returned home just in time to take part in the defense of Paris against the Germans in 1870. The navy's conservative leadership left him idle from 1871 to 1875 because of his republican views and then summarily dismissed him from command of a ship on the Pacific Station. After the return of a more liberal administration, he briefly commanded an ironclad in the Squadron of Evolutions and was then appointed rear admiral and governor of Martinique. There his wife died of yellow fever and he was again invalided home. After a few months as a titular member of the Conseil des Travaux and service as second in command of the Squadron of Evolutions, he retired to the country for about a year before taking office as minister of marine in the cabinet of Louis de Freycinet on 3 January 1886.[2]

With the exception of his last two years in the Mediterranean fleet, Aube had spent essentially his entire career in the colonies before coming to the ministry. The single greatest factor in his thought was undoubtedly his personal devotion to and connection by marriage with Faidherbe.[3] Republican, Catholic, and one of the most gifted of the late-nineteenth-century French naval literary men, he was above all a colonial fanatic. His single-mindedness, his patriotism, his ruthlessness, and even his boundless optimism all stemmed from his connection with the colonies. The conquest of French West Africa by French forces, which, although nothing more than small bands, had leaders like Faidherbe and the best weapons of the machine age, was literally a miracle of modern matériel. It is hardly surprising that Aube believed that another such miracle was possible in the art of naval warfare.

Aube expressed his naval doctrines clearly in even the earliest of his numerous writings. In particular, he took sides from the beginning in the personnel struggle within the navy that became so bitter in the heyday of the Jeune Ecole. In 1873 he came out frankly for the cause of the younger men by urging a radical reduction in the number of higher posts and honest seagoing assignments for the senior officers that remained.[4] Even then, he had little use for the massive ironclads and their noble officers. The little gunboats on the foreign stations and in the colonies and even the old sailing ships were far better for the navy. As he put it, "In the old days, one armored oneself, instead of armoring one's ship."

A second aspect of Aube's ideas was also extremely important for the future of the Jeune Ecole: he did not understand at all the movement led most recently by Gougeard for reform of the navy's organization. One of his most important writings was a defense of the port of Rochefort against Gougeard's efforts to suppress it.[5] Although leader of the Jeune Ecole and chief exponent of its personnel and military ideas, Aube did not see the need to change the organization of the French Navy, to improve either its efficiency or its image in Parliament and the public.

Aube's military ideas were based on the premise that the navy had but one function: the defense of the colonial empire against England. This was to be accomplished, as discussed above, by ruthless commerce-destroying on the high seas and by coast defenses. Aube had great confidence in the ability of modern coast defenses to defeat a landing on French shores.

> With the extreme mobility that steam gives to all warships . . . with the speed and sureness of information permitted by the electric telegraph, with the ability to concentrate forces provided by the railroad, though no point on the coast is safe from attack, there is none that cannot be strongly and rapidly defended. . . . Any army corps venturing into enemy territory appears destined to be thrust back into the sea. . . . Finally, one may ask, in our day what real effect would a corps whose strength could not exceed 30,000 men have on the ultimate outcome of the war.[6]

Aube adopted the familiar German scheme of multiple mobile defensive forces on land and sea operating from a number of fortified "garrison" bases. He added an important element to this theory, however, by describing its usefulness in high-seas warfare (a type of warfare that, ironically, he did not believe in).

> To prepare in secret powerful squadrons whose union . . . would assure numerical superiority . . . and strike a decisive blow . . . was, before Trafalgar, the very conception of the emperor Napoleon. . . . His three squadrons separated by so many diverse causes could today, thanks to steam and the electric telegraph, meet at a fixed hour at a rendezvous assigned to them at the last minute. They would only have to evade the surveillance of the blockading squadrons, an easier matter today. . . . The division of [the enemy's] battleships among a larger number of blockading squadrons will lead directly . . . to the weakening of each of these squadrons. . . . Behind the menacing screen of its maritime sharp-shooters, our battleships will pass before the blockading squadron that has been pushed back from the coast, and the high seas will be open to them . . . their junction . . . mathematically assured. Whether one accepts or rejects our ideas on . . . high-seas war, reason calls for the multiplication of centers of construction, basing, and departure of the instruments, whatever they may be, of maritime warfare. This warfare will be simultaneously high-seas war, commerce raiding, and coast defense.[7]

Thus Aube's equivalents of the German *Ausfallkorvetten* were not just coast-defenders but the parts of a dispersed fleet whose junction on the high seas would produce superiority over any portion of the blockading force. No idea in Aube's writings is more important than this claim that it was possible to ensure momentary superiority, even on the high seas, by a combination of forces from a number of naval bases. Against England, Aube believed that the multiplication of naval bases was a fundamental necessity, whether for commercial warfare, for coast defense, or even for a revival of the attempt to defeat the British at sea. In this respect he differed significantly from Gougeard, who thought in terms of a "garrison" as simply a strong point for defending its own area.

The last element of Aube's theories prior to his adoption of the torpedo boat was his view of Italy. This was, in a way, more important than his advocacy of cruiser warfare. Aube's anonymous *Italie et Levant,* written on his return from his cruise with the Mediterranean fleet, declared that Italy, which lay across the route to the "empire" in the Levant, was France's principal enemy.

> As far as Italy and France are concerned, their expansive forces have been stopped short in the north. . . . Before the impassive firmness of the Iron Chancellor [Bismarck], the one has had to renounce the dream of the *irredenta* in the Tyrol and Trieste, the other the cherished hopes summarized in the one word *revanche.* Pushed toward the south, both have as their only remaining field of external activity, at least in Europe, the great Mediterranean basin. . . . This rivalry is inescapable. For a modern people, to be condemned to act only internally, without external expansion, is to be condemned to death, slow perhaps but certain.[8]

Italy had no commerce to destroy, blockade of its coasts was impossible, and combined expeditions would be of only local value. Therefore the missions of

> a fleet superior in numbers . . . are all clear, on the condition, however, that we descend from the cloudy heights of that sentimentality which has created that monstrous association of words: "the laws of war." . . .
>
> The highest objective of war [is] to do the most possible harm to the enemy. . . . [Since] wealth is the sinew of war, everything that strikes the enemy's wealth . . . becomes not only legitimate but obligatory. We can thus expect to see the . . . masters of the sea turn their powers of attack and destruction . . . against all the cities of the coast, fortified or not, pacific or warlike; burn them, ruin them, or at least ransom them mercilessly.[9]

In this war of ruthless coastal bombardments carried out from bases at Bizerte and Toulon, Aube pointed out that the control of Corsica and the Strait of Bonifacio between Corsica and Sardinia would play an extremely important role. The efforts of Italian nationalists to persuade King Victor Emmanuel to countenance an expedition to Corsica during France's defeat in 1871 was only the most important indication of Italian interest in this part of the *irredenta.* The defense of Corsica, the middle point of the Toulon-Bizerte line, was to become a cardinal point in the doctrine of the Jeune Ecole.[10]

The main points in Aube's strategic system against France's three major enemies were perfectly clear before 1884. Against England he called for coastal defense and cruisers, with the possibility of the rapid concentration of a battle fleet from a number of fortified points. Against Italy he planned to use coastal bombardments, while against Germany his strategy was largely defensive. Technically, as in the earlier strategy of Grivel, all of these could be carried out by various combinations of the three elements in the existing French fleet: battleships, cruisers, and torpedo defenses.

AUBE AND THE TORPEDO BOAT

Aube had left Lorient for Senegal in 1858, the year in which the *Gloire* was laid down, and in the twenty-five years of matériel progress that had since elapsed, he had not once been actively connected with a technical service. He had never even commanded a modern warship before joining the Squadron of Evolutions in 1883. In that year he discovered almost simultaneously the torpedo boat and a brilliant young foreign affairs expert of the *Journal des débats,* Gabriel Charmes.

Charmes had contracted the malady that led to his death a few years later on a voyage to the Levant in 1882, and he met Aube during the latter's recovery from the illness he had caught in Martinique. The convalescents' mutual ideas on colonial expansion resulted in Aube inviting Charmes on a cruise with the Mediterranean fleet. This was the beginning of a friendship and unity of views so inseparable that it is impossible to distinguish between the ideas of the two men.

Charmes, a talented writer and student of foreign affairs but not a sailor, knew nothing whatever of naval technique. His cruise, which happened to be the one in which torpedo boats *No. 63* and *No. 64* rode out the storm with the squadron, resulted in the publication of Charmes's first naval article in the *Journal des débats,* "Les torpilleurs autonomes et l'avenir de la Marine" (Autonomous torpedo boats and the future of the navy).[11]

> A new really revolutionary event has taken place this very year in France. . . . Two torpedo boats of the new type, *63* and *64,* attached to the Squadron of Evolutions, have taken part in all its maneuvers in the Mediterranean. It is now possible to send to sea, far from the coast, torpedo boats that are self-sufficient and that can sail round the Mediterranean or cross the Atlantic alone.[12]

The storm that had overtaken the fleet was "the most complete possible" proof that the new 46-ton boats were ready "for any weather, in any sea." The torpedo boat the Boyardville Commission had called "seagoing" because it could withstand occasional high winds at sea was declared by Charmes to be an autonomous seakeeping ship.

Based on the experience of the storm off Villefranche, Aube, through Charmes, laid down a complete technical theory of naval matériel to add to his strategic system. It combined familiar tactical arguments on the importance of speed and numbers with the notion, peculiar to Charmes and Aube, that hundred-foot-long torpedo boats were *autonomes*. Aube, a seasoned seaman, should have known better, and except for his total ignorance of the history of the development of these craft, the only possible explanations for his vigorous assertion of their seakeeping abilities are psychological and social. One is his "colonial mind," which was at the same time the secret of his astounding gift of naval prophecy and his greatest weakness. The second was that the autonomous torpedo boat seemed to make possible the attainment of one of his deepest ambitions: to give the navigators, the colonials, their revenge on the ironclads and the Paris seamen at last.

> [Today] our officers no longer go to sea. The only ones to get assignments to ships are a few privileged men belonging to a maritime aristocracy outside of which there is neither hope for advancement nor opportunity to serve while acquiring experience. The inequality cries out—it is called necessary. But it will no longer be the same when, thanks to the practically indefinite multiplication of the number of ships, seagoing assignments and commands will also increase practically infinitely. The navy will immediately become what it always should have been, and no longer is today: a school of navigation where everyone finds his place. . . . Service will count more than protection.[13]

In every country, the torpedo boat, the cruiser, and little ships in general were the hope of the younger men. In France, where conditions of advancement and favoritism were particularly bad, the Jeune Ecole—literally the Young School—had found its solution, and its leader.

According to Charmes, "the principal vice of ironclads is the attempt to combine in them at one time all of the means of naval warfare: the ram, the gun, and the torpedo. The result is that they are not really suited to use any of them."[14] He therefore applied the principle of the division of labor and split up the battleship into a lot of little boats, some with torpedoes, some with guns, and the rest with rams. Thus, accompanying the torpedo boat would be the gunboat or *bateau-canon,* a vessel similar to it but armed with a single 5.5-inch gun. Designed like the torpedo boat to exploit the tactical advantages of speed, small size, and numbers, it was essentially a late development of Armstrong's unarmored gunboat. To defend against the possibility that light craft might protect the battleships, Charmes later created a third species, defensive torpedo boats, each equipped with several light automatic guns, a spar torpedo, and a ram. This flotilla, accompanied by "mother ships" to supply them with coal, water, and torpedoes, plus converted merchant cruisers for scouting, would be sufficient for any squadron combat. Torpedo boats and gunboats, augmented by fast rams and a German-style system of telegraphs, semaphores, and light scouts to assure their ability to concentrate against the enemy, would also be the principal coast defenses.

Though the tactics for such a fleet, composed mainly of small craft, had not been developed, Charmes stated that "I cannot really understand why it should be difficult for torpedo boats to arrive from all points of the horizon at once. Nothing indeed seems easier."[15] The gunboats and defensive torpedo boats would break through any defending small craft and split the line of the enemy fleet, firing at it all the while to produce a lot of smoke. The attack torpedo boats would then sneak up through the smoke and dash in and finish off the battleships. The creation of the cloud of smoke by the voluntary immolation of the defensive torpedo boats and gunboats at the start of the battle was certainly Charmes's prize-winning theory.[16]

The idea of a torpedo mother ship, along with the notion of the division of labor, had already been advanced by the torpedo experts at Boyardville. The original function of the mother ship had been to carry the torpedo boats to the scene of action. This idea, along with the idea of carrying specially built small torpedo boats on the decks of battleships, became quite common, and the French Navy's torpedo school ship, the converted merchantman *Japon,* was equipped to carry five. In 1881 the Conseil des Travaux called for plans of a special ship with the same speed and range as the squadron to carry torpedo boats and mines.[17] In 1883 the transports *Mytho* and *Annamite,* specially fitted for this purpose a couple of years earlier, took to China some torpedo boats, which carried out successful attacks under Courbet. With the development of the autonomous torpedo craft, the mother ship became essentially a floating base.

Even for offensive warfare against enemy coasts, Charmes argued that the *bateau-canon* would be superior to armored battleships. Since enemy torpedo boats would make direct blockades and landings impossible, larger ships had no function. Against a regular fortified base, whose defenses typically consisted of minefields and heavy guns to prevent the forcing of the entrance passages, small gunboats and torpedo craft would be more effective than the biggest armored fleet. The objective of the action, after all, was the destruction of the arsenal or the merchant port, not the reduction of the forts; while the chance of hitting a small gunboat with, for example, a 100-ton gun like those fitted in the forts at La Spezia was just as small as the chance of the similarly armed *Italia* defending herself against torpedo attack. Having entered the port, the torpedo boats would attack the ships at anchor while the gunboats bombarded the arsenal. At La Spezia, which was practically impregnable to an attack by a regular armored fleet, the lack of a mole opened the port to torpedo attack and left the arsenal open to light gunvessels. It could have been bombarded relatively easily by a sudden descent at the opening of a war before the barrages were gotten out.[18] Against coastal defenses, particularly in England and Italy, where the big-gun craze was worst, light, fast gunboats had exactly the same advantage that torpedo boats did against battleships.

AUBE'S NEW KIND OF NAVAL WAR

The real objectives were not naval arsenals but open coastal towns defended solely by the "so-called laws of war." Charmes stated blandly what even Aube had been too politic to mention directly.

> It is . . . clear that the bombardment of forts will be in the future only an accessory operation. . . . We will ravage above all the undefended coasts, the open cities. In a fight against England, instead of stupidly trying to silence the forts at Gibraltar and Malta, we will strike at the heart, that is at the commercial ports, and so complete the ruin of the country begun by the cruisers. In a war against Italy, what terrible disasters will inevitably accumulate along this continuous coastline which seems to offer everywhere its admirable cities to the incendiary projectiles of the enemy.[19]

The anti-Italian sentiments of the Jeune Ecole played a major role in shaping its ideas. Italy could not be attacked economically at sea—its entire foreign trade was relatively small, and the only essential element of it transported at sea (coal) was carried in neutral English ships. Though a large part of the Jeune Ecole's theory of bombardment was simply a revival of the old notion of doing a lot of indiscriminate damage, it also contained elements of a much more modern idea: working on the morale of the civilian population. According to another leading Jeune Ecole polemicist, Paul-Jean Fontin (who became Aube's personal secretary), "an ordinary bombardment" consisted of "firing on any inhabited part of a coast in order to provoke a popular movement that could oblige the defense to capitulate."[20] The ruthless destruction of Italy's coastal towns was to be the chief method of warfare against her. Indeed, in a war with the Triple Alliance of Germany, Austria, and Italy, the whole weight of the French would fall upon Italy. "If a balance is achieved on the Rhine, the navy will decide, in the Mediterranean, the fate of the Triple Alliance."[21]

The Jeune Ecole was thus ready to play any card that might overthrow the Italian state—the excitability of Italian public opinion and its tendency to split over issues such as the Roman question, the republican movement in Italy, and Neapolitan dissatisfaction with its northern Italian rulers. The moral effects of bombardments were more important than the actual destruction, for the real economic strength of Italy, the heavy industry in the northern plain, could not be touched by such means. This provides a clue to one of the outstanding characteristics of the Jeune Ecole's theory of commercial war, which so often has been described—wrongly—as the hope of "starving out England." Its major objective was not actual starvation, or stopping the raw materials and food necessary to carry on a war, but to produce an economic panic that would bring about social collapse. The reliance on economic paralysis and the threat of social revolution is the chief explanation for two other aspects of Jeune Ecole thought—its tendency to under-estimate the forces necessary to overthrow England and its absolute insis-tence on a sudden paralyzing attack at the beginning of a war. The success of the *Alabama* in causing American merchant ships to take refuge under foreign flags suggested that panic was more important than destruction. In addition, the Frenchmen of the 1880s had, just a decade previously, been the victims of one of the most amazing reversals of the European balance of power. It is not to be wondered that they thought that a single blow, sudden and ruthless but more moral than material, might have a decisive effect on the international alignment.

In many ways, the ideas of the Jeune Ecole on the social effects of modern war were more realistic than those of the statesmen who, thirty years later, so blindly led Europe into the cataclysm of World War I. In Paris during the German siege of 1870–71 and in the suppression of the Paris Commune, the group's leaders had had the experience of living through a social revo-lution. Aube's preoccupation with the social problems of modern capital-ism, which he described in 1883, was one of the bases of his whole colonial theory.

> On the condition that products of industry find remunerative prices on the world market . . . labor and capital . . . are in accord, in harmony. But . . . by the law today incontestable, which is that of the forward march of humanity, *the struggle for life,* . . . these markets are rapidly glutted. . . . Labor and capital . . . become antagonistic, and the question of labor, exacerbated by misery and hunger, . . . transforms itself into a social question, whose solution appears possible only by the advent of absolute justice in our societies, which are oriented, alas, toward the contingent and the relative. This is essentially the French solution.
>
> Wholly different is the solution sought and found by other nations, more fortunate and of a more practical spirit. . . . One must create and invent new markets, production will revive, and the menace of poverty will be averted. . . . And what are these new markets? They are the colo-nies with which England covers and transforms the world. . . . Thanks to these colonies . . . the question of labor has not become, will not be-come for a long time in England, a social question.[22]

In the 1880s social revolution in England did not appear out of the ques-tion. During the American Civil War the French had seen the panic that swept away American shipping, as well as the sufferings of the British cotton workers. At the time Charmes and Aube were writing, in 1886, Britain and the world at large were in the depths of a great depression. In 1885, after a famous bomb plot and explosions in Birmingham, Liverpool, and Glasgow, and in London at the Local Government Board, Victoria Railway Station, the Tower, Westminster Hall, and the House of Commons, the government passed an Explosives Bill. In 1886 and 1887 Henry Hyndman's Social Demo-cratic Federation made its first real progress, while in 1889 came the great

Dock Strike, probably one of Britain's most publicized labor disputes. It is not a mere coincidence that, just at this time, British official scare literature like *The Great War of 189–* began to use numerous bloodcurdling tales of anarchist outrages.

The British continued to take the threat seriously in later years. In a great investigation completed in 1905, two labor leaders testified that they could not conceal the danger of serious riots, or at least of great pressure for peace at any price, if England's trade was endangered by a serious maritime war. A number of underwriters estimated that insurance rates would rise to about 20 percent per voyage. Grain prices, normally sixty to seventy shillings a quarter, had risen five shillings during the 1885 Penjdeh crisis with Russia and the 1898 Fashoda crisis with France, and fifteen shillings during the 1878 crisis with Russia. Mr. Broomhall of the *Corn Trade Yearbook* estimated that they might run up to two hundred shillings in a major war.[23]

The Jeune Ecole claimed that the threat of commerce-destroying had caused England to give way in the *Alabama* arbitration and in the Russian crises of 1878 and 1885.[24] This view was contested by Admiral Bourgois, who wrote that it looked to him as though Russia had done the backing-down at San Stefano in 1878.[25] Whatever its soundness, the French theory of commercial war was based on the possibility of the creation of an economic panic in England by a sudden attack "to make her insurance rates rise from the very beginning. . . . The surest way of stopping English merchantmen is thus to prevent them from starting."[26]

While advocating the use of torpedo boats and their accompanying gunboats against battleships, Aube and Charmes did not lose sight of another of the main elements of Jeune Ecole thought—commercial warfare. This was to be carried out ruthlessly not only on the routes to the Indies but on every commercial sea lane on the globe.

> Doubtlessly India is one of the most precious elements of [England's] prosperity, but, if cruisers were to interrupt for many months the arrival of American cotton that flows incessantly into her innumerable factories that produce the textiles that are then spread over all the markets of the universe, could one believe that she would not suffer as much as from the interruption of her relations with India? As soon as her factories stop, thousands of workers will be plunged into misery, and a terrible economic crisis will break out. Little by little, even famine will make itself felt with all its horrors, for the grain of America is no less necessary than the products of India for feeding England.[27]

In direct contradiction to Gougeard and the partisans of a rival French route to the East, Aube saw that the heart of England was still the Atlantic. There is no more remarkable example of his extraordinary breadth of view. Although his Mediterranean thinking had led him to proclaim a ruthless war against Italy, a danger Gougeard and Ferry had scarcely perceived, he was able to see that England should be struck in the Atlantic instead of the Mediterranean. As to England blockading France, he and Charmes saw clearly enough that "today, when blockades have become illusory, it is by commerce raiding that one can interdict the seas to an enemy."[28] With a legally effective blockade no longer possible, even the navy with command of the sea would have to resort to some illegal means of blockade to stop French and neutral trade with French ports.

A year later, in 1885, Aube made his most famous prophecy and proposed the use of torpedo boats for commercial war. Given his views on war and on international law, this was scarcely astonishing. He argued:

> War is the negation of law. It . . . is the recourse to force—the ruler of the world—of an entire people in the incessant and universal struggle for existence. Everything is therefore not only permissible but legitimate against the enemy.
> In the days when . . . in theory the laws of war were accepted by even the most rebellious spirits . . . how was maritime war practiced? . . . A captured ship was taken to the nearest port if it was worth it, otherwise the captor took aboard its crew and the prize was sunk. Humanity was saved—and also safe were the laws of war. Tomorrow, war breaks out; an autonomous torpedo boat—two officers, a dozen men—meets one of these liners carrying a cargo richer than that of the richest galleons of Spain and a crew and passengers of many hundreds; will the torpedo boat signify to the captain of the liner that it is there, that it is watching him, that it could sink him, and that consequently it makes him prisoner—him, his crew, his passengers—in a word that he has platonically been made a prize and should proceed to the nearest French port? To this declaration . . . the captain of the liner would respond with a well-aimed shell that would send to the bottom the torpedo boat, its crew, and its chivalrous captain, and tranquilly he would continue on his momentarily interrupted voyage. Therefore the torpedo boat will follow from afar, invisible, the liner it has met; and, once night has fallen, perfectly silently and tranquilly it will send into the abyss liner, cargo, crew, passengers; and, his soul not only at rest but fully satisfied, the captain of the torpedo boat will continue his cruise.[29]

The Jeune Ecole thus applied the theory of the little boats to every field of naval war. Charmes proclaimed that the torpedo was being improved so rapidly that it would inevitably prevail over all defenses, and he called on Frenchmen to "bring to bear immediately all of our genius for invention and all of our budgetary resources on the side whose future is certain and inevitable. The sea is ours, at least for several years, if only we take the lead."[30] The final element in the ideas of the Jeune Ecole was thus a revival of French faith in technological progress. Against England, "let us be better, if that be possible, but in any case *we must be different,* in the adaptation to rejuvenated methods of war, of new engines, judiciously conceived and rapidly executed."[31] Perhaps this faith was an illusion, but it was certainly different from Tirpitz's dictum that "no new weapon be adopted until it has a definite tactical place." It was closer to the exhortation of the pioneer of strategic bombing, the Italian General Giulio Douhet, "in departing from the highest lessons of the last war, to look carefully around oneself, and then to leap into the future. . . . It is [the new technical means] that will give war its form and character."[32]

In summary, to avoid the loss of the second colonial empire as France had lost the first, Aube had developed a complete system of naval strategy:

In past wars:	*In the next:*
England's command of the sea had assured simultaneously:	Aube argued that:
1. The defense of English soil	1. She could be conquered without setting foot on her coasts
2. The attack on French coasts	2. Could 30,000 men succeed against a nation in arms?
3. The defense of English commerce	3. Because blockade was impossible, only the direct defense of her enormous trade would be of any use
4. The attack on French trade	4. French trade could only be attacked by violating the laws of blockade, while not seriously injuring France
5. The defense of English colonies	5. The English colonies would proclaim their separate nationality
6. The attack on French colonies	6. The French colonies would be defended by a separate colonial army

In short, "command of the sea is nothing more than an expression void of any meaning." Aube forgot only one thing—England had never fought alone.

Tactically, the Jeune Ecole called for all ships to be divided into those armed with the gun and those with the torpedo. They expected that the events of a future war would fall into four main categories:

1. The weakest fleet would rest in its bases and refuse combat.
2. The stronger would be forced to do the same for fear of the torpedo.
3. The only real activity would be commercial warfare.
4. That would be absolutely merciless.

In spite of the many arguments against these ideas, it is possible to view the events of the war of 1914–18 under exactly those four points.[33]

THE NAVY DIVIDED

By the time Aube became minister of marine in January 1886, the debate over the ideas of the Jeune Ecole was in full swing, and it was to split the navy into two contesting factions for nearly fifteen years. The navy itself was ready for an explosion: its relations with public opinion and Parliament were uncertain, and tensions within the officer corps were rising even before the technical debate came to a head. Aube, whose three greatest faults were his technical incompetence, his optimism, and his taste for resorting to the public press, enlisted Charmes as an aide in setting off the dynamite—a man even less competent technically, more optimistic, and versed in all the arts of French newspaper controversy. Instead of appealing to the public primarily on issues of administration, secondarily on general points of strategy and diplomacy, and not at all on technical matters beyond its competence, Charmes completely reversed the process. "We agree . . . that there are great economies to be made in the organization of our arsenals, but reforms must be made above all in the products of these arsenals."[34]

The incredibly doctrinaire—and incredibly French—character of the debate was at least partly due to Charmes. Like most French journalists, he believed that all things could be solved by argument, if only the polemic was violent enough. This belief was based on the view that those who did not agree with the absolute truth being presented were solely motivated by personal interests, which the French press, with its marvelous aptitude for indulging in personalities, would soon drag to light. As a result, the technical question of the torpedo boat versus the battleship soon became entangled in the rivalry of *Le Temps* versus the *Journal des débats,* the republicans versus the conservatives, the lower versus the higher officers, and a thousand other personal and political squabbles that had nothing to do with it. The whole affair was soon so lost in the mire of French journalism and politics that it is useless even to summarize the arguments used. Charmes did not go to the lengths of calling up the spirit of the great corsair of the Napoleonic Wars, Surcouf, and then quoting the ghost as a supporter, as one enthusiastic spiritualist did, but he did start the French Navy down the road to a new nadir under the ministry of Camille Pelletan (1902–5).[35]

The only possible remaining irrelevant argument was soon added by Juliette Adam, the anglophobe editor of the *Nouvelle revue.* Because of the definite anglophobia of the new theory, she opened her columns freely to its partisans. In the monthly naval section edited by Paul Fontin, the wildest anglomania and the most insensate developments of Aube's views appeared comfortably side by side. In the meantime, in another section of the press, the radical politicians Georges Clemenceau and Camille Pelletan were delivering the most scurrilous personal attacks on the ablest of the traditionalist admirals, Alfred-Albert Gervais, because the visit of his squadron to Kronstadt in 1891 had led to the conclusion of an alliance with autocratic Russia. Among other things, Gervais was blamed for the death of a sailor who slipped on the deck of one of the ships of his fleet!

After Charmes there were two French navies, that of the liberal parliamentary philosophers who supported the torpedo boats and that of the black reactionaries who supported the battleships. The *Journal des débats, Nouvelle revue, Revue des deux mondes,* and *La Marine française*—the Jeune Ecole's own "technical" publication—were on the side of light and reason, while *Le Temps* and *Le Yacht* belonged to the black cult. Indeed, when Lieutenant Robert Degouy published a heretical article in the *Revue des deux mondes,* the editor was looked upon almost as a traitor. Within the navy itself, the violence of the conflict was due to the profound dissatisfaction of the lower with the higher officers and of the younger men with the rule of the naval aristocrats. The whole situation contained many of the elements of the Dreyfus affair that polarized French politics in the 1890s, but lacked a *cause célèbre* to set it off.

With Charmes, the questions of arsenal reform, technical change, personnel, and the navy's relations with the public and Parliament were mixed into one grand hash that obscures many of his individual arguments. Of all his irrelevant contentions, however, the old financial argument undoubtedly had the most effect, for it came just at the time when the navy was involved in a great financial crisis. In the fiscal conditions of 1885 and 1886, particularly in view of the enormous expenditures of Aube's colleague, Minister of War General Georges-Ernest Boulanger, the most liberal and humanitarian of parties were willing to accept the most ruthless theories of naval war if only they could save a little money.[36] The torpedo boat offered a cheap method of warfare. Charmes, rhetorically addressing Gougeard, solemnly affirmed that "there are in this world things with which one can do a great deal with little, win a great payoff while risking a small stake."[37]

REACTIONS TO THE JEUNE ECOLE

Perhaps the most radical proposal of the Jeune Ecole was the use of torpedo boats as commerce-destroyers. On this subject the torpedo-boat fanatics like Aube, who had played no part whatever in the technical development of the new weapon, encountered their most redoubtable adversary—Admiral Bourgois, one of the greatest authorities on torpedo work in France. Designer along with the naval constructor Charles-Marie Brun of the French Navy's first submarine, the *Plongeur,* president of the commission that had recommended the adoption of the Whitehead torpedo, and chairman of the Commission on Submarine Defenses for several years after the war of 1870, he was also one of the greatest French students of naval international law. He ably summed up the legal arguments against the use of the torpedo boat for commerce-destroying. He agreed with Aube that it was absolutely impossible for a torpedo boat to lead a prize to the nearest port, to put a prize crew on her, or to take the passengers and crew on board, and that one shot from an armed merchantman would finish the torpedo boat. Yet, even admitting that an English ship could be sent to the bottom at night, in violation of the laws of war, how was the boat's captain to know that the liner he had sunk so tranquilly was English? The use of such methods would almost inevitably bring in neutral powers, not merely America or Holland but Italy and Germany, all of whose shipping passed through the very waters in which Aube's boats were to do their work. It was not mere humanitarianism that prevented the use of such methods; it was the diplomatic fact, which the "rationalists" had forgotten, that such violations of the laws of war would make the combination of England and Germany almost certain. "The admission that commercial warfare conducted by torpedo boats could lead to such excesses is the most forceful of possible condemnations of this use of the new weapon."[38]

Admiral Ernest du Pin de Saint-André, who had produced much of the new defensive system of Toulon against torpedo attack,[39] pointed out how little Charmes knew of the real conditions of torpedo war. With the certainty of being sunk without warning, merchant ships would be defensively armed to fight torpedo boats (they had no hope of fighting a cruiser). Merchant ships could see a torpedo boat as soon as the latter could see it. He concluded that any ship that went at full speed away from the danger in zig-zags while using her defensive automatic guns would have an excellent chance of escaping.[40] Thus, within a year of the proposal of the new idea, French writers had outlined not only the ways the new craft could be used for commercial warfare but also the resultant violations of the laws of war, the protests of neutrals, and the tactics merchantmen could take against the danger.

In the diplomatic environment of 1885, in which it was essential to keep the Triple Alliance neutral in a maritime war, the ideas of Aube and Charmes on commerce-raiding reflected a brand of colonial insanity that was a suitable companion for the then-popular radical nationalism of Paul Déroulède. The idea of using torpedo boats as raiders was condemned unanimously by every officer of importance who seriously considered the question. According to one, "Such piracy . . . would only be the signal for a general league of neutrals against us."[41] Another study limited torpedo boats to attacks on convoys from bases at Oran, Bizerte, and Cherbourg, which would be perfectly legal but which would perpetuate the problem of trade defense for potential enemies.[42]

The British saw the danger, and continued to worry about it into the twentieth century. In the British naval maneuvers of 1901, the "French" side under Admiral A. K. Wilson used its torpedo-boat destroyers as commerce raiders, and the London *Times* was seriously alarmed about the type of naval war it presaged. "The only way in which a destroyer can really stop the trade of an enemy in real war is by sending to the bottom every hostile merchant ship she comes across. This is a barbarous proceeding."[43] The testimony of Sir John Hopkins before the Royal Commission on Food Supplies gave an interesting view of what the English then thought was likely to happen.

> Q. Do you contemplate that a torpedo boat could possibly make a cap-
>   ture of a first-class liner?
> A. Yes.
> Q. How?
> A. By hailing her to the effect that "if you don't stop, I will sink you."
> Q. What is to become of the crew and passengers? Do you contemplate
>   that they are going to be destroyed?
> A. Certainly, if she does not stop; you can do nothing else.[44]

Fifteen years after Aube—and fifteen years before World War I—the British recognized that French public opinion might force the navy to employ drastic methods, and the English system of commerce protection that was developed in the late 1890s probably included measures to meet this contingency, such as special routings of merchant ships in the Mediterranean.[45]

It is instructive to compare the theories of Aube with the unrestricted submarine warfare unleashed by the Germans against the Allies during World War I. The French theories were based not on the destruction of commerce to starve out the enemy but on inducing the paralysis of British trade and economic life by a sudden, merciless attack at the outbreak of the war. The Germans were so wedded to Mahan, the High Seas Fleet, and Tirpitz's "Risk Theory" that they gave no thought in advance to commercial war and had to learn in wartime what France had learned over a period of three decades of peace. The result was a series of lost opportunities and misdirected actions. The German policy of not adopting a new weapon until it had a definite tactical place left them in complete ignorance of the possibility of catching England unawares by the immediate use of the submarine as a commerce raider. In the first year of the war, with the exception of sending out a few auxiliary cruisers and the cruiser squadron of Admiral Von Spee, Germany did nothing at all. It took two years for the Germans to decide to violate American neutrality; by then every other great neutral was in the war.[46] In its general naval strategy, in its estimate of the diplomatic situation, and in its tardy recognition of the possibilities of the new weapon, the German navy not only was not influenced by the theory of the French, it violated every single rule that Aube and Charmes had laid down.

THE MINISTRY OF ADMIRAL AUBE

Aube served as minister of marine from 7 January 1886 to 30 May 1887. (His flamboyant colleague, Minister of War General Boulanger, became a national hero for his anti-German sentiments during this period.) The chief faults in Aube's administration, as in his ideas, were his lack of technical experience and his optimism, plus the common liberal flaw of trusting too much in private firms. He made no effort to reform the navy's administration—his only change in the system was the creation of a separate torpedo service at the ministry and in each port. He thus followed what had become the traditional approach of adding another new organism instead of trying to reform the whole. Otherwise he concentrated simply on speeding up the functioning of the bureaucracy. He reduced the mandatory retirement age limits of commissaries, mechanics, and engineers by decree, since the bill submitted by one of his predecessors, Admiral Jauréguiberry, was then in its sixth year in a parliamentary committee. He also threw out nearly all of the officers on the navy's Paris staff and most of the ministry's bureau chiefs, and for the first time in French naval history he punished an engineer for a technical mistake. Finally, he launched what amounted to an attack on the Council of Admiralty by reducing the number of its members and calling it together more frequently. With the exception of the creation of the torpedo service, most of these measures were good, but all of them made Aube an enormous number of enemies.

All of the efforts of Aube's ministry were bent on the accomplishment of his strategic and technical program. He redistributed the navy's European forces into three main groups. The entire battle fleet was concentrated at Toulon against Italy. Since there was no danger whatever of a German offensive, Cherbourg was left with nothing but torpedo craft and old coast-defense battleships, while Brest received all the commerce-destroying cruisers. The general principles of Aube's new distribution were thus offensive in the Mediterranean, defensive in the Channel, and commercial warfare in the Atlantic.

In the Mediterranean, Aube and Boulanger definitely chose Bizerte as the site of a major base and submitted a complete plan for its development. The cabinet rejected the plan as a violation of the assurances given to England, and all that was done was some dredging to make a torpedo station in the old port.[47] Aube's projects for colonial defenses and coaling stations were financially impossible and, save for the torpedo station at Bizerte and another established at Ajaccio in Corsica, his plans for bases in the Mediterranean against Italy and a chain of coaling stations around the globe were completely unrealized. Aube also lost his main battle over coast defense when Boulanger flatly refused to turn it over to the navy, but he made considerable progress in the organization of coastal observation points and telegraphs.[48]

The first-class protected cruiser Isly *(launched in 1891). She was one of three large cruisers built under Aube's program of cruisers and torpedo boats.*

Turning to matériel, Aube completely stopped work on the four battleships of the *Hoche* and *Magenta* types begun in 1880 in order to concentrate on his cheaper methods of warfare. He requested an immediate special credit of 200 million francs for a building program that included six large and ten small cruisers, twenty large torpedo boats for use against other torpedo boats, fifty *bateaux-canons,* one hundred regular torpedo boats, and three armored coast-defense ships for use as torpedo mother ships.[49] This program went through various amputations at the hands of the Budget Committee and Aube's successors as minister of marine, but before Aube left office he was able to order three large cruisers similar to the *Sfax* but without sails; two similar, medium-sized cruisers; and six small 1,800-ton cruisers much like the *Milan.* The latter, Aube's ideal cheap cruisers, suffered from lack of staying power.[50] Three other cruisers (two large and one medium) ordered by Aube were canceled, but at least a start had been made toward the construction of a modern cruiser and commerce-destroying force. In addition, it was the magnitude of Aube's original projects, not the form in which they eventually were realized, that affected the perceptions of the English.

Construction of the torpedo boats in Aube's program was prevented by problems with the design of their predecessors, *No. 75* through *No. 125.* In June 1885 the navy had ordered thirty boats, which were to be slightly improved versions of the 33-meter boats that had so impressed Charmes; immediately upon taking office, Aube ordered twenty-one more. Completely new 35-meter plans were adopted for these boats, however, leading to extensive wrangling between designers, contractors, and the ministry. Deliveries were then delayed by major problems with the boilers and by doubts concerning the stability of the boats, which were confirmed in 1889 when

Two Davids and a Goliath: the torpedo boats No. 101 *and* No. 102 *(1887), of Aube's 35-meter type, near the battleship* Marceau, *a* Magenta-*class ship on the ways just before her launch in 1887.* No. 102 *capsized at sea two years later, revealing a major design defect in her class.*

No. 102 capsized and a wave broke *No. 110* completely in two. The class had to be entirely rebuilt, reboilered, and strengthened, and as a result its maximum speed fell to 17 knots instead of the planned 20. France did not have a torpedo boat design that it could depend on until the successful trials of *No. 126,* built by Normand, in 1889.

Aube had better luck with torpedoes and with organizational matters. He moved the Torpedo School from Boyardville to Toulon, where he also established the factory that thereafter successfully built the navy's torpedoes. In addition to forming a torpedo service and a corps of torpedo mechanics, he created the *défenses mobiles,* the organization under which torpedo boats were henceforth maintained scattered among French ports for the defense of the coasts.

Some of the other elements of Aube's program were implemented in whole or in part by his successors. Under Aube, some preliminary design work was done on an "armored coast defense ship destined to serve as center of action for a group of torpedo boats," and four ships of this general type but without the torpedo warfare function—the *Valmy* and *Bouvines* classes—were eventually ordered in 1889.[51] The next year design work began on a cruiser-sized torpedo mother ship, the *Foudre,* which was ordered in 1892.

The bateau-canon Gabriel Charmes *(1886). Designed to support attacks by torpedo boats, she proved that a 5.5-inch gun could not fire accurately from a torpedo boat hull.*

While the immediate results of Aube's administration in the area of naval matériel were either practically nil or actually unfortunate, the studies and experiments he was responsible for starting, like his strategic theories, foresaw nearly the whole range of developments in matériel for the next fifteen years. Though those on torpedo boats were the most famous, almost equally important were those on Charmes's *bateau-canon*. In April 1886 Aube ordered the construction of an experimental *bateau-canon,* which, after Charmes's death, was named for the publicist. The *Gabriel Charmes* was nothing but an enlarged 35-meter torpedo boat carrying one 5.5-inch gun. The accuracy of the gun's fire from such a small, lively platform was fully equal to the expectations of Aube's worst opponents. The fifty *bateaux-canons* were quietly dropped from the building program, and under Aube's successor, the de-gunned *Gabriel Charmes* became simply torpedo boat *No. 151.*

The most important part of Aube's experiments was the first trial in the navy of the high explosive melinite shell, which had been adopted in the army primarily for bombardments. It was a long, thin-walled projectile carrying a very large charge of explosive, and was generally fired from mortars, like those which were to be placed on Aube's bombardment gunboats. Much of the propaganda carried on by the Jeune Ecole was based on a vision of the terrible destruction that would be wrought by lobbing these big cans of melinite in the general direction of an Italian city. But Aube had wished to use his gunboats against battleships, and some of the projectiles were tried against an old battleship, the *Belliqueuse.* The effects of the enormous quantity of gases they released were appalling. The tests indicated that one shell exploding in a closed space such as that between the armored deck and the turrets of an Italian battleship would collapse scores of water-tight compartments and almost push the protective belt right out of the ship. The result of this and similar experiments abroad was to render the whole class of practically unarmored battleships, especially those like the *Duilio* and the *Italia,* whose protection depended on a cellular layer, more obsolete than the thinly plated *Gloire.* By a totally unexpected turn of fate, Aube's unarmored *bateau-canon* was responsible in a way for the revival of armor.[52]

Aube's experiments with torpedoes included studies of the resistance of hulls to underwater explosions using the old armored floating battery *Protectrice* at Cherbourg. Trials off the Hyères islands near Toulon against the new battleship *Amiral Duperré* examined Charmes's claim of the "almost absolute" certainty of hitting a full-sized moving target with a torpedo. They showed that within four hundred yards, a well-launched Whitehead already had a really fair chance—about one in three or four. Two months after his arrival in power, Aube also opened an official competition for designs for a submarine, which ultimately led to the construction of France's first viable underwater craft, the *Gymnote.*

Most publicized of all were Aube's trials of his twin theories of the auton-

Life on a torpedo boat: aboard No. 143 *(1890). The commander is peering out of his action station in the conning tower, just over the helmsman's station, and other types of crewmen, including an engineer, are also shown. The spar for the spar torpedo is on deck in the foreground.*

omy of torpedo boats and of the victory of the microbes over the giants. In February 1886, torpedo boat *No. 61* and some other boats set out from Atlantic ports to Toulon with the avowed purpose of testing their capacity to make independent cruises. A winter voyage along the coasts of the Bay of Biscay was no easy one for a 33-meter, 46-ton boat. Though the boats made the journey safely, the *torpilleur autonome* was buried silently beside the *bateau-canon*. In an average voyage of around twenty days, about that of a poor tramp steamer, the crews were so worn out from seasickness and the lack of warm food and sleep that there could be no question of their inability to fight at the end of the trip. According to one participant:

> As a rule, we lived on ham, sardines, and tinned soups; for most of the time the weather was so rough that it was as much as we could do to get a little water boiled. We had a table about 18 inches wide, but there was no point in laying it, for nothing would stay on it. The usual plan was for one man to hold the sardine tin while the other picked out sardines by their tails and transferred them to his mouth.

The commander of *No. 61* reported:

> Particularly fatiguing on a torpedo boat, and especially hard for men of nervous disposition, is the continual vibration that constantly shakes you, and with it the throbbing of the engines that produced a kind of counterstroke that made the whole stern tremble and seemed likely to cause the engine itself to become dislocated. . . . In sum, one can sail and live at sea on a torpedo boat, if one does not exaggerate the number of days to be spent in the open ocean. . . . [53]

The Boyardville Commission had concluded that torpedo boats like *No. 61* could stand a sudden blow, but Charmes should have been able to make for himself the astounding discovery that a 33-meter boat was not yet an Atlantic liner.

In a final great experiment, all the existing Davids (eleven 33-ton and eleven 46-ton boats) were pitted against the Goliaths (the whole Mediterranean fleet, representing about twenty times as much money and men) in the first French naval maneuvers. The microbes were given four problems: the defense of Toulon against bombardment without aid from the forts, the breaking of a blockade, the closing of a strait, and an attack on the squadron at anchor in a temporary base. They failed round one when the squadron carried out the bombardment without any trouble in seas heavy enough to have prevented any boats intercepting the battleships from launching their torpedoes.

In round two, the fleet was judged to have sunk the cruiser that tried to break the blockade with the aid of the torpedo boats. However, in this phase the microbes made 126 appearances, got within good range 21 times, and completely surprised the giants in 8 cases. In spite of the destruction of the cruiser, the commander concluded that "the most assiduous night watch may be set at nought by a torpedo boat. . . . Their intervention makes impracticable the keeping of a blockade." Round two thus really went to the Davids, a fact that was particularly important, since Aube's whole theory of the nullification of command of the sea was based on the impossibility of close blockade.

In round three the Goliaths, though carrying some lights, went through a strait about the width of the English Channel almost unnoticed and never in danger. For round four, they were sent to Ajaccio to improvise their own defense. Though informed by telegraph of the anchoring of the squadron, the torpedo boats were kept in Toulon by a good west wind for two days until their commander decided to leave all his small boats behind and set out with twelve boats, two cruisers, and a coast-defense ship. Six boats were forced to turn back and another broke down just before the attack, which failed even to get within range. "Five torpedo boats out of twenty-two," the commander reported, "harassed by fatigue, waterlogged, and probably incapable of launching their torpedoes, finally arrived. This odyssey in summer, on a friendly coast, may demolish the faith of the most dedicated believers in the absolute autonomy . . . of the seagoing boats, who lost three quarters of their effective strength in twelve hours in the Mediterranean."[54] In Aube's budget for 1887, money was again appropriated for the unfinished battleships.

It should be noted that the inauguration of French naval maneuvers was itself a major step forward, opening the way for perfecting and integrating into the navy's organization the equipment developed during the preceding fifteen years. Although landsmen were disposed to look on them and their "lessons" as just another means of propaganda while armchair strategists were tempted to regard them as infallible, they really began to provide once more a modest, imperfect experimental basis for naval strategy to supplement the lessons of the fifteen years between the Crimean War and the Franco-Prussian War. Impossible ground rules, outlandish conclusions, and distortions for political and even personal purposes (like the amazing feats of the Duke of Genoa in the Italian maneuvers) were certainly present, but even so, the maneuvers began to provide an experimental basis for the use of the new naval weapons.

Other experiences confirmed that the "autonomous" torpedo boats were done for. The Germans had seen that in daytime, without the help of armored ships and coastal forts, torpedo boats could not even assure an adequate coastal defense. At night, and indeed at almost any time, they could not see; and without the help of larger boats like the German flotilla leaders, they could not detect an enemy passing through a strait or maintain contact once they had found him. In 1887 thirty-two French torpedo boats, three cruisers, and one coast-defense ship tried to prevent the squadron from passing through the Balearic passage, but the squadron saw the nearest boats before the latter saw it and picked them off one by one. The rest, warned by the "mother ship" *Aréthuse,* failed to come up in time. The total bag in this debacle was two ships: a liner mistaken for a battleship, and the *Aréthuse* herself. Admiral Bergasse Dupetit-Thouars, who took command of the Mediterranean Fleet in 1888, reported that "a coast such as ours can only be defended by a fleet, or coast-defense ships accompanied by torpedo craft. The latter are useful against well-handled ships only when they act in groups. In daytime they must be hidden until the moment for action; at night they must have a leader to guide them and keep them together."[55]

The English at the time of the Russian scare of 1885 had ordered fifty-five torpedo boats as hastily as Aube had bought his a year later, and with the same results as in France. The boats were slow and too small, and the untrained crews were unable to stay very long at sea. Of twenty-two boats that started a hundred-mile trial in 1887, seven were put out of action by machinery accidents and another lost its propeller. The defensive nets used to protect the battleships proved very successful, and the British decided to build no more regular first-class torpedo boats but instead concentrate on larger "torpedo-boat catchers" or "torpedo gunboats" (equivalent to the larger French torpedo avisos) and on second-class torpedo boats to be carried by battleships and for use within harbors.[56]

THE LEGACY OF THE JEUNE ECOLE

Of the Jeune Ecole's creators, Gabriel Charmes died at the age of thirty-six at the very opening of Aube's administration, and Gougeard, fifty-nine, died in the same year. Lamy, beaten in the elections of 1881, left politics entirely at the age of thirty-eight for a career as secretary to the French Academy, while Grivel, fifty-five, had died of fever in 1882 in Senegal. When Aube himself, his health broken at age sixty-one, retired to the country for the last three years of his life, there disappeared the last of the really important figures of the Jeune Ecole, the last with the ability to keep it from degenerating into a mere naval faction. In spite of his failures and mistakes, Aube displayed all of the best personal characteristics of the handful of men who built the second French colonial empire: clarity of vision, courage, and absolute intellectual and personal honesty.

In both theory and practice, Aube's Jeune Ecole split the French Navy wide open, and the next fifteen years was a period of incredible confusion. Next to the personal bitterness involved and the complete lack of constructive relations between the navy and Parliament and public opinion, the worst legacy of the Aube ministry was the idea that every minister had to change something. In the sixteen years from the beginning of Pothuau's ministry on 19 February 1871 to the end of Aube's on 30 May 1887, there

were fifteen ministries; in the fifteen years to the fall of the Lanessan ministry on 7 June 1902 there were sixteen more. (Omitting duplications, there
were still thirteen different ministers in the first period and twelve in the
second.)

Although the average of one ministry per year holds true throughout, the
effects of ministerial turnover were vastly different in the two periods. During the first, the navy was effectively controlled by a group of higher officers
who, though occasionally differing in their political views, knew the machine and were united on questions of doctrine. Aube threw out all of the
old school at once and changed simultaneously many of the basic principles, such as the system for distributing shipbuilding orders, that gov-
erned the functioning of the ministry. As a result, while the grievances of the
younger men were many and justified and while Aube's general strategic
system was sound, his ministry ended in complete disorder.

Another change was that nine of the sixteen ministries that followed Aube
were headed by civilians. The necessary change from a military to a civilian
head for the navy thus took place at the very time in which, instead of
making the ministry simpler to administer, Aube had made it more complex. The civilian ministers, totally lost, had two choices. They could give up
entirely and let the various services and bureaus go their separate ways, or
they could tinker with the machinery as they saw fit—without any effective
check from the officers who knew how it worked. Félix Faure, for example,
attended to general political affairs (which soon made him president of the
Republic) while the navy ran itself, a course that was very popular with the
officers. On the other hand, Edouard Lockroy had ideas that were sound
enough but which he did not know how to put into effect, while the idio-
syncrasies of the brilliant but erratic Camille Pelletan proved disastrous for
the navy. Of all the civilian ministers, only Jean-Louis de Lanessan (1899–
1902), like Théophile Delcassé ten years later, had the tact and intelligence
necessary to give the naval machine a really vigorous impulsion. Under the
admirals who were ministers, the navy generally just stagnated, as the admirals were completely unable to handle either the cabinet or the Chamber
of Deputies. They did no harm, but they were unable to bring about any
improvement.

Admiral or civilian, however, nearly every minister after Aube felt the itch
to play the reformer. The admirals generally indulged in some fad in naval
construction; the civilians could at least busy themselves with the administrative machine (where, it must be admitted, the addition of a few more
organs did little harm). If they had no new ideas, they could undo what their
immediate predecessor had done.

A common pastime was changing the distribution of the fleet—relatively
harmless, since the only expenses were those of moving the coal and stores,
and one's successor could always move them back again if he wished. The

favorite version of this sport was shuffling the coast-defense ships. With the end of the possibility of undertaking the mission for which they had been designed (an offensive in the coastal waters of France's neighbors), these ships were as useless as the overseas station fleet after the appearance of fast protected cruisers like the *Esmeralda*. Aube had seen that the coastal battle-ships were largely wasted in the Channel, since there was no danger of a German offensive, and he began the attempt to use the best ones against Italy. However, the Italian coast offered no shoal water for them to operate in, while the ships had a short steaming range, were slow, and often, as in the case of the *Tonnerre,* which had been so badly bested in the storm by *No. 63* and *No. 64,* were only a handicap. Even the coast-defense ships of the *Indomptable* class that had so worried England were very mediocre in the Mediterranean, and all the coast defenders had to be written off as prac-tically useless. Without counting the five survivors from Napoleon III's days but including the four new ones of the *Valmy* group begun in 1889, the navy had no less than fourteen heavily armored ships in this obsolete cate-gory during the 1890s, and each minister used all his ingenuity in trying to find a place for them. They moved in droves from the Channel to the Medi-terranean and back again, and even the first-class battleships themselves were not exempt from this shuffling. One wanderer went between Brest and Toulon six times in six ministries.

After Aube, with an increasingly complicated ministry, an increasing con-fusion in strategic ideas, and an increasing number of civilian ministers, it is a wonder that the French had any naval policy at all. At times it is certainly difficult to find it.

> There is the classic experiment in physiology of the pigeon from which the cerebral hemispheres have been removed; the bird eats, drinks, walks, flies, performing each of its separate functions by reflex action. There is no doubt that this is not death, but it is far from life in the whole sense of the word. It is from the absence of this directing and impelling organ that the navy suffers.[57]

The single rule that appears to have been observed was that each minis-ter stayed at least long enough to upset the system.[58] When the minister was capable, the result was sometimes progress. When he was not, the best that could be hoped for was stagnation.

Eleven

〜〜〜〜〜〜〜〜〜〜〜〜〜〜〜〜〜〜〜〜〜〜〜〜〜〜〜

The Race with Italy

THE TURMOIL in the French Navy in the mid-1880s was one of the factors that helped revive the French rivalry with Italy at the end of the decade. Aube's public statements regarding the kind of war he planned and even some of his actions, including the concentration of the whole fleet in the Mediterranean, were worrisome not only for their own sake but also because they were connected with the inflamed French nationalism of the day. Aube, after all, was in the same cabinet as the highly nationalistic General Boulanger. In some ways, the new French nationalist movement resembled the liberal internationalism that had caused France to meddle in the domestic affairs of much of Europe during the revolutions of 1848. To the rest of Europe, it seemed as though France might be getting ready to explode again. The German chancellor Caprivi was obsessed by the danger of a "two-front war" against France and Russia, while the English feared that their whole commerce and coasts might be subjected to ruthless attack if the explosion should turn in their direction.

In the meantime, the French Navy was trying to make some order out of the chaos left by the Aube ministry. Aube had challenged the navy's strategy, disrupted its building program, and overextended its budget. Under these conditions, the efforts of the Italians to strengthen their navy triggered alarm in France and led to a short but intense naval race between the two countries.

THE ITALIAN NAVAL REVIVAL, 1884–88

In Italy, the rise of French nationalism was accompanied in March 1884 by the return as minister of marine of Benedetto Brin. Under his immediate predecessor, Ferdinando Acton, all preparations against Austria had ceased as a result of the formation of the Triple Alliance, and work at the new base at Taranto had proceeded very slowly, while the navy had not yet awaked to the French menace. Endless discussions had taken place on the advisability of future battleship construction, and for several years most of the new construction money had gone for protected cruisers. In 1886 the three battleships of the *Ruggiero di Lauria* class and even the *Lepanto* were not yet complete, and the navy still had only three battleships fit to fight (the *Duilio, Dandolo,* and *Italia*).[1]

The extent of the revival under Brin in the mid-1880s is indicated by the growth of the navy budget. The budget for 1883 was about the same as that of 1878. It rose about 20 percent in 1884, the year of the publication of Aube's *Italie et Levant,* and it almost doubled in 1885, the year of Brin's return to power. By 1888 it had practically doubled again. The results of Brin's second five years (1885–89) in the area of matériel were the completion of all the battleships under construction and of thirteen cruisers and the laying down of three ships similar to the *Italia* but even larger and faster, the *Re Umberto* class. When these were finished, Italy would have ten large battleships—over three times as many as she had in 1886—which were faster than and as powerful as any France had ever laid down.

Meanwhile, in the years 1882–89 the Italian Army spent 127 million lire on new defenses along the peninsula's west coast. Besides building enormous fortifications in the Alps and improving the regular naval ports, the Italians built strong defenses along the coast at Vado, Genoa, Monte Argentario, and Elba. They also set up an elaborate semaphore and telegraph system, which made it almost impossible for an enemy to slip through the Tuscan archipelago in the northern approaches to the Tyrrhenian Sea without being attacked by practically all of the Italian torpedo craft, which were concentrated in that area.[2] Both sides of the Strait of Messina were heavily fortified to prevent interruption of transport traffic between Sicily and the mainland, to form a secondary base for the fleet, and to close another of the entrances into the Tyrrhenian toward Naples and Rome. Something was also done about the problem of the vulnerability of Naples by creating a fortified anchorage at Gaeta, though the old arsenal at Naples was not moved. A fleet could thus find refuge in the Naples area, even though it could not receive repairs there or prevent the destruction of the city and arsenal.

Most important of all was the construction of permanent fortifications on La Maddalena Island, located at the northern tip of Sardinia in the Strait of Bonifacio between that island and Corsica. "A fleet that holds the Strait of Bonifacio," Aube had written, "has a foothold on Corsica, and the resources of Sardinia, which it protects, are at its disposal. It cannot be blockaded since it has two exit routes, it defends Spezia, covers Genoa, and watches or menaces Toulon and all Provence."[3] The group of islands around La Maddalena formed a perfectly defensible base of operations with passages that could be opened or closed to cruisers and torpedo craft at will. The Italians had long used the location as a secondary port, but in 1887, spurred in part by Aube's articles on the importance of Corsica, they began construction of a first-class naval base there.[4] By 1894 the work was completely finished, and the second entrance to the Tyrrhenian Sea was closed nearly as tightly as that at Messina.[5]

The intricate system of naval bases established by Italy was the first application to sea power of the German defensive principle of the control of a given area by concentration of forces from fortified points. In this respect, the forts were even more important to Italian strategy than were Brin's battleships, which were the main reason for the enormous cost of the Italian naval program. While France had one Mediterranean port (Toulon) and England two (Malta and Gibraltar, the latter being not much more than a strongly defended anchorage), Italy had Spezia (a major port of the stature of Toulon and Malta), Maddalena (equivalent to Gibraltar), plus minor ports at Gaeta, Messina, and Elba.

The Italian battleships, however, were still coast-defense garrison ships or *Ausfallkorvetten,* not a real fleet. In a well-informed scare story of 1888, the Italian battleships were divided into three main groups, one at Spezia with the *Duilio* and three older ships, one at Maddalena with the *Dandolo* and the old *Affondatore* (the flagship at the battle of Lissa in 1866), and one at Naples consisting of the *Italia* and *Lepanto.*[6] Instead of dividing their ships into a fast and a slow squadron, the Italians were still trying to leave one fast ship and a number of slow ones in each port. (One of the criticisms of the *Duilio*'s design had been that it was too fast to serve with the navy's older ships.) In this distribution, as in their tactics, Italian naval officers were remarkably behind their constructors.

But when Italy did form a fast squadron, Maddalena was its natural base, even for defensive purposes. And if Italy ever took the offensive, she had only to remember that Nelson had used Maddalena as his base of operations against Toulon. The American Alfred Thayer Mahan observed that "if we could possess Sardinia, we would want neither Malta nor any other port. It possesses at its northern end the finest harbor in the world. It is twenty-four hours' sail from Toulon . . . it covers Egypt, Italy, and Turkey."[7] Though Marseilles was not as vulnerable to attack from the sea as the great Italian ports, and though there were no other cities on the coast of Provence even half the size of Leghorn, Maddalena at least gave Italy the ability to reply to the French bombardment threat. In addition, the popular clamor that would arise following a series of rapid blows against the French coast would tie the French fleet to its bases, ending the threat to the Italian coast.

The fortification of Maddalena was also the first serious and permanent Italian threat to French control of the western Mediterranean. Directly astride the route between France and North Africa, it was also a barrier to a fleet sailing from Toulon to the eastern Mediterranean, just as Port Mahon in the Balearics was to a fleet heading for the Atlantic. It was thus a response to the still unrealized threat from Bizerte. Even more important, it increased Italy's value as an ally to England at a time when England was particularly interested in "covering Egypt and Turkey." The use of Maddalena and the Italian coastal telegraphs and the closing of the Strait of Messina to a fleet going east from Toulon would be just as important to England as would the cooperation of Brin's rapid and powerful ships. Even if Italy remained nominally neutral, the use of the Gulf of Asinara west of Maddalena as an advance base and of the Italian communications system would have been very useful to England. In the war of 1870 Britain had shown that she could allow or deny France access to the island of Heligoland without going beyond the bounds of neutrality, and the same would apply to Italy in the case of the ports of northern Sardinia.

Italy and Her Allies

French nationalism, and Bismarck's fear of it, also played a central role in a series of diplomatic agreements concluded in early 1887, which strengthened Italy's position in the Mediterranean while largely isolating France. The renewed Triple Alliance between Italy, Germany, and Austria and the First Mediterranean Agreement that associated Italy, Britain, Austria, and Spain provided for the protection against France not only of peninsular Italy but of Italian colonial ambitions in North Africa.

Italy's basic relationship to Germany and England was established by the fact that France was stronger than Italy but Italy was fairly strong against her traditional foe, Austria. To gain Bismarck's support, Italy exploited her nuisance value against Austria, Germany's ally, while to attract Britain she made the most of the prospect that if Italy were to collapse under French pressure, England would be left alone in the Mediterranean. The Italian position was further strengthened because it was Russia, not Italy or even France, that was the principal problem in European diplomacy in 1887, and both London and Berlin needed a strong Vienna as a bulwark against St. Petersburg.

Italy's basic weakness was that French seapower prevented her from mounting offensive operations overseas, forcing her to settle instead for whatever colonial crumbs Germany or England might decide to give her at the negotiating table. In a war, Italy would have had little real opportunity to seize Tunis or another colony as long as France controlled the seas, while only the ability to occupy territory would have given her a really strong position at the conference table. She was normally able to get defensive guarantees by menacing Austria, but guarantees against French colonial aggression proved to be only temporary. Soon France would make a new forward move, while Italy could only look on helplessly.

In 1887, however, the danger to peace from both Russia and a nationalistic France was so grave that Italy was able to get full support for all her western Mediterranean ambitions and the right to be heard in Balkan affairs as well. Article III of a treaty signed in February 1887 with Germany guaranteed both Morocco and Tripoli against French attack and colonization, while Article IV stated:

> If the fortunes of any war undertaken in common against France should lead Italy to seek for territorial guarantees with respect to France for the security of the frontiers of the kingdom and of her maritime position, as well as with a view to the stability of peace, Germany will present no obstacle thereto; and if need be, and in a measure compatible with circumstances, will apply herself to facilitating the means of attaining such a purpose.[8]

An exchange of notes with England on 12 February 1887, known as the First Mediterranean Agreement, provided for the maintenance of the status quo in the Mediterranean, Adriatic, and Black seas.[9] Spain adhered to this agreement on 4 May, promising not to enter into any arrangement with France regarding North Africa. The activities of the French nationalists, in a year made particularly tense by Russian activities in the Balkans, thus provoked a defensive coalition of all the Mediterranean powers against France.

Spain's appearance on the side of Italy, Germany, and England against France was motivated not by French naval or colonial policy, but by fear of French republican intriguing against the Spanish monarchy. For decades the Spanish Navy had been moribund; there was a ship still in dry dock at Ferrol that had been placed there for repairs after the battle of Trafalgar in 1805. But in the mid-1880s, under the reforming Admiral Don José Maria de Beranger, it began to show signs of revival. A Spanish Jeune Ecole planned a new fleet of cruisers (most of which were destined to be destroyed in the Spanish-American War in 1898), and a British syndicate set up a new shipyard at Bilbao to build most of the ships. At the same time, German firms planned a defensive scheme of barrier forts and strategic railways in the Pyrenees.[10] As usual, nobody cared which side the Spanish warships were on; the vital question was who would be allowed to violate Spanish neutrality. In those years there was very little doubt that it would be Britain, whose shipyard at Bilbao was in full activity and whose Channel fleet visited Santander and Ferrol. In 1890 French naval men did not seem to take the Spanish affair very seriously, but by 1900 it had become nearly as important as in the days of Nelson and Napoleon.[11]

In addition to supporting Italian colonial ambitions, the Italian-German agreement of February 1887 provided for Italy to keep as much French territory as she could take in a war: Nice "for the security of the frontiers," and Corsica and Tunis for "her maritime position." The text of the Italian-

German military convention of January 1888, however, suggests that when the two allies studied the problem in more detail, they realized that French sea power would probably be able to prevent Italy from getting any of these. The convention did not suggest an Italian attack by sea on France or her colonies, eliminating Tunis and Corsica as possible prizes. In addition, Italy never made any preparations for the transport of an army by sea. The Italian navy possessed few transports, and the merchant marine was so lacking in proper ships that carrying even a single army corps, like the one that the French Navy could throw on a hostile coast with its own transports, was regarded as quite beyond it.[12]

Italy was limited to operations on land, and one of these, an advance along the Riviera toward Nice, was rendered impossible by the French Navy. The Germans suggested that Italy try it with eight army corps covered by the English fleet, indicating that they realized Italy had even less chance of making gains anywhere else.[13] In the Alps, everything favored the French. The valleys fanned out northward from Turin, and each Italian success in advancing along them would only mean a greater separation of their forces. The mountains were studded with defenses so strong that even if the Italians had succeeded in concentrating their whole first-line army in the Alps, two active and two territorial French corps could have contained it. The situation was so impossible that the allies decided instead to use six corps of the Italian Army on the Rhine. (Four others were to remain in the Alps and five were to be held further south to defend Rome, Naples, and Spezia against a French landing.) Though the Italian troops on the Rhine would guarantee Italy's loyalty to the alliance, the Germans apparently never had the slightest confidence in their military usefulness. Because of the French control of the sea, Italy thus had literally nothing to bargain with except her nuisance value, and no chance of taking any of the territory Germany was willing to give her.[14]

The barometer of French appreciation of the Italian danger was the disposition of the army's Nineteenth Corps. According to Plan I of 1880, this crack colonial contingent was to be transported from Algeria and substituted for territorial forces along the Italian border in about twenty days. Under this plan, the French would respond to the danger of Italian intervention in a Franco-German war by keeping two corps in the Alps, at least until the first decisive engagements were over. The only immediate French reaction to the initial signing of the Triple Alliance by Italy, Germany, and Austria in 1882 was the suppression of all plans for the eventual use of the Alpine troops against Germany and their reinforcement by a reserve corps. In 1884 another corps of reservists was sent to the Alps and a corps and a half were held in the Pyrenees. This distribution remained in effect through the dangerous year of 1887.

In the meantime, all of the navy's transports had become involved in colonial operations, notably the expedition to China. After 1883 the army was forced to plan to find ships of its own to transport the Nineteenth Corps; the navy provided only the escort and advice. In early 1887 there was a head-on collision between Aube's plan for an immediate offensive against Italy and the army's plan of throwing everything against Germany on the Rhine. In September Aube's successor, Edouard Barbey, protested vigorously against diversion of the navy for direct protection of the transports and declined "all responsibility for their safety," adding that "it is impossible to assure the protection of the western basin of the Mediterranean, even after the destruction of the principal force of the enemy." Though he repeated this declaration the next month, and though England's alignment with the Triple Alliance soon strengthened the navy's case, the army did not change its plans.

Plan X of 1889 shows French fears of the Italian danger at their height, even though it reduced the forces in the Pyrenees to one division. Under this plan, the Nineteenth Corps was to remain in Algeria and the Naval Infantry was to be transformed into a new Twentieth Corps to take its place. Since under previous plans the Naval Infantry had been the expeditionary force against the Italian coast, the change meant that Brin's navy, the fortification of Maddalena, and the entente with England had fulfilled their mission of defending the peninsula. The Italians were not yet ready to attack France's colonies, but they had forced the French Navy to trade its troops for the Nineteenth Corps. In 1891, when France had recovered sufficient confidence to plan once again to transport the Nineteenth Corps to Europe, the Naval Infantry was kept in the army. As Aube had foreseen, Italy's new navy had eliminated the threat of a French seaborne assault.

Barbey and Krantz

The problems of the French Navy in 1887 included not only the Italian efforts at Maddalena but also the profound disorder left by Aube's ministry. Aube's immediate successor was Edouard Barbey, a mild-mannered clothing-maker turned senator whose only connection with naval affairs had been a short period of service in his youth. Subsequent observers have viewed Barbey as a mere reactionary whose sole thought was to undo everything that Aube had started. True, he brought back many traditionalist officers and canceled some of Aube's programs, but his primary concern during his first ministry, from May to December 1887, was not to turn back the clock but to bring some order out of chaos.

Aube had stopped the construction of France's four newest battleships, the ones begun in 1880, to order a lot of new cruisers and torpedo craft and to begin vast schemes of coast defense, naval facilities, and coaling stations. Something had to go, for in pursuing his "cheap" program Aube had overdrawn his budget by the enormous sum of 19.139 million francs. The navy owed 7 million francs to private firms and 1.24 million to Whitehead in

An early French-built high-seas torpedo boat, the Ouragan *(launched in 1887). Noticeably larger than a regular torpedo boat, she also had more torpedo tubes, some of which are shown loaded.*

Torpedo boat No. 132 *(1890). One of the early units of the successful* No. 126 *class, which became the model for future boats for the* défenses mobiles.

The coast-defense battleship Valmy *(1892). Castigated by the Jeune Ecole as an anachronism, she had her origins, ironically, in Aube's plans for an armored mother ship for torpedo boats.*

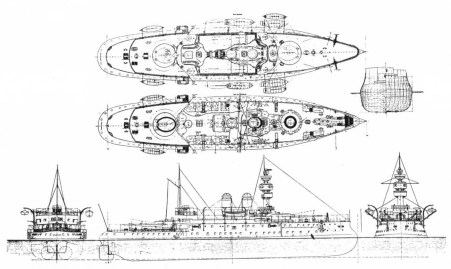

An official plan of the coast-defense battleship Bouvines *(1892). In concept she was as archaic as her half-sister* Valmy, *but in service she was more satisfactory owing to her raised forecastle. She carried two 12-inch guns instead of the two 13.4-inchers of the* Valmy.

Fiume for contracts that were impossible to cancel.[15] Additional money was also needed to rebuild Aube's 35-meter torpedo boats.

In spite of the howls of rage from the Jeune Ecole, there was only one way out of the dilemma, and in the diplomatically tense year of 1887 practically the whole force Aube had gathered in the Mediterranean and had held in commission ready for immediate war was disbanded. In the summer the Squadron of Evolutions, then under Admiral Peyron, was cut to six armored ships, and Barbey proposed cutting it further to four, the lowest number since 1874.[16] He also stopped work on the torpedo stations at Ajaccio and Bizerte. At best, Barbey seemed very tame to the fire-eaters in the navy, but some of Aube's vast schemes had to be abandoned temporarily if the navy were not to consist entirely of half-built battleships, cruisers, and naval bases. In addition, these moves helped calm the international situation, particularly since Boulanger fell at the same time as Aube and the naval reductions were accompanied by reductions in army war preparations.

Barbey did not abandon either the torpedo or the cruiser, however. He continued the experiments that definitely proved the unsuitability of "autonomous" torpedo boats for operations on the open seas, and he then ordered two larger experimental "high-seas torpedo boats," the *Avant-Garde* and *Coureur,* from the leading French and British builders, Normand and Thornycroft, respectively. (He also ordered the torpedo boats *No. 126* and *No. 127,* whose plans rectified the design problems in Aube's coastal boats.) His consultation of the Conseil des Travaux on the subject of cruiser designs led to his order in October 1887 for France's first true armored cruiser, the *Dupuy de Lôme.*[17]

The technical decision for which he was most unmercifully castigated by both the Jeune Ecole and the traditionalists, the building during his second ministry of the four obsolete coast-defense ships of the *Valmy* group, was not wholly his fault, as the project grew out of Aube's plans to build armored ships to serve as centers of action for torpedo boats. Even Aube's program of naval bases was not abandoned entirely. The plans for both Corsica and Bizerte remained under consideration, and on 19 July 1887, right in the middle of the cutbacks, the Conseil des Travaux approved the project for Ajaccio.[18]

A general revival of the navy began under Barbey's successor, Admiral Krantz, who served as minister from January 1888 to November 1889. Krantz had spent most of his career in staff work at Paris and Toulon, and was a perfect traditionalist target for the Jeune Ecole, who attacked him as unmercifully as they had Barbey. But Krantz was much abler, and he at least saw the danger from the Italian plans, while the whole navy was now aware of the importance of Brin's return. In June 1888, for example, the Conseil des Travaux called for modification of a new cruiser design so it could stand up against similar new Italian cruisers.[19]

Krantz realized that it was impossible to continue to respond to the financial problem merely by decreasing the size of the active squadron of battleships. The only possible solution appeared to be an overhaul of the completely inadequate system for mobilizing ships in reserve. In 1884 the minister had cut the time for mobilizing ships in the first category of reserve from eight days to two. The Budget Committee complained that this was largely a paper reform, however, since in 1886 there would be only two battleships in the first category while there would be thirty-six ships of various types in the other two, less ready, categories.[20]

Aube's solution had been the simple but expensive one of keeping as many ships as possible in commission. In 1886 France and England were the only powers maintaining a battle squadron in permanent commission all year round. Austria, Germany, Italy, and Russia still formed squadrons only for summer exercises, although during these they sent a fairly large number of men and ships to sea for more or less thorough practice in navigation. Because of their lack of practice in getting the fleet ready for an annual summer at sea, England and France were far behind the Germans in mobilization techniques.

Though Krantz did not solve the problem, the widespread criticism of Barbey's decommissionings led, first, to the reactivation of some of the ships and, second, to various tests of the system of mobilization.[21] The navy was becoming increasingly aware that the only middle ground between the useless expense of keeping all its ships in commission all of the time and the more or less complete disarmament of the fleet was a solution to the problem of reserves and mobilization.

The Italian Naval Scare of 1888

One unintended result of Krantz's experiments with mobilization and the increase in the number of ships in commission was a naval scare in Italy. In February 1888, a month after Krantz took office, France broke off all negotiations for a tariff treaty with Rome and opened a tariff war, which in the next decade was to do Italy incalculable harm. Italy's intensely nationalistic prime minister, Francesco Crispi, interpreted the French activities at Toulon as preparations for a sudden attack on Spezia. There is no evidence that either the French government or the French naval authorities ever had the slightest intention of doing this, but diplomatic conditions were so bad that the slightest additional irritation could have led to war.

The Italians did not have to look very hard for additional reasons for worry. For one thing, the French Navy's leaders at this time, while not members of the Jeune Ecole, shared some of its notions that alarmed the Italians the most. Krantz was, like Aube, one of the republican Catholics who would have been willing to play every card against the Italian monarchy, which had deprived the papacy of its secular possessions. The maritime prefect at

Toulon was the energetic Admiral Bergasse Dupetit-Thouars, who, although anathema to the Jeune Ecole because of his clericalism and family connections, shared Aube's views on war and on the necessity of a ruthless, immediate offensive. Undoubtedly one of the ablest line officers of his day, he subsequently commanded the squadron from late 1888 until his sudden death in 1890. He was the organizer first of the torpedo service and coast defenses at Cherbourg, then of the mobilization of reserve ships at Toulon, and finally of the first studies in France of modern battle tactics. If the order had come, the men then in actual command of the French naval forces in the Mediterranean would have struck with everything they had.

At the same time, Italy had just become aware that the defenses of its main naval base, Spezia, were incomplete, particularly against torpedo attack, and the Italian naval press was carrying on a campaign for its strengthening.[22] The Italian Navy, although heavily involved at Maddalena, had no money to do more than improvise temporary booms and barrages. Like almost every naval base in Europe except Toulon, Wilhelmshaven, Kiel, and Malta, Spezia was vulnerable to sudden torpedo attack because it lacked a permanent mole and because time was required to move the barrages into position.

Perhaps most unnerving were the polemics on either side of the Alps. For three years a vociferous French naval school, including a minister of marine, had publicly threatened Italy with unspeakable violence, including attacks on coastal positions. If its rhetoric looks a bit mild today, one must remember that Aube had been preaching an entirely new kind of naval warfare involving complete disregard of every law of war in a continent that had not experienced a real naval struggle since Trafalgar. A French scare story published in early 1888 gave an account of a French surprise attack on Spezia that corresponded perfectly with French plans.[23] The Italian press needed no urging to pick up such stories—indeed, Italian naval writers had been drumming the idea of the French threat into the minds of the excitable Italian public during the great Italian naval agitation of the 1870s, well before Aube.

Convinced of the danger of an immediate French attack, Crispi appealed to Bismarck for support, and the Germans persuaded the English to send their fleet to Genoa in February 1888. In the general exchange of resounding compliments between the naval commanders, the British admiral, Sir William Hewett, was reported to have said that "the bonds which unite us may hereafter receive a practical application by the union of the Italian and English fleets."[24] The French could no longer have the slightest doubt of the nature of the coalition against them.[25] England was ready to defend Italy when she was convinced of the danger of a French attack. In a crisis two years later, in 1890, over the status of Rome, Britain apparently gave Italy similar defensive assurances, and there is no doubt that an unprovoked attack on Italy would have led to British intervention. The majority of French naval officers were well aware of the general sentiment among the English on this point.

By 1889 peninsular Italy was fairly well protected by her fleet from an invasion and by the British from wanton bombardment of her open coastal towns. But she was never able to tie the English to anything more definite, and she did not get a naval agreement from her allies in the Triple Alliance. Although Crispi tried to get such an agreement in 1889, it would have been perfectly academic, as both the Austrian and German fleets consisted primarily of coast-defense battleships and small torpedo boats, which would have been as useless in the western Mediterranean as the French coast-defense ships had proven to be.

BIZERTE

In 1888 France began serious planning for a major naval facility at Bizerte. Aube had wanted to build a torpedo station there, but he was allowed to do nothing but a little dredging to allow the torpedo boats to get up to the old port, while plans for a much larger new port were held in abeyance. They were revived the next year with help from the champion of French colonialism, Jules Ferry. (Critics of the government claimed that Ferry's intervention was decisive, but the port would clearly have been saved even without him.)[26] Following his incognito visit to Bizerte in 1887, Ferry personally backed a move for its "commercial" exploitation. A Compagnie du Port de Bizerte was soon formed by a powerful syndicate of Paris bankers headed by Abel Couvreaux, the son of one of the Suez Canal promoters. In a series of concessions between 10 December 1888 and 13 August 1890, the syndicate received from the bey of Tunis all the harbor rights for seventy-five years, all the land reclaimed from the lakes, 2 million francs in cash, and a seventy-five-year fisheries monopoly guaranteed to be worth 200,000 francs a year. In return, the syndicate was to put a whole mountain of stone, fortunately discovered near the spot, into two great moles completely enclosing an outer harbor of about three hundred acres, and it was to dig a seven-mile deep-water canal to connect the outer harbor and the interior lake. The defensive system for the new port was worked out in detail in 1888, and a railway concession from Tunis was also under consideration. All of these negotiations and plans were carried out in the greatest secrecy. Construction began in 1891, while the first defensive works were started a year later.

The works at Bizerte were a major change in the Mediterranean status quo and a grave danger to Italy, but the only limits on France were the vague assurances made to England at the time of the Tunis expedition of 1881. The usual answer to such a situation was to upset the status quo somewhere else to produce a new balance, but the Italians under Crispi were powerless to do this, since their alliance with Germany did not provide for

Italian occupation of places such as Tripoli and they could not carry out such an operation themselves. Crispi pointed out to the British and Germans that Bizerte would menace Malta and immobilize most of the Italian Army in Naples and Sicily, but his allies could do little about it and the Italian Army was pretty much immobilized already. British and German questions in Paris only brought bland assurances that nothing but commercial dredging was going on, and the French showed only contempt for the Italian complaints.

Crispi's constant complaining also ended up by disgusting the English. The Admiralty, if Crispi can be believed, told Antonio di Rudini, the leader of the opposition to Crispi, that in any event neither England nor Italy had anything to fear, since the new base would split the French forces and be a source of weakness.[27] There is a good deal of evidence that this was really the official British theory and that even yet England did not see the danger.

The German view was contained in a memorandum on the subject of Bizerte written by the chancellor, Caprivi, only a few months after he replaced Bismarck in 1890.

> The establishment of the French in Bizerte touches the English, it seems to me, more than the Italians, because of its menace to the Suez Canal. . . . The pretension to command of the sea is untenable as long as the Suez Canal can be violated in time of war and the chain of coaling stations from Gibraltar to Hong Kong, fortified by the expenditure of millions, loses its value. A blockade of Port Said will be more easily executed from Bizerte than Toulon. . . . If she has such intentions, France must either strengthen her fleet or withdraw a good portion of it from Cherbourg and Brest. Both will be good for us; the first will weaken the army, the second give us the greater liberty of action in the North Sea and Channel. Unless England introduces military service—which she will do only after a defeat—she can build many ships but not man them. She will be menaced in Malta, paralyzed toward Constantinople, and will have the most pressing interest to strengthen her alliance with Italy if only because of Bizerte. . . . The finishing of Bizerte can only help us by holding Italy to the Triple Alliance as long as we hold England bound to this League.[28]

The belief of the new chancellor (who had been head of the navy from 1883 to 1888) that Italy's weakness against France would bind her more closely to the Triple Alliance was a change in German Mediterranean policy. As late as 1888, Bismarck was urging England with every means in his power to strengthen her own fleet and to strengthen Italy. In 1890 France was using a strong fleet, a strong army, and every economic weapon at her command to try to detach Italy from Germany, just as the new German leaders had decided to make no real efforts to save her. Occasional loans or good advice did nothing to prevent the steady deterioration of Italy's position. Caprivi's statement also shows that he was not willing to do anything even to keep the support of the greatest of naval powers, England. As a result, the Mediterranean coalition assembled by Bismarck against France in the late 1880s eventually fell apart under his successors.

TOWARD THE FRENCH PROGRAM OF 1890

Alarmed by the presumed French threat of 1888, the Italians worked on the fortifications of Maddalena and the unfinished battleships even more actively, and at last they decided to distribute their battleships as a fleet instead of a garrison force. The older ones were distributed among the ports as before, but the four big battleships, and the new ones as rapidly as they were completed, were gathered in a single squadron at Maddalena. At the same time, the English, Italian, and Austrian fleets held a demonstration in March 1888 at Barcelona in support of the First Mediterranean Agreement, whose terms had just been leaked to the press. The Italian naval officers involved were very careful to show around the numerous French journalists in attendance.

These developments touched off a violent campaign in the French press on the danger of the Italian Navy.[29] For the first time since 1878 the Budget Committee advocated a French "two-power" standard, stating that "the French Navy should have as its objective to be equal numerically to the two principal navies of continental Europe" (the German and Italian fleets).[30] In a four-day debate in the Chamber—one of the longest and certainly the ablest held in France during this whole period—the ministry was bitterly attacked by both the Jeune Ecole and the older officers.[31] While the traditionalist officers took up the slogan that "once more the Mediterranean must be made into a French lake," the mass of the deputies united in demanding more torpedo boats and the adequate defense of the coasts of Provence against the fast Italian Maddalena squadron.

In the spring of 1889, new threats of war with Italy led to an even greater outburst, and the French Navy turned its whole attention to the Italian problem.[32] The campaign did not bring out any new ideas, but it was significant in that it was the first real big-navy agitation in France. For the first time since the mid-1840s (when the issues were quite different), the representatives of the French people were demanding not a less expensive, a better administered, or a less aristocratic navy but a greater military force—albeit primarily for coast defense.

As in England in the 1860s and Italy in 1872, public interest in the navy was first aroused by the issue of coast defense. The French Navy as an instrument of prestige went back to the days of Colbert; but as an instrument of national defense, in the sense that it was demanded by general opinion and not merely by a certain class or economic interest group, it was fifteen years younger than that of Italy.

One response of the navy was a new round of maneuvers. The experiences of 1886 and 1887 had proved conclusively that the defense of a coast by torpedo boats alone, "autonomous" or not, was impossible. In 1889, in response to the criticisms by the Budget Committee, the task was given to the battleships. The chief problem examined in French maneuvers for the remainder of the period of rivalry with Italy was always the defense of an open coastline by a battle fleet and torpedo boats against an inferior but faster squadron.

In the summer of 1889 the "Italian" fleet based on Ajaccio (Maddalena) was opposed by one of nearly twice its size but two knots slower. The "French," told by one of their cruisers of the departure of the "Italians," lost contact immediately while the "Italians" leisurely bombarded Marseilles and Cette with nothing but the torpedo boats, which they destroyed, for opposition. The "French" admiral, coming up at the end of the bombardment, again lost contact with the enemy, who retired to sea beyond the eyes of the torpedo boats and returned during each of the next two days to continue his leisurely bombardments. The "French" admiral was generally able to come up in time to speed the "Italians" on their way to another depredation. "The enemy," wrote the French admiral, "due to his superior speed and his more powerful cruisers, attacked successfully all the points of the coast, when and as he wished."[33] Besides noting the additional evidence that torpedo boats alone were useless even for coast defense and recommending increasing the size of high-seas torpedo boats to 120 tons, over twice that of the *autonomes,* the arbiters concluded that only one solution to the coast-defense problem was possible: a ruthless offensive against the Italian coasts to draw the Italian fleet away from Maddalena. The maneuvers also showed that for every three battleships it was necessary to have three cruisers, and that the whole problem of using cruisers to scout an enemy at sea, as distinct from merely carrying messages, was completely unsolved.[34]

These maneuvers took place just at the time of the greatest tension in the crisis between Italy and the papacy over the status of Rome, and they were probably responsible for Crispi's fears that the danger of February 1888 might be repeated. Though Crispi's attempt to conclude a naval agreement with his allies failed, the Germans in November sent a fleet of four battleships to Maddalena for a visit. This produced a combined squadron of ten battleships: two *Duilios,* two *Italias,* two *Laurias,* and the four German ships, plus five cruisers, seven torpedo gunboats, and twenty-four high-seas torpedo boats.

The French were alarmed by the comparison between this fleet and their squadron at Toulon, which then included five battleships, three older ships with reduced crews, and three cruisers. Against Italy's seven large ships (a third *Lauria* was nearly complete but did not participate in the demonstration), France could oppose three *Redoutables,* the *Amiral Duperré,* and two

Amiral Baudins. None of the four battleships begun in 1880 were yet complete, the nine station battleships were completely useless, and only four of the ten coast-defense ships could give even mediocre assistance in the Mediterranean. In addition to thirty-five obsolete wooden cruisers, France had six modern cruisers of 16 knots' speed while Italy had seven of the same general type. Though the German fleet did not stay permanently in the Mediterranean, as some journalists had feared when they apparently got wind of negotiations for a naval convention, the French Navy was inferior in modern ships even to Italy.

According to Jean-Louis de Lanessan, the French Navy was at a low ebb in the spring of 1890. Lanessan, who a decade later became one of France's most successful ministers of marine, was a former naval doctor who had taken up politics and the colonial cause as a follower of Jules Ferry. He was not a member of either naval school but gathered his information largely from conversations with naval officers. He concluded that there was a real danger of defeat in a "secondary" combat between the Toulon and Maddalena squadrons, while the French Navy was utterly unable to perform its real duty of preventing "the destruction of merchant ships and the bombardment and burning of open towns." He agreed with Paul Fontin of the Jeune Ecole that "the Italian armored division at Maddalena is absolutely able to impose, accept, or refuse combat. It can therefore cruise the entire Mediterranean, ravage our coasts from Port Vendres to Nice and Oran to Tunis, without running the slightest risk." This description was sobering enough without raising the number of Italian ships to fifteen by counting all those built in the 1860s, as did Fontin in his polemics.[35]

Although England had just adopted a massive naval building program (the Naval Defence Act of 1889) designed to make her fleet equal to that of France and any other power, the French felt that the immediate danger in 1890 was not the British but Italy and the Triple Alliance. On 22 November 1890 the Superior Council, as the Council of Admiralty had been renamed, approved the first large French naval program since 1872. Based on the principle that "the combatant units of the French fleet must be equal in number to those of the combined fleets of the Triple Alliance," it called for a fleet of the line including twenty-four battleships, thirty-six cruisers, and forty high-seas torpedo boats; a coast-defense fleet including fifteen coast-defense battleships and 220 torpedo boats; and a foreign station fleet of thirty-four cruisers.[36] The fleet was to be brought up to this strength in ten years by an ambitious construction program of ten battleships, forty-five cruisers, over one hundred torpedo boats, and numerous other ships, in addition to others just begun. Even Aube would have gasped in amazement at the total of seventy cruisers and 260 torpedo boats.

The most important aspect of the program was what happened to the traditional three fleets. In the battle fleet there were three times as many light craft and auxiliaries as battleships—only ten years after France had decided to build its first light scout (the *Milan*). The coast-defense fleet was not the old fleet for Baltic operations; the idea of an offensive against Germany had been abandoned. Instead it consisted of the existing coast-defense battleships and a large number of new torpedo boats, and was to be used strictly for defensive purposes "to free the battle fleet entirely for offensive action." The fleet of transports, so prominent in the days of Napoleon III, had disappeared altogether, confirming that Italy was safe from a landing. Finally, the foreign station fleet contained the older cruisers that were useless for any other purpose, although as a concession to the station admirals practically all the existing station cruisers were to be replaced by new construction.

The focus of the program was solely on the Triple Alliance. The fleet was to remain on the defensive against Germany and fall with all its weight on the weakest member of the Alliance, Italy. It provided no commerce-raiders for either the home or station fleets and no money for coaling stations. When the navy and the colonies had been put under separate ministries in 1889, the Council of Admiralty had been asked to lay down a general plan for coaling stations, but it had done no more than choose the points and nothing whatever was done to put its suggestions into effect. The one base that was actively pushed toward completion was Bizerte, no longer primarily against England but against Italy.

One difference between the Program of 1872 and the Program of 1890 was that while the former had been adopted at the request of the Budget Committee, the latter was produced by the navy on its own. Like its predecessor, the new program was never approved by Parliament except vaguely in its first year, and it started out in the traditional way—23 million francs, or nearly a quarter, underfunded. The next year and the next, the deficits were only 12 million each, but by that time the program was being revised.[37] Yet as in the case of the other major naval programs of the period, including the British Naval Defence Act, its terms gave an idea of the aims and strategy of the navy. In 1890, with a strong fleet, a strong army, a ruthless tariff, and an alliance with both the clerical and republican oppositions in Italy, the French Republic intended to detach Italy from the German alliance.

Italy's Decline

In 1889 the Italian Navy was, if not quite equal to the French, at least the third in the world; a decade later it had fallen to seventh. Though the collapse was due to many causes, the economic crisis arising out of the tariff war with France was by all odds the most important. The ruthless economic warfare that France carried on against Italy for the ten years following 1888 was the chief factor in French success, not only in eliminating Italy from the naval race but also in nearly causing the fall of her monarchy. From 158 million lire in 1888, the Italian naval budget dropped to 114 million in 1890 and to 99 million in 1893. The disastrous defeat of an Italian expedition in Ethiopia at Adua in 1896 was only the coup de grâce; the Italian threat to French control of the Mediterranean had been eliminated rather earlier.

The large Italian battleships, mechanical marvels when new, suffered more than most as a result of further technological change. Their big guns shared the problems of all of the monster guns of the day, notably those built on the Armstrong system. These ships, but particularly the almost totally unprotected *Italia* and *Lepanto,* were extremely vulnerable to the new high explosives like melinite, and became even more so when rapid-firing medium-caliber (up to 6-inch) guns were developed to fire the high-explosive shells. So badly overloaded that their protective layer of watertight compartments was under water and their speed fell to 16 knots, these two great ships became nothing but huge protected cruisers whose sole chance against even a cruiser with side armor was to get in a lucky hit with one of their big guns. Ironically, against the older French battleships, which still had smaller large-caliber guns but whose large secondary battery had been replaced by quick-firing guns, they were not in much better shape. The two *Duilios* and three *Laurias* were also vulnerable because the new quick-firing guns and high explosives could destroy their unprotected ends. Remarkable as the Italian ships had been in their day, the gunnery revolution of the late 1880s and early 1890s made all but the last three, the *Re Umberto* class, obsolete. These three were saved only by the addition of a substantial amount of armor during their construction.

There is no doubt that even had the financial and technological crises not developed, the Italians would still have been in trouble. They had sunk too much money into their matériel and had not taken into account the probable costs of upkeep and repairs. Like the British, they forced their boilers to the utmost during trials to get the maximum possible speed, with the result that the ships subsequently experienced frequent major boiler problems just as the navy found itself short of money for boiler and engine repairs. With its entire naval strategy based on speed, the consequences for Italy of such a condition were very serious indeed.[38]

Yet like a family of impoverished Venetian nobles, the Italian Navy fought a heroic fight to keep up appearances, and by a remarkable system of reduced crews of brevetted mechanics and engineers, it succeeded in keeping practically the whole fleet ready to go to sea. Under Admiral Constantino Enrico Morin, minister of marine from December 1893 to March 1896, expenses were cut to the bone, construction was stopped entirely, the councils and much staff work were suppressed, and the pay of the personnel was cut to its lowest possible limit. The "A" reserve, with all its brevetted men and officers on board, even formed a special squadron of "patriotic abnegation," in which they surrendered the special pay to which they were entitled and took only ordinary garrison pay and rations.[39]

The weakest element in the Italian Navy was its personnel. In stopping target practice in order to save munitions and curtailing navigation to save coal and wear and tear on the engines, the Italian Navy was unable to maintain its level of training, at the very time that the French Navy reached its highest point of preparedness for war. The Italian torpedo craft, in which training was most needed and deterioration was fastest, were the worst of all. The high-seas torpedo boats, of which Italy had only seven of 24 knots, eventually proved entirely unable to go with the fleet and were hauled up in dock at Spezia. The coast-defense boats were largely of the "autonomous" type that had proved so unsatisfactory in both England and France.[40] In gunnery, even on the *Sardegna* of the *Re Umberto* class, a shot every five minutes was the best the Italian heavy guns could do, and as late as 1897 these were not fully supplied with smokeless powder.

Italy's reliance on a small number of brevetted mechanics meant that its crews were filled out with an unusually large proportion of common sailors, and the good men on the Italian ships were literally swamped by hordes of deckhands who furnished the muscle power whenever the fleet put to sea. Though uneducated, the Sardinians and Sicilians, like the Bretons in France, were intelligent and easily disciplined, but even the Italian officers considered the Venetians and Neapolitans to be thoroughly worthless. In time of war, even the most carefully trained permanent crew could not be merged in such a group without grave danger. In time of peace, perhaps the most important effect was that produced on English observers, who thought the deckhands were the entire crew. The officers, discouraged, poorly paid, and lacking in scientific training, had all the defects and none of the advantages of their English system of naval education. Not being able to navigate, they lacked the seagoing capabilities the English system would otherwise have given them, while the schools were incapable of giving them the scientific skill of the French.

With the departure of Brin in 1891 (he returned briefly between 1896 and 1898), the navy again returned to the control of the old school. The appointment of a number of Neapolitan ministers increased the old feud between the Neapolitans and the Sardinians, and the rule that allowed officers on active shore duty to sit in the Chamber of Deputies led to endless bickering. A minister's own subordinates at the ministry would be not only his public critics but also his possible successors. In the navy's organization, the rudimentary naval staff was placed under the permanent leadership of the Duke of Genoa, in flattering, but disastrous, imitation of Kaiser Wilhelm II's personal leadership of the Prussian military.[41]

Strategically, there was no money to solve the problem of the vulnerability of Naples, and the problem became even worse as the Neapolitan ministers of marine fought the transfer of the arsenal to Taranto. The Italian position became weaker and weaker as the French completed Bizerte, for there was no money to build the bases at Cagliari and Palermo that later were to form the reply to Bizerte. "A French naval force would find Cagliari undefended to the left, Palermo undefended to the right, and in the depth of the [Tyrrhenian] basin the defenseless Naples-Castellammare region."[42]

Between 1895 and 1900 the Italian Navy continued its decline. Naval construction stopped entirely after the army's colonial disaster at Adua in 1896, and even Italian relations with England became less cordial. England left Italy out of the international investigation of the Armenian massacres of 1895, allowed her to take a beating in the Ethiopian war and in the treaty that recognized the French protectorate over Tunis in 1896, and did not even consult her about the Anglo-French agreement that concluded the Fashoda crisis of 1898. It became clear that England was taking the first steps toward abandoning the Mediterranean, and Britain made no effort to save Italy's finances or to strengthen her diplomatically.[43]

With the growing hostility of England and Germany, her two powerful allies, Italy was forced to cultivate better relations with France. When the Fashoda crisis brought war very near in the Mediterranean, she prepared for an extremely uneasy neutrality.[44] A program of two small battleships and three small armored cruisers was finished with great difficulty, and in the mid-1890s another program was begun with no battleships at all but very good armored cruisers (the *Giuseppe Garibaldi* class) that were to take their place, in a pinch, in the line of battle. Italy adopted a truly original method of "getting experience to build them better" by designing the cruisers, letting the contracts to private yards, and then allowing the private yards to sell the ships to foreign navies and start new ones under the same contracts. As a result, the firms of Ansaldo and Orlando were kept busy, the government always had a couple of new ships nearing completion, and the designs were constantly improved without cost to the navy. Of the first seven ships, four were sold to Argentina and one to Spain, while the last two went to Italy. Subsequently two more were begun for Argentina and eventually sold to Japan, and a third was built for Italy.[45]

The Italian Navy, however, was no longer an immediately powerful factor in the Mediterranean. "You can ask the last sailor in our fleet," there was no doubt that France could whip the Italians.[46] France's response to the Triple Alliance had been to try to drive Italy out of it, and a highly organized, well-trained, rapid naval force concentrated in the Mediterranean had played a key role in their largely successful effort.

Twelve

~~~~~~

Britain Against Russia and the Jeune Ecole

BRITAIN, as well as Italy, was alarmed by the tumult in the French Navy and the resurgence of French nationalism in the mid-1880s. In addition, it was concerned about an apparent diplomatic rapprochement between France and Russia. One of the traditional objectives of British nineteenth-century foreign policy—and the main objective of British Mediterranean policy in the mid-1880s—was to prevent Russia from getting control of the Turkish Straits. The English also continued to be concerned over the safety of their maritime commerce. The improving relations between France and Russia and the increasing assertiveness of the French Navy made these difficult problems even more complex.

THE RUSSIAN THREAT TO THE TURKISH STRAITS

In the 1880s, Russia continued her policy of building large cruisers for raiding British commerce in the distant parts of the globe, but between 1886 and 1889 she also launched five first-class battleships. These were her first since the 1860s, with the solitary exception of the *Petr Veliki,* a mediocre copy of the British *Devastation.* The two new battleships built for the Baltic fleet were rather ordinary ships with some French features in their designs, but the three launched in the Black Sea were of a unique and much more powerful type. These, the *Ekaterina II* class, had a displacement of 10,300 tons and a speed of 16 knots. Their armor consisted of a complete belt topped by a huge triangular redoubt, at the corners of which were six 12-inch breech-loading guns in pairs on disappearing mountings that allowed them to be retracted into the redoubt. Four of the six guns could fire forward. There was only one explanation for this unique combination of design features: the ships were designed to engage the forts at the Bosporus. It was significant that these ships, plus two added in the early 1890s, comprised the entire Black Sea Fleet—the Russians had no cruisers there.[1]

The British could no longer count on the Turkish fleet to defend the straits. Until 1880 the Turkish Navy had been, at least in numbers, the third in Europe; by 1890 it no longer existed as a military force. After some of the ships had threatened to bombard Constantinople for their back pay, Sultan Abdul Hamid was so terrified by the sight of his own fleet that he moored it in the Golden Horn, removed essential parts of its machinery and guns, and stored them in the palace. The fleet put to sea twice during the 1880s, once at the time of the Greek war of 1886, when by a miracle of Allah it was assembled and moved as far as the Dardanelles, and once in 1889, when the sultan decided to show the flag of Turkey in Japan and decorate the mikado with the Grand Cross of Osman. In July 1889 the wood frigate *Ertogrul* set out, manned by all the naval cadets under the command of the admiral in chief. The ship spent four months in Singapore, where the English refused to clean the barnacles from her hull for fear the aged structure would not stand it. The next year she made Saigon and then Hong Kong, but in September 1890, on the last lap of the voyage, she went down in a typhoon off the coast of Japan with flag, grand cross, admiral in chief, envoy extraordinary, and most of the naval cadets.[2]

It is fairly certain that the Russian Black Sea Fleet and a small landing force could have taken the Bosporus relatively easily by a surprise attack.[3] During the 1890s the task was made even easier because, owing to the initiative and threats of the Russians, the forts on the Dardanelles were placed in fairly good condition but those on the Bosporus were left in poor shape. From the military and naval point of view, the problem of the straits became a simple matter of time—sultan, forts, and city would be in the hands of the power that got there first.

Technical factors that complicated the straits question were the disappearance of the original superiority of armored ships over land fortifications and the growing effectiveness of extemporized shore defenses. The new battleships had large unarmored portions that were vulnerable to shellfire. They were built to fight end-on with their big guns, but when thus engaged, they could not bring to bear their medium guns, normally mounted in small numbers on the broadside. The open-top barbette, used in most French ships and in major new foreign designs like the *Italia* and the Admirals, was particularly vulnerable to plunging fire. Finally, a well-laid mine field could trap a fleet under the fire of coastal batteries almost indefinitely.

The weakness of battleships against even primitive fortifications was confirmed by the small amount of damage done when the British fleet bombarded the earthwork fortifications at Alexandria in 1882. Under near target-practice conditions, five British battleships engaged the prehistoric barbette of Fort Meeks, which mounted five old muzzle-loaders, nine smoothbores, and some mortars. After three and a half hours of shooting at point-blank range, the British had not dismounted or disabled a single gun. The French had a similar experience at Sfax during the Tunis campaign of 1881. There they fired 2,002 projectiles without any opposition at all but later found the defensive power of the place practically uninjured.[4]

Though the French and Germans gave their military harbors large guns in heavy steel and concrete emplacements, both countries relied increasingly on the invisibility and mobility of a large number of smaller guns protected by mere earthworks. The lessons of every siege from Sevastopol in 1855 through Plevna in 1877 supported this decision. In 1860, when land guns could not pierce armor and when steam had just given fleets the ability to pass quickly through a narrow channel, the whole Russian Army could scarcely have prevented the British from forcing the straits. By the 1890s, thanks to the introduction of smokeless powder and other developments in gunnery, fortification, and mining, the whole British fleet could have been held at bay by extemporized land and sea defenses (as it later was in the Dardanelles campaign of 1915).

Under such circumstances, speed became increasingly important for the offensive. True, a power with a well-developed network of railways and coastal strong points could protect itself against anything that came by sea, but a relatively small landing force could still take and hold an isolated, undefended point in a *coup de main*. Constantinople was such a point, and the terrain was such that a large force would have been required to dislodge the army that got there first.

It is impossible to overemphasize the suddenness with which naval officers at the end of the nineteenth century realized the importance of speed. Army officers had learned it through a fairly constant development from Napoleon through Moltke, who demonstrated it in his amazing successes against Austria in 1866 and France in 1870. On the sea, however, there had been no real war since the uncertainty of movement under sail had nullified the plans of the master of land warfare in 1805. Instead there had been a series of punitive expeditions against every exotic ruler from the queen of Madagascar to the tsar of all the Russias, which only obscured the problem. Until the middle 1880s no one realized that the new weapons of sea warfare offered means of speed and concentration far beyond those available on land. In the fifteen years from 1885 to 1900, naval thought went through an evolution that had taken nearly a hundred years ashore, giving rise to what the older men branded as *la folie de la vitesse,* the craze over speed.

In the late 1880s, however, speed would have been of no use to the British in defending Constantinople. As long as France and England were not on good terms and France had a large fleet at Toulon, England would never have dared send her fleet up the straits. The main fear expressed by British statesmen and in the press, particularly in the early 1890s, was that France and Russia would combine forces to eliminate the British Mediterranean

Fleet. The British prime minister, Lord Rosebery, explained to the Austrians in 1894 that it would be impossible for England to defend Constantinople because "we should be unable to allow our Mediterranean fleet to run the risk of a catastrophe by finding itself between the Russian and French fleets."[5] These fears were largely illusory—even though France and Russia had signed an alliance in 1892, they did not enter into naval conversations until 1900, and the French naval command not only never considered the possibility of a union between the two fleets but was unanimously opposed to it. Instead, the French planned to concentrate their fleet against the British Channel squadron, a weak force that was used primarily for training, before it could combine with the stronger Mediterranean squadron. In any case, it would have been madness for England to detach up the straits enough ships to meet the Russians while there were strong hostile French forces in their rear. As long as the naval forces of France and Russia were even close to equal to those of England, Britain's only hope of saving Constantinople was its diplomatic promises to Italy, which freed Austria to concentrate on holding back the Russians. It is worth noting that the signing of the Franco-Russian Alliance in 1891 did not create this situation but simply formalized a strategic reality that had already existed for at least half a decade. As an anonymous French publicist noted in 1885, France held the key to Constantinople.[6]

THE NAVAL DEFENCE ACT OF 1889

It is clear that the British naval propagandists of the late 1880s were right when they stated that the British navy had fallen to its lowest strength compared to its rivals since the days of Nelson.[7] In numbers it was more than equal to those of France and Russia, but in armor, guns, projectiles, tactics, and organization for war, it was behind the revived French Navy. It was literally "no fleet, but an assembly of heterogeneous ironclads."[8] The Spithead Jubilee Review of 1887, which brought together many of these ships, revealed to the public the consequences of the policy Britain had followed since the early 1870s of simply building bigger copies whenever a new ship appeared abroad. The dockyards were crammed with half-built ships or with new ships waiting for their guns. Most important, it was just at this time that most of the technical weaknesses in British equipment were fully revealed, not only in Admiralty tests but in the sensational successes of French arms firms and equipment in competitions abroad. (America's adoption of the whole French ordnance system was particularly disturbing.) In the face of the danger of a nationalistic political explosion in France, British writers claimed that the time had come for English action.

> Considering the condition of stability in French affairs, which is represented by the at least imminent possibility which has occurred of the advent of Boulanger to power, is it the least unlikely that, if he does not, some other man of his type may come into power very shortly? If such an incident should occur, would it be safe for us to depend on his not

carrying out by war the policy which Admiral Aube has prepared for during peace time?[9]

In the summer of 1888, the British navy held comprehensive naval maneuvers to test its capabilities against the French. In July, immediately after the maneuvers, the naval members of the Board of Admiralty were asked three questions: 1) What force would be required to protect the coasts of England against invasion or bombardment by France? 2) What would give a reasonable defense to Gibraltar, Malta, and British trade routes and coaling stations? 3) What would be required, without allies, to defend Constantinople against France and Russia?[10]

The board concluded that Britain's navy "should at least be equal to the naval strength of any two other countries."[11] Using statistics provided by the newly created Intelligence Office, the Board proposed that Britain adopt a multiyear building program. France had had many such programs, including those of 1857 and 1872, but this was England's first. As passed, the Naval Defence Act of 1889 provided for a veritable fleet: eight battleships, two station battleships, nine first-class cruisers, thirty-three second-class cruisers, and eighteen torpedo gunboats, all financed by a special loan.

The Naval Defence Act signaled the start of a naval arms race between England and France that lasted through the 1890s. Its main cause was not a conspiracy of admirals and arms firms, as many polemicists and historians have claimed, but the complex colonial situation that produced the propaganda of the Jeune Ecole. (Not only were the "vested interests" not responsible for the agitation of the Jeune Ecole, they were actively opposed to it and proved to be one of the main obstacles encountered by Aube during his ministry.) The theories of the Jeune Ecole were based primarily on the burning conviction that France could not live without colonies and that Britain would not give up her monopoly of the world beyond the seas without a struggle. British authors confirmed these French fears:

> The command of the sea is not merely the tenure by which alone we hold the Empire, it is also the title, the indefeasible title by which we can at any time claim the transmarine possessions of any European Power which cannot defeat us at sea. Every Power in the world holds all its transmarine possessions merely as the caretaker of the Ultimate Naval Power.[12]

As in the time of Palmerston and Napoleon III, the English and French conceptions of security were incompatible. Faced by the Russians and the resurgent French and unable to count on either the Italians or the Germans for naval support against them, the British adopted an unequivocal two-power standard and, in the Naval Defence Act, set about making it a reality.

The Naval Defence Act was a watershed in naval technology as well as

The British battleship Resolution *(launched in 1892), of the* Royal Sovereign *class. This photo clearly shows the pairs of barbette-mounted 13.5-inch guns at the ends and the 6-inch secondary battery on the sides, a layout that soon became standard for battleships.*

policy, for it marked the end of the era of sample ships. For the previous twenty years or more, rapid technological change and paucity of funds had caused navies to build battleships a few at a time to designs that often differed radically from one another. By building seven of the eight battleships of the Naval Defence Act to a single design, Britain set a new standard for battleship design that endured until the development of the *Dreadnought* in 1904. Sir William White achieved a balanced design for the *Royal Sovereign* class by throwing to the winds the caution of his predecessors and increasing tonnage nearly 4,000 tons over that of the Admirals and the *Victoria*. (At 14,150 tons, the new ships were also 4,000 tons larger than France's most recent battleships, the four of the *Magenta* type begun in 1880 and not yet completed.) He thus produced Britain's first "engineer's" battleships, relatively untrammeled by political or fiscal limits on size, and also began the tendency to increase displacements as improvements in detail were made in successive designs.

The main technical problem confronted by White was the protection of the new ships against the new high-explosive shells. As the Italians had done in their *Re Umberto* and as the French were doing in a battleship ordered in 1888, the *Brennus,* he protected part of the hull above the main belt with 4-inch armor, thick enough to detonate the new projectiles outside the ship. He also provided a strong secondary battery of ten 6-inch guns to fire the new projectiles. The high displacement enabled him to combine the best features of earlier Italian and French designs without also inheriting their weaknesses in protection; the new ship's 18-knot speed and 5,000-mile steaming range were Italian in origin, while its high freeboard and good seakeeping qualities were French. The new design also abandoned once and for all oversized guns—White would have gone even below the 13.5-inch caliber adopted if a gun had been available. Finally, the arrangement of the four big guns in two barbettes, one at each end of the ship, marked the abandonment of end-on fire in favor of a strong broadside armament. White duplicated these features in the two station battleships, *Barfleur* and *Centurion,* which had a higher speed and 4,000 tons less displacement. Throughout the 1890s, evolution everywhere was along the lines defined by the *Royal Sovereign:* abandonment of end-on fire, smaller heavy guns and larger secondary armament, higher speed, a greater proportion of the hull protected by armor, and improved seakeeping. The change in only four years from the low-freeboard, practically unarmored *Victoria* with its two 16.25-inch guns in a single forward turret was remarkable.[13]

The most striking thing about the Naval Defence Act, however, was not its battleships but its cruisers. In the agitation that led up to the act, worry about the French battleship program (which had been the basis of the agitation leading to the Northbrook program in 1885) was completely overshadowed by concern over commerce protection. "If one *Alabama* . . . could cause a loss of trade of over £50,000,000, what loss would be inflicted on our trade if half a dozen, or a dozen, or two dozen French . . . cruisers were let loose on the immense ocean-going trade of England?"[14] English forebodings were aroused by the rice blockade and other infringements on international law by the French in their war with China in 1884–85, and they were deepened in 1885 when a serving French admiral—Aube—publicly advocated even greater violations in European waters. Apparently the British officially questioned the French ambassador about Aube's article, for which the ambassador repudiated all responsibility.

Within six weeks Aube became minister of marine and started a vast program of cruisers and torpedo craft.[15] Sir Geoffrey Hornby told the London Chamber of Commerce that England needed 140 new cruisers and expressed the fear that it would be almost impossible to blockade French raiders in Brest under any conditions.[16] The London *Times,* in a leading article mentioning Aube by name, pointed out the gravity of the danger.[17] The whole debate over the Navy Estimates for 1889 showed the British preoccupation with the problem of trade protection in European waters.[18]

The Admiralty fared much better with its cruiser program than Aube did with his. The French advocate of ruthless cruiser warfare wanted to order sixteen cruisers and ultimately got only eleven (of which six were very small), while the British experts asked for forty-two and got them all. The nine first-class cruisers of the *Edgar* class, of 7,300 tons and 20 knots, were like previous large British cruisers designed to run down raiders on overseas trade routes. However, the thirty-three second-class cruisers of the *Pallas, Apollo,* and *Astraea* classes, of around 3,500 tons and 20 knots, were clearly built to protect commerce in British waters against Aube's cruisers

The British second-class protected cruiser Terpsichore *(1890), of the* Apollo *class.
She was one of thirty-three ships provided by the Naval Defence Act of 1889 to
protect British trade against the Jeune Ecole's commerce raiders based at Brest.*

concentrated at Brest. As in the case of battleships, the Naval Defence Act
produced large numbers of ships to standardized designs; the *Apollo* class
contained twenty-one ships. It also opened the cruiser era—eight years
later, British naval enthusiasts were asking for 200 cruisers. The remaining
ships of the Naval Defence Act—the eighteen torpedo gunboats, or torpedo-
catchers, of the *Sharpshooter* and *Alarm* classes—were large boats of
around 750 tons and 19 knots designed both to defend a fleet against other
torpedo craft and to attack an enemy squadron.

The Naval Defence Act was only part of England's defensive effort against
France and Russia. The Imperial Defence Act of 1888 and the Barracks Act of
1890 added close to 10 million pounds to the 21.5 million pounds of the
Naval Defence Act—a staggering armaments program. The additional acts
provided for completion of the fortifications of the overseas coaling stations, primarily against Russia, and additional coastal defenses in England,
primarily against France. The older coastal defenses, consisting of vast ma-
sonry forts with guns up to 100 tons, were completely inadequate against
bombardments by the Jeune Ecole's fast gunboats, and they were supplemented or replaced by mobile batteries, guns on disappearing mountings
(like those in the Russian *Ekaterina II*-class battleships), quick-firing guns,
mines, moles, and floating barriers. England's coast guard stations, established at the time of the Armada, were also gradually converted into a real
network like those of the continental powers; as late as 1891, 300 of the
680 stations were from four to thirty-five miles from a telegraph station and
not one was connected directly.[19] To be sure, the British stations were always far behind the French and German ones—in the maneuvers of 1900 it

took Admiral Sir Harry H. Rawson three quarters of an hour to wake one of them up and all night to send a telegram—but at least they were given some of the new equipment.[20]

The new fortifications were needed to respond to a new threat. In 1862 the purposes of fortifications had been defined as 1) the protection of military harbors against a siege like that of Sevastopol in the Crimean War, 2) the covering of points where the French could make a landing, and 3) the defense of London. In 1888 the danger was no longer that of an invasion but that of a *coup de main* against an arsenal or the bombardment of an open commercial center. The money of the act of 1888 was spent for 1) the protection of major bases against torpedo attack, bombardment, or a short siege "if the fleet were lured away"—i.e., to Constantinople, and 2) the estuaries of the Tyne, Clyde, and Mersey. Since the Thames was already defended, the new fortifications completed the defenses of the chief mercantile ports of the United Kingdom.[21]

BRITAIN AND THE IDEAS OF THE JEUNE ECOLE

Did England and Italy, or Russia and France, start the great naval competition of the 1890s? England and Italy began the augmentation of naval expenses, but fears of the Jeune Ecole clearly motivated both the English and the Italian programs. The revolutionary factor was not the new battleships, torpedo boats, or cruisers, or even the Russian Black Sea Fleet—it was the Jeune Ecole, which was preaching a new kind of naval war. Their whole system, right up to the final conclusion that *l'empire de la mer n'est qu'une expression vide de sens* (sea power is nothing more than an expression empty of meaning), was based on two fundamental hypotheses: that blockade was impossible, and that it was also impossible to give effective direct protection to Britain's enormous floating commerce.

The British were acutely aware of the new ideas. The major naval maneuvers that they held in 1888 before formulating the Naval Defence Act were designed specifically to test them. These maneuvers were the first in which the British navy set itself a strategic problem. (The maneuvers of 1885 were nothing but torpedo-boat exercises.) The problem was to determine if blockade was possible under modern conditions—a question the British navy had not considered since the days of Horatio Nelson. For the first—and last—time since the introduction of the ironclad, the British tried a Nelsonian close blockade, with battleships actually standing off the "enemy's" ports.

The maneuvers involved a "defending" (British) fleet and an "attacking" (French) fleet. The superiority of the defending over the attacking fleet was representative of that of Britain over France. The defenders blockaded the attackers in two ports representing Brest and Cherbourg. The "French" admiral, Sir George Tryon, was secretly ordered not to attempt to break the

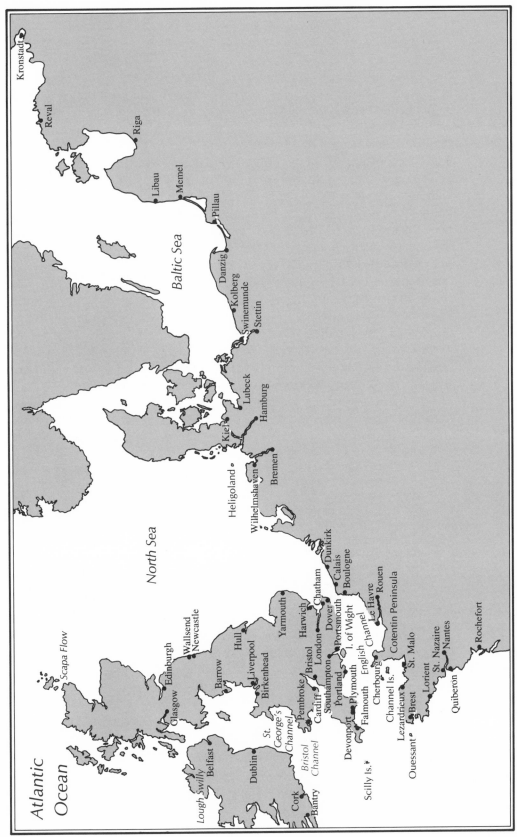

Atlantic
Ocean

Kronstadt

Reval

Riga

Libau
Memel

Pillau

Danzig

Baltic Sea

Kolberg
Swinemunde
Stettin

Lubeck
Hamburg

Kiel

Heligoland
Wilhelmshaven
Bremen

North Sea

Dunkirk
Calais
Boulogne
Rouen

Yarmouth

Chatham
Harwich
Dover
London
Portsmouth Le Havre
Scapa Flow   Wallsend   I. of Wight   Cotentin Peninsula
Edinburgh   Newcastle   English Channel
                                                              Rochefort
            Barrow   Hull   Southampton   St. Malo   Nantes
Glasgow   Liverpool Bristol   Portland   St. Nazaire
                 Birkenhead Cardiff Plymouth Cherbourg Lorient
            St.   Devonport Falmouth Channel Is. Brest
Lough Belfast George's Pembroke   Lezardrieux   Quiberon
Swilly   Channel   Ouessant
        Dublin Bristol   Scilly Is.
                Channel
Cork
Bantry

Europe—Northern Waters

blockade until "British" staying power was tested. If Tryon had waited long enough, the "British" fleet would have practically put itself out of commission, like the French off the German coast in 1870, merely by trying to stay off the ports. The torpedo boats gave up first, and all the ships found that they were unable to coal except by returning to port. Tryon maintained constant contact with his opponent and finally sent three cruisers out of "Cherbourg" without their ever coming under fire. Worse still, the "British" were not even able to tell the strength of the fugitives. For fear that this unknown force would catch the blockaders off "Brest" in conjunction with the fleet blockaded there, the "British" admiral did the only thing possible. Raising both blockades immediately, he took up a defensive position in the Channel. Meanwhile, the "French" continued uncaught on a career of commerce-destroying and bombardment of the coast.[22]

The British regarded the results of the maneuvers with dismay, for they knew of no other strategy to use against the French except maintaining a close blockade with their battleships. The official report acknowledged that Tryon's commerce-destroying and bombardments of unfortified towns had been realistic. "There can be little doubt that any Power at war with Great Britain will adopt every possible means of weakening the enemy. We know of no means more efficacious for making an enemy feel the pinch of war than thus destroying his property and touching his pocket."[23] The chief conclusions were, first:

> Under the altered conditions which steam and the development of attack by locomotive torpedoes have introduced into naval warfare, it will not be found practicable to maintain an effective blockade of an enemy's squadron in strongly fortified ports by keeping the main body of the fleet off the port to be blockaded, without the blockading battleships being in the proportion of at least 5 to 3 to allow a sufficient margin for casualties to which the enemy's vessels in a secure harbor would not be exposed and the necessary periodical absence of a portion of the blockading squadron for the purpose of replenishing fuel.[24]

The report concluded, second, that the ratio of cruisers should be at least 2 to 1, and, third, that "if a suitable anchorage . . . in the immediate neighborhood of the enemy's stronghold" could be found and British light forces could watch the enemy, it would be possible to reduce the battleship ratio to 4 to 3. The battleship ratio of 5 to 3 and the cruiser ratio of 2 to 1 were the basis of the Naval Defence Act.

If England set the pace for extravagant naval construction by adopting these ratios, she did so because technological advances and the new system of warfare preached in France had overthrown the very bases of the naval strategic system on which the British Empire had been founded. The maneuvers had shown that with nothing but ironclads, unable to coal at sea, without light craft rugged enough to stand the strain of constant steaming, and no wireless or any other means of communication, blockade was impossible.

Defense of Britain's trade also promised to be a colossal problem. In 1887 an attack on England's commerce would truly have hit her "at the heart," for her maritime trade had changed since the days of Napoleon not only in volume but in type. It was no longer a trade in luxuries but in the necessities of industrial life. The rapidity of the transformation was as startling as its magnitude: in 1851 Britain was still reasonably self-sufficient; in 1885 she was completely dependent on outside supplies. By 1903 over 80 percent of British wheat was imported, and during sixty weeks in the ten-year period 1894–1904 her domestic stocks were below a ten-week supply.[25] England's merchant ships were also highly vulnerable, for although the British merchant marine began to undergo a major renewal around 1886, much of it still consisted of sailing ships or old, slow steamers. Just when England's old enemy was again threatening to attack, it had at last "become fully true of the men of Britain and their ships what was said in the seventeenth century of the Dutchmen and theirs: 'which except they stir, the people starve.'"[26]

The enemy who was promising to attack British trade was neither Russia, whose one ice-free port suitable for cruiser use was in the Pacific, nor Germany, which had equally poor access to the sea, but France, the only European power with colonies astride every imperial sea route. Far more important, France was the only power whose continental position itself was a standing threat to English trade. With Dunkirk on the North Sea, Cherbourg in the Channel, Brest in the Atlantic approaches, and a thousand miles of Mediterranean coast, France had access to every one of the narrow seas. Brest was especially valuable, for it lay right at the entrance to the zone through which all Britain's communications with the outer world had to pass. The Mediterranean could be bypassed by most British ships, but the Atlantic approaches could not. Curiously, the French colonialists, entranced by India and the idea of making commercial war on foreign stations, did not appreciate the value of Brest, which they dismissed as "condemned by its geographical position."

British naval thinkers may have thought that building five battleships to every three of the enemy's might make blockades feasible, and that construction of additional cruisers and coaling stations might defeat Russian raiders, but it is not too much to say that they were stunned by the problem of commerce protection against France. Sir Charles Dilke, a prominent British student of imperial defense, declared:

> By the unanimous admission of the naval authorities, it would be either difficult or impossible to defend that trade against sudden attack

by France, aided by another considerable naval power. Our enormous resources would be almost useless in the case of such a sudden
attack. . . .[27]

The parliamentary and financial secretary to the Admiralty, Arthur B. Forwood, himself a shipowner, frankly told a group of shipowners at Liverpool
that British commerce under the British flag would disappear in time of
war.[28] Admiral Sir Arthur Hood stated that it was "utterly impossible" to protect it "thoroughly."[29]

The corollary to the proposition that British trade could not be protected
was the transfer *en bloc* of all of Britain's shipping to neutral flags at the
outbreak of the war. Though there was little hope that a fictitious sale of
three quarters of the world's merchant marine would be recognized by a
powerful belligerent, and though the transfer itself would have meant the
ruin of England's greatest industries, it was the only solution Dilke, for one,
could see, for "it would be doubtful if our enemies would dare to declare
food to be contraband."[30] According to another authoritative commentator,
Lord Brassey, "no amount of construction which the country would approve
in time of peace would prevent the transfer, on the outbreak of war, of a
large portion of our trade to a neutral flag, under protection of which our
supplies of food would be brought to us."[31] The president of the Board of
Trade later asked, "If, then, we start with the fact, with the assumption that
corn is not contraband of war, what chance is there that we should be reduced to starvation when the corn can come in as freely as in time of peace,
so long as it comes in neutral bottoms?"[32] The same assumption had previously been the chief point raised by the few opponents of the Naval Defence
Act.[33] The neutral flag, protected by international law, would cover the British food supply.

The threat of French commerce-destroying contributed powerfully to a
campaign to reverse Britain's traditional position on international law at sea.
English international lawyers began to join the movement to restrict the definition of contraband and even to abolish completely the right of capture at
sea. After the Crimean War, English liberals led by Richard Cobden and
joined by the Italians and Germans had pressed for the abolition of all right
of capture of private property at sea, and in 1866 the main belligerents in
the Seven Weeks' War—Prussia, Italy, and Austria—had exempted enemy
property from capture. The French legislature was ready to vote a similar
law on 9 July 1870, shortly before the fall of Napoleon III, and in 1875 the
International Maritime Congress at Naples adopted the thesis.[34] In 1876 Lord
Brassey wrote that "if, therefore, any future naval contest in which we may
be involved is confined to the fighting ships on either side . . . we shall be
the greatest gainers by the adoption of the new rule of international law . . .
and the necessity for the construction of the costly ships of the *Bacchante*

type disappears."[35] In 1885 France's blockade of rice, a foodstuff, in her war with China provoked violent controversy: England steadily refused to agree to the idea, while French international lawyers began to prepare the way for it.[36] French cruisers were instructed to destroy their Chinese prizes systematically, although it was recognized that crews were to be taken on board the cruiser or put on a neutral ship.[37] By this time France had become a steady opponent of the movement to exempt private property from capture, and it remained so until the entente with England ended the rivalry between the two countries in 1904.

The elements of Aube's theories were not new, but their combination amounted to a genuinely New School of naval war in the very country most likely to endanger the peace of Europe. There were other reasons for the Italian building program of the late 1880s and the British Naval Defence Act of 1889, but the chief one was that France was preaching a new kind of war, the logical result of the introduction of modern naval weapons. There was nothing material, like a lot of new French ironclads or specialized commerce-raiding cruisers, to explain the British actions of 1888 and 1889. A comparison of the Naval Defence Act and the ideas on which it was based with the Northbrook program of 1884–85 shows clearly that the danger at the end of the decade was much more basic—a new theory of naval war.

Thirteen

French Matériel and Tactics in the Early 1890s

T HE FRENCH NAVY entered the 1890s with a new naval program, a powerful school of naval thought that disapproved of many of the elements of that program, a powerful opponent in the north that was increasing its strength, and an opponent in the south that, although less powerful, was of more immediate concern. While endeavoring to fulfill its building program and resolve the split between the Jeune Ecole and the traditionalists, the French Navy responded to Britain and Italy by making significant advances in several aspects of naval warfare. These included artillery, mobilization, ship speed, and naval tactics.

ARTILLERY

In naval matériel, the main development of the early 1890s was not the confirmation of the supremacy of the torpedo but the revival of the gun. During the 1880s the French had led the way in abandoning oversized battleship guns in favor of smaller guns using slow-burning powders of high power. The result of this decision was the development of a type of gunpowder nearly three times as efficient as any previous powder. While the early slow-burning powders had still been only variations of the original black powder, Vielle's "Powder B" was entirely new. The first successful guncotton propellant, it was manufactured by dissolving guncotton in a base that later evaporated. (The English cordite was similar but was dissolved in nitroglycerin.)[1] The smokeless nature of the new powders was initially only a byproduct of the search for high power; since the powder was all consumed in the bore of the gun, it left only a thin blue haze instead of spewing out vast masses of unburnt matter in a thick cloud of smoke.

This quickly became one of the most important advantages of the new powder, because it freed battleships from the shroud of smoke that formed around them after only a few minutes of firing with the old powder. The new powder was adopted as fast as it could be manufactured, and the stocks of old powder were given to the army. By 1893 the change was complete in the French Navy.[2]

There were two great disadvantages to the new powders: the high combustion temperature of cordite caused great wear in the bore of the gun, while Powder B was dangerously unstable unless kept at a low temperature. With the old foolproof black powder, the magazines were put in almost any space that was left over under the armored deck. On the ships built after 1872, a favorite place had been next to the boilers, and steam pipes had been led through the magazines with reckless abandon. Long studies with the new powder showed that it began to be unsafe if exposed to a temperature of more than 95 degrees Fahrenheit, and a series of minor "incidents" on various battleships resulted in careful regulations for the refrigeration and flooding of the magazines. From the very first, the navy recognized that the new powder could not be abused.[3]

Since the new powder was originally more "slow burning" than "smokeless," the first result of its development was a new gun to utilize its power. Tests by the Gâvres Commission with an experimental 90-caliber, 45-foot-long gun led to the development of a new Model 1887 gun 45 calibers in length to replace the older 30-caliber guns. A 12-inch, 44-ton, 40-caliber gun of the similar but simplified Model 1893–96 obtained a penetration of 43 inches of iron armor with a projectile of 750 pounds. With the same powder, the largest gun the navy had built, a 16.5-inch, 76-ton Model 1875 weapon, obtained a penetration of only 32 inches with a projectile of 1,750 pounds. The light, long guns of the 1887 type were the logical answer to the huge blunderbusses. Many of the old guns were secretly rechambered to give them the greatest possible power. With the new and refitted older models, France had a new system of artillery, firing relatively light projectiles with a very high muzzle velocity. With the single exception of the aberrant Model 1875, French naval artillery followed a steady evolution from 1870 down to the dreadnought era.[4]

In developing modern large guns, the French were far ahead of the British. England was too busy fixing the defects in its artillery of the 1880s to follow the French example, which they considered "very bold." The British did not commission their first battleship with a 40-caliber main armament until 1901 and did not build 45-caliber heavy guns until 1904.[5]

The French, however, were badly outdistanced in the second development that followed the introduction of the new powder—the application to the medium-sized gun (up to 6 inches) of the quick-firing principle used in machine guns. Though Armstrong's 4.7-inch quick-firer had given good results in trials at La Spezia in 1886 and his *Piemonte,* a cruiser sold to Italy in 1889, had carried a complete armament of quick-firing guns, these became really effective weapons only with the introduction of smokeless powder. On its first trials with the new powder, the Armstrong gun fired ten rounds in forty-seven seconds; an ordinary gun of the old type fired the same number in five minutes and seven seconds.[6] Though the new quick-firer was no longer a mere light weapon for use against torpedo boats but a medium gun that could fire high-explosive shells at other ships, its most important principle, the balanced mounting with a shoulder piece that enabled the gunner to point the gun continuously at a moving target, was derived from the anti-torpedo-boat machine gun.

The development of such weapons in France was probably delayed because the designs of the new guns were worked out abroad at a time when the demands of colonial service and French budgetary difficulties were particularly severe. The success of the British and Italian guns caused a great clamor in the French press, and the first result was the reestablishment of a separate naval artillery department in the ministry like one that had been suppressed in 1872. The new department was too far behind the competition, however, and for the first time the French Navy had to go to private companies for its artillery. The Canet quick-firing gun, tried and adopted after considerable difficulty in 1892, was two years behind the equivalent Royal Navy gun and three or four behind the Italian Armstrongs.[7]

Once again, however, the strong and simple construction of the Model 1870 and 1881 guns and the patient experimentation with them over the years yielded increasing benefits. Despite initial doubts based on bad experiences with conversions in 1875, the navy decided that while the Canet and Schneider firms were developing the new quick-firers, it would convert all its old medium artillery into the quick-firing type.[8] Although the converted guns had less muzzle velocity than the new ones, France thus obtained a large number of quick-firing guns quickly and cheaply. Conversion of all the 3.9-inch, 5.5-inch, and 6.4-inch guns was completed in 1894.[9]

France was also helped because it, almost alone among the major naval powers, had continued to install large batteries of medium-sized guns in its battleships even during the height of the big-gun craze. The conversion of these medium guns to quick-firers gave the French ships an important advantage over their English counterparts, whose smaller medium-caliber batteries were not converted. For example, the main armament of the British *Sans Pareil,* two 16.25-inch, 100-ton guns, was still roughly as powerful as the four 13.4-inch, 52-ton guns of the French *Marceau,* but the twelve 6-inch guns of the British ship's secondary battery fired only two rounds per minute per gun, while the seventeen converted 5.5-inch guns of the French ship each fired seven rounds in the same time.[10] In spite of Armstrong's initiative in developing the first quick-firer, the British were again behind.

The new powder produced two movements, which eventually converged in the single-caliber armament that made the *Dreadnought* of 1905 revolutionary. To gain increased power, big guns were becoming smaller and smaller, while little guns, based on the quick-firing principle, were growing larger and larger. The latter also led to the adoption of the principle of continuous aim, which became one of the bases for modern gunlaying and fire control.

Along with the new guns and propellant powders came new projectiles. The melinite shell, a relatively thin-walled projectile loaded with high explosives, made a sensational debut in tests in the late 1880s, but a long series of experiments was required to make it practicable for naval use. Because of the danger of explosions in the gun's bore, the big thin-walled shells used by the army for bombardments could not be used in the high-pressure, high-velocity naval guns.[11] Only in 1895 did the French Navy become the first navy in Europe to issue regular high-explosive shells that could be fired with full battle charges.

The importance of the melinite experiments was that they reopened the question of shells versus armor-piercing projectiles. Ship designers suddenly rememberd that the original purpose of armor in the 1850s had been not to render a ship invulnerable to solid shot but to keep out the explosive shells that had been developed by General Henri-Joseph Paixhans in the 1820s. Critics of the *Duilio* and *Inflexible* had long claimed that the soft, unarmored ends of these giant ships would quickly be shot away in a battle, but this premise had not been tested until the melinite experiments showed that, indeed, these and other ships like the *Italia* with their armor concentrated in small areas were completely vulnerable to light guns firing explosive projectiles. The search for invulnerability through use of ever thicker armor had reached the *reductio ad absurdum* of invulnerable patches so small that the invulnerability of the ship itself disappeared.[12] The new developments gave France a great advantage over Italy: the Italian ships could now be overwhelmed by a hail of light projectiles, while the new French artillery, with its smokeless powder, new guns, and new and converted quick-firers, was "without a doubt, the best in the world."[13]

Studies by the French naval constructor Emile Bertin during the 1890s revealed additional weaknesses in the earlier battleships. He showed conclusively that every warship of the preceding period was vulnerable, not because the destruction of its unarmored ends would cause it to sink, but because the damage would probably make it capsize. In earlier studies of the effects of battle damage, the question of stability had been dangerously neglected. Only a few months before the relatively new British battleship *Victoria* capsized in June 1893 owing to collision damage in its unarmored bow, Bertin's studies showed that in case of such an injury a soft-ended ship would invariably turn over. In English ships, which had their armor concentrated amidships, Bertin demonstrated experimentally that safety depended largely on the percentage of the waterline that was armored: armor over two thirds of the ship's length was fairly safe, while armor over only half of the length was very dangerous. The *Inflexivle,* with less than half its waterline armored, seemed certain to be in danger, while even the new *Royal Sovereign,* with 66 percent of its length protected, was close to the line of safety.

More surprising were his findings regarding French ships, with their narrow but complete armor belts on the waterline and high barbette towers for the guns. Bertin was the first to point out that such a ship, once its unarmored parts had been destroyed, was essentially a low freeboard monitor with four tall towers. The lower the belt and the higher the towers, the greater the danger, for the ship would be unable to right itself once water came over the armor belt and its associated armored deck. Extra, unplanned weights on such a ship would make it even less stable. Using a model of the American armored cruiser *Brooklyn* (a quintessentially French-style design), extra weights that reduced the height of the belt above the waterline by only one half reduced the ship's stability to just one fifth of normal.[14]

Under these conditions, the constant tinkering with the designs of the four battleships that had been begun in 1880 and were still completing proved to be little short of disastrous. The *Magenta,* the worst of them all, was rendered dangerously unstable even without any injuries by an enormous superstructure, which successive Conseils des Travaux had built up bit by bit much as successive bishops had built Gothic cathedrals. Her tremendous "three-storied château," rising thirty-five feet above the armor belt and bristling with sixty guns of five different calibers, would have been certain to pull her over. The only thing her captain could find to say in defense of this edifice was that "a ship may go into battle only once in its life, and for thirty years it will be inactive. The superstructures, annoying during battle, notably improve habitability for ordinary life."[15] When the *Magenta*'s heavy guns were trained to one side and the ship was turning, she heeled over as much as twelve degrees, and even her captain admitted that some of his officers were "a little surprised." At five degrees' heel, the belt was completely under water on one side and two-thirds exposed on the other, and at fifteen degrees the water would have run out of the boilers. Even when some of the château was razed, the ship was still overloaded, but it would have been possible to put her back to her designed waterline by taking the heavy guns out of her.[16] The *Hoche,* a half sister of the *Magenta,* was described by a foreign critic as resembling "a half-submerged whale with a number of laborer's cottages built on its back," while others called her, somewhat more charitably, the *Grand Hôtel.*[17]

Practically all the French ships built during the preceding period were dangerously overweight because of design changes and lack of general oversight of design during their construction. In the *Brennus,* begun in 1889 and completed for trials in 1894, a five-degree heel completely submerged the armor belt and disabled the hydraulic mechanisms that worked the heavy guns. (Her superstructures were drastically reduced before she was accepted into service.)[18] The overloading of the French ships, their low belts, and their great superstructures that seemed designed to catch enemy shells made them as vulnerable as the British and Italian ships, though for different reasons.[19] French designs continued to have some of these problems through the 1890s, and the Russian battleships that were copied from them were even worse because of the heavy character of the work done by the Russian dockyard workers. The Russian ships that went into the battle of Tsushima against Japan in 1905 were so overloaded with coal that their belts were submerged, and practically all of them capsized before going down.[20]

In summary, all the battleships built in the 1880s were seriously defective, but the French, who succeeded in putting quick-firers on their old ships, gained an initial advantage over the Italian types, which everyone recognized as disastrously unprotected, and over the soft-ended English ships, confidence in which was shaken by the loss of the *Victoria* in 1893. In 1894 and 1895, just as the French began to realize that their ships were as vulnerable as those of their rivals, they found themselves faced by a large number of new English ships of the *Royal Sovereign* and later classes which had both extensive side armor and batteries of quick-firers.

NEW ARMOR AND SHIP DESIGNS

Fortunately for the naval architects trying to cope with the appearance of high-explosive shells and quick-firers, there was another great advance in armor technology around 1890. The general adoption of steel in place of compound armor after 1886 was followed by the appearance of Creusot nickel steel in trials at Annapolis in 1890. The very next year, an American toolmaker, Augustus Harvey, adapted his process for hardening tool steel to armor production, and in 1895 Friedrich Krupp's improvement of the Harvey process laid the basis for a complete Krupp armor monopoly. Ten inches of steel treated with the Harvey or Krupp process was as good as twenty-three inches of wrought iron or eighteen inches of the original Creusot steel.[21]

The new armor made it possible to provide reasonable protection (although not invulnerability) against large projectiles while responding to the main problem of the day: protecting nearly the entire hull against smaller high-explosive shells.[22] Accounts of tests outside France in which high-explosive shells were said to have penetrated five inches of iron without exploding proved to be greatly exaggerated, and it soon became apparent that light armor would render the shells fairly harmless. When the first naval shells were tested in 1891, steel armor only an inch thick succeeded in exploding them.[23]

At first, designers simply added thin side armor to armor schemes developed earlier. The armor of the British *Royal Sovereign,* for instance, consisted essentially of the short belt and barbette towers of the earlier Admiral class with an additional thin belt amidships above the thick one. In the Italian *Re Umberto* class, Brin retained the armor deck and minutely subdivided cellular layer of the *Italia* but added relatively thin armor on the sides to protect the cellular layer from high explosives. This arrangement proved particularly satisfactory because all three elements of the hull protection (light side armor, deck, and compartmentation) reinforced each other, and it became the standard scheme after it was improved and adopted in the nine ships of the British *Majestic* class in 1893.[24]

French battleship construction had stagnated during most of the 1880s. In 1887 the most recent French battleships under construction were the four of the *Magenta* group begun in 1880. In 1884 work had begun on two improved ships of this type, the *Brennus* and *Charles Martel,* but Aube had canceled them before much progress had been made. Aube's successor, Barbey, revived the *Brennus* and had the Conseil des Travaux prepare entirely new plans for her to respond to the new developments in naval architecture. She emerged with a number of features that were revolutionary for French battleships: a main armament on the centerline in two turrets, a new

The battleship Brennus *(launched in 1891) in her original configuration. France's first battleship with protection against high-explosive shells, she was top-heavy when completed, and her after military mast and part of her superstructure were removed before she entered service.*

The battleship Carnot *(1894). Begun in response to the* Royal Sovereigns, *she and her four half-sisters were characterized by a lozenge arrangement for their main batteries and by pronounced tumble-home to their high, relatively unprotected hulls.*

type of boiler (the Belleville water-tube type), abandonment of the ram, and the addition of a belt of armor 4.7 inches thick above the main belt.

In 1890–92 the French began five more battleships: the *Jauréguiberry, Charles Martel, Carnot, Bouvet,* and *Masséna.* These repeated most of the new features of the *Brennus* but reverted to the gun arrangement of the *Magenta,* which also ensured that they received another now-traditional feature of French battleships: high hull sides with pronounced tumble-home, which reduced their stability when damaged. In this group, France also failed to follow the British example of building battleships in uniform classes: while designed to the same specifications, every one of the five was built to plans by a different engineer. They were all of around 12,000 tons (2,000 tons less than the *Royal Sovereigns*) and 18 knots, and they carried eight 5.5-inch quick-firers in addition to two of the new long 12-inch guns and two similar 10.8-inch guns.

The main innovation of French naval architects at the end of the 1880s was the world's first true armored cruiser. This was perhaps the only important design for which the Conseil des Travaux could claim most of the credit. Even before Aube left the ministry, the Conseil, "considering the progress made by explosive shells," called for ships with more speed and better protection than those Aube wished to build.[25] In answer to questions from Aube's successor, the Conseil proposed the specifications for a cruiser of its own, which the minister accepted. The senior naval constructor of the day, Louis de Bussy, drew the plans for the ship, which was named *Dupuy de Lôme.*[26] Of 6,500 tons and 20 knots, she was the first large warship with three propellers and carried an armament of two 7.6-inch guns and six 6.4-

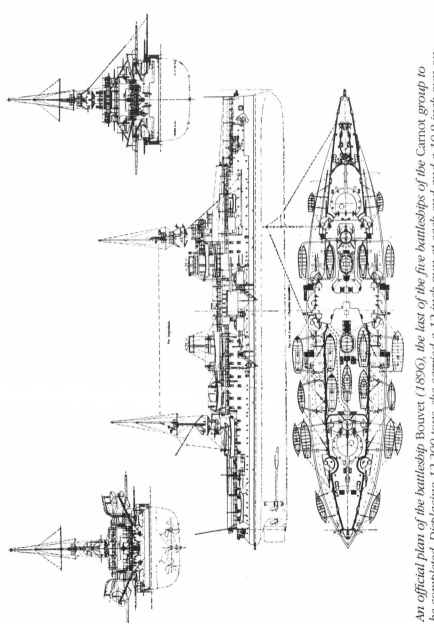

An official plan of the battleship Bouvet (1896), the last of the five battleships of the Carnot group to be completed. Displacing 12,200 tons, she carried a 12-inch gun at each end and a 10.8-inch gun on each side, and was protected by a narrow armor belt along the waterline.

The armored cruiser Chanzy *(1894), of the* Charner *class, fitting out at Bordeaux with two torpedo boats of the group* No. 192 *through* No. 194. *The* Chanzy *was similar in appearance to the pioneering armored cruiser* Dupuy de Lôme *(1890), of which she was a diminutive version.*

inch quick-firers. Most important, her hull, with its armored deck and cellular layer, was completely encased with light 3.9-inch steel armor on the sides. Thus, although the French failed to adopt the new Italian armor scheme for their battleships, they independently developed something very much like it for their cruisers.

The *Dupuy de Lôme* was the first armored cruiser that really fit the formula "faster than the strongest, stronger than the fastest." It was designed for an entirely different purpose than the earlier armored cruising ships— the station battleships and their successors, the belted cruisers. In scouting, its great superiority to the new English and Italian protected cruisers (which had no side armor) enabled it to either penetrate the enemy's cruiser screen or force the enemy cruisers to break contact with the French. It was fast enough to escape from new battleships like the *Royal Sovereign,* while it was strong enough to stand up in battle against older battleships that were vulnerable to quick-firers. (The completely armored *Dupuy de Lôme* with mostly quick-firing guns was the antithesis of the nearly unarmored *Italia* with its 100-ton guns.) Temporarily abandoning Aube's protected cruisers altogether, the Conseil des Travaux in 1889 approved plans for a "second-class armored cruiser," which were used to build the four 4,700-ton, 19-knot ships of the *Charner* class.

The new developments in artillery and armor gave France a commanding lead over Italy, particularly as that country was in no position financially to replace the battleships that were so vulnerable to the new weapons. The French innovations, notably the introduction of a revolutionary new type of cruiser, also gave France an opportunity to improve its position relative to

England. It remained to be seen whether France could exploit this opportunity by building the new ships in quantity and by remedying the design defects that remained in its battleships.

SPEED IN MOBILIZATION

Another key French advance in the late 1880s and early 1890s was the adoption of the cult of speed. Borrowed from and initially directed primarily against the Italians, it called not only for speed in the ships themselves as a tactical weapon against the fast Italian battleships but also for speed in mobilization to permit launching an immediate offensive.

Admiral Gervais, head of the naval staff in Paris from 1887 to 1889 and again between 1892 and 1894, reorganized the whole French naval mobilization system along the lines indicated by studies begun in 1888. Previously, in both England and France, ships in the "first reserve" were manned by most of their officers and skilled ratings and needed only new recruits to put to sea. However, the English ships were scattered along the coast as coast guards and did not train routinely in squadron navigation and tactics, while the French ships did not put to sea at all.

The essential point of the Gervais system, which was put into operation around 1893, was the organization of these ships into a permanent fleet, which was sent to sea each summer under its own commanders. To the permanent squadron, kept in full commission year-round like the British Mediterranean Fleet, was thus added a reserve fleet that cruised in the summers like the German and Italian fleets. Indeed, one of the main reasons for this arrangement was to meet the danger from the fleets of the Triple Alliance, which were up to full strength only at that period of the year.

New men came on board the reserve fleet ships in April and the vacancies in the permanent fleet were filled from the reserve squadron in October. Instead of being something of a disgrace, good work in the reserve fleet became the only way to get into the main fleet. In addition, the minister was given full control of the number of men in the reserve crews, which meant that in a diplomatic crisis the whole French first reserve could quietly be put on a full war footing without raising delicate questions in the Chamber.[27] With Gervais's system of reduced crews, the French reserve fleet was essentially ready within forty-eight hours of mobilization.[28] (This was nearly the same system that Admiral Fisher adopted ten years later in England amid great ballyhoo.)[29] At Toulon during the 1895 maneuvers, when the permanent squadron coaled and took all its stores on board in a day, the reserve fleet left port forty-eight hours after the mobilization order was given. The system, generally considered to be thoroughly satisfactory, was the only possible compromise between the old practices of keeping a ship in full commission or completely disarming it.[30]

Since Britain had the money to build new ships and keep them in full commission, mobilization was one of the weakest aspects of the Royal Navy.

The coast guard ships, England's first reserve, were scattered along the coast, where they were open to a quick blow from Brest before they could be concentrated into a fleet.[31] The mobilization of the so-called Fleet Reserve, which was theoretically possible in forty-eight hours, was a complete sham. The mobilization of the Flying Squadron during the crisis with Germany in 1896 over the Kruger telegram (in which the Kaiser seemed to be supporting the Boers against England) took a week.[32] In 1900 and 1901, "mobilizations" to reassure the public were entirely faked. In 1900 the mobilization date was fixed a month and a half ahead and the whole arsenal staff set to work on the fleet, while in 1901 over 3,000 men worked at Devonport for three months before the maneuvers, and even the ships' compasses were inspected ahead of time.[33] But when, after all this, a destroyer broke down and returned to Devonport and its crew was sent by train to Portsmouth to commission another, the French concluded "that the Fleet Reserve at Devonport had not a single destroyer at its disposal. . . . The rapidity of the mobilization of Fleet Reserve A has not the slightest connection with its ordinary state of readiness."[34] The French system, developed primarily to provide a first-line force against England year-round and to keep the whole navy ready during the summer against the Triple Alliance, was one of the chief sources of French strength against England, the concentration of whose first-line fleet in the Mediterranean left the Channel dangerously open to a sudden attack.[35]

Another area, intimately connected with mobilization, in which France was also ahead of England was the organization of the naval high command. The French Naval General Staff, founded after the Tunis expedition of 1881, was much better than the rudimentary information service that the British set up two years later. Additional factors such as the influence of the French Army, the high level of education of French naval officers, and the large number of them without commands and available for staff work, all combined to put France a good decade ahead of England in adapting to sea power the methods of careful preparation for war that had been introduced by Germany on land. The decisive influences were probably the German example and, curiously, the cult of coastal warfare, which led to minute, detailed studies of the German and Italian coastal defenses. The need to compete with the Triple Alliance and match the German navy in mobilization and preparation for war led France to build a military organization that became one of the chief elements of her naval strength after 1890.[36]

The British navy remained far behind until the coming of Sir John Fisher and a younger generation in 1904 with the slogan of "detailed minute attention to minutiae and the consideration of trifles."[37] Its great weaknesses were the overconfidence and mental laziness of the older school of officers trained exclusively in navigation and the belief that mere bravery in the Nelsonian tradition was sufficient. The response of the London *Times* in 1883 to alarm over the state of the navy was that "in all these comparisons, no account whatever is taken of the one thing that has secured our naval supremacy in the past, namely the discipline, daring, gallantry, and other high qualities of our seamen. . . . After all, gunners and stokers are Englishmen."[38] Another commentator noted, however, that Trafalgar and Nelson had been gone for some eighty years, and the British were no longer opposed by the untrained crews and hastily improvised officer corps of the French Revolution.[39] Only the coming of new men to power and the agitation arising from the failures of the army in the Boer War really inaugurated the modern war organization of the British navy.

The task of preparing for war was complicated by the inception of modern secrecy in naval warfare in the late 1880s. In 1888, for the first time, a French naval mission to England saw no official plans of warships.[40] In the old free and easy days, information had been readily available; even in Germany, a ministry had published a set of maps with the outlines of the coastal fortifications on them. The British were incredibly careless with their documents—in Berlin a cabinet minister left a very confidential War Office memorandum in his hotel, and when the Prussian War Office returned it a fortnight later, it had not even been missed in London.[41] Throughout the 1890s secrecy remained intermittent, and anyone with a sufficient staff to cull information from open sources could find out practically everything he wanted to know.[42] The American Office of Naval Intelligence published much of what it culled in its *Information from Abroad* series between 1885 and 1902. The British naval intelligence service, however, was minuscule— in 1886 it consisted of one young officer of marines. He was responsible for liaison with the War Office, for detailed knowledge of the defenses of all the harbors of the British Isles, the armor of foreign ships, the use of electricity abroad, and finally the general subject of "British and Foreign Trade: Defence and Attack."[43] Down to 1900, the British had one naval attaché for all the continental powers, and the most reliable information they had was chiefly gathered from the American series.[44]

SPEED IN SHIPS

Fifteen years after the laying down of the *Duilio,* both France and England suddenly began to recognize the importance of speed in ships. The period of the early 1890s saw prodigious developments in warship machinery and boilers due to the great effort put into light torpedo craft and fast cruisers. While the British pushed their ships to the limit in their trials, the French developed a new type of boiler and both countries made efforts to improve the manning of their engine rooms.

The British saw the importance of the problem of speed in ships even before the French, and on the completion of the *Italia* and two Russian belted cruisers in 1885, the British public demanded speed, just as a few years before it had demanded 100-ton guns. Chief Engineer Richard Sennett

was able and ambitious, and he saw that forced draft, just introduced in torpedo boats, offered a way to satisfy the public's desires. Forced draft consisted of closing a ship's boiler rooms and forcing additional air into them
to increase the firing rate in the boilers.

Moderate forced draft was extremely useful, but its undue application in
the British navy of the late 1880s in order to answer the public demands for
high trial speeds was disastrous. Throughout the 1880s and early 1890s, this
"invention of the Evil One," as an admiral called it, was responsible for the
practical ruin of the boilers of many new British ships on their trials.[45] British trials—especially those of private shipbuilders—had always been vigorously criticized by foreign observers as faked, since they were undertaken with only about half the normal equipment on board and with picked
coal and special stokers, but the introduction of forced draft aggravated the
previous practice of "forcing the engines and boilers to the utmost extent of
their capacities."[46] The third-class cruiser *Barham,* for example, was so
abused in her trials in 1890 that at the end of her first commission there was
"hardly a tube in her condensers but leaks."[47] Even in 1914, the British
cruisers that were chasing the German *Goeben* and *Breslau* in the Mediterranean failed to make their trial speed, while the German ships, which had
never been pushed to the limit, did two full knots over anything they had
ever made before.

Even without forced draft, British trial practices allegedly weakened the
navy's ships. During the Russian scare of 1885, the old battleship *Monarch,*
with the admiral commanding the Mediterranean Fleet on board, broke
down so completely on a rush voyage from Port Said to Malta that she had
to be towed into port by a merchant ship after lying completely helpless
for two days.[48] Perhaps even more important, the achievement of high trial
speeds by such methods caused the Admiralty to retain its old types of boilers and postpone experiments with the new types being developed abroad.

French trials consisted of an eight-hour run with the emphasis on sustained speed, and in spite of the clamor of the Jeune Ecole for high trial
speeds like the English, the navy steadily refused to allow more than a moderate use of forced draft.[49] It recognized the impossibility of successfully
forcing the old-type boilers used in ships like the *Hoche* and *Marceau* to
attain high speed and decided to adopt an entirely new design—the water-
tube boiler.

The old boilers, sometimes called fire-tube boilers, were still direct developments from the Scotch boilers of the early days of steam. In them, a
relatively large quantity of water was heated in a tank or in a box containing
pipes through which the flames were led. In the new water-tube boiler, the
water was led in many small steel tubes through a large fire box. The new
boilers exposed a much greater surface of water to the fire and therefore
provided a much more efficient means of heat transfer. They were also,

however, difficult to manufacture because of the numerous tubes and connections, all of which had to be leak-free.

Water-tube boilers were developed by Joessel and Du Temple in the late 1860s and were fitted in the dispatch boat *Actif* in 1866 without success. They were reintroduced in the dispatch vessel *Voltigeur* in 1879. Du Temple's boilers in torpedo boat *No. 130,* the Belleville boilers in the cruiser *Milan* and the torpedo aviso *Léger,* and the d'Allest boilers in the torpedo aviso *Bombe* were among many tried in light craft in the mid-1880s. In 1887 the decision was made to fit water-tube boilers in the battleship *Brennus,* the first large ship so equipped, and they were soon also fitted in the four coast-defense battleships of the *Valmy* group, the four armored cruisers of the *Charner* class, and the five battleships of 1890–92. Though a few more ships, including the *Dupuy de Lôme,* were fitted with the older type, the French had practically abandoned it by 1889. Like the jump to long guns, many conservatives considered the rapid adoption of water-tube boilers rash and imprudent.[50] Indeed, there were a number of bad accidents, of which the most notable was an explosion during the trials of the battleship *Jauréguiberry* with the loss of six lives, but the new boilers were at least no more dangerous than the British overdoing forced draft.[51]

The British soon realized that the new boilers offered significant advantages. They eliminated some of the troubles peculiar to the Scotch boiler and offered a saving of weight (around 400 to 700 tons on the 14,200-ton cruisers of the *Powerful* class). Perhaps most important, they made it possible to get up steam in a short time, an especially important consideration in cruiser work. The five or six hours needed to raise steam in the old boilers was cut to one or two or even less: the torpedo gunboat *Sharpshooter* got up steam in twenty minutes starting with cold water and fires out, and the cruiser *Terrible* was able to reach full speed in forty-three minutes without injuring the machinery.[52] In 1893, as a result of a visit by Sir William White to Toulon, the British adopted water-tube boilers for the large cruisers *Powerful* and *Terrible.*[53] The final introduction of water-tube boilers for all ships in the British navy came in 1898, ten years behind the French, after studies of the French trials. This step was far from trouble-free, however. The British boiler interests were bitterly hostile to the new invention, and there was a great controversy in 1901–2 after several failures of the new boilers. These breakdowns occurred largely because the boilers adopted were a British "improvement" of a type that had gone out of favor in France in 1895. In addition, they had been poorly constructed during an engineers' strike and badly handled by unskilled men.

The new importance of engines, boilers, and speed created an acute manning problem in both the British and French navies. The public was wrong in believing that stokers could be picked up almost anywhere because all they needed was the ability to shovel coal.[54] In England, affairs were complicated by the general expansion of the navy, and at the Spithead Review of 1887 there was hardly a ship that was not undermanned at the engines. Conditions were made worse by the bad ventilation of the stoke-holds; the whole engine crew of the belted cruiser *Orlando* was put out of action on an eight-hour speed trial, and sailors who would have had other duties in case of war were frequently called to help out the raw recruits that filled the stokeholds during the maneuvers.[55] In the late 1890s the Admiralty was forced to start a great advertising campaign to man the new ships. The lack of reserves was another major weakness. During the maneuvers of 1901, when the Sheerness and Chatham dockyards took the new sloop *Es-piègle* out for some preliminary trials, arsenal workers had to man the en-gine rooms, as there was not a single engine or stoking hand available in the two ports. In spite of statements to the contrary, marines had to serve the guns on warships.[56] Britain had sufficient personnel for the first-line fleet but would not have been able to man it after a number of battles. The most serious deficiency was in engine-room men.[57]

In France, the *Inscription maritime* always provided enough conscript seamen, but the engine rooms had to be manned by volunteers. In 1901 the *Inscription* provided 66 percent of the brevetted gunners and 68 percent of the riflemen but only 6 percent of the mechanics and 14 percent of the stokers.[58] With each development of light craft and each new mechanical invention, the problem of the poor education of the Breton seamen became more serious, for the men from the interior lacked the sea legs while the Bretons lacked the mechanical aptitude for torpedo-boat work. The navy could get along by training the Bretons carefully in one thing, but this mi-nute division of labor into simple tasks was not very satisfactory. Every time a crew needed to put in a light bulb, they had to call on a torpedoman to do it.[59] Even in 1910, 20 percent of the *inscrits* came on board absolutely illiter-ate and 50 percent more had only a rudimentary education.

At the same time, the presence of volunteers from the interior raised se-rious problems of discipline. Like the contingents from the colonies, they were largely from the least desirable portions of the population and, as in England, their relations with the trade unions were a constant source of trouble. The claims, both real and imaginary, of the stokers and mechanics were now mixed by the left parties with the claims of the arsenal workers to form another element in the agitation of the Jeune Ecole, while the new men were unable to get along with either the Bretons or the officers.

By their whole training and temperament, the officers were unable to understand or handle the more intelligent but less easily disciplined me-chanics and stokers. The most unruly elements, the common stokers from the interior who could not stand torpedo-boat work, were put on the battle-ships, the precise place where the steam-yacht group among the officers was most prominent and the difference between the quarters of the officers and men the most glaring. In every navy the problems were much the same, and mutinies in the Austrian Navy and the mutiny of the Russian battleship *Potemkin* in 1905 presaged much more widespread discontent during World War I. The poor education of the *inscrits,* the inability of the officers to handle the new type of men, and the latter's relations with the politicians were all important problems raised by the rapidly increasing mechanization of the 1890s.

The related problem of the status of the engineer officers, another discontented group, was also very serious in France. Practically all these officers were former petty officers, and their low pay and the social treatment accorded them by the lordly regular officers caused much friction. The number of higher positions available in the engineer corps was completely inadequate, the engineer officers had no right to discipline their own men, and no matter what their seniority, they ranked below the lowest line officer of their grade on board.[60] In every navy, the line officers' resentment of the growing importance of the engineers and their different social origins showed itself in a mass of petty distinctions. Here again, because of the predominance of upper bourgeois and lower noble elements in the regular officer corps, conditions were worse in France than in any other navy in Europe except the Russian, and the vague resentment the line officers showed toward the naval constructors of the Génie maritime became concrete discrimination when applied to the mechanics and engineers aboard the ships. The discontent among the engineers was another element behind the agitation of the Jeune Ecole, and from the beginning the Jeune Ecole took up the cause of the stokers, the mechanics, and their officers.[61]

Fleet Tactics

Fleet actions assumed new importance for France at the end of the 1880s, primarily because of the Italian threat in the Mediterranean.

> Obsessed by the fear of seeing the coast of the Mediterranean menaced, that of Algeria and Tunis insulted, and the mobilization of the Nineteenth Corps compromised . . . we demanded speed for our battleships and cruisers, and our great annual maneuvers and our ordinary squadron exercises rested on the one invariable theme: "To cover a coast attacked by a rapid fleet, with a slow squadron."[62]

Ironically, Aube's bombardment propaganda had ultimately tied the French fleet to its own coasts, while the building of the fast Italian battleships and the fortification of Maddalena had raised a real danger to French control of their own coastal waters. For France there was only one real solution. In response to an army demand to dedicate ships to the protection of troop transports, the ministry stated that "our naval force must be concentrated and constantly ready for the offensive, for the destruction of the enemy fleet will render everything else easy."[63]

The new advances in technology posed three major problems in naval tactics: the revival of tactics suited to the gun, the use of torpedo craft in a squadron action, and scouting and maintaining contact with an enemy at sea. The French made considerable progress with each in the late 1880s and early 1890s.

Just as the French had been most logical in working out the tactical consequences of the adoption of the ram, they now completely abandoned it and turned to the tactics of the gun. Beginning under Admiral Bergasse Dupetit-Thouars in 1888, the Mediterranean Squadron worked out a new "code of evolutions," which was adopted in 1892. Making a complete break with the elaborate formations then in vogue, Dupetit-Thouars returned to the principle of "natural tactics" first suggested by an earlier tactical innovator, Admiral Jean-Pierre-Edmond Jurien de la Gravière. These consisted of doing away with all battle signals and adopting a simple "follow the leader" line ahead in which each ship followed the example of the flagship. "Victory would be more certain . . . through very simple, brutal, and well practiced movements, than by any multiple, learned combinations."[64] The guiding idea of the new signal book of 1892 and of the final version of the new tactics, the signal book of 1905, was to let the admiral rule.[65] The old divisions and squads and movements in squares and triangles that looked so good in time of peace were thus discarded in favor of the simple line ahead. The wonderful combinations that were so secret that an admiral in command of the British Mediterranean fleet was afraid to whisper them to his pillow were replaced by constant practice of a few simple movements.[66]

The tradition of French tactical superiority held true throughout the 1890s, and the French were not boasting when they concluded after the maneuvers of 1894 that "it is not too bold to assert that in France, due to the zeal and initiative of everyone, we are in advance, from a tactical point of view, of the other maritime powers, and particularly England."[67] One reason for this excellence was that the younger officers, for whom staff work now offered a real opportunity even in the battle fleet, devoted the same attention to tactics as they had to working out the details of mobilization. Although the French ships with their dull gray paint impressed Queen Victoria as "certainly not smart looking," the American naval lieutenant Bradley A. Fiske, who was allowed to attend the French maneuvers, "acquired an enormous admiration for the French navy."[68] In passing, it might be remarked that in those days, American observers were on a par with missions from Chile: it was perfectly safe to let them see everything that was going on.

In England, the French method of evolutions without signals in a single line ahead was apparently first adopted by Admiral Sir George Tryon, but the tragic loss of the battleship *Victoria*, for which he was responsible, discredited his system of tactics as well.[69] Here, too, the mental inertia of the British higher officers in the 1890s took its toll, and only the younger admirals such as Fisher and Wilson were really interested in tactical problems. As late as 1901, Wilson won a brilliant victory over Admiral Sir Gerard Noel, then regarded as the "coming man" at the Admiralty, by using the simple French line ahead against a formation in columns that was "a relic of Trafalgar."[70]

The tactics for using torpedo craft with a fleet also received much attention. All the continental navies quickly realized that in actions between battleships, whose quick-firing guns were generally unprotected, the most effective use of torpedo craft would come after the battle had begun. The French initially adopted the idea of hiding one torpedo boat behind each battleship (as the Austrians had done as early as 1884). By 1892 they had developed the maneuver of gathering all the boats at the head and tail of the battle line to charge the enemy in groups (a tactic also developed by the Germans in the mid-1880s).[71] In the French maneuvers of 1896 this use of torpedo boats in a group was very successful, six out of eight torpedoes making hits from a standard firing range of around 400 yards.[72] In Britain in 1901, incredible as it seems, Admiral Wilson had had the idea of "springing a surprise" on the enemy by using his torpedo boats, one behind each battleship. He got the idea from Fisher, "but it proved impracticable." (The French Navy's account of this episode simply remarked that "neither of the two admirals could find any use for his destroyers.")[73]

The third tactical problem, scouting and maintaining contact with an enemy at sea, was of particular importance against Italy. The French officers who studied it also appreciated its complexity:

> The study [of scouting] was first limited to surveying as large as possible a zone around the squadron itself, but the necessity rapidly appeared of separating the scouting division from the battle force and putting it under a separate command. Since then . . . we have studied the different problems of joining and keeping contact with the enemy, of communication with the body of the fleet, and of rendezvous. The commander of the light forces, if he has under his orders a sufficient force, will maneuver to maintain contact with the enemy, fight enemy cruisers if need be, and detach dispatch vessels to report to his chief the position of the enemy and the route that he is making.[74]

In four years, French ideas on scouting advanced from a simple screen of cruisers spread out in a circle around the battle fleet to the formation of what might be called an antenna for the battle force—cruisers deployed in a T-shaped formation. The head of the T was the cruiser division, which sent back smaller dispatch vessels to pass the news to the commander. This system presaged that used in World War I; all that was needed was to replace the dispatch vessels by wireless radio. The French were fairly successful even in keeping contact at night.

Initially the French had hoped to use ships as small as torpedo avisos in scouting, but these proved hopelessly inadequate, and the need for endurance caused the tonnage of scouts to rise constantly. In the Program of 1890 and its successors, dispatch vessels turned into 2,300-ton third-class cruisers, while the second- and first-class cruisers in the advance cruiser squadron also grew in size. Missing from these plans was any provision for specially-built commerce destroyers (even Aube's cruisers were now seen primarily as fleet scouts), and commerce-raiding tactics were totally ignored.[75]

Abroad, the Germans used large torpedo craft like the *Zieten* for scouting, but they also made the move from a simple screen to deployment of cruisers in front of the squadron and others as a rear guard.[76] England was behind even in 1901:

> Last year, Rawson let an enemy get away within three miles of him. This year, in the Channel, Noel's cruisers failed even to find the enemy in six days. The Admiralty has certainly neglected the service of scouting . . . and, still more, except during the maneuvers, their fleets do not possess sufficient cruisers to allow the study of the problem.[77]

In light cruiser work, as in squadron tactics and in the use of torpedo craft with the fleet, the British navy had the elements of sea power but not the will to organize them and undertake the hard study of their use.

COAST DEFENSE TACTICS

The three points in Aube's strategy had been the offensive in the Mediterranean, the defensive in the Channel, and commerce-raiding from Brest. While commerce-raiding was completely neglected by his successors, the development of fleet tactics in the Mediterranean was matched by a vigorous development of coastal defenses along the Channel, primarily against a *coup de main* by the German fleet. The main features of the new French organization were all copied from the Germans: a few strong points with coast-defense ships and fortifications, a large number of torpedo boats scattered along the coast in *défenses mobiles,* and cruisers and observation points for scouting and communications.

Few advances were made in torpedoes during this period—400 yards remained the effective launch range until 1898, and new torpedoes were not much different from those of Aube's day except that they carried a double charge of explosive. The main effort in torpedo work was put into practice and organization. By 1896, after 1,400 firings at 400 meters, the *défense mobile* at Toulon was getting 82 percent hits, while the boats accompanying the squadron were making over 50 percent steaming at full speed against a moving target.[78]

The extent of the development of torpedo warfare in general may be seen in the following statistic: in the dozen years after Aube came to power, the number of torpedoes in every major navy but those of Austria and Russia increased between six and eight times. (In France the increase between 1886 and 1898 was from 500 to 3,000.)[79] In spite of continued failures during maneuvers of attempts to use torpedo boats for scouting, carrying orders, or even guarding wide passes, this was a torpedo-boat age. With the introduction of the German idea of using a light cruiser to lead flotillas of torpedo boats, true tactics for torpedo boats now replaced the vague ideas about "coming from all points of the compass" that had been the stock in trade of the original torpedo-boat enthusiasts.[80]

Major advances were made in torpedo-boat design during the period. Due to the complete failure of the 35-meter, 58-ton boats built under Aube, the Conseil des Travaux decided that no future torpedo boat, even for coast defense, would be less than 80 tons, while the high-seas boats to accompany the squadron were to be of around 125 tons, two or three times the size of Charmes's *autonomes*. All of the torpedo boats built under the Program of 1890 fell into these two categories.

The decision proved to have an unanticipated but important impact on the speed of the boats. The towing-tank experiments of the British naval architects William and Edmund Froude after 1872 indicated that the power required to drive a ship does not rise steadily with speed. Naval architects concluded that, for a ship of a given length, there were certain speed ranges in which each increase in power brought only a slight increase in speed and in which it was possible to multiply the horsepower substantially without getting much result. On the other hand, for the same ship there were other speed ranges in which each increase in power produced substantial increases in speed. (This theory was partly responsible for the length of the giant ocean liners of the 1930s—the *Queen Mary, Queen Elizabeth,* and *Normandie.*) The point of lowest efficiency for craft of 80 tons was 18 knots; for larger boats it was 21. In 1877 Thornycroft's torpedo boats were making 18 to 19 knots; in 1889 the fastest boat in the world was doing barely 21, an increase of two knots in twelve years. The decision to build the larger boats was made in 1889, about the same time that some French companies began making satisfactory water-tube boilers. In 1892–93 the French successfully tried a 24-knot, 37.8-meter, 80-ton boat (*No. 147*) and a 27.5-knot boat (*Chevalier*) of the larger size, and two years later Normand's 136-ton, 44-meter *Forban* reached a trial speed of 31 knots, a jump of ten knots in five years. Much of the progress was due to the better boilers, engines, and propellers used, but some of it was attributable to the shift to longer, larger boats.[81]

The seagoing boats built before the *Forban* had a steaming range of 5,000 miles, and several of them accompanied the fleet on diplomatic visits to Kronstadt and Portsmouth in 1891. The 80-ton boats for coast defense had less range and were not intended to keep the sea with the squadron, although their speed was now high enough to be useful with it in French waters.

In spite of the complaints of the Jeune Ecole, even the traditionalists did not stop building torpedo boats. After a pause in the late 1880s due to de-

Two fast high-seas torpedo boats: the Chevalier *(1893) with Normand's master-piece, the 31-knot* Forban *(1895), in the background.*

sign problems with the earlier boats, between 1890 and 1893 they ordered twenty-five seagoing boats and fifty-four coast-defense boats. In 1894 the French had in service about fifty of the large new coast-defense boats. Twenty of them were stationed at Cherbourg but spent much time at sea, using protected refuges at Le Havre and Dunkirk and five other coaling and watering points along the coast. Eight operated from Brest, two each from Lorient and Rochefort, and only about sixteen in the Mediterranean: ten at Toulon, three in Corsica, and three in Algiers. There were fifty-one smaller torpedo craft at Toulon, but most of these were of the 35-meter type that spent most of their time in boiler or other repairs. French torpedo strength, outside of the boats with the squadron, was concentrated in the north, particularly at Dunkirk, which served as an advance station against a German squadron trying to force its way into the English Channel.[82]

The French coasts, like the German and Italian, were surrounded by a cordon of information-gathering and distribution points. The French semaphore system, which eventually included 127 posts in France and 17 in Algeria, Tunisia, and Corsica, was organized into a kind of centralized news service.[83] The ports condensed the news they received into special dispatches, which they sent to all the news distribution posts. In six days of maneuvers, Toulon made 600 telegrams into thirty-six bulletins. Before the days of wireless, the news distribution function was extremely important—in the maneuvers, the semaphores succeeded in signaling the enemy thirty-five miles at sea.[84] The lighthouses were organized with similar care. They could be extinguished or lighted on command, and a cruiser creeping along the coast at night had only to signal its arrival to any station to be given secret guide lights at a port four or five hours away.

In artillery, ship design, tactics, mobilization, torpedo work, and coast defenses, the key characteristic of the French Navy after 1889 was careful organization and minute attention to detail. The navy's primary concern during these years was to meet the danger of the Triple Alliance. It never lost sight of England, however, and both the French and the British soon realized that the advances made during this period substantially improved France's position at sea relative to its historic adversary as well as its new rival.

Fourteen

The Franco-Russian Alliance and the 1893 Mediterranean Scare

IN THE EARLY 1890s, European diplomats focused much of their attention on the new alliance between France and Russia, which counterbalanced the Triple Alliance of Germany, Austria, and Italy. The new alliance was one of the factors that produced a naval scare in England in 1893 and impelled the Admiralty to undertake another major shipbuilding effort comparable to the Naval Defence Act of 1889. In informed English circles, however, the main cause of the scare was not the possibility of cooperation between England's two main maritime rivals but the increased effectiveness of the French Navy, which became evident at the same time.

THE FRANCO-RUSSIAN ALLIANCE

In 1891 a French fleet under Admiral Gervais made an unprecedented visit to the Russian naval base at Kronstadt, where on one of the French warships the autocratic tsar listened to the revolutionary "Marseillaise." Two years later a Russian squadron made a return visit to Toulon. These visits made it clear to all Europe that France and Russia had concluded some sort of treaty of alliance. The two powers in fact signed a secret convention a month after the Kronstadt visit and concluded a military convention at the end of 1893.

Although the navy's visits and receptions played an important role in the conclusion of the alliance, the new agreement did not greatly alter the naval balance of power in the Mediterranean. No naval convention was concluded that might have led to combined action by the Russian and French fleets; indeed, there were no naval conversations until 1900. There was also no real danger of Russia's becoming an effective Mediterranean power. In short, French and Russian forces were unlikely to combine to attack the British in

Egypt or to take the Suez Canal. On the other hand, it had been apparent as early as 1887 that, alliance or no alliance, England would have difficulty sending its ships up the Turkish Straits with an unfriendly force at Toulon and that, in a war between France and England, England would have to immobilize a portion of her force at Malta to watch the Russians.[1]

In his critique of the French Navy in the spring of 1890, the deputy and future minister of marine Jean-Louis de Lanessan examined the Russian Navy thoroughly. Lanessan was already close to the navy; his ideas came largely from conversations with French naval officers, and his policy of concentrating against the Triple Alliance had largely been adopted by the navy in 1890. Lanessan noted that the Russian Baltic Fleet consisted of the old battleship *Petr Veliki* and three smaller battleships still under construction. In the Black Sea, three of the peculiar *Ekaterina II* type, designed to take Constantinople, had been completed and another was building. The Russians had six mediocre armored cruisers similar to the old station battleships, one good one (the *Pamyat Azova*), and a solitary protected commerce destroyer (the *Admiral Kornilov,* built in France). He concluded rightly that the real help Russia could give to France was very little.[2]

The Russian building programs after 1890 gave the Black Sea Fleet three ships that were totally different from the *Ekaterina II,* while the Baltic got a remarkable collection of disparate types which can be loosely described as three small ships resembling the British Admiral class, a small imitation of the *Royal Sovereign,* three battleships quite similar to the French *Brennus,* a turret ship like the British *Nile,* and a Russian creation, the *Gangut,* whose loss during firing practice in 1897 was rumored to have occurred because she was badly put together and the strain of firing opened her seams.[3] There were only three new cruisers: the protected cruiser *Svetlana* (built in France), which was also fitted as a yacht, and two giant armored cruisers that caused much concern in England, the *Ryurik* and *Rossiya.*

The list of the Russian Navy was impressive enough on paper, but its ships had no homogeneity as to speed, size, range, protection, or anything else. Russia's allies frankly confessed that they could not see what the Russians wanted from such a heterogeneous collection, in which the Black Sea Fleet, with only two major types of battleships, came off the best.[4] Against England the Russians had no real cruisers, against Germany they could not match even the old *Sachsen*-class battleships with their German crews, and against Turkey they had no need for all that power. Most of their torpedo craft were old, slow, and too small to accompany the fleet. These craft were also so badly handled that nothing could be expected from them against the Germans.[5] The newer Russian artillery, a Canet pattern made foolproof and heavier for the Russian sailors, was pretty fair after French shells and powder were supplied, but the quick-firer came in slowly and Russian gunners were not well adapted to its use.[6]

Owing to the Russification policies of the late 1890s, which drove many Finns and Baltic Germans from the navy, the fleet's personnel deteriorated before the outbreak of the disastrous war with Japan in 1904. However, even in 1890, Russian officers were either brave and incompetent aristocrats who spent their time navigating on the imperial yacht, or Baltic Germans who did all the work and were denied any hope of advancement. Outside of the same Baltic Germans, good petty officers were few and far between. The common sailors were utterly hopeless. They were conscripted peasants, completely uneducated and uninterested in the sea. "After seven years of service, having learned nothing whatever," they went back to their villages as ignorant as they had left them.[7] They were wholly unsuited to torpedo-boat work, and the Russian stokers and engine-room men were reputed to be the worst in Europe.

The Russians were at their worst in exactly the areas on which the French Navy was working the hardest after 1890: tactics, speed, mobilization, organization, and the use of light craft and cruisers. The French appreciated this, as they were no fools; they had the best chance to see inside the Russian Navy, and they had one of the best intelligence services in existence. One reason French naval officers avoided any suggestion of joint action with the Russian fleet was because they were fully aware of its shortcomings.

But the Russians were good advertisers (far better than the British Admiralty), and all sorts of wonders were always being announced as ready to come forth from the shipyards at Sevastopol and Kronstadt. In 1894, for instance, they announced a twenty-year program for twenty-four battleships and thirteen cruisers.[8] In 1896 they grandly promised that they would match England ship for ship with a Russian example of superior or equal strength.[9] The British public swallowed these stories whole, and even the Admiralty, which in any event had no reason for quieting the public alarm, occasionally fell for them.

The clearest case was that of the two big armored cruisers, *Ryurik* and *Rossiya,* of 11,000 and 12,000 tons, 18 knots, and a stupendous 19,000-mile range clearly intended for commerce-destroying. In actual fact, these ships were both perfect shams: neither made any speed whatever, and their artillery, which was enormous on paper, was so badly arranged that the French thought it had been stuck on as an afterthought.[10] Yet what little information the British did get on the two cruisers led them to believe that ten of them were actually planned and that they were probably bigger than the published figures. The result was the laying down of two enormous protected cruisers, the *Powerful* and *Terrible,* of 14,200 tons and 22 knots, to chase them.[11] In the debate in the House of Commons on the 8-million-pound British reply to the Russian building program of 1898, the first lord, George Goschen, practically admitted that the Admiralty was not certain of the exact extent of the program it was answering.[12]

The French had a much better opportunity to see the Russian Navy from the inside, and their general appreciation of the Russian fleet after 1898, when the Russians began to show more interest in the Far East, was not greatly different from what it had been before.

> As far as we are concerned, the resolution taken by our ally to accumulate the best part of his fleet in China is not displeasing, for it will take certain naval forces from the Mediterranean and the Channel. History has taught us the grave inconvenience of too close cooperation of allied fleets operating in concert side by side. It is necessary, therefore, to avoid them for the future, whatever be the allied nation. This principle, true in every case, applies especially to the Russian squadrons. They are so poorly handled that their cumbersome mass could do nothing but weigh down and paralyze our own. That, in short, is our general appreciation of the navy we have just been studying.[13]

From the naval point of view, the chief advantage of the alliance for each party was that it made it more certain that the forces of the other would immobilize part of the British fleet. It would give the Russians time to establish themselves at Constantinople, which the Black Sea fleet could have taken at any time. In the meantime, the luring of the British toward the Turkish Straits would give the French a golden opportunity to head not toward Egypt but toward the Atlantic. In direct contradiction to the colonial school of thought, France was now thinking of using this chance not to hit England in the Mediterranean, but to revive her traditional strategy of getting her Toulon squadron out past Gibraltar into the open ocean.

The French tested this strategy in their 1893 maneuvers, which were held at exactly the time of the visit of the Russian squadron to Toulon. One of the problems in the maneuvers was the blockade of a "French" force at Toulon by an "enemy" at Ajaccio (which represented the Maddalena and Gulf of Asinara area, open to either Italy or England). The "enemy's" chain of scout cruisers got the message of the "French" departure to Ajaccio in five hours, but the "enemy" lost touch with the "French," who were heading through the Balearic passage instead of toward Bizerte. Even in naval maneuvers, one does not go to Egypt from Toulon by way of the Balearics.[14] The 1895 maneuvers studied the problem of a "British" force at Ajaccio (this time the combined Mediterranean and Channel fleets) preventing the union near Algiers of the Toulon and Brest squadrons.[15] In the meantime, the theme of the British maneuvers of 1894 had involved the Channel fleet being met near Gibraltar by the whole French Mediterranean force, which then united with the Brest battleships to smash the British Mediterranean fleet coming from Malta.[16]

The Russians apparently chose the area near Mount Athos in Greece as an advance base in the Aegean, and they issued charts of the eastern Mediterranean to the Black Sea Fleet.[17] There was, however, little danger of their coming beyond Constantinople or establishing a permanent force in the Mediterranean. The French were never greatly alarmed about the prospect of the Russians becoming supreme in the Levant, since without French help they would surely be in for a terrible beating from the English. If their Black Sea Fleet were caught in the open sea by a squadron of British *Royal Sovereigns*, it would have been just too bad for the Russians. Exactly as later happened at Tsushima in 1905 against the Japanese, the Russians would have come bowling along, badly overloaded, brave, ill organized, and without scouts, while the British would have had nothing to do but wait and "cut them up at leisure."[18]

The French Navy steadily eluded all Russian hints about the use of Bizerte by a Russian squadron, and only in 1903, under pressure from the Foreign Office, were they willing to let the Russians coal there regularly.[19] In 1894 the canal to the new port at Bizerte was not yet completed and the port was totally defenseless. The guns for the fortifications were kept at Bône in Algeria, ready to be rushed to their positions if a crisis broke out; the coal supply was around 500 tons; and the port was guarded by one torpedo boat. Further to the west, the Russian designs on Tangier and on the Chafarinas Islands (near the Spanish enclave of Melilla in Morocco) were, like the ten armored cruisers of the *Rossiya* type, mostly in the Slavic imagination.[20] As for the Chafarinas, French naval propagandists were equally sure that Spain had ceded them to England.[21]

French naval industries found a lucrative market in Russia. In a few things, such as the famous gunnery school at Kronstadt, where a few gunners carried on many interesting experiments with dummy guns and moving targets, the Russian Navy was very good, and visitors in St. Petersburg were mightily impressed. In general, however, things were pretty poor, particularly at the time the alliance was concluded. Under the tutelage of the French, the Russians made considerable progress in the introduction of Creusot armor, Canet guns, Belleville water-tube boilers, and French-type engines.

The French arms firms soon put their British predecessors in Russia out of business. MacPherson's engine works went bankrupt and Baird's works were taken over by the Société anonyme des Usines franco-russes. The American builder Cramp was also gradually squeezed out of the Russian business. Partly because of a big engineers' strike, England got none of the numerous Russian orders in 1898 for ships from foreign builders at estimated profits running up to 30 percent.[22]

Though it is difficult to say just when the transition took place, French capitalists controlled Russian shipbuilding by 1914 as they did the rest of the steel, war materials, and engineering trades. From the mine to the completed ship, French arms firms got most of the profits from Russian naval orders. The Union parisienne, the bank backing Creusot in France, controlled the Putilov iron works, the Russo-Baltic works, and the Northwestern

Metallurgical Machine and Shipbuilding Company; while a second great syndicate controlled the Franco-Russian company, the St. Petersburg Metal Works, the Russian Shipbuilding Company, and the Nikopol Shipyards.[23] Most of the Russian ships of the late 1890s were French in type, and the French arms firms generally enjoyed fat orders.

THE MEDITERRANEAN SCARE OF 1893

Three new factors had appeared in the Mediterranean naval situation by 1893, of which the one just discussed, the increased strength of the Russian Navy and the danger of cooperation between it and the French Navy, was no more important than the others, the weakening of Italy and of Britain's bonds with the Triple Alliance, and the increased efficiency of the French fleet. All three may be seen at work in the so-called Mediterranean scare, which followed the highly publicized visit of a Russian squadron to Toulon in October 1893 in response to the French visit to Kronstadt in 1891.

It is curious to note that on the eve of the outburst, the English appreciation of the Russian danger was generally sound. They believed that the Russians were ready for an expedition to Constantinople but felt that, as the London *Times* remarked on 14 October 1893, their fleet, without cruisers, would be hopelessly lost in the open sea, while the French themselves would not be eager to assist Russian adventures any farther than Constantinople. But the unprecedented extent and enthusiasm of the celebrations at Toulon carried England, including the *Times,* completely away only two weeks later.

> All that we know is that we have just beheld perhaps the most remarkable outburst of international feeling ever witnessed, and that the demonstration points directly to joint action between the fleets of France and Russia in the waters of the Mediterranean.[24]

At the same time, the Russians announced that they were establishing a permanent Russian squadron in the Mediterranean. Rumors quickly spread that it would be based at Bizerte and would consist of the *Ryurik* and *Pamyat Azova,* Russia's two best armored cruisers. The press, at least, was certain that the actual cooperation of the two fleets had been decided upon. Various Italian papers announced the establishment of a permanent German squadron at Maddalena as a reply, and the English and Italian navies staged a demonstration at Taranto. Even the Spanish became very concerned.[25] The situation was curiously like the alarm raised in France by the visit of the German fleet to Maddalena in 1889, which also aroused speculations that the presence of the visiting fleet might become permanent.

Another factor that became important in 1893 was the state of Anglo-Italian relations. Though the Italian premier, Francesco Crispi, had been unable to get support from England or Germany against the French development of Bizerte, the outward signs of German-Italian and Anglo-Italian friendship did not immediately weaken after the naval demonstrations of 1888 and 1889 but instead grew even stronger. When Crispi fell in 1891, his successor, Marquis Antonio Starabba di Rudini, tried to reach an understanding with France. Italy's need to maintain good relations with England, however, made it impossible for Rudini to accept the French demands for a secret guarantee that Italy would not take part in a war of the Triple Alliance against France, and he instead initiated negotiations for a premature renewal of the Triple Alliance. In the new alliance, signed in May, Italy gained a conditional promise of German support for Italian ambitions in Tripoli in compensation for the French activity at Bizerte. Although Germany was not in a position to give much support, it would at least be better than mere protests. (The previous treaty had simply pledged the three powers to maintain the status quo in the western Mediterranean basin.)

Rudini's greatest hope was to tie England more closely to the new alliance. Rumors of his efforts to accomplish this surfaced just as the announcement was made in the Italian Parliament of the renewal of the Triple Alliance. This, plus a visit of the British fleet to Fiume and Venice and a state visit by the German kaiser to London, convinced the French and Russians that England had actually joined the Triple Alliance. One of the first results of these fears was the decision to send the French fleet to Kronstadt in July 1891.[26]

This, however, was the high point of Anglo-Italian friendship. In 1889 the leader of the English Liberal Party, Gladstone, had branded Italy's connection with the Triple Alliance as a "gigantic piece of political tomfoolery."[27] The rumors of 1891 led to a second and stronger stand by the liberals against the policy of binding England to Italy. The explanations of the matter by the conservative government convinced no one, and another leading liberal, Henry Labouchere, stated in the House of Commons that under a liberal government England would not consider binding any agreements made by the preceding ministry.[28] This public discussion by a party that returned to power only a year later naturally weakened Italian confidence in England, as well as French fears of Anglo-Italian cooperation.

The Mediterranean coalition of the late 1880s fell apart after the liberal electoral victory in 1892. The new liberal foreign minister, Lord Rosebery, wanted to keep alive England's association with Italy and the Triple Alliance in order to save Constantinople, but he did not dare raise the matter with his liberal colleagues in the cabinet. The best he could give the Italians was a personal note renewing England's purely defensive pledge of help against a direct French attack. There was no guarantee that the divided liberal cabinet would be able to make up its mind immediately in a serious crisis; there was nothing about North Africa or even Tripoli, and there was nothing very definite about England's attitude in case of a general war between the two alliances.[29] Perhaps the key factor was Germany's well-founded lack of confidence in the new liberal government. The Germans saw no reason to promise England to pressure France to stay neutral in the case of a Russian push toward the straits unless England was willing to give something in return to Italy.

Another factor in the dissolution of the coalition was Italy's growing weakness—and the German miscalculation that Italy's feebleness would hold her more strongly to the Triple Alliance. Even the technical failings of the Italian fleet possibly played a role. The vulnerability of the Italian ships to shellfire, their state of disrepair, and the poor quality of their crews were all "warnings which Englishmen, who are tempted to lean upon the Italian alliance, will do well not to ignore."[30] A high-ranking English officer wrote,

> I do not know what is amiss with the Italian navy. . . . It is not in ships, it is not in officers . . . yet there is something amiss, something that I can't help being conscious of. And the upshot of it all is that, if I had a heavy job on hand here, I would rather, even if I had a very inferior force of my own, attempt it without than with the Italian help.[31]

THE FRENCH THREAT IN THE EARLY 1890s

The danger of the French Mediterranean squadron defeating either the British Channel or Mediterranean Fleet, if it caught them before they could join, was already well known to English naval experts. In 1891 Captain Lord Charles Beresford reported to Captain Rawson that "in my opinion, if the French fleet were to attack us in the Mediterranean, we should stand a very poor chance."[32] In response to such comments, the chancellor of the exchequer, Sir William Harcourt, claimed that the admirals were "up to their well-known tricks and manners" and that the British navy was really a match for all the others in the world. "We can build when we please four ships to their one, and we can man ten ships to their one with mariners who understand their work, which theirs do not."[33] Even so, it was clear by 1892 that the British Mediterranean Fleet was slightly inferior to the French squadron.[34] In addition, when Sir William White visited Toulon to study watertube boilers, he left impressed both with the efficiency of the French Navy and the danger from their new torpedo craft.

The Russian fleet's visit to Toulon was instrumental in revealing to the British public both the danger from Russia and something previously known only to the experts—the efficiency of the French. The French allowed the English newspaper correspondents to circulate freely at Toulon, which, of course, was in its best possible condition for the visit of the Russians. The impression made on the English, particularly William Laird Clowes of the London *Times,* was much like the impression made on French newspapermen at the 1888 Anglo-Italian-Austrian naval demonstration at Barcelona. To

The battleship Jauréguiberry. *One of the five battleships begun between 1890 and 1892, her launch in late 1893 during the visit of the Russian fleet to Toulon helped trigger the British Mediterranean scare.*

please the Russians, the French held a gala launching of their newest battleship, the *Jauréguiberry*. Her designer, the naval constructor Antoine-Jean-Amable Lagane, was already well known in England as the designer of two of the most successful French-built battleships sold abroad, the Chilean *Capitan Prat* and the Spanish *Pelayo*. The description of the *Jauréguiberry*, with her perfectly balanced turrets and full use of electricity, triggered the Mediterranean scare in England.[35]

Four days later, in a long article on "Toulon and the French Mediterranean Fleet," Clowes pointed out the strength of Toulon: the mountains of stores, the arrangements for mobilization, the training of the officers and men, and the excellence of the fleet reserves.[36] "'Ready' was the motto which seemed to be writ large on every piece of machinery, on every storehouse, on every magazine." In spite of the usual exaggerations in such accounts, most of his statements were perfectly true. England had finally discovered the danger produced by the superior French preparation for war.[37]

The solution proposed by Clowes to England's Mediterranean problem was to withdraw entirely from the Mediterranean in time of war and to close the entrances to the sea, at Gibraltar and at either Aden or Suez. In this respect, the scare of 1893 was only an extension of that of 1887. Then a similar proposal had been frowned upon because, first, it was impossible for England to abandon Italy and Austria, and, second, it would probably be possible to protect English commerce even in those waters by returning to the old convoy system. (The proposal to form convoys in the Mediterranean to protect troops going to India was an important step toward developing a strategy for commerce defense.)[38] Clowes's revival of the idea of abandoning the Mediterranean stemmed from the three new factors in the situation: the impossibility of assuring the safety of British commerce when a combined French and Russian fleet was equal to the British, the impossibility of risking the destruction of the Channel fleet by keeping the Mediterranean squadron separated from it at Malta, and the fact that Italy was now too weak to be of much help.[39] The idea of getting out of the Mediterranean may have been backed by Beresford and was supported by a large number of other writers.[40]

The responses were immediate and numerous, although some were wide of the mark. After 1890, writers commonly quoted the maxim that "the sea is one," supposedly derived from Mahan. "The idea of abandoning the Mediterranean is quite inadmissible. If our navy is sufficiently strong to command the sea, this covers the Mediterranean." Against commerce raiders, it was only necessary to build "additional cruisers of the *Powerful* type, to cope with these vessels on at least equal terms."[41] Philip Colomb offered the contention that it would be harder to blockade the Straits of Gibraltar than Toulon because the former were wider.[42] Sir George Clarke gathered together a large number of historical and sentimental arguments without adding any new ideas.[43] One thing emerged clearly from the discussion: England's naval position was gravely threatened.

COMMERCE PROTECTION

Even more difficult than retaining military control of the Mediterranean was the problem of defending British commerce there. Nearly all of the new small French scout cruisers were based in the inland sea. In spite of the number of British bases there, a royal commission under Lord Carnarvon concluded in 1887 that "it is evident that circumstances may arrive when the sea route through the Mediterranean will be attended with such risks that it may have to be abandoned by ships not prepared to defend themselves."[44] In another royal commission appointed in 1905 to examine similar problems, both shipping officials and naval officers were preparing for the commercial abandonment of the Mediterranean route in wartime.[45] The most superficial consideration of the problem was sufficient to show the practical impossibility of defending trade there thoroughly.[46]

Although the British had recognized that they might lose the use of the Mediterranean sea lanes, they had done nothing to prepare for such an event. No one even knew how much commerce there was to be protected in the Mediterranean or how much of it could be diverted via the Cape of Good Hope. At that time, even if the French had not captured a single ship, the diversion of the Suez Canal trade to the Cape would have been a terrible blow to English commerce. The greater time needed to go around the Cape

The third-class protected cruiser Troude *(launched in 1888). She was one of six small cruisers ordered by Aube that, stationed in the Mediterranean in the early 1890s, were seen as a menace to British trade there. The masts of the battleship* Hoche *are in the background.*

(which required three ships to do the work of two on the shorter route) was not the only relevant factor. Before the introduction of a larger size of tramp steamer in the years immediately before World War I, the majority of British merchant ships were still too small to carry paying freight on the long Cape route, which was, at this time, practically abandoned by all but a few liners and the sailing trade.[47] In 1893, before the development of the Natal coal mines and before the peak in the South African–Transvaal economic boom, the lack of coaling and port facilities on the Cape route alone would have presented a very serious problem.[48]

But was the route that England held "dearest," her Mediterranean "lifeline," also the "most vital"? It is impossible to say, but an analysis of British trade figures for the years 1888 to 1892, the results of which are reported in Table 2, shows that British trade was divided remarkably evenly between three great routes: North America, the Baltic and North Sea, and the Far East.[49]

These figures suggest that Britain's trade with all of Mediterranean Europe, including the Mediterranean parts of Spain, was little more important than her trade with France, although a suprisingly large percentage of her raw materials still came from that region. The portion of her trade with India and the Far East that went by Suez, along the so-called "lifeline" of the empire, was little more than that to North America. The loss or diversion of these two elements of her trade would indeed be a terrible blow, but the

TABLE 2

BRITISH TRADE, 1888–92

Route	Imports	Exports	Raw Materials
North Atlantic	26.0%	19.8%	40.3%
Baltic & North Sea	24.4	24.3	13.4
France	10.7	7.9	1.7
Mediterranean littoral	10.1	8.5	12.8
East of Suez	16.2	20.8	18.6
Total: Suez route	26.3	29.3	31.4
Africa and Cape	5.3	8.3	5.5
South Atlantic	4.6	7.6	5.3
East Atlantic	2.6	2.8	2.3
Total: Cape route	12.5	18.7	13.1

"lifeline" of Britain's industrial system already ran elsewhere. With the opening of the Panama Canal in 1914, the proportions were to change still more. Even at the height of its importance in the British system, the Suez Canal was still only one of three great roads.

In World War I, England survived the total loss of her Baltic trade and the diversion of most of the trade that went through the Mediterranean. The trade warfare that brought her within two months of disaster was waged, as Charmes had predicted, in the Atlantic approaches within 200 miles of Brest. In 1893 British experts like Clowes were beginning to consider abandoning the Mediterranean, at least as far as trade was concerned, to concentrate Britain's efforts on protecting the real heart of the imperial system.

By the 1890s, British ideas on commerce protection had advanced beyond the old "hare and hounds" theory of cruisers hunting down raiders on the sea lanes. But the British still saw no alternative to accepting the loss of much of their merchant marine to foreign flags in the panic that would follow the outbreak of war, and they counted on neutrals to bring in England's food. In May 1890 Admiral Sir George Tryon made the first concrete suggestion for a means of avoiding the panic itself in an article entitled "National Insurance: A Practical Proposal."[50] Tryon proposed that the state should pay the costs, subject to regulation, of destruction by the enemy, on the ground that the real value of the cargo destroyed was nothing in comparison to the cost of a panic. He showed that no navy could provide protection against a panic, and he demanded that the system be prepared in peacetime before the outbreak of war brought imminent danger of disaster. Tryon's proposal went to the root of the problem, for he saw, as did the French, that the real danger was not the destruction of tonnage but the accompanying economic turmoil.

Even Tryon did not appreciate the real danger of a panic, in that he apparently did not understand the link between marine insurance and the fabric of British banking. In the system of international trade as it existed in 1890 and in World War I, goods actually in transit were the property neither of the ultimate buyer nor of the seller but of the great financial houses, which discounted bills of exchange drawn against the goods and held as security both the bill of lading and the insurance against the risks of the voyage. A panic in marine insurance would not only cause a rise in prices but might trigger the collapse of the banking houses who really owned the cargoes. Marine insurance was the key to the whole complex system, for no bank that was looking for secure investments and was not interested in speculating on a rise in prices would advance money against an uninsured cargo. Unless the system could be kept functioning, there was "grave danger that the movement of British shipping would be brought to a general standstill by the outbreak of war." Even a temporary interruption held the potential for disaster, for the whole internal economy of the United Kingdom depended on a continuous, regular stream of supplies from abroad, and a paralysis of trade for only a few months would inevitably lead to serious shortages.[51]

The reception of Tryon's ideas showed how far most British naval men were from understanding the basics of commerce protection.[52] Beresford cheerfully advanced to Tryon's "demolition." "I do not believe the country would ever allow the State to interfere in a matter so entirely commercial." It would be subsidizing one class at the expense of the rest; those not affected by it "would rise as one man against it"; it would not protect sailing or slow steam tonnage; and Britain would need her fast ships for fleet auxiliaries. In a final flourish, he concluded that "the Naval Estimates form the sole and, I believe, the only effective insurance for this country in time of war."[53] A royal commission reported favorably on the idea in 1905, only to see it turned down by the timidity of a treasury committee. After years of effort by the shipowners themselves, who voluntarily created a machinery for its operation, the government finally passed the measure on the day Britain entered World War I.

THE SPENCER PROGRAM

The result of the 1893 Mediterranean scare was a new surge in British naval construction. John, Earl Spencer, and his successor as first lord of the Admiralty, George Goschen, began a program within the annual Estimates that made the Naval Defence Act look modest. Never made public, the program itself provided for completion by 1898 of seven to ten new battleships (the number depending on the actions of foreign navies), twenty to thirty cruisers, and almost 120 torpedo craft. The Estimates during the first three years of the program alone (1894–96) included eleven battleships (six *Majestic* and five *Canopus* class), ten first-class cruisers (two *Powerful* and eight *Andromeda* class), sixteen second-class cruisers of the *Talbot* and later classes, eight third-class cruisers of the *Pelorus* class, and eighty-four "torpedo-boat destroyers."

In the design of the *Majestic* class, of 15,000 tons and 18 knots with a range of 7,000 miles, the English completed the evolution begun with the *Royal Sovereign* class. The four 13.5-inch, 67-ton big guns of the earlier class were replaced by an entirely new type of 12-inch, 46-ton gun, and the secondary battery contained twelve 6-inch quick-firers instead of ten. The armor was only a fifth of the weight of the ship instead of a quarter, thanks to the Harvey process, and was spread over much of the hull in relatively thin plates in accordance with the system developed simultaneously by France and Italy for the *Dupuy de Lôme* and *Re Umberto*. The emphasis in the design was clearly on offensive power and, even more important, sturdiness and range. The big, solid, seaworthy *Majestic*s were constructed not to reinforce the Mediterranean fleet, but for the Channel Squadron.[54]

The 11,000-ton first-class cruisers of the *Andromeda* class were reduced editions of the enormous commerce protectors *Powerful* and *Terrible*. Despite their size, they and the *Powerful* class relied on heavy armored decks for protection rather than using side armor as in the *Dupuy de Lôme*. They were, however, highly seaworthy ships with great endurance. The second- and third-class cruisers, also protected by armored decks, were improved versions of the cruisers provided by the Naval Defence Act for commerce protection in European waters as well as overseas.

Perhaps the most important development in English ship design at this time was the introduction of the torpedo-boat destroyer. Just as the French were making a remarkable jump in the speed of their torpedo boats from 20 knots to 28 or 30, the British were finding their torpedo gunboats totally inadequate in their intended role as torpedo-boat catchers.

Most of England's efforts in torpedo vessel construction between 1888 and 1892 had gone into the torpedo gunboat. The first large group was the thirteen *Sharpshooter*-class vessels of 735 tons. All of these failed to make their designed 21 knots on trials, their old-style locomotive boilers were weak, their hulls were bad, and they were so slow in service that in the maneuvers of 1890, one of them was captured by the torpedo boats. The eleven ships of the *Alarm* class, ordered in 1890–91, made all of 19 knots, and the five *Dryads* begun the following year failed to make even 20.[55] The regular torpedo boats, completely neglected, were remarkable chiefly for the trouble they caused in the maneuvers.[56] The British had entirely given up the idea of having the torpedo boats accompany the fleet. Defensively,

The torpedo-aviso Leger *(1891). Like her British contemporaries, the torpedo gun-boats of the* Sharpshooter *class, she was intended as a torpedo-boat catcher but proved deficient in both speed and seakeeping abilities.*

the torpedo nets carried by large ships, in which the British had placed a great deal of stock, were also becoming less and less useful.[57]

Even the parsimonious liberal prime minister, Gladstone, was ready to admit that the British needed an answer to the French torpedo boats in the Channel. In 1892 a private firm, Yarrow, proposed plans for a ship that, instead of following the lines of the catchers, was designed as a bigger version of the French high-seas torpedo boats. The first of these destroyers, the 240-ton *Havock,* made 26.8 knots on her trials. The success of the new type was obvious, and the British soon built large numbers of this logical development of the big French torpedo boats.[58] The catchers, on the other hand, were entirely abandoned. Although England and France continued to build torpedo boats for another decade, the days of these small craft were also numbered. Destroyers soon proved capable both of hunting down torpedo boats and of executing most of the traditional torpedo-boat missions as well.

Fifteen

The Jeune Ecole in the 1890s

THE JEUNE ECOLE did not die with Aube and Charmes. The constant advances in torpedo warfare and cruiser design ensured continued interest in its ideas, within and outside the navy. More important, the association of the question of torpedo boats versus battleships with the social struggle within the navy between the older and younger officers had won the Jeune Ecole a large following on the left in Parliament and the press. This politicized Jeune Ecole focused its attention during the 1890s on France's coast defenses and on the areas in which the navy had most successfully resisted change—its arsenals and its administration.

THE SUCCESSORS TO THE JEUNE ECOLE

Although the founders of the Jeune Ecole were all gone by the early 1890s, their followers achieved considerable popularity. The most prolific were Paul Fontin (writing under the pseudonym Commandant Z), Aube's former private secretary; Lieutenant Mathieu-Jean-Marie Vignot (writing as H. Montéchant), a member of the Fiume Commission in 1884 whom Aube had placed in charge of the work at Bizerte; and Lieutenant Emile Duboc, one of the heroes of the China campaign of 1884–85 who had been passed over for promotion because he did not belong to the inner group.

These and other Jeune Ecole writers of the 1890s followed Aube's ideas to their logical conclusions. Their theory, as that of the traditionalists, focused on coast defense. For this they combined the "laws of speed and numbers," the common currency of all the battleship opponents, with Aube's idea of multiplying the number of naval bases. They proposed to split the whole Mediterranean fleet into six or eight distinct parts, since it would compel the English to navigate everywhere in force and would permit torpedo

The torpedo-boat transport Foudre *(launched in 1895). An extreme product of France's infatuation with the torpedo boat, she had a cruiser-type hull to allow her to accompany the fleet, and large gantries to handle the brood of small torpedo boats built especially for her.*

boats and cruisers to raid Britain's commerce.[1] (Bases were proposed at Toulon, Marseilles, Cette, Bizerte, Bône, Philippeville, Oran, and Algiers.) Since every blockade was likely to be broken, the blockaders would need to have in front of each port a fleet equal to the total force of the divided enemy, unless they wanted to run the risk of being crushed by the sudden combination of the enemy's forces. Thus if the French fleet were split into six portions, England would have to keep a total force six times as large.[2] "The dispersion of every combatant unit, including battleships, cruisers, scouts, and above all torpedo boats, constitutes the first defensive measure at sea, contrary to what takes place on land, where it is agreed that armies, on the defensive as well as the offensive, should only operate in masses."[3]

Under this strange new guise, the theory of scattering torpedo boats in every creek revived the essence of the English idea of the 1860s of stationing coast-defense ships like watchdogs in every port, as well as the more developed garrison battleship theory of the Germans and Italians in the 1870s. It was remarkably attractive to the deputies from the commercial ports, and the ministry was endlessly trying to quiet demands from them for just one or two torpedo boats so that the good citizens (who were also voters) could sleep in peace. In England, the theory even got mixed up with the traditional English penchant for volunteering, and writers claimed that each port should be given a couple of torpedo boats, the most delicate engines of modern naval warfare, to be manned by volunteers.[4]

The battleship, of course, was finished. Although there was relative silence about Charmes's "autonomous" torpedo boats after 1886, enthusiasts heralded every new improvement as the final doom of the giants. Even in

England, where such ideas were less popular, the appearance of the destroyer gave a final opportunity in the presubmarine period to predict the end of the battleship. No less an expert than Admiral Philip Howard Colomb made a sensational prediction in 1900 that naval warfare of the future would be between destroyers.[5]

For cruisers, the new Jeune Ecole spokesmen felt that speed was the sole quality that counted. In their concept of "shamelessly attack the weak; shamelessly fly from the strong," the purpose of speed was not to give a ship the choice of fighting, but merely to enable it to run away. The only contribution of these writers to the theory of commerce-destroying was their recognition that the rise of German commerce, which emerged as a distant but significant threat to the British during the 1890s, made raiding a possible weapon against Germany as well as England. They thus began to get around the old criticism that a policy of nothing but commerce-destroying would have no effect on a continental enemy.[6]

Their ideas on the rights of neutrals made those of Aube and Charmes look mild, especially after the Fashoda crisis of 1898 further embittered Anglo-French relations. "There are no neutrals. At least in time of war, and on the sea. Neutrals are a subtle invention of peacetime."[7] France could sink every ship in the Channel, because nineteen out of twenty would be English and the remaining one twentieth was a percentage of error too small to invalidate the theory scientifically.[8] Even the worst ideas of Aube and Charmes were revived—the *bateau-canon* became the *aviso mortier,* and as late as 1904 one hardy soul was reviving the theory of *décuirassement.*[9]

The traditionalists never understood the importance of combating such ideas by educating the public to their way of thinking. Instead, the admirals took refuge behind a wall of silence, which, reinforced by the navy's profound distrust of the army, soon formed a barrier so strong that the average Frenchman could not have penetrated it if he had wished.[10] At the very time that the Germans under Admiral Tirpitz, following the example set by the Italians in 1872, began a concerted effort to educate the public on the need for a large navy, the French officers withdrew still further into their shell. They thus moved away from the only policy that, as Grivel and Gougeard had pointed out, could save them from disaster at the hands of the amateurs.

The traditionalists never tried to woo either the press or Parliament. When the president of the republic reviewed the fleet at Villefranche, the deputies who accompanied him were allowed to look on from a liner a long way off. At the Spithead review in 1887, on the other hand, the British navy specially fitted out two large transports with abundant refreshments for members of Parliament.[11] Likewise, French naval literature never rose above a narrowly technical approach. Tirpitz's Navy League, founded in 1898, soon grew to really enormous proportions, but the French Ligue maritime et coloniale, founded a year later, remained just another organization within the little group of people already active in naval and colonial life. As late as 1914 it had only 28,000 members, and its importance in spreading the naval gospel in France was practically nil.

The fate of the French naval movement paralleled that of the colonial movement. In the 1880s, the English, French, and German colonial movements were all still limited to a relatively small group of enthusiasts. During the great imperialist movement of the 1890s, those in England and Germany expanded remarkably, but the French colonial movement signally failed to widen the base of its popular support.

The contrast between the writings of Pierre Loti and Rudyard Kipling illustrates the different approaches of the French and English to the outside world. To some extent, both men responded to the same desire to get away from Europe and the same discontent with European civilization. There was a world of difference, however, in the breadth and nature of their appeals. Kipling became an enormously popular mainstay of the British imperial movement. Loti, on the other hand, never stirred the masses, and with the exception of *Pêcheur d'Islande,* he did not write of reality at all. Popular as they were, his works never became a literature of the new colonial empire but were simply a sort of travel literature with which he calmed the restless spirits of his time.

One of the key changes in the Jeune Ecole of the 1890s was its separation from the colonial movement. The school of Aube and Charmes had arisen directly out of the necessities of colonial defense, but the Jeune Ecole of the 1890s became the property of a group of deputies who had led in bringing about the fall of the leading colonial exponent, Jules Ferry. Chief among these men were Edouard Lockroy, Camille Pelletan, and Georges Clemenceau. Their primary ideas were, first, to reduce the navy to a force for coast defense against the Triple Alliance, and, second, to save as much money as possible on the navy in order to build up the army. They wholeheartedly adopted the Jeune Ecole's slogan of coast defense at little expense, while showing scant interest in its ideas on cruiser warfare against England.[12] They also revived the movement of Lamy and Gougeard, which Aube and Charmes had completely forgotten, for more economical naval administration.

As the politicians of the Jeune Ecole went further and further to the political left, they took up more vigorously the cause of the arsenal workers, the stokers, the engineers, and the discontented officers against the old naval aristocracy. Their propaganda took on a more and more personal tone against the navy's leadership. The "monarchist and religious ceremonies" on board French men-of-war and the haughty airs of the more prominent officers moved the left to veritable frenzies, as did the navy's association with the new French alliance with autocratic Russia. When Admiral Louis-Henri Brown de Colstoun gave a ball on his flagship at Saint-Malo and neglected to invite a prominent family of the local bourgeoisie, he gave the left a splendid opportunity to review all of the errors that the admirals had ever made. The accidents that were bound to occur with the delicate, complex machinery of the day also provided numerous occasions for criticism; Lockroy, for one, published a list of all the fatal accidents on French warships since the beginning of the ironclad fleet. The left also vigorously attacked the practice of carrying chaplains on French men-of-war at a time when the republic was trying to laicize French society. When Admiral Jules-Marie-Armand, count de Cavelier de Cuverville, was unfortunate enough to visit a missionary bishop, the whole left press demanded that he be relieved of his command.

The most famous exploit of the left against the navy was the theft of some documents from the Ministry of Marine by hired spies of Clemenceau. The documents revealed a shortage of wine and olive oil at Toulon and the stealing of twenty sacks of flour by an employee of the commissary department there. At the end of a long series of articles in *La Justice* sensationalizing this *affaire du blé,* Clemenceau came to the astonishing conclusion—in the year when French mobilization was the most efficient in Europe—that the French fleet would not be able to put to sea in case of war. This press agitation in France was contemporary with the agitation in England that led to the Spencer Program of 1893, but while the English, under the influence of the American prophet of sea power, Alfred Thayer Mahan, were becoming more and more concerned with questions of general naval strategy, the Clemenceau-Pelletan group was dragging the navy into a mucky mass of petty scandals in order to gain political advantage for their faction.

The *affaire du blé* was largely responsible for the calling of a great parliamentary investigation of the navy, the Commission extra-parlementaire de la Marine, whose hearings ran from 1894 to 1897. To a large extent, they simply produced a voluminous indictment of all the navy's sins while the left press, notably *La Justice* and the *Lanterne* of Toulouse, beat the war drums from the sidelines. The Extra-Parliamentary Commission made a full investigation of the *affaire du blé* and produced a special report on the defects of the *Magenta* (although it would have been much more to the point to examine the defects in the navy's organization, which had taken fourteen years to produce such a monstrosity). The poor condition of the 35-meter torpedo boats at Toulon, many of which the maritime prefect there had wisely decided to quit patching up, was also blamed on the traditionalists.

For their part, the navy's chiefs did little to add to the enlightenment of the commission. Some, notably Admiral Gervais, then chief of the Naval Staff, and Admiral Charles-Edouard, Count de la Jaille, testified as grand seigneurs dealing with a group of importunate petty tradesmen. Others, like the engineers of the Génie maritime at Toulon, spent all their time blaming one another. One of the leading members of the commission, Charles Cabart-Danneville, publicly stated that Gervais and his staff were doing everything in their power to block the investigation. One reason for the popularity among the deputies of another admiral, François-Ernest Fournier, was the simple fact that he was one of the few higher officers who attempted to get on with them. Gervais's accusation that Fournier was trying to play the role of a naval Boulanger just because he retained cordial social relations with the deputies and the press is a clear indictment of the attitude of most of the aristocratic officers.

The Jeune Ecole, with its new emphasis on coast defense and economy, soon completely conquered the Chamber of Deputies. During most of the 1890s, each year's discussion of the naval budget, like the parliamentary investigation, became the occasion for a sanguinary struggle between the minister and the admirals on the one hand and the Budget Committee and the Chamber on the other.

COAST DEFENSE

The most confused battle of all was waged over coast defense. There was, first of all, a fight between the Budget Committee and the ministry over the howls of the Channel merchants who wanted to scatter torpedo boats one or two to a port. The differences on this subject were so great that in 1891 the Chamber had to set up a special committee to work out a compromise.[13] Even the parliamentarians, however, soon came to accept the contention that little groups of torpedo boats would be, as the English boasted, mopped up in forty-eight hours by cruisers and destroyers.[14]

The main fight was between the army and the navy. Since time immemorial, one of the chief efforts of the navy had been to obtain control of coast defense from the army, and the attempt of Gougeard during his ministry in 1881 was only the latest of many. In 1884 the Conseil des Travaux took up the cause and produced the proposals that were the basis of Aube's effort to get coast defense away from General Boulanger.[15] Aube was not merely turned down. In the general reorganization of the army in 1888, the old joint commission of five naval and five army officers that had controlled coast defense was discontinued, and all of the coast defenses were taken over by the army's Superior Council. With the navy no longer represented, the army proceeded to a great purge of coastal fortifications. In one session the council closed no less than 320 batteries and forts, and whenever part of the army budget had to go, the coastal batteries felt the axe. In 1893 the army gave up a million and a half francs and in 1894 nearly a million that were to have been devoted to coastal fortifications.[16]

This change was sound enough militarily. Most of the razed fortifications were in small towns or on islands, and the important points along the coast were not seriously affected. The Jeune Ecole predictably demanded the reestablishment of the coastal batteries at each fishing hamlet; Cabart-Danneville even made a moving plea on behalf of the peasants who would be afraid to work in the fields along the coasts.[17] More important, this wholesale destruction of the old coastal works, just at the time that the Jeune Ecole was advocating the ruthless use of coastal bombardments against Italy, was one of the factors that aroused fears that Italy might respond in kind and tied the French fleet to the defense of its own coasts.[18]

The real trouble with French coast defenses was in their organization and manning. There was no lack of guns; France had over 3,000 at various points along the coast, including 360 at Cherbourg alone. The problem was an unhappy compromise arrived at in 1890 to resolve the conflict for authority between the navy and the army. As in the eighteenth century, all guns that pointed toward the interior of a port belonged to the navy, while those firing away from it were the army's. A single battery of six guns might contain three different calibers of guns under two different authorities. A naval gun, manned by the navy, would fire on one side of an imaginary line at a target, while the gun next to it, an army gun with different personnel, munitions, and firing techniques, was shooting on the other side of the mythical line.[19] The army was in charge of the general coast-defense organization outside the ports, but at the moment of mobilization the maritime prefect became supreme commander of all coast defenses in his arrondissement—over army troops whose organization he had not controlled and under the orders of the minister of war, not the minister of marine. In this remarkable arrangement, the prefect did not know either his new subordinates or his new chief.[20] At the same time, the general who controlled the coastal works under the prefect was given command of the torpedo boats stationed in the commercial ports. Thus, on mobilization, the prefect would hand over his torpedo boats to the general, who was at the same time passing under his command, while the prefect was becoming responsible to the Ministry of War. The general became an admiral and the admiral a general.

The garrisons of the naval ports were furnished, in time of peace, by the Naval Infantry, which was being bled white in colonial service. In time of war, these troops would become the army's Twentieth Corps and would be replaced in the coastal batteries by territorials. The ports would thus be nearly denuded of troops until the territorials could get there, while the territorial gunners were completely unused to hitting a moving object and were generally unable to tell a battleship from an ocean liner, let alone a French man-of-war from an English or Italian one. In 1900, when the territorials were actually tested, they spent most of their time blazing away at fishing boats or at friendly ships.[21]

The whole problem, which became a pitched battle between the army and the navy, was complicated by the navy's having more reservists than it needed in wartime. In 1891 Lockroy estimated that the number of *inscrits maritimes* aged between eighteen and fifty was around 100,000, with another 25,000 men available to the navy in the active and reserve volunteer forces. He estimated that no more than 50,000 men would be needed to man all the ships and forts that the navy possessed. Although Lockroy's estimates were pessimistic, at least 40,000 *inscrits* had no definite function in time of war, while the army required around 30,000 men to man the coastal forts.[22]

Lockroy's 1891 proposal to give all the extra *inscrits* to the army met with violent opposition from the naval men. The navy and the Jeune Ecole enthusiastically supported the countersuggestion of giving the coastal forts to the navy.[23] The army violently attacked this idea, charging that all the navy wanted was a place to settle worn-out officers.[24] In his counteroffensive, the minister of war now demanded the extra *inscrits* as categorically as Aube had demanded the coastal forts.[25] Through the 1890s the matter was left unresolved, with each service muttering at the other.

The result was that French coast defenses remained woefully unready. In March 1898, at the peak of a crisis with England over access to the navigable portion of the Niger River and four months before the start of the much larger Fashoda crisis, the French hurriedly tested the manning of the coastal forts. They found that at Brest no more than 1,500 untrained men of the 5,520 that were required were ready.[26] The secret tests, whose results were later publicly revealed by Lockroy, also showed that the territorials would arrive only five to ten days after mobilization and that the troops in the ports at the outbreak of war would be able to man only a third of the guns. The army had completely abandoned some islands that the British might be able to use as advance bases for a blockade, and the island of Ouessant, the old English base near Brest, was garrisoned by only 60 pensioners and 55 *inscrits*.[27]

There was special concern over Cherbourg, which was not only uncomfortably close to England but also within range of the German fleet. There was a great clamor over the Cherbourg defenses at the time of the opening of the Kiel Canal in June 1895, even though the situation there was later found to be not as bad as at Brest. There was clearly no way to protect the arsenal from bombardment, but the prospect of leaving the growing German navy completely unopposed in the Channel raised fears that the Germans would attempt to land an army corps to take the place in the rear. The port was at the end of the Cotentin peninsula, with rugged topography reminiscent of Corsica, and the navy feared that "it would be as easy to separate Contentin from France as Gibraltar from Spain."[28] The army boasted that its mobile troops would "emerge from the soil . . . and throw the enemy back into the sea," but these troops would not be concentrated at Rennes until twenty-two days after the outbreak of the war and there was only a single-track railway from Caen to Cherbourg for their transportation.[29] French fears of a sudden German attack on Cherbourg (which dated back to 1814) were not entirely without foundation. At the Kiel ceremonies and elsewhere, German naval officers talked about the project rather freely, and Tirpitz planned a torpedo-boat attack at the outbreak of a war. It is hard to see, however, how the German navy could have obtained an army corps for a landing.

The general rise of the German navy was responsible for a number of important changes in French strategic dispositions. It began a shift to the north, from the Mediterranean to the Channel. In the Channel itself, Cherbourg, which was too open, lost much of its importance. Dunkirk, an ideal torpedo and cruiser station behind its sandbanks, became the advance base and defensive center against Germany, while Brest was the natural point of concentration for both cruisers and the Channel Squadron against England.[30] The result was that Brest increased greatly in importance, becoming the main port in the north; Cherbourg stagnated; and Dunkirk, entirely new, became an important secondary point. This is illustrated by the coal supplies in each port in 1896: Cherbourg had only 29,000 tons, while Brest's 50,000 tons was nearly equal to Toulon's 54,000.[31]

In 1892, after a sensational reversal by the Jeune Ecole of its earlier slogan of "torpedo boats, not dikes," the deputies revived in various private bills the proposals for port improvements that had originally been offered by Gougeard in 1881 and had been in committee ever since.[32] Work was started on a vast project at Brest that was as important as that at Bizerte. Gougeard's plan called for nothing less than the closing of the long channel leading to the port by erecting a dike over a mile in length, giving a completely defended anchorage in which, as in the lake at Bizerte, a blockaded fleet could practice squadron evolutions. With the construction of a whole series of coaling piers for the rapid refueling of cruisers and large additions to the arsenal itself, Brest was undergoing a complete transformation. Nevertheless, the Fashoda crisis of 1898 caught the navy with the works still incomplete, and in its coast defenses, mobilization, coastal forts, offshore islands, and harbor works, the French Navy's state of preparation to meet the danger of war "was practically nil."[33]

Bizerte, officially opened on 4 June 1895 as a reply to the opening of the Kiel Canal, was still practically undefended three years later during the Fashoda crisis. The guns had been kept waiting at Bône in Algeria until the summer of 1897, after the conclusion of a treaty that resolved the conflicting claims of France and Italy over Tunis. In the meantime, there was a long fight with the army over the defenses, which was still raging when the crisis broke. The original army plans called for defending the port "largely" with sixteen guns, of which none was larger than 10-inch. In contrast, the Italians had 101 heavy guns at Maddalena and England over 100 at Malta. During the Fashoda crisis there were probably about a dozen guns actually in position, served by army officers who sent posthaste to Paris for all the naval men they could get, since none of them could tell the difference between a French ship and a British one.[34]

In 1898 there were still no docks or stores at Bizerte because the navy naturally refused to leave them there for the British to take. Even the harbor works proved insufficient. A strong current in the channel created grave danger in night navigation.[35] The near success of the Americans in scuttling a ship across the channel at Santiago showed the danger of Bizerte's being blocked by a *coup de main*. A bridge that had foolishly been put across the canal near its entrance offered another splendid means of blocking the port. The canal was also too narrow, and the arsenal and the nearby city of Ferryville were still to be created.[36]

Corsica, the middle point in the French line of bases against Italy, had no harbors fitted for a naval base. In spite of the complaints of the Jeune Ecole, nothing was attempted but the fortification of Ajaccio as a temporary coaling point and the establishment of a torpedo station at Bonifacio. This latter station was in a good position but was too small, and the good harbor of Porto-Vecchio, which Lockroy and the Jeune Ecole hoped to make a base, was on the wrong side of the island and could be isolated by forces at Maddalena and Spezia. In fortifying Maddalena, the Italians had chosen the one spot in the whole region to which the French could make no adequate reply.[37]

DEFENSES OUTSIDE EUROPE

In these years, nobody cared whether the colonies were defended or not. The so-called systems of colonial defense that followed one another with each change in government were designed primarily to save money. These usually gave two or three authorities a voice in colonial defense, although generally the navy was made responsible for it while the bills were paid from the colonial budget.

The actual work of colonial defense was done by the Naval Infantry, which by now was an army with as many officers as the fleet had line officers. The Naval Infantry was the one service within the Ministry of Marine that had not attained autonomy and control over its own personnel. Since the colonial office paid its expenses, it had very few higher officers. In 1894 a sudden economy move suppressed two of the three generals in Tonkin, and the remaining one found himself in charge of the defense of a territory as big as France, Belgium, and Italy with a command including 26,000 men plus a native militia.[38]

The main trouble with the Naval Infantry was not so much the lack of troops as the complete absence of any general plan. The corps had grown with the colonies—a company here, a battery there—without any system of railways, fortifications, or points of concentration. Like the American army of its day, it was a fairly large force scattered in little posts over a wide area, fairly efficient in putting down the natives, but nearly useless for anything else.[39]

While neglecting colonial defense, the Jeune Ecole continued to look on

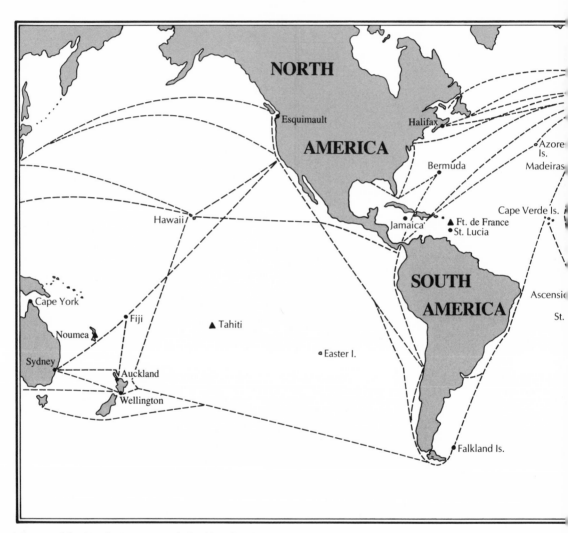

The World—Trade Routes and Coaling Stations

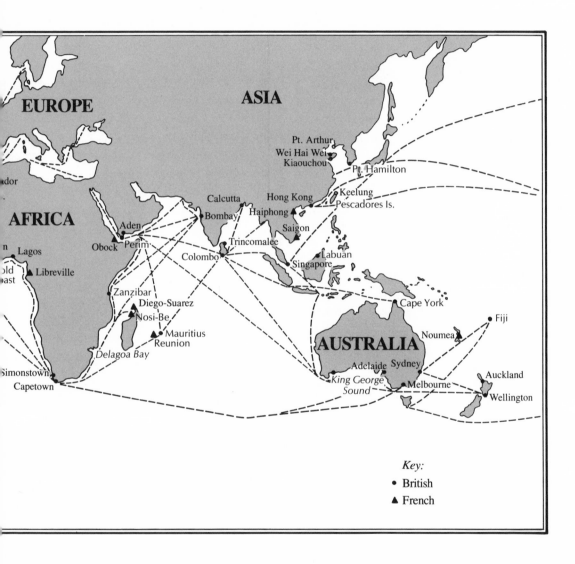

EUROPE

ASIA

AFRICA

AUSTRALIA

Pt. Arthur
Wei Hai Wei
Kiaouchou
Pt. Hamilton
Calcutta
Hong Kong
Keelung
Pescadores Is.
Bombay
Haiphong
Aden
Saigon
Obock
Perim
Trincomalee
Labuan
Lagos
Colombo
Singapore
Libreville
Zanzibar
Diego-Suarez
Nosi-Be
Cape York
Mauritius
Reunion
Fiji
Noumea
Delagoa Bay
Simonstown
Adelaide
Sydney
Capetown
King George Sound
Melbourne
Auckland
Wellington

Key:

● British

▲ French

every tropical island as a potential coaling station or even a "new Gibraltar," though with less enthusiasm than in the 1880s. In a major discussion of the issue in 1890, which produced no results whatever, no less than fifteen different points were at one time or another selected as coaling stations. The question of France's undeveloped foothold on the Red Sea, Obock, and of the alternative position across the Bab-el-Mandeb straits, Shaykh Said, came up again during the Italian expedition to Ethiopia in the mid-1890s and during a dispute with Turkey in 1901.[40] Easter Island, Tubuai, and the rest of the route across the Pacific were kept in mind, although it was not wise to talk about Panama after a great financial scandal in 1892 over investments in the canal project there tarred many politicians. At the time of the Fashoda crisis in 1898, someone had the bright idea of getting a coaling station at Muscat at the entrance to the Persian Gulf, where France had no interests whatever.[41] The state of mind of the French was the same as that of the Russians when they were figuring out how to despoil the British in 1900—one got out a map, looked for likely islands, sent a cruiser there, and presto! a naval base.

One result of this casual policy was that France squandered some real opportunities in China. The Pescadores, which the French had briefly occupied in 1885, slipped away with Formosa to the Japanese in the negotiations following the Sino-Japanese War in 1895. France was too late in making her demand that Japan return the islands to China—the great European powers had already forced Japan to give up most of her other conquests and could not decently ask for more. The most France could get was a promise that the islands would not be fortified or ceded by Japan to any other European power.[42]

Two years later, when the powers scrambled for bases on the China coast, the French had nothing staked out and came out almost as empty-handed as the Italians (who got nothing). The island of Hainan, which had looked like a likely point, turned out to have no harbors at all, and Admiral Jean-Olivier de La Bonninière, count de Beaumont, whose orders could accurately be summarized as "take anything, but take it quickly," reluctantly settled for the nearby port of Kwangchow. A thorough examination of the spot in 1899 showed that both as a naval port and as an entrance to the interior of China, it was inferior to Haiphong, which the French already possessed. (The British did no better at Wei Hai Wei in the north, but the Germans converted their position at Kiaochow into a useful base.)[43]

The French neglected the defenses of the tropical islands and other bases that they already had until the dispute with England over the Niger River triggered a general awakening. Toward the end of 1897, the ministry issued a general manual for the defense and organization of coaling stations.[44] General Borgnis-Desbordes, sent out on a hurried mission to examine them, found that after a decade of complete neglect, defenses were wholly lacking. Saigon in Indochina, which was fairly easily defended due to its location on a river, was the French Navy's sole usable base of operations outside France. Its shops could make engine repairs and it had five dry docks, although none of these was big enough for a first-class cruiser.[45] Saigon had only five antiquated torpedo boats, left there in 1885 after Courbet's campaign in China.

In Madagascar, Diégo-Suarez possessed nothing but a barracks, a coal supply, and a hospital, all left over from France's 1885 expedition to the island. It had no dock, and its port was defended by only a dozen 5.5-inch Model 1870 guns.[46] The army expedition that completed the conquest of the island in 1895 was perhaps the worst-managed colonial affair France ever conducted.[47] The French only began construction of adequate defenses at Diégo-Suarez in 1898 at the time of the Fashoda crisis.[48]

Dakar, which like Brest had been ignored by the advocates of Tunis, Tonkin, and Madagascar, was defended by sixteen 9.4-inch guns (four Model 1870 and twelve Model 1864) and had no dry dock, repair shop, or even an enclosed anchorage.[49] Construction of jetties and dry docks there began in 1899.[50] Fort de France in Martinique, which was to be a major base in spite of the difficulty of defending so small an island, had France's only dry dock outside of France that was able to take a first-class cruiser, but was otherwise undefended. A fine plan for its defense, which included three forts that had not even been begun in 1897, was abandoned after the terrible eruption of the volcano of Mount Pelée in 1902.[51] In general, the efforts begun in 1897 to make up lost ground came far too late, and during the Fashoda crisis of 1898 the French Navy did not possess a single modern coaling station.

Even if France had had some coaling stations overseas, there would have been no ships to use them. As a matter of deliberate policy, the French had done almost nothing to provide new ships for the old station fleet. In 1891, the Chamber vigorously protested any policy that would catch good ships away from home in case of war.[52] The new cruisers, built for scouting in the Mediterranean, were all too small to be sent to foreign stations. In 1898 the Far East station had two old station battleships, one newer armored cruiser, and three second-class cruisers. There was not a single modern cruiser on any other foreign station.[53]

Organizational Reforms

The haphazard state of French maritime defenses resulted in part from an unsatisfactory relationship between the navy and Parliament. Despite all the polemics, the main feature of this relationship was apathy, at least on the part of the politicians. Most deputies showed little interest in the navy unless it could be used against their political enemies. Though the naval budget never passed through the Chamber so fast that the minister did not have time to reach his seat (as happened in 1937), the annual budget discussions were stuck into the schedule wherever there was room left over. Although

The first-class protected cruiser D'Entrecasteaux *(1896). She was one of the few cruisers ordered for service on the foreign stations during the 1890s.*

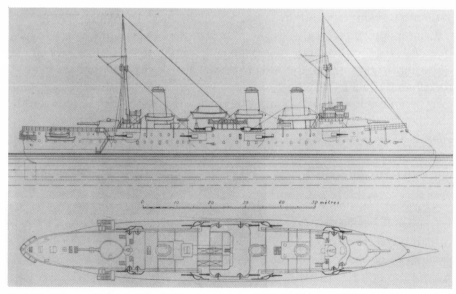

A contemporary plan of the D'Entrecasteaux. *This 8,000-ton, 19-knot ship carried two 9.4-inch and twelve 5.5-inch guns and was protected by a 3.3-inch-thick armored deck at the waterline.*

there were a couple of pretty fair debates, the discussions were generally sterile. Typically there were two or three speeches by leading members of the Jeune Ecole calling attention to all the sins of the admirals, and then someone submitted an amendment to raise the pay of the arsenal workers. Each of the port deputies put in a few words, the amendment was voted down, and the Chamber passed the budget as reported out by the Budget Committee and went on to other matters. In 1893 the report of the Budget Committee contained a number of errors, but the minister did not reply, since the cabinet was anxious to get the whole budget through and told him to be quiet.[54]

Although the navy maintained detailed financial accounts, these were of little practical use to the deputies. The navy generally put together the budget nearly a year before the start of the financial year and published the accounts of the money actually spent as much as three years after the year's end. The accounts for 1879 were distributed before the Easter recess in 1883, six months after the minister responsible for them had died.[55] The delays made little difference, for in spite of the constant demands of the Budget Committee, the navy did nothing to make either its budget or its accounts intelligible. The department claimed, with some truth, that it would have to modify the whole naval organization to make them clear. In effect, throughout the 1890s the navy withdrew behind a bulwark of figures and defied every effort of the deputies to drag its affairs to light.[56]

The response of Parliament was to subdivide the navy's budget. True Parliamentary control of expenses in France was relatively recent. Until 1831 the legislature had voted only on the total expenditures of the government and each of its departments, without having any control over the contents of the budgets. The division of departmental budgets into chapters subject to parliamentary scrutiny began in 1831, was abolished by Napoleon III in 1851, and was reestablished only in 1869. In the face of the obstinate refusal of the navy to establish clear accounts, Parliament demanded increased subdivision of the budget. In 1881 the navy budget contained eighteen sections, in 1887 it had forty, and in 1905 it had sixty-three.[57] One of the Budget Committee reporters explained that "it is a truth of an elementary sort that the possibility of control by Parliament is measured by the numbers of chapters the budget contains. The more tightly the minister is bound by numerous specialized chapters, the more he is held accountable for his acts."[58]

Unfortunately, the remedy only aggravated the disease. For the school system or the postal service, which had a small number of standard types of expenses, extensive budget subdivision worked fairly well. But the French Navy was an increasingly complex industrial system, and more important, it was unable to estimate expenses in the way Parliament wanted as long as its archaic organization remained unchanged. Due to the arbitrary separation of personnel from matériel and labor from raw materials in French accounts, expenditures for a battleship were never totaled but were entered under five or six different headings: naval construction—personnel, naval construction—matériel, artillery—personnel, artillery—matériel, and so forth. The parliamentary budget reformers left this basic structure intact and simply added more chapters within each of these groups. As early as 1882, there were four chapters devoted to salaries under the single heading of naval construction. Personnel expenses were divided so that the port deputies could be sure that the navy was not cheating the arsenal workers, and new subdivisions in the matériel divisions enabled the Jeune Ecole to ensure that the traditionalists were spending enough on the torpedo service.[59] The deputies could tell to a centime whether the workers in their ports were getting their share of the booty, but no one knew (or cared) whether a French battleship cost half or twice as much as an English one.

No matter how hard they tried, the ministers could not present really accurate estimates in their budgets. Yet once passed by the legislature, the estimates for each chapter became legally binding. Thus, if the expenses for a particular chapter happened to be under the budget estimate, the ministry had to spend the money somehow in order to get any at all the next year. Ministerial dispatches of 1883 stated:

> The justifications that the department will henceforth have to furnish when presenting the budget make it absolutely necessary that the estimates of the preceding year be punctually fulfilled.
> Out of a total credit of 9,700,000 francs, the directors of hydraulic works in the naval ports still have available, for the year 1883, two million. This situation is profoundly regrettable and, to attenuate it to a certain degree, I asked you in my dispatch of yesterday to undertake immediately various projects to be paid for under the present year's budget.[60]

On the other hand, when the estimates were too low, the navy was forced to come to the Chamber for special credits, which further angered the deputies. Money could not be transferred between chapters, and the navy often found itself throwing away money to use up funds in some chapters while begging for additional funds for others.

The crowning absurdity came when the Chamber attempted to keep the navy from using too much of its supplies. Etienne Lamy's criticism in the 1879 budget report that the navy's personnel was eating up its matériel led the Chamber to take to its bosom that wonderful organization, the fictitious general magazine. The process began in 1887, when Parliament established both maximum and minimum limits for coal supplies in order to prevent the admirals from secretly stocking up on coal by not navigating enough or burning it without confessing to the Chamber. After a long period of development, the Chamber on 13 April 1898 founded a remarkable system consisting of *crédits-matières* and *crédits-achats*. The *crédit-achat* was the amount of money given to the general magazine to expend for supplies. An exactly equal amount of *crédits-matières* was given to the various departments to be used for drawing supplies from the magazine. Parliament thus converted one of the ministry's more absurd accounting devices into another legal barrier against waste by the admirals and naval constructors.[61]

The trouble was not so much the complexity of the budgetary system, the inexperience of the deputies, or even their interest more in the salaries of the arsenal workers than in the good of the navy. It was the ineradicable distrust on both sides. In spite of the advantages of allowing the naval constructors to keep their own accounts, the Chamber decided to retain a special corps of accountants because of "the utility of a contradiction between the directors and an organ representing more especially the financial interests."[62] The Chamber was just like the mistress of a bourgeois household who kept the accounts and discussed the menu and prices with the cook every morning.

Within the arsenals, organizational complexity continued to grow in the absence of true reforms. Responsibility under the maritime prefect for ship construction continued to be divided between two main commissaries, one for personnel and labor and one for matériel. The Extra-Parliamentary Commission distinctly opposed any change in this arrangement because it saw competing responsibilities as a safeguard. In the meantime, the navy had created a separate torpedo service, and most of its other services had achieved substantial autonomy. As a result, Toulon consisted of not one arsenal but four: one for naval construction, one for torpedoes, one for naval works, and one for artillery. Each had its own personnel, its little submagazine, and even its own repair shops. Critics complained that it had never occurred to anyone in the navy that a gun mounting and a torpedo might be repaired in the same shop with one machine.[63] Red tape was also growing as a result of the Chamber's demands on the accounting system, and in the middle 1890s the administrative services of the arsenals alone employed 8 admirals, 21 captains, 66 commanders, 110 lieutenants, 236 commissary officers, 542 commissary subalterns, and a little army of over 3,000 clerks and guards.[64] There was even a special corps of 432 firemen, although the risk of fire had declined with the replacement of wooden ships by steel ones. The regulation firemen stood solemn guard on the steel-hulled battleship *Magenta* throughout the thirteen years she was under construction.[65] In Germany, each admiral's staff consisted of a captain and four or five lieutenants, and if there was a fire they called the city fire department.[66]

Much of the machinery acquired in the late 1870s was wearing out in the late 1890s, and this compounded the problems in the arsenals. At a time when the English were replacing practically the entire industrial plant in their dockyards, the Budget Committee consistently refused to invest in new equipment.

Even the unduly cheap supply of labor that the arsenals had enjoyed was disappearing. The syndicalist movement, with its demands for shorter hours, higher pay, and the exclusion of all outside labor, began in the arsenals with the organization of a workers' committee at Brest in 1892. Six years later, the minister of marine recognized a union at Toulon. The pressure of the workers on the port deputies became even heavier, and when the minister tried to discharge 4,500 extra workers taken on during the conflict with the Boxers in China in 1900, the Chamber forced him to transfer contracts from private firms to the arsenals to keep them employed. Both workers and constructors refused to have anything to do with piecework, and it would have been impossible to adopt the English flexible hiring system, due not only to the unions but to the lack of sufficient trained workers in France. Indeed, the only means that the navy had of ensuring an adequate labor supply in wartime was to enroll most of its labor permanently in time of peace. Workers in the shipbuilding trade had been removed from the *Inscription maritime* in 1866, and there was no other way to keep them away from the army chiefs in an emergency.[67]

The net effect of these factors—poorer machinery, the workers' demands for higher wages and shorter hours, their political influence, and the large number of them kept permanently employed—was that the individual worker in French dockyards produced much less than his more highly paid English competitor. In 1892, 19,000 English workers turned out 33 million francs' worth of work, while 21,000 French workers were employed on only 18 million francs' worth of construction.[68]

The number of arsenals was also a problem. Germany was contented with two major bases and England with three, but France continued to keep all five of its naval ports in full operation. When the Extra-Parliamentary Commission looked at the less productive ports of Rochefort and Lorient, the port deputies worked hand in glove with the admirals who happened to be stationed there at the time to protect them. (Indeed, the admirals outdid even the local deputies in their efforts.)[69] As a result, the commission pronounced for the retention of Lorient as a full military port and for the deepening of its channel as a cruiser base.

Rochefort, which Gougeard in 1881 had given up as hopeless, also made a remarkable comeback. The maritime prefect there in 1889, Admiral Adrien-Barthélémy-Louis Rieunier, submitted a great project for the deepening of the Charente River, which led to the port. The Rochefort deputies made him minister of marine in 1893 to put through the preliminary studies, and he was then selected deputy on the sole platform of bringing home the bacon to Rochefort. The Extra-Parliamentary Commission approved his plan, which led to not only the appropriation of 6 million francs for a third new port (while the works at Brest, Bizerte, Dunkirk, and all the coaling stations were still incomplete) but also the retention of all the arsenal staff and administrative machinery. Indeed, the strategic position of Rochefort was excellent as the first point of refuge for a fleet coming toward the Channel from the Mediterranean and as a cruiser base. The retention of a whole staff of administrators, however, was just another expensive victory of the deputies over the navy.[70]

These were the really fertile years of reform and counterreform in the central administration in Paris. Edouard Lockroy, a particularly capable deputy from the left who became minister in 1896, continued the tradition begun by Aube ten years earlier of throwing out most of the naval staff and department heads. He made a torpedo specialist, Admiral Eugene-Charles Chauvin, his chief of staff; gave the Service of Accounts to one of Aube's intimates, Louis-Charles-Jean-Baptiste Châtelain; and turned over the naval library to Aube's former personal secretary and an avid Jeune Ecole publicist, Paul Fontin. He also made the entirely logical move of replacing the old administrative distinction between personnel and matériel by one separating the fleet under construction from the fleet already built. His successor, Admiral Armand-Louis-Charles-Gustave Besnard, returned things to the status quo of 1894 and suspended a number of officers who had supported Lockroy. Fontin even received a visit from the police.[71] Lockroy's return in 1898 meant a new shuffle of the same sort, since "it was in the rules of the game."[72]

In the confusion, the autonomous technical services generally went their several ways. The most interesting part of the discussion of the problem of the central services in the Extra-Parliamentary Commission was the ferocity with which the head of the Naval Artillery and the chief of the special torpedo branch defended their independence. A special commission for purchases set up in Paris did good work, compensating for the lack of a true purchasing division, but all the separate little purchasing departments in the ports continued to buy small items. It was easier to order a new battleship at Paris than a peck of beans for the commissary department at Brest, but at least all the administrative officials continued to enjoy their usual functions.[73] Taking into account all the navy's administrative organizations, including the central administration, the arsenals, and the *Inscription,* the Budget Committee of 1902 estimated that 33 percent of the French naval budget went into general expenses, compared with 26 percent in Italy, 22 percent in England, and 14 percent in Germany.[74]

The 1890s were also good years for special councils and commissions, thanks to the "irresistible penchant" of the French Navy for such bodies.[75] They flourished, not only in the ministry, but also in the arsenals and even in the fleet. The Conseil des Travaux continued to deliberate on ship designs. While it had created successes like the *Dupuy de Lôme* and failures like the *Magenta,* these ships had been designed by committee, and it was therefore impossible to fix credit or blame on any one individual. The Superior Council was responsible for the general strategic policy of the navy. The successor to the Council of Admiralty, it was frequently reformed by adding or subtracting a pair of admirals, and its decisions sometimes reflected a lack of consistency. For example, in January 1898, during the dispute over the Niger River, the Council deliberated what became the Program of 1898—France's third naval program in four years. They included in it, among other things, twelve armored cruisers.

> Why twelve? The minutes of the meeting are silent as to the reasons for this conclusion. Some months later . . . at another meeting, held for quite another purpose, a member observed that the number of armored cruisers seemed to him insufficient, especially in view of the exigencies of our colonial policy, and he proposed to increase the number to twenty-four. After a confused discussion, the Council pronounced for eighteen. No serious argument was advanced for that number any more than for the others.[76]

Little was accomplished in the way of planning for war. The Naval General Staff was entirely occupied with the details of mobilization and collection of information. Lockroy had the idea of separating it from the multitude of technical burdens that fell to it owing to its position within the cabinet of the minister, but he did not know how to implement the idea and nothing came of it. As a result, the development of a general plan of operations was always left to the discretion of the commander on the spot. The ministry had no plan for a war with England when the Fashoda crisis broke out in 1898.[77] The best the minister could do was to give the Mediterranean Fleet commander the general order "Take your whole squadron and cruise off Algiers."[78] In 1903, as the Russo-Japanese War approached, the commander of the China Station, Admiral Eugène-Albert Maréchal, cabled that he was without instructions except those given to his predecessor in 1900. He added that he was expecting his recall at any time and that the second in command was in such poor health that he would be unable to take charge.[79]

MARITIME INDUSTRIES

In the eleven years between 1891 and 1901, British public and private shipyards launched thirty-five battleships, all but three of which displaced over 13,000 tons. In the same years, France launched eleven, none of which was as big as 13,000 tons. Thanks largely to the strength of English industry and finance, the Admiralty was able in the 1890s to reestablish a crushing superiority over France in battleships, a superiority that Britain never again lost.

English industry was still a little behind when the *Royal Sovereign*–class battleships were begun in 1889. The ships were equipped with old-style

The British battleship Hannibal *(1896), of the* Majestic *class. This nine-ship class reestablished England's undisputed supremacy at sea.*

13.5-inch guns and compound armor because the English could not wait for the technical men to catch up. In the next big class, the *Majestics*, begun in 1893, the full force of English industry and of the navy's admirable organization came into play. At a time when French yards had to sign on skilled men full time to be sure of having them when needed, a single British shipbuilding region, the Clyde, disposed of 200,000 to 300,000 men in the shipbuilding trades who moved from plant to plant doing piecework, certain of finding the kind of work in which each specialized.[80] British efficiency also improved. The French *Redoutable* and *Duperré,* built in about five years during the 1870s, had cost about the same in time and money as contemporary British ships. The *Majestics*, built when Childers's dockyard organization really began to be put to use, were completed on the average in two years, at prices about 30 to 40 percent less than the best French prices.

Ironically, the Admiralty's success was due in part to the success of the French arms combine and some big German firms in entering the international arms trade in the late 1880s and breaking a monopoly that the British arms companies had enjoyed for years. The British firms thus became more dependent on government orders just at the time the Naval Defence Act was signed. Then came the collapse of the merchant shipbuilding boom, during which many of the older British merchant ships dating from the 1860s had been replaced with new ones during the early 1890s. Competition for foreign orders became still more intense during the 1890s. Even the

Italians became a factor, as the Italian government made strenuous efforts in the later 1890s to win foreign orders for an arms industry that was clearly ailing (Schwarzkopf's torpedo factory at Venice was closed and for sale and Armstrong's gun works at Pozzuoli was completely deserted). The leading Italian firms merged into two combines, led by Orlando and Ansaldo, and won a number of orders.[81]

The Admiralty was thus buying in an unusually favorable market, and it took full advantage of the cutthroat competition between the shipbuilders. The government held the shipbuilders in a vise; there was no merchant shipbuilding, and the prerequisite for success abroad was Admiralty orders as proof of competence. The smaller companies could either take Admiralty orders at disastrous prices or leave them. Six of the oldest firms in the islands went to the wall, not from lack of Admiralty orders but from too many contracts at cutthroat prices.[82] Around 1900, these financial conditions inevitably resulted in the combination of many of the larger firms into an arms trust, which took its turn at milking the Admiralty in the decade before World War I.[83] For the moment, however, the Admiralty was both enjoying the full benefits of an efficient organization and using a particularly favorable price situation for all it was worth.

The formation of a French arms syndicate in 1886 to enter the international arms trade was also a turning point for the French Navy, but in the opposite direction from the English. In the 1890s the Chamber of Deputies delivered the navy and its constructors into the hands of the most pitiless arms ring in Europe.[84] Responsibility for the navy's plight lay not with the conservatives, but with the liberal republicans like Thiers, Lamy, Gougeard, Aube, the Extra-Parliamentary Commission of 1894, and the liberal majority in the Chamber. Beginning with the Parliamentary Mixed Commission of 1879, which suppressed the gun foundry at Nevers without even looking at it, everything went in the direction of the private firms. Admiral Jauréguiberry, the minister of marine who put the commission's recommendation into effect, became a year later one of the directors of the Forges et Chantiers de la Méditerranée and got an order for the parts for three hundred naval guns at 15 percent more than the government had paid at Nevers.[85]

The government still had some control over gun costs, since it still made naval guns at the foundry of Ruelle. It had no control over armor costs, and following the traditional policy, Admirals Peyron and Galiber, ministers of marine between 1883 and 1886, drew up a plan for a government armor works at Guérigny.[86] Peyron's request for 400,000 francs in 1885 and Galiber's for 100,000 in 1886 were both beaten in the Budget Committee on the grounds of economy—though the Committee allotted 3 million francs for a new dry dock at Saigon. A counterattack by the "economists" then closed Guérigny altogether. The drafter of the Budget Committee's report for both years, Paul Ménard-Dorien, deputy from Nevers, was the head of the Unieux works, which furnished all the pig iron to the armor plant of Marrel Frères. He was also a brother-in-law of the chief owner of another big firm, Holtzer's. In 1882 the government had set a relatively high price of 1,600 to 1,800 francs a ton for compound armor in order to repay the manufacturers for their investment in new machinery. On the failure of the navy's plan for the compound armor plant at Guérigny, this price rose to 2,000 francs for the armor for the battleship *Hoche*.[87] Even before the formation of the arms syndicate for foreign orders, the politicians had opened the way for the profitable exploitation of the home market.

By 1886 the arms ring was ready for action. The only firms not in the combine were Normand (the leading torpedo-boat builder) and the works of the Messageries Maritimes and other shipping companies that built nothing but merchant steamers.[88] The union of Canet and Creusot under the same management in 1896 to form the only private naval gun factory in France was merely a matter of form; they had already been cooperating for a decade.

While the arms firms were combining, the merchant shipbuilding market was disappearing. The law of 1881 that established maritime subsidies produced a small boom between 1881 and 1886, but then the French merchant marine took a nose-dive, which landed it in 1900 in fifth place among the world's merchant navies, with Italy and Norway about to overtake it. French merchant shipping was literally subsidized to death. The French taxpayer between 1881 and 1902 paid out a total of construction and navigation bounties of 433.5 million francs.[89] Between 1874 and 1895 the government also distributed 1.2 billion francs in harbor work to at least seventy ports—instead of concentrating on three or four to compete with foreign centers like Antwerp and Genoa.[90] It added 27 million francs more per year (about half a billion over a comparable twenty-year period) in subsidies for auxiliary cruisers.[91]

Following a period of collapse between 1887 and 1892, Parliament passed a law in 1893 that actually favored sailing ships over steamers. (Their owners persuaded the Chamber that sailing ships, being slower, should get higher subsidies in order to compete with steam. There were legends of French sailing ships cruising in the Pacific in ballast and stopping only to collect their bounties.)[92] By the mid-1890s, over half of the total net income of many shipping companies was derived from the subsidies, but in the decade from 1886 to 1896, when English steam tonnage increased 53 percent, Italian 68 percent, and German 107 percent, that of France actually decreased. There were handouts to the builders and to the operators of the French-built ships, lesser ones to those who imported ships, to the sailing-ship owners, to the fishermen, to everybody; but there was no merchant marine.

The law of 1881 pauperized the French merchant marine and the law of

The battleship Gaulois *(1896). In this class, the French definitively adopted the armament layout that had become standard abroad with the* Royal Sovereign *class. The French ships, however, were still considerably smaller than their English contemporaries.*

1893 utterly demoralized it. By the 1890s the navy was again getting no help whatever from this potentially gigantic industry. The French auxiliary cruisers built under the first law no longer compared with those furnished Germany by the North German Lloyd. While the German merchant marine was a powerful factor in promoting the growth of the German navy, French maritime trade was less important than ever in national life. It provided almost no economic basis for public interest in the navy. The French companies were not even interested in the heart of the merchant shipping business—tramp freighters—but concentrated on luxury liner services. They also played into the hands of the arms trust by deliberately agreeing to prices that would absorb most of the construction bounties as well as those for navigation.[93] The result was an inefficient industrial base—even the commonest of articles in Britain had to be made to order in France.

The navy's constructors, caught in the middle, complained that the Chamber had "delivered us with our hands tied" to a gang of highway robbers and that it was impossible to see a single means of escape.[94] While complaining about waste in the arsenals, the protectionist Chamber had set up an enormous tariff, and every attempt by the navy to buy abroad to beat down prices provoked a tremendous outcry among the deputies about "treason to the national industries." One crusty aristocrat noted bitterly that Ménard-Dorian's brother-in-law had no compunction about delivering Holtzer shells, which had been developed in tests conducted by the Gâvres Commission, to the English.[95]

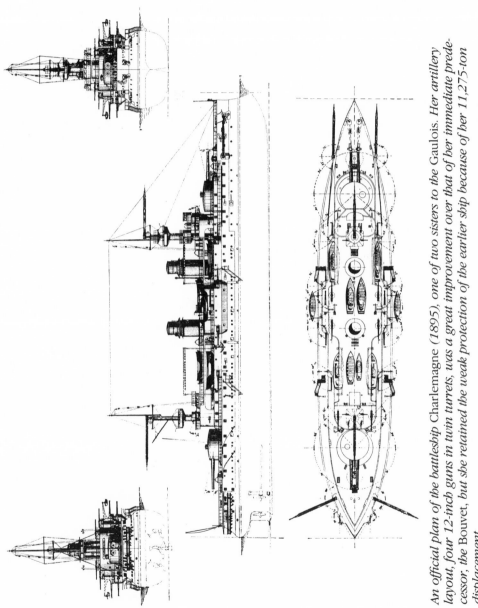

An official plan of the battleship Charlemagne (1895), one of two sisters to the Gaulois. Her artillery layout, four 12-inch guns in twin turrets, was a great improvement over that of her immediate predecessor, the Bouvet, but she retained the weak protection of the earlier ship because of her 11,275-ton displacement.

The real plunder came not in the price of completed ships, which the navy could build in its arsenals, but in the raw materials. The navy could not buy its steel abroad, the refusal of the Chamber to set up a government armor plant prevented it from making its own steel, and the partisans of "economy" in the Extra-Parliamentary Commission succeeded in blocking the Guérigny project a second time.[96] Finally, the ministry got enough money to make the 900-ton deck armor of the battleship *Gaulois* at Guérigny at 570 francs a ton. Since the lowest price quoted by the steel companies was 1,720 francs per ton, the saving on this item alone on one ship was 1,035,000 francs.[97]

Before the limited revival of Guérigny and threats in 1898 from the minister of marine, Lockroy, had succeeded in bringing the steel prices down a little, the cost figures were perfectly fantastic. Creusot armor had originally been quoted at 1,400 francs a ton. Harvey steel averaged 2,700 francs for a whole ship, with some of the special shapes running up to 4,200. The cheapest French battleships, built in the late 1890s after the French had begun building ships in classes and had streamlined the naval construction bureaucracy in 1895 with the formation of a Technical Section, cost 2,240 francs per ton, compared to 1,560 for the British *Majestic*s and 1,750 for the *Royal Sovereign*s. The cheapest French protected cruisers cost 2,000 francs per ton, compared with prices ranging from 1,250 to 1,310 for similar British ships. Labor costs in the two countries were roughly similar: 436 francs per ton of displacement in France, 396 in England. The difference was in materials: 928 francs per ton in France against only 557 in England.[98]

The arms firms did well. The Aciéries de Saint-Etienne, a typical firm in the armor business with capital of 4 million francs, in the decade 1891–1900 declared a regular annual dividend of 12 percent, spent 6.5 million francs on new plant, and built up a reserve of 6,623,000 francs.[99] This tidy ten-year profit seems to have been about average, though Holtzer hit the record with a 1900 dividend of 40 percent.[100] General steel prices were high in the 1890s in France and England compared with Germany because of high transportation costs for both pig iron and finished products and the high price of coking coal in France, but there is no doubt that the French steel men, particularly before the establishment of a light armor plant at Guérigny, were holding up the navy for all they could get.[101]

Partly because of the formation of the French arms trust and its activities in the Chamber, and partly because of the wearing out of the Loire companies' equipment and serious labor trouble, which accompanied similar developments in the arsenals, France's former price advantage over England was completely reversed by the end of the century.

Sixteen

The Decline of French Matériel

U P TO 1894, it is at least possible to find some policy for the navy of the Third Republic. In the years immediately before the Fashoda crisis of 1898, however, while England was working out the general strategic system on which she fought World War I, the French showed signs of only reflex action in most naval fields. Perhaps the most important result of this lack of a coherent French naval policy in the mid-1890s was the continued drift in the development of French naval matériel. By the end of the decade, the French were hopelessly behind England in both the quantity and quality of their battleships and cruisers.

THE POLICY VOID: THE RESPONSE TO GERMANY

In the early 1890s, the French had difficulty responding to some major changes in German naval power. In a colonial treaty with the English in 1890, Germany acquired the island of Heligoland, just off her northwestern coast. Heligoland filled in the last gap in the naval defensive structure of the German empire, freeing the future German armored fleet for offensive action. Five years later the kaiser opened the Kiel Canal, which connected the Baltic and North Sea elements of the German fleet, and a year later the whole German fleet passed through in thirty hours. Since the defenses at Heligoland covered the approaches to the western end of the canal, the two developments were intimately connected.[1] The opening of the canal and the fortification of Heligoland gave Germany what was essentially a single giant naval base, comprising Kiel, the canal, Brunsbüttelkoog, Cuxhaven, Heligoland, and Wilhelmshaven.[2]

Although later the decision to cede Heligoland was much criticized in England, it is hard to see what else the British prime minister, Lord Salisbury, could have done. The retention of the island during another Franco-German war would have led to serious bickerings with both belligerents because of the possibility that the French would use the waters nearby as a fleet anchorage, as they had in 1870. Since the anchorage extended outside the three-mile limit, the English would be unable to prevent the French coaling there. The island's lights, pilots, and fog warnings were indispensable to all navigation in the area. No matter what the British did, the very situation of the island made unambiguous neutrality impossible. Even before the German ambassador in London, Count Hatzfeldt, obtained Salisbury's consent to the cession, the British recognized the force of the German argument in an informal verbal assurance that the French would not be allowed to coal there.[3]

A new German naval building program developed in 1888 by Admiral Friedrich Hollmann provided the nucleus of a high-seas fleet in the form of four ships of the *Brandenburg* class, Germany's first full-sized battleships since the early 1870s. It also provided eight small coast-defense ships of the *Siegfried* class to defend the entrance to the Kiel Canal. The new fleet still lacked cruisers, and scouting was to be provided by torpedo boats and auxiliary cruisers.

The cession of Heligoland deprived the French of their only advance base against the German coasts, and although there was still a slight possibility of a *coup de main* against the mouth of the canal, it ruled out a landing by France and Russia on the Baltic coast, like the one the French had planned in 1870.[4]

In the meantime, the building of the new ships and their concentration with the ships of the *Sachsen* class at the western end of the canal, just when Germany's whole army was more clearly devoted to the west, led to an outcry in the mid-1890s over the state of France's northern coast defenses much like that which the fortification of Maddalena had caused in the south.[5] There were complaints from chambers of commerce and vigorous criticisms by the Budget Committee.[6]

The navy conducted several maneuvers with the theme of defending the Channel coast against a German attack. The results were always the same. The torpedo boats failed to stop the enemy fleet in the Strait of Dover; the ports of Boulogne, Dieppe, Havre, and Cherbourg were bombarded; the "torrential" daytime attacks of the torpedo boats failed miserably; and the defending squadron spent most of its time hurrying to the places where the enemy had last been reported. Had it intercepted the new German ships, the weak Channel squadron would scarcely have been able to stand up to them. The results of the maneuvers were essentially the same, on a smaller scale, as those held in the Mediterranean.

Under these circumstances, the Superior Council met to provide what had become the one infallible remedy—a new naval program.[7] It appears that the Program of 1894, which replaced the Program of 1890 and was still focused on the Triple Alliance, despite England's renewed activity and France's alliance with Russia, was the navy's response to a suggestion by the Budget Committee of 1893 for a "compromise program." The Committee thought that everybody would be made happy by a program that included a few scout cruisers and some battleships for the admirals and a lot of torpedo craft and some special commerce-raiding cruisers for the Jeune Ecole. As most of these had been provided in the earlier program, the only differences between the Program of 1894 and that of 1890 were the requirement that all first-class cruisers be armored, the abandonment of torpedo-boat mother ships (of which the only example, the *Foudre,* was under construction), and the addition of two special commerce-destroying cruisers, the *Guichen* and *Châteaurenault.* The changes showed how unimportant French naval programs had really become, and the addition of the two commerce destroyers, which even Aube would not have deemed sufficient to do harm to England, inaugurated the complete confusion of the next four years.[8]

Confusion in Naval Matériel

During the 1890s the French, crippled by the complete lack of a coherent shipbuilding plan, lost much of the technical advantage they had held over England during the 1880s. With the introduction of Longridge wire-wound twelve-inch guns in the *Majestic* class, the English once again had guns nearly as good as those on the continent.[9] English projectiles were still not quite as good, the *Majestic* still had to train its guns fore and aft for loading, and fifteen men had to help out the electric motor that trained them, but such defects were resolved in later classes. Although English ships retained shells filled with black powder, an important trial in 1896 against the old station battleship *La Galissonnière* showed, much to the French surprise, that against thin armor, black powder shells were as good as melinite. The melinite shells were detonated by the armor plate, and much of their explosive force was dissipated outside the target.

Though the trials did not destroy French faith in the superiority of armored cruisers over protected ones, they added to the blue funk of the French Navy in the summer before the Fashoda crisis.[10] (Around 1900, the French completed experiments with a "semi-rupture" armor-piercing high-explosive shell, their answer to this problem and the culmination in the evolution of French projectiles.)

More significant still, the *La Galissonnière* trials also proved that the combination of armored deck, watertight compartments, and relatively thin side armor used to protect the *Majestics* and the Italian *Re Umbertos* was superior to the system used in the new French battleships. Although French armored cruisers beginning with the *Dupuy de Lôme* had been armored on the new plan, the efforts of Emile Bertin to persuade the Conseil des Travaux to adopt it for battleships had failed.[11] (Bertin's scheme was finally adopted in the *Patrie* class of 1900.) Finally, the arrangement adopted by the British for their heavy guns (a twin turret on the centerline forward and another aft) was superior to the lozenge pattern the French had adopted twenty years earlier to give end-on fire and were still using. Only in the three ships of the *Gaulois* class, begun in 1894, did the French adopt the gun arrangement of the *Royal Sovereign.*

Although the English had developed the destroyer directly from the successful French high-seas torpedo boats, the French in 1894 were still trying to make the large torpedo aviso type into a torpedo-boat catcher. The Conseil des Travaux decided that the ideal craft would be a catcher of 375 tons. The Superior Council, on the other hand, wanted a high-seas torpedo boat of 245 tons.[12] They compromised in a typically French manner by accepting a proposal of Jacques-Augustin Normand, supported by the minister, for a destroyer of 300 tons that became the *Durandal.* Normand's proposal involved giving the little craft two armaments. When they were to face German torpedo craft, they would carry their guns, but against English battleships they would embark their supply of torpedos. Over the next decade, the French Navy built fifty-five boats of this successful type.

No less than four different authorities—the Superior Council, the Conseil des Travaux, the minister of marine, and the Budget Committee—fought over French cruiser policy from the mid-1880s through the mid-1890s. The Jeune Ecole wanted commerce-destroying cruisers with a long range, a light armament, and the ability to run from better armed ships. The older admirals wanted ships for cruising on the foreign stations, while the more modern officers wanted armored *Dupuy de Lômes* plus a lot of very small scout cruisers, all for operations with the battle fleet. Round one went to the Jeune Ecole when Aube in 1887 laid down a group of cruisers with relatively light protection and armament. Round two, extending from the late 1880s into the early 1890s, generally went to the modern admirals, who got six armored cruisers of the *Dupuy de Lôme* and *Charner* types. The foreign station men, however, managed to slip in the *D'Entrecasteaux,* a big 8,000-ton, 19-knot protected cruiser.

The Jeune Ecole began a comeback in 1895 with two equally large commerce destroyers of 24 knots, the *Châteaurenault* and *Guichen,* whose designs were copied right down to the hull lines from the American cruisers *Columbia* and *Minneapolis.* Carefully built to resemble ocean liners, they were never really able to make enough speed to catch one, while they were too expensive to use against tramp steamers and could do nothing but run away, like an ordinary auxiliary cruiser, from a real ship of war.[13]

A liberal minister, Edouard Lockroy, came to power in November 1895 but did not have time to fight with the traditionalists over cruiser policy dur-

The large commerce-raiding cruiser Châteaurenault *(launched in 1898) fitting out at La Seyne. She was designed to resemble an ocean liner when seen at a distance.*

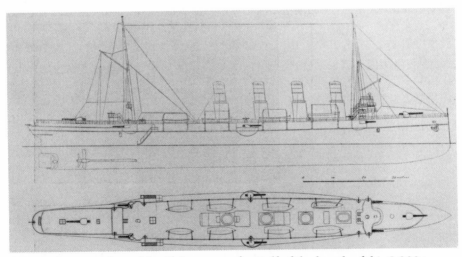

A contemporary plan of the Châteaurenault. *Half of the length of this 8,000-ton ship was occupied by machinery designed to give her a speed of 23 knots for commerce-raiding. She carried only two 6.4-inch and six 5.5-inch guns and had a 2.4-inch protective deck.*

The large armored cruiser Jeanne d'Arc *(1899). Bigger and more expensive than many battleships, she was the first of a series of nineteen armored cruisers of various types ordered by the French between 1895 and 1905.*

ing his first ministry, which lasted only to April 1896. He and his allies in the Chamber made a major change to the 1896 budget proposal, however, replacing a second ship of the *D'Entrecasteaux* class with an enormous armored cruiser of 11,400 tons, 22 knots, and 13,500 miles steaming range. He built this ship, the *Jeanne d'Arc,* without ever consulting the Conseil des Travaux. The only thing that he built that the Conseil des Travaux actually refused to approve was the coast-defense battleship *Henri IV,* a unique 8,700-ton ship that combined the low-freeboard hull of a monitor with the traditional high superstructures of French battleships and used Bertin's new protection scheme.[14]

The battle over cruisers was fully joined under Lockroy's successor, Admiral Besnard. Besnard, of the really old school, wanted a special type of cruiser for foreign stations, and though the Chamber of Deputies had refused to accept a second ship of the *D'Entrecasteaux* type in the budget for 1896, it decided it would take something smaller in the 1897 budget. But the Conseil des Travaux, now in the hands of the partisans of the *Dupuy de Lôme,* flatly rejected a proposed 5,700-ton station protected cruiser with the general declaration that it would turn down any more protected cruisers or any other ships that could only run away.[15] Just at this time, the Superior Council was engaged in drawing up another program, the Program of 1896, which took England somewhat into account. It joined with the Chamber and the foreign station men in allotting four new armored cruisers and two protected ones to the station fleet. At the end of 1896, Besnard ordered the construction of the *Jurien de la Gravière,* the protected cruiser that had been accepted by the Chamber and turned down by the Conseil des Travaux.

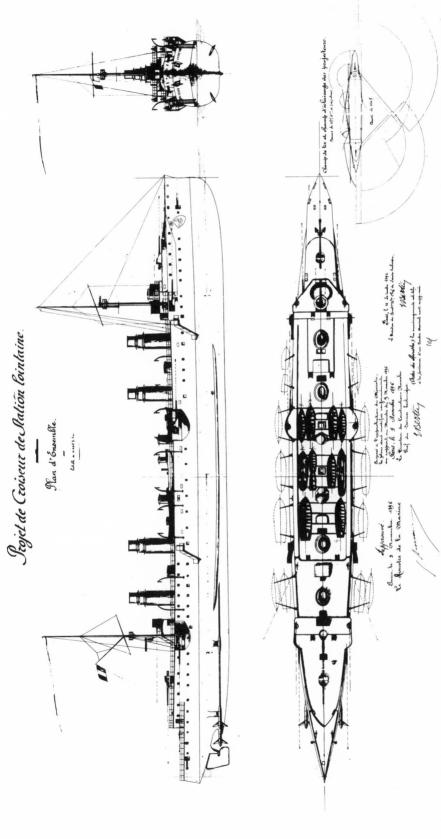

Emile Bertin's design for the second-class protected cruiser Jurien de la Gravière (1899) as approved by the minister of marine on 9 November 1896. This ship was designed for overseas service, and was also given enough speed to be a dangerous commerce raider.

The armored cruiser Montcalm *(1900) running trials. She was designed for service in European waters along the lines advocated by Admiral Fournier.*

In the meantime, Lockroy, who controlled the Budget Committee, had been converted to the ideas of Admiral Fournier, perhaps the best French naval theoretician of his generation. Among other things, Fournier called for using armored cruisers somewhat smaller than the *Jeanne d'Arc* for most naval tasks, including commerce-destroying. The Budget Committee was also becoming more alarmed about England, and when Besnard proposed in his 1898 budget to begin one battleship, two armored cruisers, and two protected cruisers, the committee replied by striking out the battleship and offering him 120 million francs for armored cruisers, 60 million for torpedo boats and submarines, and more if he got to work on Bizerte.[16]

Besnard initially exchanged the plans of the battleship for the "C-3," an enlarged *Jeanne d'Arc,* which was turned down by the Conseil des Travaux as of "very problematical" utility.[17] Ultimately, the grant from the Chamber for armored cruisers gave Besnard a chance to build three of his favorite station type, the 7,600-ton *Kléber* class, which the Conseil des Travaux approved although it maintained that there was "no need to create a special class of station armored cruisers."[18] In return, Besnard gave the Chamber three 9,500-ton Fournier armored cruisers of the *Montcalm* class, to which the Conseil objected with equal lack of success.[19]

When Lockroy returned to the ministry in June 1898, just after the settlement of the dispute with England over the Niger River and just before the Fashoda crisis, he and Fournier planned five slightly improved *Montcalms,* the *Gloire* class. These, also built without the Conseil's blessing, completed what became a really formidable group of eleven relatively homogeneous armored cruisers begun between 1897 and 1899.[20]

French naval construction during these years lacked a guiding hand. During the entire period, the Conseil des Travaux had done nothing but raise objections. It was flouted as effectively by the ultraconservative Besnard as by the Superior Council, the Chamber, and the reforming minister, Lockroy.

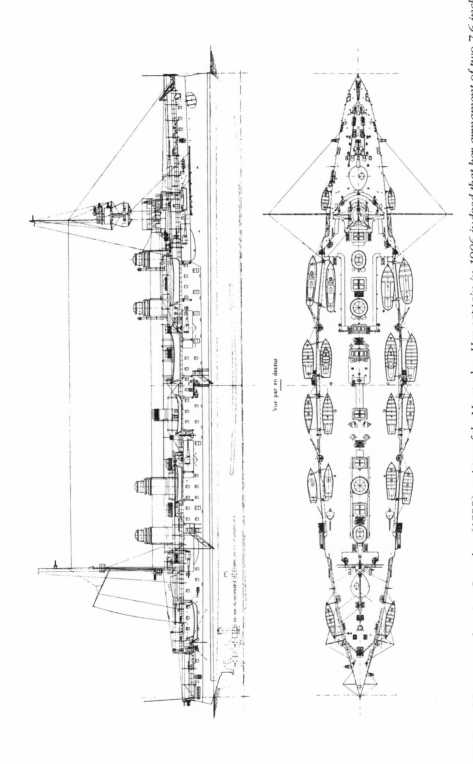

Vue par en dessus

An official plan of the armored cruiser Gueydon (1899), a sister of the Montcalm. Her captain in 1906 judged that her armament of two 7.6-inch and eight 6.4-inch guns was insufficient for her size of 9,500 tons. She made 21 knots and had 5.9-inch side armor.

In England the designs for ships were prepared down to the very last details in a central technical division under Sir William White. The French, despite Gougeard's attempt in 1881 to establish a similar central planning bureau, did not establish a Technical Section in the ministry until 1895, just before Lockroy's first administration.

Once the plans were completed, the Admiralty normally built a large number of identical ships in classes from them while the French often built only a single ship. One reason why the French avoided both a central design authority and large ship classes was the rather dubious results of extreme centralization under Napoleon III. In his last years in the navy, Dupuy de Lôme not only had turned out some unsatisfactory designs but also, like most geniuses, had used no ideas but his own. The Council of Admiralty formally decided in 1871 that "ships of new types should be laid down individually and never in classes, and they should be reproduced only after sufficiently prolonged and conclusive trials."[21] The rapid changes that had rendered all of Dupuy de Lôme's ships obsolete at one time made a very deep impression, and in 1878, when the whole fleet of early ironclads was rotting away together, Lamy's Budget Committee report strongly condemned building ships in classes, stating that "as long as [France] builds her fleet in groups of identical ships, any progress in the naval art will weaken several elements of her naval strength at the same time."[22]

During the period of indecision over battleship designs that extended throughout the 1880s, French ships were all custom built. The Conseil des Travaux and the ministry worked out the general specifications of a design and invited all engineers of the Génie maritime who were interested to submit plans that conformed to them. By encouraging the engineers to incorporate their own ideas in the plans, the system was partly responsible for the progress made by the French during the decade.

Once a standard type of ship had been evolved, the industrial disadvantages of this approach, despite the opinion of the Génie to the contrary, far outweighed its benefits.[23] Between 1890 and 1892, while England was building eight *Royal Sovereign*s to identical plans, the French began five battleships (*Masséna, Carnot, Jauréguiberry, Charles Martel,* and *Bouvet*) to plans drawn to the same specifications by five different designers. The result of the designers' "initiative" was five ships that differed completely in appearance and varied in a thousand and one details.[24] If the officers and crew of the *Carnot* had been transferred to the *Bouvet,* they would have had to spend most of the first month learning where the different gadgets were and how to manipulate them. The crew of one *Royal Sovereign,* on the other hand, could take over another ship of the same class almost as easily as one can step from one Ford to another and drive away.

A French ship was generally referred to by the name of her designer, as that of Monsieur X or Monsieur Y. Each engineer occupied himself with the problem he found most interesting. The ships of one would be famous for their guns, those of another for their speed, and those of a third for the ingenious distribution of the coal bunkers to get more theoretical range.[25] The ideas of strength, simplicity, and reasonable cost were entirely forgotten. A complicated gadget that saved ten pounds of weight in the engine room would generally cost twice as much as the old type, would break down at sea, and would take ten men to repair it. A French historian later attributed the relative failure of French submarines in World War I to "the ingenuity with which we had studied the technical problems of submarine navigation and to the elegant solutions chosen for the sake of elegance itself. . . . Our submarines were more perfect in detail than the English and German submarines, but in practical warfare they were no match for them."[26]

The French artillerists were as ingenious as the engineers of the Génie. By 1899 the navy was using fifteen different calibers of guns firing forty-five different charges and using 128 different projectiles. The battleship *Charles Martel* carried guns of six calibers, with a seventh for the ship's boats. Her 5.5-inch guns alone had nine types of projectiles, while her main armament consisted of two 12-inch and two 10.8-inch guns. If the 12-inch guns were put out of action, the 10.8-inch guns would be totally unable to use the rest of the ammunition supply. It was almost impossible to know what kind of ammunition to place in stock at coaling stations.[27] Even the gun mountings, built by different firms according to their own ideas, could be different for the same types of guns on ships of the same general type.

In England, at least two and sometimes three ships of the same class were always built in a single port: one would be completing, one in the middle of construction, and one just beginning. The experience acquired on the first would enable the second and third to be built nearly a third faster, while the steady work would keep each worker busy in his specialty. In France, the port deputies always made sure that the work was spread around, and when a program was given out, one ship of each type would be given to each port.

Even if two ships of the same type had been built in the same port, the details of the designs would have been so different that things would not have speeded up very much. English ships were designed down to the smallest details in London—White's staff worked for a year on the *Canopus*-class battleships of the 1896 estimates before a single contract was let. Once construction started, the English pushed it as rapidly as possible and allowed no design changes. In France, even after the Technical Section was established at the ministry, the Chamber gave money for only four engineers for it. In the meantime, the minister (Lockroy) was demanding complete plans in only two or three months so that he could let the contracts and start the ships before his successor could upset things. In these conditions, even with the Technical Section, it was necessary to leave some details to the engineers in the ports and to arrange others after the ships were started.[28]

When the British finished the first ship of a class, they sent her to sea for long and thorough trials. If nothing untoward occurred, the other ships of the same class only had to go through short engine and firing trials and a general inspection. In each new French ship, every gadget was the subject of long and complex trials, and endless reports were made on minor matters that could just as well have been studied while the ship was in actual service with the fleet.

The Spithead Review of 1897, in which the British paraded long lines of their new battleships and cruisers, showed the French their real weakness on the eve of the Fashoda crisis. In a remarkable report, the naval engineer Maxime Laubeuf stated that apart from the general power of the *Majestic-*class battleships, the most profound impression of all was the remarkable uniformity of the fleet in the overall designs, the armament, the internal details, and even in the position of the masts and funnels. "We can only envy the unity of the plan . . . its execution . . . the simplicity of its details . . . and the stability in the direction of the navy. The results of the British efforts are indeed profoundly impressive." Laubeuf argued that there was only one solution for France: ships of one program should be built on the same plan, the details should be exactly the same, and at least two of a kind should be laid down at the same port and worked on continuously.[29]

A detailed look at the condition of the French Navy on the eve of the Fashoda crisis leaves one astounded not only at the magnitude of the disorder but at the multiplicity of its causes. The state of the navy in 1898 reflected confusion in French diplomacy, politics, and industry in general. Who was the chief enemy of the navy: Italy, England, or Germany? Should war against England be waged by the battle fleet or by the cruisers, in the Mediterranean or in the Channel? Were the colonies worth defending directly? Such questions were all left to the admiral on the spot. The Chamber of Deputies, while trying to gain general control over naval expenditures, had not only passed from a strategy of coast defense to one of commerce-raiding with large cruisers but had also intervened in the case of an actual design to decide that a *D'Entrecasteaux* was too large but that a *Jurien de la Gravière* was acceptable. What naval bases were necessary? While Bizerte, Brest, and all the coaling stations overseas were still incomplete, the supporters of the inefficient ports of Rochefort and Lorient had carried out a remarkable raid to the tune of six million francs. The arsenal workers, the stokers, the discontented officers, and the engineers all had their own representatives in the Chamber. In the design of a single ship, the technical services wanted one thing, the minister another, the Superior Council a third, and the Conseil des Travaux a fourth. The ingenuity of the designer only completed the confusion started by the conflicts in Paris. Finally, the navy had to battle with the army to settle questions such as the problem of coast defense, the distribution of extra *inscrits* and shipbuilding workers, and the defense of coaling stations.

The English looked on the French scene much as the French looked on the Italians. One English writer classed the situation as a general "cholera morbus," while a second, more charitable, simply expressed the surprise that "any navy worthy of the name exists."[30]

During this period France was in a state of general disorder due to the Dreyfus affair, a long and bitter political struggle that came to a head in 1898 and 1899. The navy avoided direct involvement in the affair, and its main problems stemmed instead from its failure to establish a satisfactory relationship between itself and public opinion. The French Navy had stubbornly refused to implement the changes that the public demanded in its industrial organization, and it had made no effort to educate the public in the importance of the navy as part of a general system of national defense or in the general principles of war on the sea. As a result, the public and its elected representatives were now interfering in every conceivable way, not only in general strategy but also in technical matters.

THEORY: TOWARD THE ARMORED CRUISER

The writings of Alfred Thayer Mahan gave England not only a definitive naval history but also an explanation for her importance in the world's affairs. In Germany the uncritical acceptance of Mahan's ideas provided the basis for construction of the High Seas Fleet. Meanwhile, the French Navy remained split between two contending schools, while the general public, tired of the whole business and occupied with internal affairs, turned away from the idea of empire and from the sea.

Gougeard's 1881 project for a higher naval school had almost been forgotten during the period of Aube, but the idea was revived in 1895, and on 27 December of that year Lockroy established the Ecole supérieure de la Marine.[31] It aroused violent opposition at the outset, largely because it was less a school than a means of forcing the Chamber's Jeune Ecole ideas on the recalcitrant admirals. Lockroy himself, after a number of high-sounding statements as to the value of the school for the study of tactics and strategy, let the cat out of the bag when he added that it was a great step against "favoritism."[32] Lockroy appointed Admiral Fournier, the best thinker of the Jeune Ecole, to be the first commandant, and he chose the students from among the lieutenants who had been placed on the advancement list but not advanced. Fournier, left in charge of the general organization of the school, decided that it should be afloat to permit the study of both tactical and theoretical matters. The ministry gave him two cruisers with which to go to work.

The actual aims of the school were fairly clear: to give the "neglected" officers a chance, to teach them Fournier's version of the Jeune Ecole strategy, and to set up a little rival Squadron of Evolutions in which Fournier could demonstrate his tactical ideas. The main course, taught by Fournier himself with aid from the officers in the two cruisers, was in four parts:

Naval Tactics, Tactics of Scouting and Squadron Cruisers, Battle Tactics, and Naval Strategy.[33] A historian of the school later explained:

> Only the general theme of operations can be foreseen and regulated . . . and the aim of strategy must be therefore to assign in peacetime an initial direction to the offensive action of each distinct fraction of the fleet. The lectures . . . study especially the qualities of the cruisers that are our instruments for foreign action and the organization of their bases of operation.[34]

Fournier's idea of naval strategy involved nothing more than the choice of the field of operations. The kind of operations conducted there was a matter of one's individual faith: commercial war for the Jeune Ecole, high-seas war for the traditionalists. French naval theory was still so split by warring factions that it was now on a level lower than of Grivel's day in the late 1860s. Grivel, at least, had seen that the first necessity was the impartial examination of the kind of warfare that France should use against a given enemy. Also forgotten was Gougeard's original idea in 1881 of the school as a place for frank and public discussion and as a common ground on which the public and the officers would thrash out the general strategic problems of the functions and aims of the navy. Without such a forum, there would simply be a long series of pitched battles between the public and the officers. In the school's first year, the "unity" that the partisans of the Jeune Ecole sought meant only the triumph of their own particular ideas, and the public was never invited to participate.[35]

Admiral Besnard returned as minister of marine in April 1896 and allowed Fournier's school to finish out its term, although the commander of the squadron, Admiral Gervais, was demanding his two cruisers back to take part in the annual maneuvers. When the classes were over, the ministry sent Admiral Rieunier, the defender of Rochefort against the reformers and the most redoubtable champion that the traditionalists possessed, to "inspect" the school. The Superior Council recommended its suppression for two reasons: "it appears to wish to direct tactical and strategical studies without submitting them to the test of experience, and to annihilate the Squadron"; and "it tends to create a special body of a General Staff which will soon be tempted to take over the direction of the navy"—i.e., to annihilate the traditionalists.[36]

But with Lockroy entrenched in the Budget Committee, Besnard could not suppress the school entirely. Instead, rightly abandoning the idea of trying to work out tactical problems with two cruisers, Besnard deprived the school of its chief and its warships, gave it a new name, and set it up as a kind of adjunct of the Naval General Staff in Paris. The attitude of the higher officers was so unfavorable that the younger men were afraid to apply for admission: in 1899 it failed to open because only eleven acceptable candidates presented themselves.[37] In spite of this attitude and despite additional reorganizations when Lockroy returned to the ministry in June 1898 and departed in June 1899, the school remained alive until the great awakening of 1900 made it a real factor in French naval thought.

The first courses at the school, consisting mostly of documents hastily chosen from the archives by the members of the staff who were told off to give the lectures, were both fearfully dull and amazingly ill-organized. Even in the floating school, besides Fournier's "The French Navy: Tactics and Strategy," there were "Mobilization," "Foreign Navies," "Naval Construction," "Machinery," "Administration," "International Law," "Electricity," and "Naval Hygiene." Though the traditionalists merged the course on mobilization with the main one in 1897, they added "Theoretical Artillery," "Torpedoes," "History," "Political Geography," "Meteorology," "Nautical Instruments," "Oceanography," "Astronomy," and "Terrestrial Magnetism." This was by no means all, since they added six more before 1902, including "Carrier Pigeons."

Besides showing the general tendency of the French Naval Staff to mix in everything even remotely connected with the navy, this curriculum must have given some of the students a fearful case of mental indigestion. All twelve students in 1897 apparently took all the courses. The "strategy" of the main course in 1897 consisted of nothing but long accounts of French and foreign naval maneuvers.[38] Not until the next year was the first hesitant attempt made to study naval strategy by examining the lessons of naval history as well.[39] But, although the French started fully fifteen years behind, their naval theory, which flowered with writers like René Daveluy (1909–10) and Raoul Castex (1920–30), evolved largely in connection with the school.

In 1894 the Japanese defeated the Chinese in the battle of the Yalu, the first fleet action in twenty-eight years. The battle gave a great impetus to the latest fad of the Jeune Ecole, the building of armored cruisers. As usual, what happened was much less important than what some people thought had happened. The victory of the Japanese fleet, led by the three big protected cruisers designed by Emile Bertin in the late 1880s, over a Chinese fleet, led by two German-built battleships similar to the British *Inflexible,* was taken to mean the definite triumph of the quick-firing gun over the blunderbuss, the line-ahead formation over the line abreast, and almost any fast ship over any slow one. There was really not much to the battle: the Japanese fleet, circling around the Chinese and carrying on an afternoon's target practice with their quick-firers, destroyed all the Chinese cruisers, ruined the unprotected ends of the battleships, ran out of ammunition, and then went home. The Chinese, who had fired all their ammunition long before, went into the armored centers of the two battleships, where the officers spent their time taking pictures and putting out fires (partly caused by the mandarins' economizing on paint by thinning it with kerosene instead of linseed oil), and then went home likewise.

The battle did at least give an indication of the damage that quick-firing guns could do to the unprotected portions of older ships and definitely buried the fallacies of the one-punch school. (The large guns of the Chinese battleships failed to sink any Japanese ships, and the single 12.6-inch Canet guns on the three Japanese cruisers seem to have fired only one shot an hour because of the failure of their mountings.)[40]

In his book *La flotte nécessaire* (1896), Admiral Fournier ably presented the idea that a fleet of armored cruisers like the *Dupuy de Lôme,* accompanied by torpedo craft, would be sufficient for every kind of naval warfare. In direct contrast to the theory of the early 1890s, which called for the "division of labor" between specialized ships—battleships, coast-defense ships, scouts, gunboats, commerce-destroyers, and special ships for foreign stations—Fournier proposed a modified *Dupuy de Lôme* as a ship *bon à tout faire* (able to do anything). Completely cased in Harvey steel armor, with great speed and range, carrying almost nothing but large quick-firing guns using melinite shells, and using their speed to control the range at which engagements were fought, Fournier's armored cruisers would conquer the English or Italian ships by ruining their unprotected portions and demoralizing their personnel. For scouting, a commander would detach a few units of the regular squadron. For commercial warfare (the chief method of attacking England), the new ships would be fast enough to catch the majority of English merchantmen and notably superior to any English protected cruiser that tried to drive them off. In addition, their steaming range would enable them to be used on foreign stations where current scouting cruisers could not go. All of France's naval needs would be satisfied by 117 of them, with 300 torpedo boats.[41] By devoting practically all of France's new construction budget, 83 million francs a year, to this program, it would be possible to start six armored cruisers each year.

Even the partisans of the battleship recognized the utility of the armored cruiser for scouting and commercial war. While not wishing for a fleet composed entirely of armored cruisers, they hoped to use them as a reserve to finish off damaged enemy ships or to put them in the line of battle against older battleships that were vulnerable to high explosives.[42] Italy planned to use her new armored cruisers of the *Giuseppe Garibaldi* class against France in the same way that Fournier planned to use his against England. The adoption of Fournier's cruiser by the Jeune Ecole and Parliament, however, was the decisive factor that led to the large armored cruiser program in the late 1890s.

The old belief that cruisers offered a cheaper method of naval war than battleships was belied by the fact that armored cruisers eventually became almost as large as battleships. The 6,500-ton *Dupuy de Lôme* and the 4,700-ton *Charner* were followed in the late 1890s by the 9,500-ton *Montcalm* and the 11,400-ton commerce destroyer *Jeanne d'Arc*. After 1900 these gave way to the 12,350-ton *Léon Gambetta* and ultimately the 14,000-ton *Edgar Quinet*. The English joined the race in 1898 with the 12,000-ton *Cressy* and followed a year later with the 14,100-ton *Drake*. By this time, armored cruisers were little smaller than battleships: the contemporary battleship to the *Drake* was the 15,000-ton *Formidable*. The real arms race during these years was in armored cruisers: British battleships grew only 2,500 tons between the *Royal Sovereign* of 1889 and the *King Edward VII* of 1902.

Maneuvers soon showed that Fournier's idea of a ship *bon à tout faire*, like his exaggerated opinion of the tactical (as distinct from the strategic) value of speed, was unsound. Fournier had claimed that speed would enable a weaker ship to defeat a stronger one in battle, but a test in 1900 of a fast squadron representing French armored cruisers against a slow one representing English coast-defense ships revealed that if the slow ships were even reasonably well handled, they could avoid destruction by the weaker fast ones, which could merely circle around them.[43] Nonetheless, the ideas of speed and the importance of offensive power became firmly rooted in naval thought in these years.

The late 1890s nearly saw the development of an "all-medium-gun ship," a precursor in some ways of the all-big-gun *Dreadnought* of 1905. Especially in the continental navies, quick-firing guns grew larger and big guns grew smaller until they nearly met. In the early 1880s Benedetto Brin had designed Italian battleships with 17.7-inch guns, but by 1897 Italy, Russia, and Germany were all building new battleships with no guns larger than 10-inch. The German *Kaiser Friedrich III* class, begun in 1895, carried this evolution to an extreme with its main battery of four 9.4-inch guns and secondary armament of eighteen well-protected 5.9-inch quick-firers. This class was really armed with nothing but quick-firers, which in five minutes could launch the then enormous quantity of twenty-two tons of projectiles on the broadside and sixteen ahead or astern. The British *Majestic,* on 4,000 tons greater displacement, fired only seventeen tons on the broadside and seven tons ahead or astern.[44] In this design the Germans practically gave up the effort to pierce their opponents' armor in the belief that a hail of relatively light projectiles would completely demoralize the enemy by razing all the unarmored portions of his ship. The battleships of the *Kaiser Friedrich III* class were only 500 tons larger than the armored cruiser *Fürst Bismarck,* built under the same program, and they were really big Fournier cruisers.

Proposals to take the next step and build an armored battleship carrying nothing but large quick-firers were numerous. The Italian artillerist Albini, who earlier had been partly responsible for Brin's ideas on big battleship guns, had proposed such a ship as early as the first trials of the Armstrong

The German battleship Kaiser Karl der Grosse *(1899), of the* Kaiser Friedrich III *class. This type relied on a high rate of fire from its 9.4-inch main guns and numerous 5.9-inch quick-firers to overwhelm its opponents.*

quick-firers in 1887.[45] In 1898 the naval constructor attached to the French Mediterranean fleet called for a ship of the same type with ten 9.4-inch guns.[46] A Russian engineer published a similar idea in 1900.[47] The 8,000-ton ship proposed in 1899 by the Italian naval constructor Vittorio Cuniberti, which was later regarded as a direct ancestor of the *Dreadnought,* was armed only with twelve 8-inch quick-firers and some small anti-torpedo-boat guns.[48] At this time, Admiral Fisher, who later developed the *Dreadnought,* was also a partisan of the smallest large gun and the largest small gun possible.[49] Although none of these all-medium-gun ships was ever built, they represent the culmination of the ideas that began with the *Dupuy de Lôme* and extended through Fournier's writings.

GUNNERY AND TORPEDOES, 1895–1905

The problem of hitting a moving target from a ship at sea was so complex that a competent British writer of the 1880s was able to identify and discuss eleven different important sources of error.[50] Of the various aspects of this problem, only the question of the gun itself had been fairly satisfactorily solved by the mid-1890s. The advances in gun design and fabrication ensured that with a given projectile and powder charge, the new guns would send the shell in a scientifically predictable direction. The question of how to modify the direction of aim to compensate for the wind and the motion of the target was also one of the less troublesome aspects of the problem.

The great difficulty was in determining the range to the target, and then in firing the gun from a rolling platform with the elevation necessary to reach it. None of the hundred or more different devices used in the 1890s for measuring the distance to an enemy ship was satisfactory. (The most common of them was a sextant used to measure the angle formed by the enemy's mast and waterline, or that formed by the waterline and the horizon.) In addition, the range could change so much during the fifteen minutes between rounds from the older big guns that each shot required an entirely new estimate of the distance.[51]

The prevailing practice was to set the elevation and direction of aim of the gun and then to have the gunner fire when the rolling of the ship itself brought the sights—a front and a rear nick sight like those on an ordinary rifle—in line with the target. The difficulty of firing at the right moment, and not just before or just after the target crossed the sights, was by far the greatest cause of error. A tenth of a second's misjudgment in a ship rolling ten degrees would cause the shot to be thirty feet above or below the point aimed at, given a range of 1,000 yards. The differences in reaction time for an individual gunner might run from four to eight tenths of a second and would vary with factors such as the state of his health and his excitability. Each gunner had to learn by incessant practice just when to fire as the roll of the ship brought his three reference points—the rear sight, the front sight, and the target—into line. For a few men, mastery of this problem of physical coordination became instinctive after long practice, but it was generally agreed that good gunners were born and not made. Even with the best possible training, the errors from this source alone were such that it was regarded as practically impossible for the average ship to fire in battle with any accuracy at ranges of more than 1,000 yards.

Of course, if the ship was scarcely rolling at all and was firing at a known distance, very good results could be obtained. Such conditions, approaching those typical of artillery on land, were the only ones under which the rolling of the ship did not practically neutralize the accuracy of the new naval guns. During Aube's ministry, the very stable ships of the *Redoutable* and *Amiral Duperré* types conducted firing trials against a target, the old station battleship *Armide,* anchored in a perfectly calm sea. They fired 625 shots at an average distance of 3,000 yards and obtained the remarkable result of 23.2 percent hits. The conditions were so exceptional, however, that they gave no indication of the probable effectiveness of even the most carefully trained gunners in the world at that time.[52] At Santiago during the Spanish-American War in 1898, the comparatively well-trained American gunners, under practically target-practice conditions, fired some 6,000 projectiles at ranges from 2,000 to 6,000 yards but got only 130 (2.2 percent) hits.[53]

The new revolution in naval gunnery began when innovators applied to heavy- and medium-caliber guns the entirely different principles used in firing anti-torpedo-boat quick-firers. These were essentially large machine guns that were manned not by regular gunners but by brevetted riflemen. These men judged the range empirically by the fall of shot in the water. They also attempted to keep their guns continuously on the target: instead of waiting for the rolling of the ship to bring the sights in line with the target, they attempted to compensate for the ship's motion by slight movements of the gun's shoulderpiece, similar to movements required for riding a bicycle.[54] Because of the size of the new medium-caliber quick-firers, the first of these new principles, judging the range by observation of the fall of shot, was applied before the second, continuous aim.

In 1891 the French began to study the problem of controlling the fire of the new quick-firing guns. They realized that smokeless powder had done away with the smoke that formerly obscured the battlefield and that the new guns fired rapidly enough to provide sufficient shell splashes for observation. Under the direction of Admiral Auguste-Eléonore-Marie de Penfentenyo de Kervéréguin, they took up two related problems—observing the fall of shot and controlling the fire from an entire ship in order to make observation possible.

The preliminary instructions of 27 February 1898 established the essentials of a modern system of fire control: the ship was no longer a platform carrying a certain number of individual guns but a unit using its artillery according to a specified system of command, with one observer directing the fire of all the artillery on board. At the opening of an action, the observer in the mast estimated the distance to the enemy as closely as he could with his unsatisfactory range-finder. Then a number of shots, of which the first was to be obviously short, were fired from the medium guns in rapid succession, at ranges that stepped up—1,000 yards, 1,050, and so on—to the target. When two successive shots "straddled" the enemy, all the guns opened fire at the range thus determined. Continuous observation of the fall of shot was then used to make subsequent adjustments. The range, direction, and speed of the enemy were sent by the observers to a central post (with a duplicate system of posts and lines in case the first was shot away) and then transmitted automatically to the guns. The gunners were required to use the range indicated on the dials of the automatic order transmitter, and only if this mechanism failed was an individual gun section allowed to direct its own fire. Though the guns did not fire together in salvos as they did under later systems, they were all firing at the same range under the command of the observer.[55]

The two stages of stepping up the range to the target and the continuous rapid fire of all the guns were the essentials of the new fire-control system. A third method, a curtain of fire at a given range through which the enemy must pass, was to be used when the range was changing very rapidly. Speed of fire was important not only for overwhelming the enemy but to provide a greater number of splashes to help find and keep the range.[56]

The final trials prior to the appearance of the new instructions took place in 1897 in the squadron, which was completely equipped with the new order transmitters. These trials caused some disappointment (which, like several other disappointments, came on the eve of the Fashoda crisis). The chief difficulties were that the short-shot method of finding the range was too slow and that considerable confusion resulted when several ships in the squadron fired at the same target. It was also hard to find a proper target for firing practice—individual ships usually used a large rock, but squadrons of islands arranged in line ahead were very scarce.[57]

The new instructions were permanent, however, and were accompanied by a general order requiring at least three major firing practices each year. The result was great activity in training gunners and successful trials ranging up to 4,000 yards; the battleships *Brennus, Neptune,* and *Marceau* got 26 percent hits at 3,000 to 4,000 yards with the new method in the 1897 trials.[58] As part of the new emphasis on gunnery, the French even produced a careful regulation on the kind of projectiles that should be fired against certain parts of English ships.[59] The high velocity and flat trajectory of French projectiles enabled them to increase the point-blank range of the large guns and to cover the enemy with a storm of light projectiles, which could do a great deal of damage at short range.

Nevertheless, the French did not discover a satisfactory range-finder, their sights were still only an elaboration of the old type, and they did not apply the principle of continuous aim. French gunners still fired "when the sights pass the target in the middle of the roll."[60] In short, they still had not solved the problem of long-range fire. The Fournier cruisers and the all-medium-gun ships like the *Kaiser Friedrich III* class found the new methods of controlling fire effective at short ranges but could not extend them to longer ranges because of the methods used to fire the guns.

In England the later 1890s were the height of the reign of "spit and polish," in which the chief efforts of British captains went into making their ships look smart in the great reviews, culminating in the Spithead Review of 1897, which showed Queen Victoria and the British public that they were getting their money's worth from the Naval Defence Act. In these years, "prettiness was necessary to promotion,"[61] and it was said that the French could always tell of the approach of the British Mediterranean Fleet by the glitter. The watertight doors of British ships were often polished until they were no longer tight, the entire chases of the guns were burnished, the nuts and bolt heads were gilded into fancy patterns, and even extra gauges that were supposed to be kept in the engine room were brought to the upper deck for more convenient polishing and then hung in long and shining rows. The ratings were kept so busy with such matters that they had to leave even minor repairs to the dockyards.

Firing a gun on such a beautiful ship (for which the officers bought extra white paint with their own money) was a real disaster. While the flag officers went on shore to get away from the required gunnery practice, the ships got rid of the regulation ammunition as fast as they could, with the least possible damage to the paint. Firing practice on the gunnery training ship *Excellent* was still carried on with smoothbores in 1884, and "the idea of teaching a man how to lay a gun with the idea of hitting anything was the last thing that had entered anyone's head. There were so many rounds of ammunition to be gotten rid of. Some ships conscientiously put them into the sea—through the guns—others put them into the sea without troubling to use the guns for the purpose."[62] The flagship of the Mediterranean Fleet, which had to be the most beautiful ship in the navy, was next to last in the firing trials, and it was only surpassed in lack of practice by that of Admiral Lord Charles Beresford.[63]

The new era in British gunnery began in 1899. In that year the fleet's average in prize firing (which cannot be compared directly with the French percentages) was 30 percent. The little cruiser *Scylla,* under the command of Percy Scott, a fifty-year-old captain waiting for retirement at fifty-five, turned in a figure of 80. Scott repeated the performance the next year in the much larger cruiser *Terrible.* "One cannot tell exactly what happened in England, but pushed on by English public opinion a veritable revolution took place."[64] By 1902, with a skillful use of the English sailor's love for competition, the whole British navy was applying itself as avidly to gunnery as it had before to polish and reviews.

Scott's three famous devices—the dotter, the deflection teacher, and the loading machine (a dummy gun with which picked crews from the ships on the China station held challenge matches at Hong Kong and Singapore)—were essentially methods of teaching quickness in loading and firing. With them came the application of the principle of continuous aim to heavy guns.

Scott had adopted the training devices with excellent results in the *Scylla,* until one day's practice in a heavy sea produced perfectly wretched scores for all but one man. Scott's careful observation of this one gunner provided the key to the whole problem: the man had learned by instinct to work his elevating wheel so rapidly that in spite of the rolling of the little *Scylla,* his sights were on the target all the time.[65] In the completed Scott system for a heavy gun, one man worked the elevating wheel, one the training mechanism, and the pointer kept the sights continuously on the target.

The new principle, in addition, made it possible to adopt a form of the telescopic sight; previously, the long experiments of the French and Americans with sighting tubes and telescopes had always failed when the ship's rolling carried the narrow field of vision of such mechanisms off the target. The telescopic sight not only provided a better image of the target but also simplified the job of the pointer, whose eye was certain to be at the same spot all the time and who had only two points, the crosshairs and the target, instead of three to keep in line. Under Scott's system, almost anybody with

good eyes and coordination could aim a heavy gun, and the revolution practically doubled the efficiency of the British fleet, as measured in the number
of shots it could lay on a given target in a given time.

The French were as stunned by the results of the British gunnery revolution as they had been by the whole Naval Defence Act. By 1903 the most
careful comparison that could be made between the prize firing of the two
navies showed that the number of hits per minute from the English ships,
instead of being a half to a quarter less, was nearly double that of the French.
In the training of individual gunners, the Scott system was a really formidable element of British sea power.[66]

The British still put the emphasis on the "man behind the gun" firing at a
fixed range in great firing contests. The first attempt to have a whole ship
fire at a given target, the trials of the *Majestic* against the old battleship *Belleisle* in 1900 to test the effect of projectiles, was carried out at a range that
was known in advance. Otherwise, it was "unlikely that the *Belleisle* would
have been hit very often."[67] When the commander of a turret wanted to
know the range, he hailed a messenger boy, who shouted to a midshipman,
who measured the range with a fixed-base rangefinder (the English were
the first to adopt this device) and sent another messenger boy back with the
results. As an experiment, the battleship *Canopus* was fitted with automatic
order transmitters, but in 1902 the sole means of communication on English ships was still armored speaking tubes. These had been shown to be
entirely useless in the Battle of the Yalu in 1894, when the temporary deaf-
ness of the men made it necessary to write orders on the deck with chalk.

Although a few English captains tried to work out a system of central gunnery control for their ships, the general British fire orders of 1902 divided
each ship into sections (similar to those which were to take over fire control in French ships after the communications systems had been shot away).
The captain of each section took the range and controlled the fire of his
portion of the battery. This system of splitting a big battleship into several
little ones would have made it as impossible to control the range by observing the fall of shot as it had been in the French trials of 1897 when several
ships happened to fire on the same target. The whole reason for adopting
central fire control was that splashes meant nothing unless one knew which
guns fired the shots that made them.[68]

In 1902 the state of gunnery in all the major navies was about the same,
except in the Italian, which used the British system of individual fire without
the sea-training of the gunners. The Russians and the Germans (the only
navy on whose methods of fire the French had no information whatever and
which may have discovered the principles of fire control independently)
were using the French system.[69]

The *Dreadnought,* the all-big-gun battleship of 1905, was the result of the
union of the two principles of ranging on the fall of shot and continuous

aim. The Americans, in a remarkable gunnery development after the Spanish-American War, were apparently the first to put the two together aboard their old battleships.[70] In 1903 the British published their first system for fire control, which added to the emphasis on the "man behind the gun" the idea that "it is not the individual gun, but the whole ship which is the fighting unit of the fleet."[71] The rest of the new system practically repeated the French Instructions of 1898, even down to the stepping method of finding the range.

With a method of finding the range at a long distance and improved means of pointing guns, it was now possible to fire at the enormous distances of 8,000 to 10,000 yards. This made the all-big-gun ship inevitable. A *Dreadnought* could overwhelm an all-medium-gun ship like that proposed by Cuniberti or built by the Germans without the latter getting close enough for its light shells even to reach the target accurately or to penetrate if they did hit. The *Dreadnought* combined some of the best ideas of the previous thirty years. Her speed came from Brin's idea of punishing the enemy by keeping outside the fire of his guns while holding him under one's own. The single-caliber armament made the best use of the fire control system first worked out by the French. The big guns were the result of the possibility opened by Percy Scott of hitting something at long range. Finally, the ship's large tonnage, as in the *Duilio* of the 1870s, resulted from all the other factors.

I have considered this matter in detail, simply because there is no single point in the naval history of this period that is more misunderstood. The *Dreadnought* was not due to the megalomania of Sir John Fisher, nor did it spring full-armed from his brain.[72] None of its elements were due to him, and his chief contribution was the boldness with which he resolved to combine them. In this case, as in his other innovations (the reform of the foreign stations, the new tactics, and the system of reduced crews), Fisher, a man of remarkable energy with a flair for advertising, represented a whole group of other men to whom he did not give credit in the footnotes. Fisher's originality (except in his harebrained World War I scheme for operations in the Baltic) and his importance have been greatly exaggerated all along the line, and the legend has been added to by his biographer, Admiral Sir Reginald Bacon, who does not even mention Scott in his account of the *Dreadnought*'s designing.[73] Men like Admiral Beresford were able propagandists, and Fisher was an extremely energetic adapter, but the new strength of the British navy in these years came as much from the efforts of officers such as Admirals Tryon, Wilson, and Rawson and Captain Scott (to mention those whom the French considered the most able) to prepare for war as from the more flamboyant personalities.

One factor that hastened the decision to adopt longer gunnery ranges (although it was not a factor of the first importance) was the increase in range of the automobile torpedo.[74] While gunnery ranges increased from 1,000 to 8,000 yards between 1898 and 1905, the range of torpedos increased proportionally, from 400 to 3,000 yards.

As was usual in torpedo work, the improvement came from the White-head firm, where Ludwig Obry applied to the torpedo the principle of the gyroscope. His simple apparatus, invented in 1894, weighed only eight pounds and cost about 1,000 francs, of which 750 were for patent rights. It could be applied to any torpedo in service to suppress the errors in direction due to the torpedo itself and to bring the torpedo back to the desired course, no matter what deviations took place when it fell into the water from the launch tube. In Austrian trials in 1896, a torpedo fired at 25 knots with but one of its screws working did not vary in direction more than 12 degrees. A torpedo could be fired from an underwater tube at any speed and any angle, and the Obry would bring it back on a course that was so constant that in the first new 2,000-yard Whitehead torpedo, it did not vary more than fifteen yards throughout. There was no need to wait for new torpedoes—all that was necessary was to buy and regulate enough Obrys. The latter point was the one still unsettled in 1898: a well-regulated Obry was infallible, but on one not properly regulated (about 3 percent of the time in the first trials), the action of the gyroscope infallibly caused the torpedo to turn in a perfect circle and come back at the firing ship.[75]

When the Obry entered service after 1898, the torpedo became practically like the gun, a scientifically perfected weapon that was nearly certain of hitting the mark if it were properly fired. In addition, its range, which had remained essentially the same since the days of the *autonomes* in the mid-1880s, could now be increased almost indefinitely merely by giving the torpedo greater compressed-air capacity.

Similar progress was made in mining by the adoption of the Austrian automatic mine, which could be laid by a cruiser or other fast ship in water of unknown depth. Offensive mining had previously been impractical owing to the need to take detailed soundings before laying mines.[76] By the early 1900s, as the new era in gunnery opened, the chief elements of a much improved torpedo and mining system were also falling into place.

Seventeen

Fashoda and British Sea Power

THE FASHODA CRISIS of 1898 was another major turning point in the development of the navy of the Third Republic, comparable in importance to the Aube ministry of 1886. The crisis brought England and France close to war and revealed to the French the major progress that England had made in naval plans and preparations while the French had been squabbling among themselves in the mid-1890s. It convinced the French, beyond any doubt, that in its current state, their navy would be overwhelmed if France chose to fight England.

FASHODA

On 10 July 1898, a French colonial expedition of about 150 men under Captain Jean-Baptiste Marchand arrived at the town of Fashoda on the Nile and raised the French flag. The expedition had set out more than two years earlier, despite a public warning from the British foreign secretary that England would regard any French presence in the Nile basin as an unfriendly act. On 18 September 1898 the advance guard of an English army of 20,000 men under Lord Kitchener appeared off Fashoda after completing the reconquest of the Sudan from the native mahdi. Marchand refused to abandon his position and lower his flag, and the two leaders referred the dispute to London and Paris. An intense diplomatic crisis ensued, marked by violently nationalistic press campaigns and political statements on both sides, but only one outcome was possible. On 3 November the French cabinet, realizing that France was not ready for war with England, gave the order for Marchand to withdraw.

Fortunately for the cause of peace, the Fashoda crisis found the French Navy not only unprepared but also, equally important, thoroughly aware of its condition. This awareness was due to the Niger crisis, a dispute between France and England over a portion of the Niger River that had embittered relations through most of 1897 and caused a war scare in February and March 1898. The public pressure that had led to initiation of a great armored cruiser program in 1897 was paralleled by the realization within the navy that it would have to plan to meet England.

In January 1898 the Superior Council drew up the Third Republic's first naval program directed solely and specifically at England.[1] The program turned out to be little different from its predecessors of 1896, 1894, and 1890. The most important thing about it was the realization of the odds that France faced. France could expect no help from the Russians; and England, like Italy and Germany, was ready to pass from the defensive to a revival of her old offensive naval policy using a navy of tremendous power that was ready for an immediate blockade of the French coasts.[2] France's only hope lay in an active defense of her coasts and in commerce-destroying supported by the battle fleet.[3]

The Fashoda crisis came just as Edouard Lockroy was beginning his second term as minister of marine. It caught him in the midst of redistributing the coast-defense battleships and reorganizing the Naval General Staff, actions that by now traditionally accompanied changes in ministers. Lockroy assigned as chief of staff Admiral Cavelier de Cuverville, the original advocate of the large commerce-raiding cruisers *Guichen* and *Châteaurenault,* and he gave Admiral Fournier command of the Mediterranean Squadron. His preparations during the crisis, however, were purely defensive.[4] He reinforced the troops in the ports, on the strategic islands off France's coasts, at Bizerte, and in the colonies. He also hastened ship construction and repairs in the ports, and he ordered the wooden decks of the old battleships to be covered with thin steel plates. The French officers were completely convinced of the danger of war and were prepared for the worst, but after the debates following the Niger crisis they clearly had little hope of success against the English.

BRITISH STRATEGY: THE CHANNEL

Throughout the crisis, the British Channel fleet cruised off Brest, ready to attack the unfinished works there, and off the island of Ouessant. At both spots, the French had feared a British attack during the Niger affair the year before.[5] The English apparently prepared an expedition of 20,000 men at Southampton for use against one of those points.[6] The Admiralty positioned another fleet at Gibraltar and readied the Mediterranean fleet for a *coup de main* against Bizerte by preparing another expeditionary force at Malta. The British probably also planned expeditions in the colonies against Diégo-Suarez in Madagascar and Fort de France in Martinique, although the evidence is less definite either way. Saigon and Dakar were the only French colonial posts with sufficient men to resist very long.[7] Perhaps most important, these war preparations gave a glimpse of the whole new strategic system that England had developed in the ten years since 1888.

The British, in fact, were so confident in their new strategy that there was actually some danger they might start a preventive war. Every new development in France in the summer before the crisis, from the internal political situation to the disappointing trials of melinite shells against the *La Galissonnière,* seemed designed to completely discourage the French. Everything in England in 1897, from the teachings of Mahan through the Spithead Review to a successful naval demonstration off Crete, raised the confidence of the British in their remarkable new navy to new heights. The British navy was "absolutely unrivalled."[8] A leading officer heartily congratulated the authors of the Naval Defence Act, stating that "now we look upon a navy of which we may well be proud, and which, in all human probability, ensures the safety of the Empire."[9] For the first time in modern history, not only the general British public but also the commercial interests seemed to welcome the idea of a war.[10] The idea became widespread that the time had come to settle with France once and for all. The French chargé d'affaires reported later that around this time "one frequently heard English men and women remark, 'We need a war: other nations need to know our strength and how much it is necessary to reckon with us.'"[11]

But while the English public and admirals such as Fisher were talking in the good old way about immediate offensives against the enemy's coasts, the British were developing the elements of the strategic system that they later used against Germany in World War I. Commander (later Admiral) George Alexander Ballard presented some of the key ideas in an essay that won the 1897 Gold Medal of the Royal United Service Institution, "The Protection of Commerce in War."[12] (The French even referred to the new British ideas as the *système Ballard.*)

The main differences between the old and new strategies lay in their methods of blockade. The increasing power of the torpedo boat gave the coup de grâce to the old system of having blockading battleships stand off the enemy's ports. The British used this system for the last time in their maneuvers of 1888, although the Americans used it successfully in the Spanish-American War of 1898 against weak torpedo opposition. In the old days, when protection of commerce was not a vital matter, British commanders detached their frigates from the blockading force only after the battle fleet had obtained command of the sea. The blockaders themselves caught most of the enemy marauders as they attempted to get in and out of port. During World War I, on the other hand, the battleships remained in their own bases, light craft observed the entrances to the enemy's harbors, and from the outset, cruisers provided direct protection to a now vital commerce against raiders the light blockading forces could not stop.

The British battleship Vengeance *(launched in 1899). Under construction during the Fashoda crisis, this unit of the* Canopus *class was one reason for British confidence in their control of the sea.*

By 1898 torpedo craft (Aube's *tirailleurs maritimes,* or naval sharpshooters) were so formidable that an attempt to carry out a close blockade might have caused such attrition to the blockaders that they would become no stronger than the blockaded fleet. With the appearance of the torpedo boat,

> our most dearly cherished strategical traditions were shaken to the bottom. The "proper place" for our battle fleet has always been "on the enemy's coasts," and now that was precisely where the enemy would be best pleased to see it.[13]

The British Grand Fleet commander in World War I, Admiral Sir John Jellicoe, realized that in advancing directly to an enemy's coast, a blockading force would expose itself to the wasting power of torpedo craft. "The policy of attrition of our Battle Fleet might thus be carried out with such success as to produce equality, or even inferiority, on the part of the British Fleet as compared with the German, in a comparatively short space of time."[14] In 1914 the Germans were not afraid of a British close blockade. Instead they hoped that Fisher, who was actually considering an offensive in the Baltic, would try one so the kaiser's submarines, mines, and torpedo boats could give the High Seas Fleet numerical equality with the British and produce circumstances favorable for a massive counterattack.[15] There was one catch:

Fisher did not command the Grand Fleet, which blockaded Germany without ever coming within sight of the German coasts.

The same factors were all present in 1898, including Fisher with his call to take the offensive, the cautious men in control who had no intention of doing so, and the French hope that the British would try it.

> The aim of the French fleets is to force the enemy to maintain before [French ports], if he wishes to keep the liberty of the sea, very important forces, and to use every occasion to menace that possession of the sea, so that the blockade of our coast will become an operation in which the enemy uses up his material and expends his forces while ours are maintained intact.[16]

The torpedo altered the whole question of naval strategy. In the old days, each fleet consisted almost exclusively of battleships, and the only problem was how to concentrate them on a specific field of action. By the late 1890s each fleet consisted of not only battleships, to be concentrated as before, but also torpedo craft, which were effective against battleships but could not proceed far to sea. Now it was desirable to lure the enemy as far away from his bases as possible, so that more and more of his torpedo craft would drop out, toward a friendly base whose torpedo craft would add their strength to that of the friendly battleships.[17] In their 1895 maneuvers, the French attempted a close blockade of Brest and Quiberon and proved once more the practical impossibility "of blockading a port provided with a *défense mobile.* The large ships, due to the mere fact of the existence of that defense, are always forced to retire during the night to a distance so great . . . that the passage is entirely open."[18] In his 1898 article, Ballard did not propose to blockade Toulon at all, and the tight blockade of Brest was also done for.[19]

The only kind of blockade now possible was a loose one, in which light craft watched the enemy fleet while the main force remained in its bases.[20] The torpedo-boat destroyer, which had only been introduced by the British in 1894, now emerged as a crucial ship. The destroyers were the first craft small enough to be built in sufficient numbers to set up a real surveillance cordon but large enough to keep the seas and to threaten both the battleships and the torpedo boats inside the blockaded ports. The curious proposal to give the first French destroyers interchangeable armaments shows that they were seen as both torpedo boats and gunboats. "They are dangerous adversaries for both our battleships and our torpedo craft . . . and the presence of such craft at the entrance to our ports will prevent our battleships from coming out in the same way that the presence of torpedo craft inside our ports prevents his battleships from approaching them during the night."[21]

To carry out such a blockade of Brest, Ballard proposed to take the island

The destroyer Rapière *(1901). Similar to the first French destroyer, the* Durandal, *she carried a mixed armament of guns for use against torpedo boats, and torpedo tubes for use against battleships.*

of Ouessant as an advance base. At the time the island was entirely unprotected, and the French could not have retaken it since it was ten miles offshore and could be considered an island in the open sea rather than a point on the French coast.[22] Ballard did not make it clear whether the British would try to keep their battleships there, protected from the French torpedo boats by an elaborate system of mines and booms. (Later French maneuvers proved this was possible only in favorable weather.)[23] After Fashoda, the French spent 85 million francs for permanent fortifications to replace the trenches thrown up on this French Heligoland during the crisis.[24] The plan to take Ouessant was, in fact, only a temporary project due to the French foolishly leaving the island undefended, and once the new fortifications were in place the British gave up the idea.[25] By 1903 the British planned to keep their fleet in the well-defended home bases that had been prepared during peacetime and to use temporary bases only for light craft and cruisers.

From 1889 to 1903 British ideas on bases thus passed through three stages of evolution. The English first recognized that it was impossible to keep the fleet directly off an enemy port without an advanced base for coaling. They then realized that the danger from the torpedo boat was so great that it was nearly impossible to improvise sufficient protection for the fleet off enemy shores. They finally concluded that it was better to keep the main fleet at home in major bases prepared in peacetime.

After 1895 the British spent enormous sums on metropolitan bases for use as defended anchorages for offensive blockades. By 1902 the amount spent under the Naval Works Loan Act of 1895 had risen to 27.5 million pounds (6 million more than the Naval Defence Act), while the War Office budget for a single year, 1897–98, contained 7 million more.[26]

The positions and relative importance of these bases reflected the new English strategy. In 1886 the British had three bases opposite the French pair of Cherbourg and Brest. In order of importance (and also moving from east to west), these were Portsmouth, Portland, and Plymouth. The main projects between 1886 and 1898 were a great increase in the importance of Plymouth and the building of a new deep-water harbor at Dover opposite the new French secondary base at Dunkirk. The previous fortifications at Dover had been designed simply to prevent a landing. The new port, which at 3.5 million pounds was second in cost only to Gibraltar in the program, was intended as a base for the blockade of Dunkirk.

For offensive operations against Brest, the British built not one base but a whole system. The main base at Plymouth, with the extension of the nearby facilities at Devonport Dockyard and Keyham, became nearly as important as Portsmouth. In addition, the English built two entirely new secondary bases further to the west, at Falmouth and in the Scilly Islands, to push the line of British operations fully fifty miles closer to the French port. To the east, they gave Portland, now entirely secondary in importance, an advance base near France in the Channel Islands. It is not clear how extensive the fortifications in the Channel Islands were, but there was at least a new cable that so worried the French that they sent out fishing boats to attempt to drag it up to discover its position.[27]

BRITAIN IN THE MEDITERRANEAN

The tangled question of controlling the western access to the Mediterranean completely overshadowed other aspects of Mediterranean strategy from the mid-1890s until the Entente of 1904 ended the Anglo-French naval rivalry. Just as the British realized that the main aim of the French Mediterranean Fleet was to break out into the Atlantic, the problem was enormously complicated by the simultaneous weakening of Spain and Morocco, both of which were clearly falling into the French diplomatic orbit. The key British strategic decision in the Mediterranean was to undertake a vast program of works at Gibraltar.

The popular idea in England that Gibraltar closed the straits with its guns was a remnant of sailing days, when the currents and winds forced all ships passing the straits to hug the European shore. By 1893 careful French studies had made it perfectly clear that ships passing at night on a course close to the African shore would encounter no difficulty whatever from the guns. They would also not be seriously threatened by British torpedo craft, which would have difficulty even coming out of the harbor in some weather. (The problem there was exactly like that at Dunkirk, where without advance

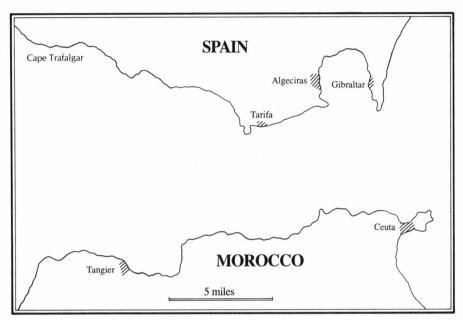

The Straits of Gibraltar

knowledge that the enemy was coming, it was almost impossible for torpedo boats to sortie fast enough to do any damage.) As long as the main British fleet was at Malta and there was no fleet at Gibraltar, all the guns the British could cram into the Rock would make little difference.[28]

If there were a fleet inside Gibraltar with cruisers patrolling outside, however, the straits would be harder to force than even the much narrower Strait of Bonifacio between Corsica and Sardinia. The important factor was the length of the straits, not their width. The area that could be controlled from Gibraltar was not just the short narrow passage between Gibraltar and Ceuta but the entire Alborán Sea, a long funnel that extended almost as far to the east as the line between Oran and Cartagena and narrowed as one approached the Rock. The French would have to pass some part of this distance in daytime, and the British would find it fairly easy to maintain a cruiser watch over the narrower portions at night.[29] It was relatively easy to avoid the guns at Gibraltar, but against a fleet it would be almost impossible to pass without fighting an action.

The French maneuvers of 28 June 1900 proved conclusively that the diagnosis of the situation made in 1893 had been correct. In a carefully worked-out secret exercise, the Mediterranean Squadron under Admiral Gervais tried to force the passage against three cruisers representing a British patrol. In the most famous of all Gervais's feats of navigation, the entire squadron, in line ahead without even the secret running lights that had been used in every previous French maneuver, passed through the dangerous currents close to the African shore at practically full speed without an accident. The British did not signal the French passage, but all three of the little French cruisers apparently saw the fleet before it got to Gibraltar. The official French report concluded,

> The problem of guarding the straits is so easy to solve by stationing a naval force at Gibraltar that the hope of escaping its notice without the aid of exceptional atmospheric conditions, such as a thick fog, is illusory. . . . The risk of battle is almost inescapable if the enemy is in force in the Bay of Gibraltar.[30]

In the early 1890s Gibraltar was only an impregnable anchorage like Aden, not a base for fleet operations. Although the Rock was crammed with guns of every description, it lacked practically everything else. It had no dry dock, and ships with underwater damage had to go to either Malta or England for repairs. It had no reserve stocks of naval ammunition, and its coaling wharves were so small that only two battleships could coal at one time. Gibraltar's situation as a commercial coaling port was declining rapidly on account of the rise of Algiers, and if the alarmists could be believed, there was not more than half enough coal there for the Mediterranean Fleet in 1893.[31] In that year the British examined various proposed strategies for the Mediterranean, including pulling out of it entirely in time of war. They concluded that their greatest need was to create a base of operations in the straits.[32] They subsequently undertook works at Gibraltar, including dry docks, a small arsenal, and a mole for protection against torpedo boats.

The fact that it was the fleet and not the guns at Gibraltar that controlled the straits limited the importance of three other ports in the area: Algeciras, Tangier, and Ceuta. The British and French each suspected the other of designs on these and would have been ready to fight to prevent them from falling into the hands of the other, but the real value of these positions was less than was generally imagined. The possession of both sides of the straits would not enable Britain to close them more effectively than she could by stationing ships at Gibraltar. For the French, a move on Tangier would have been the height of folly. Their whole problem was to elude a blockade by British destroyers, and there was no point in building a military port right where the British could most effectively watch it. Instead, they could build a base to the east at Oran, which was sufficiently close to provide every advantage of a position in the straits except the unimportant one of having guns that could fire at passing ships. The reason for the eventual Franco-British compromise on Tangier was simply that neither power had enough to gain from a forward move to warrant making trouble.

The proximity of Algeciras to Gibraltar made it the most important of the three lesser ports for the British. A number of Spanish artillery officers had claimed during a nationalist revival in Spain in 1883–84 that mobile siege artillery placed in the hills north of Gibraltar and around Algeciras could render the port untenable. The new Krupp field guns like those which had proven so effective at the battle of Plevna in 1877, firing from emplacements and earthworks prepared in peacetime and using smokeless powder that rendered them invisible, could easily do tremendous damage to a target as large as a dockyard, though no one contemplated reduction of the Rock it-self.[33] The English who studied the problem admitted that the danger was real, and its importance was increased by the placement of the new works begun at Gibraltar in the 1890s on the west side of the Rock facing the Spanish port.[34]

The British kept mountain guns and field artillery at Gibraltar, not for a *coup de main* on Tangier or Ceuta but for operations in Andalusia.[35] In 1898 a Spanish attempt to use the American danger as an excuse to place some of the guns in position at Algeciras provoked a vigorous British response. A statement by the British prime minister, Arthur Balfour, in 1903 that every measure had been taken for the security of the new works could only have meant that England was ready to take the Spanish territory around Algeciras to prevent such a bombardment.[36]

The danger from Spain gave rise to numerous proposals to trade Gibraltar for Tangier or Ceuta. The earliest of these seems to have been made in 1868.[37] These discussions, in turn, provoked French fears that Britain was ready to take one of the two ports in order to gain possession of both sides of the straits. In fact, the governors at Gibraltar had standing instructions to take Tangier on the receipt of telegraphic orders from London.[38] It appears, however, that the danger of such an offensive move on England's part was largely nonexistent. As long as France made no move, Britain was unlikely to make one. In the Entente of 1904, the two countries settled the question of Tangier, to the complete surprise of the Germans, who had considered it a source of permanent conflict.[39]

Strategically, the Balearic Islands were much more important than Tangier, and a British move against them appeared more likely. In 1898 Ballard proposed taking the Balearics as an advanced observation point against a French fleet moving from Toulon toward the straits.[40] Alfred Thayer Mahan advised the English to retake Port Mahon on Minorca (which they had held for most of the period from 1708 to 1803). Sir Charles Dilke and Admiral Beresford were the leading partisans of the idea, and the designs of the English were more publicly expressed with regard to the Balearics than any other point in the Mediterranean.[41] The danger of a British move was real, not imaginary. "While war between France and England appeared to be the greatest impending danger, Spain was well aware that the Balearic Islands, and possibly the Canaries, would almost inevitably fall into the hands of one of the combatants."[42]

The prize was weakly defended. The principal port in the Balearics, Port Mahon, was protected by some fairly strong fixed fortifications put up by the Spanish equivalent of the Jeune Ecole in the 1880s. By the time of Fashoda, these would have been useful, like the fortifications of Constanti-nople, chiefly to the first great power to arrive there. Port Mahon com-pletely lacked men and ammunition, and there were no mines whatever, although this was a long, narrow port where defenses with mines could have been improvised very quickly. The military capital of the Balearics was on a different island, and the *défense mobile* of the whole Balearic group consisted of one twenty-two-year-old spar torpedo boat.[43]

To the French, the question of the Balearics was second in importance only to that of Gibraltar itself.[44] In the maneuvers of both 1900 and 1901, the French examined the problem of getting past a British fleet operating just off Minorca. Both maneuvers ended with the defeat of the "French" force. In 1900 the "British" lost contact with the "French" just off Toulon but caught them again in the Balearic passage, as Ballard had predicted. In 1901 the "British" off the Balearics battered a force from Brest that was creeping north along the coast toward Toulon and then caught and held the Toulon squadron.[45] It was nearly as impossible to get past an advance force at Port Mahon as it would have been to force the passage of the straits against an alert fleet inside Gibraltar.

The English proposals to Spain at the time of the Algeciras episode in 1898 are further proof of how badly Britain wanted the Balearics. On 30 October, with the authority of the cabinet, Sir Henry Charles Drummond-Wolff submitted to the Spanish government the following four points:

1. In case of war, Spain shall not side with England's enemies, but give aid to England to the best of her ability and resources. . . .

2. Spain will defend Gibraltar from all land attack, undertaking not to con-struct any works of fortification or batteries, or mount any guns other than field guns within gunshot of Gibraltar—that is, for the present, 7 miles.

3. England may enlist Spanish soldiers in time of war.

4. If Spain becomes involved in war, England will assist her by preventing any hostile force from landing in the Bay of Algeciras or on the coast within gunshot of Gibraltar, and by undertaking the defence on the part of Spain of the Balearic and Canary Islands.

In rejecting the British proposals, Spain offered the following counter-proposals, which the British in turn rejected as "possibly restrictive of Brit-ish freedom of action in the event of war."

1. Spain will guarantee that Gibraltar shall not be attacked by Spanish forces, or by the forces of a Power at war with England operating from Spanish territory. . . .

2. England will undertake that, in time of war, she will not conduct military operations on Spanish territory, continental or insular, and that on the demand of Spain, but not otherwise, she will navally assist to prevent violation of Spanish territory.[46]

While the British and French were able to compromise on the Tangier-Morocco question during the negotiations that produced their 1904 Entente, the British flatly rejected the French proposal for a guarantee of the territorial status quo within a circle of five hundred miles of the Straits of Gibraltar, which included the Balearics. The French ambassador admitted that the English had not been taken in by his explanation that it was the German danger that worried France in the Balearics.[47]

The French and British also displayed considerable activity in the eastern part of the great inland sea, but neither power undertook anything as concrete as the real plans both had for the spoliation of the Spanish. The French colonial school that advocated developing a French route to the Indies with strong points at Tunis, Tonkin, and Madagascar was dead, and with it died the old notion of a French offensive into the eastern Mediterranean. (It was the diplomats, not the navy, that demanded the reestablishment of the navy's Levant Squadron.) Though both the French and the British would have readily accepted a share in the Turkish empire, the question was not nearly as important for either as that of Morocco and Spain.

England demonstrated her lack of real strategic interest in the Near East by completely abandoning Italy in the 1890s and by her willingness to compromise with Russia on the question of Constantinople after 1900. In 1903 the British Defence Committee unanimously decided that while Russia would get some advantage from having free use of the Turkish Straits and being able to close them to all other powers, "it would not fundamentally alter the present strategic situation in the Mediterranean."[48]

In 1898 the British still planned to retain military forces in the Mediterranean in case of war, but they had accepted that merchant shipping would have to go around the Cape of Good Hope. Ballard was even willing for Britain to blow up the Suez Canal if she had to.[49] The British did send a coast-defense ship to Alexandria (in effect, taking possession of the place), establish a 54,000-ton coal supply there, lay a new cable to Malta and Gibraltar, and reorganize the Egyptian Army. The French interpreted these moves correctly as simply an attempt to close the canal to other powers, not as a British effort to establish a new center of power in the eastern Mediterranean.[50] The British did nothing to develop Cyprus and made no concrete moves at the desirable port of Suda Bay in Crete. The really important new strategic works undertaken by the British after the mid-1890s were those at Dover, Plymouth, and Gibraltar.

The armored cruiser Kléber *(1902). Part of the large French armored cruiser program of 1897–98, this ship and her two sisters were also the last cruisers designed specifically for service overseas.*

THE SEA LANES

In accepting the principle of the loose blockade, the British admitted one of Admiral Aube's main contentions: the necessity for the direct protection of English commerce. Initially the British had responded to the threat to their commerce with the theory that they could simply transfer most of their merchant marine to foreign flags, but Ballard, in the second part of the system he proposed in 1898, attempted to provide direct support to British trade by a combination of "sweeping the seas," cruiser patrols, and convoys.

By the time of Fashoda, the transfer theory was clearly unworkable. The McKinley tariff of 1890 in the United States and a new protective law in Italy made transfer of tonnage more difficult, and the French were clearly prepared to refuse to recognize transfers anyway. Even in cases where transfers were genuine and in good faith, French cruisers were to sequester the ships and tie them up in French harbors, and even to sink them when they could not take them into port. "A few indemnities more or less" would certainly not be too high a price for stopping both the real and the fake neutrals from leaving their ports. The French now planned an immediate attack on British commerce at the outbreak of war to create an insurance panic with rates that they hoped would go as high as 25 percent of the total value of ship and cargo.[51] When the French embarked on armored cruiser construction in 1897, they also clearly decided to go the limit in cruiser warfare by ruthlessly destroying prizes, declaring food contraband of war, and even possibly declaring a paper blockade of England as Germany did in 1915.[52]

The whole French navy's all-out embrace of commercial warfare in the late 1890s was essentially due to the change in the relations between England and Germany. Only the extremists would have been ready for such a war in 1886, for at that time such methods would have led to an immediate German intervention against France. In 1898 the French felt they could

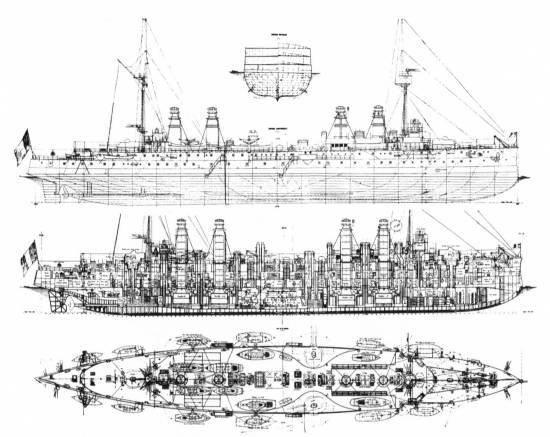

An official plan of the armored cruiser Kléber *(1902). A diminutive version of the*
Gueydon *type designed for overseas stations, this 7,600-ton, 21-knot ship had side
armor only 3.9 inches thick and carried her eight 6.4-inch guns in four twin
turrets.*

count on "benevolent and interested" German neutrality, though not actual
German help. The new factor was the dramatic rise of the German merchant marine and of German economic competition with England in the
decade before Fashoda. By 1898 there were in Europe

> two great, irreconcilable, opposing forces, two great nations who would
> make the whole world their province, and who would levy from it the
> tribute of commerce. England . . . and Germany . . . compete in every
> corner of the globe. . . . Is there a mine to exploit, a railway to build, a
> native to convert from breadfruit to tinned meat, from temperance to
> trade gin, the German and the Englishman are struggling to be first.[53]

Ultimately, the question of going the limit in commercial warfare depended on only one factor: the interests and attitude of the neutrals. The
wrangling of England and Germany in the 1890s, notably the furor over the

Kruger telegram of 1896 in which the kaiser appeared to be inciting resistance to the British in the Transvaal, made it clear that the Germans would not intervene against France in an Anglo-French commercial war. Instead, a general French attack on English commerce would give Germany an unequaled opportunity to ruin British trade and shipping in every part of the world.

A French observer noted that "Germany will not only not supply England, she will be only too glad to stop the transport of English goods, while the German coal barons, the German merchants, the German shippers, and the German shipbuilders" ascended to the heights of an unequaled prosperity.[54] Germany, the most powerful neutral, had "too great an interest, in case of an Anglo-French war, in substituting herself for Britain as common carrier on the seas to think of creating any trouble for us."[55] Ballard perceived the danger and noted that even Germany's joining France and Russia in a war against England would "not prove an unmixed evil, as it would free us of a possible rival for commercial supremacy at a critical period." In addition, it would permit closing the Suez Canal to all shipping, which would be to England's benefit. By their control of the coal and ports on the Cape route, the British could "put under considerable and perhaps prohibitive difficulties" any neutral shipping that tried to supplant them.[56]

British trade in 1898 would have been highly vulnerable to the French. Of the total of 9 million tons, one third was sailing ships—the product of a new revival of sail in the 1890s—which would disappear immediately on the outbreak of the war. Of the 6 million tons of steam shipping, only 28 ships made over 18 knots, 300 from 14 to 18, and the vast majority, 8,000, from 8 to 12. For the French, these last were "our cruisers' inevitable prey," for the tramp steamer "is not only an organ essential to [England's] material existence, but even an absolute necessity for the actual support of life."[57]

Ballard's main proposal for commerce defense was the "patrol of focal zones," a sort of midpoint between "sweeping the seas" and the convoy system. Even the captain of the *Alabama,* Raphael Semmes, had concluded after the Civil War that with "a few more ships on the chief highways," the "old gentlemen" would have protected the Union commerce pretty thoroughly.[58] Under Ballard's proposal, a double line of cruisers was to patrol the four main trade routes from England to Newfoundland, Bermuda, Gibraltar, and the Azores, while the entrances to the Mediterranean and the Baltic were to be tightly closed. For example, on the Newfoundland route one cruiser would start on the seven-day voyage from each end each day at a speed of 15 knots. With two days for rest and coal between voyages, it would be possible to maintain a constant stream of ships going in both directions with no gap ever greater than 160 miles. A merchant ship, on sighting an enemy, would make full speed away along the route toward the next cruiser, while the nonarrival of expected ships would show where the raider was at work.[59] Large, fast cruisers like the *Powerful* were to be held in reserve until one of the few fast raiders like the *Châteaurenault,* which the patrolling cruisers could not catch, was signaled. When this happened, four pursuers guided by telegraphic reports would start from Plymouth, one along each of the four main lines, to end the raider's career before she had time to coal.

The British dedicated two new bases especially to commerce protection. Cork and Pembroke already protected the two sides of the southern entrance to the Irish Sea. The new protected points at Bantry Bay and Lough Swilly in the south and north of Ireland opened the possibility of diverting much traffic around the north of Ireland. They also provided refuges where groups of old battleships could be formed to escort merchant shipping through the narrow seas around the British Isles.

The Admiralty, in fact, appeared to be moving toward adoption of convoys at least for the narrow seas, and possibly for wider areas in case the patrol system failed. It refitted several old battleships, whose armor was now too thin for the battle fleet, with new guns and boilers for use against armored cruisers. Though there was much opposition to convoy in the 1880s and early 1890s (largely due to the great variation in the speeds of merchant ships during the height of the transition from sail to steam), there was more opinion in its favor than is commonly supposed. Admiral P. H. Colomb defended it very ably in 1887, and men like Sir Thomas Brassey and Sir Charles Dilke both saw the necessity of returning to it as a last resort—as the French were convinced they would.[60]

The mid-1890s, however, were the high point in British planning for commerce protection before World War I. The English soon began to regress, in part because of the general overconfidence of such men as Fisher that "the Admiralty had gone to the bottom of the matter," and in part because Mahan's historical proof that commercial warfare was impossible was too reassuring.[61] Ballard led the way: he seems to have accepted the idea of patrol rather reluctantly and to have put most of his faith in the pursuit of individual marauders. He objected to convoys, and the Royal Commission on the Supply of Food and Raw Material in Time of War gave official sanction to his objections by repeating them in 1905.[62] Around the same time, the British practically abandoned the idea of national insurance for shipping in wartime.

Instead of fearing for their trade, the English after Fashoda actually seem to have believed that any opponent would come out for one big battle, according to Mahan's rules. The Admiralty memorandum to the Commission of 1905 was a perfect example of the glosses on Mahan, full of phrases like "the fleet in being" and "the sea is one," which passed for naval strategy in Britain at the time.

The memorandum even took a step backward from Ballard's position, for it rejected the idea of direct protection of commerce entirely. The command of the sea was essential for the successful attack or defense of commerce, and concentration of force was the best way to gain that command. "A dispersion of strength for either of those objects is the strategy of the weak, and cannot materially influence the ultimate result of the war." Admiral Sir Cyprian Bridge categorically agreed with the proposition that "the policy of attack upon commerce upon the great scale cannot take place before the actual effect of battle power on naval predominance has been secured and ascertained."[63] The French report on the British maneuvers of 1900 noted that "the sole objective of both admirals was concentration for the one big battle. [The "French" admiral's] conception was not even criticized in England, *though it contained absolutely no provision for the destruction of enemy commerce.*"[64]

From 1898 to 1914 the Admiralty made no progress whatever on the general problem of commerce protection besides establishing the Trade Section of the Intelligence Department in 1903, which supplied the "plodding, methodical, daily" collection of trade information for which Sir John Colomb had pleaded in 1881.[65] The British only elaborated on the Ballard system of patrol.

As long as Britain's enemies accepted Britain's rules, such a policy did little damage. Indeed, no one was more surprised than the Germans when they suddenly found that wartime circumstances actually forced them into the "errors of the French."[66] Once World War I was under way, Ballard, an admiral at Malta in 1916, was one of the first to abandon the patrol system. As late as 1917, the Admiralty had no idea of how many convoys would be required.[67]

BRITISH STRATEGY AGAINST FRANCE, 1898

The English war plan of 1898, known in France as the *système Ballard,* cowed the French during Fashoda and shaped their naval effort after the crisis. Its elements can be summarized as follows:

1. Defensive in the Mediterranean by eighteen battleships, twenty-two cruisers, and fifteen destroyers against the main French fleet of fifteen battleships and fifteen cruisers at Toulon. Diversion of commerce to the Cape, where the works at Simonstown were the third largest project in the works program after Plymouth and Gibraltar.

2. The blockade of Brest by a *coup de main* against Ouessant. Communications between the destroyers off Brest and the main force at Plymouth to be provided by a cable to Ouessant or by an old cruiser fitted with a special apparatus that played out a light cable as she went along. At Plymouth, a rapid squadron of the nine *Majestics* plus fourteen cruisers and twenty destroyers.

3. Portsmouth and Dover to watch Cherbourg and Dunkirk using a slow squadron of ten battleships, seven cruisers, twelve torpedo gunboats, and twenty destroyers.

4. Direct protection of commerce from Cork, Pembroke, Bantry Bay, and Lough Swilly using thirteen old battleships, ten large cruisers of the *Powerful* type for chasing, twenty-five second-class cruisers for patrol, and thirty third-class cruisers for the narrow seas.

5. Mopping up the French colonies: Bizerte from Malta, Fort de France from the new garrison at Port Castries in St. Lucia, New Caledonia by the newly organized Australian militia, and other expeditions (with less chance of success) against Diégo-Suarez, Dakar, and Saigon.

As nearly as can be told, France had literally no chance against this juggernaut in 1898. The French realization of this fact helped keep the peace during the Fashoda crisis and impelled France to lay aside her politically motivated bickering long enough to start putting her naval house in order.

Eighteen

After Fashoda

BEFORE FASHODA there were two French navies: that of the Jeune Ecole and that of the traditionalists. After the crisis, the most striking development was the union of the moderates of both schools in the Chamber and elsewhere against the extremists on both sides. The moderates first came to power in June 1899 in the ministry of Jean-Louis de Lanessan, who, appropriately enough, was part of a cabinet whose mission was to heal the wounds of a much larger struggle, the Dreyfus affair. In 1900 this cabinet proposed to Parliament five basic laws, including a new building program, which provided the foundation for a new balanced maritime policy. The moderates returned to power permanently in January 1905 and continued to work toward a major revival of the French Navy, which, however, was interrupted by the outbreak of World War I.

THE LAST OF THE EXTREMISTS

In its early years, the movement toward unity encountered strong opposition from both extremes. In a striking epitaph for the traditionalist ideas of the 1890s, Admiral Rieunier launched violent attacks in the Chamber of Deputies in 1899 and 1900 against the policies of the Lockroy ministry. He defended the battleships, the lack of homogeneity in the fleet, and even the *Magenta,* as well as the archaic arsenal administration and the councils that had produced them. At the same time, he attacked the torpedo boats, the submarines, the Ecole supérieure de la Marine, the idea of a civilian minister of marine, the Jeune Ecole's journal *La Marine française,* Lockroy's career as a journalist, and "all the insults of the Jacobins against an ancient and honorable organization."[1]

On the left, the extremists of the Jeune Ecole retained control of the press during Lanessan's ministry. They helped launch a violent newspaper campaign against England when that country began fighting the Boers in South Africa a year after Fashoda. Their propaganda contained nothing new and simply rehashed all of Aube's old extravagances, such as the assertion that twenty cruisers could ruin English trade. Lanessan and the navy were fortunate that the politicians who in the 1890s had attacked the admirals every time a sailor hit his thumb with a hammer now turned their unrivaled gifts for name-calling against the British.[2]

A cruel twist of fate brought the Jeune Ecole back to power one last time in 1902, interrupting the movement toward unity for a fateful two and a half years. In June 1902 Camille Pelletan, who had used the ideas of the Jeune Ecole against his political enemies throughout the 1890s, became minister of marine in a cabinet dedicated to defending the Republic against its enemies on the right. Pelletan faithfully based his administration on the worst of the Jeune Ecole ideas of the 1890s: that the welfare of the arsenal workers, the common sailors, and the republican officers was more important than the welfare of the navy as a whole. There was nothing new about such an approach—thirty years earlier the traditionalists had refused promotion to republicans like Gougeard in the belief that the navy existed to serve the interests of the aristocrats of the port towns.

Some of the incidents during the Pelletan ministry were so outrageous as to be amusing. In 1903 the destroyer *Espingole* was sunk in a collision near Toulon, and Pelletan gave the contract for her salvage to two wine merchants of the proper political faith. These worthies had no equipment for the task, and the minister lent them men and machinery from Toulon. Even so, they were unable to raise the ship.

Pelletan's supporters could defend other of his actions only as "stamping out clericalism and aristocracy in the navy." Some of these political actions were merely puerile. For example, he suppressed the dress uniforms of the officers and, instead of giving new ships "aristocratic" but traditional names such as *Dupleix, Suffren,* and *Dupuy de Lôme,* he assigned good "republican" names like *Justice, Liberté,* and *Ernest Renan.*

Some of his political actions threatened to undermine discipline in the service. When a sailor named Kermovant was sentenced to the usual thirty days in the brig for drunkenness, Pelletan released him as part of "the general justice due to the common sailor." The minister also relieved Admirals Amédée-Pierre-Léonard Bienaimé, Edmond-Baptistin Ravel, and Eugène-Albert Maréchal from their commands for their previous relations with Lockroy and Lanessan. He raised the pay of the arsenal workers, but as an economy measure he put on half pay ashore many stokers and common sailors, whose cause he also claimed to foster but who had no votes.

The minister's technical competence was on the same level. To prove the outmoded theory of *décuirassement,* he ordered a test in which a battleship fired point-blank at the turret of the *Suffren,* a new battleship that had not yet even started its sea trials. He met a Swiss chemist named Raoul Pictet at a summer resort and gave him a staff of naval engineers to work out a new type of submarine. He did not bother to appoint new members to the Conseil des Travaux to replace the "aristocrats" he had retired, and the only two new projects he submitted to that body in 1903 and 1904 were by his socialist friends from Basse Colombes. One of these called for a ship with inclined armor; the other (which the minister submitted officially) was for an invulnerable ram.[3]

Pelletan's ministry provoked widespread reactions. The reports that France's ally, Russia, officially demanded some action on Pelletan's weakening the navy cannot be confirmed.[4] The English were relieved, and even amused, by actions that clearly degraded the strength of what had once been their main naval rival.[5] French experts were deeply disturbed.[6] But the most important reaction was the reaffirmation of the unity of the French naval moderates, which had first appeared in 1899. The striking unanimity of the press campaign that was raised against Pelletan, with Lockroy and Lanessan both attacking him in the Chamber, and the contempt of the republican officers themselves for those who became the "spies of the minister" by reporting on the clericalism of their superiors, were signs of a new spirit.[7] Pelletan's "republican" ardor, like Rieunier's speech, was simply a fitting, if belated, climax to an era in which party politics were more important than the good of the navy. Both extremes had clearly outlived their day, and the remarkable work of the Lanessan administration, which happened to come before that of Pelletan in time, was the real beginning of the unity of the modern French Navy.

THE LANESSAN MINISTRY

Lanessan's ministry was less a victorious return of the traditionalists than it was the beginning of an official realization that public (and parliamentary) opinion was generally right in matters of administration and generally wrong in matters of naval strategy and building programs. In the administrative area, Lanessan implemented many reforms that the navy's critics had demanded for years. Retaining most of Lockroy's reforms in the central administration and the arsenals, he separated the Naval General Staff from the minister's cabinet and made a modest attempt to reduce the number of services within the navy and to free them from the worst features of the Chamber's straitjacket accounting system of *crédits-achats* and *crédits-matières.* He also restructured the budget to eliminate the traditional but meaningless separation between personnel and matériel expenses and replaced it with a distinction between the fleet under construction and the operational fleet.

French naval strategies since the mid-1880s had provided for either war against nobody but the Triple Alliance (Germany, Italy, and Austria) or nobody but England. The most striking characteristics of Lanessan's strategy were its flexibility and its close integration with the cautious diplomacy of Théophile Delcassé, France's minister of foreign affairs from 1898 to 1905. Like that diplomacy, the new strategy was entirely without that *grand fracas* so dear to Kaiser Wilhelm II, the taste for which in naval affairs went back to Aube. But like the German strategy, it was based on the seemingly permanent mutual hostility of all three western powers: France, Germany, and England. France could not hope for a permanent understanding with either England or Germany, but the mutual aversion of her prospective opponents was so strong that it was nearly certain that France would be able to strike a neutrality agreement with one or the other. In fact, France would be safer attempting such an agreement than trying to count on her own ally, Russia.

During Lanessan's ministry the most immediate danger was a preventive war launched by England, and his first move would have been to seek an agreement with the Germans. Since Delcassé's policy was, for the moment, strictly defensive, there was no question of forming a new Continental League to overthrow England. Even so, the feeling in the navy in favor of coming to terms with the Germans was very strong. The French recognized that "ship for ship and man for man" the German navy was "equal to any in the world," while the English were still repeating the hoary argument that "Germany had ships but no sailors to man them."[8] However, the French never hoped for a naval alliance, but only for an assurance of German neutrality in a French war with England. This would allow France to leave sufficient troops in the colonies—an important consideration, since France, in adopting a policy of active defense, had to depend on direct protection of the colonies.[9] England's lack of troops and a large French army massed in the Channel ports would paralyze English offensive action. Even more important, the lid would be off for ruthless French commercial warfare.

The navy did not state its ideas in public, since it had always been suspect to the advocates of revenge against Germany, but there was a surprising unanimity within it as to the need for some arrangement with Germany. Even Lockroy, who formerly had bitterly criticized Jules Ferry for diverting French attention from Alsace and Lorraine to his colonial schemes, now came out in public with a cautious statement that recent German actions "tend to lay the basis for a future accord, which might not be concluded but which also might be concluded."[10] As in Ferry's ministry (1883–85), the danger of attack by England seemed so great "that, though we may not abandon, we must at least adjourn all ideas of revenge in the East."[11] "We must come to some understanding with Germany with regard to this specific point [an attack by England]. Alliance, entente, accord, convention—

the name does not matter. The policy of emotion has outlived its day, and we have been its victims. Let us, like the others, follow a policy in line with our interests."[12]

Yet all of the French Navy's new leaders would really have preferred a settling of France's difficulties with England. None of them had any sympathy with the attempt to create the kind of permanent antagonism between France and "our real hereditary enemy" that the professional anglophobes were preaching. Lockroy, the most hostile to England, had also been among those most concerned with revenge against Germany. Delcassé, who was foreign minister while Lanessan was minister of marine and who later himself became minister of marine, was equally opposed to the permanent estrangement of France and England and was anxious, even during the crisis of 1898, to come to an understanding.[13] Lanessan, under whom the navy formulated its most complete plan for warfare against England, had been the founder of the Entente Cordiale Society of 1897, which worked to produce the understanding that was reached in 1904.

Admiral Fournier, whose revised idea of a fleet containing both battleships and cruisers that could be used against both England and Germany was the basis of Lanessan's Program of 1900, had always been on the best of personal terms with the English.[14] When King Edward VII broke the diplomatic ice by visiting Paris in 1903, Fournier was his naval host; and when a Russian fleet shot up some British fishing vessels on the Dogger Bank in 1904, he was selected to serve as president of the arbitration commission on account of his personal popularity in English naval circles.[15]

The remarkable reawakening of the French Navy after 1900 thus did not come from French hostility to England or from Anglophobia in the navy's leadership. Instead it resulted from a realization by both the Chamber and the navy itself that the navy was not the property of republicans or monarchists but an essential instrument of national defense. The Chamber also came to realize that it could no longer allow the navy to expand or contract according to whims in diplomatic policy or changes in the amount of money available.

Of the two big naval programs of 1900, the German naval law (Tirpitz's second) is much more famous, but the Lanessan program in France was almost equally important, not in the history of international relations, but in the history of naval policy. On 30 January 1900 the government of which Lanessan was part submitted five bills: one to increase the number of ships in the fleet, one to improve arsenals and port facilities in the metropole and overseas, one to improve French coast defenses, one to improve colonial defenses in order to give the navy secure operating bases overseas, and one to extend France's network of overseas submarine cables. A month earlier, the government had submitted a bill transforming the colonial troops into a semi-independent army. All but the coast defense and cable bills became law, and the Pelletan administration left all but the fleet law essentially intact. This legislation collectively became the basis for the new French Navy.

THE FLEET LAW OF 1900

In his "bill relative to the augmentation of the fleet," Lanessan asked Parliament to increase the fleet to a strength of 28 battleships, 24 armored cruisers, 52 destroyers, 263 torpedo boats, and 38 submarines. To do this, France would have to build 6 battleships (the *Patrie* and *Liberté* classes), 5 armored cruisers (the *Jules Ferry* and two later classes), 28 destroyers, 112 torpedo boats, and 26 submarines in the next eight years at a cost of 476,836,000 francs. The Chamber not only accepted the program, battleships and all, but reduced the time limit to seven years, added 50 million francs for submarines and torpedo boats (on an amendment by Pelletan), and relaxed the usual accounting rules to permit unspent sums to be carried over to later years. The contrast between these changes and the mauling that the Chamber had given the program submitted a few years earlier by Admiral Besnard was striking. The approval of the fleet law by the Chamber was the first indication of the beginning of the new unity in French naval policy.[16] Perhaps the most damaging act of the subsequent Pelletan ministry was to delay the construction of many of the new ships at a time when Germany was carrying out its program with remarkable regularity.

The English interpreted the new law as being directed solely against the German menace, as the definite end of the Jeune Ecole, and as the French adoption of the theory that the English found so comforting, that commercial war "never brings an opponent to her knees."[17] In fact, the new program with its battleships and large cruisers meant nothing of the kind. At this time, as in 1869, French thinkers were making an effort to work out a comprehensive French naval strategy that could meet both England and Germany.[18] (An indication of the size of the effort is that the number of candidates for admission to the Ecole supérieure de la Marine rose from twenty in 1899 to sixty-six in 1900.) Led by Fournier, they came up with the only possible solution: the one developed by Baron Grivel in 1869. The French fleet would contain elements for both high-seas and commercial war, and the choice of the kind of operations would depend upon the enemy to be met.

Within the navy itself, from the extreme Jeune Ecole to those who practically reproduced the ideas of Mahan, every serious writer came to the same conclusion. "In a conflict with England, industrial warfare will develop parallel to that on the high seas and be solidly supported by it."[19] Although Mahan taught that, historically, commercial warfare had failed,

> he has failed to show how a people which does not have a navy comparable in quantity to that of England can fight with that country. Reason

The battleship Patrie *(launched in 1903). For this and the other five battleships of the Program of 1900, Emile Bertin was allowed a substantial increase in tonnage, and he produced a design fully as good as its British contemporaries.*

> refuses to believe that an insular position alone should be for any country a guarantee of universal tyranny.[20]

Commerce-raiding remained a key element in the new French naval strategy. However, another element was also necessary.

> It would be an illusion to believe that we could successfully wage war on England by launching only isolated cruisers, or even divisions of them, without immobilizing on her coasts or on ours an important part of her fleet, with a relatively powerful force ready for instant action at her least sign of weakening. Without this diversion, our most admirable cruisers would soon succumb to the efforts of the whole British navy. ... With it, I have the firm conviction that we can impose on England sufferings out of all proportion to the benefits of the war, and such as in consequence will force her to respect the peace.[21]

Against England's battle fleet, the task of the French battleships would be "to wear down the forces of our enemy by an active defensive until we can strike the decisive blow,"[22] and "to force the enemy to risk his battleships on a tight blockade" until an equality of numbers was reached.[23] In the war of fleet against fleet, the French planned to use Aube's principle of dispersing their forces among numerous bases and suddenly concentrating them at the right moment to attain at least numerical equality. "In the presence of the multiple obligations which the development of the Empire has imposed upon [England], we may be permitted to hope that on certain days our ships

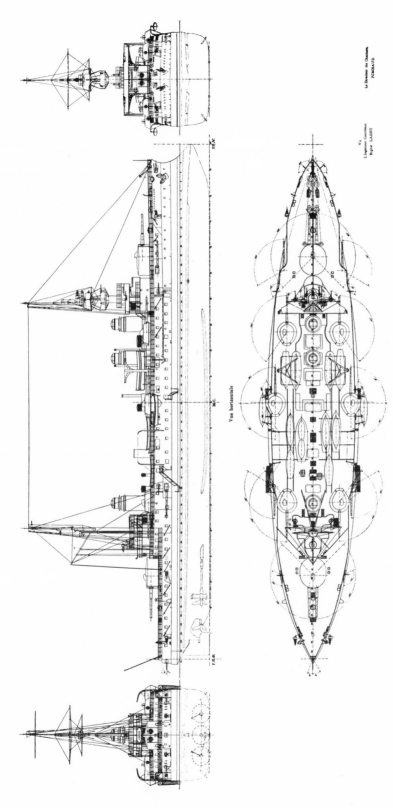

Vue horizontale

Vu
L'ingénieur Contrôleur
Signé LADET

Le Directeur des Chantiers
RIMBAUD

An official plan of the battleship Justice, one of the later ships of the Program of 1900. She and her three sisters were essentially identical to the two ships of the Patrie type except for a modified secondary armament.

The armored cruiser Victor Hugo *(1904), of the* Jules Ferry *class. One of the first three armored cruisers built under the Program of 1900, she was an enlarged version of the* Montcalm *with double the armament and a slight increase in speed.*

will be more numerous, or at least as numerous, as hers on the battle-field."[24] With French coasts and colonies protected by one of the strongest armies in the world, the fleet was to go on the offensive, now against England's battle fleet, now against her commerce.[25]

The key to the new strategy was that, against England, France would do both. Carrying on nothing but commercial war with none of England's main force tied down in a blockade of the French battle fleet would have been as disastrous as trusting in ingenious concentration without attempting to tie down much of Britain's fleet in commerce defense. The combination of fleet and cruiser warfare gave the French the true advantage of the offensive, which, as the French had learned in their long efforts to counter the Italians, was the ability to keep the enemy in suspense as to the point where the blow will fall. The British appreciated their dilemma. Sir Julian Corbett concluded that no matter how advantageous it was to concentrate forces at the outbreak of a war for a decisive battle, England would find it absolutely impossible to leave either her commerce or her home islands without im-mediate, direct protection as long as the enemy might attack either one or the other.[26]

As its proponents realized, the new policy was curiously like the policy of the Italians under Brin. "The acts of a less powerful but more rapid fleet will always have the character of *coups de main* . . . which, without being de-cisive, will worry our enemy nonetheless. They are adapted perfectly to . . . a power which has made its principal ports secure from insult and which,

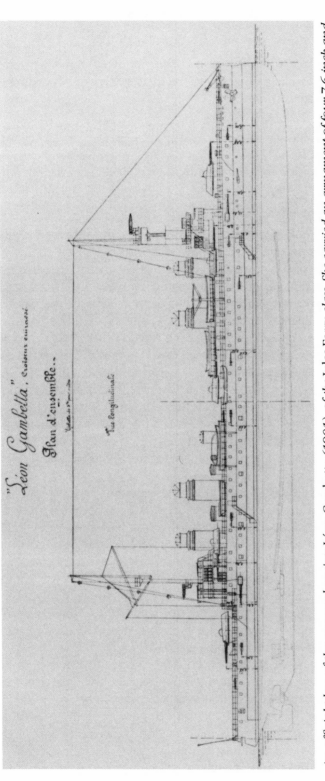

An official plan of the armored cruiser Léon Gambetta (1901), of the Jules Ferry class. She carried an armament of four 7.6-inch and sixteen 6.4-inch guns, exactly twice that of the Gueydon type, on a 12,350-ton hull. Her side armor was also increased to 6.7 inches and her designed speed to 22 knots.

with little commerce to protect, can consecrate itself entirely to offensive acts."[27] It also had a clear similarity to the ideas of Grivel. According to one of its chief advocates,

> There are two sorts of war, employed either simultaneously or one to the exclusion of the other . . . war on the high seas . . . against the armed forces of the enemy . . . or war against commerce. . . . Naval strategy has for its object the determination of the kind of war one will employ against a given enemy and in what measure one will use each of them simultaneously.[28]

Or, as a Jeune Ecole writer put it, "A sound strategy prepares for itself, not an abstract victory, but the specific powerlessness of a given enemy."[29]

Another aspect of the new strategy was that by giving coast defense and colonial protection to the army, it delegated some traditional naval tasks to another service in a war with England in order to reserve the navy for the offensive. Unlike England, France could not concentrate all her resources in a single service, and she had to find some way to render the army a part of naval strength in a war with British sea power. Against Germany the navy, by defeating the enemy fleet as Mahan and Grivel taught, would protect French coasts, commerce, and colonies, and make France the base of operations for the army offensive that would decide the outcome of the war. Against England, the two services would switch roles: the army would take over the defense of coasts and colonies and ensure the base of action of the navy, which would be free to take the offensive against England's battle fleet and commerce.

The Program of 1900 contained all the elements of the new theory: a battle fleet to conduct an active defense, commerce-destroyers to force the enemy to blockade French ports and bring its ships within range of French torpedo craft, and a new colonial army to provide direct protection of the colonies. This remarkably complete theory for a *marine des pauvres* (poor men's navy), which was developed between 1897 and 1902, was completely ignored even by later French writers, because no single author ever summarized it all and because the Entente Cordiale of 1904 diminished the English danger and opened the way for French versions of Mahan, ably introduced by René Daveluy and Gabriel Darrieus.[30]

During the period from 1870 to 1914 there were four navies in Europe that could be called "modern," in the sense that a definite matériel was built according to a general set of definite strategic ideas. They were the English navy, whose theory was expressed in the writings of Colomb and Mahan; the Italian Navy designed by Brin, Saint Bon, and the Commission of 1872 to prevent an invasion of the peninsula; the German coast-defense navy started by Moltke in the 1870s and brought to its highest perfection by Caprivi in the 1880s; and the French Navy begun under the five laws of 1900. Curiously, the most famous new navy of this period, Tirpitz's High Seas Fleet of 1900, does not fall into this category.

Initially, Tirpitz and the kaiser based their new High Seas Fleet on the dangerous illusion (which they shared with the Jeune Ecole) that when it came to a crisis, England probably would not fight. They also based it on a curious anachronism: they and their popular backers saw the fleet not as an instrument of national defense but as "a symbol of added power."[31] In other words, they began building it for *prestige à bon marché* (prestige on the cheap), exactly as the French bourgeoisie in the 1860s and early 1870s had built the navy designed by Dupuy de Lôme. Tirpitz himself stated that "the navy never seemed to me to be an end in itself, but always a function of [our] maritime interests."[32] The idea that a navy should be proportionate to the maritime interests of a country was a relic of the days when it was necessary to police the seas against the Barbary pirates or force civilization on the Chinese. As a doctrine for national defense against another first-rate European power, it was as irrational as the notion that an air force should be proportional to the "air interests" created by a Lufthansa or a Pan American.

The French program of 1900 combined a fleet that was ready to go to the limit against either England or Germany, though not both, with a diplomacy that would have been ready to make far-reaching concessions for the neutrality of the other power. The German navy, militarily speaking, was explicitly designed to be second best, unable to stand up against England alone in an unlimited war. The Germans continued building it long after the disappearance of any reasonable hope that England would not fight for fear of French intervention. They were also unwilling to pay much for a neutrality agreement with either country and apparently hoped to continue to blackmail both alternately. Tirpitz never developed a strategy to offset the crushing superiority of English numbers in case his bluff failed, and in World War I the German navy's only accomplishment (outside of the magnificent improvisation of the submarine war) was to prove the truth of the adage that a second-best navy is like a second-best poker hand, useless when called. It was unable to keep its trade routes open or to close those of its enemy, and to the very end the kaiser futilely clung to the idea of using it for bargaining at the peace conference.

French thinkers also eventually followed the English and the Germans in adopting the ideas of Mahan. Daveluy's theory of neglecting commercial warfare entirely at the outset of a war was pure Mahan. "Destroy the enemy and you will have all the results at one time."[33] But he also perceived the problem that the Germans never solved:

> We must therefore employ our forces to defeat the enemy fleet on the battlefield which will offer us the greatest chance of success. If we win, we shall shift our forces onto the field of commercial war. The final ob-

jective thus shall only be reached after a duel, of which it will be the
fruit of victory.
    I see here the objection: we shall be beaten.
    That is probable![34]

When Daveluy wrote this in 1908, France no longer really faced the problem of meeting England, and against any other power Mahan's theory was
perfectly sound. A French commentator noted, however, that against a Germany that lacked its own naval strategy, "Mahan's system is part of the arsenal of Britain. Whether the English believe it themselves or not, it is to
their advantage to persuade the world that a war against them is scientifically and historically hopeless."[35] Perhaps that accounts for the vigor with
which a prominent English writer complained in 1893 that France, in cling-
ing to at least some of the "immoral" theories of the Jeune Ecole, "wicked as
they were foolish," was "alone among the Nations in refusing to accept the
law of sea power as it had been formulated and demonstrated by Captain
Mahan."[36]

BASES AND ALLIES

The emphasis on dispersing elements of the battle fleet made naval bases
as important in French naval thought as in earlier Italian planning. The second bill presented by Lanessan in 1900 provided for the improvement of
the navy's arsenals and operating bases in France, in North Africa, and overseas. The main debate over Lanessan's naval base bill was between advocates of concentration in the Mediterranean and the Channel. In 1900 the
French were as divided over this issue as the British had been in the early
1890s. The main problem was whether French forces, which could clearly
weaken England's hold on the Mediterranean, would be sufficient to overthrow her. Some, citing the evidence that France would not be able to force
the Straits of Gibraltar, revived Gougeard's idea of attacking Egypt in cooperation with Russia.[37] Others argued for concentrating entirely in the Channel. The decision, as in the case of commercial versus fleet warfare, was to
do both, on the grounds that the essential thing was to keep the English in
suspense by preparing bases that would permit both kinds of action.

The naval base law allotted almost 170 million francs for naval works during the eight years originally proposed for the fleet law. It did not concentrate on either the Mediterranean or the Channel but looked toward a completed system in both regions.[38]

In the north, the works at Brest, Rochefort, and Cherbourg were completed under the law while Dunkirk became the chief center for action in
the North Sea. Dunkirk had a strongly defended sea front, an active torpedo
boat force, and three exits through its sandbanks (one in Belgian waters).[39]

In the Mediterranean, Parliament voted money for a complete arsenal at

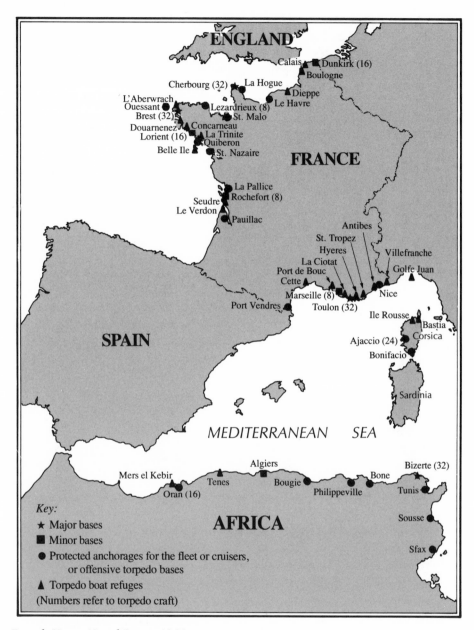

French Home Naval Bases, 1902

Bizerte while the navy studied the problem of developing an adequate base to counter Gibraltar. Algiers had important resources in the form of docks and coal, but it was too open to bombardment for use as a regular naval base.[40] After a long series of studies, the French decided to give heavy fortifications and a strong torpedo-boat defense to Oran, only 228 miles east of Gibraltar. Oran's existing fortifications, dispersed according to the new ideas on the subject, were already considered formidable, and the navy decided that Oran should replace Algiers as its secondary Mediterranean base until the completion of Bizerte would permit beginning construction of a third major base on the scale of Toulon and Bizerte.[41] The site chosen for this new base appears to have been Rachgoun, about fifty miles west of Oran. There a breakwater harbor, a canal following the bed of the Tafna River, and a moderate amount of excavation in a dried-up lake would make an artificial harbor much like that of Bizerte at the reasonably small cost of 23 million francs. The three French Mediterranean bases—Toulon, Bizerte, and Rachgoun—would form a strategic triangle right across the route to India.[42] The Entente Cordiale of 1904, however, ended the need for the third port before work began.

France also strengthened her position in the Mediterranean through diplomatic action. An Italian naval visit to Toulon in 1901 and Italian statements accompanying the renewal of the Triple Alliance in 1902 made it clear that Italy put rapprochement with France ahead of her formal ties with Germany and Austria. This did not produce major changes in Mediterranean strategy, as Italy had been moving toward France since the latter part of the 1890s.[43] Given the deteriorating state of Anglo-German relations, Italy's action in coming to terms with France was only a matter of common prudence. The Italian Navy was still an important force, and the completion of Bizerte made it easier for France to launch an expedition against Naples, but the French now considered the likelihood of war with Italy in the Mediterranean as very remote.

More important strategically was the situation in Spain. As Italy's attitude became more and more neutralist, England's eagerness to secure the use of the Balearics naturally increased. The attitude of the English during the Spanish-American War and London's ill-concealed views on the Spanish colonies, however, resulted in the complete French diplomatic conquest of Spain. The first idea of the Spanish Queen Mother, Maria Cristina, had been to obtain a joint guarantee of her territories by all the powers, but when that failed, the Spanish threw themselves wholeheartedly into the power of the French. In 1903 the prime minister, Augustino Silvela, made an outright proposal of an alliance under which France and Russia would guarantee Spain's position in the Straits of Gibraltar. Although nothing definite was done, France was ready to join, and even Russia might have come reluctantly trailing along. Instead, the French fleet paid one of its great ceremonial visits to Cartagena, and Silvela followed it up with a resounding declaration of friendship for France.[44]

But France's chief interest in Spain was negative, not positive. Reflecting general French opinion, the French ambassador in Madrid, Jules Cambon, wished solely to keep the English out of the Balearics and Ceuta. He noted that "Ceuta, in the Straits of Gibraltar, and Mahon, in the center of the routes that link Algiers and Oran to Toulon and Corsica," were the two important points. He added that "any arrangement that would deliver them, and especially the latter, to an important maritime power would be so dangerous to us as to constitute a real *casus belli.*" However, he felt that only "the maintenance of the status quo in the Balearics would justify an entente with Spain."[45] With bases at Oran and Ajaccio, the French were not interested in taking either the Balearics or Ceuta for themselves, and they prompted Spain to reinforce the Canaries, Ceuta, Algeciras, Mahon, and Majorca in 1904 strictly to keep out the English.[46]

The French Navy examined the naval advantages to be drawn from the new Franco-Spanish connection and found that they were meager. Mobile field guns in Algeciras could attack Gibraltar, and the only way to cut the Gibraltar cable was from Spain, but such actions would go beyond the "benevolent neutrality" that Spain was likely to offer.[47] Studies in the French maneuvers of 1900 and 1901 of "the interesting question of the licit or illicit use of ports and territorial waters of neutrals" did not come to very much.[48] The French had hoped to use the Spanish semaphore system to communicate with Paris, but found it utterly hopeless. One message took five hours and another eight and a half to go from ship to shore, and the French were reduced to sending a cruiser into port and telegraphing through the consul's office.[49] The colliers sent out from Spanish ports to meet the fleet got lost and then proved poorly equipped for rapid transfer of their cargo. Finally, the Spanish customs officials at Lagos and Vigo Bay showed great alarm at such open friendliness and apparently did their best to gum up the proceedings.[50] Spain was literally teeming with English spies, especially in the telegraph service, and it was well not to risk anything very important on the Spanish. The most France would probably have gotten from Spanish "benevolent neutrality" was the ability to coal isolated cruisers in her territorial waters.

The problem of getting French forces past Gibraltar remained unsolved. The French revealed the extent of their frustration at this by the seriousness with which they revived the old project of a deep-water canal across the south of France. French canal enthusiasts in the 1880s and 1890s supported the idea with rosy predictions of its commercial value. Militarily it would probably have proved to be the "mousetrap" that Admiral Martin Fourichon had nicknamed it when it was first proposed in the 1870s, but many officers supported it, including Admirals Pierre, Jurien de la Gravière, Bergasse

Dupetit-Thouars, and Fournier.[51] The success of the Kiel Canal in 1895 and the tsar's vast project for a canal across Russia from the Black Sea to the Baltic produced considerable sentiment in the navy for the *canal des deux mers* (the two-seas canal). Between 1899 and 1901, three committees of the Chamber reported favorably on this gigantic project that would finally "annihilate Gibraltar."[52]

Outside the Mediterranean, the growth of the fleet of France's notional ally, Russia, promised to alter the strategic picture. The Russian fleet had long since overtaken the Italian as the third largest in Europe. In the ten years from 1894 to 1904 the Russians laid down eighteen battleships (more than France) and three armored cruisers. A single program, initiated in 1898, contained about half of this considerable new fleet, much of which was intended to support Russia's ill-fated ambitions in the Far East. The Russians spent huge sums on the bases of Port Arthur and Vladivostok, and they did much work on a new ice-free port in the Baltic at Libau (which was eventually curtailed owing to the success of the icebreaker *Ermak* in freeing Kronstadt itself). The Russians did not increase their Black Sea Fleet and displayed little real activity in the Mediterranean, but the tsar's proposed Black Sea–Baltic canal would reportedly enable the whole fleet to be concentrated at will in either the north or the south. As usual, there were clouds of other rumors concerning Russia, such as her construction of one hundred submarines all at once.

Britain continued to show her extreme sensitivity to maritime developments in Russia. The considerable Russian effort in the Baltic increased English anxiety about home waters, and they began a new base on their east coast against both Russia and Germany.[53] The prospect of an overwhelming Russian force in the China Sea was at least one important element in Britain's decision to conclude an alliance with Japan in 1902.[54] Finally, the 1898 supplementary estimates, Viscount Goschen's second special building program, were directed publicly at Russia.

The French were more cautious in their appraisal of Russia. When the two members of the Dual Alliance finally negotiated a military accord in 1901, the tsar and the French foreign office also accepted a preliminary naval convention. This document could not be considered a binding agreement—it was simply a carefully worked-out plan for the division of the activity of the allied fleets in case the two powers found themselves opposing England, which might come in useful but which committed neither side.

According to this plan, France was to concentrate her fleet in the Mediterranean while her second-class battleships, *défenses mobiles,* and army threatened an invasion of England in order to keep Britain's army and navy in home waters. Russian forces in the Baltic were to remain on the defensive while eight battleships in the Black Sea and three in the Mediterranean forced the Turkish Straits and moved with an army corps toward Egypt, their liberty of action assured by the main French fleet. In the east, Russia would prepare for a march on India while the French fleet withdrew to Diégo-Suarez to cut off Britain's supplies to the subcontinent and allowed the Russians to use Saigon.[55]

The whole French effort at the turn of the century was on a long-range plan for developing their navy which would take some years to work out, under the control of men who were anxious to avoid any immediate trouble. Russia, on the other hand, was desperately preparing for her reckless Far East adventure of 1904–5, and the policies of the two navies soon diverged entirely. In a war with England, the French would probably have placed as high a price on German neutrality as on Russian help.[56] In addition, the French had no higher an opinion of the new Russian fleet than they had had of the old. The new ships still lacked homogeneity and their armor belts were too low—a fatal flaw when the ships were overloaded, as was the Russian habit. Russian scouting and torpedo work were also frankly miserable. The dominant theme in French discussions of the Russian navy in these years was that Russia "must be given a different theater of action," and, above all, that any plan was dangerous "which counts too much on the Russian navy."[57] The French accounts of the Russian defeats by the Japanese in 1904–5 seemed to have been written by simple spectators, not allies.[58]

COASTAL WARFARE

The third of the bills of 1900, submitted by the army but never passed, was designed to provide solid defenses for France's coasts and naval ports.[59] The army now had entire responsibility for coast defense, and the bill would have given the Ministry of War 82.2 million francs to make the necessary improvements.

Even without this bill, the army carried out some major reforms. It established large peacetime garrisons at such points as the mouths of the Loire and Gironde rivers and the island of Ouessant, near Brest. (The need for a garrison at Cherbourg was largely removed by construction of a railroad.) It also changed its whole system of mobilization. Formerly the Ministry of War had plans to replace the troops in coastal defenses with territorials in the event of a war with Germany, but it had no mobilization plans for a strictly maritime war. It now made provisions for the immediate reinforcement of coast-defense garrisons with forces from the regular army in case of war with England.[60]

At about the same time, in a series of reforms beginning with the naval base bill of 1900 and culminating in a ministerial decree of 1 April 1902, the navy completely reorganized the torpedo boats of the *défenses mobiles*. It provided quick-firing guns to defend the refuges of the boats against cruisers and destroyers, and it created secret defended stations on each flank of the great military ports to meet the destroyer danger by making it impos-

The high-seas torpedo boat Rafale *(1901), one of the last built by the French before the Program of 1900 and the advent of the destroyer ended construction of the type and relegated it to the* défenses mobiles.

sible to blockade both battleships and torpedo boats at the same time. Finally, it divided the coastal boats into offensive and defensive flotillas and assigned the offensive flotillas the additional task of always being ready to operate with battle squadrons in their vicinity. They would thus supplement the destroyers, which accompanied the battle fleet all the time as the earlier high-seas torpedo boats had done.

For the first time, torpedo boats scattered in small bases along the coast enhanced the strength of the main fleet. A squadron moving from base to base would be able to pick up offensive torpedo-boat flotillas, already organized but not able to go far to sea. Thus a fleet with a dozen destroyers would find eight additional torpedo boats at Ajaccio, ready to aid the fleet in any operations in the Corsican region, with whose waters they were thoroughly familiar. The Ajaccio boats did not have sufficient range to accompany the fleet to Bizerte, but the fleet would pick up another set of sixteen boats permanently stationed there, and so on. The new organization provided five offensive torpedo-boat groups outside the regular military ports. In addition to supporting the fleet, the flotillas of Ajaccio, Bizerte, and Oran were to act against English convoys in the Mediterranean, while that of Dunkirk was to bar the Channel to either an English or a German force. The navy also created a fifth, entirely new, offensive center at Lézardrieux, at the northern tip of Brittany. Its task was to attack Channel convoys or the anchorages at Falmouth and Scilly, cutting British sea lanes much as the Channel Islands cut the French route between Brest and Cherbourg.[61]

The 232 torpedo boats in France and North Africa now became part of a cordon of steel along the whole French coast. France's coast defenses no longer consisted of a few great ports, like battleships without auxiliaries, but of an integrated system of major and minor refuges for cruisers and light craft of all kinds. The difference between the system proposed by the Jeune Ecole and the new system was the same as the difference between a chain of naval garrisons and an active fleet operating as a unit from several points. Instead of having a torpedo boat in each fishing hamlet, France now had groups of them working from a complex system of bases and refuges, which could be guided by the telegraph and semaphores in a coordinated war of concentration, dispersion, and reconcentration.

Offensive coastal warfare, an idea that had been the excess baggage of French naval theory since the Crimean War of 1854, gradually declined in importance relative to fleet actions and commercial warfare. Its two constituent parts, bombardment and combined expeditions, also changed places in the navy's priorities. The navy was sick and tired of listening to the howls of the merchants in the Channel ports about the tremendous damage a bombardment could wreak, an agitation that had been strengthened by the propaganda of the Jeune Ecole against Italy. It also realized that the effect of the demands of French public opinion for protection against bombardment was to immobilize most of the French fleet in useless efforts to chase the elusive Italians or Germans.

In response, the French naval artillery corps actually launched a counter-attack. In 1894 its leader, General Borgnis-Desbordes, gave the classic reply to the bombardment propagandists when he pointed out that lobbing a can or two of high explosive in the general direction of a city or arsenal would not accomplish much, and that the coverage necessary for real damage would require such an expenditure of munitions that it was not worth the trouble. Suppose a chance cruiser should fire all of its 400 or 500 projectiles against a city seven miles away. A few houses would probably be seriously damaged, a few women and children killed, and the firemen would be given a few active hours of putting out a number of isolated blazes. But "war no longer consists of each side inflicting indiscriminate damage on the other and then negotiating on the basis of the balance between the results obtained by each. Today it involves armed nations which clash with the objective of reducing the other to impotence."[62] Such methods might have been effective against the tribes of Madagascar, but they would be clearly useless against a first-class European power. The whole idea of solitary cruisers going in to destroy places like Liverpool or Glasgow was, in fact, pretty well finished.

The other forms of coastal bombardment advocated by the Jeune Ecole were even less feasible. The addition of quick-firing guns and moles to the defenses of military ports now prevented small gunboats from getting close enough to destroy the arsenals and kept torpedo boats from attacking the battleships in them. The Jeune Ecole made one more attempt to revive its *bateau-canon,* in the form of the *aviso mortier.*[63] Lockroy took up this idea, already several years old, in 1896, during his first ministry. He fitted one of

The torpedo aviso Dague *(1885), of the* Bombe *class, one of many semi-experi-
mental ships of the 1880s that were largely useless by 1900. Her sister* Dragonne
was fitted with a mortar in the mid-1890s in an attempt to revive Charmes's
bateau-canon.

the early torpedo avisos of the *Bombe* class, the *Dragonne,* with a 5.9-inch
mortar that made acceptable practice at 1,500 yards. The navy decided to
place mortars on the seven remaining vessels of this class, which were
useless for anything else, but subsequently gave up the idea.[64] The British
thought the French Navy was putting mortars on new ships for high-angle
fire against the decks of enemy battleships, and modified the armor decks of
their new *Canopus* class accordingly.[65]

   Of all the subjects ever offered to armchair strategists, that of the invasion
of England has always had the greatest fascination for the continental mind.
The Boer War of 1899–1902 provided a marvelous opportunity to thrash
out the whole hypothetical situation. During the summer of 1900 the British
Isles were practically denuded of troops and the Channel fleet was at Gibraltar watching French activities in the Mediterranean. Under these conditions, the British had much greater reason to be worried than at any other
time between 1870 and 1914. Most British invasion scares, such as the one
accompanying the proposal for a Channel tunnel in 1882, the one preceding the passage of the Naval Defence Act of 1889, or the numerous ones
during the Anglo-German arms race, had no basis in any actual preparations
by continental states but were concocted of pure hot air by either the army,
the navy, or both as a prelude to an assault on the taxpayers' pocketbooks.[66]

In 1900 the French were at least actively considering the question, and if the Channel force had actually been defeated or absent, they might have tried it.

The idea of combined warfare had changed considerably during the previous decade. After the French Navy lost its naval troops to the army in 1887, it finally realized that the special fleet of transports that had survived from the days of Napoleon III was as useless as the Germans had always claimed.[67] The success of the Japanese in landing their armies in China in 1894 by improvised methods such as towing fishing junks across the Bo Hai Gulf threw an entirely new light on the problem. In both Germany and France, the idea of transporting a large number of troops using the merchant marine caused the abandonment of the old special transports. Both armies began to indulge in speculations as to what would happen if the English Channel was clear long enough to get the troops across. The Germans, who had a longer distance to cover, usually proposed using the ample merchant tonnage now in their ports.[68] The French tended to revive the idea of Napoleon's Boulogne Flotilla. The author of an anonymous article in the *Revue des deux mondes* in the spring of 1899 hoped to convoy canal or fishing boats across the narrow passage from Dunkirk or Boulogne.[69] Soon afterward, the Conseil des Travaux examined a proposal for a transport ram similar to the special canal boats suggested in the article.[70] There were numerous variations, but officers in both countries seemed to agree that an army of around 100,000 men could be embarked and started on its way within twenty-four hours of the decision to move.[71]

In 1898, under the direction of Colonel (later Marshal) Ferdinand Foch, the French Army and Navy held modest combined maneuvers in the Mediterranean, and in the same year they instituted a course in combined operations at the Ecole supérieure. In 1900 the army organized its maneuvers to test the whole railway system on the Belgian border. Dunkirk was now a well-developed port connected with the rest of the industrial part of French Flanders by a network of commercial railways. With the new system of mobilization for reinforcing coastal defenses and the general attention then being given to the problem of invading Belgium, it is pretty certain that the French also studied the problem of concentrating troops in the Channel ports. The first discussions and projects for a combined expedition against England came before the Boer War, however, and the new interest in cross-Channel operations probably resulted from new conditions rather than England's temporary weakness in 1899 and 1900.

England's defenses against the new threat were completely inadequate. The British Isles had absolutely no system of coastal semaphores, torpedo boats, and railways comparable to the *défenses mobiles*. At least 100 miles of the British coasts were perfectly open to a landing, and a well-equipped army of 100,000 men with light field guns would have had little between it and London.[72] The ten old battleships of the Reserve Fleet were open to

The coast-defense battleship Requin *(1885) after a total reconstruction carried out between 1898 and 1901. This and some other ships dating from the 1870s and 1880s were given a modern armament and new boilers to enhance their usefulness against the older British battleships.*

torpedo attack in their dispersed stations before they could be concentrated, and they had very little training in squadron navigation. Old ships of six different classes (including four Admirals and two *Niles*), they were completely unsuited to work together.[73] They also still had their old one-punch guns and, even worse, had the Admiralty "boiler disease," which forced them to spend most of the day getting up steam—when the boilers worked at all.

The French in the summer of 1899 were engaged in the usual shuffle of coast-defense ships that accompanied changes in ministers (and which in this case aroused severe English worries about the Mediterranean). If they had been planning a war, they would probably have stationed in the north five of the first-class battleships designed in the early and mid-1870s (the *Redoutable, Dévastation, Courbet, Duperré,* and *Baudin*), two *Magentas*, and enough armored cruisers from the commerce-destroying force at Brest to make up the numerical inequality. Most of these battleships had been hastily overhauled with quick-firing secondary guns and modern water-tube boilers at the time of Fashoda, and even a good armored cruiser with its quick-firers was a match for an Admiral-class battleship. Assuming the Channel Fleet had been lured away, there seems to be little question that the French Channel force, combined with the armored cruisers and torpedo boats always available in the Channel ports, could have whipped the British Reserve Fleet.

Beginning with considerable comment about the 1899 article in the *Revue des deux mondes* and encouraged by articles by the alarmist journalist W. T. Stead, the British gradually built up to a full-blown invasion scare in 1900.[74] One unique characteristic was that no higher army or navy officer apparently had anything to do with the agitation. In 1901 the British hastily reorganized the reserve and decided that it was to be sent to sea three times a year for squadron navigation. They also sent down Admiral Noel with a special staff from the Admiralty to take it over. The theme of the maneuvers of that year seems to have been to test the efficiency of the new force, but due in part to his own ineptitude, Noel was disastrously beaten by Admiral A. K. Wilson's faster but less numerous battleships and armored cruisers maneuvering in the French single line ahead with the armored cruisers as a battle-line reserve. No good accounts of these maneuvers ever reached the press, inspiring the French to speak of a "quasi-censorship."[75]

Entirely aside from the specific situation created by the Boer War, preparation for the invasion of England was extremely important in French naval theory, not because France ever hoped to carry it out, but because everybody agreed that it was an excellent way of tying the British army and at least part of the fleet to the English Channel. Even the partisans of commercial warfare concluded that "the menace of a landing has such an unreasonable influence on the English" that it was necessary to make elaborate and not-too-secret preparations.[76] Without an army, the naval offensive of which the English boasted "reduces itself to the efforts of a beleaguered garrison that is attempting to clear the environs."[77] The fixing of the British army to the home islands was also an essential part of French colonial defenses. With the exception of Indochina (which after 1902 was endangered by Britain's ally, Japan), Martinique, and New Caledonia, none of the French colonies was seriously threatened by a British dominion. All the rest would have to be conquered by an army from Europe. The invasion idea in this light was perfectly sound. Like the retention of the possibilities of both commercial and high-seas operations, the chief point of the invasion project was to keep the British guessing.

The Submarine

In 1900 Parliament added 50 million francs to Lanessan's fleet law for additional submarines and torpedo boats. In the same year the "submersible" *Narval,* designed by the naval constructor Maxime Laubeuf, proved that the submarine had become a practical instrument of war.

Considering the generally excited state of French public opinion during the Boer War, the most curious thing about the appearance of the submarine in France was that comparatively little notice was taken of it. The rabidly Anglophobe newspaper *Le Matin* succeeded in raising funds by public subscription for two boats, *Le Français* and *L'Algérien,* but the Jeune Ecole generally had a hard time drumming up much enthusiasm for its latest discovery. Most people saw the submarine as just another form of torpedo boat that these gentry were taking up, just as they had taken up every other naval fad for the last fifteen years. In 1902 Paul Fontin demanded a whole fleet of gunboats, torpedo gunboats, torpedo boats, and submarines, including special submarine transports and fast cruisers with portable submarines for commerce-destroying.[78] However, by then even a reasonably well-versed layman could tell that Fontin had simply added another item to the Jeune Ecole's now worn-out collection.

If there was one certain characteristic of French naval opinion in 1900, it was that it was sick of doctrinaires. In addition, there had been so many earlier false alarms from the Jeune Ecole that people probably doubted that anything really serious had happened. (Lockroy had proclaimed the triumph of the submarine in 1891 and Fontin had done so a year earlier.)[79] The Anglophobes were so busy predicting England's downfall by commercial warfare, by invasion, or by a Continental League, that they largely neglected the submarine. As a result, there was nothing that could be called either a "submarine rage" in France or a "submarine scare" in England.

Another unusual characteristic of the history of the submarine was its late integration into general naval theory. The appearance of the torpedo boat as an effective weapon in the early 1880s had caused a great flurry among the faddists, but a great number of officers of all opinions had also immediately recognized that the new weapon deserved study and integration into the general system of naval war. Indeed, the appearance of the new weapon had practically caused the cessation of battleship-building in Europe for five years. The submarine, whose potential strengths and weaknesses were very different from those of the surface torpedo boat, was acclaimed only by the faddists and did not receive really serious attention from general students of naval war until the outbreak of World War I. In 1900 it was at least as effective as the first torpedo boats had been, but the theorists ignored it and battleship-building went on untroubled anywhere. Navies also showed much less concern over it than they had over the torpedo boat. In the 1880s they had quickly responded to the torpedo boat by equipping their ships with nets and quick-firers. Although Laird Clowes proposed both the depth bomb and the underwater "annunciator" in 1901, navies still lacked any countermeasures to the submarine in 1914.[80]

One final reason for the slow integration of the submarine into naval warfare was that the new craft became practical just in the years when France became the ally instead of the open or latent enemy of England. French hostility to England had been the driving force behind practically every innovation in naval war in the nineteenth century, and the tenacity with which the French applied themselves to the technical problem of perfecting the submarine is an indication of the way in which they would have developed ways to use it in support of national strategy if the diplomatic shift of the entente and the disorders of the Pelletan ministry had not intervened.

The submarine Gymnote *(1888) under way. The experiments conducted with this diminutive vessel gave the French the lead in the development of submarine designs and tactics.*

The development of the submarine in France was the result not of the propaganda of the Jeune Ecole, but of patient experimentation by a long series of naval officers. France's first practical submarine, the *Gymnote,* which Admiral Aube accepted for trials in 1886, was the product not of the Jeune Ecole but of Dupuy de Lôme's last years. Most boats at this time, like the *Holland No. 1* (1881) and the Nordenfelt series (1885–90), were steam-propelled even underwater: these craft put out the fires in the boiler, pulled in the smokestack, and used the remaining hot water in the boiler to run the engine. They got along more or less satisfactorily until they submerged, when they nearly suffocated the crew. Dupuy de Lôme's fundamental idea was to use electricity. "We are going to recommence the study of the submarine boat, and we will end the conflict of the torpedo boats and the battleships by suppressing both of them."[81] In developing what he hoped would be a submarine transport, Dupuy de Lôme also hoped at last to make possible the invasion of England.

Dupuy de Lôme died in 1884 before leaving any specific plans for a boat, and his friend Gustave Zédé, another retired "relic" of the remarkable period of the 1860s, drew up the plans for the *Gymnote,* which Gaston Romazotti built under his direction in the arsenal at Toulon. Launched in 1888, she displaced only 30 tons and had no military apparatus at all because the Conseil des Travaux wanted as cheap an experimental boat as possible. Her essential principles were, first, the use of the electric storage battery, and, second, use of excess buoyancy to control movement underwater. When running submerged, the *Gymnote,* like later submarines and the Whitehead torpedo, maintained a reserve of positive buoyancy and was kept at depth by the constant action of horizontal rudders. The batteries worked fairly well, though innumerable troubles in keeping the boat on course underwater required many changes in her control surfaces.

The trials of 1888 to 1890 were so promising that the navy decided to start immediately two real fighting submarines. Both Romazotti's 267-ton *Sirène* (renamed *Gustave Zédé* on that engineer's death in 1891) and his 142-ton *Morse* were equipped with torpedo tubes. These two boats, however, revealed so many new difficulties because of their increase in size that initially they were comparative failures.

While the first French combatant submarines were under construction, the little *Gymnote* was used to study their possible tactical employment. The studies were carried out by Lieutenant (later Admiral) Gabriel Darrieus along lines drawn up by Lieutenant Marie-Joseph Baudry-Lacantinerie, who had been in charge of the boat's first dives. The first problem was to select a weapon, and it was only after some consideration of Darrieus's proposal for a controllable electric torpedo that went through the water ahead of the boat that it was decided that the Whitehead would, after all, be the best. In the trials, the *Gymnote* was very successful in forcing a blockade and in coming up to attack the blockading ships from the seaward side. Other trials, against a dummy *Gymnote,* showed that the new boat could stand the explosion of 220 pounds of guncotton from a mine or its own torpedo as close as seventy-five yards. "Enemy" ships could not see the *Gymnote* beyond a mile, even when she had her conning tower out of the water in a calm sea and approached at a given hour from a given direction. Ordinary quick-firing guns were unable to hit the dummy *Gymnote*'s conning tower. A covering of only four inches of water over the rest of the boat proved sufficient to ricochet everything fired at long range and to explode the shells of quick-firing guns at short range.

Solid, invisible, and invulnerable to the quick-firer, the *Gymnote*'s one great fault was its blindness. Without a periscope, the only possible way to see anything was to poke the conning tower itself out of the water, and the only way to attack an enemy was to bob up along its course to see where it was going. The *Gymnote* approached to within a mile of her target with the conning tower exposed. She then dived and came in to 1,800 yards, emerged to correct her position, dived again and moved to 800 yards, emerged once more, and came up finally at 400 yards to launch her fictitious Whitehead. In all the attacks, the submarine was never seen before the 800-yard mark, and since practice eventually reduced the length of time necessary for the emerging maneuver to twenty seconds, there was not much hope of hitting her conning tower.

The practical demonstration of the invisibility of so small an object and of the ineffectiveness of the quick-firing gun against a target that was even slightly submerged resulted in a shift from the "submarine" toward the "submersible." The torpedo-shaped submarine *Gymnote* was built to navigate underwater most of the time but had to emerge whenever she wanted to be of any use. Some engineers proposed developing a submersible boat that would normally navigate on the surface and that, when making an attack, would submerge only partially, leaving an armored conning tower out of the water.

As a result of the first experiments with the *Gymnote,* Darrieus proposed three kinds of underwater craft. The first was a small submarine of 10 tons and 8 knots with a crew of three men, to be carried by a warship to the battlefield, where, thanks to its solid hull, it could be dropped in the water. The second was a larger submarine of 100 tons for port defense, and the third was an "offensive-defensive" submersible torpedo boat with an armored conning tower. He added that even if an "autonomous submarine" were possible, "it is as yet impossible to see exactly what use it would be."[82]

In 1896 Laubeuf won a public contest for a new submarine design. His *Narval,* designed as a submersible, merged the French electric and the American Holland types to produce what became the more or less standard submarine, a vessel with a petroleum-fueled motor for surface navigation and batteries for underwater work. However, it was the little *Gymnote* that paved the way for her acceptance. In eight years of service, the *Gymnote* carried out the first methodical experiments in submarine warfare without any serious accidents, though the flimsy construction of the first improved conning tower gave the crew some narrow escapes.

Before the *Narval* was even complete, four more submersibles of her type were ordered, along with six small electric submarines like the *Morse.* Shortly before Fashoda the Conseil des Travaux asked that more submersibles be built "without delay," and it already envisaged the general adoption of the submarine. "If we do not march boldly along this road and do not accept some of the obvious weaknesses still existing, years may pass before a really useful type is reached."[83] The submarine had thus already been accepted in one of the last redoubts of the traditionalists.

By 1900 the navy was on the way to solving the problem of the periscope, and it hoped to make the submarine a practical weapon for coast defense and for attacking a blockading squadron. In the maneuvers of 1901 it tested the new device in the *Gustave Zédé.* The little submarine was towed from Toulon to within two miles of Ajaccio, where she was cast off to attack the battleships "blockading" the port. No one was looking for her, and the first sign of her presence was the shock of the torpedo striking the flagship *Charles Martel,* on which the minister of marine was eating his dinner. The crowing of the Jeune Ecole over this exploit made it appear as though the *Zédé* had sunk the whole Mediterranean fleet.[84] However, the keynote of the Lanessan ministry was hard work and little advertising, and in spite of the remarkable progress made, both in the construction of the new weapon and in the development of the tactical ideas of its use to break a blockade and of a submarine screen over which surface ships would lure the enemy fleet, the new development created little disturbance. Pelletan's proposal to build nothing but submarines and cruisers was, like the rest of his ideas, only a throwback to the heyday of party politics in the 1890s.

COLONIAL AND COMMERCIAL WARFARE

The fourth of the bills of 1900, submitted by the minister of colonies, supplied 61 million francs for warfare outside of Europe.[85] Along with the naval base bill of 1900, it provided five fortified bases overseas to serve both as strong points for land defense and as coaling stations and supply points for commerce-destroying. It came at a time when France was establishing a new colonial army of long-service European and strong native contingents for direct defense of the colonies and reestablishing an expeditionary division of colonial troops to be rushed to any threatened point.[86]

In 1890 the navy's Superior Council had proposed ten coaling stations, in a kind of reflex action against the English Naval Defence Act of 1889. The new laws reduced these to five: Dakar, Diégo-Suarez, Fort de France, Saigon, and Nouméa. (Parliament also added some money for Réunion.) This marked the end of the policy of establishing a rival French route around the globe with centers at Tunis, Madagascar, and Tonkin and with stocks of coal in a large number of points which, being nearly unprotected, would be useful chiefly to the English in event of war. The new bases were to be strong enough "to defend themselves, without any help from our naval divisions."[87] The new, small arsenals at Dakar, Diégo-Suarez and Fort de France became France's key positions overseas. Saigon and a second point in Indochina not included in the law, Port Courbet or Haiphong, were important primarily as fortresses against a Japanese invasion of Indochina. Since Russia was to take over Saigon in case of war, this port declined in importance in the commerce-destroying system to a level only slightly above Obock, Nouméa, Tahiti, and Libreville, all of which except Nouméa were left out of the new program entirely.

Dakar had been entirely neglected in previous colonial schemes, notably by those who, following Gougeard, advocated cutting Britain's road to India in the Mediterranean. Under the new law it was to become the French Navy's chief colonial fortress outside of North Africa and a part of the strategic triangle on which French cruiser operations in the Atlantic were to be based. (The other points of the triangle were Brest and Fort de France in Martinique, which was also to be made into a major base.)

The marvelous position of Dakar, completely secure from land attack from an English colony, was right at the intersection of the routes to Cape Horn and the Cape of Good Hope. As such, it was a standing threat to the routes that English commerce would have to follow during a war in Europe.[88] It also happened to be right in the middle of the weakest link in the whole British chain of coaling stations, the long stretch from Gibraltar to Simonstown, where Britain possessed neither a satisfactory major base nor the prospects of establishing one in a British colony. In response, the British showed sudden interest in the territories of third countries where their merchantmen routinely coaled, notably the Portuguese possessions of Cape Verde, Angola, and Madeira. In 1898 Ballard proposed taking one of these to complete his commerce defense system.

During the Boer War, the French hastily fortified their position at Diégo-Suarez in Madagascar. Diégo-Suarez was purely an offensive base for cruiser warfare, and it had no importance in the defense of Madagascar itself. Its growth, and the navy's withdrawal from Saigon, were the result of the first real French studies of English trade routes and English preparations for diverting their commerce around the Cape in wartime.[89]

> "Tactics alter, but principles of strategy do not," says the gospel of the day. It is not true. Tactics remain much as they were, because the old idea of a warship still remains—strategy on the other hand has completely changed. . . . In the old days the fleet not the base was the heart of things: to-day the base is the heart pure and simple. . . .[90]

Another essential element in naval warfare was communications, which in prewireless days meant cables. With over 80 percent of the world's cables and thirty-one out of its forty-four cable ships, the English had a monopoly of the world's communications system.[91] At the time of the Niger crisis in 1898, not a single French foreign station commander could communicate with Paris or with another station without the message passing through British hands.[92]

Napoleon III had established the first French cable to America in 1869, but the Republic had sold it to the English in 1872. France did not re-establish its communications with the New World until 1890 because of the stupidity of the Chamber, which tried to milk prospective cable companies at the same time that it was pouring money into the merchant marine. The two French cables established to America in the 1890s were not very satisfactory: the most prosperous of them touched English soil, service on the other was frequently interrupted for weeks before the company could get money for repairs, and the vital link between Martinique and the United States passed through a British station at Havana.

France had no line by land or sea to Senegal, and the Franco-Russian line through Denmark passed close to the German shore. Heroic French bribery of the Portuguese Chamber took the concession for the South American cable by way of the Azores right out of English hands, but the French Chamber turned down the contract and the English got the line anyway. While France did practically nothing, Joseph Chamberlain, the English colonial secretary from 1895 to 1900, extended the "all-red" line around the world, and the British based their whole system of commerce protection, with patrol and chasing instead of convoy, on the "cruiser at the end of a telegraph wire."

In time of war, the weak French foreign stations would be entirely isolated, and during periods of diplomatic tension France could not move a ship in the colonies without the English getting word. Some of the reports from Courbet's campaign in China in 1884 and 1885 were printed in the British press before the telegrams ever reached the Ministry of Marine. In the Siam crisis of 1893 the Bangkok cable opportunely "broke down," forcing the French to send their messages via China and Siberia. Even this connection was precarious, for British "fishermen" in the North Sea dragged up its last link, the Franco-Danish cable, several times.[93] In 1897 the French were reduced to sending fake commercial messages, but the British during the Transvaal crisis countered this expedient by stopping commercial traffic entirely.[94]

It was essential for the French to break this English stranglehold, and they laid the foundations for a solution when the Chamber accepted a Brest-Boston-Antilles line and the ministers of commerce, colonies, and finance proposed a major cable bill in January 1900.[95] Under the bill, land lines from Oran to Senegal and from Indochina to the Russian cables in China and Siberia would at least connect Saigon and Dakar with Paris. Shorter lines were planned between Madagascar and Réunion and between Dahomey and the French Congo. Proposed lines between Bizerte and Turkey (with a branch to Russia), between Diégo-Suarez and Saigon, and between Dakar, Brazil, and the Antilles were still unprovided for, however.[96]

The French had not even begun to study the related problem of attacking cables. This was not as easy as it looked. Near the shore, a big cable weighed from 10 to 12 tons per mile and was built to resist tensions up to 24 tons. Even an ordinary grappling apparatus weighed nearly 100 tons, meaning it would have to be carried by a specialized cable ship. The English companies that had laid many French cables knew their exact position, while the French knew only the approximate location of British cables, which were constantly being moved by dragging for repairs. Even if the French succeeded in dragging one up, the chance that it would be the wrong one or simply a dead end left from the numerous failures, splices, and repairs would be about one in three.[97] Experiments after 1900 finally developed a light tackle for fishing boats or destroyers that would at least damage a cable by exploding a light mine against it, but it was clear that a systematic attack to isolate a given point, such as Gibraltar, whose cable fortunately ran off Ouessant, would be a long operation to be undertaken by a cable ship guarded by military force.[98]

The last major reform of the Lanessan ministry, implemented in ministerial decrees of 1 and 23 April 1902, was the replacement of the dozen-odd French overseas stations still hanging on from the days of Napoleon III by two flying squadrons of cruisers. The little river gunboats had gradually come under the control of the Colonial Service, and the French now gathered all the remaining modern ships on their foreign stations into an Atlantic and a single Indian Ocean and Pacific squadron. The first, based on the strategic triangle of Dakar, Fort de France, and Brest, was the nucleus of a wartime commerce-destroying squadron. The second, based in peace on Nouméa, Saigon, and Diégo-Suarez, was to operate in wartime from Diégo-Suarez. Several years before Admiral Fisher ended many of the useless British stations in his famous "recall of the legions," the Lanessan regime thus inaugurated a much more radical reform as part of a new general theory of commercial warfare by groups of cruisers.[99]

The chief reasons for this reform were the importance that the French attached to their armored cruisers, the return to favor of armed merchant cruisers after the Spanish-American War, the comparative failure of special commerce-raiding cruisers like the *Guichen* and *Châteaurenault,* and the problem of coal. Under the new plans, armored cruisers, armed merchantmen, torpedo boats, and even minelayers and cable ships would attempt a series of raids in the Irish Sea. Other commerce-raiding fleets of armed merchantmen, colliers, and armored cruisers would operate from a number of bases rather than using a single point. For example, a division from Brest would follow the North Atlantic trade route to Dakar, where it would have the choice of returning to Brest or of going around the Cape to Diégo-Suarez.[100] A carefully planned attack on English commerce at the outbreak of a war, with divisions of cruisers based on the regular ports and neutral colliers providing coal, formed the last part of the Lanessan system.[101]

Possibly the chief reason for the new grouping of the commerce destroyers was the ease with which they could be refueled in groups.[102] With the average cruiser carrying no more than a ten days' supply of coal, the problem of coaling was the most serious confronting a raider.[103] A number of long experiments with the Temperley coaling apparatus showed that it was at least possible to transfer coal between ships in a sheltered anchorage or in a very quiet sea. In areas where the navy possessed no bases, colliers would accompany the commerce-raiding fleet, some coal would be taken from captured steamers, and some would be sent out in neutral colliers to secret rendezvous. In World War I, 55 percent of the coal supplied to the German commerce-raiders came from the colliers sent out by the German secret organization in neutral countries and 30 percent, a surprisingly large amount, came from prizes. In contrast, only 12 percent came from regular German coaling stations and 3 percent was taken on in neutral ports.[104]

A BALANCE SHEET

On 8 April 1904 France signed the Entente Cordiale with England. The diplomatic steps toward a rapprochement between the two traditional rivals had begun in 1902, and the movement gathered strength in mid-1903 with an exchange of visits by the two heads of state, King Edward VII and President Emile Loubet. The initial purpose of the Entente was to improve relations between the two countries by resolving all their colonial disputes, in places as diverse as Egypt, Morocco, and the Newfoundland fishing grounds. Within a year the relentless expansion of the German navy under Tirpitz's naval laws and Berlin's assertive colonial policies gave the Entente a new purpose and transformed it into a de facto alliance for the containment of the kaiser.

To a substantial degree, France's willingness to conclude the Entente was a result of her experiences in her naval rivalry with England during the previous decade. In the years immediately before the Fashoda crisis of 1898, England had built up an overwhelming advantage in modern battleships and cruisers while the French advocates of torpedo boats, cruisers, and battleships fought among themselves. The Fashoda crisis revealed the full implications of the disparity in maritime power and made it evident that any direct French challenge to English sea power would be sheer folly. France's perception of her weakness, England's perception that France was no longer a major threat, and the skillful diplomacy and flexibility of France's foreign minister, Delcassé, led to a diplomatic revolution that most of the leaders of the French Navy had hoped for since the late 1890s.

In mid-1903 the parliamentary Budget Committee, in its report on the 1904 budget, compared the French fleet one last time with the Royal Navy. Although the French Navy had clearly made great progress, the reporter noted that it was actually further behind England in battleships in 1903 than in 1898 despite the Program of 1900. He made no mention of the impressive growth of the German battle fleet during the same period, which was also apparent in his figures (see table 3).[105] In contrast, the report on the 1905 budget, compiled after the signature of the Entente, compared the French Navy only with the German navy and ignored the British.

On 1 January 1904 the ships of the French Navy were distributed essentially along the lines laid down by Lanessan between 1900 and 1902. The nucleus of the fleet was the Mediterranean Squadron at Toulon, which included six of the navy's most modern battleships and three of its older armored cruisers. Three older battleships formed a ready reserve at Toulon. Another squadron, centered around two battleships, three coast-defense ships, and three large cruisers, was in the north at Brest. Lanessan's two flying squadrons of cruisers now consisted of a division with three cruisers in the West Indies and a squadron with five cruisers and nine other ships in

TABLE 3

EUROPEAN NAVIES, 1898 AND 1903

	1898				1903			
	Britain	*France*	*Germany*	*Italy*	*Britain*	*France*	*Germany*	*Italy*
Battleships								
Over 10,000 tons	28	16	4	3	40	19	13	5
Under 10,000 tons	1	10	8	0	0	10	0	2
Obsolete	23	11	5	7	7	8	13	7
Armored Cruisers								
Modern	9	6	1	3	23	16	2	4
Obsolete	7	0	3	0	4	0	3	1
Protected Cruisers								
Over 3,500 tons	55	17	8	0	57	20	6	0
Under 3,500 tons	53	11	9	14	27	13	10	7
Obsolete	15	1	9	2	35	1	19	7
Destroyers								
Modern	135	124	58	100	191	199	34	10
Obsolete	90	92	36	37	85	74	47	100
Submarines	0	3	0	0	9	14	0	0

the Far East. Small naval divisions and detachments still existed on the foreign stations and in the colonies, but they no longer had modern ships. Finally, France and her principal possessions were ringed by *défenses mobiles* consisting of roughly two hundred torpedo boats and twenty larger torpedoboat leaders at about a dozen bases, with more bases ready in case of war. France also led the world with almost twenty operational submarines in her ports.[106]

From 1871 to 1904, France, although nominally at peace, had engaged in a "silent war of steel and gold" with her maritime rivals. This had been a war not only of great naval programs but of strategic and tactical theory and preparation for war, in which every factor of industry, finance, and public opinion had played a part. In 1904 the evolution of the modern French Navy was not complete, as the Pelletan ministry showed. But by the time of the Entente the navy had resolved many of the questions raised during the previous decades of rapid technological and political change and had developed the foundations of the strategic system that was to guide it until World War I.

The navy of 1904 retained most of its traditional strengths. Its seagoing personnel remained among the most proficient in Europe. It also remained fully competitive in many aspects of naval technology, just as it had in the days of Dupuy de Lôme. Its artillery, torpedoes, submarines, and steam machinery were generally of very high quality, thanks in part to the scientific methods of its naval construction and artillery corps. French ship designs had been adversely affected by the uncertainty over naval tactics in the 1880s and 1890s, but when Bertin was allowed a substantial increase in the size of the ships in the Program of 1900, he quickly restored France to a leading position in naval architecture.

One of the most important new strengths of the French Navy of 1904, developed largely after 1870, was its high state of preparation for war. It had created a naval general staff, undertaken detailed studies of various types of naval warfare, and established a school in which its officers could study tactics and strategy. Perhaps the most impressive result of these efforts was the development of a coherent naval strategy, one specifically designed for a weak maritime power confronted by a strong one. This strategy, embodied in the Program of 1900, drew the best ideas from the theories of the several schools of thought that had fought each other so intensely during the previous fifteen years. Although this strategy was soon modified as a result of the Entente, the spirit of unity in naval ideas generated by Lanessan endured the disruptive Pelletan interlude. It led eventually to the reforms of Delcassé, minister of marine from 1911 to 1913, and to the Program of 1912, which but for the outbreak of World War I would have completed the revival of the French Navy.

The navy of 1904 also had some serious weaknesses. Some of these, such as the cumbersome organization of the central administration in Paris and of the arsenals, were inherited from the old navy. Others were relatively new. The Pelletan regime was particularly unfortunate in that it caused France to slow down her building program at the very time that the naval arms race between England and Germany was getting under way. Under budgets for 1903–5, Britain authorized sixteen new battleships and armored cruisers, Germany approved nine, and France began two (both cruisers). The French Navy also apparently failed to understand the implications of the revolution in naval gunnery that led to the all-big-gun battleship. When it resumed construction of new battleships in 1906, a year after the keel laying of Fisher's *Dreadnought,* it built the six-ship *Danton* class with mixed-caliber armaments that were obsolete before the ships were begun. (Several of these ships remained in service into the 1930s, prolonging the effects of this lapse.) Finally, there were some hidden flaws in France's naval technology. For instance, its gunpowder, "Powder B," proved to be unstable, and accidental explosions caused the loss of two modern battleships, the *Iéna* in 1907 and the *Liberté* in 1911.

Perhaps the greatest weakness of the French Navy in 1904 was the continued lack of understanding between its leaders on the one hand and the public and its representatives in Parliament on the other. The navy's failure to resolve the traditional problem of its relations with public opinion was a major cause of the survival of its antiquated administration, of the public apathy that permitted the ruinous regime of Pelletan, and of the continued failure of the public and military men to see the importance of sea power in a continental war. In a democratic society like France, it is as impossible for the public to escape its responsibility toward the navy as it is for the navy to exclude it by reconstituting the old closed corporation of experts of aristocratic days. While the French experience proved the public's incompetence in technical matters such as ship design and naval tactics, it also proved that the abstention of the public, which owes far more to the navy than mere financial support, will show up eventually in flaws in the navy's industrial and general strategic system, even if the navy is run by some of the ablest experts in the world.

Appendix

~~~~~~

French Naval Building Programs 1857–1900

LISTED below are the main building programs of the French Navy between 1857 and 1900. These programs were the results of efforts by the navy's leadership to determine how many ships of each type the navy needed and to obtain the funds to build them. In some cases, the way in which the naval staff laid out the programs (reproduced here) also revealed how the ships in the fleet were related to the navy's principal missions. Only the programs of 1857 and 1900 were sanctioned by special legislation, but all were used for planning within the Ministry of Marine and for planning and justifying annual budgets.

For each program, the left-hand column (*Plan*) shows the planned strength of the navy upon completion of the program. The next column (*Build*) shows the number of ships that would have to be built during the program period to reach and maintain this planned strength. The program period upon which these calculations were based is indicated at the top of each listing.

THE PROGRAM OF 1857[1]
(PERIOD AS APPROVED: 1858–71)

Plan Build
The Combat Fleet

Plan	Build	
25	11	Line-of-battle ships, large (900 horsepower, 90 guns)
15	15	Line-of-battle ships, small (700 horsepower, 70 guns)
20	7	Frigates (650 horsepower, 40 guns)
30	24	Corvettes (400 horsepower, 14 guns)
30	21	Avisos, first class (250 horsepower, 4 guns)
30	4	Avisos, second class (150 horsepower, 4 guns)

Plan   Build

The Transport Fleet (To carry 40,000 men)

27	0	Sail frigates converted to screw transports (200–250 horse-power, 4 guns)
20	0	Paddle frigates
47	22	Screw transports

The Transition Fleet (Existing: to be maintained but not replaced)

(26)	Sail line-of-battle ships converted to steam
(3)	Screw corvettes (slow)
(7)	Paddle corvettes
(40)	Paddle avisos

The Sail Fleet (Existing: to disappear in eight years)

(10)	Line-of-battle ships
(20)	Frigates
(115)	Other

THE PROGRAM OF 1872[2]
(PERIOD: 1872–81. PROGRAM DURATION INDEFINITE)

Plan   Build

Combat Ships

16	7	Battleships, first class (formerly armored frigates)
12	2	Battleships, second class (formerly armored corvettes)

Ships for Coast Defense and Attack

20	15	Coast-defense battleships, first and second class
32	20	Coast-defense gunboats (unarmored, *Crocodile* type)

Commerce Raiders

8	7	Cruisers, first class (formerly frigates)
8	0	Cruisers, second class (formerly corvettes)

Avisos

18	1	Avisos, first class (later third-class cruisers)
18	14	Avisos, second class (later station avisos and gunboats)

Steam Transports

10	10	Large transports for horses
10	0	Small transports for matériel
5	4	Large transports for Cochinchina

THE PROGRAM OF 1879[3]
(PERIOD: 1880–85)

Plan	Build	
26	6	Squadron battleships (including 7 former first-class coast-defense battleships)
10	0	Station battleships
12	4	Coast-defense ships (including 8 former second-class coast-defense battleships and 4 proposed fast, lightly protected torpedo vessels)
10	4	Cruisers, first class
16	0	Cruisers, second class
16	0	Squadron avisos (formerly third-class cruisers; replacement of some older ships might become necessary)
16	0	Station avisos and gunboats
10	0	Large transports
16	0	Small transports for matériel and the stations
40	25	Flotilla craft and paddle vessels
60	5	Torpedo boats

THE PROGRAM OF 1881[4]
(PERIOD: NOT SPECIFIED)

Plan

Battleships

20	Squadron battleships
8	Station battleships

Rams and Coast-Defense Ships

6	Squadron battleships classified before 1879 as first-class coast-defense battleships
6	Coast-defense battleships (formerly second class)

Gunboats

12	Armored gunboats (new type)

Torpedo Boats

70	Torpedo boats and larger torpedo vessels (new type)

Cruisers

12	Cruisers, first class
12	Cruisers, second class

Plan

Avisos

16	Squadron avisos
16	Station avisos and gunboats

Transports

2	Transports to carry small torpedo boats (new type)
28	Transports for matériel and the stations
6	Sail transports

Subsidiary Services and Flotilla Craft

50	Various auxiliary and small craft

THE PROGRAM OF 1890[5]
(AS FINALIZED IN JULY 1891. PERIOD: 1892–1901)

Plan Build

European Waters

Plan	Build	
24	10	Squadron battleships
12	1	Cruisers, first class
12	7	Cruisers, second class
12	5	Cruisers, third class
4	3	Supply transports
4	4	Torpedo-boat transports
2	2	Repair ships
12	5	Torpedo cruisers and large torpedo avisos acting as squadron torpedo-boat destroyers
40	19	High-seas torpedo boats
45	45	Torpedo launches for the torpedo-boat transports

Coast Defense

Plan	Build	
17	1	Coast-defense battleships (17 in program, 14 on hand, but only one new one planned)
8	0	Armored gunboats (4 first class, 4 second class)
10	0	Torpedo avisos (small)
110	71	Torpedo boats, first class
110	27	Torpedo boats, second class
?	?	Submarines

Overseas Stations

Plan	Build	
10	8	Flagship cruisers (formerly station battleships)
12	12	Station cruisers, second class
12	12	Station cruisers, third class

Plan   Build

Overseas Stations (continued)

12	8	Avisos, first class
12	7	Gunboats

THE PROGRAM OF 1894[6]
(PERIOD: 1895–1904)

Plan   Build

European Waters

24	5	Squadron battleships
12	6	Armored cruisers
12	0	Protected cruisers, second (and old first) class
12	1	Protected cruisers, third class
12	3	Torpedo-boat destroyers (torpedo cruisers and large torpedo avisos, ca. 1,000 tons)
16	16	Squadron torpedo boats (new type, ca. 220 tons)

Coast Defense

(22)		Coast-defense battleships and armored gunboats (existing, not to be replaced)
30	20	Torpedo avisos (small, ca. 300 tons)
200	130	Torpedo boats (ca. 80 tons, as recent first class)

Overseas Stations

10	7	Station armored cruisers
12	8	Station protected cruisers, second class
12	12	Station protected cruisers, third class
12	9	Avisos, first class
12	6	Gunboats

Supplementary Program

2	2	Fast cruisers for commerce-raiding

THE PROGRAM OF 1896[7]
(PERIOD: 1897–1904)

Plan   Build

European Waters

28	8	Squadron battleships (four squadrons of 6 plus 4 replacements)
12	5	Armored cruisers
12	1	Protected cruisers, second (and old first) class
12	1	Protected cruisers, third class
30	16	Torpedo-boat destroyers (ca. 300 tons, as *Durandal*)
30	29	Squadron torpedo boats (ca. 150 tons, as *Cyclone*)

Plan   Build

Coast Defense

Coast-defense ships that can be formed into another squadron

(9)		Coast-defense battleships (*Valmy, Indomptable,* and *Furieux* types. Existing, not to be replaced)
3	3	Armored cruisers
3	3	Protected cruisers, second class
3	3	Protected cruisers, third class
9	9	Torpedo-boat destroyers
9	9	Squadron torpedo boats

Coast-defense ships assigned to the defensive

(14)		Coast-defense battleships and armored gunboats (existing, not to be replaced)
20	10	Torpedo avisos (small, ca. 400 tons)
200	62	Torpedo boats (as recent first class)

Overseas Stations

4	3	Station armored cruisers
2	0	Station protected cruisers, first class (raiders)
6	0	Station protected cruisers, second class
5	3	Station protected cruisers, third class
7	3	Avisos, first class
10	4	Gunboats
7	0	Transport avisos

THE PROGRAM OF 1898[8]

This "program" consisted of a single modification to the program of 1896: increasing the number of armored cruisers for European waters from 12 to 18. Including the 3 listed with the coast defense squadron and the 4 on the overseas stations, the total number of armored cruisers planned for the navy thus rose to 25.

THE PROGRAM OF 1900[9]
(PERIOD AS APPROVED: 1900–1906)

Plan   Build

First-line Fleet

28	6	Squadron battleships (four squadrons of 6 plus 4 replacements)
24	5	Armored cruisers (eight divisions of 3)
52	28	Torpedo-boat destroyers
263	112	Torpedo boats
38	26	Submarines

Note: The Chamber of Deputies added 50 million francs to the government request, which added an estimated 74 torpedo boats and 18 submarines to the above totals. At the end of the program period, the navy would also still have numerous ships of types not included in the building program, notably 14 coast-defense battleships and 34 protected cruisers.

Notes

I. Introduction: The Second Hundred Years' War

1. Joannès Tramond and André Reussner, *Eléments d'histoire maritime et coloniale contemporaine (1815–1914)* (Paris, 1924), p. 62.

II. The Navy of Napoleon III

1. Joannès Tramond and André Reussner, *Eléments d'histoire maritime et coloniale contemporaine (1815–1914)* (Paris, 1924), p. 44.

2. Ibid.

3. Commandant Houette, "Marine française," vol. 1 (Course, Ecole supérieure de la Marine, 1897), p. 156.

4. S. M. Eardley-Wilmot, *The Development of Navies During the Last Half Century* (London, 1892), p. 3; Sir William White, "History of the Institution of Naval Architects and of Scientific Education in Naval Architecture," *Transactions of the Institution of Naval Architects* vol. 53, part 2 (July 1911).

5. Since *Polytechniciens* chose their careers in order of final class standing, much-coveted appointments to small corps like the Génie maritime or the Naval Artillery were normally filled by the best men, while the less popular and more numerous field artillery got a good proportion of the laggards. Paul Dislère, "Génie maritime," in Ecole polytechnique, *Livre du Centenaire* (Paris, 1894), vol. 2; Dislère, "L'histoire du corps du Génie maritime" (Ecole d'Application du Génie maritime, 1922); Nathaniel-Lucien-Louis-Jean-Jacques Villaret, "Notions historiques sur le Service des Constructions navales dans les ports militaires," *Mémorial du Génie maritime* (1902, no. 3); James Russell Soley, *Report on Foreign Systems of Naval Education* (Washington, 1880), p. 140.

6. The Royal Dockyard School of 1813 trained leading hands and foremen. E. C. Millington, *Seamen in the Making: A Short History of Nautical Training* (London, 1935), p. 83.

7. Frederic Manning, *The Life of Sir William White* (London, 1923), p. 91.

8. André-Simon-Eugène Dupont, *Les arsenaux de la Marine de 1689 à 1910: Leur organisation administrative* (Paris, 1913), p. 211.

9. Admiral R. Vesey Hamilton, *Naval Administration* (London, 1896).

10. Lieutenant Colonel Spencer Childers, *The Life and Correspondence of the Right Hon. C. E. Childers, 1827–1896,* vol. 1 (London, 1901), pp. 160ff.

11. Raoul-Victor-Patrice Castex, "La modernisation de l'éperon," *Revue maritime,* n.s., 97 (1928): 1.

12. Lieutenant Moreau, "Lissa (1866)" (Thesis, Ecole supérieure de la Marine, 1928), pp. 16–59.

13. Admiral Philippe-Victor Touchard, "A propos du combat de Lissa," *Revue maritime* 19 (1867): 199.

14. Admiral Jean-Pierre-Edmond Jurien de la Gravière, "Considérations générales sur la tactique navale à propos de la révision du livre des signaux" (manuscript, Paris, 1870). Pownall Pellew, *On Fleet Maneuvering* (London, 1868), and Foxhall A. Parker, *Squadron Tactics under Steam* (New York, 1864), described English and American ram tactics.

15. The battle line of sailing days and of the dreadnought era, with the two opposing fleets following the leader in parallel courses, is technically known as line ahead. In line abreast, the ships lined up and charged like cavalry on land, with their bows pointing toward the enemy.

16. Paul Dislère, "Historiques des différents types de la flotte, 1858–1875" (manuscript prepared for the members of the Conseil des Travaux, in the library of the Service historique de la Marine). The letter of Lord Armstrong to the London *Times,* 14 October 1893, shows how long it took the idea of the small armored ram to die.

17. Jules-Marie-Armand Cavelier de Cuverville, *Progrès réalisés par l'artillerie navale de 1855 à 1880* (Paris, 1881), p. 13.

18. "L'artillerie et les murailles cuirassées," *Mémorial de l'Artillerie de la Marine* 2 (1874): 63 and later; "Résumé des principales expériences de tir contre les cuirassées exécutées à l'étranger," ibid. 7 (1879): 285 and later.

19. These principles were first laid down in Félix Hélie, *Ballistique expérimentale* (1865). L. Patard, *Historique de la Commission d'Expériences de Gâvres (1829–1930)* (Paris, 1930).

20. *Mémorial de l'Artillerie de la Marine* 1 (1873): 25; 4 (1876): 129.

21. Admiral Touchard was the most distinguished partisan of *décuirassement* in France, while Sir William Armstrong took up the cause in England. Touchard, *La question du décuirassement* (Paris, 1873) and *Encore la question du décuirassement* (Paris, 1876); Armstrong, "Our National Defences," *Colburn's United Service Magazine* 158 (1882): 125.

22. Armstrong, "Our National Defences."

23. A curious expression of this nostalgia for the comfortable, safe, sure sailing days is in Richild Grivel, "Mission militaire et nouveau programme de la flotte," *Revue maritime* 40 (1874): 864 and 41 (1874): 31. For more on Grivel, see note 28 below.

24. Raoul Castex, *Théories stratégiques,* vol. 1 (Paris, 1929), p. 181.

25. E. von Mantey, *Histoire de la Marine allemande* (Paris, 1930), p. 117.

26. *Résumé analytique des affaires examinées par le Conseil des Travaux de la Marine,* items 13638 (2 June 1868), 13812–28 (5 January 1869), and 13914 (20 April 1869). This collection of annual annotated indexes is hereafter referred to as *Conseil des Travaux.* See also *Engineering* 9 (1870): 119 and Grivel, "Mission militaire," 40: 869. The French had endless trouble with the *Dunderberg:* Victor-André Daymard, "Mémoire sur le garde-côtes cuirassé, le *Rochambeau,*" *Mémorial du Génie maritime* (1872, no. 6): 487.

27. "Naval Warfare," *Colburn's United Service Magazine* 124 (1870): 496.

28. Richild Grivel, *De la guerre maritime avant et depuis les nouvelles inventions . . .* (Paris, 1869). He had already presented some of his technical ideas in an earlier work, *La guerre des côtes: Attaque et défense des frontières maritimes* (Paris, 1864). His 1874 work, cited in note 23 above, shows clearly how little his ideas changed as a result of the Franco-Prussian War and the extent to which they dominated the Program of 1872. The work of his father, Vice Admiral Baron Jean Grivel, *De la Marine militaire considérée dans ses rapports avec le commerce et avec la défense du pays* (Paris, 1837), is a remarkable examination of the position of France in the maritime world, of the importance colonies and sea power would have in the economic development of the Old World, and of the way in which command of the sea was necessary in order to be able to choose the theater of strategic operations.

29. Grivel, "Mission militaire," 40: 866.

30. Grivel, *De la guerre maritime,* p. 278.

31. Ibid., p. 277.

32. Ibid., p. 279.

33. Ibid., p. 6.

34. Ibid., p. 277.

35. Grivel, "Mission militaire," 40: 867.

36. Grivel, *De la guerre maritime*, p. 281.

37. Ibid., p. 277.

38. Edouard Chevalier, *La Marine française et la marine allemande pendant la guerre de 1870–71* (Paris, 1873), p. 13.

39. The legend of the complete unpreparedness of the navy was thoroughly exploded by archival research, which confirmed the account of the minister of marine, Admiral Rigault de Genouilly. See Olivier Guihéneuc, "L'Expédition combinée de la Baltique en 1870," *Revue maritime,* n.s., 51 (1924): 328; and Lieutenant Fave, "Les projets de débarquement sur les côtes allemandes en 1870" (Thesis, Ecole supérieure de la Marine, 1931). For earlier accounts see the report of the Commission d'Enquête parlementaire sur les Actes du Gouvernement de la Défense nationale in the *Annales de l'Assemblée nationale* 23: 112ff.; and Charles-Jules Layrle, "Les opérations maritimes dans la Baltique et la Mer du Nord pendant la guerre de 1870," *Revue des deux mondes* (15 July 1872): 241.

40. The quarrel was continued after the war and was the origin of the legend of the unreadiness of the navy. The chief supporters of Bouët-Willaumez were Félix Julien, his aide-de-camp, and René de Pont-Jest, a journalist who accompanied the squadron. Félix Julien, *L'amiral Bouët-Willaumez et l'expédition dans la Baltique* (Paris, 1872); Louis-René Delmas de Pont-Jest, *Les escadres françaises dans la Mer du Nord et la Baltique: Campagne de 1870* (Paris, 1871).

41. Lieutenant Ruyssen, "L'escadre de l'amiral de Gueydon, 1870–1871" (Thesis, Ecole supérieure de la Marine, 1936).

42. Edouard Lockroy, *La Marine de guerre: Six mois rue Royale* (Paris, 1897), p. 6.

43. Paul Knaplund, *Gladstone's Foreign Policy* (New York, 1935), p. 58.

44. See Auguste-Antoine Thomazi, *La Marine française dans la Grande Guerre, 1914–1918,* vol. 5 (Paris, 1933), p. 25; Charles de La Roncière, *La Marine au siège de Paris* (Paris, 1872); *The Men of the Third Republic; or, The Present Leaders of France* (Philadelphia, 1873, from the London *Daily News*), p. 319.

45. François Dahirel, "Rapport . . . sur l'état de la Marine," *Revue maritime* 31 (1871): 528, 546.

III. The Program of 1872

1. W. Vernon Harcourt, "Our Naval and Military Establishments Regarded with Reference to the Dangers of Invasion," *Journal of the Royal United Service Institution* 16 (1872): 574.

2. Sir Nathaniel Barnaby, "On Ships of War," *Transactions of the Institution of Naval Architects* 17 (1876): 1.

3. Frederick Harvey, *Instructions for the Management of Harvey's Sea Torpedo* (London, 1871).

4. Victor Touchard, *La question du décuirassement* (Paris, 1873), p. 25; Sir George Elliot, *A Treatise on Future Naval Battles* (London, 1885), p. 7.

5. Paul Dislère, *La marine cuirassée* (Paris, 1873), p. ii. The discussion that followed Barnaby's address "On Ships of War," op. cit., and the testimony of the experts to the Committee on Designs are also very interesting examples. "Report of the Committee on the Designs upon Which Ships of War Have Recently Been Constructed," Great Britain, House of Commons, *Parliamentary Papers, Accounts and Papers* (1872, vol. 14). (This series is cited hereafter as *Parliamentary Papers.*)

6. Graf von Moltke, *Die deutschen Aufmarschpläne, 1871–1890* (Berlin, 1929), p. 31.

7. Lieutenant Degouy, "Marines étrangères," vol. 1 (Course, Ecole supérieure de la Marine, 1897), p. 337.

8. The best contemporary French description of the German system is Charles-François-

Edouard Didelot, *La défense des côtes d'Europe* (Paris, 1894), pp. 12ff. See also Degouy, "Marines étrangères" p. 114; United States Office of Naval Intelligence, *Information from Abroad* 7 (1888): 24.

9. The most famous of the British alarmist works caused by German successes is Sir George Tomkyns Chesney, *The Battle of Dorking: Reminiscences of a Volunteer* (London, 1871). Two examples of the alarm of the 1870s and its rapid decline are Major W. P. Jones, "The Invasion of England," *Colburn's United Service Magazine* 129 (1872): 363, and "The Growth of German Naval Power," *Edinburgh Review* 144 (1876): 1. For French commentary see "Développement de la Marine imperiale allemande," *Revue maritime* 39 (1873): 517, and Paul Marruau, "La Marine militaire de la Russie: La flotte et les arsenaux," *Revue des deux mondes* (1 June 1876): 665.

10. Paul Dislère, "Les Marines de la Mer du Nord et de la Baltique," *Mémorial du Génie maritime* (1877, no. 2): 73.

11. Admiral Alfred von Tirpitz, *My Memoirs,* vol. 1 (New York, 1919), pp. 32 and 36; Ulrich von Hassell, *Tirpitz: Sein Leben und Wirken mit Berücksichtigung seiner Beziehungen zu Albrecht von Stosch* (Stuttgart, 1920), p. 35. See also *Revue maritime* 75 (1882): 469.

12. Gaston Moch [Patiens], "La défense nationale et la défense des côtes," *Revue de Paris* (1 May 1894): 187.

13. Edouard Lockroy, *La Marine de guerre: Six mois rue Royale* (Paris, 1897), p. 4.

14. Théophile Aube, "L'avenir de la Marine française," *Revue des deux mondes* (1 July 1874): 175.

15. François Dahirel, "Rapport . . . sur l'état de la Marine," *Revue maritime* 31 (1871): 529.

16. Daniel Ancel, "Rapport fait au nom de la Commission du Budget sur le budget des dépenses de l'exercice 1871," *Revue maritime* 31 (1871): 555. (These reports, published in the official series of parliamentary documents and during part of the 1870s in *Revue maritime,* are cited hereafter as "Rapport, Commission du Budget" followed by the budget year and preceded by the name of the *rapporteur.*)

17. Daniel Ancel, "Rapport, Commission du Budget, 1872," *Revue maritime* 33 (1872): 567.

18. Ibid., p. 571.

19. "Budget de la Marine et des Colonies pour l'exercice 1872: Note préliminaire," *Revue maritime* 32 (1872): 158.

20. *Annuaire de la Marine,* 1872. The stations, with the number of ships on each, were as follows: Algeria, one; Egypt, one; Constantinople and Danube, one; Antilles and Newfoundland fisheries, four; Martinique, one; Guadeloupe, one; St. Pierre and Miquelon, three; Guiana, four; Iceland fisheries, one; South Atlantic, six; Gabon, two; Senegal, five; Pacific, three; Tahiti, one; China and Japan, seven; Cochinchina, eleven; Indian Ocean, two; Réunion, one; Mayotte, two; New Caledonia, three; police of the French coast, nine; schools and transport of convicts from the 1871 Commune of Paris, sixteen; port service, five; and the diplomatic mission at Civita Vecchia, one.

21. Commandant Houette, "Marine française," vol. 1 (Course, Ecole supérieure de la Marine, 1897), p. 61.

22. "Budget de 1872: Note préliminaire," *Revue maritime* 32 (1872): 176.

23. Louis de Bussy, "Projet de garde-côtes cuirassé de 2e classe," *Mémorial du Génie maritime* (1873, no. 12): 469, 514.

24. Viktor Ernst Karl Rudolf von Scheliha, *A Treatise on Coast Defence* (London, 1868); John C. Paget, *Naval Powers and Their Policy* (London, 1876), p. 5.

25. Robert Degouy, *Etude sur les opérations combinées des armées de terre et de mer: Attaque et défense* (Paris, 1882); Charles Bride, *Notions sur les opérations combinées de l'armée et la flotte* (Paris, 1898).

26. Louis de Bussy, "Projet de cuirassé de 1er rang," *Mémorial du Génie maritime* (1873, no. 11): 332.

27. Ibid., p. 337.

28. Nathaniel Barnaby, "On Iron and Steel for Shipbuilding," *Transactions of the Institution of Naval Architects* 16 (1875): 131; Barnaby, *Naval Developments of the Century* (Lon-

don, 1904), p. 52; Sir Henry Bessemer, *An Autobiography* (London, 1905), p. 245; Marc Berrier-Fontaine, "On the Use of Mild Steel for Shipbuilding in the Dockyards of the French Navy," *Transactions of the Institution of Naval Architects* 22 (1881): 87.

29. The creation of "centers of naval power" was suggested by the British Committee on Designs, *Parliamentary Papers* (1872, vol. 14).

30. H. W. Wilson, "The Protection of Our Commerce in War," *Nineteenth Century,* February 1896; "Report of the Royal Commission on the Supply of Food and Raw Material in Time of War," *Parliamentary Papers* (1905, vol. 39): 29.

31. Lieutenant Le Franc, "L'organisation des croisières sudistes: La croisière de l'*Alabama*" (Thesis, Ecole supérieure de la Marine, 1923); Lieutenant Lepotier, "La protection du commerce pendant la Guerre de Sécession par les flottes des Etats du Nord" (Thesis, Ecole supérieure de la Marine, 1933).

32. Richild Grivel, "Mission militaire et nouveau programme de la flotte," *Revue maritime* 40 (1874): 873.

33. William Hovgaard, *Modern History of Warships* (New York, 1920), p. 165; James W. King, *The War-Ships and Navies of the World* (Boston, 1880), p. 246.

34. Admiral Aristide-Louis-Antoine-Maximilien-Marie Vallon called for sails in cruisers as late as 1890: Chambre des Députés, *Annales, Débats parlementaires* 32 (13 November 1890). (Hereafter cited as Chambre, *Débats,* the concurrent series of parliamentary documents being Chambre, *Documents.* Similar series existed for the senate.)

35. Grivel, "Mission militaire," p. 876; Nathaniel Barnaby, "On Some Recent Designs for Ships of War," *Transactions of the Institution of Naval Architects* 15 (1874): 1–10.

36. *Conseil des Travaux,* 15391 (27 April 1875).

37. Grivel, "Mission militaire," p. 873.

38. Paul Dislère, "Historiques des différents types de la flotte, 1858–1875" (manuscript prepared for the members of the Conseil des Travaux, in the library of the Service historique de la Marine), p. 54.

39. *Conseil des Travaux,* 15431 (22 June 1875).

40. Daniel Ancel, "Rapport, Commission du Budget, 1873," *Revue maritime* 36 (1873): 508, and Charles Lambert de Sainte Croix, "Rapport, Commission du Budget, 1874," ibid. 40 (1874): 442.

41. Lambert de Sainte Croix, "Rapport, Commission du Budget, 1874," p. 414.

42. Léon Say in Chambre, *Débats* (1876, vol. 6, 6 November 1876).

43. Admiral Baron Camille de la Roncière Le Noury, "Rapport, Commission du Budget, 1875," *Revue maritime* 42 (1874): 934.

IV. The Heritage

1. James Russell Soley, *Report on Foreign Systems of Naval Education* (Washington, 1880), p. 117.

2. E. C. Millington, *Seamen in the Making: A Short History of Nautical Training* (London, 1935), p. 54.

3. "Report of the Admiralty Committee on the System of Training Naval Cadets on Board H.M.S. *Britannia,*" *Parliamentary Papers* (1875, vol. 15): 347.

4. Soley, *Report on Foreign Systems of Naval Education,* p. 89. Soley's report caused a considerable stir in England, where a special committee practically endorsed his views and recommended a thorough reform of the whole system: "Report of the Committee on the Education of Naval Executive Officers," *Parliamentary Papers* (1886, vol. 13): viii.

5. Admiral Jules-François-Emile Krantz in Chambre, *Débats* 26 (29 October 1888).

6. G. de Tannoy, "L'Ecole navale," *Revue maritime* 147 (1900): 73; Admiral E. Drujon, "L'Ecole navale," *Revue des deux mondes* (1 August 1930), pp. 570–90.

7. Lieutenant Degouy, "Marines étrangères," vol. 1 (Course, Ecole supérieure de la Marine, 1897), p. 275, and the "Report of the Committee on the Education of Naval Executive Officers," p. 75, both recognized the superiority of the Germans. See also Edmond-P. Dubois, *Le surmenage intellectuel à l'Ecole navale et l'instruction des officiers de vaisseau* (Paris, 1889).

8. Commandant Lephay, "Marines étrangères," vol. 1 (Course, Ecole supérieure de la Marine, 1902), p. 168; Degouy, "Marines étrangères," vol. 1, p. 63.

9. Théophile Aube, "L'avenir de la Marine française," *Revue des deux mondes* (1 July 1874): 193. The French ranks cited were capitaine de vaisseau, capitaine de frégate, and lieutenant de vaisseau respectively.

10. Chambre, *Débats* 14 (6 December 1872) and 33 (25 July 1874).

11. See table attributed to the U.S. Office of Naval Intelligence in *Revue maritime* 121 (1894): 154. See also table on promotions in Thomas Brassey, *The Naval Annual, 1893* (Portsmouth, 1893), p. 82.

12. Gaston Gerville-Réache, "Rapport, Commission du Budget, 1886," Annexe 3882, Chambre, *Documents* 16 (22 June 1885): 166; *Journal de la Marine: Le yacht* (hereafter cited as *Le yacht*) 8 (1885): 349; "Rapport sur les cadres," Annexe 1684, Chambre, *Documents* 21 (26 March 1887); Gabriel Charmes, *La réforme de la Marine* (Paris, 1886), p. 308. See also Rouzier, *Notre Marine de guerre, comment sont employés nos officiers de vaisseau?* (Nevers, 1899).

13. Charmes, *La réforme de la Marine,* p. xxix; Edouard Lockroy, *La Marine de guerre: Six mois rue Royale* (Paris, 1897), p. 85.

14. Etienne-Louis-Jean Tréfeu, *Nos marins* (Paris, 1888), pp. 101, 343; Henri Buchard, *L'amiral Cloué: Sa vie, récits maritimes contemporains* (Paris, 1893).

15. G. de Tannoy, "L'Ecole navale," p. 73; Tréfeu, *Nos Marins.*

16. Emile Weyl, *La flotte de guerre et les arsenaux* (Paris, 1894), p. 326; *Le yacht* 21 (1898): 485.

17. See also André-Henri Chassériaud [Ancien officier de la Marine], "L'avancement dans la Marine," *Nouvelle Revue* 16 (1 June 1882): 481, and Commission extra-parlementaire de la Marine (1894–98), *Délégations,* vol. 1, p. 87.

18. Including Fred T. Jane and Admiral Sims. French commentators on foreign navies such as Lieutenants Degouy, Charlier, and Lephay all mention, though in different connections, the "over-familiarity" of the English.

19. For example, see Bouchard in Commission extra-parlementaire de la Marine, *Commissions,* vol. 3, p. 220; Francis Mury, "Nos officiers de Marine," *Revue politique et littéraire: Revue bleue* (1 February 1902), pp. 132–36.

20. Annexe 1625, Chambre, *Documents* 35 (18 July 1891); Annexe 1933, Chambre, *Documents* 37 (27 February 1892); Chambre, *Documents* 49 (7 March 1896).

21. U.S. Office of Naval Intelligence, *General Information Series: Information from Abroad* 7 (1888): 47; Lephay, "Marines étrangères," vol. 2, p. 69.

22. Paul Dislère, "Les budgets maritimes de la France et de l'Angleterre," *Revue maritime* 57 (1878): 90.

23. Lionel Yexley, *The Inner Life of the Navy* (London, 1908); and the "Rapports de fin de campagne" for 1898, 1899, and 1900 by the chief engineer of the squadron, the naval constructor Just-Lucien Maurice.

24. Lockroy in Chambre, *Débats* 45 (11 March 1895).

25. Commission extra-parlementaire de la Marine, *Délégations,* vol. 6, p. 661.

26. Admiral Touchard, "Rapport sur l'instruction élémentaire dans les équipages de la flotte . . . ," *Revue maritime* 58 (1878): 18.

27. Auguste-Antoine Thomazi, *La Marine française dans la Grande Guerre, 1914–1918,* vol. 5 (Paris, 1933), p. 58.

28. Weyl, *La flotte de guerre et les arsenaux,* p. 6.

29. Auguste Gougeard, *Les arsenaux de la Marine,* vol. 1 (Paris, 1882), p. 110.

30. Paul Ménard-Dorien, "Rapport, Commission du Budget, 1885," Annexe 3147, Chambre, *Documents* 14 (23 October 1884): 107; Charles Ferrand [Georges Michel], *Le budget de la Marine: Les vices de l'organisation de la Marine en France* (Paris, 1891), p. 8.

31. *Le yacht* 11 (1888): 30.

32. Lord George Hamilton, *Parliamentary Reminiscences and Reflections,* vol. 2 (London, 1922), p. 87.

33. Admiral Aristide-Louis-Antoine-Maximin-Marie Vallon, "Rapport sur le *Magenta*," in

Commission extra-parlementaire de la Marine (1894–98), *Commission plénière,* vol. 2, pp. 45ff., and *Délégations,* vol. 1, p. 349.

34. Sir John Henry Briggs, *Naval Administration, 1827 to 1892* (London, 1897), p. 22; "The Story of the Battle of Port Said," *Engineering* 36 (1883): 1.

35. Dislère claimed that they were even less: "Les budgets maritimes de la France et de l'Angleterre," *Revue maritime* 57 (1878): 309. However, they were probably equal: see Lord Brassey's speech at Portsmouth in the London *Times,* 13 August 1884.

36. Philip Hichborn, *Report on European Dockyards* (Washington, 1886), pp. 27–30, 47; *Engineering* 22 (1876): 466; Marc Berrier-Fontaine, "On the Hydraulic Machinery in the Iron Shipbuilding Department of the Naval Dockyard at Toulon," *Institute of Mechanical Engineers: Proceedings* (1878): 346; Henry Robinson, *Hydraulic Power and Hydraulic Machinery* (London, 1893), p. 114.

37. Jacques Fonlupt-Espéraber, "Etude historique et critique sur le recruitement et le salaire des ouvriers des arsenaux" (Doctoral dissertation, Paris, 1913), p. 90; Hichborn, *Report on European Dockyards,* p. 67.

38. Ferrand, *Le budget de la Marine,* p. 7.

V. NEW FACTORS: FRENCH MARITIME INDUSTRIES

1. L. Lefol, *La protection de la construction navale en France et à l'étranger* (Paris, 1929), p. 36.

2. Joannès Tramond and André Reussner, *Eléments d'histoire maritime et coloniale contemporaine (1815–1914)* (Paris, 1924), p. 651.

3. He summarized his ideas in a speech in the senate on 27 January 1881, which was published under the title *Marine marchande* (Paris, 1881).

4. Royal Meeker, *History of Shipping Subsidies* (New York, 1905), p. 50.

5. Comité des Forges de France, *La sidérurgie française, 1864–1914* (Paris, n.d.), p. 141.

6. James Dredge, *Modern French Artillery* (London, 1892), p. 7.

7. *Engineering* 26 (1878): 258.

8. Comité des Forges de France, *La sidérurgie française,* p. 228; *Engineering* 65 (1898): 3ff.; J. Lavainville, *L'industrie du fer en France* (Paris, 1922), p. 81; J. Barba, "Creusot et les usines de la Loire," *Mémorial du Génie maritime* (1876, nos. 5 and 6); Delévêque, "Métallurgie du fer dans le bassin du Rhône," ibid. (1878, no. 5); and "Métallurgie du fer dans l'Allier et dans la Saône et Loire," ibid. (1881, no. 1).

9. J. H. Clapham, *An Economic History of Modern Britain: Free Trade and Steel, 1850–1886* (Cambridge, 1932), p. 88.

10. *Engineering* 68 (1899): 600.

11. Lucien Brocard, *La grosse métallurgie française et le mouvement des prix de 1890 à 1913* (Paris, 1923), p. 174.

12. "Résumé des essais faits à Gâvres pendant les cinq années 1886–1890," *Mémorial du Génie maritime* (1892, no. 2): 101, gives a summary of every lot of armor, from every company, for every ship.

13. L. Baclé, *Les plaques de blindage* (Paris, 1900), p. 83; Léon Lévy (manager of Chatillon-Commentry) in Commission extra-parlementaire de la Marine, *Délégations,* vol. 5, p. 319; L. Patard, *Historique de la Commission d'Expériences de Gâvres (1829–1930)* (Paris, 1930), p. 262.

14. *Mémorial de l'Artillerie de la Marine* 8 (1880): 13; *Conseil des Travaux,* 15491 (26 October 1875) and 15861 (19 June 1877).

15. Baclé, *Les plaques de blindage,* p. 85; *Mémorial de l'Artillerie de la Marine* 13 (1885): 549; "Historique de la fabrication des projectiles de rupture pour canons de 34 cent.," ibid., p. 131.

16. *Engineering* 38 (1884): 479.

17. *Mémorial de l'Artillerie de la Marine* 12 (1884): 540.

18. Baclé, *Les plaques de blindage;* W. H. Jaques, *Modern Armor for National Defense* (New York, 1885); and Edward W. Very, *The Development of Armor for Naval Use* (Annapolis, Md., 1883), sketch developments discussed more fully in countless technical papers.

19. Dredge, *Modern French Artillery,* p. 8.

20. *Report of the Gun Foundry Board* (Washington, 1884), p. 23.

21. *Rapport annuel technique au sujet de la situation de l'Artillerie* (Paris, 1895–96), p. 43; Colonel Cerf, "Artillerie," vol. 1 (Course, Ecole supérieure de la Marine, 1897), p. 534.

22. Lefol, *La protection de la construction navale,* p. 15.

23. F. Laur, *Les mines et usines au XX° siècle: Les mines et la métallurgie à l'Exposition universelle de 1900* (Paris, 1901), vol. 3.

24. Admiral Motoki Kondo, "The Progress of Naval Construction in Japan," *Transactions of the Institution of Naval Architects* 53 (1911, part 2): 50.

25. *Le yacht* 13 (1890): 373.

26. Captain Togari, *Louis-Emile Bertin: Son rôle dans la création de la Marine japonaise* (Paris, 1935).

27. *General Information Series: Information from Abroad* 8 (1889): 359.

28. H. E. Deadman (Admiralty chief constructor), "On the Application of Electricity in the Royal Dockyards and Navy," *Institution of Mechanical Engineers: Proceedings,* July 1892. The *Capitan Prat* was the model for the ship in W. L. Clowes's fictional *The Captain of the Mary Rose* (7th ed., London, 1898).

29. Jaques, *Modern Armor for National Defense,* p. 13.

30. *Report of the Gun Foundry Board,* p. 47.

31. W. H. Smith speech in *Hansard Parliamentary Debates,* 3rd ser., 294 (2 December 1884): 469; *Engineering* 42 (1886): 426.

32. *General Information Series: Information from Abroad* 6 (1887): 332.

33. Alfred-Maxime Laubeuf and Emmanuel-Marie-Victor Petithomme, "Mission en Angleterre," *Mémorial du Génie maritime* (1890, no. 5): 823.

VI. New Factors: Italy and Russia

1. Commandant Ceillier, "Les idées stratégiques en France de 1870 à 1914: La Jeune Ecole" (Thesis, Ecole supérieure de la Marine, 1928), p. 6.

2. *Al Mare! Al Mare! La difesa navale delle coste* (Genoa, 1872); "Difesa delle coste e dello isole," *Rivista militare italiana* (July 1873).

3. *Revue maritime* 33 (1872): 595.

4. See Commissione permanente per la Difesa generale dello Stato, *Relazione a corredo del Piano generale di Difesa dell'Italia* (Rome, 1871), p. 29.

5. Carlo de Amezaga, *Il pensiero navale italiano* (Genoa, 1898), p. 166; J. Avice, *La défense des frontières maritimes* (Paris, 1922); "Mediterranean Politics," *Edinburgh Review* 176 (1892): 388, 393.

6. *Piano generale di Difesa dell'Italia,* p. 23.

7. Charles à Court Repington [Charles Martel], *Military Italy* (London, 1884), p. 375; Commandant Marga, *Géographie militaire,* vol. 2 (3rd/4th ed., Paris, 1884–5), pp. 11 and 301.

8. Repington, *Military Italy,* p. 219; Graf von Moltke, *Die deutschen Aufmarschpläne, 1871–1890* (Berlin, 1929), p. 33.

9. W. A. H. Hare, *The Armed Strength of Italy* (London, 1875; translation of an account of the German General Staff); Victor Roll, *Encyclopedie des gesamten Eisenbahnwesens* (Vienna, 1893); and a long, officially inspired article from the *Augsburg Allgemeine Zeitung* translated in *Journal of the Royal United Service Institution* 24 (1880): 123.

10. Cristoforo Manfredi, "Guerra offensiva o difensiva?," *Rivista marittima* (1902, no. 1): 45; Repington, *Military Italy,* p. 309.

11. Carlo Rossi, *Il racconto di un guardiano di spiaggia: Traduzione libera della Battaglia di Dorking* (Rome, 1872). A historical work that was part of the movement was Alberto Guglielmotti's great *Storia della marina pontifica nel medio evo,* 10 vols. (Rome, 1886–93).

12. A. V. Vecchi, *Al servizio del mare italiano* (Turin, 1928), is an excellent account by "Jack La Bolina," one of the most active of the propagandists, as is his "La letteratura nello sviluppo della marina," *Rivista marittima* (1897, no. 2): 331.

13. Commandant Lephay, "Marines étrangères," vol. 2 (Course, Ecole supérieure de la Marine, 1901–3), p. 416.

14. Lephay, "Marines étrangères," vol. 2, p. 405; Colonel G. Russo, "Fifty Years' Progress of Shipbuilding in Italy," *Transactions of the Institution of Naval Architects* 53 (1911): 252; Vecchi, *Al servizio del mare italiano;* and Vecchi, "Naval and Maritime Industries in Italy," in Thomas Brassey, *The Naval Annual, 1908* (Portsmouth, 1908), p. 161.

15. Paul Dislère, "Rapport sur une mission dans les arsenaux étrangers de la Méditerranée, de la Mer Noire et de l'Adriatique," *Mémorial du Génie maritime* (1875, no. 6): 379 and 460; Arthur-François-Alphonse Bienaymé, "Rapport sur une mission effectuée en Italie," ibid. (1880, no. 1).

16. Lieutenant Charlier, "Marines étrangères," (Course, Ecole supérieure de la Marine, 1898), p. 301; Randaccio, "Arsenaux maritimes italiens," *Revue maritime* 142 (1899): 388; S. M. Eardley-Wilmot, "Italy as a Naval Power," *United Service Magazine,* n.s., 7 (1893): 692; A. Palermo, *Il golfo di Spezia ad il nuovo regno italiano* (Milan, 1860).

17. De Amezaga, *Il pensiero navale italiano,* p. 70.

18. "Report of the Committee on the Designs upon Which Ships of War Have Recently Been Constructed," *Parliamentary Papers* (1872, vol. 14): x.

19. Benedetto Brin, ". . . alla stabilità del *Duilio* e del *Dandolo,*" *Rivista marittima* (1876, no. 2): 4.

20. Sir Nathaniel Barnaby in "Official Documents Relating to the Design of H.M.S. *Inflexible,*" *Parliamentary Papers* (1877, vol. 52): 1.

21. "Official Documents Relating to the Design of H.M.S. *Inflexible,*" p. 673; "Report of the Committee on the *Inflexible,*" *Parliamentary Papers* (1878, vol. 49): 143; Sir Edward Reed, *Modern Ships of War* (New York, 1888), p. 45; Letters to the London *Times* of 19 February 1885 and 3 November 1893.

22. William Hovgaard, *Modern History of Warships* (New York, 1920), p. 47.

23. Simone Pacoret de Saint Bon, *La questione delle navi* (Turin, 1881), and Benedetto Brin, *La nostra marina militare,* 2nd ed. (Rome, 1881). The line officers' views are given in Paolo Cottrau, "Maris Imperium Obtinendum," *Rivista marittima* (1882, no. 3): 33, and E. Algranati, "Considerazioni sulle nostre grandi navi," ibid. (1882, no. 3): 75.

24. Dislère, "Rapport sur une mission dans les arsenaux étrangers de la Méditerrannée," p. 425.

25. Paul Dislère, "Mission en Angleterre," *Mémorial du Génie maritime* (1879, no. 5): 97.

26. Augustus C. Buell, *The Memoirs of Charles H. Cramp* (Philadelphia, 1906), p. 209; Leonid L. Strakhovsky, "Russian Privateering Projects of 1878," *Journal of Modern History* 7 (1935): 22.

27. In his famous defense of the treaty, Lord Clarendon claimed that the abolition of privateering was of the "utmost advantage" to England. *Hansard Parliamentary Debates,* 3rd ser., 142 (22 May 1856): 501.

28. W. M. Robinson, *The Confederate Privateers* (New Haven, 1928).

29. Hubert Haines, "Privateering and International Law," *United Service Magazine,* n.s., 1 (1890): 422.

30. Grivel discussed this point in "Mission militaire et nouveau programme de la flotte," *Revue maritime* 40 (1874): 873, but did not suggest official central preparation of such data.

31. The complete Russian cruiser theory was given by Captain Zelenyi in *Revue maritime* 61 (1878): 33.

32. Translated by C. J. Cook (London, 1887).

33. "Report of the Committee on the Designs upon Which Ships of War Have Recently Been Constructed," p. 153.

34. Letter to the London *Times,* 20 October 1884.

35. "Naval Supremacy and Naval Tactics," *Edinburgh Review* 171 (1890): 146.

36. "Extracts from Reports of the Royal Commission on the Defence of British Possessions and Commerce Abroad," *Parliamentary Papers* (1887, vol. 56): Appendix, p. 295.

37. Sir Samuel Baker, "Cyprus as a Strategical Position," *Journal of the Royal United Service Institution* 26 (1882): 72.

38. Sir Samuel Baker, "Maritime Dangers and Defense," *National Review* 11 (1888): 585.

39. "On the Fighting Power of the Merchant Ship," *Transactions of the Institution of Naval Architects* 18 (1877): 1; "Merchant Service and Royal Navy," ibid. 28 (1887): 197.

40. Sir Thomas Brassey, "Mercantile Auxiliaries," *Transactions of the Institution of Naval Architects* 43 (1901): 224.

41. Sir John Henry Briggs, *Naval Administration, 1827 to 1892* (London, 1897), p. 234; Frank C. Bowen, *History of the Royal Naval Reserve* (London, 1926), p. 423.

42. *General Information Series: Information from Abroad* 6 (1887): 284.

43. William L. Langer, *The Diplomacy of Imperialism,* vol. 1 (New York, 1935), p. 70.

VII. The Revival of French Naval Matériel

1. *Conseil des Travaux,* 13847 (2 February 1869), 14208 (17 May 1870), and 15122 (5 May 1874).

2. *Conseil des Travaux,* 14704 (13 August 1872) and 14789 (19 November 1872); Paul Dislère, "Historiques des différents types de la flotte, 1858–1875" (manuscript, 1875), pp. 12–13, 28; Louis-Emile Bertin, *Evolution de la puissance défensive des navires de guerre* (Paris, 1907), p. 27.

3. Paul Dislère, "Rapport sur une mission dans les arsenaux étrangers de la Méditerranée, de la Mer Noire et de l'Adriatique," *Mémorial du Génie maritime* (1875, no. 6): 388.

4. Small disks of compressible metal were placed in the bore of the gun. The size of these "crushers" after the gun had been fired indicated the maximum pressure at various locations.

5. *Conseil des Travaux,* 15355 (23 March 1875).

6. Colonel Jean-Pierre-Raymond de la Rocque, "Etude historique de la résistance des canons rayés," *Mémorial de l'Artillerie de la Marine* 12 (1884): 161. See also *Mémorial de l'Artillerie de la Marine* 1 (1873): 31; 2 (1874): 581; 5 (1876): 426; and Prosper-Jules Charbonnier, *L'Artillerie de la Marine* (Paris, 1904), p. 13.

7. Chambre, *Débats* (1878, vol. 10, 29 November 1878).

8. *Conseil des Travaux,* 16212 (7 January 1879). They wanted a 17.6-inch, 120-ton gun with a 2,420-pound projectile: 15818 (1 May 1877).

9. The most reliable comparative figures, which are cited throughout this work, were provided in Commission extra-parlementaire de la Marine, *Commission plénière,* vol. 1, p. 107, by Admiral Marie-Edgard de Maigret, who attempted to exclude non-naval expenses from the French figures and include expenditures for coastal fortifications in the Italian ones to match French accounting.

10. Arthur-François-Alphonse Bienaymé, "Rapport sur une mission effectuée en Italie," *Mémorial du Génie maritime* (1880, no. 1): 36.

11. In addition to Lamy (discussed below), there was apparently some naval sentiment for a new policy: Commandant Houette, "Marine française," vol. 1 (Course, Ecole supérieure de la Marine, 1897), p. 61.

12. *Répertoire des affaires soumises au Conseil d'Amirauté du 1 janvier 1871 au 4 novembre 1890* (Paris, 1891).

13. They were quite similar to a design for a first-class battleship of 8,500 tons (the size of the *Redoutable*) and with two 100-ton guns recommended by the Conseil des Travaux in lieu of a proposed 10,500-ton ship: *Conseil des Travaux,* 16083–16089 (30 July 1878).

14. Colonel Cerf, "Artillerie," vol. 2 (Course, Ecole supérieure de la Marine, 1897), p. 562.

15. Cerf, "Artillerie," vol. 2, pp. 560ff.; *Mémorial de l'Artillerie de la Marine* 10 (1882): 533; La Rocque, "Etude historique de la résistance des canons rayés."

16. *Conseil des Travaux,* 17084 (4 January 1881).

17. Louis-Emile Bertin, "Mission en Angleterre," *Mémorial du Génie maritime* (1885, no. 4): 13; Commandant Gabriel Janet, "Mission en Angleterre," *Mémorial du Génie maritime* (1885, no. 1): 1.

18. Thomas Brassey, *The Naval Annual, 1886,* (Portsmouth, 1886), p. 67.

19. Vice Admiral Siméon Bourgois, "La défense des côtes et les torpilleurs," *Nouvelle revue* 49 (1887): 489.

20. P. H. Colomb, *Memoirs of Sir Cotley Cooper Key* (London, 1898), p. 431.

21. Among contemporaries, almost the only reasoned explanation of the propaganda campaign behind the naval scare was Sir William White's anonymous letter to the London *Times* of 14 October 1884.

22. The French were very skeptical: *Mémorial de l'Artillerie de la Marine* 8 (1880): 122; but they had already said bad things about this gun earlier: Ibid. 2 (1874): 340.

23. *Mémorial de l'Artillerie de la Marine* 9 (1881): 130.

24. The powder charges had to be reduced. La Rocque, "Résistance des canons rayés," *Mémorial de l'Artillerie de la Marine* 13 (1885): 11.

25. Ibid., p. 87.

26. *General Information Series: Information from Abroad* 9 (1890): 76.

27. Rear Admiral Robert A. E. Scott, "The Big Gun Question," *United Service Magazine,* n.s., 2 (1891): 321.

28. Letter of 12 June 1888 in G. E. Buckle, ed., *The Letters of Queen Victoria,* 2nd ser., vol. 1 (London, 1926), p. 416.

29. Alfred-Maxime Laubeuf and Emmanuel-Marie-Victor Petithomme, "Mission en Angleterre," *Mémorial du Génie maritime* (1890, no. 5): 810.

30. Sir Nathaniel Barnaby, *Naval Development of the Century* (London, 1904), p. 146.

31. La Rocque, "Etude historique de la résistance des canons rayés," *Mémorial de l'Artillerie de la Marine* 13 (1885): 93; Lieutenant Alfred-François Devoir, "Etude comparative des flottes de combat," *Bulletin des travaux des officiers* 4 (1898): 413.

32. C. C. FitzGerald, "Side Armour *v.* Armoured Decks," *Journal of the Royal United Service Institution* 29 (1885–86): 63, and *Le yacht* 14 (1891): 458, gave estimates of twenty and fifteen minutes between rounds for the Italian.

33. Admiral Sir George Elliot, *A Treatise on Future Naval Battles and How to Fight Them* (London, 1885); G. H. U. Noel, *The Gun, Ram and Torpedo,* 2nd ed. (London, 1885); H. von Amymeyer, *Seetaktik und Seekrieg mit dem Kriegsmitteln der Neuzeit,* 2 vols. (Pola, 1875–78); and W. B. Huff, *Modern Naval Tactics* (Washington, 1884), are good examples of thought in this period.

34. Enrico Morin, *Degli ordini e delle evoluzioni d'una flotta* (Rome, 1873). All five prize-winning tactics in a contest in *Rivista Marittima* in 1881 were standard ramming tactics.

35. Fred. T. Jane, "The Navy: Is All Well?," *Fortnightly,* n.s., 71 (1902): 445.

36. The most notable were Admiral Siméon Bourgois, *Etudes sur les manoeuvres des combats sur mer* (Paris, 1876); Commandant Amédée-Anatole-Prosper Courbet, *Conférences sur la tactique* (Cherbourg, 1872); and Lieutenant Auguste-Eléonore-Marie de Penfentenyo de Kervéréguin, "Projet de tactique navale pour les béliers à vapeur," *Revue maritime* 35 (1872): 622. The exception was Admiral Jérôme-Hyacinth Penhoat, *Eléments de tactique navale* (Paris, 1879).

37. Commission de révision de la tactique navale, *Instructions générales et code d'évolutions* (Paris, 1875–79).

38. Admiral Grigori Butakov in Russia was the founder of this "exact and geometrical science of evolutions": Grégoire Boutakov, *Nouvelles bases de la tactique navale* (Paris, 1864). See also Léon-Charles-Eugène Lewal, *Principes des évolutions navales et de la tactique des combats de mer pour les flottes cuirassées à hélice* (Paris, 1868).

39. Admiral Jean-Pierre-Edmond Jurien de la Gravière, "Considérations générales sur la tactique navale à propos de la révision du livre des signaux" (manuscript, Service historique de la Marine, Paris, 1870).

40. Ibid.

41. A good example of this image is in Philip Howard Colomb et al., *The Great War of 189–* (London, 1893).

42. Richild Grivel, *De la guerre maritime avant et depuis les nouvelles inventions* (Paris, 1869), p. 25.

43. *Conseil des Travaux,* 16013 (26 March 1878).

44. Bertin, *Evolution de la puissance défensive des navires de guerre,* p. 57.

45. *Conseil des Travaux,* 17994 (10 July 1883) and 18319 (20 May 1884).

46. *Journal des débats,* 28 December 1889, p. 1.

47. Jean-Louis de Lanessan, *La Marine française au printemps de 1890* (Paris, 1890), p. 144.

48. *Conseil des Travaux,* 15966 (8 January 1878). See also Houette, "Marine française,"

vol. 1, p. 345; de Freycinet, "La marine de commerce et la guerre navale," *Bulletin des travaux des officiers* 5 (1899): 873.

49. Two important contemporary accounts are J. S. Barnes, *Submarine Warfare: Offensive and Defensive* (New York, 1869), and Viktor von Scheliha, *A Treatise on Coast Defence* (London, 1868).

50. Commandant Le Camus, "Historique sommaire des défenses sous-marines" (Thesis, Ecole supérieure de la Marine, 1926), p. 27.

51. Lieutenant Seaton Schroeder, "The Development of Modern Torpedoes," *General Information Series: Information from Abroad* 6 (1887): 18.

52. Lieutenant Richard, "Torpilles," vol. 4 (Course, Boyardville, 187–), p. 297.

53. *Revue maritime* 14 (1865): 690.

54. Richard, "Torpilles," vol. 4, p. 205.

55. Ibid., vol. 5, p. 542.

56. Le Camus, "Défenses sous-marines," p. 53.

57. Richard, "Torpilles," vol. 5, p. 542.

58. Ibid., vol. 5, p. 550.

59. These complaints were catalogued in Joseph-Marie-Suzanne Audic, *Torpilles,* vol. 3 (Paris, 1880), p. 242.

60. Dislère, "Rapport sur une mission dans les arsenaux étrangers de la Méditerranée," p. 439.

61. G. E. Armstrong, *Torpedoes and Torpedo-vessels* (London, 1896), p. 15.

62. Jules-Marcel Brossard de Corbigny, *Considérations sur l'emploi des bateaux torpilleurs* (Paris, 1880), p. 26.

63. Audic, *Torpilles,* vol. 3, p. 229.

64. *Instructions sur l'emploi, la manoeuvre et la tactique des torpilles divergentes* (Paris, 1875).

65. Le Camus, "Défenses sous-marines," p. 47.

66. Richard, "Torpilles," vol. 4, p. 355.

67. "Rapport de la sous-commission chargée d'expérimenter les canots silencieux," *Mémorial du Génie maritime* (1875, no. 5): 378.

68. Le Camus, "Défenses sous-marines," p. 60.

69. Lieutenant Seaton Schroeder, "The Development of the Modern Torpedo Boat," *General Information Series: Information from Abroad* 5 (1886): 121.

70. Audic, *Torpilles,* vol. 3, p. 152.

71. C. W. Sleeman, "Torpedoes in the Late War," *Engineering* 26 (1878): 439.

72. "The Torpedo Scare," *Blackwood's Edinburgh Magazine* 137 (1885): 737.

73. Armstrong, *Torpedoes and Torpedo-vessels,* p. 171.

VIII. The Navy Under the Republicans

1. Etienne Lamy, "Rapport, Commission du Budget, 1879," Annexe 926, Sénat et Chambre des Députés, *Annales* (21 November 1878, vol. 10): 129, 130.

2. Ibid., pp. 129, 135.

3. Ibid., pp. 129, 130.

4. Ibid., pp. 126, 129.

5. A. Dupont, *Les arsenaux de la Marine de 1689 à 1910: Leur organisation administrative* (Paris, 1913), p. 237.

6. Joseph Reinach, *Le ministère Gambetta: Histoire et doctrine* (Paris, 1884), p. 203.

7. Henri Durassier, *La réforme maritime: Souvenirs du ministère de M. Gougeard* (Paris, 1884), p. 15. Durassier was Gougeard's secretary.

8. Auguste Gougeard, *Les arsenaux de la Marine* (Paris, 1882).

9. Gougeard, *Les Troupes de la Marine depuis leur origine jusqu'à nos jours* (Paris, 1875); Idem, *La Marine de guerre: Ses institutions militaires depuis son origine jusqu'à nos jours* (Paris, 1877).

10. Gougeard, *La Marine de guerre: Son passé et son avenir. Cuirassés et torpilleurs* (Paris, 1884), p. 102.

11. Gougeard, *Les arsenaux,* vol. 1, p. 151.

12. Ibid., vol. 1, p. 130.

13. Ibid., vol. 2, p. 137.

14. Ibid., vol. 2, p. 232.

15. Lieutenant Fénard, "L'évolution de l'enseignement à l'Ecole supérieure de la Marine de 1895 à 1921" (Thesis, Ecole supérieure de la Marine, 1922), p. 1.

16. Gougeard, *La Marine de guerre: Son passé et son avenir,* p. 6.

17. Fénard, "L'évolution de l'enseignement," p. 5.

18. Chambre, *Débats* 26 (29 October 1888): 243.

19. Gougeard, *Les arsenaux,* vol. 1, p. 149.

20. Raoul Castex, *Questions d'état-major: Principes, organisation, fonctionnement,* vol. 1 (Paris, 1923), p. 269.

21. Théophile Aube, "Italie et Levant," reprinted in his *A terre et à bord: Notes d'un marin* (Paris, 1884), pp. 55–56. For his reaction to the *Alabama* see his "Un nouveau droit maritime internationale" of 1873 reprinted in the same volume and his *De la guerre maritime* (Paris, 1873).

22. Gougeard, *La Marine de guerre: Son passé et son avenir,* p. 20.

23. Ibid., p. 23.

24. Gougeard, *Les arsenaux,* vol. 2, p. 155.

25. *Conseil des Travaux,* 16789 (7 April 1880).

26. *Conseil des Travaux,* 16866 (25 May 1880).

27. *Conseil des Travaux,* 16380 (3 June 1879).

28. *Conseil des Travaux,* 16013 (26 March 1878).

29. *Conseil des Travaux,* 17255 (31 May 1881).

30. Gougeard, *La Marine de guerre: Son passé et son avenir,* p. 48.

31. Ibid., p. 62.

32. A. V. Vecchi [Jack La Bolina], *Al servizio del mare italiano* (Turin, 1928), p. 395; Paolo Cottrau, "Maris Imperium Obtinendum," *Rivista marittima* (1882, no. 3): 578.

33. *Conseil des Travaux,* 17760 (24 October 1882).

34. *Conseil des Travaux,* 18259 (25 March 1884). V. Morazzani, "Explosion des torpilles et leurs effets sur les carènes," *Bulletin des travaux des officiers* 2 (1895): 297, gives a detailed description of the defenses of each port.

35. *Conseil des Travaux,* 18140 (27 November 1883).

36. George Sydenham-Clarke, *Fortification: Its Past Achievements, Recent Development, and Future Progress* (London, 1890), p. 170.

37. Sir George Ashton, *Memories of a Marine* (London, 1919), p. 25.

38. Joseph-Marie-Suzanne Audic, *Torpilles* (Paris, 1880), vol. 3, p. 162. The new boats respectively were *Numbers 8–30.*

39. G. E. Armstrong, *Torpedoes and Torpedo-vessels* (London, 1896), p. 172.

40. "Conférences sur les torpilles" (Boyardville, 1885–86), p. 507.

41. "Etudes sur le tir des torpilles Whitehead," report dated 17 September 1884 produced on board the torpedo-school ship *Japon.*

42. Laurent-Gaston Drouet, "Conférences sur le tir de torpilles Whitehead," and Marie-Joseph-Edmond de Geis de Guyon de Pampelonne, "Etudes sur un nouveau procédé de visée à bord des torpilleurs," both in ibid.

43. "Rapports de la commission française envoyée à Fiume," (Boyardville, 1884–86).

44. Ibid., report of 30 December 1884, p. 51.

45. Letter of 12 October 1877 in Ulrich von Hassell, *Tirpitz: Sein Leben und Wirken mit Berücksichtigung seiner Beziehungen zu Albrecht von Stosch* (Stuttgart, 1920), p. 65.

46. Commandant Lephay, "Marines étrangères," vol. 2 (Course, Ecole supérieure de la Marine, 1901–3), p. 172.

47. Paschen, *Aus der Werdezeit zweier Marinen* (Berlin, 1908), p. 171.

48. Admiral E. von Mantey, *Histoire de la Marine allemande* (Paris, 1930), p. 148; Admiral Alfred von Tirpitz, *My Memoirs,* vol. 1 (New York, 1919), p. 39; Eckart Kehr, *Schlachtflottenbau und Parteipolitik, 1894–1901* (Berlin, 1930), p. 257.

49. "Rapports de la commission française envoyée à Fiume" (Boyardville, 1884–86), Report of 23 July 1884.

50. Paul Brière, *Un grand français: Le vice-amiral François-Ernest Fournier* (Paris, 1931), p. 121.

51. "Conférences sur les torpilles" (Boyardville, 1885–86), p. 509.

52. Alfred Yarrow, "Torpedo-Boats, Having Special Reference to Those Built by Messrs. Yarrow and Co.," *Journal of the Royal United Service Institution* 28 (1884): 693.

53. *Mémorial de l'Artillerie de la Marine* 6 (1878): 69.

54. *Conseil des Travaux,* 19299 (10 May 1887).

55. E. de Pampelonne, *Etude sur la tactique des torpilleurs* (Toulon, Ecole des Torpilleurs, 1888), p. 41.

56. Admiral Edward E. Bradford, *Life of Admiral of the Fleet Sir Arthur Knyvet Wilson* (London, 1923), p. 103.

57. E. de Pampelonne, *Etude sur la tactique des torpilleurs,* p. 56.

58. Robert Fulton, *De la machine infernale maritime, ou de la tactique offensive et défensive de la torpille* (Paris, 1812).

59. Chambre, *Débats* 12 (13 December 1884).

60. William Hovgaard, *Modern History of Warships* (New York, 1920), p. 54.

61. *Hansard Parliamentary Debates,* 3rd ser., 290 (10 July 1884).

62. Ibid. 306 (10 June 1885): 1386.

63. Gougeard, *Les arsenaux,* vol. 2, p. 14.

64. Commandant Houette, "Marine française," vol. 1 (Course, Ecole supérieure de la Marine, 1897), p. 41.

IX. New Factors: Colonial Expansion

1. The colonial administration moved from the navy to the Ministry of Commerce in the Gambetta ministry in 1881, reverted to the navy in 1882, returned to Commerce in 1889 and reverted in 1892, passed to Commerce for the third time in 1893, and became a separate ministry in 1894.

2. Gabriel Charmes, *La Tunisie et la Tripolitaine* (Paris, 1884), p. 20; *L'avenir de la Turquie: La Panislamisme* (Paris, 1883), p. 2.

3. Théophile Aube, "Italie et Levant," reprinted in his *A terre et à bord: Notes d'un marin* (Paris, 1884), p. 47.

4. Raoul Castex, "L'expansion coloniale et la stratégie navale," *Académie de Marine: Communications et mémoires* 9 (1930).

5. Charles W. Porter, *The Career of Théophile Delcassé* (Philadelphia, 1936), p. 66; Etienne-Esprit Farret, "Etude sur la stratégie maritime," *Bulletin des travaux des officiers* 6 (1900): 212.

6. Exposition coloniale internationale de Paris de 1931, *L'artillerie aux colonies* (Paris, 1931); Idem, *Les grands soldats coloniaux* (Paris, 1931).

7. Commission extra-parlementaire de la Marine (1894–98), *Délégations,* vol. 6, p. 193.

8. P. Fournier, "Administration" (Course, Ecole supérieure de la Marine, 1898), p. 76.

9. Prosper-Jules Charbonnier, *L'Artillerie de la Marine* (Paris, 1904), p. 61.

10. La Rocque in Commission extra-parlementaire de la Marine, *Délégations,* vol. 1, p. 46.

11. L. Patard, *Historique de la Commission d'Expériences de Gâvres (1829–1930)* (Paris, 1930), p. 188.

12. Pietro Silva, *Il Mediterraneo dall' unità di Roma all' unità d'Italia* (Milan, 1927), p. 345; Giuseppe Di Luigi, *Il Mediterraneo nella politica europea* (Naples, 1925), p. 161.

13. *The Memoirs of Francesco Crispi,* vol. 2 (London, 1913–14), p. 100.

14. Lord Thomas Wodehouse Legh Newton, *Lord Lyons: A Record of British Diplomacy,* vol. 2 (London, 1913), p. 139.

15. Colonel G. A. Furse, "French Ports in North Africa," *Journal of the Royal United Service Institution* 43 (1899): 1113.

16. It received the support of de Lesseps and Jurien de la Gravière: E. Roudaire, "Une mer intérieure à rétablir en Algérie," *Revue des deux mondes* (15 May 1874): 323.

17. *Journal of the Royal Geographical Society* 16 (1845): 245.

18. Trevelyan in *Hansard Parliamentary Debates,* 3rd ser., 260 (3 May 1881): 1661.

19. Lieutenant Bataille, "L'expédition de Tunisie" (Thesis, Ecole supérieure de la Marine, 1936), p. 56.

20. Lieutenant Mazen, "L'expédition de Tunisie" (Thesis, Ecole supérieure de la Marine, 1926), p. 12.

21. Bataille, "L'expédition de Tunisie," p. 18.

22. Mazen, "L'expédition de Tunisie," p. 17.

23. Ministère des Affaires étrangères, *Documents diplomatiques: Affaires de Tunisie* (Paris, 1881), no. 282 (16 May 1881), p. 54. An unofficial denial of such intentions had appeared on 5 May: "Tunis, No. 2," *Parliamentary Papers* (1881, vol. 99): 501.

24. Letter to the London *Times,* 16 May 1881; *Hansard Parliamentary Debates,* 3rd ser., 241 (16 May 1881): 568; Hobart Pasha, Letter to the London *Times,* 26 May 1881.

25. René Pinon, *L'empire de la Méditerranée* (Paris, 1904), p. 343. Ferry made his statement during a visit to Bizerte in 1887.

26. [Admiral Jules-François-Emile Krantz], "La vérité sur la Marine," *Revue politique et littéraire,* 3rd ser., 42 (1888): 233.

27. S. M. Eardley-Wilmot, "Italy as a Naval Power," *United Service Magazine,* n.s., 7 (1893): 695.

28. "Naval Armaments," *Edinburgh Review* 179 (1894): 457.

29. Commandant Juge, "La campagne de l'amiral Courbet en Chine" (Thesis, Ecole supérieure de la Marine, 1927), p. 171.

30. Ministère des Affaires étrangères, *Affaires de Chine et du Tonkin, 1884–1885* (Paris, 1885); Lieutenant Quiquandon, "Les opérations de Courbet dans la rivière Min" (Thesis, Ecole supérieure de la Marine, 1922); Maurice Loir, *L'escadre de l'amiral Courbet* (Paris, 1894); Juge, "Campagne de l'amiral Courbet," p. 81.

31. Captain S. P. Oliver, *Madagascar,* vol. 2 (London, 1886), p. 470, is the best contemporary account. See also Hué, *La France et l'Angleterre à Madagascar* (Paris, 1885).

32. *Hansard Parliamentary Debates,* 3rd ser., 294 (2 December 1884): 395 and 447 respectively.

33. The mass of literature on this period is summarized in Angela von Schönberg, *Um den Twopowerstandard: Englische Flottenpolitik, 1880–1895* (Stuttgart, 1933).

34. Castonnat des Fosses, *La France, l'Angleterre, et l'Italie dans la Mer Rouge* (Lille, 1889).

35. Un marin [pseud.], *Les colonies nécessaires: Tunisie, Tonkin, Madagascar* (Paris, 1885).

36. Ibid., p. 8.

37. Ibid., p. 25.

38. Chambre, *Débats* 14 (29 July 1885): 1670.

39. *Les colonies nécessaires,* p. 20.

40. Paul Deschanel, *La politique française en Océanie à propos du canal de Panama* (Paris, 1884). The promoter of the canal, Ferdinand de Lesseps, wrote the introduction.

41. "Défense nationale, défense des colonies," in *Atlas colonial,* edited by Henri Mager (Paris, 1885).

42. Ibid.

43. Baron de Cambourg in *Atlas colonial.*

44. Henri Mager in *Atlas colonial,* p. 4.

X. The Jeune Ecole

1. T. Aube, "Manille et les Philippines: La domination et la société espagnoles dans l'archipel," *Revue des deux mondes* (1 May 1848): 329–55.

2. Etienne-Louis-Jean Tréfeu, *Nos marins* (Paris, 1888), p. 312.

3. See "La pénétration dans l'Afrique centrale," in Aube, *A terre et à bord: Notes d'un marin* (Paris, 1884), p. 65.

4. Aube, "L'avenir de la Marine française," *Revue des deux mondes* (1 July 1874): 175.

5. "La guerre maritime et les ports militaires de la France," originally published in 1882, reprinted in Aube, *A terre et à bord: Notes d'un marin* (Paris, 1884), p. 127.

6. Ibid., pp. 163–64.

7. Ibid., pp. 185–89.

8. Aube, "Italie et Levant," in his *A terre et à bord,* pp. 31–32.

9. Aube, "La guerre maritime et les ports militaires de la France," pp. 161–63.

10. René Pinon, *L'empire de la Méditerranée* (Paris, 1904), p. 28.

11. Also published separately in Paris in 1885.

12. Gabriel Charmes, *Les torpilleurs autonomes et l'avenir de la Marine* (Paris, 1885), p. viii.

13. Ibid., pp. 72–73.

14. Ibid., p. 162.

15. Ibid., p. 169.

16. Gabriel Charmes, *La réforme de la Marine* (Paris, 1886), pp. 142–43.

17. *Conseil des Travaux,* 17431 (18 October 1881).

18. Lieutenant Degouy, "Marines étrangères," vol. 1 (Course, Ecole supérieure de la Marine, 1897), p. 460.

19. Charmes, *Les torpilleurs autonomes,* pp. 154–55.

20. Paul Fontin [Commandant Z], "Les crédits extraordinaires de la Marine et la défense du littoral," *Nouvelle revue* 61 (1889): 192.

21. Preface by Admiral Paul-Emile-Marie Reveillère to Paul Fontin [Commandant Z] and Mathieu-Jean-Henry Vignot [H. Montéchant], *Les guerres navales de demain* (Paris, 1891), p. v.

22. Aube, "La pénétration dans l'Afrique centrale," pp. 66–68.

23. "Royal Commission on Food Supplies and Raw Materials in Time of War," *Parliamentary Papers* (1905, vol. 39): 37.

24. Aube, "La guerre maritime et les ports militaires de la France," p. 159; and Charmes, *La réforme de la Marine,* p. 97.

25. Vice Admiral Siméon Bourgois, "La guerre de course," in his *Les torpilleurs: La guerre navale et la défense des côtes* (Paris, 1888), p. 39. Originally appeared in *Nouvelle revue* in July 1886.

26. Henri-Paul-Louis-Camille Desaulses de Freycinet, "La marine de commerce et la guerre navale," *Bulletin des travaux des officiers* 5 (1899): 51.

27. Charmes, *Les torpilleurs autonomes,* p. 143.

28. Ibid., p. 150.

29. Aube, "Défense nationale, défense des colonies," in *Atlas colonial,* edited by Henri Mager (Paris, 1885), pp. 11–12.

30. Charmes, *Les torpilleurs autonomes,* p. 80.

31. Degouy, "Marines étrangères," vol. 1, p. 226.

32. Colonel P. Vauthier, *La doctrine de guerre du général Douhet* (Paris, 1935), p. 12.

33. Commandant Ceillier, "Les idées stratégiques en France de 1870 à 1914: La Jeune Ecole" (Thesis, Ecole supérieure de la Marine, 1928), p. 47, is a particularly good analysis.

34. Charmes, *Les torpilleurs autonomes,* p. 152.

35. Guihéneuc collection (1886, vol. 1): 56.

36. Paul Leroy-Beaulieu, "Le budget de 1884 et la situation financière de la France," *Revue des deux mondes* (15 May 1883): 352.

37. Charmes, *Les torpilleurs autonomes,* p. 142.

38. Bourgois, *Les torpilleurs: La guerre navale et la défense des côtes,* p. 44.

39. Du Pin de Saint André, *La rade de Toulon et sa défense* (Paris, 1882).

40. Du Pin de Saint-André, "La question des torpilleurs," *Revue des deux mondes* (15 June 1886): 880 and (15 July 1886): 343.

41. Joseph-Eugène-Albert Wilhelm, "Droit maritime international" (Course, Ecole supérieure de la Marine, 1898), p. 125.

42. X [pseud.], "Stratégie navale," *Bulletin des travaux des officiers* 4 (1898): 249.

43. London *Times,* 10 August 1901.

44. "Report of the Royal Commission on the Supply of Food and Raw Material in Time of War," *Parliamentary Papers* (1905, vol. 39): 322.

45. G. A. Ballard, "The Protection of Commerce During War," *Journal of the Royal United Service Institution* 42 (1898): 374.

46. Admiral Arno Spindler, *Der Handelskrieg mit U-booten,* vol. 1 (Berlin, 1932), p. 8.

47. Hennique, "Conférence sur le port de Bizerte" (Ecole supérieure de la Marine, 1898), p. 6; Commandant Davin, "Bizerte, arsenal maritime et port marchand," *Revue des deux mondes* (15 March 1915): 425; Ludwig Salvator (archduke of Austria), *Benzert und seine Zukunft* (Prague, 1881). The latter was the best study of the military possibilities of the port, and a second magnificently illustrated edition appeared in 1897.

48. *Conseil des Travaux,* 19167 (26 December 1886).

49. *Le yacht* 9 (27 November 1886); Annexe 1111, Chambre, *Documents* 20 (14 October 1886): 112–13.

50. A. Mallarmé, "Emploi des bâtiments légers en temps de guerre," *Travaux des officiers* 1 (1895): 49.

51. *Conseil des Travaux,* unnumbered (26 January 1887).

52. Colonel Cerf, "Artillerie," vol. 1 (Course, Ecole supérieure de la Marine, 1897), p. 447.

53. Lieutenant Antoine-Auguste Le Roy, "Rapport de mer du *Torpilleur 61,*" *Revue maritime* 89 (1886): 9–10, 21.

54. Commandant Lucien-Joseph Berryer, "Marine française" (Course, Ecole supérieure de la Marine, 1898), p. 355.

55. Berryer, "Marine française," p. 354.

56. "Statement Explanatory of the Navy Estimates 1887–1888," *Parliamentary Papers* (1887, vol. 52): 17.

57. Gabriel Darrieus, *War on the Sea: Strategy and Tactics* (Annapolis, Md., 1908), p. 17.

58. Archibald S. Hurd, "French Friendship and Naval Economy," *Fortnightly Review,* n.s., 74 (1903): 654.

XI. The Race with Italy

1. Thomas Brassey, *The Naval Annual, 1886* (Portsmouth, 1886), p. 20.

2. Lieutenant Charlier, "Marines étrangères" (Course, Ecole supérieure de la Marine, 1898–1900), p. 294.

3. Aube, "Italie et Levant," in his *A terre et à bord: Notes d'un marin* (Paris, 1884), p. 36.

4. A. V. Vecchi [Jack La Bolina], *Al servizio del mare italiano* (Turin, 1928), p. 351.

5. Lieutenant Degouy, "Marines étrangères," vol. 1 (Course, Ecole supérieure de la Marine, 1897), p. 472; "L'importance stratégique de La Maddalena," *Revue maritime* 149 (1901): 1129; *Revue maritime* 123 (1894): 647.

6. Charles Rope, *Rome et Berlin: Opérations sur les côtes de la Méditerranée et de la Baltique au printemps de 1888* (Paris, 1888), p. 24.

7. Alfred Thayer Mahan, *The Life of Nelson: The Embodiment of the Sea Power of Great Britain,* vol. 2 (Boston, 1897), p. 202; Carlo Marchesi, "L'ammiraglio Nelson alla Maddalena e la marina Sarda di quei tempi," *Rivista marittima* (1902, no. 4): 5.

8. Alfred F. Pribram, *The Secret Treaties of Austria-Hungary, 1879–1914,* vol. 1 (Cambridge, Mass., 1920), p. 104.

9. Ibid., vol. 1, p. 95.

10. *Revue maritime* 98 (1888): 188; Un Marino, *Estudios sobre el porvenir de la marina militar en España* (1876); and a collection of Spanish Jeune Ecole articles: *Opinion de la prensa respecto de la Marina militar de España* (Seville, 1882).

11. Albert Mousset, *L'Espagne dans la politique mondiale* (Paris, 1923), p. 73; A. Marvaud, "La politique extérieure de l'Espagne," *Revue des Sciences politiques* 50 (1927): 41.

12. *Revue maritime* 58 (1878): 243; Charles à Court Repington [Charles Martel], *Military Italy* (London, 1884), p. 313.

13. *Die grosse Politik der europäischen Kabinette, 1871–1914,* vol. 6 (Berlin, 1922), doc. 1302.

14. Ibid., vol. 6, docs. 1290ff.; François Charles-Roux, "Les conventions militaires italo-allemandes sous la Triple Alliance," *Revue de Paris* (1 August 1926): 608; Waldersee, "Von Deutschlands militärpolitischen Beziehungen zu Italien," *Berliner Monatshefte* 7 (1929): 636; Cristoforo Manfredi, "Guerra offensiva o difensiva?," *Rivista marittima* (1902, no. 1).

15. *Le yacht* 10 (1887): 308.

16. *Le yacht* 10 (1887): 223.

17. Conseil des Travaux, 19374 (20 July 1887).

18. Conseil des Travaux, 19368 (19 July 1887).

19. Conseil des Travaux, 19715 (26 June 1888).

20. Gaston Gerville-Réache, "Rapport, Commission du Budget, 1886," Annexe 3882, Chambre, *Documents* 16 (22 June 1885): 176.

21. For criticism see Paul Ménard-Dorien, "Rapport, Commission du Budget, 1888," Annexe 2039, Chambre, *Documents* 23 (25 October 1887): 77–79.

22. Carlo de Amezaga, *Il pensiero navale italiano* (Genoa, 1898), p. 129.

23. Rope, *Rome et Berlin,* p. 40.

24. London *Times,* 15 February 1888.

25. William L. Langer, *European Alliances and Alignments, 1871–1890* (New York, 1931), pp. 474ff.

26. Two key critics were Paul Deschanel in Chambre, *Débats* 26 (29 October 1888) and Paul Fontin [Commandant Z], "Le péril maritime," *Nouvelle revue* 52 (1888): 837. See also Lieutenant Fay, "Etude sur l'établissement de la Marine à Bizerte," *Bulletin des travaux des officiers* 19 (1913): 789.

27. Francesco Crispi, *The Memoirs of Francesco Crispi,* trans. Mary Prichard-Agnetti, vol. 2 (London, 1913), p. 450, and vol. 3, p. 98.

28. *Die grosse Politik,* vol. 8, doc. 1862 (15 May 1890).

29. Fontin, "Le péril maritime," p. 829; and the official defense, *La vérité sur la Marine* (Paris, 1888).

30. Gaston Gerville-Réache, "Rapport, Commission du budget, 1889," Annexe 3022, Chambre, *Documents* 26 (15 October 1888): 191.

31. Chambre, *Débats* 26 (29 and 30 October and 6 and 8 November 1888).

32. Chambre, *Débats* 28 (17 June 1889); V. de Gorloff, "La flotte italienne en 1887–88," *Nouvelle revue* 58 (1889): 110.

33. Commandant Berryer, "Marine française" (Course, Ecole supérieure de la Marine, 1898), p. 358.

34. Ibid., p. 359.

35. Jean-Louis de Lanessan, *La Marine française au printemps de 1890* (Paris, 1890), pp. 4, 90; Fontin, "Le péril maritime," p. 821.

36. Commandant Houette, "Marine française," vol. 1 (Course, Ecole supérieure de la Marine, 1897), p. 81.

37. Ibid., vol. 1, p. 85.

38. A. Devoir, "Etude comparative des flottes de combat," *Bulletin des travaux des officiers* 4 (1898): 413; Commandant Lephay, "Marines étrangères," vol. 2 (Course, Ecole supérieure de la Marine, 1901–3), p. 358; S. M. Eardley-Wilmot, "Italy as a Naval Power," *United Service Magazine,* n.s., 7 (1893): 692.

39. Lephay, "Marines étrangères," vol. 2, p. 387.

40. Ibid., vol. 2, p. 373.

41. Ibid., vol. 2, p. 208; Degouy, "Marines étrangères," vol. 1, p. 423; Kerhelleuc, "Les vicissitudes de la Marine italienne," *Le yacht* 26 (1903): 457.

42. Charlier, "Marines étrangères," p. 299.

43. James L. Glanville, *Italy's Relations with England, 1896–1905* (Baltimore, 1934).

44. A. Cangemi, *L'Italia e le lotte avvenire sul mare* (La Spezia, 1899).

45. Lephay, "Marines étrangères," vol. 2, p. 269; Thomas Brassey, *The Naval Annual, 1900* (Portsmouth, 1900), p. 40.

46. Admiral Charles-Edouard de la Jaille in Commission extra-parlementaire de la Marine, *Délégations,* vol. 3, p. 21 (Testimony in May 1895).

XII. BRITAIN AGAINST RUSSIA AND THE JEUNE ECOLE

1. Commandant Lephay, "Marines étrangères," vol. 3 (Course, Ecole supérieure de la Marine, 1901–3), p. 90.

2. *Le yacht* 13 (1890): 326.

3. William L. Langer, *The Diplomacy of Imperialism,* vol. 1 (New York, 1935), p. 340.

4. George Sydenham-Clarke, *Fortification: Its Past Achievements, Recent Development, and Future Progress* (London, 1890), p. 180.

5. Wiliam L. Langer, *The Franco-Russian Alliance* (Cambridge, Mass., 1929), p. 379.

6. Un marin [pseud.], *Les colonies nécessaires: Tunisie, Tonkin, Madagascar* (Paris, 1885).

7. Lord George Hamilton, *Parliamentary Reminiscences and Reflections,* vol. 2 (London, 1922), p. 292; Angela von Schönberg, *Um den Twopowerstandard: Englische Flottenpolitik, 1880–1895* (Stuttgart, 1933), p. 37.

8. Sir Thomas Symonds, letter to the London *Times,* 6 September 1884.

9. Colonel J. F. Maurice, "Two Years of Naval Maneuvers," *Contemporary Review* 56 (1889): 516.

10. Frederic Manning, *The Life of Sir William White* (London, 1923), p. 234.

11. Lord George Hamilton in *Hansard Parliamentary Debates,* 3rd ser., 333 (7 March 1889): 1172.

12. G. S. Clark and J. R. Thursfield, *The Navy and the Nation* (London, 1897), p. 151.

13. William Hovgaard, *Modern History of Warships* (New York, 1920), p. 79; Sir William White, "On the Designs for the New Battleships," *Transactions of the Institution of Naval Architects* 30 (1889): 150; "Action Taken by the Board of Admiralty with Regard to the Preparation of Designs for First Class Battle-Ships," *Parliamentary Papers* (1889, vol. 50): 671; Maxime Laubeuf and E.-M.-V. Petithomme, "Mission en Angleterrè," *Mémorial du Génie maritime* (1890, no. 5): 601.

14. Frank Harris, "What Our Navy Should Be," *Fortnightly Review,* n.s., 44 (1888): 557.

15. "The Naval Maneuvers," *Fortnightly Review,* n.s., 44 (1888): 381.

16. London *Times,* 29 May 1888.

17. London *Times,* 17 August 1888.

18. *Hansard Parliamentary Debates,* 3rd ser., 326 (4 June 1888); von Schönberg, *Um den Twopowerstandard,* p. 68.

19. A. Stenzel, *The British Navy* (London, 1898), p. 109. This was an English translation of a volume in the German "Die Heeren und Flotten der Gegenwart" series.

20. *Manoeuvres navales anglaises* (1900): 47.

21. "Report of a Committee . . . to Consider the Fortification and Armament of Our Military and Home Mercantile Ports," *Parliamentary Papers* (1888, vol. 15): 5.

22. "The Naval Maneuvers," *Fortnightly Review,* n.s., 44 (1888); Maurice, "Two Years of Naval Maneuvers"; Sir John Colomb, "The Naval Maneuvers," *Nineteenth Century* 24 (1888): 595.

23. "Extracts from the Report of the Committee on the Naval Maneuvers, 1888," *Parliamentary Papers* (1889, vol. 50): 8.

24. Ibid., p. 6.

25. "Report of the Royal Commission on the Supply of Food and Raw Material in Time of War," *Parliamentary Papers* (1905, vol. 39): 17.

26. J. H. Clapham, *An Economic History of Modern Britain: Free Trade and Steel, 1850–1886* (Cambridge, 1932), p. 529.

27. Sir Charles Wentworth Dilke, *Problems of Greater Britain,* vol. 1 (London, 1890), p. 4.

28. Forwood, "Naval Defence," *Edinburgh Review* 168 (1888): 402.

29. "Select Committee on the Navy Estimates," *Parliamentary Papers* (1888, vol. 13): 34.

30. Dilke, *Problems of Greater Britain,* vol. 1, p. 676.

31. Letter to the London *Times,* 23 October 1884.

32. *Hansard Parliamentary Debates,* 4th ser., 66 (16 February 1899): 1165.

33. Henry Labouchere and Jacob Bright, *Hansard Parliamentary Debates,* 3rd ser., 326 (4 June 1888): 1050, 1082.

34. *Revue maritime* 38 (1873): 1070. This article provoked Aube's "Un nouveau droit maritime international" in the same journal, 44 (1875): 60–81.

35. Sir Thomas Brassey, "On Unarmoured Vessels," *Transactions of the Institution of Naval Architects* 17 (1876): 13. The three *Bacchantes* were unusually large cruisers for their day.

36. A. Le Moine, *Précis de droit maritime international* (Paris, 1888), p. 180; *Hansard Parliamentary Debates,* 4th ser., 66 (16 February 1899): 1165; Raoul Bompard, "Le blé contrabande de guerre," *Revue politique et parlementaire* 20 (1899): 302.

37. Joseph-Eugène-Albert Wilhelm, "Droit maritime international" (Course, Ecole supérieure de la Marine, 1898), p. 125; A. Pillet, *Les lois actuelles de la guerre* (Paris, 1898), p. 13; X [pseud.], "Stratégie navale," *Bulletin des travaux des officiers* 4 (1898): 301.

XIII. French Matériel and Tactics in the Early 1890s

1. Colonel Cerf, "Artillerie," vol. 1 (Course, Ecole supérieure de la Marine, 1897), p. 194; L. Patard, *Historique de la Commission d'Expériences de Gâvres (1829–1930)* (Paris, 1930), p. 227.

2. Cerf, "Artillerie," vol. 1, p. 543.

3. *Conseil des Travaux,* 21375 (24 April 1894) and 21521 (20 November 1894). The lessons were not fully learned, however, as shown by the loss to magazine explosions of the battleships *Iéna* in 1907 and *Liberté* in 1911.

4. Prosper-Jules Charbonnier, *L'Artillerie de la Marine* (Paris, 1904), p. 14; Cerf, "Artillerie," vol. 2, p. 587.

5. Thomas Brassey, *The Naval Annual, 1903* (Portsmouth, 1903), p. 382.

6. Captain H. Garbett, *Naval Gunnery: A Description and History of the Fighting Equipment of a Man-of-War* (London, 1897), p. 170; Maxime Laubeuf and E.-M.-V. Petithomme, "Mission en Angleterre," *Mémorial du Génie maritime* (1890, no. 5): 810; "Mitrailleuses et canons à tir rapide," *Mémorial de l'Artillerie de la Marine* 17 (1889): 1.

7. *Mémorial de l'Artillerie de la Marine* 20 (1892): 1 and 881.

8. General Gustave Borgnis-Desbordes, "Considérations générales sur les canons à tir rapide," *Mémorial de l'Artillerie de la Marine* 20 (1892): 303; and idem, "Répartition et protection de l'artillerie à bord des cuirassés," ibid., p. 681.

9. *Mémorial de l'Artillerie de la Marine* 21 (1893): 307 and 22 (1894): 1011.

10. London *Times,* 12 November 1894.

11. *Mémorial de l'Artillerie de la Marine* 23 (1895): 558.

12. Colonel Bonnier, "Artillerie" (Course, Ecole supérieure de la Marine, 1898), p. 308.

13. *Rapport sur l'artillerie,* 1895–96, p. 41.

14. Bernard de Courville, "Constructions navales," vol. 2 (Course, Ecole supérieure de la Marine, 1898), p. 339; Louis-Emile Bertin, *Evolution de la puissance défensive des navires de guerre* (Paris, 1907), p. 43.

15. Commandant Léon Valéry in Commission extra-parlementaire de la Marine (1894–98), *Délégations,* vol. 1, p. 92.

16. Admiral Aristide-Louis-Antoine-Maximin-Marie Vallon, "Rapport sur le *Magenta*," in idem, *Commission plénière,* vol. 2, pp. 45–68.

17. William Laird Clowes, "Some Lessons from Kiel," *Nineteenth Century* 38 (1895): 165.

18. *Conseil des Travaux,* 21960 (15 June 1897).

19. Alfred-François Devoir, "Etude comparative des flottes de combat," *Bulletin des travaux des officiers* 4 (1898): 413.

20. William Hovgaard, *Modern History of Warships* (New York, 1920), p. 120.

21. L. Baclé, *Les plaques de blindage* (Paris, 1900), p. 117; C. E. Ellis, "Recent Experiments in Armour," *Transactions of the Institution of Naval Architects* 35 (1894): 215; E. Weyl, *Les essais d'Annapolis* (Paris, 1891); E. Vallier, *Cuirasses et projectiles de la Marine* (Paris, 1897), p. 125.

22. Sir Andrew Noble, "The Rise and Progress of Rifled Naval Artillery," *Transactions of the Institution of Naval Architects* 41 (1899): 235; Sir Nathaniel Barnaby, "The Protection of

Buoyancy and Stability in Ships," ibid. 30 (1889): 316; "Armour for Ships," *Institution of Civil Engineers: Minutes of Proceedings* 98 (1889): 1.

23. *Mémorial du Génie maritime* (1891, no. 5): 681.

24. *Conseil des Travaux,* 19381 (26 July 1887), 20827 (1 December 1891); Courville, "Constructions navales," vol. 2, p. 167; Bertin, *Evolution de la puissance défensive des navires de guerre,* p. 57; Gaston Clauzel, "Cours d'artillerie navale, canon, protection, engins sous-marins" (Course, Ecole d'Application du Génie maritime, 1898), p. 287.

25. *Conseil des Travaux,* 19312 (24 May 1887).

26. *Conseil des Travaux,* 19374 (20 July 1887).

27. Maurice Loir, "L'armement de la réserve navale," *Revue de Paris* (1 November 1894): 146.

28. Commandant Houette, "Marine française," vol. 1 (Course, Ecole supérieure de la Marine, 1897), p. 344.

29. Lord Charles Beresford, *Memoirs,* vol. 1 (London, 1914), p. 465.

30. *Manoeuvres navales françaises* (1895): 65 and (1897): 5.

31. Lieutenant Degouy, "Marines étrangères," vol. 1 (Course, Ecole supérieure de la Marine, 1897), p. 164.

32. William Laird Clowes, "The Naval Teachings of the Crisis," *Nineteenth Century* 39 (1896): 448.

33. *Manoeuvres navales anglaises* (1900): 5.

34. Ibid. (1901), p. 10.

35. Lieutenant Charlier, "Marines étrangères" (Course, Ecole supérieure de la Marine, 1898–1900), p. 56; E. R. Fremantle, *The Navy as I Have Known It* (London, 1904), p. 456.

36. Bradley A. Fiske, *From Midshipman to Rear Admiral* (New York, 1919), p. 140. His efforts to introduce his rangefinder abroad got him access to all three of the major navies in the early 1890s.

37. Admiral Sir Reginald Hugh Spencer Bacon, *The Life of Lord Fisher of Kilverstone* (London, 1929), vol. 1, p. 165.

38. London *Times,* 3 October 1883.

39. H. W. Wilson, "Trafalgar and Today," *National Review* 28 (1896): 354.

40. Laubeuf and Petithomme, "Mission en Angleterre," p. 813.

41. W. H. H. Waters, *Secret and Confidential: The Experiences of a Military Attaché* (London, 1926), p. 54.

42. Degouy, "Marines étrangères," vol. 1, p. 10, gives a thorough account of the working of the French Intelligence Service.

43. Sir George Ashton, *Memories of a Marine* (London, 1919), p. 73.

44. H. W. Wilson, "Our Navy Against a Coalition," *Fortnightly Review,* n.s., 63 (1898): 898; "The War Training of the Navy," London *Times,* series beginning 26 December 1901.

45. Admiral Mayne in *Engineering* 53 (1892): 356.

46. J. W. King, *The War-Ships and Navies of the World* (Boston, 1880), p. 254; *Mémorial du Génie maritime* (1898, no. 5): 736.

47. R. C. Oldknow, *The Mechanism of Men of War* (London, 1896), p. 39; R. C. Hawtrey, "The Speed of Warships," *Fortnightly Review,* n.s., 62 (1897): 435.

48. F. C. Marshall, "Progress and Development of the Marine Engine," *Transactions of the Institution of Naval Architects* 29 (1888): 26.

49. Guillaume, "Chaudières," vol. 1 (Course, Ecole supérieure de la Marine, 1898), p. 23.

50. E. Weyl in Thomas Brassey, *The Naval Annual, 1892* (Portsmouth, 1892), p. 18; Commission extra-parlementaire de la Marine, *Délégations,* vol. 6, p. 695.

51. Guillaume, "Chaudières," vol. 1, p. 49; De Maupeou d'Ablièges, "De la puissance des chaudières," *Bulletin de l'Association technique maritime* 2 (1891): 2; H. H. P. Powles, *Steam Boilers: Their History and Development* (London, 1905), p. 195.

52. C. C. F. Fitzgerald, "Water-Tube Boilers for Warships," *Transactions of the Institution of Naval Architects* 38 (1897): 165.

53. Frederic Manning, *The Life of Sir William White* (London, 1923), p. 287.

54. "Naval Armaments," *Edinburgh Review* 179 (1894): 471.

55. "Extracts from the Report of the Committee on the Naval Maneuvers, 1888," *Parliamentary Papers* (1889, vol. 50): 23; R. Appleyard, "We Always Are Ready," *Fortnightly Review,* n.s., 68 (1900): 430.

56. *Manoeuvres navales anglaises* (1901): 19.

57. Commandant Lephay, "Marines étrangères," vol. 1 (Course, Ecole supérieure de la Marine, 1901–3), p. 165; Degouy, "Marines étrangères," vol. 1 (Course, Ecole supérieure de la Marine, 1897), p. 83; Frank C. Bowen, *History of the Royal Naval Reserve* (London, 1926), p. 33; Sir Thomas Brassey, "Manning the Navy in Time of War," *Nineteenth Century* 40 (1896): 861.

58. Georges Le Bail, "Rapport fait au nom de la Commission de la Marine chargée d'examiner le projet de loi sur le recruitement de l'Armée de Mer," Chambre, *Documents* 81–82 (1911): 87.

59. Ibid., p. 103.

60. J. M. Farinacci, *Etude sur le corps des officiers mécaniciens,* 2nd ed. (Nevers, 1899).

61. Gabriel Charmes, *La réforme de la Marine* (Paris, 1886), p. 256; Paul Fontin [Commandant Z] and Mathieu-Jean-Henry Vignot [H. Montéchant], *Les guerres navales de demain* (Paris, 1891), p. 27.

62. E. Farret, "Etude sur la stratégie maritime," *Bulletin des travaux des officiers* 6 (1900): 214.

63. Lieutenant Laurin, "Le transport du XIXe corps et des troupes coloniales en 1914" (Thesis, Ecole supérieure de la Marine, 1931), p. 7.

64. Admiral François-Ernest Fournier, preface to J. de la Faye, *Une famille de marins: Les Du Petit-Thouars* (Paris, 1893).

65. *Instructions générales et code d'évolutions* (Paris, 1892); *Manoeuvres de combat sans signaux et sans compas d'une ligne de bataille* (Paris, 1905).

66. Admiral Sir Cyprian Bridge, "Fifty Years' Architectural Expression of Tactical Ideas," *Transactions of the Institution of Naval Architects* 53 (1911): 34.

67. *Manoeuvres navales françaises* (1894): 86.

68. G. E. Buckle, ed., *The Letters of Queen Victoria,* 3rd ser., vol. 2 (London, 1932), p. 62; Fiske, *From Midshipman to Rear Admiral,* p. 140.

69. A Captain of a Battleship [pseud.], "Some Remarks on Modern Naval Tactics," *Engineering* 58 (1894): 479.

70. *Manoeuvres navales anglaises* (1901): 55; H. W. Wilson, "Our Navy Against a Coalition," *Fortnightly Review,* n.s., 63 (1898).

71. Degouy, "Marines étrangères," vol. 1, p. 321.

72. *Manoeuvres navales françaises* (1896): 67; Jules-Eloi Guilhon, "Essai sur la tactique des torpilleurs," *Bulletin des travaux des officiers* 5 (1899): 1.

73. Admiral Edward E. Bradford, *Life of Admiral of the Fleet Sir Arthur Knyvet Wilson* (London, 1923), p. 171; *Manoeuvres navales anglaises* (1901): 58.

74. *Manoeuvres navales françaises* (1894): 85.

75. "Emploi tactique des divisions légères, 1893," *Bulletin des travaux des officiers* 4 (1898); Homey, "Essai de tactique des croiseurs," *Bulletin des travaux des officiers* 4 (1897): 11; *Manoeuvres navales françaises* (1895): 55, (1897): 179, and (1900): 178.

76. Degouy, "Marines étrangères," vol. 1, p. 321.

77. *Manoeuvres navales anglaises* (1901): 58.

78. Lieutenant Sénès, "Cours de torpilles," vol. 1 (Course, Torpedo Service, Paris, 1900), p. 185.

79. Joseph-Louis-Léon Tissier, "Sous-marins, torpilles" (Course, Ecole supérieure de la Marine, 1898), p. 154. Other figures were: England, 800 to 5,000; Germany, 300 to 2,000; Austria, 200 to 500; Russia, 300 to 1,300; Italy, 200 to 1,600; and total (including other countries), 3,000 to 18,000.

80. E. de Pampelonne, *Etude sur la tactique des torpilleurs* (Toulon, Ecole des Torpilleurs, 1888).

81. Jacques-Augustin Normand, "Le problème de la vitesse," *Bulletin de l'Association*

technique maritime 6 (1895): 19; Bernard de Courville, "Les Torpilleurs" (Course, Ecole supérieure de la Marine, 1898), 20.

82. *Manoeuvres navales françaises* (1894): 3; Commission extra-parlementaire de la Marine, *Délégations.* Volumes 1, 2, and 6 are partly devoted to a long examination of the Torpedo Service.

83. Commandant Rouyer, "Marine française," vol. 1 (Course, Ecole supérieure de la Marine, 1901), p. 210; *Conseil des Travaux,* 20740 (28 July 1891).

84. Commandant Aubry, "Marine française," vol. 1 (Course, Ecole supérieure de la Marine, 1902), p. 161; Commandant Adigard, "Etude de nos côtes au point de vue maritime" (Course, Ecole supérieure de la Marine, 1898), p. 307.

XIV. The Franco-Russian Alliance and the 1893 Mediterranean Scare

1. William L. Langer, *The Franco-Russian Alliance* (Cambridge, Mass., 1929) is the classic account of the negotiations.

2. Jean-Louis de Lanessan, *La Marine française au printemps de 1890* (Paris, 1890), p. 170.

3. These ships were respectively, in the Black Sea, the *Dvenadtsat Apostolov, Tri Svyatitelya,* and *Rostislav;* and in the Baltic, the three *Admiral Senyavin*-class, the *Sisoy Velikiy,* the three *Sevastopol*-class, the *Navarin,* and the *Gangut.*

4. Lieutenant Degouy, "Marines étrangères," vol. 2 (Course, Ecole supérieure de la Marine, 1897), p. 95.

5. R.-P.-M. Vittu de Kéraoul, "Considérations sur l'emploi des torpilleurs dans les Marines française et étrangères," *Bulletin des travaux des officiers* 4 (1898): 63.

6. *Rapport annuel technique au sujet de la situation de l'Artillerie* (1895), p. 37.

7. Commandant Lephay, "Marines étrangères," vol. 3 (Course, Ecole supérieure de la Marine, 1901–3), p. 25.

8. N. Monasterev and S. Terestchenko, *Histoire de la Marine russe* (Paris, 1932), p. 214.

9. *Revue maritime* 129 (1896): 129.

10. Maxime Laubeuf, "Mission à Spithead," *Mémorial du Génie maritime* (1898, no. 5): 779.

11. Frederic Manning, *The Life of Sir William White* (London, 1923), p. 307.

12. *Hansard Parliamentary Debates,* 4th ser., 62 (22 July 1898): 854, 911. George Sydenham-Clarke, *Russia's Sea Power, Past and Present* (London, 1898), is a pretty good account. Fred T. Jane, creator of *Jane's Fighting Ships,* was taken in rather badly by the Russians in his *The Imperial Russian Navy: Its Past, Present, and Future,* 2nd ed. (London, 1904).

13. Lephay, "Marines étrangères," vol. 3, p. 91.

14. Commandant Berryer, "Marine française" (Course, Ecole supérieure de la Marine, 1898), p. 371.

15. *Manoeuvres navales françaises* (1895): 112.

16. William Laird Clowes, "Our Warning from the Naval Maneuvers," *Nineteenth Century* 26 (1894): 341.

17. *Die grosse Politik,* vol. 9, doc. 2145; Degouy, "Marines étrangères," vol. 2, p. 106.

18. Lieutenant Charlier, "Marines étrangères" (Course, Ecole supérieure de la Marine, 1898–1900), p. 353.

19. Ministère des Affaires étrangères, *Documents diplomatiques français, 1871–1914,* 2nd ser., vol. 4 (Paris, 1929–), doc. 22 (20 October 1903).

20. "Die zaristische Diplomatie über Russlands Aufgaben in Orient im Jahre 1900," *Berliner Monatshefte* 6 (1928): 638; Gibson Bowles in *Hansard Parliamentary Debates,* 4th ser., 115 (4 December 1902): 1322.

21. *La Marine française* 16 (15 January 1893): 21.

22. *Marine Engineer and Motorship Builder* 20 (1898): 230.

23. L. J. Lewery, *Foreign Capital Investments in Russian Industries and Commerce,* U.S. Department of Commerce, Bureau of Foreign and Domestic Commerce, Miscellaneous Series, no. 124 (Washington, D.C., 1923), p. 10.

24. Editorial in the London *Times,* 28 October 1893, p. 9.

25. Sir Henry Drummond Wolff, *Rambling Recollections,* vol. 2 (London, 1928), p. 401.

26. William L. Langer, *The Diplomacy of Imperialism,* vol. 1 (New York, 1935), p. 18.

27. Gladstone [Outdianos], "The Triple Alliance and Italy's Place in It," *Contemporary Review* 56 (1889): 469.

28. *Hansard Parliamentary Debates,* 3rd ser., 355 (7 July 1891): 546.

29. Paul Knaplund, *Gladstone's Foreign Policy* (New York, 1935), p. 14; Richard Dietrich, "England und Italien, 1887–1902," *Historische Vierteljahrschrift* 39 (1935): 768.

30. John Leyland, "The Italian Navy and Its Recent Maneuvers," *United Service Magazine,* n.s., 8 (1894): 357; Thomas Brassey, *The Naval Annual, 1893* (Portsmouth, 1893), p. 41.

31. William Laird Clowes, "The Millstone Round the Neck of England," *Nineteenth Century* 37 (March 1895): 369.

32. Geoffrey Rawson, *Life of Admiral Sir Harry Rawson* (London, 1914), p. 82.

33. A. G. Gardiner, *The Life of Sir William Harcourt,* vol. 2 (London, 1923), p. 201.

34. Brassey, *The Naval Annual, 1893,* p. 70.

35. London *Times,* 27 October 1893.

36. London *Times,* 31 October 1893.

37. Clowes's "Toulon and the French Navy," *Nineteenth Century* 34 (December 1893): 1023, repeats much of his earlier letter. Angela von Schönberg, *Um den Twopowerstandard: Englische Flottenpolitik, 1880–1895* (Stuttgart, 1933), p. 95, is a good discussion of the scare but pays too little attention to its technical aspects.

38. Thomas Brassey, *The Naval Annual, 1887–88* (Portsmouth, 1887–88), p. 6; P. H. Colomb and Sir Samuel Baker, letters to the London *Times,* 17 August 1887.

39. Clowes, "The Millstone Round the Neck of England."

40. *Die grosse Politik,* vol. 9, doc. 2135 (6 November 1893, on Beresford); E. Ashmead Bartlett in the London *Times,* 20 November 1893; J. W. Gambier, "An Exchange for Gibraltar," *Fortnightly Review,* n.s., 53 (1893): 722; Lieutenant Colonel H. Ellsdale, "Should We Hold On to the Mediterranean in War," *Nineteenth Century* 37 (1895): 215; W. L. Clowes, "Braggadocio About the Mediterranean," ibid., p. 875.

41. "The British Navy," *Quarterly Review* 178 (1894): 295.

42. P. H. Colomb, "Our Strategic Position in the Mediterranean," *North American Review* 158 (1894): 583; and, under the same title, in Thomas Brassey, *The Naval Annual, 1894* (Portsmouth, 1894), p. 141.

43. Sir George Clarke, "England and the Mediterranean," *Nineteenth Century* 37 (1895): 541.

44. "Extracts from Reports of the Royal Commission on the Defence of British Possessions and Commerce Abroad," *Parliamentary Papers* (1887, vol. 56): 299.

45. "Report of the Royal Commission on the Supply of Food and Raw Material in Time of War," *Parliamentary Papers* (1905, vol. 39): 321.

46. Admiral Hornby, letter to the London *Times,* 22 December 1893; Admiral Richard C. Mayne, "On Lessons to be Learnt from Naval Maneuvers," *Journal of the Royal United Service Institution* 34 (1890): 339; Sir Charles Nugent, "The Advantages and Disadvantages of the Different Lines of Communication with Our Eastern Possessions in the Event of a Great Maritime War," ibid. 31 (1886): 509.

47. Admiral Samuel Long, "On the Present Position of Cruisers in Naval Warfare," *Transactions of the Institution of Naval Architects* 34 (1893): 10.

48. E. Loze, *Les charbons britanniques et leur épuisement,* vol. 2 (Paris, 1900), p. 962; U.S. Office of Naval Intelligence, *Coaling, Docking and Repairing Facilities of the Ports of the World* (Washington, 1892).

49. The principal source for the table is Great Britain, Board of Trade, "Trade, Navigation, and Shipping," *Parliamentary Papers* (1893, vol. 88). Other material was found in "Statement of the Trade of British India . . . for the five years 1888–89 to 1892–93," ibid. (1893, vol. 65); "Statistical Tables (Colonies)," ibid. (1894, vol. 92) and (1897, vol. 97); "Return Showing What Proportion of the Trade of the United Kingdom with the East Goes Through the Suez Canal," ibid. (1883, vol. 64): 773; and "Report of the Royal Commission on the Supply of Food and

Raw Materials in Time of War," ibid. (1905, vols. 39 and 40). Other statistics on the Suez Canal are in J. Charles-Roux, *L'Isthme et le Canal de Suez,* vol. 2 (Paris, 1901); C. W. Hallberg, *The Suez Canal* (New York, 1931); Lincoln Hutchinson, *The Panama Canal and International Trade Competition* (New York, 1915); and A. J. Sargeant, *Seaways of Empire* (London, 1918).

50. *United Service Magazine,* n.s., 1 (1890): 184.

51. C. Ernest Fayle, *The War and the Shipping Industry* (London, 1927), p. 53; Sir Norman Hill, *State Insurance Against War Risks at Sea* (London, 1927), p. 15.

52. A long series of articles on this subject ran in every issue of the *United Service Magazine* from May to December 1890. Participants included S. M. Eardley-Wilmot and Sir George Clarke (both of whom were rather favorable), Lord Charles Beresford, T. G. Bowles, Lord Clarence Paget, Herbert Haines, Sir George Elliot, and Captain James Bruce.

53. See Tryon, "National Insurance," *United Service Magazine,* n.s., 1 (1890): 290.

54. Degouy, "Marines étrangères," vol. 1, p. 118; Laubeuf, "Mission à Spithead," p. 723.

55. G. E. Armstrong, *Torpedoes and Torpedo-vessels* (London, 1896), p. 226.

56. R.-P.-M. Vittu de Kéraoul, "Considérations sur l'emploi des torpilleurs dans les Marines française et étrangères," *Bulletin des travaux des officiers* 4 (1898): 74; U.S. Office of Naval Intelligence, *General Information Series: Information from Abroad* 13 (1894): 336.

57. *Conseil des Travaux,* 21350 (6 March 1894).

58. Manning, *The Life of Sir William White,* p. 323; Lady Yarrow, *Alfred Yarrow: His Life and Work,* 2nd ed. (London, 1928), p. 80.

XV. The Jeune Ecole in the 1890s

1. Paul Fontin [Commandant Z] and Mathieu-Jean-Henry Vignot [H. Montéchant], *Les guerres navales de demain* (Paris, 1891), p. 57.

2. Fontin and Vignot, *Les lois du nombre et de la vitesse dans l'art de la guerre: Le travail des armées et des flottes* (Paris, 1894), p. 44.

3. Fontin and Vignot, *Les guerres navales de demain,* p. 35.

4. Sir George Baden-Powell, "Mosquito Defence," *Fortnightly Review,* n.s. 44 (1888): 546; H. O. Arnold-Forster, "How to Utilize the Naval Volunteers," *Nineteenth Century* 30 (1891): 112.

5. P. H. Colomb, "Naval Warfare of the Future," *National Review* 29 (1897): 916. See also Fred T. Jane, "The Apotheosis of the Torpedo," *Fortnightly Review,* n.s., 70 (1901): 261.

6. Emile-Charles Duboc in *Le yacht* 20 (1897): 2, 37; Fontin and Vignot, *Essai de stratégie navale* (Paris, 1893), p. 25; J.-L. de Maconge, *Une Marine rationelle: La flotte utile, les réformes nécessaires de notre organisme naval* (Paris, 1903), p. 24.

7. Lieutenant X [pseud.], "La guerre de course et la défense navale," *Revue de Paris* (15 May 1900): 361.

8. X [pseud.], *La guerre avec l'Angleterre: Politique navale de la France* (Paris, 1900), p. 150.

9. A. Duquet, "La faillite du cuirassé," *Revue maritime* 161 (1904): 153.

10. Vice Admiral Pierre-Alexis-Marie-Antoine Ronarc'h, in his preface to Auguste-Antoine Thomazi, *La Marine française dans la Grande Guerre, 1914–1918,* vol. 1 (Paris, 1925), p. 9.

11. *Le yacht* 13 (1890): 145.

12. Georges Weill, *Histoire du movement social en France,* 3rd ed. (Paris, 1924), p. 303; Lucien Herr, *Choix d'Ecrits* (Paris, 1932), vol. 1, p. 20; Louis Soule, *La vie de Jaurès, 1859–1892* (Paris, 1921), p. 65.

13. The results were reported by Georges Cochery in Annexe 1745, Chambre, *Documents* 36 (21 November 1891): 249ff.

14. Cabart-Danneville, "Rapport sur la défense des côtes," in Commission extra-parlementaire de la Marine, *Délégations,* vol. 6, p. 607. His earlier ideas are in his *La défense de nos côtes* (Paris, 1895).

15. Commandant J. Avice, *La défense des frontières maritimes* (Paris, 1922), p. 74.

16. Cabart-Danneville, "Rapport sur la défense des côtes," p. 636.

17. Cabart-Danneville, *La défense de nos côtes,* p. 192.

18. An early example of such fears is Henri Leleu, "Marseille et la prochaine guerre maritime," *Bulletin de la Société scientifique industrielle de Marseille* 13 (1885): 1.

19. Commandant Aubry, "Marine française," vol. 1 (Course, Ecole supérieure de la Marine, 1902), p. 234.

20. Edouard Lockroy, *La défense navale* (Paris, 1900), p. 341.

21. *Manoeuvres navales françaises* (1900): 28.

22. Annexe 1625, Chambre, *Documents* 35 (18 July 1891).

23. Annexe 1945, Chambre, *Documents* 37 (5 March 1892); Annexe 178, Chambre, *Documents* 42 (15 December 1893); and Annexe 935, Chambre, *Documents* 45 (27 October 1894); Cabart-Danneville, "Rapport sur la défense des côtes," p. 635; Million d'Ailly de Vereuil, "Le service des batteries de côte en temps de guerre," *Mémorial de l'Artillerie de la Marine* 18 (1890): 213.

24. Gaston Moch [Patiens], "La défense nationale et la défense des côtes," *Revue de Paris* (1 May 1894): 203.

25. Commandant Houette, "Marine française," vol. 1 (Course, Ecole supérieure de la Marine, 1897), p. 319.

26. Aubry, "Marine française," vol. 1, p. 234.

27. Lockroy, *La défense navale,* p. 133.

28. Quoted by Cabart-Danneville, "Rapport sur la défense des côtes," p. 572.

29. Lockroy, cited in Cabart-Danneville's report on Lockroy's coast defense bill of 15 December 1893, Annexe 935, Chambre, *Documents* 45 (27 October 1894).

30. Lieutenant Degouy, "Marines étrangères," vol. 1 (Course, Ecole supérieure de la Marine, 1897), p. 373.

31. Commandant Lucien-Joseph Berryer, "Marine française" (Course, Ecole supérieure de la Marine, 1898), p. 469.

32. Annexe 2386, Chambre, *Documents* 24 (7 February 1888); Annexe 2657, Chambre, *Documents* 25 (24 April 1888); Annexe 2936, Chambre, *Documents* 25 (10 July 1888); and Annexe 1450, Chambre, *Documents* 47 (4 July 1895). For the earlier Jeune Ecole position see Paul Fontin [Commandant Z], "Un programme d'armements," *Nouvelle revue* 53 (1888): 648.

33. Commandant Davin, "Marine française" (Course, Ecole supérieure de la Marine, 1900), p. 105.

34. Lieutenant Fay, "Etude sur l'établissement de la Marine à Bizerte," *Bulletin des travaux des officiers* 19 (1913): 804.

35. *Manoeuvres navales françaises* (1898): 59.

36. Emile-Charles Duboc, "Bizerte, point d'appui de la flotte," *Questions diplomatiques et coloniales* 3 (April 1898): 479; Davin, "Marine française," p. 75; Lieutenant Colonel Georges-F. Espitallier, "Travaux du port de Bizerte et de l'arsenal de Sidi-Abdallah," *Le Génie civil* 42 (1902): 33.

37. Lockroy, *La défense navale,* p. 157; Davin, "Marine française," p. 118.

38. General Charles-Auguste-Frédéric Begin in Commission extra-parlementaire de la Marine, *Sous-commissions,* vol. 1, p. 48.

39. Cabart-Danneville, "Rapport sur les Troupes de la Marine," Commission extra-parlementaire de la Marine, *Délégations,* vol. 6, p. 167; B . . . [pseud.], *Les Troupes de la Marine* (Paris, 1897); Colonel Pierre-Paul Famin, *L'Armée coloniale* (Paris, 1897); General Auguste-Paul-Albert Duchemin, *Les troupes coloniales et la défense des colonies* (Paris, 1905); Captain Louis-Michel-Jean-Baptiste Ferradini, *Essai sur la défense des colonies* (Paris, 1905).

40. Lieutenant Alvarez, "Obock et Abyssinie," *Revue maritime* 121 (1894): 59; *La Marine française* 15 (1901): 468.

41. *Die grosse Politik,* vol. 14, docs. 3934ff.

42. *Die grosse Politik,* vol. 9, docs. 2260ff.

43. A. A. Fauvel, "Les bases navales en Chine," *Revue politique et parlementaire* 20 (1899): 484; J. Silvestre, "La France à Kouang-Tcheou-Ouan," *Annales des Sciences politiques* 17 (1902): 472; Davin, "Marine française," p. 171.

44. France, Ministry of Marine, *Organisation de la défense des points d'appui de la flotte* (1897).

45. Houette, "Marine française," vol. 1, p. 241.

46. B. Brun, "L'artillerie de la Marine à Madagascar," *Mémorial de l'Artillerie de la Marine* 17 (1889): 393; Houette, "Marine française," vol. 1, p. 251.

47. Lieutenant Chrétin, "L'expédition de Madagascar" (Thesis, Ecole supérieure de la Marine, 1926).

48. Davin, "Marine française," p. 160; E. Fichot, "Les côtes de Madagascar," *Revue maritime* 153 (1902): 1017.

49. Houette, "Marine française," vol. 1, p. 246.

50. *Conseil des Travaux,* 22175 (17 October 1899).

51. Houette, "Marine française," vol. 1, p. 248; Davin, "Marine française," p. 153.

52. Georges Cochery, "Rapport, Commission du Budget, 1892 modified," Annexe 1745, Chambre, *Documents* 36 (21 November 1891): 249ff.

53. Lockroy, *Défense navale,* p. 234.

54. Emile Weyl in *Le yacht* 17 (1894): 25.

55. Emile Weyl in *Le yacht* 6 (1883): 116.

56. Bériel, M. Lachenaud, and Pierre-Louis Soleil, *Le contrôle du Parlement sur le budget de la Marine* (Paris, 1906).

57. Ibid., p. 17.

58. Paul Ménard-Dorien, "Rapport, Commission du Budget, 1887," p. 18.

59. A. Dupont, *Les arsenaux de la Marine de 1689 à 1910: Leur organisation administrative* (Paris, 1913), p. 240.

60. Gaston Gerville-Réache, "Rapport, Commission du Budget, 1889," Annexe 3022, Chambre, *Documents* 26 (15 October 1888): 189.

61. Bériel et al., *Le contrôle du Parlement sur le budget de la Marine,* p. 20.

62. A. Dupont, *Les arsenaux de la Marine de 1689 à 1910,* p. 257; Hamelin, "Administration économique et maritime de la France" (Course, Ecole supérieure de la Marine, 1897).

63. Charles Ferrand [Georges Michel], *Le budget de la Marine: Les vices de l'organisation de la Marine en France* (Paris, 1891), p. 7.

64. Emile Weyl, *La flotte de guerre et les arsenaux* (Paris, 1894), p. 86.

65. Ibid., p. 87.

66. Camille Pelletan, "Rapport, Commission du Budget, 1896," Annexe 1540, Chambre, *Documents* 47 (13 July 1895): 404.

67. Jacques Fonlupt-Espéraber, "Etude historique et critique sur le recrutement et le salaire des ouvriers des arsenaux" (Doctoral dissertation, Paris, 1913), p. 112; Gerville-Réache, "Rapport, Commission du Budget, 1889," p. 191.

68. Weyl, *La flotte de guerre et les arsenaux,* p. 95.

69. Commission extra-parlementaire de la Marine, *Délégations,* vol. 4, p. 17, and vol. 5, pp. 85 and 183 (Admirals Edouard Pottier, Emile Parrayon, and Auguste-Pascal Blanc).

70. Admiral X [pseud.], *L'arsenal de Rochefort* (Paris, 1895); *La défense nationale et le port de Rochefort* (Paris, 1895); *Le port de Rochefort devant la Commission du Budget* (Paris, 1877); Commission extra-parlementaire de la Marine, *Commission plénière,* vol. 3, p. 163.

71. Charles à Court Repington, "French Naval Policy in Peace and War," *Nineteenth Century* 41 (1897): 146.

72. Raoul Castex, *Questions d'état-major: Principes, organisation, fonctionnement,* vol. 1 (Paris, 1923), p. 186.

73. Ferrand, *Le budget de la Marine,* p. 13.

74. Edouard Lockroy, "Rapport, Commission du Budget, 1902," Annexe 2636, Chambre, *Documents* 60 (6 July 1901): 1372.

75. Castex, *Questions d'état-major,* vol. 2, p. 520.

76. Gabriel Darrieus, *War on the Sea: Strategy and Tactics* (Annapolis, Md., 1908), p. 8.

77. Edouard Lockroy, *La Marine de guerre: Six mois rue Royale* (Paris, 1897), p. 168.

78. Darrieus, *War on the Sea,* p. 22.

79. *Documents diplomatiques français,* 2nd ser., vol. 3, doc. 339.

80. For some of the French problems, see testimony of Augustin Normand in Commission extra-parlementaire de la Marine, *Délégations,* vol. 5, p. 351.

81. The Orlando combine included firms at Ancona, Muggiano, and Palermo, which had united as the Cantieri Riuniti, plus the Terni steel works, which had absorbed its chief competitors, Savona and Elba. Its rival was formed by the union of Ansaldo and Pozzuoli.

82. Palmer's Shipbuilding Co., Thames Ironworks, Wallsend Slipway and Engineering Co., London and Glasgow Shipbuilding Co., Earle's Shipbuilding Co., and the great engine works of Maudslay Sons and Field built between them five battleships and eight cruisers complete, furnished one battleship without its engines, and engined twelve battleships and eight cruisers before going under.

83. The first great combinations occurred in 1897 with the formation of Armstrong-Whitworth and the union of Vickers Naval Construction and Armaments, Maxim-Nordenfelt, and William Beardmore into Vickers Sons and Maxim. Swan-Hunter and Wigham-Richardson was formed in 1903, and the great hook-up of Cammell, Laird, Mulliner-Wigley, John Brown, Clydebank, Firths, Fairfield Shipbuilding, and Coventry Ordnance was completed in 1905.

84. Lockroy, *La Marine de guerre,* p. 52.

85. Gaston de Laporte, *Les usines de la Marine et la féodalité industrielle* (Nevers, 1886), p. 17.

86. *Conseil des Travaux,* 18174 (8 January 1884).

87. Laporte, *Les usines de la Marine,* p. 23.

88. *Engineering* 42 (1886): 426.

89. Royal Meeker, *History of Shipping Subsidies* (New York, 1905), p. 57.

90. Ambroise Colin, *La navigation commerciale au XIXᵉ siècle* (Paris, 1901), p. 130.

91. *General Information Series: Information from Abroad* 6 (1887): 287.

92. P. Charliat, *Trois siècles d'économie maritime française* (Paris, 1931), p. 181.

93. Roger Lambelin, *Notre marine marchande: Sa décadence, sa législation, son avenir* (Paris, 1898), p. 16.

94. Degouy, "Marines étrangères," vol. 1, p. 59.

95. Henri-Joseph Dugué de la Fauconnerie in Chambre, *Débats* 24 (27 February 1888).

96. Commission extra-parlementaire de la Marine, *Délégations,* vol. 5, p. 51.

97. Bernard de Courville, "Constructions navales," vol. 1 (Course, Ecole supérieure de la Marine, 1898), p. 295. This is a long and detailed study of the problem.

98. Courville, "Constructions navales," vol. 1, p. 292; Charles Vignot, "Les prix de revient des bâtiments de guerre," *La Marine française* 13 (1900): 20. James-Marie-Antoine de Kerjégu, "Rapport, Commission du Budget, 1897," Annexe 2039, Chambre, *Documents* 50 (11 July 1896): 139, put the average cost of French ships at 25 percent more than the British cost, while Degouy, "Marines étrangères," vol. 1, p. 59, put it at 30 to 50 percent.

99. F. Laur, *Les mines et usines au XXᵉ siècle: Les mines et la métallurgie à l'Exposition universelle de 1900,* vol. 1 (Paris, 1901), p. 330.

100. *Annuaire générale des sociétés françaises par actions* (1904).

101. Lucien Brocard, *La grosse métallurgie française et le mouvement des prix de 1890 à 1913* (Paris, 1923), p. 171.

XVI. The Decline of French Matériel

1. Ulrich von Hassell, *Tirpitz: Sein Leben und Wirken mit Berücksichtigung seiner Beziehungen zu Albrecht von Stosch* (Stuttgart, 1920), p. 88.

2. "La stratégie du canal de Kiel," *Revue de Paris* (15 June 1895): 701; Lieutenant Degouy, "Marines étrangères," vol. 1 (Course, Ecole supérieure de la Marine, 1897), p. 349; *Die grosse Politik,* vol. 4, docs. 738–42 and 946–53, and vol. 8, docs. 1684–88; and the long discussion in *Journal of the Royal United Service Institution* 35 (1891): 1109.

3. *Die grosse Politik,* vol. 4, doc. 949 (13 April 1889).

4. Degouy, "Marines étrangères," vol. 1, p. 349.

5. Eckart Kehr, *Schlachtflottenbau und Parteipolitik, 1894–1901* (Berlin, 1930), p. 26; Lieutenant Charlier, "Marines étrangères" (Course, Ecole supérieure de la Marine, 1898–1900), p. 238; Commandant Lephay, "Marines étrangères," vol. 2 (Course, Ecole supérieure de la Marine, 1901–3), p. 161.

6. Henri Brisson, "Rapport, Commission du Budget, 1895," Annexe 965, Chambre, *Documents* 45 (8 November 1894): 345.

7. Commandant Berryer, "Marine française" (Course, Ecole supérieure de la Marine, 1898), p. 370.

8. Commandant Houette, "Marine française," vol. 1 (Course, Ecole supérieure de la Marine, 1897), p. 89; E. Farret, "Etude sur la stratégie maritime," *Bulletin des travaux des officiers* 6 (1900): 221.

9. Colonel Bonnier, "Artillerie" (Course, Ecole supérieure de la Marine, 1898), p. 287; Maxime Laubeuf, "Mission à Spithead," *Mémorial du Génie maritime* (1898, no. 5): 747; J. Delahet, "L'artillerie de la Marine anglaise," *Revue maritime* 147 (1900): 465.

10. Colonel Cerf, "Artillerie," vol. 1 (Course, Ecole supérieure de la Marine, 1897), p. 341.

11. Cerf, "Artillerie," vol. 1, p. 343.

12. *Conseil des Travaux,* 21337 (13 February 1894), 21458 (27 July 1894), 21544 (18 December 1894), 21651 (28 March 1895), and 21787 (14 April 1895).

13. Cavelier de Cuverville, "Les croiseurs," *Revue maritime* 116 (1893): 481; *Conseil des Travaux,* 21543 (18 December 1894).

14. *Conseil des Travaux,* 21815 (9 June 1896).

15. *Conseil des Travaux,* 21868 (20 October 1896).

16. James de Kerjégu, "Rapport, Commission du Budget, 1898," Annexe 2039, Chambre, *Documents* 50 (11 July 1896): 136–38.

17. *Conseil des Travaux,* 21920 (17 March 1897).

18. *Conseil des Travaux,* 21954 (4 May 1897).

19. *Conseil des Travaux,* 21970 (27 July 1897).

20. *Conseil des Travaux,* 22059 (20 August 1898).

21. Etienne Lamy, "Rapport, Commission du Budget, 1879," p. 135.

22. Ibid.

23. Testimony of J.-A. Normand in Commission extra-parlementaire de la Marine, *Délégations,* vol. 5, p. 345; Marc Berrier-Fontaine in ibid., vol. 3, p. 21; and Inspector General Bienaymé in Commission extra-parlementaire de la Marine, *Sous-commissions,* vol. 1, p. 24.

24. A. Croneau, "La complication des navires de guerre: Ses causes et ses remèdes," *Bulletin de l'Association technique maritime* 6 (1895): 102.

25. René Daveluy, *L'esprit de la guerre navale,* vol. 1 (Paris, 1909), p. 319.

26. Auguste-Antoine Thomazi, *La Marine française dans la Grande Guerre, 1914–1918,* vol. 1 (Paris, 1925), p. 76.

27. Commandant Nicol, "Artillerie pratique" (Course, Ecole supérieure de la Marine, 1898), p. 31.

28. X [pseud.], "Notre marine de guerre," *Revue de Paris* (1 May 1899): 45; Bernard de Courville, "Constructions navales," vol. 1 (Course, Ecole supérieure de la Marine, 1898), p. 294; "Les millions de la Marine," *Le Temps,* 1897 (Guihéneuc collection, 1897, vol. 1); Edouard Lockroy, *La défense navale* (Paris, 1900), p. 267.

29. Laubeuf, "Mission à Spithead," pp. 725 and 736.

30. Charles à Court Repington, "French Naval Policy in Peace and War," *Nineteenth Century* 41 (1897): 146; Archibald S. Hurd, "French Friendship and Naval Economy," *Fortnightly Review,* n.s., 74 (1903): 654.

31. A private bill by Emile Chautemps was the first revival of the idea after the Gougeard period: Annexe 1300, Chambre, *Documents* 30 (12 March 1891).

32. Edouard Lockroy, *La Marine de guerre: Six mois rue Royale* (Paris, 1897), p. 250.

33. Paul Brière, *Un grand français: Le vice-amiral François-Ernest Fournier* (Paris, 1931), pp. 138ff. Brière apparently used Fournier's own copy of the course, which must have been the last remaining one since a long search in Paris failed to reveal either the main or the minor courses of the first year. In any event, Fournier's strategic ideas are all expressed in his *La flotte nécessaire: Ses avantages stratégiques, tactiques et économiques* (Paris, 1896).

34. Lieutenant Fénard, "L'évolution de l'enseignement à l'Ecole supérieure de la Marine de 1895 à 1921" (Thesis, Ecole supérieure de la Marine, 1922), p. 45.

35. Emile Duboc in *Le yacht* 19 (1896): 445.

36. Fénard, "L'évolution de l'enseignement," p. 9.

37. Ibid., p. 1.

38. Houette, "Marine française."

39. Berryer, "Marine française."

40. Charles Ferrand, "La bataille du Yalu et ses conséquences dans la construction des bâtiments de guerre," *Bulletin de l'Association technique maritime* 6 (1895): 83; "A Great Naval Need," London *Times,* 12 November 1894; Jules-Martial-Stanislas Lephay, "La bataille navale du Yalu," *Revue maritime* 124 (1895): 5.

41. Fournier, *La flotte nécessaire,* pp. xxiv and 39–41; X [pseud.], *La guerre avec l'Angleterre: Politique navale de la France* (Paris, 1900), p. 85; Commandant Chassériaud in *Nouvelle revue* 106 (1897): 304.

42. Berryer, "Marine française," p. 317.

43. *Manoeuvres navales françaises* (1900): 120 and (1898): 25.

44. "Le navire de combat de l'avenir," *Revue maritime* 137 (1898): 508.

45. Carlo Felice Albini, *Uno sguardo all avvenire navale* (Fano, 1887), p. 40.

46. Just-Lucien Maurice, "Rapport de fin de campagne" (1898–1900), p. 40.

47. "Organisation de la flotte à venir," *Revue maritime* 145 (1900): 82.

48. Vittorio Cuniberti, "Il nuovo tipo di nave da battaglia," *Rivista marittima* (1899, no. 4): 39.

49. Admiral Sir Reginald H. S. Bacon, *The Life of Lord Fisher of Kilverstone,* vol. 1 (London, 1929), p. 173.

50. "On Hitting Objects at Sea," *Engineering* 35 (1883): 362ff.; "Gun Practice at Sea," *Engineering* 37 (1884): 213; and "British Naval Gunnery," ibid., p. 1.

51. Jacob de Marre, "Instruments pour la mesure des distances," *Mémorial de l'Artillerie de la Marine* 6 (1878): 371.

52. M. Gobert, "Etude relative au tir sur mer," *Mémorial de l'Artillerie de la Marine* 6 (1878): 371.

53. Gabriel Darrieus, *War on the Sea: Strategy and Tactics* (Annapolis, Md., 1908), p. 137.

54. A. Mallarmé, "Notes sur l'exercice à bord du branlebas de combat," *Bulletin des travaux des officiers* 1 (1894): 28.

55. The British did not adopt salvo firing until 1909, out of fear that gunners would fire whether their sights were on the target or not to avoid being left out. Admiral Sir Percy Scott, *Fifty Years in the Royal Navy* (London, 1922), p. 180.

56. The whole question was thrashed out in 1898, in the vigorous criticisms of Amiral Bienaimé, "Contributions à l'étude de la pratique de tir à la mer," *Bulletin des travaux des officiers* 4 (1898): 629; Admiral de Penfentenyo's defense in ibid., 665; and a long note of the Naval General Staff, which closed the discussion.

57. Cerf, "Artillerie," vol. 2, p. 1065; Nicol, "Artillerie pratique," p. 103.

58. Cerf, "Artillerie," vol. 2, p. 1068.

59. Louis-Adolphe Mottez, "Réflexions sur le réglage du tir de l'artillerie à bord," *Bulletin des travaux des officiers* 3 (1897): 472; Victor-Gabriel Voitoux, "Instruction spéciale de pointage," ibid. 6 (1900): 116; A. Laporte, "Etude sur le tir de combat aux grandes distances," ibid. 2 (1895): 1; Paul-Louis-Théodore Freund, "Essai d'un manuel de tir à bord," ibid. 8 (1902): 25; Charles-Pierre-Marie Poidloüe, "Des conditions de tir à terre et en mer," ibid. 1 (1894): 59; *Carnet de combat* (Paris, 1900).

60. *Manuel de canonnier breveté,* 17th ed. (Paris, 1907), p. 261.

61. Scott, *Fifty Years in the Royal Navy,* p. 60.

62. Lionel Yexley, *The Inner Life of the Navy* (London, 1908), p. 38; Bacon, *Fisher,* vol. 1, p. 95.

63. Jean Nogues, "Etude sur la question du tir dans la Marine anglaise," *Bulletin des travaux des officiers* 10 (1904): 24; Arnold White, "Gunnery vs. Paint," *National Review* 40 (1902): 389.

64. Marie-Maxime-Augustin Banal, "De l'entrainement au tir," *Bulletin des travaux des officiers* 9 (1903): 58. Banal was on the China station with Scott and describes Scott's system in detail.

65. Scott, *Fifty Years in the Royal Navy,* p. 87.

66. Nogues, "Etude sur la question du tir dans la Marine anglaise."

67. Ibid., p. 68.

68. Commandant Merveilleux de Vignaux, "Artillerie pratique" (Course, Ecole supérieure de la Marine, 1902), p. 301.

69. Ibid., p. 341.

70. Ibid., p. 325.

71. Rapidan, *The Tactical Employment of Naval Artillery* (London, 1903), p. 12. Admiral Fisher experimented with continuous fire in 1902, but still used the section captains to determine the range. See also Scott, *Fifty Years in the Royal Navy,* p. 162; and Maurice-Henri Mercier de Lostende, "Les tirs de la Marine anglaise," *Bulletin des travaux des officiers* 12 (1906): 217.

72. Admiral Sir Herbert Richmond, *Sea Power in the Modern World* (New York, 1934), p. 109, ably lends his support to this old error.

73. Bacon, *Fisher,* vol. 1, p. 255.

74. Ibid., p. 249.

75. Joseph-Louis-Léon Tissier, "Sous-marins, torpilles" (Course, Ecole supérieure de la Marine, 1898), p. 149; Marie-Joseph-Gervais Sénès, "Cours de torpilles," vol. 1 (Course, Torpedo Service, 1900), p. 87; "Rapport sommaire des travaux de la Commission supérieure d'Expériences des Torpilles, 1899," *Bulletin des travaux des officiers* 6 (1900): 130.

76. "Instructions sur le montage, le chargement, et le mouillage des torpilles automatiques mécaniques" (Torpedo school ship *Algesiras,* 1893–95).

XVII. Fashoda and British Sea Power

1. The Anglophobe ideas within the navy in this period are reflected in Etienne-Esprit Farret, "Etude sur la stratégie maritime," *Bulletin des travaux des officiers* 6 (1900): 185; and two important articles written before Fashoda: J. Simon, "Quelques réflexions sur la Marine française," ibid. 4 (1898): 383; and Etienne-Pierre Lesquivit, "Etude historique et stratégique sur la guerre de course," ibid. 5 (1898): 473.

2. Lieutenant Degouy, "Marines étrangères," vol. 1 (Course, Ecole supérieure de la Marine, 1897), p. 63.

3. X [pseud.], "Stratégie navale," *Bulletin des travaux des officiers* 4 (1898): 249. Another Anglophobe study written before Fashoda.

4. Edouard Lockroy, *La défense navale* (Paris, 1900), p. 183.

5. Paul Brière, *Un grand français: Le vice-amiral François-Ernest Fournier* (Paris, 1931), p. 148.

6. Lieutenant Charlier, "Marines étrangères" (Course, Ecole supérieure de la Marine, 1898–1900), p. 114.

7. For the details of the military preparations and the diplomacy, see William L. Langer, *The Diplomacy of Imperialism* (New York, 1935), chapter 16, and Charles W. Porter, *The Career of Théophile Delcassé* (Philadelphia, 1936), pp. 130ff.

8. William Laird Clowes, "Our Naval Demonstration," *Contemporary Review* 81 (1897): 631.

9. Admiral C. C. P. Fitzgerald in the London *Times,* 29 June 1897.

10. *The Economist* (15 October 1898): 482.

11. *Documents diplomatiques français,* 2nd ser., vol. 1, doc. 493, p. 582.

12. *Journal of the Royal United Service Institution* 42 (1898): 365.

13. Julian S. Corbett, *Some Principles of Maritime Strategy* (London, 1911), p. 122.

14. Admiral Sir John Jellicoe, *The Grand Fleet, 1914–1916* (New York, 1919), p. 19.

15. Paul Sethe, *Die Ausgebliebene Seeschlacht: Die englische Flottenführing, 1911–1915* (Berlin, 1932), p. 9.

16. Commandant Berryer, "Marine française" (Course, Ecole supérieure de la Marine, 1898), p. 432.

17. René Daveluy, "Utilisation militaire des sous-marins," *Bulletin des travaux des officiers* 6 (1900): 81. He used nearly the same words in his *L'esprit de la guerre navale,* vol. 1 (Paris, 1909), p. 59.

18. *Manoeuvres navales françaises* (1895): 41.

19. The RUSI Gold Medal Essay for 1903 came to exactly the same conclusion. See Lieutenant A. C. Dewar, "In the Existing State of Development of Warships, and of Torpedo and Submarine Vessels, in What Manner Can the Strategical Objects Formerly Pursued by Means of Blockading an Enemy in His Own Ports, Be Best Attained?" *Journal of the Royal United Service Institution* 48 (1904): 329.

20. H. W. Wilson, *Ironclads in Action: A Sketch of Naval Warfare from 1855 to 1895,* vol. 1 (London, 1896), p. 207; Sir John Hopkins in "Report of the Royal Commission on the Supply of Food and Raw Material in Time of War," *Parliamentary Papers* (1905, vol. 39): 321.

21. *Manoeuvres navales françaises* (1895): 42.

22. Carl Didelot, "Etude sur l'utilisation de nos côtes pour la guerre sur mer," *Bulletin des travaux des officiers* 7 (1901): 40. (Written in 1899.)

23. *Manoeuvres navales françaises* (1900): 141.

24. Commandant Davin, "Marine française" (Course, Ecole supérieure de la Marine, 1900), p. 123.

25. Dewar, "In the Existing State of Development . . . ," p. 329.

26. Brassey, *The Naval Annual, 1903* (Portsmouth, 1903), chapter 5; Commandant Lephay, "Marines étrangères," vol. 1 (Course, Ecole supérieure de la Marine, 1901–3), p. 307.

27. Major J. M. Macartney in *The United Service Magazine,* n.s., 22 (1901): 446; and H. O. Arnold Forster in *Hansard Parliamentary Debates,* 4th ser., 86 (23 July 1900): 863.

28. Didelot, "Etude sur l'utilisation de nos côtes," p. 150.

29. Louis-Marie-Saint-Ange de Francq, "Préparation du combat, ou Manouevre du combat," *Bulletin des travaux des officiers* 3 (1897): 203. (Written in 1893.)

30. *Manoeuvres navales françaises* (1900): 67 and 72. René Pinon, *L'empire de la Méditerranée* (Paris, 1904), heard of the maneuvers but drew the wrong conclusion from them.

31. H. O. Arnold Forster in *Hansard Parliamentary Debates,* 4th ser., 18 (28 November 1893): 1899.

32. H. O. Arnold Forster in the London *Times,* 2 September 1893; Lord Brassey in ibid., 10 December 1886 and leader of 4 December 1893.

33. José Navarette, *Las llaves des estrecho: Estudio sobre la reconquista de Gibraltar,* 2nd ed. (Madrid, 1882): Colonel Camilo Valles, *Gibraltar y la bahia de Algeciras* (Barcelona, 1889); A. Fernandez y Garcia, *Gibraltar, Ecos de la Patria* (Malaga, 1884).

34. The most important of these studies was the 1884 report of General J. F. Crease of the Royal Engineers, whose essentials are contained in "Ceuta and Gibraltar," *Journal of the Society of Arts* 50 (1902): 462.

35. Pinon, *L'empire de la Méditerranée,* p. 397; Z [pseud.], "Les puissances maritimes en Méditerranée," *Annales des sciences politiques* 19 (1904): 76.

36. Balfour in *Hansard Parliamentary Debates,* 4th ser., 118 (4 March 1903): 1363. He was responding to a scare aroused by T. G. Bowles, *Gibraltar: A National Danger* (London, 1901).

37. *A Memoir of Sir John Drummond-Hay* (London, 1896), p. 231.

38. *Die grosse Politik,* vol. 17, doc. 5171 (18 September 1900).

39. The many discussions of Tangier are not very illuminating. These include Graham H. Stuart, *The International City of Tangier* (Stanford, 1931); and Jean Sibieude, *La question de Tanger* (Montpellier, 1927).

40. Commander George Alexander Ballard, "The Protection of Commerce in War," *Journal of the Royal United Service Institution* 42 (1898): 398. Dewar made a similar proposal in 1903.

41. Spencer Wilkinson, *The Command of the Sea* (Westminster, 1894), p. 124; a series of discussions in *Journal of the Royal United Service Institution* 47 (1903): 78; and *Revue maritime* 143 (1899): 394.

42. *British Documents on the Origin of the War, 1898–1914,* vol. 3, doc. 445 (27 April 1907).

43. "Défense maritime des Baléares," *Revue maritime* 145 (1900): 333.

44. Charles Nouette d'Andrezel, "La guerre contre l'Angleterre," *Bulletin des travaux des officiers* 6 (1900): 249; X [pseud.], *La guerre avec l'Angleterre: Politique navale de la France*

(Paris, 1900): p. 122; Z [pseud.], "Les puissances maritimes en Méditerranée," *Annales des sciences politiques* 19 (1904): 97.

45. *Manoeuvres navales françaises* (1900): 13 and (1901): 16.

46. *British Documents on the Origin of the War, 1898–1914,* vol. 7, doc. 1.

47. *Documents diplomatiques français,* vol. 4, docs. 119–20; *British Documents on the Origin of the War, 1898–1914,* vol. 2, docs. 373, 378, and 380.

48. *British Documents on the Origin of the War, 1898–1914,* vol. 4, no. 55, annex; Langer, *The Diplomacy of Imperialism,* vol. 1, chapters 10 and 11.

49. George Hooper, "How the Political and Military Power of England Is Affected by the Suez Canal," *United Service Magazine,* n.s., 1 (1890): 505. The whole question, even to the idea of forcing neutral shipping to go around the Cape, was thrashed out in a long discussion after the paper of Colonel Sir Charles Nugent, "The Advantages and Disadvantages of the Different Lines of Communication with Our Eastern Possessions in the Event of a Great Maritime War," *Journal of the Royal United Service Institution* 31 (1887–88): 509. At about the time of Fashoda, a French writer was proposing that a "collision" would be the easiest way to block the canal in time of war. X [pseud.], "Stratégie navale," *Bulletin des travaux des officiers* 4 (1898): 294.

50. Charlier, "Marines étrangères," p. 103.

51. Degouy, "Marines étrangères," vol. 1, p. 25.

52. Ibid., vol. 1, p. 21.

53. *The Saturday Review* (11 September 1897): 278.

54. Degouy, "Marines étrangères," vol. 1, p. 24; and, for a remarkable consideration of how far France could go, Wilhelm, "Droit maritime international" (Course, Ecole supérieure de la Marine, 1898).

55. Just-Lucien Maurice, "Rapport de fin de campagne" (1898–1900), p. 58.

56. Ballard, "The Protection of Commerce in War," p. 376; H. W. Wilson, "The Protection of Our Commerce in War," *Nineteenth Century* 39 (1896): 218.

57. Degouy, "Marines étrangères," vol. 1, p. 18.

58. Raphael Semmes, *Service Afloat* (Baltimore, 1887), p. 629.

59. Ballard, "The Protection of Commerce in War," p. 377; "Naval Supremacy and Naval Tactics," *Edinburgh Review* 171 (1890): 146.

60. P. H. Colomb, "Convoys: Are They Any Longer Possible," *Journal of the Royal United Service Institution* 31 (1887): 297; W. C. Crutchley and H. L. Swinburne, "Suggested Lines of Convoy in Wartime," ibid. 39 (1895): 19; Admiral Samuel Long, "On the Present Position of Cruisers in Naval Warfare," *Transactions of the Institution of Naval Architects* 34 (1893): 1. The French opinion is in Charlier, "Marines étrangères," p. 115.

61. *Die grosse Politik,* vol. 15, doc. 4274 (28 June 1899).

62. "Report of the Royal Commission on the Supply of Food and Raw Material in Time of War," *Parliamentary Papers* (1905, vol. 39): 34.

63. Ibid., vol. 39, p. 28 (Report) and p. 413 (Minutes of Evidence).

64. *Manoeuvres navales anglaises* (1900): 43.

65. John Charles Ready Colomb, *Naval Intelligence and Protection of Commerce in War* (London, 1881); "The War Training of the Navy," London *Times,* 26 December 1901; "Report of the Royal Commission on the Supply of Food and Raw Material in Time of War," vol. 39, p. 35.

66. Germanicus [pseud.], "Frankreichs Flottenfrage und die junge Schule," *Preussische Jahrbucher* 96 (1899): 258.

67. Archibald Hurd, *The Merchant Navy,* vol. 1, History of the Great War Based on Official Documents (London, 1921), p. 225.

XVIII. AFTER FASHODA

1. Chambre, *Débats* 57 (18 March 1899).

2. Jean de la Poulaine, *Le colosse aux pieds d'argile* (Paris, 1899); Emile-Charles Duboc, *Le point faible de l'Angleterre,* Paris (1899); Duboc, "Après Fashoda: La politique navale de la

France," *Questions diplomatiques et coloniales* 9 (1900): 338, and in the same number, O'Cabe, "Considérations sur une guerre entre la France et l'Angleterre," p. 353; X [pseud.], *La guerre avec l'Angleterre: Politique navale de la France* (Paris, 1900), p. 9.

3. *Conseil des Travaux,* 22411 (28 April 1903) and 22436 (11 August 1904).

4. London *Times,* 20 November 1902.

5. Letter of Monson to Lansdowne in Lord Newton, *Lord Lansdowne: A Biography* (London, 1929), p. 270; Thomas Brassey, *The Naval Annual, 1904* (Portsmouth, 1904), p. 10; John Leyland, "French Naval Personnel," in Brassey, *The Naval Annual, 1908* (Portsmouth, 1908), p. 111; and a cartoon in *Punch,* 24 September 1902.

6. Charles W. Porter, *The Career of Théophile Delcassé* (Philadelphia, 1936), p. 199; Paul Brière, *Un grand français: Le vice-amiral François-Ernest Fournier* (Paris, 1931), p. 113.

7. Lockroy reprinted his letters to *Le Temps* in his *Les Marines française et allemande* (Paris, 1904). Lanessan published a similar series in *Le Siècle.*

8. Commandant Lephay, "Marines étrangères," vol. 2 (Course, Ecole supérieure de la Marine, 1901–3), p. 168.

9. Commandant Berryer, "Marine française" (Course, Ecole supérieure de la Marine, 1898), p. 433; X [pseud.], "Stratégie navale," *Bulletin des travaux des officiers* 4 (1898): 305; Lieutenant Laurin, "Le transport du XIXe corps et des troupes coloniales en 1914" (Thesis, Ecole supérieure de la Marine, 1931), p. 3.

10. Edouard Lockroy, *La défense navale* (Paris, 1900), p. 54.

11. Etienne-Esprit Farret, "Etude sur la stratégie maritime," *Bulletin des travaux des officiers* 6 (1900): 195.

12. Commandant Davin, "Marine française" (Course, Ecole supérieure de la Marine, 1900), p. 563.

13. Porter, *The Career of Théophile Delcassé,* p. 118.

14. François-Ernest Fournier, *La flotte de combat* (Paris, 1899).

15. Brière, *Un grand français,* p. 183.

16. Annexes 1375, 1599, and 1677, Chambre, *Documents* 58 (30 January, 10 April, and 7 June 1900); Farret, "Etude sur la stratégie maritime," p. 225; P. Collard, "Une loi navale," *Revue politique et parlementaire* 33 (1902): 18; Henry Fleury-Ravarin, "La réorganisation de notre Marine militaire," *Revue politique et parlementaire* 23 (February 1900): 255.

17. John Leyland in Thomas Brassey, *The Naval Annual, 1901* (Portsmouth, 1901), p. 40; Archibald S. Hurd, "French Friendship and Naval Economy," *Fortnightly Review,* n.s., 74 (1903): 654.

18. Lockroy, *Du Weser à la Vistule: Lettres sur la Marine allemande* (Paris, 1901), first published in 1900, is the best French account of the German danger.

19. Farret, "Etude sur la stratégie maritime," p. 210. The extreme Jeune Ecole was represented by X [pseud.], "Stratégie navale," p. 289.

20. Berryer, "Marine française," p. 250.

21. Ibid., p. 251.

22. Lephay, "Marines étrangères," vol. 1, p. 374.

23. Commandant Rouyer, "Marine française," vol. 1 (Course, Ecole supérieure de la Marine, 1901), p. 401; and Lieutenant Charlier, "Marines étrangères" (Course, Ecole supérieure de la Marine, 1898–1900), p. 112.

24. Berryer, "Marine française," p. xi.

25. X [pseud.], "Stratégie navale," p. 255.

26. Julian S. Corbett, *Some Principles of Maritime Strategy* (London, 1911), p. 162.

27. X [pseud.], "Stratégie navale," p. 255; Louis-Marie-Saint-Ange de Francq, "Préparation du combat, ou Manouevre du combat," *Bulletin des travaux des officiers* 3 (1897): 385.

28. Rouyer, "Marine française," vol. 2, p. 363.

29. X [pseud.], "La guerre de course et la défense navale," *Revue de Paris* (1 May 1900): 73.

30. René Daveluy, *L'esprit de la guerre navale* (Paris, 1909–10); Gabriel Darrieus, *War on the Sea: Strategy and Tactics* (Annapolis, Md., 1908).

31. William L. Langer, *The Diplomacy of Imperialism,* vol. 2 (New York, 1935), p. 655.

32. Admiral Alfred von Tirpitz, *My Memoirs,* vol. 1 (New York, 1919), p. 77.

33. Daveluy, *L'esprit de la guerre navale,* vol. 1, p. 8.

34. Quoted from ibid. by Commandant Ceillier, "Les idées stratégiques en France de 1870 à 1914: La Jeune Ecole" (Thesis, Ecole supérieure de la Marine, 1928), p. 40.

35. J. Legrand, "La guerre sur mer et ses leçons," *La Marine française* 13 (1900): 89.

36. William Laird Clowes, "Sea Power, Its Past and Its Future," *Fortnightly Review,* n.s., 54 (1893): 713.

37. Commandant Dennis-Marie-Charles de Champeaux La Boulaye, "Comment faire la guerre à l'Angleterre," *Bulletin des travaux des officiers* 7 (1901): 182; Rouyer, "Marine française," vol. 2, p. 473; Charlier, "Marines étrangères," p. 117.

38. Annexes 1376, 1548, 1677, and 1716, Chambre, *Documents* 58 (30 January, 26 March, 7 June, and 15 June 1900).

39. Commandant Aubry, "Marine française," vol. 1 (Course, Ecole supérieure de la Marine, 1902), p. 185.

40. *Manoeuvres navales françaises* (1901): 25.

41. *Manoeuvres navales françaises* (1900): 33.

42. M. G. Milsom, *Rachgoun: Port militaire et port de commerce* (Algiers, 1897); Colonel G. A. Furse, "French Ports in North Africa," *Journal of the Royal United Service Institution* 43 (1899): 1113; Aubry, "Marine française," vol. 1, p. 203.

43. James L. Glanville, *Italy's Relations with England, 1896–1905* (Baltimore, 1934), p. 110.

44. Porter, *The Career of Théophile Delcassé,* pp. 120ff.; *Die grosse Politik,* vol. 13, doc. 3580; vol. 15, docs. 4211–12; vol. 18, doc. 5884; *Documents diplomatiques français,* 2nd ser., vol. 3, docs. 81, 144, 163, 358; Albert Mousset, *L'Espagne dans la politique mondiale* (Paris, 1923), p. 109.

45. *Documents diplomatiques français,* 2nd ser., vol. 3, doc. 144, Annex II (16 March 1903).

46. Ibid., vol. 4, doc. 290 (18 February 1904).

47. Pierre Ronarc'h, "Etude sur l'attaque des cables sous-marins," *Bulletin des travaux des officiers* 5 (1899): 203.

48. *Manoeuvres navales françaises* (1901): 32.

49. Ibid. (1900): 123.

50. Ibid. (1900): 19.

51. Admiral François-Ernest Fournier, *La flotte nécessaire* (Paris, 1896), p. 10; Davin, "Marine française," p. 531.

52. Paul Canet, *Le canal des deux mers* (Toulouse, 1932); Annexe 1136, Chambre, *Documents* 46 (14 January 1895); Annexe 934, Chambre, *Documents* 56 (12 May 1899); Chambre, *Documents* 57 (27 December 1899); Annexe 2861, Chambre, *Documents* 61 (23 December 1901); Charles Vignot, "Stratégie du canal des deux mers," *La Marine française* 12 (1899): 465.

53. K. Reinhardt, "La défense des côtes des états de la Baltique," *Revue maritime* 156 (1903): 535; N. Monasterev, "Le premier brise-glace, l'*Ermak,*" *Revue maritime,* n.s., 196 (1936): 453.

54. Fred T. Jane, *The Imperial Russian Navy: Its Past, Present, and Future,* 2nd ed. (London, 1904), pp. 368, 414; "Russia's Great Naval Enterprise," *Fortnightly Review,* n.s., 65 (1899): 899; Thomas Brassey, *The Naval Annual, 1899* (Portsmouth, 1899), p. 51.

55. *Documents diplomatiques français, 1871–1914,* 2nd ser., vol. 3, Annex III (21 December 1901).

56. Davin, "Marine française," p. 563, said so in so many words, although this was an isolated instance.

57. Rouyer, "Marine française," vol. 2, p. 475; Davin, "Marine française," p. 561.

58. Darrieus, *War on the Sea,* p. 144; "Compte-rendu de la guerre russo-japonaise," *Bulletin des travaux des officiers* 13 (1907): 287.

59. Annexes 1371 and 1698, Chambre, *Documents* 58 (30 January and 11 June 1900).

60. Commandant J. Avice, *La défense des frontières maritimes* (Paris, 1922), p. 95; Davin, "Marine française," p. 107.

61. Sénès, "Cours de torpilles," vol. 1 (Course, Torpedo Service, 1900), p. 236; Rouyer, "Marine française," vol. 1, p. 250.

62. Géneral Gustave Borgnis-Desbordes, "Des opérations maritimes contre les côtes et des débarquements," *Mémorial de l'Artillerie de la Marine* 22 (1894): 27. This remarkable study was later apparently printed for the benefit of the Jeune Ecole investigators on the Extra-Parliamentary Commission of 1894. See also Berryer, "Marine française," p. 340.

63. Illustrated in the frontispiece to Paul Fontin [Commandant Z] and Mathieu-Jean-Henry Vignot [H. Montéchant], *Essai de stratégie navale* (Paris, 1893).

64. Berryer, "Marine française," p. 347.

65. Frederic Manning, *The Life of Sir William White* (London, 1923), p. 352.

66. Grip, *How John Bull Lost London* (London, 1882); Lord Dunsany, "The Proposed Channel Tunnel," *Nineteenth Century* 11 (1882): 128; "The Proposed Channel Tunnel: A Protest" (by a whole group of lords), ibid., p. 493; Colonel H. M. Hozier, "Our Actual Military Strength," ibid. 23 (1888): 799; Angela von Schönberg, *Um den Twopowerstandard: Englische Flottenpolitik, 1880–1895* (Stuttgart, 1933), p. 65.

67. Borgnis-Desbordes, "Des opérations maritimes contre les côtes," p. 68.

68. F. Edelsheim, *Operations on the Sea* (New York, 1914). This work, originally published in 1901, was written by an officer of the General Staff. Also: Freiherr von den Goltz, "Seemacht und Landkrieg," *Deutsche Rundschau* 102 (1900): 355; Vice Admiral Livonius, "Die deutsche Nordseeflotte und die englische Seemacht," *Deutsche Revue* 27 (1902): 196.

69. "Les descentes en Angleterre," *Revue des deux mondes* (15 March 1899): 275.

70. *Conseil des Travaux,* 22119 (20 June 1899).

71. Commandant Houette, "Marine française," vol. 1 (Course, Ecole supérieure de la Marine, 1897), p. 218, thought 120,000 men could be carried on fishing boats, and Davin, "Marine française" (1900), p. 576, estimated 110,000 on regular Channel shipping.

72. W. L. Clowes, "A System of Coast Defence," *Fortnightly Review,* n.s., 57 (1895): 551; Davin, "Marine française," p. 568.

73. Thomas Brassey, *The Naval Annual, 1900* (Portsmouth, 1900). The other ships were the *Sans Pareil, Colossus, Thunderer,* and *Alexandra.*

74. H. W. Wilson, "The Invasion of England," *National Review* 33 (1899): 653; H. W. Wilson, "Are We Misled About the Fleet?," *Nineteenth Century* 47 (1900): 574; Capt. W. E. Cairnes, "The Problem of Invasion," *National Review* 36 (1900): 341; *The New Battle of Dorking* (London, 1900); Arnold White, "Shall Britain be Ladysmithed?," *Navy League Journal* 5 (1900): 154.

75. *Manoeuvres navales anglaises* (1901): 51.

76. Henri-Paul-Louis-Camille Desaulses de Freycinet, "La marine de commerce et la guerre navale," *Bulletin des travaux des officiers* 5 (1899): 85; X [pseud.], "Stratégie navale," p. 294; Charles Nouette d'Andrezel, "La guerre contre l'Angleterre," *Bulletin des travaux des officiers* 6 (1900): 265.

77. Lephay, "Marines étrangères," vol. 2, p. 48.

78. Paul Fontin, *Les sous-marins et l'Angleterre* (Paris, 1902).

79. Lockroy in Chambre, *Débats* 35 (7 December 1891) and 57 (17 March 1899); Fontin in *Nouvelle Revue* 67 (1890): 846. For other prophecies see Maxime Laubeuf [d'Armor], *Les sous-marins et la guerre contre l'Angleterre* (Paris, 1899).

80. William Laird Clowes, "The Government and the Submarine Boat," *Navy League Journal* 6 (1901): 5.

81. Tissier, "Sous-marins, torpilles" (Course, Ecole supérieure de la Marine, 1898), p. 17.

82. Lieutenant Gabriel Darrieus, *Etude sur les bateaux sous-marins* (Paris, 1895), gives the whole history of the experiments with the *Gymnote.* The other indispensable account is Commandant Joseph-Charles Baudry-Lacantinerie, "Etude sur les torpilleurs submersibles," *Bulletin des travaux des officiers* 1 (1895): 115.

83. *Conseil des Travaux,* 22047 (5 July 1898).

84. *Manoeuvres navales françaises* (1901): 57.

85. Annexes 1377, 1489, and 1686, Chambre, *Documents* 58 (30 January, 6 March, and 8 June 1900).

86. Annexe 1245, Chambre, *Documents* 57 (1 December 1899), and Annexe 1347, Chambre, *Documents* 58 (18 January 1900, 2 parts); General Auguste-Paul-Albert Duchemin, *Les Troupes coloniales et la défense des colonies* (Paris, 1905), p. 9.

87. *Organisation de la défense des points d'appui de la flotte* (1897), p. 1.

88. One of the many discussions during the 1890s of the importance of Dakar was Camille Sabatier, *Touat, Sahara et Soudan* (Paris, 1891).

89. Rouyer, "Marine française," vol. 2, p. 475, and Houette, "Marine française," vol. 1, p. 234. Exposition coloniale internationale de Paris de 1931, *L'artillerie aux colonies* (Paris, 1931), p. 261, gives a good summary of the whole problem.

90. Fred T. Jane, *Heresies of Sea Power* (London, 1906), p. 139. See also "Les conditions nouvelles de la guerre navale," *Nouvelle revue* 79 (1892): 456; Renaut d'Oure-Seille, "L'évolution du problème des bases navales," *Communications et mémoires de l'Academie de Marine* 11 (1932): 117.

91. Carlyon Bellaire in Thomas Brassey, *The Naval Annual, 1903* (Portsmouth, 1903), p. 97.

92. Lieutenant Degouy, "Marines étrangères," vol. 1 (Course, Ecole supérieure de la Marine, 1897), p. 219.

93. Wilhelm, "Droit maritime international" (Course, Ecole supérieure de la Marine, 1898), p. 40.

94. Berryer, "Marine française," p. 478.

95. Annexes 1374 and 1727, Chambre, *Documents* 58 (30 January and 19 June 1900).

96. The pioneer systematic work is Lieutenant Pierre-Jean Verlynde, "La question des cables télégraphiques au point de vue militaire," *Bulletin des travaux des officiers* 2 (1896): 228. The chief public sources were the articles of the promoter of the Azores line: J. Depelley, *Les cables sous-marins et la défense de nos colonies* (Paris, 1896), and "Les cables télégraphiques en temps de guerre," *Revue des deux mondes* (1 January 1900): 181. See also E. Watbled, "Communications télégraphiques de la France avec ses possessions d'outremer," *Nouvelle revue* 101 (1896): 77; and a German study, Otto Wachs, "Les cables sous-marins considérés comme arme de guerre," *Revue maritime* 143 (1899): 423.

97. Berryer, "Marine française," p. 482.

98. Pierre-Alexis-Marie-Antoine Ronarc'h, "Etude sur l'attaque des cables sous-marins," *Bulletin des travaux des officiers* 5 (1899): 203; L. Mascart, "Mémoire sur l'attaque des cables sous-marins," *Bulletin des travaux des officiers* 9 (1903): 59; Commission supérieure d'Expériences des Torpilles, "Etudes et Travaux, 1903," ibid., p. 223; P. G. McGrath, "Our Defenceless Cables," *Fortnightly Review,* n.s., 72 (1902): 513.

99. "La Marine française dans les mers d'Orient," *Revue de Paris* (15 August 1902): 813; Archibald S. Hurd, "The New Flying Squadrons of France," *Fortnightly Review,* n.s., 72 (1902): 321.

100. Etienne-Pierre Lesquivit, "Etude historique et stratégique sur la guerre de course," *Bulletin des travaux des officiers* 5 (1899): 415–79; X [pseud.], "Stratégie navale," p. 249; Desaulses de Freycinet, "La marine de commerce et la guerre navale," p. 51; Degouy, "Marines étrangères," vol. 1, p. 224; D'Andrezel, "La guerre contre l'Angleterre."

101. Rouyer, "Marine française," vol. 2, p. 471.

102. Houette, "Marine française," vol. 1, p. 231; *Conseil des Travaux,* 22286 (5 February 1901).

103. C. Ernest Fayle, *Seaborne Trade,* vol. 1 (London, 1920), p. 23; "Report of the Royal Commission on the Supply of Food and Raw Material in Time of War," *Parliamentary Papers* (1905, vol. 39): 34.

104. J. Duroché, "Le ravitaillement des croiseurs corsaires sur les théâtres extérieurs d'opérations," *Revue maritime,* n.s., 166 (1933): 481.

105. Adolphe Messimy, "Rapport, Commission du Budget, 1904," Annexe 1201, Chambre, *Documents* 64 (4 July 1903), Annexe II.

106. France, Ministère de la Marine, *Annuaire de la Marine pour 1904* (Paris, 1904), pp. 773–818. See also Messimy, op. cit.

APPENDIX

1. Some of the planned conversions for the transition and transport fleets were never undertaken. In addition, unlike later programs, the list of ships to be built did not include replacements for existing ships that would reach the end of their useful lives before the end of the program period. (The program provided money for such replacements, however.) "Rapport de son exc. M. le Ministre de la Marine à l'Empereur sur la transformation de la flotte," Conseil d'Etat, Document No. 657 (8 January 1857), Bibliothèque de la Marine call number 29.L.4; Franklin Whittelsey Wallin, "The French Navy during the Second Empire: A Study of the Effects of Technological Development on French Governmental Policy," Doctoral dissertation, University of California at Berkeley, 1953, pp. 75–78. An imperial decree of 23 November 1857 implemented the program.

2. "Budget de la Marine et des Colonies pour l'exercice 1872: Note préliminaire," *Revue maritime* 32 (1872): 176. The headings are from the minutes of the Council of Admiralty for 29 August 1871 in the Archives de la Marine, BB8-901. The numbers of ships to be built during the first ten years of the program were calculated from Annexe 7 of the budget submitted by the navy for 1874.

3. Minutes of the Council of Admiralty (16 August 1879), Supplementary register of secret deliberations (1843–1879), Archives de la Marine (Archives nationales), BB8-853.

4. Minutes of the Council of Admiralty (6 May 1881), Archives de la Marine, BB8-910. The primary purpose of the Program of 1881 was to reclassify ships already afloat or under construction, and it did not specify how many additional ships were to be built.

5. "Note pour l'Etat-major général" by the Director of Matériel (2 July 1891), Archives de la Marine, BB8-2424/2.

6. Minutes of the Superior Council (5, 7, 10, and 11 December 1894), Archives de la Marine, BB8-2424/2.

7. "Programme adopté pour la constitution de la Flotte" (ca. January 1897), and Minutes of the Superior Council (17, 18, and 21 December 1896), Archives de la Marine, BB8-2424/4.

8. Minutes of the Superior Council (17 January 1898) and supporting papers, Archives de la Marine, BB8-2424/5 and 4.

9. [Jean-Louis de Lanessan], *Le programme maritime de 1900–1906* (Paris, 1902), especially pp. 188–89 and 259. The program became law on 9 December 1900.

Bibliography

THIS BIBLIOGRAPHY is in three sections. The first is a list of materials from the libraries of the Service historique de la Marine and the Ecole d'Application du Génie maritime, which, when this study was written, were confidential. The second lists most of the published sources cited in the footnotes. Omitted are works on less important technical subjects that are cited only once, most books on general history, most biographies, works on subjects connected with all foreign navies except the Italian (where an attempt was made to indicate the main works in a field previously entirely untouched by historians), and items on certain technical matters such as naval tactics, coast defense, gunnery, naval construction, descriptions of individual ports, et cetera. For these, see the notes for the relevant sections of the text.

The third section of this bibliography, added by the editor, is a supplement listing the few major works on the French Navy of this period which have appeared since this research was completed, along with the principal published works of the author.

Throughout this work, the French Navy's School of Naval War is referred to as the Ecole supérieure de la Marine without making any attempt to follow its numerous and bewildering changes of name. The courses given at this school and the theses produced there and at the Historical Section were the most important groups of materials used in this research. Hastily thrown together in the earlier years from the documents of the General Staff, the courses must have been positively deadly to the students of the school, but they are extremely valuable to the historian. For this research, the complete files of the major courses from 1897 to 1904 were consulted, although none of those for the first year, 1896, seem to have been kept.

Also of great importance was the Guihéneuc Collection, sixty-three scrapbooks of pamphlets and newspaper clippings collected by Olivier Guihéneuc from 1882 to 1918 and purchased by the Harvard University Library, arranged according to years without the exact date of individual articles being given.

Naval titles used in this work are normally forms of address, not ranks. Ensigns and lieutenants were addressed as Lieutenant; capitaines de corvette, capitaines de frégate, and capitaines de vaisseau as Commandant; and rear admirals and vice admirals as Admiral.

THE LIBRARY OF THE SERVICE HISTORIQUE DE LA MARINE

Serial Publications

Bulletin des travaux des officiers (1895–1913). An extremely valuable monthly periodical for articles that could not be inserted in the *Revue maritime* and for other materials of a confidential nature which it was desired to publish for officers of the fleet.

Manoeuvres navales françaises (1894–1901); and in the same series, *Manoeuvres navales anglaises* (1898–1901).

Mémorial de l'Artillerie de la Marine (2nd series, 1873–1904).

Mémorial du Génie maritime (1872–1904). The technical publications of the two auxiliary corps.

Répertoire des affaires soumises au Conseil d'Amirauté du 1 janvier 1871 au 4 novembre 1890 (1891). A mere index.

Résumé analytique des affaires examinées par le Conseil des Travaux de la Marine (1866–1904). Very valuable for all periods but rather uneven. At times it gives a full account of the major points in each discussion; at others it only indicates the nature of the proposal and the general reasons for acceptance or rejection. Cited in the notes as *Conseil des Travaux,* with index numbers and dates for individual discussions.

Signal Books and Instructions

Carnet de combat. 1900.

Commission de révision de la tactique navale. *Instructions générales et code d'évolutions.* Paris, 1875–79, 1884, and 1892. These are the official tactics of which the official explanation was given in Admiral Jean-Pierre-Edmond Jurien de la Gravière, "Considérations générales sur la tactique navale à propos de la révision du livre des signaux," manuscript, Service historique de la Marine, Paris, 1870. The tactics of 1892, contained in the *Instructions générales et code d'évolutions* of that year, evolved into the *Manoeuvres de combat sans signaux et sans compas d'une ligne de bataille de groupes divisionnaires autonomes à intervalles de déploiement,* 1905.

"Emploi tactique des divisions légères, 1893." *Bulletin des travaux des officiers* 4 (1898).

Manuel de canonnier breveté. Many editions, 1883–1915.

Organisation de la défense des points d'appui de la flotte. 1897.

Rapport annuel technique au sujet de la situation de l'Artillerie. 1895, 1896.

Courses at the Ecole supérieure de la Marine

"Marine française: Tactique et stratégie" (the main course) was given by Commandants Pascal-Auguste-Alfred Houette (1897, 2 vols.), Lucien-Joseph Berryer (1898), Louis-Joseph-Albert Davin (1900), Albert Rouyer (1901 and 1903–5), and Etienne-Jean-Isidore Aubry (1902, 2 vols.). Berryer provided long summaries for the officers of the Ecole supérieure of all the French naval maneuvers before 1894, the year in which accounts began to be issued to the fleet under the title *Manoeuvres navales françaises.*

"Marines étrangères" (the most interesting secondary course) was given by Lieutenant Jean-Baptiste-Charles-Robert-Mathieu Degouy (1897, 2 vols.), Lieutenant Charles-Timothée-Louis Charlier (1898 and 1900), and Commandant Jules-Martial-Stanislas Lephay (1901–3).

Adigard, Commandant Paul. "Etude de nos côtes au point de vue maritime." 1898.

Bernard de Courville, Maurice-Henri-Marie. "Constructions navales." 2 vols. 1898. Also a separate course bound with these, "Les torpilleurs."

Bonnier, Colonel François-Xavier-Louis-Henry-Marie-Gaëtan. "Artillerie." 1898.

Cerf, Colonel Louis-Georges-Simon. "Artillerie." 2 vols. 1897.

Fournier, P. "Administration." 1898.

Guillaume. "Chaudières." 2 vols. 1898.

Hamelin. "Administration économique et maritime de la France." 1897.

Merveilleux du Vignaux, Commandant Marie-Benjamin-Gaston-Jean. "Artillerie pratique." 1902.

Nicol, Commandant Ernest-Eugène. "Artillerie pratique." 1898.

Tissier, Joseph-Louis-Léon. "Sous-marins, torpilles." 1898.

Wilhelm, Joseph-Eugène-Albert. "Droit maritime international." 1898.

The Ecole d'Application du Génie maritime

Clauzel, Gaston. "Cours d'artillerie navale, canon, protection, engins sous-marins." 1898. The only course of this school that contained anything of interest.

Publications of the Torpedo Service

Audic, Joseph-Marie-Suzanne. *Torpilles: Cours de torpilles à l'usage des officiers, professé à Boyardville.* 3 vols. Paris, 1878 (vols. 1–2) and 1880 (vol. 3).

"Conférences sur les torpilles." Boyardville, 1885–86.

Darrieus, Pierre-Joseph-Gabriel-Georges. *Etude sur les bateaux sous-marins.* Paris, 1895. Produced on board the torpedo-school ship *Algesiras.*

"Etudes sur le tir des torpilles Whitehead." Reports produced on board the torpedo-school ship *Japon,* 1884–85.

"Instructions sur le montage, le chargement, et le mouillage des torpilles automatiques mécaniques." 1893–95. Produced on board the torpedo-school ship *Algesiras.*

"Instructions sur l'emploi, la manoeuvre et la tactique des torpilles divergentes." 1875.

Poggiale. "Conférences sur la description et le fonctionnement de la torpille Whitehead." Toulon, 1887.

"Rapports de la commission française envoyée à Fiume." Boyardville, 1884–86.

Richard, Lieutenant. "Torpilles." 5 vols. Boyardville, 187–.

Roussell. "Torpilles automobiles." Boyardville, 1885.

Sénès, Lieutenant Marie-Joseph-Gervais. "Cours de torpilles." 2 vols. Paris, 1900.

Theses of the Ecole supérieure and the Historical Section

Bataille, Lieutenant Marie-Joseph-Gaston. "L'expédition de Tunisie." 1936.

Ceillier, Commandant Marie-Raymond. "Les idées stratégiques en France de 1870 à 1914: La Jeune Ecole." 1928. A brilliant analysis of the strategic ideas of the Jeune Ecole. It was the only effort up to its time to try to do justice to the Jeune Ecole or to show how many ideas originating with that movement later became part of French strategic theory. Ceillier did not attempt to analyze the conditions in the officer corps that were behind the movement or to point out its place in the general naval thought of the time.

Chrétin, Lieutenant Louis-Gabriel. "L'expédition de Madagascar." 1926.

Fave, Lieutenant Robert-Charles-Joseph. "Les projets de débarquement sur les côtes allemandes en 1870." 1931.

Fénard, Lieutenant Raymond-Albert. "L'évolution de l'enseignement à l'Ecole supérieure de la Marine de 1895 à 1921." 1922.

Juge, Commandant René-Clément. "La campagne de l'amiral Courbet en Chine." 1927.

Laurin, Lieutenant Joseph-Elisée-Auguste. "Le transport du XIXe corps et des troupes coloniales en 1914." 1931.

Le Camus, Commandant Charles-Auguste-Joseph. "Historique sommaire des défenses sous-marines." 1926.

Le Franc, Lieutenant Paul-Marie-Ernest-Adrien. "L'organisation des croisières sudistes: La croisière de l'*Alabama*." 1923.

Lepotier, Lieutenant Adolphe-Auguste-Marie. "La protection du commerce pendant la Guerre de Sécession par les flottes des Etats du Nord." 1933.

Mazen, Lieutenant Antoine-Nathalis-Charles-Georges. "L'expédition de Tunisie." 1926.

Moreau, Lieutenant Jacques-Hector-Charles-François. "Lissa (1866)." 1928.

Quiquandon, Lieutenant Charles-Jean-René. "Les opérations de Courbet dans la rivière Min." 1922.

Ruyssen, Lieutenant Henri-Joseph-Auguste. "L'escadre de l'amiral de Gueydon, 1870–1871." 1936.

Other Official Articles and Studies

"L'artillerie et les murailles cuirassées." *Mémorial de l'Artillerie de la Marine* 2 (1874): 63.

Banal, Lieutenant Marie-Maxime-Augustin. "De l'entrainement au tir." *Bulletin des travaux des officiers* 9 (1903): 58.

Barba, J. "Creusot et les usines de la Loire." *Mémorial du Génie maritime* (1876, nos. 5 and 6).

Barradini, Commandant. "Notice historique sur l'emploi des mortiers et des canons courts à bord des bâtiments." *Mémorial de l'Artillerie de la Marine* 32 (1904): 197.

Baudry-Lacantinerie, Commandant Marie-Joseph. "Etude sur les torpilleurs submersibles." *Bulletin des travaux des officiers* 1 (1895): 115.

Bertin, Louis-Emile. "Mission en Angleterre." *Mémorial du Génie maritime* (1885, no. 4).

Bienaimé, Admiral Amédée-Pierre-Léonard. "Contribution à l'étude de la pratique du tir à la mer." *Bulletin des travaux des officiers* 4 (1898): 629.

Bienaymé, Arthur-François-Alphonse (Génie maritime). "Rapport sur une mission effectuée en Italie." *Mémorial du Génie maritime* (1880, no. 1).

Borgnis-Desbordes, General Gustave. "Des opérations maritimes contre les côtes et des débarquements." *Mémorial de l'Artillerie de la Marine* 22 (1894): 1.

———. "Répartition et protection de l'artillerie à bord des cuirassés." *Mémorial de l'Artillerie de la Marine* 20 (1892): 681.

Boyer, Lieutenant. "Idées qui ont cours en Italie sur l'emploi des torpilleurs." *Bulletin des travaux des officiers* 2 (1896): 285.

Bussy, Louis de. "Projet de cuirassé de 1ᵉʳ rang." *Mémorial du Génie maritime* (1873, no. 11): 395. This is the designer's description of the *Redoutable* and the use of steel in her construction.

———. "Projet de garde-côtes cuirassé de 2ᵉ classe." *Mémorial du Génie maritime* (1873, no. 12): 469.

Courville, de. "Mission en Angleterre." *Mémorial du Génie maritime* (1888, no. 5): 1.

Daveluy, Marie-Isidore-René. "Utilisation militaire des sous-marins." *Bulletin des travaux des officiers* 6 (1900): 74.

Delevaque, Charles. "Métallurgie du fer dans le bassin du Rhône." *Mémorial du Génie maritime* (1878, no. 5).

———. "Métallurgie du fer dans l'Allier et dans la Saône et Loire." *Mémorial du Génie maritime* (1881, no. 1).

De Poyen-Bellisle, Isidore-Henry. "Du rôle de l'artillerie navale depuis la création de la marine cuirassée." *Mémorial de l'Artillerie de la Marine* 8 (1879): 457.

Desaulses de Freycinet, Lieutenant Henri-Paul-Louis-Camille. "La marine de commerce et la guerre navale." *Bulletin des travaux des officiers* 5 (1899): 51.

Devoir, Lieutenant Alfred-François. "Etude comparative des flottes de combat." *Bulletin des travaux des officiers* 4 (1898): 413.

Didelot, Lieutenant Charles-François-Edouard [Carl], baron. "Etude sur l'utilisation de nos côtes pour la guerre sur mer." *Bulletin des travaux des officiers* 7 (1901): 40.

Dislère, Paul. "Historiques des différents types de la flotte, 1858–1875." Manuscript, 1875. In the library of the Service historique de la Marine, call number 27.L.13. This work, which gives the main reasons for the various changes in French naval ship designs between 1858 and 1875 from a military point of view, is probably the most interesting of the many writings of the secretary of the Conseil des Travaux, although all, including those below, are of great value.

Dislère, Paul. "Rapport sur une mission dans les arsenaux étrangers de la Méditerranée, de la Mer Noire et de l'Adriatique." *Mémorial du Génie maritime* (1875, no. 6): 379.

———. "Les Marines de la Mer du Nord et de la Baltique." *Mémorial du Génie maritime* (1877, no. 2): 73.

———. "Mission en Angleterre." *Mémorial du Génie maritime* (1879, no. 5): 97.

———. "L'histoire du corps du Génie maritime." Written for the Ecole d'Application du Génie maritime in 1922.

Farret, Commandant Etienne-Esprit. "Etude sur la stratégie maritime." *Bulletin des travaux des officiers* 6 (1900): 185. An Anglophobe account summarizing the theories of the Program of 1900 printed the month after it was written.

Fay, Lieutenant. "Etude sur l'établissement de la Marine à Bizerte." *Bulletin des travaux des officiers* 19 (1913): 789.

Francq, Lieutenant Louis-Marie-Saint-Ange de. "Préparation du combat, ou Manoeuvre du combat." *Bulletin des travaux des officiers* 3 (1897): 203.

Gobert. "Etude relative au tir sur mer." *Mémorial de l'Artillerie de la Marine* 15 (1887): 313.

Hennique, Commandant Privat-Agathon-Benjamin-Arthur. "Conférence sur le port de Bizerte." Ecole supérieure de la Marine, 1898.

Homey. "Essai de tactique des croiseurs." *Bulletin des travaux des officiers* 4 (1897): 11.

Kéraoul, Commandant Roger-Pierre-Marie Vittu de. "Considérations sur l'emploi des torpilleurs dans les Marines française et étrangères." *Bulletin des travaux des officiers* 4 (1898): 63.

La Rocque, Colonel Jean-Pierre-Raymond de. "Etude historique de la résistance des canons rayés." *Mémorial de l'Artillerie de la Marine* 12 (1884): 161–286, 361–435, and 13 (1885): 1–130.

Laubeuf, Alfred-Maxime. "Mission à Spithead." *Mémorial du Génie maritime* (1898, no. 5): 723.

———, and Petithomme, Emmanuel-Marie-Victor. "Mission en Angleterre." *Mémorial du Génie maritime* (1890, nos. 5 and 6).

Marchal, Théodore-Jean-Maurice. "Etude comparative des cuirassées les plus récents et des croiseurs anglais." *Mémorial du Génie maritime* (1875, no. 9): 201.

Mascart, Lieutenant Léon-François. "Mémoire sur l'attaque des cables sous-marins." *Bulletin des travaux des officiers* 9 (1903): 59.

Maurice, Just-Lucien. "Rapport de fin de campagne." Annually 1898, 1899, and 1900. He was engineer in chief of the squadron.

Mercier de Lostende, Lieutenant Maurice-Henri. "Les tirs de la Marine anglaise." *Bulletin des travaux des officiers* 12 (1906): 217.

Mottez, Lieutenant Louis-Adolphe. "Réflexions sur le réglage du tir de l'artillerie à bord." *Bulletin des travaux des officiers* 3 (1897): 472.

Nogues, Lieutenant Jean. "Etude sur la question du tir dans la Marine anglaise." *Bulletin des travaux des officiers* 10 (1904): 24.

Pampelonne, Marie-Joseph-Edmond de Geis de Guyon de. *Etude sur la tactique des torpilleurs.* (Toulon, Ecole des Torpilleurs, 1888).

Penfentenyo de Kervéréguin, Admiral Auguste-Eléonore-Marie de. "Réflexions suggérées par la lecture du mémoire intitulé 'Contribution à l'étude du tir à la mer.'" *Bulletin des travaux des officiers* 4 (1898): 665. Of the greatest importance as a defense of and explanation of the new system of fire control.

"Résumé des principales expériences de tir contre les cuirassés exécutées à l'étranger." *Mémorial de l'Artillerie de la Marine* 7 (1879): 285.

Ronarc'h, Lieutenant Pierre-Alexis-Marie-Antoine. "Etude sur l'attaque des cables sous-marins." *Bulletin des travaux des officiers* 5 (1899): 203.

Verlynde, Lieutenant Pierre-Jean. "La question des cables télégraphiques au point de vue militaire." *Bulletin des travaux des officiers* 2 (1896): 228. The most thorough and important study of this question, it was printed without the usual delay.

Villaret, Nathaniel-Lucien-Louis-Jean-Jacques. "Notions historiques sur le Service des Constructions navales dans les ports militaires." *Mémorial du Génie maritime* (1902, no. 3).

Voitoux, Lieutenant Victor-Gabriel. "Instruction spéciale de pointage . . ." *Bulletin des travaux des officiers* 6 (1900): 116.

X [pseud.]. "Stratégie navale." *Bulletin des travaux des officiers* 4 (1898): 249. A violently Anglophobe study by a member of the Jeune Ecole that was printed without the usual delay.

PUBLISHED MATERIALS

Government Publications

Annales de l'Assemblée nationale: Compte rendu in extenso des séances, with annexes, 1871–76. Superseded by *Annales du Sénat et de la Chambre des Députés,* with annexes, 1876–80, and, beginning in 1881, by *Chambre des Députés, Annales, Débats parlementaires* and *Documents parlementaires,* with a similar series for the Senate. The various titles in this series are referred to throughout the notes as Chambre (or Sénat), *Débats* (or *Documents*). The reports of the Budget Commission contained in the *Documents* (and, during part of the 1870s, in *Revue maritime*) are noted as "Rapport, Commission du Budget" followed by the budget year and preceded by the name of the *rapporteur*. French parliamentary debates and documents were also published in the *Journal officiel* with different pagination and volume identifications.

Commission extra-parlementaire de la Marine. *Commission plénière* (3 vols., of which vol. 3 is the Rapport général), *Sous-commissions* (2 vols.), *Délégations* (6 vols.), and *Table général* (1 vol.). Paris, 1896–98.

Ministère des Affaires étrangères. *Affaire de Tunisie.* Paris, 1881.

———. *Affaires du Tonkin.* Parts 1 and 2. Paris, 1883.

———. *Affaires de Chine et du Tonkin, 1884–1885.* Paris, 1885.

———. *L'alliance franco-russe.* Paris, 1918.

———. *Documents diplomatiques français, 1871–1914.* Paris, 1929–.

Great Britain. House of Commons. *Parliamentary Papers. Accounts and Papers.* Referred to in the notes as *Parliamentary Papers.* The key reports in this series are the following:

"Report of the Committee on the Designs upon Which Ships of War Have Recently Been Constructed" (1872, vol. 14).

"Report of the Admiralty Committee on the System of Training Naval Cadets on Board H.M.S. *Britannia*" (1875, vol. 15).

"Official Documents Relating to the Design of H.M.S. *Inflexible*" (1877, vol. 52).

"Report of the Committee on the *Inflexible*" (1878, vol. 49).

"Report of the Committee on the Education of Naval Executive Officers" (1886, vol. 13).

"Extracts from Reports of the Royal Commission on the Defence of British Possessions and Commerce Abroad" (1887, vol. 56, Appendix, pp. 295–338). This, the report of the Carnarvon Commission of 1882, was published in the Proceedings of the Colonial Conference of 1887.

"Report of a Committee . . . to Consider . . . the Fortification and Armament of Military and Home Mercantile Ports" (1888, vol. 25).

"Action Taken by the Board of Admiralty with Regard to the Preparation of Designs for First Class Battle-Ships" (1889, vol. 50).

"Extracts from the Report of the Committee on the Naval Maneuvers, 1888" (1889, vol. 50).

"Report of the Royal Commission on the Supply of Food and Raw Material in Time of War" (1905, vols. 39 and 40).

British Documents on the Origin of the War, 1898–1914. Edited by G. P. Gooch and Harold Temperley. 11 vols. London, 1926–.

Die grosse Politik der europäischen Kabinette, 1871–1914. Edited by Johannes Lepsius, Albrecht Mendelssohn-Bartholdy, and Friedrich Thimme. 40 vols. Berlin, 1922–26.

Bibliographies

Etat-major de l'Armée, Service historique. *L'Afrique française du Nord: Bibliographie militaire des ouvrages français ou traduits en français et des articles des principales revues françaises relatifs à l'Algérie, à la Tunisie et au Maroc de 1830 à 1926.* 4 vols. Paris, 1930–35. Useful in connection with North African problems such as Bizerte, Tunis, etc. Contains a multitude of periodical references.

Favitski de Probobysz, Commandant de. *Répertoire bibliographique de la littérature militaire et coloniale française depuis cent ans.* Paris, 1935. Does not list periodical articles, but omits few other important naval works. Contains French materials only.

New York Public Library. *A Selected List of Works in the Library Relating to Naval History, Naval Administration, etc.* New York, 1904. Useful for British titles in the absence of a systematic bibliography of British naval history.

Revue maritime et coloniale. Contains very complete monthly reviews of contemporary literature.

Tramond, Joannès. *Bibliographie d'histoire coloniale, 1900–1930.* Paris, 1932. Largely superseded by the first two, above.

Annuals and Periodicals

Académie de Marine: Communications et mémoires. Paris, 1922–.
Bulletin de l'Association technique maritime. Paris, 1890–.
Engineering. London, 1870–1904.
General Information Series: Information from Abroad. U.S. Office of Naval Intelligence, Washington, 1885–1898.
Journal de la Marine: Le yacht. Paris, 1879–. Normally referred to as *Le yacht.*
Journal of the Royal United Service Institution. London, 1870–.
La Marine française. Paris, 1888–1914. The organ of the Jeune Ecole. Interesting, but not particularly important because of the propagandist nature of its articles.
The Naval Annual. Edited by Sir Thomas Brassey. Portsmouth, 1886–. This and *Information from Abroad* are the great mines of accurate information on all naval subjects for these years. Far superior to the continental naval manuals because of the range of topics covered and the accuracy of its figures.
Revue maritime et coloniale. 1861–. After the separation of the colonies from the Ministry of Marine it became *Revue maritime.* Always valuable, although its quality fluctuated.
Rivista marittima. 1870–. Under the editorship of the brilliant Eugene Pescetto, it changed overnight from a dull collection of official documents to by far the best official naval magazine in Europe.
Transactions of the Institution of Naval Architects. 1870–.
The United Service Magazine. London, 1870–. Of rather mediocre quality during the 1870s and 1880s, but a change in management around 1890 made it a source of the first importance for British naval policy during the next decade.

Retrospective General Accounts

Avice, Commandant J. *La défense des frontières maritimes.* Paris, 1922. An excellent work, published by the Historical Section.

Bargone, Charles [Claude Farrère]. *Histoire de la Marine française.* Paris, 1934. Good drawings and a remarkably unreliable text by the leading member of the interwar school of naval novelists.

Baxter, James Phinney 3rd. *The Introduction of the Ironclad Warship.* Cambridge, Mass., 1933.

Castex, Raoul-Victor-Patrice. *Synthèse de la guerre sous-marine de Pontchartrain à Tirpitz.* Paris, 1920.

———. *Questions d'état-major: Principes, organisation, fonctionnement.* 2 vols. Paris, 1923–24.

———. "La modernisation de l'éperon." *Revue maritime,* January 1928.

———. "L'expansion coloniale et la stratégie navale." *Académie de Marine: Communications et mémoires* 9 (1930): 203.

Castex, Raoul-Victor-Patrice. *Théories stratégiques.* 5 vols. Paris, 1929–30. Curiously, this great naval thinker is very unfair to the Jeune Ecole.

Charliat, P. *Trois siècles d'économie maritime française.* Paris, 1931. An excellent history of the French merchant navy.

Di Luigi, Giuseppe. *Il Mediterraneo nella politica europea.* Naples, 1925.

Exposition coloniale internationale de Paris de 1931. *L'artillerie aux colonies.* Paris, 1931.

———. *Les grands soldats coloniaux.* Paris, 1931. Very well done commemorative volumes containing a great deal of information on the whole problem of colonial defense.

Fayle, C. Ernest. *Seaborne Trade.* 3 vols. History of the Great War Based on Official Documents. London, 1920–24.

———. *The War and the Shipping Industry.* Economic and Social History of the World War, edited by James T. Shotwell. London, 1927.

Fénard. "Le bâtiment de ligne a-t-il vécu?" *Académie de Marine: Communications et mémoires* 6 (1927), supplement. One of the best French accounts of the Jeune Ecole.

Frothingham, Thomas G. *The Naval History of the World War.* 3 vols. Cambridge, Mass., 1924–26.

Haffner, Léon. *Cent ans de marine de guerre.* Paris, 1931. A popular account by a marine painter. Deserves mention for its excellent sketches.

Hill, Sir Norman. *State Insurance Against War Risks at Sea.* Part 2 of War and Insurance, in Economic and Social History of the World War, edited by James T. Shotwell. London, 1927.

Hovgaard, William. *Modern History of Warships.* New York, 1920.

Hurd, Archibald. *The Merchant Navy.* History of the Great War Based on Official Documents. London, 1921.

———, and Castle, Henry. *German Sea Power: Its Rise, Progress, and Economic Basis.* London, 1913.

Jouan, René. *Histoire de la Marine française de la Révolution à nos jours.* 2 vols. Paris, 1932. A brief popular account, though very good as such.

Kehr, Eckart. *Schlachtflottenbau und Parteipolitik, 1894–1901.* Berlin, 1930. Very good, though the present writer does not accept his interpretation of the general reasons for the rise of the German naval agitation.

Langer, William L. *European Alliances and Alignments, 1871–1890.* New York, 1931.

———. *The Franco-Russian Alliance.* Cambridge, Mass., 1929.

———. *The Diplomacy of Imperialism.* 2 vols. New York, 1935.

La Roncière, Charles de, et al. *Histoire de la Marine française.* Paris, 1934. Similar to Bargone but slightly better.

L'Illustration. Histoire de la Marine. Paris, 1934. A popularized account with magnificent illustrations.

Mantey, Admiral E. von. *Histoire de la Marine allemande.* Translated from the German. Paris, 1930. A mediocre general account.

Meurer, Admiral Alexander. *Seekriegsgeschichte im Umrissen.* Berlin, 1925.

Monasterev, N., and Terestchenko, S. *Histoire de la Marine russe.* Paris, 1932. A brief but fairly good general account.

Richmond, Admiral Sir Herbert. *Sea Power in the Modern World.* New York, 1934.

Salaun, Admiral Henri. *La Marine française.* Paris, 1934. This account by a former chief of staff of the navy is very good on the World War I period, but for the earlier years it does nothing more than repeat the account given in Tramond and Reussner.

Schönberg, Angela von. *Um den Twopowerstandard: Englische Flottenpolitik, 1880–1895.* Stuttgart, 1933. Very good from the political side, very poor from the technical.

Sethe, Paul. *Die Ausgebliebene Seeschlacht: Die englische Flottenführung, 1911–1915.* Berlin, 1932.

Silva, Pietro. *Il Mediterraneo dall' unità di Roma all' unità d'Italia.* Milan, 1927.

Spindler, Admiral Arno. *Der Handelskrieg mit U-booten.* 3 vols. Der Krieg zur See. Berlin, 1932–.

Thomazi, Auguste-Antoine. *La Marine française dans la Grande Guerre, 1914–1918.* 5 vols. Paris, 1925–33. Probably the least satisfactory of the official histories.

Tramond, Joannès, and Reussner, André. *Eléments d'histoire maritime et coloniale contemporaine (1815–1914)*. Paris, 1924. In its day, practically the only account of the naval-colonial movement in France. References to the French Navy *per se* are necessarily scattered throughout a mass of other material.

Wilson, H. W. *Ironclads in Action: A Sketch of Naval Warfare from 1855 to 1895*. 2 vols. London, 1896.

Woodward, E. L. *Great Britain and the German Navy*. Oxford, 1935. Official and disappointing because of its pro-English bias. Does not go very far behind the picture revealed in the official documents.

Contemporary General Accounts

Balincourt, Marie-Maurice-Clément-Raoul Testu de. *Etude sur les navires d'aujourd'hui*. Paris, 1892.

Barnaby, Sir Nathaniel. *Naval Development of the Century*. London, 1904.

Batsch, Admiral, and Meuss, Captain. *Frankreich: Die Flotte*. Die Heere und Flotten der Gegenwart. Berlin, 1900.

Brassey, Sir Thomas. *The British Navy: Its Strength, Resources, and Administration*. 5 vols. 1882–83.

Didelot, Charles-François-Edouard [Carl]. *La défense des côtes d'Europe*. Paris, 1894. Very thorough, with excellent maps of all the major European bases.

Dislère, Paul. *La marine cuirassée*. Paris, 1873.

———. *Les croiseurs, La guerre de course*. Paris, 1875.

———. *La guerre d'escadre et la guerre des côtes*. Paris, 1876.

Eardley-Wilmot, S. M. *The Development of Navies During the Last Half Century*. London, 1892.

Jane, Fred T. *The Imperial Russian Navy: Its Past, Present, and Future*. 2nd ed. London, 1904.

King, James W. *The War-Ships and Navies of the World*. Boston, 1880.

Kronenfels, J. F. von. *Das schwimmende Flottenmaterial der Seemächte*. Vienna, 1881.

Loir, Maurice. *La Marine française*. Paris, 1893. An able and well illustrated popular description.

Paget, John C. *Naval Powers and Their Policy*. London, 1876.

Reed, Sir Edward. *Modern Ships of War*. New York, 1888.

Report of the Gun Foundry Board. Washington, 1884.

Sydenham-Clarke, George. *Russia's Sea Power, Past and Present*. London, 1898.

Biographies and Memoirs

Ashton, Sir George. *Memories of a Marine*. London, 1919.

Bacon, Admiral Sir Reginald Hugh Spencer. *The Life of Lord Fisher of Kilverstone*. 2 vols. London, 1929. The facts are correct, but the author gives so much credit to Fisher as to give a thoroughly misleading impression of the Fisher revolution.

Barbou, Alfred. *L'amiral Pothuau*. Paris, 1882.

Beresford, Lord Charles. *Memoirs*. 2 vols. London, 1914.

Bradford, Admiral Edward Eden. *Life of Admiral of the Fleet Sir Arthur Knyvet Wilson*. London, 1923.

Brière, Paul. *Un grand français: Le vice-amiral François-Ernest Fournier*. Paris, 1931. The one really good French naval biography for this period, and with one of the period's most interesting men for its subject.

Briggs, Sir John Henry. *Naval Administration, 1827 to 1892*. London, 1897.

Buchard, Henri. *L'amiral Cloué: Sa vie, récits maritimes contemporains*. Paris, 1893.

Buckle, G. E., ed. *The Letters of Queen Victoria*. 2nd series: 3 vols., London, 1926–28. 3rd series: 3 vols., London, 1930–32.

Buell, Augustus C. *The Memoirs of Charles H. Cramp*. Philadelphia, 1906.

Dartige du Fournet. *A travers les mers: Souvenirs d'un marin*. Paris, 1929.

Dominique, L. C. *Un gouverneur général de l'Algérie: L'amiral de Gueydon*. Algiers, 1908.

Durassier, Henri. *Le vice-amiral Bergasse Du Petit-Thouars: Sa vie militaire (1832–1890)*. Paris, 1890.

Faye, J. de la. *Une famille de marins: Les Du Petit-Thouars*. Paris, 1893. Preface by Admiral Fournier.

Fiske, Bradley A. *From Midshipman to Rear Admiral*. New York, 1919.

Grandin, Commandant Léonce. *Histoire d'un marin: Le vice-amiral Jurien de la Gravière*. Paris, 1895. Much better than the average French naval biography.

Guichen de Grandpont, Alfred. *Le vice-amiral cte. de Gueydon*. Brest, 1887.

Hamilton, Lord George. *Parliamentary Reminiscences and Reflections*. 2 vols. London, 1916–22.

Hassell, Ulrich von. *Tirpitz: Sein Leben und Wirken mit Berücksichtigung seiner Beziehungen zu Albrecht von Stosch*. Stuttgart, 1920.

Hopman, Admiral. *Das Logbuch eines deutschen Seeoffiziers*. Berlin, 1924.

Julien, Félix. *Un marin: Le contre-amiral baron Grivel*. Paris, 1883.

Lockroy, Edouard-Etienne-Antoine Simon. *Au hasard de la vie: Notes et souvenirs*. Paris, 1913. The first volume, of his projected memoirs, of great interest.

Manning, Frederic. *The Life of Sir William White*. London, 1923.

Porter, Charles W. *The Career of Théophile Delcassé*. Philadelphia, 1936.

Révillon, Tony. *Camille Pelletan, 1846–1916*. Paris, 1930.

Scott, Admiral Sir Percy. *Fifty Years in the Royal Navy*. London, 1922.

Taylor, Charles C. *The Life of Admiral Mahan*. London, 1920.

Tirpitz, Admiral Alfred von. *My Memoirs*. 2 vols. New York, 1919.

Togari, Captain. *Louis-Emile Bertin: Son rôle dans la création de la Marine japonaise*. Paris, 1935. A small pamphlet.

Tréfeu, Etienne-Louis-Jean. *Nos marins*. Paris, 1888. A collection of short sketches of all the general officers of the French Navy as of 1888. Extremely well done for such a volume, it is indispensable in view of the general poverty of French naval biography. Most of the other French biographies mentioned in this section are of little historical value.

The Steel Industry and the French Arms Trade

Baclé, L. *Les plaques de blindage*. Paris, 1900.

Bauer, Lothar. "Die Rustungsindustrie der Welt." *Wirtschaftskurve* 11 (1932): 149. Contains some material on Creusot.

Berrier-Fontaine, Marc. "On the Use of Mild Steel for Shipbuilding in the Dockyards of the French Navy." *Transactions of the Institution of Naval Architects* 22 (1881): 87.

Bresson, G. *L'industrie métallurgique dans ses rapports actuels avec les constructions navales*. Paris, 1880.

Brocard, Lucien. *La grosse métallurgie française et le mouvement des prix de 1890 à 1913*. Paris, 1923.

"Canet vs. Krupp guns." *Engineering* 53 (1892): 69. By "a French artillerist."

Comité des Forges de France. *La sidérurgie française, 1864–1914*. Paris, n.d.

Dredge, James. *Modern French Artillery*. London, 1892. A collection of articles from *Engineering*.

Jaques, Lieutenant William H. *Modern Armor for National Defense*. New York, 1885.

Laporte, Gaston de. *Les usines de la Marine et la féodalité industrielle. L'ancienne fonderie de canons de Nevers. Les usines de La Chaussade à Guérigny*. Nevers, 1886.

Laur, F. *Les mines et usines au XXᵉ siècle: Les mines et la métallurgie à l'Exposition universelle de 1900*. 5 vols. Paris, 1901.

Lavainville, J. *L'industrie du fer en France*. Paris, 1922.

"Messrs. Schneider and Co.'s Works, Creusot." *Engineering* 59 (1898): 245ff. A series of eighty articles.

Very, Lieutenant Edward W. *The Development of Armor for Naval Use*. Annapolis, Md., 1883.

The Italian Navy

Algranati, E. "Considerazioni sulle nostre grandi navi." *Rivista marittima* (1882, no. 3): 75. By one of Brin's critics.

Al Mare! Al Mare! La difesa navale delle coste. Genoa, 1872.

Amezaga, Carlo de. *Il pensiero navale italiano.* Genoa, 1898. A collection of propaganda articles of great interest for the history of the early years.

Bettolo, Captain. "Le navi da guerra." *Rivista marittima* (1884, no. 4): 351. Another of Brin's critics.

Bonamico, D. *I primi elementi della guerra marittima.* Turin, 1880. A tactical study with some insights into Italian theory.

———. *Il problema marittimo dell'Italia.* Turin, 1880.

Brin, Benedetto. ". . . alla stabilità del *Duilio* e del *Dandolo,*" *Rivista marittima* (1876, no. 2): 4.

———. *La nostra marina militare.* 2nd ed. Rome, 1881.

Cangemi, A. *L'Italia e le lotte avvenire sul mare.* La Spezia, 1899.

Clowes, William Laird. "The Millstone Round the Neck of England." *Nineteenth Century* 37 (1895): 369.

Commissione permanente per la Difesa generale dello Stato. *Relazione a corredo del Piano generale di Difesa dell'Italia.* Rome, 1871. The basic report for the whole system of the following years.

Cottrau, Paolo. "Maris Imperium Obtinendum." *Rivista marittima* (1882, no. 3): 33. Another of Brin's critics.

Eardley-Wilmot, S. M. "Italy as a Naval Power." *United Service Magazine,* n.s., 7 (1893): 692.

Fincati, Luigi. *Studi sui combattimenti in mare.* Rome, 1882. A tactical study with insights into theory.

———. *Aforismi militari.* Rome, 1882.

Glanville, James L. *Italy's Relations with England, 1896–1905.* Baltimore, 1934.

Hare, W. A. H. *The Armed Strength of Italy.* London, 1875. Translation of an account by the German General Staff.

Kerhelleuc. "Les vicissitudes de la Marine italienne." *Journal de la Marine: Le yacht* 26 (1903): 457. Short, very unfriendly, but interesting.

Manfredi, Cristoforo. *L'Italia dev'essere potenza terrestre o marittima?* Rome, 1899.

———. "Guerra offensiva o difensiva?" *Rivista marittima* (1902, no. 1): 45. Focuses on tactics, with theoretical insights.

Molli, Giorgio. *L'Italia in mare.* Rome, 1888. Another of Brin's critics.

Pescetto, E. "La difesa delle coste per mezzo di batterie galleggianti." *Rivista marittima* (1873, no. 3): 265. The official reply to the coast-defense school and its floating batteries.

Randaccio. "Arsenaux maritimes italiens." *Revue maritime* 142 (1899): 388.

Repington, Charles à Court [Charles Martel]. *Military Italy.* London, 1884. A very valuable discussion of the whole Italian problem.

Rossi, Carlo. *Il racconto di un guardiano di spiaggia: Traduzione libera della Battaglia di Dorking.* Rome, 1872. Scare story.

Russo, Colonel G. "Fifty Years' Progress of Shipbuilding in Italy." *Transactions of the Institution of Naval Architects* 53 (1911): 252. An important short account.

Saint Bon, Simone Pacoret de. *La questione delle navi.* Turin, 1881.

Sechi, G. *Elementi di arte militare marittima.* 2 vols. Leghorn, 1903–6. An Italian version of Mahan's ideas, the first general treatise on naval strategy produced in Italy.

Vecchi, A. V. [Jack La Bolina]. *Al servizio del mare italiano.* Turin, 1928. A very good volume of memoirs.

———. "La letteratura nello sviluppo della marina." *Rivista marittima* (1897, no. 2): 331.

———. "Naval and Maritime Industries in Italy." In Thomas Brassey, *The Naval Annual, 1908.* Portsmouth, 1908, p. 161.

Naval Strategy and Policy

Precursors of the Jeune Ecole Through the Gougeard Ministry

Armstrong, Sir William. "Our National Defences." *Colburn's United Service Magazine* 158 (1882): 125.

Durassier, Henri. *La réforme maritime: Souvenirs du ministère de M. Gougeard.* Paris, 1884. The official apologia for Gougeard's ministry, by his secretary.

Fulton, Robert. *De la machine infernale maritime, ou de la tactique offensive et défensive de la torpille*. Paris, 1812.

Gougeard, Auguste. *Les Troupes de la Marine depuis leur origine jusqu'à nos jours*. Paris, 1875.

———. *La Marine de guerre: Ses institutions militaires depuis son origine jusqu'à nos jours*. Paris, 1877.

———. *Les arsenaux de la Marine*. 2 vols. Paris, 1882.

———. *La Marine de guerre: Son passé et son avenir. Cuirassés et torpilleurs*. Paris, 1884.

Grivel, Baron Jean-Baptiste. *De la Marine militaire considérée dans ses rapports avec le commerce et avec la défense du pays*. Paris, 1837.

Grivel, Baron Louis-Antoine-Richild. *La guerre des côtes: Attaque et défense des frontières maritimes; les canons à grande puissance*. Paris, 1864.

———. *De la guerre maritime avant et depuis les nouvelles inventions . . .* Paris, 1869.

———. "Mission militaire et nouveau programme de la flotte." *Revue maritime* 40 (1874): 864ff.

Paixhans, Henri-Joseph. *Nouvelle force maritime, ou exposé des moyens d'annuler la force des marines actuelles du haut bord, et de donner à des navires très petits assez de puissance pour détruire les plus grands vaisseaux de guerre*. Paris, 1821.

Touchard, Admiral Philippe-Victor. *La question du décuirassement*. Paris, 1873.

———. *Encore la question du décuirassement*. Paris, 1876.

———. *La défense des frontières maritimes*. Paris, 1877.

Un marin [pseud.]. *Les colonies nécessaires: Tunisie, Tonkin, Madagascar*. Paris, 1885. Possibly written by Ferry's minister of marine, Admiral Alexandre-Louis-François Peyron, or his successor, Admiral Charles-Eugène Galiber.

The Jeune Ecole and Its Critics

Aube, Théophile. *De la guerre maritime*. Paris, 1873.

———. "L'avenir de la Marine française." *Revue des deux mondes* (1 July 1874): 175.

———. *Entre deux campagnes: Notes d'un marin*. Paris, 1881.

———. *A terre et à bord: Notes d'un marin (deuxième série)*. Paris, 1884. By far the most important of Aube's works, it reprinted the following: "Un nouveau droit maritime international" (1873), "La guerre maritime et les ports militaires de la France" (1882), "La pénétration dans l'Afrique centrale" (1883), and "Italie et Levant: Souvenirs d'un marin" (1883).

———. "Défense nationale, défense des colonies." In *Atlas colonial,* edited by Henri Mager. Paris, 1885. The most quoted of Aube's writings.

Bourgois, Vice Admiral Siméon. *Les torpilleurs: La guerre navale et la défense des côtes.* Paris, 1888. An extremely able reply to the Jeune Ecole, this work originally appeared in *Nouvelle revue* between April 1886 and February 1888.

Charmes, Gabriel. *La Tunisie et la Tripolitaine*. 2nd ed. Paris, 1884.

———. *Politique extérieure et coloniale*. Paris, 1885.

———. *Les torpilleurs autonomes et l'avenir de la Marine*. Paris, 1885.

———. *La réforme de la Marine*. Paris, 1886.

Chassériaud, André-Henri [Ancien officier de la Marine]. "L'avancement dans la Marine." *Nouvelle revue* 16 (1 June 1882): 481.

———. "Torpilleurs et torpilles." *Nouvelle revue* 32 (1885): 42.

———. "La guerre navale par escadres cuirassées." *Nouvelle revue* 33 (1885): 710.

———. "Le torpilleur et le droit des gens." *Nouvelle revue* 40 (1886).

Deschanel, Paul. *La politique française en Océanie à propos du canal de Panama*. Paris, 1884. Introduction by Ferdinand de Lesseps.

Du Pin de Saint-André, Admiral Ernest. "La question des torpilleurs." *Revue des deux mondes* (15 June 1886): 880 and (15 July 1886): 343. A devastating critique of the Jeune Ecole, though not as broad as that of Admiral Bourgois.

Fontin, Paul [Commandant Z]. "Le péril maritime." *Nouvelle revue* 52 (1888): 821.

———. *Les sous-marins et l'Angleterre*. Paris, 1902.

Fontin, Paul [Commandant Z], and Vignot, Mathieu-Jean-Henry [H. Montéchant]. *Les guerres navales de demain.* Paris, 1891.

———. *Essai de stratégie navale.* Paris, 1893.

———. *Les lois du nombre et de la vitesse dans l'art de la guerre: Le travail des armées et des flottes.* Paris, 1894.

———. *Réformes navales.* Paris, 1899. It was supposed to be their crowning work, but their ideas were all completely out of date when it appeared.

Guierre, Alphonse-Alexis. *L'avenir de la torpille et la guerre future.* Paris, 1898.

Pène-Siefert, Jocelyn. *La Marine en danger (1870–1888).* Paris, 1888.

———. *Flottes rivales: Programme de demain.* Paris, 1890.

Reveillère, Admiral Paul-Emile-Marie [Paul Branda]. *La conquête de l'Océan.* Paris, 1894.

The Moderates, Fashoda, and the Program of 1900

Demigny, A. *La faillite de la Marine.* Paris, 1899.

[Dez, R.]. *Etude sur la Marine de guerre: La stratégie navale . . . la constitution logique de la force navale française.* Paris, 1898.

Duboc, Emile-Charles. *Le point faible de l'Angleterre.* Paris, 189–.

———. "Après Fashoda: La politique navale de la France." *Questions diplomatiques et coloniales* 9 (1900): 338.

Duquet, A. "La faillite du cuirassé." *Revue maritime* 161 (1904): 153.

[Ferrand, Charles]. *Notre Marine de guerre en 1899: Les vices de son organisation; un programme de réformes.* Paris, 1899. Reprinted under its author's name in 1908.

Fleury-Ravarin, Henry. *Notre défense maritime et coloniale.* Paris, 1900.

———. "La réorganisation de notre Marine militaire." *Revue politique et parlementaire* 23 (February 1900): 253. The theory of the Program of 1900, by the reporter of the Budget Committee.

Fournier, Admiral François-Ernest. *La flotte nécessaire: Ses avantages stratégiques, tactiques et économiques.* Paris, 1896.

———. *La flotte de combat.* Paris, 1899.

La Rocque, General de. "Esquisse d'un programme naval en 1900." *Revue des deux mondes* (15 February 1900): 758–91.

Lanessan, Jean-Louis de. *La Marine française au printemps de 1890.* Paris, 1890.

Laubeuf, Maxime [d'Armor]. *Les sous-marins et la guerre contre l'Angleterre.* Paris, 1899.

Lockroy, Edouard. *M. de Moltke: Ses mémoires et la guerre future.* Paris, 1892.

———. *La Marine de guerre: Six mois rue Royale.* Paris, 1897. His account of his first ministry.

———. *La défense navale.* Paris, 1900. His second ministry.

———. *Du Weser à la Vistule: Lettres sur la Marine allemande.* Paris, 1901.

———. *Les Marines française et allemande.* Paris, 1904.

Maconge, J.-L. de. *Une Marine rationelle: La flotte utile, les réformes nécessaires de notre organisme naval.* Paris, 1903.

O'Cabe. "Considérations sur une guerre entre la France et l'Angleterre." *Questions diplomatiques et coloniales* 9 (1900): 353.

Weyl, Emile. *Les grandes manoeuvres de l'escadre française.* Paris, 1886.

———. *La Marine militaire (1888–1889).* Paris, 1889.

———. *La flotte de guerre et les arsenaux.* Paris, 1894.

X [pseud.]. *La guerre avec l'Angleterre: Politique navale de la France.* Paris, 1900.

X, Lieutenant [pseud.]. "La guerre de course et la défense navale." *Revue de Paris* (1 May 1900): 62 and (15 May 1900): 351.

Later Theoretical Writings

Carfort, René de. "Introduction à l'étude de la tactique navale." *Revue maritime* 140 (1899): 5.

Castex, Raoul-Victor-Patrice. *Théories stratégiques.* 5 vols. Paris, 1929–30. Contains a classic short sketch in volume 1, chapter 2: "Historique succinct de la stratégie navale théorique."

Cloarec, P. "Les points d'appui." *Journal de la Marine: Le Yacht* 25 (1902): 505.

Colomb, Philip Howard. *Naval Warfare*. London, 1891.

———. "The English Channel and War." *United Service Magazine,* n.s., 5 (1892): 225. A good example of his realistic attitude toward the torpedo boat.

Corbett, Julian S. *Some Principles of Maritime Strategy*. London, 1911.

Darrieus, Gabriel. *War on the Sea: Strategy and Tactics*. Annapolis, Md., 1908. First published in French in 1907.

Daveluy, René. *L'esprit de la guerre navale*. 3 vols. Paris, 1909–10.

Farret, Etienne. "Questions de stratégie navale." *Revue maritime* 131 (1896): 205. One of the first French adaptations of Mahan.

Jane, Fred T. *Heresies of Sea Power*. London, 1906.

Mahan, Alfred Thayer. *The Influence of Sea Power upon History, 1660–1783*. London, 1892.

Sydenham-Clarke, George. "The Limitations of Naval Force." *Nineteenth Century* 46 (1899): 180.

Miscellaneous

Armstrong, G. E. *Torpedoes and Torpedo-vessels*. Royal Navy Handbooks. London, 1896.

Ballard, Commander George Alexander. "The Protection of Commerce in War." *Journal of the Royal United Service Institution* 42 (1898): 365.

Barnes, J. S. *Submarine Warfare: Offensive and Defensive*. New York, 1869.

Bériel; Lachenaud, M.; and Soleil, Pierre-Louis. *Le contrôle du Parlement sur le budget de la Marine*. Paris, 1906. Very valuable.

Bertin, Louis-Emile. *Evolution de la puissance défensive des navires de guerre*. Paris, 1907. Bertin's own account of his ideas on naval matériel; indispensable.

Bowen, Frank C. *History of the Royal Naval Reserve*. London, 1926. An excellent account of the whole British manning problem.

Bridge, Admiral Sir Cyprian. "Fifty Years Architectural Expression of Tactical Ideas." *Transactions of the Institution of Naval Architects* 53 (1911): 34.

Brossard de Corbigny, Jules-Marcel. *Considérations sur l'emploi des bateaux torpilleurs*. Paris, 1880.

Candace, Gratien. *La marine marchande française et son importance dans la vie nationale*. Paris, 1930.

Chadwick, French Ensor. *Report on the Training Systems for the Navy and Mercantile Marine of England, and on the Naval Training System of France*. Washington, 1880.

Charbonnier, Prosper-Jules. *L'Artillerie de la Marine*. Paris, 1904. An excellent account by the future commander of the navy's artillery corps and one of the greatest of French ballistics experts.

Clapham, J. H. *An Economic History of Modern Britain: Free Trade and Steel, 1850–1886*. Cambridge, 1932.

Claudeville, Commandant. "L'importance des mines sous-marines dans les guerres maritimes." *Revue maritime,* March 1926.

Clowes, William Laird. "Some Lessons from Kiel." *Nineteenth Century* 38 (1895): 165.

Colomb, John Charles Ready. *Naval Intelligence and Protection of Commerce in War*. London, 1881.

Delauney and Guittard. *Historique de l'Artillerie de la Marine*. Paris, 1889.

Dewar, Lieutenant A. C. "In the Existing State of Development of Warships, and of Torpedo and Submarine Vessels, in What Manner Can the Strategical Objects Formerly Pursued by Means of Blockading an Enemy in His Own Ports, Be Best Attained?" *Journal of the Royal United Service Institution* 48 (1904): 329.

Dilke, Sir Charles Wentworth. *Problems of Greater Britain*. 2 vols. London, 1890.

Dislère, Paul. "Les budgets maritimes de la France et de l'Angleterre." *Revue maritime* 57 (1878): 90.

Duchemin, General Auguste-Paul-Albert. *Les Troupes coloniales et la défense des colonies*. Paris, 1905.

Dupont, André-Simon-Eugène. *Les arsenaux de la Marine de 1689 à 1910: Leur organisation administrative*. Paris, 1913.

Ecole polytechnique. *Livre du Centenaire.* 3 vols. Paris, 1894. Very valuable for its biographies and its short accounts of the various corps.

Farret, Etienne. "Etudes comparatives de tactique navale." *Revue maritime* 77 (1883): 59.

Ferrand, Charles [Michel, Georges]. *Le budget de la Marine: Les vices de l'organisation de la Marine en France.* Paris, 1891.

Fonlupt-Espéraber, Jacques. "Etude historique et critique sur le recrutement et le salaire des ouvriers des arsenaux." Doctoral dissertation, Paris, 1913.

Furse, Colonel G. A. "French Ports in North Africa." *Journal of the Royal United Service Institution* 43 (1899): 1113.

Garbett, Captain H. *Naval Gunnery: A Description and History of the Fighting Equipment of a Man-of-War.* Royal Navy Handbooks. London, 1897.

Germanicus [pseud.]. "Frankreichs Flottenfrage und die junge Schule." *Preussische Jahrbucher* 96 (1899): 258.

Hichborn, Philip. *Report on European Dockyards.* Washington, 1886.

Hurd, Archibald S. "French Friendship and Naval Economy." *Fortnightly Review,* n.s., 74 (1903): 654. Although extremely critical, this is one of the best British accounts of the French Navy.

Knaplund, Paul. *Gladstone's Foreign Policy.* New York, 1935.

Loir, Maurice. *L'escadre de l'amiral Courbet.* Paris, 1894.

Long, Admiral Samuel. "On the Present Position of Cruisers in Naval Warfare." *Transactions of the Institution of Naval Architects* 34 (1893): 1.

Marchand, A. *Plans de concentration de 1871 à 1914.* Paris, 1926.

Marga, Commandant. *Géographie militaire.* 5 vols. and 2 atlases. 3rd and 4th eds. Paris, 1884–85.

Meeker, Royal. *History of Shipping Subsidies.* New York, 1905.

Millington, E. C. *Seamen in the Making: A Short History of Nautical Training.* London, 1935.

Moch, Gaston [Patiens]. "La défense nationale et la défense des côtes." *Revue de Paris* (1 May 1894): 180.

Moltke, Graf von. *Die deutschen Aufmarschpläne, 1871–1890.* Forschungen und Darstellungen aus dem Reichsarchiv, vol. 7. Berlin, 1929.

Mousset, Albert. *L'Espagne dans la politique mondiale.* Paris, 1923.

Oultre-Seille, Renault d'. "L'évolution du problème des bases navales." *Académie de Marine: Communications et mémoires* 11 (1932): 117.

Patard, L. *Historique de la Commission d'Expériences de Gâvres (1829–1930).* Paris, 1930.

Pinon, René. *L'empire de la Méditerranée.* Paris, 1904.

Pribram, Alfred F. *The Secret Treaties of Austria-Hungary, 1879–1914.* 2 vols. Cambridge, Mass., 1920–21.

Rope, Charles. *Rome et Berlin: Opérations sur les côtes de la Méditerranée et de la Baltique au printemps de 1888.* Paris, 1888.

Roussin, Alfred. "Les arsenaux de la Marine: Réformes dans leur organisation administrative." *Revue des deux mondes* (15 May 1897): 320–39.

Sallström, Emilio. *Estado actual de la cuestion torpederas.* Buenos Aires, 1887.

Scheliha, Viktor Ernst Karl Rudolf von. *A Treatise on Coast Defence.* London, 1868. The experience of the Confederacy, 1861–65.

Schroeder, Seaton. "The Development of Modern Torpedoes." *Information from Abroad* 6 (1887): 1.

———. "The Development of the Modern Torpedo Boat." *Information from Abroad* 5 (1886): 117.

Sleeman, C. T. *Torpedoes and Torpedo Warfare.* Portsmouth, 1889.

Soley, James Russell. *Report on Foreign Systems of Naval Education.* Washington, 1880.

Sydenham-Clarke, George. *Fortification: Its Past Achievements, Recent Development, and Future Progress.* London, 1890.

Yexley, Lionel. *The Inner Life of the Navy.* London, 1908.

Z [pseud.]. "Les puissances maritimes en Méditerranée." *Annales des sciences politiques* 19 (1904): 76.

Supplementary Bibliography

Bueb, Volkmar. "Die 'Junge Schule' der französischen Marine: Strategie und Politik, 1875–1900." Boppard am Rhein: Harald Boldt, 1971.

Coat, Paul. *Les arsenaux de la Marine de 1630 à nos jours.* Brest: Editions de la Cité, 1982.

Crouzet, François. "Recherches sur la production d'armements en France (1815–1913)." *Revue historique* (1974, no. 1): 45–84. Also: "Remarques sur l'industrie des armements en France (du milieu du XIXe siècle à 1914)." *Revue historique* (1974, no. 2): 409–422.

Del Vecchio, Edoardo. "Il fallimento delle trattative maritime fra Italia e Francia." *Storia e Politica* 8 (1969, no. 4): 617–61.

——. *Di Robilant et la crisi nei rapporti marittimi italo-francesi (1862–1888).* Milan, 1970.

Dousset, Francis. *Les navires de guerre français de 1850 à nos jours.* Brest: Editions de la Cité, 1975.

Ganiage, Jean. *L'expansion coloniale de la France sous la Troisième République.* Paris: Payot, 1968.

Jenkins, Ernest H. *A History of the French Navy from Its Beginnings to the Present Day.* Annapolis, Md.: Naval Institute Press, 1973.

Le Masson, Henri. "Douze ministres, ou dix ans d'hésitations de la Marine française." *Revue maritime,* n.s., 233 (June 1966): 710–33.

——. *Histoire du torpilleur en France.* Paris: Académie de Marine, 1966.

——. *Les sous-marins français des origines (1863) à nos jours.* Edited by Francis Dousset. Brest: Editions de la Cité, 1980.

Lepotier, Adolphe-Auguste-Marie. *Cherbourg: Port de la Libération.* Paris: Editions France-Empire, 1972. Also: *Brest: Porte océane,* Paris, 1968; *Toulon: Porte du Lévant,* Paris, 1972; and *Lorient: Porte des Indes,* Paris, 1970.

Luce, Emile. "La Marine française et le Président Félix Faure dans la crise de Fachoda." *Académie de Marine: Communications et mémoires* (1959–60): 5–37.

Masson, Philippe. "La politique naval française de 1850 à 1914." *Revue maritime,* n.s., 251 (February 1968): 183–203.

——. *Histoire de la Marine.* 2 vols. Paris: Lavauzelle, 1981–83.

Polak, Jean. *Bibliographie maritime français depuis les temps les plus reculés jusqu'à 1914.* Grenoble: Editions des 4 Seigneurs, 1976. Also a supplement with index, Grenoble: Jean-Pierre Debbane, 1983.

Randier, Jean. *La Royale.* 3 vols. Brest: Editions de la Cité, 1972–78.

Roberts, Stephen S. "The Introduction of Steam Technology in the French Navy, 1818–1852." Doctoral dissertation, University of Chicago, 1976.

Ropp, Theodore. "Continental Doctrines of Sea Power." In *Makers of Modern Strategy,* edited by Edward Mead Earle, pp. 446–456. Princeton: Princeton University Press, 1941.

——. "German Seapower: A Study in Failure." In *Dreadnought to Polaris: Maritime Strategy since Mahan,* edited by A. M. J. Hyatt, pp. 12–18, 112–14. Annapolis, Md.: Naval Institute Press, 1973.

——. *History and War.* Augusta, Georgia: The Hamburg Press, 1984.

——. "The Modern Italian Navy." *Military Affairs* 5 (1941): 32–48, 104–16.

——. *War in the Modern World.* Durham, N.C.: Duke University Press, 1959.

Rouyer, Admiral, *et al.* "Un 'compact' documentaire pour shiplovers et modélistes." *Triton* 36 (1956) through 50 (1959). The only good published plans of French ships of this period; one or two per issue. Appeared simultaneously in *Neptunia.*

Taillemite, Etienne. *Dictionnaire des Marins français.* Paris: Editions maritimes et d'Outre-mer, 1982.

Thomazi, Auguste-Antoine. *Marins bâtisseurs d'empire.* Paris: Horizons de France, 1946–47.

Vichot, Jacques. *Répértoire des navires de guerre français.* Paris: Association des Amis des Musées de la Marine, 1967. Originally appeared serialized in the magazines *Triton* and *Neptunia.*

Wallin, Franklin Whittelsey. "The French Navy during the Second Empire: A Study of the Effects of Technological Development on French Governmental Policy." Doctoral dissertation, University of California at Berkeley, 1953. An article drawn from this dissertation is in *Revue maritime* (April 1958): 486.

Walser, John Raymond. "France's Search for a Battlefleet: French Naval Policy, 1898–1914." Doctoral dissertation, University of North Carolina, 1976.

Wolff, Robert. *Marins et navires de la flotte française de guerre d'avant 1914.* Paris: SED4, 1983. Photos of navy life.

Index